158-4574

Political Parties and Party Systems

Political Parties and Party Systems

Editors

Ajay K. Mehra

D.D. Khanna

Gert W. Kueck

SAGE Publications
New Delhi • Thousand Oaks • London

In association with

 Konrad Adenauer Foundation

 Centre for Public Affairs

 Society for Peace, Security and Development Studies

First published in 2003 by

Sage Publications India Pvt Ltd
B-42, Panchsheel Enclave
New Delhi 110 017

Sage Publications Inc
2455 Teller Road
Thousand Oaks, California 91320

Sage Publications Ltd
6 Bonhill Street
London EC2A 4PU

Published by Tejeshwar Singh for Sage Publications India Pvt Ltd, typeset by S.R. Enterprises, New Delhi in 10/12 Palatino and printed at Chaman Enterprises, New Delhi.

Library of Congress Cataloging-in-Publication Data

Political parties and party systems/edited by Ajay K. Mehra, D.D. Khanna, and Gert W. Kueck.
   p.   cm.
Includes index.
1. Political parties—India. 2. India—Politics and government—1947. 3. Political parties—Germany. 4. Political parties—European Union countries. I. Mehra, Ajay K. II. Khanna, D. D. III. Kueck, Gert W.

JQ298.A1P57   324.254—dc21   2003   2003003671

ISBN: 0–7619–9709–1 (US-Hb)   81–7829–185–1 (India-Hb)

Sage Production Team: Jaya Chowdhury, Praveen Dev, Sushanta Gayen and Santosh Rawat

Dedicated to

Professor Pradeep Kumar,
an intense scholar and a loving friend,
who unfortunately is no longer
in our midst

CONTENTS

List of Tables   9
List of Figures   11
List of Abbreviations   13
Preface   16

1. Introduction   21
   Ajay K. Mehra

2. Historical Development of the Party Systems in India   49
   Ajay K. Mehra

3. Federalisation of India's Party System   83
   Balveer Arora

4. The Party System in Germany and Party
   Fragmentation in the European Union   100
   Karl-Rudolf Korte

5. Social, Cultural and Economic
   Dimensions of the Party System   129
   Amit Prakash

6. How Many Parties are too Many?   162
   Pran Chopra

7. The Electoral Framework, Process
   and Political Parties   181
   Madhav Godbole

8. Parties, Civil Society and the State in India   209
   S.K. Chaube

9. The Congress and the BJP:
   Struggle for the Heartland   224
   Partha S. Ghosh

10. The Third Front or The Third Force:
    A Political Maze or an Ideological Oasis?   244
    Bidyut Chakrabarty

11. The Third Force: As an Ideology and as a Reality   270
    Muchkund Dubey

12. The National Parties and the Regional
    Allies: A Study in the Socio-Political Dynamics   288
    Pradeep Kumar

13. The Regional Parties and Democracy:
    Romantic Rendezvous or Localised Legitimation?   306
    Suhas Palshikar

14. The Contest for the Marginal Space:
    Parties and Politics in Small Indian States   336
    Sajal Nag

15. Mediating Economic Reforms: Party Politics
    from Bangalore to Chennai   366
    Harish Khare

16. Local Democracy and Political Parties in India   384
    Sandeep Shastri

About the Editors and Contributors   397

Index   400

LIST OF TABLES

3.1: Number of Parties Successful in
Lok Sabha Elections (1991–99)   84

3.2: Twenty Principal Parties
in 13th Lok Sabha (1999)   86

3.3: Lok Sabha Seats of Five Main National
Parties (1977–99)   87

3.4: Seats and Votes (%) won by Categories of
Parties in the Lok Sabha, 1996–99   88

3.5: State-wise Distribution of Seats between
Parties in the 12th Lok Sabha, 1998   90

3.6: Parties and Alliances in the 13th Lok Sabha, 1999 91

5.1: Vote Share Polled by National and Regional
Political Parties/Formations in the General
Elections, 1996, 1998 and 1999   150

9.1: Performance of BJS in Parliamentary
Elections (1952–71)   228

9.2: Vote Share of BJP in Hindi States
(1989 and 1991 elections)   233

9.3: Tally of Seats by Political Parties and
Alliances, 1999 Elections   236

9.4: Social base of the BJP and allies (Samata Party,
Shiv Sena and the Haryana Vikas Party) and
the Congress and allies (AIADMK), 1996   237

10.1: Electoral Performances of the Third Front:
1989, 1991, 1996, 1998 and 1999   263

12.1: 'Do You Feel Close to Any Political Party?'   304

12.2: Lok Sabha Elections: Votes Polled in Percentages 305

13.1: Regional Parties in the Lok Sabha: 1952–71 310

13.2: Regional Parties in the Lok Sabha: 1977–89 311

13.3: Regional Parties in the Lok Sabha: 1991–99 312

13.4: Social Profile of Voters of Akali Dal (1999) 317

13.5: Social Profile of Voters of DMK
and AIADMK (1999) 318

13.6: Social Profile of Voters of BJD (1999) 320

13.7: Social Profile of Voters of RJD (1999) 322

13.8: Social Profile of Voters of Samajwadi Party (1999) 323

13.9: Social Profile of Voters of Shiv Sena
and NCP (1999) 325

13.10: Social Profile of Voters of TDP (1999) 327

13.11: Social Profile of Voters of Trinamool
Congress (1999) 328

13.12: Performance of Some Regional Parties:
1995–1999 334

14.1: Order of States and Union Territories
in terms of Area 338

14.2: Order of States and Union Territories
in terms of Population (1991 Census) 339

16.1: Representation to Different Castes in Karnataka
Legislative Assembly and Local Bodies 395

LIST OF FIGURES

5.1: Support for Main Political Parties
in 1996 Elections According to Gender   131

5.2: Support for Main Political Parties
in 1998 Elections According to Gender   132

5.3: Support for Main Political Parties
in 1996 Elections According to Locality   133

5.4: Support for Main Political Parties
in 1998 Elections According to Locality   134

5.5: Support for Main Political Parties
in 1999 Elections According to Locality   135

5.6: Support for Main Political Parties in 1996
Elections According to Educational Levels   136

5.7: Support for Main Political Parties in 1998
Elections According to Educational Levels   137

5.8: Support for Main Political Parties
in 1996 Elections According to Occupation   138

5.9: Support for Main Political Parties
in 1998 Elections According to Occupation   140

5.10: Support for Main Political Parties
in 1996 Elections According to Caste   141

5.11: Support for Main Political Parties
in 1998 Elections According to Caste   143

5.12: Support for Main Political Parties
in 1999 Elections According to Caste   144

5.13: Support for Main Political Parties
in 1996 Elections According to Religion   145

5.14: Support for Main Political Parties
in 1998 Elections According to Religion   146

5.15: Support for Main Political Parties in 1996
Elections According to Economic Class   147

5.16: Support for Main Political Parties in 1998
Elections According to Economic Class   148

LIST OF ABBREVIATIONS

AC	Arunachal Congress
AGP	Asom Ganatantra Parishad (1957), Asom Gan Parishad (1984–)
AD	Akali Dal/Party (all factions mentioned together)
AIADMK	All India Anna Dravida Munnetra Kazhagam
APHLC	All Party Hill Leaders' Conference
ASDC	Autonomous State Demand Committee
BC	Bangla Congress
BJD	Biju Janata Dal
CJ	Congress (Jagjivan Ram)
CS	Congress (Socialist)
CSJ	Chhota Nagpur and Santhal Pargana Janata Party
CT	Congress (Tiwari)
CW	Commonweal
DMK	Dravida Munnetra Kazhagam
EITU	Eastern Indian Tribal Union
FB	Forward Bloc
GNLF	Gorkha National Liberation Front
GP	Gantantra Parishad
HLD/INLD	Haryana Lok Dal/Indian National Lok Dal
HLS	Haryana Lok Shakti
HVC	Himachal Vikas Congress
HVP	Haryana Vikas Party
IPF	Indian People's Front
IUML	Indian Union Muslim League
JDG	Janata Dal (Gujarat)
JKP/D	Jharkhand Party/Dal
JMM	Jharkhand Mukti Morcha
JP	Janata Party
KCP	Karnataka Congress Party
KC*	Kerala Congress (all factions)

LC	Loktantrik Congress
LD	Lok Dal
LS	Lok Shakti
MADMK	MGR Anna Dravida Munnetra Kazhagam
MDMK	Marumalarchi DMK
MGP	Maharashtrawadi Gomantak Party
MGRK	MGR Munnetra Kazhagam
MIM	Majlis-E-Ittehadul Musalmeen
ML	Muslim League
MML	Madras Muslim League
MP	MahaGujarat Parishad
MPVC	Madhya Pradesh Vikas Congress
MSC	Manipur State Congress
NC	National Conference
NCP	National Congress Party
NNO	Naga National Organisation
NPC	Nagaland People's Council
PDF	People's Democratic Front
PMK	Pattali Makkal Kachi
PWP	Peasants' and Workers' Party
RJD	Rashtriya Janata Dal
SCF\RPI	Scheduled Castes Federation (1952–57), Republican Party of India (all factions)
RRP	Ram Rajya Parishad
RSP	Revolutionary Socialist Party
SDF	Sikkim Democratic Front
SJP	Samajwadi Janata Party
SKJP	Sikkim Janata Parishad
SMP	Samata Party
SP	Samajwadi Party
SS	Shiv Sena
SSP	Sikkim Sangram Parishad
TC	Trinamool Congress
TDP	Telugu Desam Party
TMC	Tamil Maanila Congress
TNT	Tamil Nadu Toilers' Party
TPS	Telangana Praja Samiti
TRS	Tamil Nadu Rajiv Congress
TTC	Tamil Nadu & Travancore Congress

UC	Utkal Congress
UFN	United Front of Nagas
UGDP	United Goan Democratic Party
UG (S)	United Goan (Sequeria)
UMF	United Minorities Front
VHP	Vishwa Hindu Parishad

PREFACE

The evolution of political parties and the party systems in the world's largest, most complex and volatile democracy reached a critical stage at the turn of the century. The 20th century, that brought independence to the 'brightest jewel in the British Crown' and unleashed democratic process under a republican constitution in a society with bewildering social plurality, mass poverty and illiteracy, in its last decade witnessed the decline of the Indian National Congress. Despite having ruled the country for most of the time since 1947, the party that had become synonymous with the national movement had to finally make way for coalition politics at the national level. That it could no longer hold the kaleidoscopic nation with carefully constructed social coalition under its umbrella became clear. However, in the process of this 'federalisation' of national politics, a complex pattern of party systems began to emerge. The process is a dynamic one and still pregnant with innumerable possibilities. This volume is a modest attempt to study and understand this complex process in comparison with similar processes going on in Germany and the European Union.

This collaborative work emerged out of common concerns of the three participating institutions—the Centre for Public Affairs, the Society for Peace, Security and Development Studies and the Konrad Adenauer Foundation. Concerned with existing and emerging political processes that influence life of common people and their political institutions in their respective countries, these organisations joint hands together to team up for a comparative study of the Indian and the German party systems. The focus and structure of the volume were designed in consultations with leading political and social scientists. Obviously, the federalisation process in the party system in India at the national, state and local levels emerged as the focus of this volume and the stage was set for a study of intricate political interactions and alliances. The scholars identified to write chapters under this project were invited to present the findings of their research, which generated a lively and intense debate on various related issues. In the light of these discussions, the authors revised their contributions that have been edited and presented in this book. Of course, many scholars felt that some more issues could have been included, but a focused edited volume has to avoid peripheral concerns.

Naturally, the revision of 15 substantive chapters by as many different scholars and editing of the respective research papers, rich in analysis and data, often takes more time than is intended. However, the recent trends in Indian party politics reinforce several insights offered by the collection of essays brought together here. The widely held perception that the fortress of the National Democratic Alliance was crumbling and the emerging possibilities of new political alliances as the 14th general elections inches closer, enormous volatility in state politics across the country, concerns about and discourse on electoral reforms in the wake of the Supreme Court ruling and the Election Commission's initiative, the debate on the constitutional limits of the powers of the Election Commission to determine the suitable time for holding poll and, of course, the democratic energies released with the strengthening of widened local democracy make the analyses presented in this volume relevant for some time to come. In any case, these analyses are meant to initiate further debate and encourage more scholars to carry on discovery of new trends in Indian party politics.

The analysis of the German party system incorporated in this volume deserves to be updated with fresh facts emerging out of elections on 22 September 2002, when more than 60 million voters in that country went out to elect a new *Bundestag*, the German Parliament. Total voter turnout was at 79.1 per cent, which is slightly less than that experienced in the previous elections that took place in 1998. It was a very close race, but at the very end Mr Gerhard Schroeder, who had succeeded Mr Helmut Kohl as Federal Chancellor in 1998, and his coalition of Social Democrats and Greens came out on top.

Mr Schroeder's SPD gathered 38.5 per cent of the vote, which is a loss of 2.4 per cent in comparison to the previous election in 1998. His conservative challenger, the Minister-President (equivalent to Chief Minister in India) of the German federal state of Bavaria, Mr Edmund Stoiber, and the combined Christian Democratic Union/Christian Social Union (CDU/CSU) received just a few thousand votes less and also achieved exactly an equal (38.5 per cent) share, which is an improvement of 3.4 per cent as compared to the 1998 figure. The Green Party of Germany's most popular politician of the moment, Foreign Minister Mr Joschka Fischer, could celebrate a surprising success of 8.6 per cent (plus 1.9 per cent compared to 1998) of his party. In contrast to that, the Free Democratic Party ('The Liberals') came in as fourth runner up with 7.4 per cent votes, which is gain of 1.2 per cent over 1998, but, nevertheless, is well below the target it aimed to achieve. For months before the elections, the FDP had entertained an ambitious goal of 18 per cent and was widely expected to at least overpower the Greens. According to most observers, it was this unlikely weakness of the liberal party that precluded a change in government. Even unexpected was the complete defeat of the left-wing Party of Democratic Socialism (PDS)—the successor to the erstwhile Socialist Unity Party which ruled the former German Democratic Republic—that will no longer be part of the *Bundestag* since it could garner only 4 per cent and thus clearly missed the '5 per cent debarring clause', which stipulates that only parties gaining at least 5 per cent of the valid second votes or at least three constituency seats can be represented in the parliament as a parliamentary group (voters have two votes, the first of which is given to a candidate in the respective constituency, whereby the successful candidate is elected on a first-past-the-post basis; the second vote is given to one of the campaigning parties). However, because of the German system of personalised proportional representation, two PDS candidates who won the majority of votes in their constituency are members of the new *Bundestag*.

Translated into mandates, this means that the SPD remains the strongest parliamentary group with 251 seats (but minus 47 compared to 1998). CDU/CSU achieved three more than in 1998, which amounted to 248 seats in total. The Greens could win 55 seats (plus 8), the FDP 47 seats (plus 4), and—as it was mentioned earlier—the PDS 2 (minus 34) seats. Thus, the weakened Red-Green coalition still controls a razor-thin majority of 306 out of 603 seats, four more than what the so-called chancellor-majority requires, and will therefore be in government for some time.

For a long time during the campaign, many if not most of the observers were assuming that the election would bring a change in government. Only in the last weeks, Chancellor Schroeder could turn this trend around, due to three crucial events and issues: his populist performance in the second TV-debate between him and Mr Stoiber, his federal government-backed management of the flood disaster that occurred in August 2002, and last but not least, his strong stance against any military intervention in Iraq. Indeed, it may have been the first time that foreign policy issues and an appeal to strong pacifist feelings that had developed in many parts of that country's population after World War II, at least partly decided a German election. Obviously, the party system in Germany too appears to be in a state of flux, though the changes at the moment appear to be only temporary.

Finally, the editors want to stress that this volume would not have been possible without the valuable assistance of several supporters. Of course, first and foremost the three partners in this venture would like to thank all the reputed scholars who participated in consultations and the brainstorming that preceded to give this project a definite and cogent shape. While asking for the kind understanding of the respected reader for not being able to mention them all, the editors should be allowed to refer especially to Dr Partha S. Ghosh and Dr O.P. Sharma of the Centre for Public Affairs, as well as to Dr Prashant Agarwal of the Society for Peace, Security and Development Studies who offered intellectual and managerial help, without which the project would not have been completed successfully. The same is true for the unmatched organisational skills of Mr Pankaj Madan of the Konrad Adenauer Foundation that were always a highly regarded asset. The editors would like to record their appreciation for it. The authors of each chapter deserve our most profound thanks for their co-operation and for tolerating unending nagging of the editorial team. Expressing trust in the project at the highest degree, Sage Publications India Pvt Ltd agreed to publish this volume even before the editors received a single paper. We feel deeply obliged to thank them for their faith in the editors and the contributors to the volume.

A tragedy struck while this volume was being edited. Prof. Pradeep Kumar, one of the scholars involved in the project, unfortunately and unexpectedly passed away in Chandigarh, where he taught political science at Punjab University. An eminent scholar, a perceptive student of Indian politics and an exuberantly pleasant company at any time was snatched away from our midst. We dedicate this volume to him in appreciation of his scholarship, which added a rich empirical and analytical base to the study of political parties and party systems in India.

New Delhi
January 2003

Ajay K. Mehra
D.D. Khanna
Gert W. Kueck

1

INTRODUCTION

Ajay K. Mehra

The essays in this volume review and analyse political parties and party systems in India and put them in a comparative perspective with Germany and the European Union (EU). Such a review is necessitated at this crucial period in time not just because of the dawn of a new century, which has coincided with India completing half-a-century of volatile democratic politics (1997), the republic (2000) and parliamentary electoral politics (2002) under the present Constitution. After the 13th general elections in 1999, India also embarked on a distinctly different phase of her democratic journey, with a distinct change in party politics in the country. The country witnessed a significant transformation in the political sociology of her democracy 53 years after her independence at the close of the 20th century, naturally effecting comprehensive changes in political parties—their leadership, ideological profile, support base, programmatic content, their spread and reach across the country and above all their numbers—as well as in the texture of the party system in the country.

The need for such a review at this particular juncture in India's political history also arises because the 13th general elections heralded a new political era in the country. In fact, three general elections—the 11th (1996), the 12th (1998) and the 13th (1999)—in a matter of three years were crucial for political parties individually and for the party systems collectively, for two reasons. On the one hand, they conclusively laid to rest any possibility of return of the Indian National Congress (INC, hereafter Congress) to its post-independence dominant position in the foreseeable future, despite the fact that the Congress still remains the only truly national party with presence practically in all parts of the country and its return to power in New Delhi is a distinct possibility. On the other hand, the Bharatiya Janata Party (BJP) not only emerged as the single largest party in the Lok Sabha and the second largest national party (though still far behind the Congress in its national reach), but having failed to create a winning social alliance (*a la* Congress) that could propel it to power on its own, it also created a new basis for a winning political alliance to capture power at the Centre in two successive general elections—1998 and 1999. In the process, it overcame the limitations of being the political pariah that it has been due to a distinct communal/ sectarian tilt in its politics, which had come in the way of its attracting any ally with any party in 1996 to win the confidence of the Lok Sabha even after forming the government. The emergence of the BJP has not only created the basis for bi-nodal party politics in India in the near future, since the Third Front remains in total disarray, it has also paved the way for coalition politics based on a federalised party structure with participation from national and regional parties alike. Indeed, in whatever form it remains, the Third Front too is a federalised idea of a party system. Should it revive itself, either due to the collapse of the BJP-led coalition or otherwise, federalisation of the party system in India appears a reality. Obviously, a federalised party system at the national level creates a new basis for interactions amongst the parties and lends a fresh meaning to their role in the states. Simultaneously, their role at the local level as well as the role of the 'local' in the state and national party systems is still in the process of crystallisation. Surely, in the years to come it is bound to impact the party system.

A comparative perspective on parties and party systems with Germany and the EU in a volume focusing on India is as much due to the collaboration with the Konrad Adenauer Foundation as to the perception of the editorial team that at this particular juncture when the parties in Germany and the EU are undergoing collaborative and federalising experiences, a comparison would provide useful analytical perspectives in the Indian context.

This volume is structured to study the developments in the Indian party systems at four levels. First, it surveys the status and strategies, interaction pattern and processes of political parties as well as issues and key questions governing the party system in the country. Second, it reviews the texture and pattern of political alliances from the national perspective, i.e., how alliances with the regional parties are viewed and made from the perspective of the national parties. Third, it evaluates the process of making alliances from the perspective of the regional parties. Finally, it attempts to study parties and politics in small states and at the local level since the introduction of the 73rd constitutional amendment.

A word of explanation is due here for treating the Indian party system in the plural, i.e., as 'party systems'. Obviously, the question arises whether it is possible for one country and one political system to have more than one party system. In order to answer this question it would be worthwhile at this stage to remind ourselves how and when parties make a 'system'. 'Parties', according to Sartori, 'make for a "system" ... only when they are parts [in the plural]; and a party system is precisely the *system of interactions* resulting from inter-party competition. That is, the system in question bears on the relatedness of parties to each other, on how each party is a function (in the mathematical sense) of the other parties and reacts, competitively or otherwise, to the other parties.'[1] While for Sartori, parties and the system they form are parts of the larger political system, for Jean Blondel, '... parties which exist in a given community tend to share common characteristics: they form in the widest sense of the word, a *system*, both with respect to their internal structure and to their interrelationships'.[2] The party system, thus, refers to complex social and political processes that go beyond individual leaders, societal associations, political groups and organisations to the intricate pattern of their interactions and interrelationships. These interaction patterns are governed not only by constitutions, statutes, rules, regulations and institutions, but a whole range of live issues that shape political attitudes and behaviours at critical stages of evolution in a society and polity. The pattern of interactions is reflected in ideologies and personalities, party building and fragmentation, coalescence and split, cooperation and opposition, support and protest, voter mobilisation and electoral competition. More particularly, it reflects how parties relate to each other at the ground level as well as in legislatures and power situations. The expression 'party system' acquires a special connotation in situations where parties represent multiple interests and identities and need to continuously build coalitions at social and political levels. And, in a multi-cultural society like India, coalition building takes place at more than one level, with each level having its own distinct identity. There is a process of coalition building at the state and regional levels, which is driven by compulsions of power at those levels. There is a similar process at the national level, which has a dual character. In the Indian case, thus, several levels of interaction, inter-party competition and relatedness of parties make more than one system of interactions. Obviously, political parties in India have more than one systemic ingredient to make for 'systems' in the plural.[3]

---

[1] Giovanni Sartori, *Parties and Party Systems: A Framework for Analysis, Vol. I*, Cambridge: Cambridge University Press, 1976, p. 44.

[2] Blondel underlines societal links of the party system while locating it within the larger political system:

> Basically, a party exists in order to win battles against other parties or groups. Parties which compete overtly necessarily come to resemble each other through this competition. Similarly, when a party stands alone, its characteristics are a function of the latent opposition which it must fight or repress. The nature of the competition thus markedly influences the nature of the party system.

Thus, the many links which exist between parties in a society lead to a party system. Jean Blondel, *Political Parties: A Genuine Case for Discontent*, London: Wildwood House, 1978, pp. 76–77. Obviously, in exploring the links between society and party system Blondel has not concerned himself with a complexly heterogeneous society like India. Yet, his basic logic creates justification for treating the party system in India in the plural.

[3] Myron Weiner too has argued that it is useful in the Indian case to distinguish between the national party system and the state party system. Myron Weiner, 'Party Politics and

Accordingly, the structure of the study explains this question. The three levels of the alliance pattern in contemporary Indian politics (national to regional, regional to national and within a region; indicating the level from which the alliance is being sought) among a score of political parties which have national, inter-regional and region-specific presence, also indicate the presence of an intricate party system at each level. They also operate at two or three different levels; many a times each level operates independent of the other. As stated earlier, two more levels of interaction patterns—rural and urban local levels—are emerging with the 73rd and 74th Amendments to the Constitution. While both would prove crucial in the long run for the structure, texture and processes related to the party systems in the country, the Panchayati Raj would have deeper impact on the party systems in India in the years to come.

James Manor explains the presence of the 'party systems' (i.e., network and interaction patterns of and amongst the parties in the plural) in India in terms of its most complex social heterogeneity 'on earth' which has 'so far made it impossible for a single set of alternative parties to emerge right across the country'. While the emergence of national parties indeed has had its own dynamics, 'the constellation of social groups and sentiments which gave rise to regional parties in different Indian states varied considerably' from time to time, which naturally had an impact on the party system in the country. Manor traces the complexity of the national and state party systems in India to the emergence in recent times of regional parties, i.e., explicitly regional parties, and substantially autonomous units of supposedly regional parties, which, he rightly argues, 'should not be seen as a political pathology, but partly as symptom of the fundamental problem that has lately afflicted the federal system: over-centralization by national leaders and governments'.[4]

A Party System at the Outset

The institutionalisation of the Indian National Congress in the first-ever meeting of the Indian National Union on 28 December 1885 in Bombay (now Mumbai), which subsequently became an annual event, evolving first as the organisational base for India's nationalist movement against British imperialism and graduating in course of time to an all-embracing political party, is

Electoral Behaviour: From Independence to the 1980s', in Myron Weiner and Ashutosh Varshney (eds), *The Indian Paradox*, New Delhi: Sage Publications, 1989, p. 192. The underlying argument in Weiner's suggestion is that different levels of political sociology operating at two different levels, where the state level too is not uniform, but highly diverse, unleash political processes that create more than one party system.

[4] James Manor, 'Regional Parties in Federal Systems', in Balveer Arora and Douglas Verney (eds), *Multiple Identities in a Single State: Indian Federalism in Comparative Perspective*, New Delhi: Konark, 1995, pp. 107 and 111.

rightly considered as the moment of the founding of a political party and the beginning of party politics in the Indian context. Of course, a whole range of factors came into play before the untiring efforts of A.O. Hume and some prominent personalities of the Indian intelligentsia led to a coordination among associations existing in the three Presidency capitals and other prominent towns, resulting in the formation of the Congress. The feeling within the colonial establishment following the revolt in 1857, that in order to prevent such an eventuality in the future a forum needed to be created for 'controlled' public participation and ventilation of public sentiments, deserves underlining here.[5] Hume, an 'eccentric' to his colleagues, stressed this point time and again with his fellow countrymen in administration as he went around tirelessly to organise the 'Congress'. Of course, the motives and objectives of the colonial government remained unaltered; the Indian National Congress was to become an instrument for it to keep its finger on the public's pulse. Also, the emerging intelligentsia and political leadership, very limited at that stage, could be kept in good humour. Yet the Congress and political parties and organisations in India, as they evolved, developed and got rooted in society and emerging democratic polity remained an outgrowth of a historical process, not a foreign transplant.[6]

As the Congress consolidated organisationally and gained in legitimacy both with the government and the people, a political process conducive for the crystallisation of political parties and political groups was set in motion. Thus, in the process of articulating nationalist sentiments and mobilising the masses—at times highly diverse groups of people socially, economically and politically—political beliefs and political culture were also shaped. The founding of the INC deserves to be regarded as the birth of a party system in India because it set in motion processes that, on the one hand, were a signal to a number of ideas to bloom, on the other hand, in the process of its evolution and growth, rules of political mobilisation and competition were written. Throughout this process, it remained the pivot on which the party system hinged before and after independence; of course, the context and processes differed in the two respective periods.

---

[5] The motives, circumstances and events leading to the founding of the Congress conform to the formulation of LaPalombara and Weiner that political parties emerge in a political system 'whenever the notion of political power comes to include the idea that the mass public must participate or be controlled'. Their emergence at any given time also reflects the situation that 'the tasks of recruiting political leadership and making public policy could no longer be handled by a small coterie of men unconcerned with public sentiments'. Joseph LaPalombara and Myron Weiner, 'The Origin and Development of Political Parties', in Joseph LaPalombara and Myron Weiner (eds), *Political Parties and Political Development*, Princeton, NJ: Princeton University Press, 1966, pp. 3–4.

[6] Weiner, 'Party Politics', p. 185.

There is an agreement among students of political parties in India about their evolutional route through the social reform movements, social, literary, religious and other associations, to the founding of the Indian National Congress, the Muslim League and sprouting of other political groups within and outside the two main streams of parties. The path thereafter becomes automatically clear as the Congress evolves from an elite club meeting annually and petitioning the colonial government to the vanguard of a robust anti-colonial nationalist movement, taking with it a critical mass from the heterogeneous society. In the process, it developed elements of a party system within itself. In tracing the historical development of the party system in India (Chapter 2), from the available data and analysis on Indian nationalism and the growth of political parties in India, I have attempted to identify 'competitive interaction patterns among parties'[7] and 'the forms and modes of their coexistence'[8] as well as political processes and the institutional framework that led to the development of a party system in the country; the foundation that became a solid basis for the growth of the party system as the Indian democracy took firm roots. I have identified the processes and inter-relationships at four levels, which created the base for a party system in India.

First, even as various associations were sprouting and taking firm roots during the 19th century, both before and after the revolt, there were interactions, not always collaborative, amongst them. The Brahmo Samaj, which did not shy away from protesting against the East India Company under the leadership of Raja Ram Mohun Roy, had several schisms within it. The growth of organisations, social and political consciousness and overt political activity based on political demands like representation throughout the decades of the 1960s and 1970s meant collaboration, debates, differences, splits and coalescence. While dealing with communitarian issues each association had concerned itself with, in pursuing their respective goals they were dealing with a shrewd colonial government as well, which carefully used any schism to divide and weaken the 'opposition'. As associations emerged and grew in the three Presidencies, they not only attempted to tie up their objectives and activities with each other, some of them also approached the British Members of Parliament (MPs) to garner support within the establishment. The Indian Association's reformist role as well as representation and the accommodation of conflicting interest by it carried constitutionalism to its highest point, obviously bequeathing the legacy of parliamentarism and liberal democracy in the process to the future generations. Indeed, the party system is a part of this legacy. It is equally important to note that even

---

[7] Harry Eckstein, 'Party Systems', *International Encyclopaedia of Social Sciences*, vol. 11, Macmillan, 1968, p. 436.

[8] Maurice Duverger, *Political Parties: Their Organisation and Activity in the Modern State*, New Delhi: B. I. Publications, 1979 (first Indian edition, a reprint of the third English edition), p. 203.

as the first Indian National Congress was being organised in Bombay, there were moves to isolate Surendra Nath Banerjea and his associates responsible for activities of the Indian Association in Calcutta (now Kolkata), though by the second Congress in 1886 in Calcutta they all came together. The processes thus set in motion had created conditions for political interactions that make a party system.

Second, as the Congress graduated from being an elite debating club and transcended the 'politics of mendicancy' during the first decade of the 20th century, the conflicts within the organisation, a hallmark of a democratic organisation, and organisational efforts to manage such conflicts, aided evolution of a party system. The second stage of the evolution of the Congress (1905–16), when the great debate between the moderates and the extremists took place over strategy, was one of the reflections of such a process. With the institutionalisation of this process within the organisation, political cohabitation in the face of differences, democratic dissent as well as splits and coalescence became part of its organisational culture. As the Congress got transformed into a mass movement by 1916, the rules of the game for the operation of the party system were defined as much from within the Congress as around it. Almost simultaneously and as a part of this process, rival groups developed. These processes intensified as the Muslim League's competitive politics versus the Congress, despite moments of coalescence (e.g., the Lucknow Pact), created opportunity for the British government to play the role of the rival axis.

Third, with elections becoming more and more competitive with each Act since 1909, political groups began to take the shape of parties, and the parties together of a party system. We have already cited the example of the Lucknow Pact. Not only did parties learn the ground rules of electoral competition, they also shaped into a system by learning to operate in the legislative councils. The emergence of the Swaraj Party (1922) from within the Congress to contest the legislative council elections of 1923 on the one hand, was a learning experience for the party as the Swarajists went back to the party. On the other hand, it highlighted the features of a party system within the Congress.

Finally, I have attempted to look at the interface of conflicting interests at the intra-party and inter-party levels—their political competition, the forms and modes of their coexistence and parties' capacity to resolve conflicts—as the emergence of the party system. The operation of several interests within the Congress is very well documented. The signposts begin with moderate extremist debate and split, Gandhi's differences with Jinnah and Subhash Chandra Bose and their parting of ways, the emergence of the Swaraj Party and the Forward Block and the formation of the Congress Socialist Party within the Congress. In fact, the resolutions of the All India Congress Committee (AICC) over the years provide a good view of various interests operating therein.

Institutionalisation of the Indian Party Systems

Independence, and partition, created a vacuum of sorts in the party system operating for close to four decades, in which the Congress and the All India Muslim League (AIML) emerged as political rivals, with the British government playing the third party of the system, taking advantage of their bitter rivalry. As the Muslim League became a Pakistani party due to the process and logic of partition, the Congress was left virtually by itself monopolising the political arena, as it were. Though the Congress emerged as the 'dominant party' by virtue of its identification with the independence movement,[9] the seeds of a party system, as I have argued (Chapter 2), were sown during the pre-independence politics both within and around the Congress. Thus, by 1951, a year after the new Constitution was put into effect and the time when preparations for the first general elections were on, four major groups of parties had emerged in the Indian political arena. One group 'more or less accepted the basic democratic, secular state provided for in the Constitution'. The Congress, the parties that came out of it, like the Socialist Party, the Kisan Mazdoor Praja Party (KMPP), and several small state parties, formed part of this group. The Communist Party of India (CPI) and various Marxist parties that rejected the western-type parliamentary democracy and advocated the Soviet or the Chinese model formed another group. A third group consisted of the Hindu sectarian parties like the Bharatiya Jan Sangh (BJS), the Hindu Mahasabha, Ram Rajya Parishad and so on. A fourth group of parties were indifferent to the constitutional framework and concentrated on parochial or regional demands. They included the Akali Dal, the Scheduled Caste Federation, the Jharkhand Party, the Tamilnad Congress and such other regional groups.[10]

The Congress, expected to do well in the first general elections, won 45 per cent of the national vote and 73 per cent of the seats (357 out of 489) in the Lok Sabha, the House of People. In the State Assemblies, the Congress won 68.47 per cent seats (2,248 out of 3,283) with 42.2 per cent of the vote. The Congress managed to get absolute majority in all but three State Legislative Assemblies, but it emerged as the single largest party in them too. Only four other parties could manage to get 3 per cent or more votes to get the status of a national party—Socialist Party (10.6 per cent), KMPP (5.8 per cent), and CPI (3.3 per cent) and BJS (3.1 per cent). Thus, out of 14 parties that entered the

---

[9] Duverger's description of a dominant party is apt in the Indian context, 'A party is dominant when it is identified with an epoch; when its doctrines, ideas, methods, its style, so to speak, coincide with those of the epoch.' Duverger, *Political Parties*, p. 308.

[10] Myron Weiner, *Party Politics in India: The Development of a Multi-Party System*, Princeton: NJ: Princeton University Press, 1957, pp. 16–17.
It is worth noting here that whatever their relative strength, regional parties emerged virtually at the outset of the electoral competition.

elections as national parties, only five could retain this status.[11] Obviously, since the Congress emerged as the single dominant party and retained that status unchallenged till the mid-1960s, the party system and political discourse on the Indian political system continued to be determined by this characterisation as the single party dominant system till then. For despite some of the opposition parties improving their strength in Parliament and some of the State Assemblies in subsequent elections, neither any single party, nor a combination of them, seemed to be emerging as an alternative to the Congress. The emergence of a non-Congress coalition in Kerala in as early as 1956 was an exception.

The Chinese debacle, Nehru's fading charisma, developing organisational lethargy in the party, Nehru's deteriorating health and the possibility of a succession tussle, were the trying factors for the Congress during the first half of the 1960s. The Congress system[12] was under severe strain despite the fact that there were two smooth successions to the post of prime minister within 18 months in this period.[13] Yet, the complexities and ambiguities of Indian society,[14] social coalition built by the Congress which were buttressed by traditional values and the party's conciliatory role in society,[15] and quick adaptation to modern representative politics by the traditional structure and elements of the caste system,[16] helped the party sustain itself through the adversity. No less important were the facts that the Congress had an excellent organisation[17] and '(t)he Congress organization was also the main instrument

---

[11] Weiner, 'Party Politics', pp. 16–20.

[12] Rajni Kothari in his celebrated essay 'The Congress "System" in India' published in the *Asian Survey*, 4 (December 1964, pp. 1161–73), characterised the single party dominant system in India as the Congress system. He developed his thesis further in *Politics in India* (New Delhi: Orient Longman, 1970), where he has argued that the system provided inter-party competition but no alteration of power and that the usual functions of opposition parties in a democracy were in India shared between opposition parties and groups within the Congress.

[13] Though independently, W.H. Morris-Jones too developed a similar thesis. India's party system during this period, according to him, was characterised by 'dominance coexisting with competition but without a trace of alternation'; in this 'competitive party system ... the competing parts play(ed) rather dissimilar roles'. W.H. Morris-Jones, 'Dominance and Dissent: Their Inter-relations in the Indian Party System', also 'Parliament and Dominant Party: The Indian Experience', in W.H. Morris-Jones, *Politics Mainly Indian*, Madras: Orient Longman, 1978, pp. 196–232.

[14] Morris-Jones, 'Dominance and Dissent', pp. 219–20.

[15] Myron Weiner, 'Traditional Role Performance and the Development of Modern Political Parties: The Indian Case', *Journal of Politics*, 26:4, November 1964, pp. 830–49.

[16] I. Lloyd and Susanne Hoeber Rudolph, *The Modernity of Tradition: Political Development in India*, Chicago: University of Chicago Press, 1967, p. 1.

[17] James Manor, 'Parties and the Party System', in Atul Kohli (ed.), *India's Democracy: An Analysis of Changing State-Society Relations*, Princeton, NJ: Princeton University Press, 1988, p. 65.

that knit together state and society, which is to say that it was India's central integrating institution'.[18]

This strain became visible in the fourth general elections in 1967 when the Congress, facing the first post-Nehru election, returned to Parliament with 40.78 per cent of votes and 54.62 per cent of seats.[19] The party also lost power in eight states to coalitions of assorted national and regional parties. Except in Haryana and Madhya Pradesh (MP), where it gained in votes and seats, it lost 1.5 per cent to 18 per cent seats in the states where it retained power.[20] Obviously, the Congress was shaken badly by the electorate. The closing years of the decade were even more eventful for the Congress as well as for the party system in the country, as the growing schism within the Congress leadership led to a vertical split in the party in 1969. Thus, at the close of the 1960s the Congress was under severe strain and neither any single political party, nor any cohesive coalition of parties, was in sight to fill this political space. As the two factions of the Congress battled for the party's political legacy and popular support base, with Mrs Gandhi's Congress claiming a definite edge, the emerging contour of the party system in the country was still hazy.[21] While neither of the Congresses appeared in the pink of their political health to claim the dominance the party had enjoyed for two decades since independence, others had yet to emerge above political squabbles to work out an effective strategy to claim the space the Congress appeared to be vacating. What emerged as a result was 'a market polity' in which political competition and bargaining transcended the Congress structures and came into the realm of inter-party competition by the participation of new groups

---

[18] James Manor, 'Indira and After: The Decay of Party Organization in India', *The Round Table*, vol. LXIII, No. 272, October 1978, pp. 315–24. Also see his 'Party Decay and Political Crisis in India', *The Washington Quarterly*, 4:3, Summer 1981, pp. 25–40.

[19] These percentages for earlier elections were 44.99 and 74.44 (1952), 47.78 and 75.10 (1957), 44.72 and 73.08 (1962).

[20] The Congress lost majority in Bihar (40.25 per cent seats), Kerala (6.77 per cent seats), Madras (later named Tamil Nadu) (21.37 per cent seats), Orissa (22.14 per cent seats), Punjab (45.19 per cent seats), Rajasthan (48.37 per cent seats), UP (46.82 per cent seats) and West Bengal (45.36 per cent seats). In the states where it retained power, its biggest loss of seats was in Assam (18.3 per cent), Mysore (now Karnataka) (8.2 per cent) and Maharashtra (6.25 per cent). Thus, out of 15 states, the party suffered losses in 13.

[21] Rajni Kothari thus articulated the changes:

> The socio-economic and demographic profile of the polity is changing fast.... The mobilization of new recruits and groups into the political process ... has given rise to the development of new and more differentiated identities and patterns of political cleavage ... [leading to] the expectation of freer political access ... and a greater insistence on government performance. Intermediaries and vote banks, while of continuing importance, have become increasingly circumvented as citizens search for more effective participation in the political market place and develop an ability to evaluate and make choices.

in government; the result was the onset of coalition politics.[22] The Dravida Munnetra Kazhagam (DMK) led by C.M. Annadurai in Madras (now Chennai)/ Tamil Nadu was the only exception.[23]

The party system went through three significant developments in India during the decade of the 1970s. First, a new-look Congress, led by Mrs Indira Gandhi and a bunch of leaders described as 'Young Turks', appeared strong and robust enough to warrant a review that 'the end of the dominant party had been too readily proclaimed in 1967'.[24] However, the implications of Mrs Gandhi's new 'political process' with a 'pyramidal decision-making structure'—which emphasised her own image, undermining and disman- tling established structures of the party, making direct plebiscitary appeals to the voters—for the Congress and the party system in India began to appear in less than half-a-decade, but was fully realised only at the close of the 1980s, as it 'proved unable to manage the tensions and cleavages of a hetero- geneous party operating in a heterogeneous society, federally governed'.[25]

Second, the space for the opposition still appeared limited, for Mrs Gandhi's approach towards the opposition parties, which were mauled badly in the 1971 general elections, and the state governments run by them, was confron- tationist. However, a determined opposition effectively used the contradic- tions within a centralised but weakened Congress government to put it on the mat taking advantage of rising corruption and mounting popular dis- content. And, following an 18-month (June 1975–January 1977) internal emergency, just a decade after the Congress was challenged in several states, a 'quickfix' coalition of several non-left parties ascended to power in New Delhi under the banner of the Janata Party (JP). By voting for old political 'wines' rebottled hurriedly with a new label, the voters demonstrated politi- cal discretion and their option for polarisation of parties, bringing in a new competitive element into the party system. The power struggle within the Congress, which had witnessed yet another vertical split, clearly reflected that 'the influence of people at the apex of national and regional political

Rajni Kothari, 'Continuity and Change in the Indian Party System', *Asian Survey*, vol. X, No. II, November 1970, pp. 937–48.

[22] Aside from the intense political competition that emerged after 1967, the reference here is also to defections and 'horsetrading' in legislators, which emerged as significant charac- teristics of politics in India in the years to come. W.H. Morris-Jones, 'From Monopoly to Competition in India's Politics', in Morris-Jones, *Politics Mainly Indian*, p. 156.

[23] It is significant that not only has the DMK sustained its dominance in Tamil politics since, it has also created its own opposition through a vertical split in 1977 resulting in the formation of the All India Anna DMK.

[24] W.H. Morris-Jones, 'From Monopoly to Competition in India's Politics', in Morris-Jones, *Politics Mainly Indian*, p. 187.

[25] Stanley A. Kochanek, 'Mrs Gandhi's Pyramid: The New Congress', in Henry C. Hart (ed.), *Indira Gandhi's India*, Boulder: Westview Press, 1976, pp. 104–5.

systems penetrates down through the systems most effectively by means of compromise. Attempts to rule by diktat paradoxically weaken the centralizers, as happened to Mrs Gandhi.'[26]

Third, the collapse of the Janata experiment within two years meant that despite a visible change in the texture of the party system, a final social and political realignment to give a definite shape to the Indian party system was still far away. Of course, a remarkable awakening among the voters regarding power of the ballot was clearly visible. The resulting expectations and pressures had thrown political calculations of the parties and leaders awry, who were either deinstitutionalising the established organisational framework (Congress), or were unable to create one (Janata Party). The only exceptions were parties on the left and right edges of the political spectrum. A related development, which has become a trend since, was that parties and governments increasingly became unable to meet social expectations.

The 1980s began with the baggage of the political developments of the 1970s. On the one hand, fragmentation of the Janata Party had become an unending process, on the other, personalisation and deinstitutionalisation of the Congress by Mrs Gandhi, if anything was left of this process after she had unabashedly imposed personal and dynastic rule on the political system and the party, had become more brazen, signified by the suffixation of Indira (I) to the Indian National Congress. Since many of her trusted colleagues and supporters of 1969–71 had deserted her in 1975 and between 1977–80, she placed a premium on personal loyalty. Aside from the return of Mrs Gandhi with an overwhelming majority, which again gave the impression of the return of the one party dominant system, 1980 witnessed another significant development—the creation of the Bharatiya Janata Party (BJP). The dual membership (of the party and the Rashtriya Swayamsevak Sangh [RSS]) issue concerning the former members of the (BJS), which had rocked the Janata Party in 1979 leading to the split by Charan Singh and his supporters, caused another significant (in retrospect) split in the party.

The 1980s too proved crucial for political parties and the party system in India in several respects. First, despite apparently maintaining its dominance from 1980 to 1989, Congress (I)'s organisational base and structure were corroded from within due to factionalism rampant in most of its units. It is a matter of conjecture how the Congress (I) would have done in the 1984 elections had Mrs Gandhi not been assassinated that year. Though Rajiv Gandhi promised to free the Congress (I) of 'powerbrokers' and made a blistering critique of his own party during the party's centenary celebration in Bombay on 28 December 1985, he did little to improve the state of affairs during the

---

[26] Manor, 'Party Decay and Political Crisis in India', p. 25.

seven years that he was at the helm in the party.[27] In fact, bizarre though it was, weaknesses in the party structure made him think of establishing direct communion and formal links with the local self-government and the district administration. The same was true of most political parties, except BJP and the left, though the BJP's rout in the 1984 elections (it won only two seats in the Lok Sabha) was also caused because RSS grassroots workers worked for the Congress (I).

The second, and related, development was that Mrs Gandhi was virtually on a confrontational course with the opposition throughout her tenure, which included the national parties as well as regional parties; particularly those who dared to oppose her. In a way this was an extension of her pre-Emergency and Emergency period politics. Her confrontational politics in Punjab, Jammu and Kashmir, Assam and West Bengal (on the Darjeeling Hill Council issue) and the attempts to dismiss the opposition-controlled governments in Karnataka, Jammu and Kashmir, Sikkim, and Andhra Pradesh, were heavily criticised. She did not hesitate to brand the opposition parties as anti-national for criticising her. In fact, the shrill election campaign, depicting the opposition as anti-national, by the Congress (I) led by Rajiv Gandhi in 1984 was planned during Mrs Gandhi's lifetime.[28] Though Rajiv Gandhi authored the Punjab and Assam accords, the party maintained a similar posture under his leadership.

Third, the national parties had begun to resemble each other in the 1980s in several respects. The Janata Party and its variants were competing with the Congress (I) for centrist space. The BJP began by shedding the BJS skin of a communal rightist party as it attempted to position itself on the right of the centre under the leadership of Atal Behari Vajpayee by adopting 'Gandhian socialism' as its new mantra. The Congress (I) too shifted its ideological posture 'to court the votes of the Hindu majority across North India by making appeals based on Hindu chauvinism and the notion that India's unity was in jeopardy'.[29] The dangers of this portentous political posture were visible in the anti-Sikh riots of 1984. However, political compulsions of the Congress (I) and the Gandhis made them compete with the BJP. While the Congress (I) could manage the support of the RSS grassroots workers in 1984,[30] the compulsion manifested itself again at the height of the Vishwa

---

[27] He was critical of 'cliques ... enmeshing the living body of the Congress in their net of avarice'. He virtually condemned Congress members' 'self-aggrandizement, their corrupt ways, their linkages with vested interests ... and their sanctimonious posturings ...' and rued that in the party 'corruption is not only tolerated ... but even regarded as a hallmark of leadership'. *The Times of India* (Bombay), 29 December 1985.

[28] Manor, 'Parties and the Party System', p. 85.

[29] Ibid., p. 86.

[30] Ibid., p. 97.

Hindu Parishad (VHP)-Sangh Parivar's Ayodhya (Ram *mandir*) campaign. In 1986 the padlock of the disputed site was opened on lower court orders, allegedly at the behest of the Union government, and the *darshan* of the deity was allowed; in 1989 Rajiv Gandhi felt compelled to allow *shilanyas* at the site and promise *Ram Rajya* if reelected, a complete U-turn from the promise of leading India into the 21st century in the previous elections. This blurring of boundaries heightened prospects of political migrations across parties. No wonder, an alarmed Rajiv Gandhi and his advisors felt compelled to bring in the anti-defection law.

The emergence and consolidation of the DMK (and Dravidian politics) after 1967 in Tamil Nadu, and the virtual monopoly of the Communist Party of India (Marxist) (CPM) under Jyoti Basu's leadership in West Bengal after 1977 were not isolated events. On the one hand, to the extreme discomfiture of political parties at the state and national levels, social bases of Indian politics were clearly transcending political boundaries; on the other, these changes were beginnings of 'a growing divergence between the logic of politics at the national level and the political logic in various state-level arenas'.[31] As this trend consolidated, the 1980s witnessed the emergence of regional parties in many states. In fact, state and regional units even of some of the national parties seemed to have a political compulsion to function as regional parties. Many of these parties played a crucial role in national politics in the coming decade.

In order to set the immediate background for the emerging party systems, let us briefly capture the party politics of 1989–96, the period which witnessed three governments—the V.P. Singh-led National Front coalition government with outside support from the Left Front and the BJP, Chandrashekhar's rump government with outside support from the Congress (I) and a full-term Congress (I) government led by P.V. Narasimha Rao, which began as a minority government, but managed majority in the Lok Sabha through defections, allegedly by bribing the defecting MPs. The assassination of Rajiv Gandhi by the Liberation Tigers of Tamil Eelam (LTTE) while campaigning for the 1991 elections had far-reaching impacts both on the Congress (I) and the party system. The Congress (I) came under the microscope, as it were, for the party's ability to emerge out of the shadows of the Nehru-Gandhi family; as Rajiv Gandhi's children were not old enough to step in and his widow, Italy born Sonia Gandhi, was reluctant to join politics.

Four major developments deserve to be underlined in this context. First, the data on election turnouts collected by the Centre for the Study of Developing Societies in Delhi has pointed out that there has been a dramatic change in the social composition of voters and active participants in politics. Characterised as the 'second democratic upsurge', it refers to 'a participatory

---

[31] Ibid., pp. 73–74.

upsurge among the socially underprivileged, whether seen in terms of caste hierarchy, economic class, gender distinction or the rural-urban divide. They do not lag far behind the socially privileged as they did in the past; indeed in some respects they are more active today than the former.'[32] V.P. Singh's use of the 'Mandal' card in 1990 and its long-term implication for party politics in India was a part of this trend. Whether he was just taking advantage of this trend or his move precipitated the trend is still being debated. However, that the erstwhile largest Indian state, Uttar Pradesh (UP), has been ruled more than once in the 1990s by parties and coalitions representing the backward castes and dalits clearly shows the silent revolution taking place through the ballot in India. Not only do these social groups have leaders and parties representing their cause, increasingly, national parties also resort to ethnic strategies of political mobilisation to seek their support and draw them out.[33]

Second, given a second chance by the voters in 1989–91, the non-Congress centrist parties frittered away the opportunity once more. Of course, the mandate given to the hastily glued together Janata Dal (JD) (and the National Front coalition) was much less clearer than to its predecessor, the Janata Party, in 1977. It also did not have the Hindu right—BJS in 1977 and BJP in 1989—with it, but aside from the left, the BJP had entered into seat adjustment with the Front and gained from it. Internally, the story of 1977–80 was repeated with different actors in the JD, which failed to create a viable party organisation once again and disintegrated during and after their short reign.[34] The BJP's outside (critical) support proved too costly to V.P. Singh's National Front government. It is a moot point what other strategy or pretext the BJP would have adopted had V.P. Singh not gambled on implementing the Mandal Commission report on protective discrimination to the backward castes. On its part, JD lost the opportunity to consolidate its position as the second largest political configuration, if not the party, and handed the space on a platter to the BJP.

Third, despite Rajiv Gandhi's assassination and lack of absolute majority in 1991 in the Lok Sabha, the Congress (I) had a historic opportunity to resurrect itself. Having sorted out the leadership question in the absence of the Nehru-Gandhi legacy with relative ease, the party and its leaders could

---

[32] Yogendra Yadav, 'Understanding the Second Democratic Upsurge: Trends of Bahujan Participation in Electoral Politics in the 1990s', in Francine R. Frankel, Zoya Hasan, Rajeev Bhargava and Balveer Arora (eds), *Transforming India: Social and Political Dynamics of Democracy*, New Delhi: Oxford University Press, 2000, p. 120.

[33] Zoya Hasan, 'Representation and Redistribution: The New Lower Caste Politics in North India', in Frankel et al. (eds), *Transforming India*, pp. 146–75.

[34] Ajay K. Mehra, 'Political Parties and Party System in India', in D.D. Khanna and Gert W. Kueck (eds), *Principles, Power and Politics in India*, New Delhi: Macmillan, 1999, pp. 238–69.

not devote their collective energies to party building as factionalism and personal ambitions got the better of them. Narasimha Rao retracted his steps after holding organisational elections. The party also suffered because Rao attempted to gain majority through defections, allegedly by bribing the defecting MPs. In any case, few leaders of the party seemed to have grasped the full import of the drastic changes in the political and social dynamics of elections.

Finally, the progressive rise and consolidation of the Hindu 'right' between 1989 and 1996 too has had significant and far-reaching implications for the party system in the country. The BJP's political stock soared due to its seat adjustments with the National Front in 1989. L.K. Advani's (then BJP president) *rath yatra* (pilgrimage on a chariot) in 1990 for the Ram temple in Ayodhya, a small town in UP known as the birth place of Lord Ram, made it the main opposition in the 10th Lok Sabha. However, the *rath yatra* also heightened religious schism across north and west India and gave the BJP a new ideological belligerence, which it has sustained since then.[35] The BJP emerged as the single largest party in the 11th Lok Sabha in 1996 and succeeded in receiving the presidential invitation to form the government. However, still short of absolute majority, it could not attract any ally to sustain it. This experience was crucial for its coalition strategies later.

Federalisation of Parties

'*Kahin ki eeint kahin ka roda, Bhanumati nay qunba joda*'[36] and a '13-legged animal'[37] is how BJP had described the United Front governments during 1996–98. It is a different matter that no party was in a position to form the government in 1996, 1998 or 1999 on its own and even BJP would have worked out a similar coalition structure had it succeeded in attracting allies to bridge the deficit in the Lok Sabha. Naturally, the BJP worked harder in 1998 and succeeded in putting together a 24-party coalition, known since then as the National Democratic Alliance (NDA). It is equally necessary to remember that the BJP-led NDA government fell in 1999 by one vote because one of the allies pulled out of the coalition. As a result, the effort by the BJP and NDA to secure itself in 1999 was far greater.

Obviously, the party systems in India have become highly competitive, in which parties, depending on their social bases, internal organisations and

---

[35] For details, see Partha S. Ghosh, *BJP and the Evolution of Hindu Nationalism*, New Delhi: Manohar, 1999.

[36] A proverb in Hindi literally meaning 'brick from somewhere, mortar from somewhere else; that is how Bhanumati (an imaginary maternal figure) has put together her clan'. In this context it is self-explanatory.

[37] Derogatory description of the 13-party United Front coalition government. This did not include the Congress (I) which had extended 'outside' support to the Front.

ideologies, have developed complex modes of interactions and/or coexistence. Balveer Arora assiduously underscores this process through an intensive analysis of the electoral data of recent years. As he grapples with complex questions of fragmentation of voters and political parties,[38] apparently visible in the Indian polity in recent years, he discovers processes both of federalisation and renewal. It is obvious from his analysis that the days of Congress-style centralised 'federalism' in party structure are over, a reality that the Congress is finding hard to adjust to. Though both the Congress (I) and the BJP are naturally aspiring for parliamentary majority, if not Congress-type dominance, the BJP has been able to grasp the reality of coalition and federalisation better than the Congress (I), which it has adopted as the party's policy in the Chennai declaration.[39]

Balveer Arora has looked at the processes of renewal of parties from three sources—intra-party democracy, statutory processes in which the Election Commission of India is playing an important role and the 73rd and 74th Amendments to the Constitution. Arora has rightly argued that the compulsions of the emerging federalised party system are compelling the parties to look at new strategies of renewal. Legal and statutory processes addressing major infirmities, including the Election Commission's initiatives, are also compelling enough for the parties to look into organisational weaknesses and aberrations. Finally, as the local self-government and its democratic processes get institutionalised, a major change in the party systems could be expected. Thus, the process as Arora outlines it, includes democratisation, 'fragmentation' and federalisation, both politically and socially a highly optimistic scenario.

In a Comparative Perspective

Balveer Arora has meticulously outlined the crucial changes taking place in parties and the party systems in India. It would indeed be worthwhile to put the processes in India in a comparative perspective, even though a limited one, to comprehend these processes in a larger perspective. The chapter by Karl-Rudolf Korte looks at the party system in Germany and, what he calls, 'party fragmentation' in the European Union. Since the party systems in both the contexts are witnessing changes in social and political contexts that are integrational, their political processes would be useful comparisons with

---

[38] Francine R. Frankel, 'Contextual Democracy: Intersections of Society, Culture and Politics in India', in Frankel et al. (eds), *Transforming India*, pp. 12–13.

[39] The BJP realistically accepted the coalition era as a 'natural phenomenon' in its Chennai meeting and promised a 'positive evolution of coalition politics by ensuring that regional and sectional aspirations are properly harmonised with national imperatives'. Bharatiya Janata Party, *Chennai Declaration*, January 2000, p. 4.

the transformations taking place in the Indian party systems. Of course, we have to keep in mind the proliferation of parties in India, despite a movement towards a bi-nodal party system in recent years as highlighted by Balveer Arora, in comparison to just five parties in Germany, though in the initial years of the Federal Republic there were a much larger number of parties. We also must keep in mind different social contexts of the three cases, which have a bearing both on the number of parties and the nature of the party systems.

The German Basic Law (constitution) makes explicit mention of the constitutional and political role of political parties (Article 21) in German polity. It also makes a provision for the federal government to enact laws for the parties to adhere to constitutional objectives. Thus, unlike in India, political parties in Germany find their legitimacy from the constitution and have to adhere to the norms set by the Basic Law, and the Federal Constitutional Court, not the executive, rules on the question of unconstitutionality of parties by determining whether they 'seek to undermine or abolish the free democratic basic order or to endanger the existence of the Federal Republic of Germany'.[40] Yet, the Federal Republic has been referred to as a 'party state', at times even skeptically implying too much influence of parties in German political life.[41]

Thus, Article 21 and the Political Party Act of 1967 provide an explicit legal context for the shaping of the party system in Germany. On the one hand, Article 21 led to the banning of two parties in 1952 and 1956 and, on the other, the 5 per cent rule (or three consecutive mandates) has restricted the proliferation of parties.[42] Interestingly, akin to the process Arora has suggested as emerging bi-nodality in the Indian party system, 'the transformation of the two largest parties, the combined CDU-CSU and the SPD, into "catch-all parties" (*Volksparteien*), enabling them to appeal to voters beyond the confines of their traditional church-related or working-class environments' led to a reduction in the numbers of the German parties.

The reunification did not have any major impact on the German party system and the broad framework of the party system so far remains fundamentally

---

[40] Political parties in India find a place in the constitutional system indirectly through the People's Representation Act, Anti-Defection Act and rules laid down by the Election Commission of India. Considering the fact that the need has been felt from time to time to ban political organisations or ultra-left parties, which is currently done through an executive order, a place in the Constitution for an institution that plays a constitutional role is worth visualising. The German Basic Law can provide us with a model.

[41] Dieter C. Umbach, '50 Years of German Basic Law: Roots, Experience, Import', in Subhash C. Kashyap, D.D. Khanna, Gert W. Kueck, (eds), *Reviewing the Constitution*, New Delhi: Shipra, 2000, p. 230.

[42] The 5 per cent rule has been recommended by some experts for India too. However, others advise caution referring to fallacy of designs, as social diversity in India would militate against such a rule. See Yogendra Yadav, 'Which Reforms? Whose Democracy? A Plea for Democratic Agenda of Electoral Reforms', in Kashyap et al. (eds), *Reviewing the Constitution*, pp. 296–317.

unchanged. However, voter dissatisfaction leading to loss of votes to major parties and a decrease in partisan identification of the German electorate from 80 per cent to 50 per cent are some of the features of the German party system today.

Korte's brief account of the emerging party system in the EU presents some insights to (con)federalisation of the party system in an emerging confederation based on economic rather than political or social interests. Federalisation of parties within the European Parliament is taking place along transnational lines. Naturally, Social Democrats, Christian Democrats, Liberal Democrats and the Greens, who have a presence in most member countries, have emerged as important players in the political systems of the EU. However, what could cause discontinuity in the party politics of the EU is the level at which the parties operate—the EU, national, regional—as in each of these theatres party competition may take different forms. As the EU is taking more definite shape and gaining roots, the parties too seem to be defining their new role and the party system is taking shape in the process. Korte's conjecture is that '(t)he development of *Volksparteien* (the party system) in a largely de-ideologised environment is on the cards. Party profile will no longer be determined by the ideological leanings of the party leadership but rather by the socio-economic interests and political and cultural aspirations of its voters.'

Despite its size and variety, the Indian case cannot be easily compared with a multi-nation organisation like the EU. However, the convergence to established party structures in a de-ideologised environment could be an important level of comparison for two extremely dissimilar situations. Second, it would also be worthwhile to look at the functioning of parties at different theatres with theatre-specific interests, interacting with and representing theatre-specific interest groups. This indeed creates a new agenda for research and enquiry for the theorists of party sytems.

Socio-economic Bases

The analysis of polling data and voting patterns between the 1996, 1998 and 1999 elections clearly shows a decline in support for the Congress, which according to Balveer Arora is one of the two nodes of the emerging bi-nodal party system in the country. More than an expansion for the BJP, the other node of the bi-nodal system, according to Amit Prakash, the decline is 'partially a product of its alliance with a wide range of regional and socio-cultural parties in the 1998 and 1999 elections'. The data clearly indicates 'a greater voter preference for regionally based socio-culturally located parties with mobilisation base in a distinct economic grouping in the society'. The alliances also helped the BJP to create and expand its rural support base. Larger urban support base for the BJP also meant a larger support base for the party amongst the educated middle class. However, the 1998 elections witnessed a swell in support for the BJP amongst the illiterate voters as well. On the other hand, the INC was not able to increase its vote share across any of the educational category, as it was unable to offer anything to counter the cultural nationalism plank of the BJP.

During these three elections the stereotype of the BJP as an urban-based middle class and traders' party also seemed to break down, when no occupational interlinkages with political support could be witnessed. The analysis of the relative electoral support bases of political parties demonstrates that the support base of all political parties, including the national parties is fluid and prone to changes along the lines of socio-cultural and economic fractures in the society.

Both Balveer Arora and Amit Prakash emphasise the point that during the half-century since independence not only has the one party dominance declined, but regional socio-cultural or economic interests have been asserting themselves and carving out a political space for themselves. Important in this context have been the strategies of political parties to increase their support base. Amit's conclusions have processual, if not theoretical, linkages with what Korte has described for the EU. The emergence of the regional parties is a reflection of the assertion of 'smaller' communities and their demand for 'political recognition and at times, autonomy, by mobilising on India's electoral scene. The social support for these demands is expressed in the form of rising electoral support for regional socio-cultural political parties and the decline of support for national parties.' However, the process of federalisation is a reflection of the desire to establish links with the national theatre.

Arguing in a similar vein and supporting the arguments of Amit, Pran Chopra does not see any problem with a number of parties as long as they do not fragment the voters. This trend he perceives as a nexus between the results of elections and the socio-political reality surrounding them. The growing number of parties representing India's socio-political (even economic) reality, have found their answers in coalition politics, or what Arora calls federalisation; its managerial dimension, according to Chopra, is in reviewing 'the systems we have for electing legislatures and governments'. Succinctly, he blames bigger parties for instability rather than smaller parties.

Party Structures and Institutional Framework

Two kinds of concerns have emerged over the past decade-and-a-half over party structures and institutional frameworks supporting them. The first set of concerns deal with organisational dimensions of political parties and the institutional framework supporting them. The second set of concerns emerges from interventions, or lack of them, from the civil society.

We have noted the changing contour of political participation and its impact on the party system in terms of 'fragmentation' and 'federalisation' which sound paradoxical, but have progressed *pari passu*, indicating a dynamism in Indian society, polity and democracy. As the centre stage of Indian politics becomes more competitive with a larger number of claimants and actors having different aspirations and expectations from the state and the wielding of political power, the rules of the political game get redefined, sometimes with a no-holds-barred attitude, resulting in distortions. The discussion on the German party system highlights the merits of a constitutionally defined role for political parties which play the central role in representing popular will. A whole range of reforms have been discussed in official as well as public fora.

Madhav Godbole presents a comprehensive review of issues and suggestions. He sees merit in incorporating 'a proper and sustainable framework' for political parties in the Constitution on the lines of Article 21 of the German Basic Law. Considering the proliferation of political parties with the disintegration and degeneration of the Congress as a mega-coalition, or a catch-all party and the failure of any other party to rise to that status, he underlines the need for 'a proper Constitutional and legislative framework' to deal with emerging distortions both in the electoral framework and the organisational framework of the parties. Indeed, the rising cost of elections, the use of black money and muscle power, utter disregard amongst political parties, leaders and candidates for the rule of law, criminalisation of politics and politicisation of crime, increasing number of candidates and elected representatives with alleged criminal antecedents, etc., have had a corrosive influence on Indian democracy, polity and society. Detailed analyses and suggestions by Godbole deserve a prime place in the discourse on the Indian party system.

Focusing on the dilemmas of the liberal state and the civil society in coming to terms with imperatives of power politics and civilised social ethos, S.K. Chaube succinctly brings out the increasing disjuncture between the two. Since political parties form an important link between the two, representing citizens and the civil society in the portals of power; not only exercising political power on behalf of the civil society, but also acting as the countervailing force when the state uses the power against the society it draws its power and legitimacy from Civil Society in a democracy. However, when attainment, retention and wielding of political power become the sole aim, parties end up tampering with societal balance and civilisational values to the detriment of the cohesion that civil society stands for. In such a case, not only a party, but also the state turns sectarian, directing its political force as well as legitimised state power against a section of the civil society. Chaube's incisive analysis and candid formulations, derived from political theory and current political developments in the country, expose the ideological hollowness pervading the Indian party system. Indeed, the need for political reforms running through the arguments of most contributors gets further buttressed by Chaube's analysis.

The National Parties

Balveer Arora's thesis of a 'bi-nodal' party system emerging in India, as coalitions are gradually coming of age in the country, indeed has its validity. However, that does not undermine aspirations of each of the two nodes—the Congress and the BJP—to capture political power on its own. While the Congress, despite all the limitations, has pushed itself into difficulties during the past couple of decades in spite of being in power for 15 years and an ally of the ruling coalition for two-and-a-half years during this period, aspires to return to power on its own, as so far it has spurned the suggestions of entering into coalitional arrangements, the BJP, having fulfilled its immediate objective of ascending to power in New Delhi through coalition politics, is striving hard to create its own countrywide independent constituency.

The Hindi heartland, consisting of nine Hindi-speaking states—Bihar, Chhattisgarh, Haryana, Himachal Pradesh, Jharkhand, Madhya Pradesh, Rajasthan, Uttaranchal and Uttar Pradesh—has traditionally played a crucial role in the electoral battle for New Delhi. Partha S. Ghosh takes a critical look at this crucial struggle for the heartland between the Congress and the BJP. In his own style of comprehensive empirical data-based analysis of historical facts and electoral performance, Ghosh sharply brings out the complexities of battle at the hustings in India's civilisational society. It was perhaps easier for the Congress to garner a complex of social support due to its epochal role in the nationalist movement and pan-Indian organisation for the first couple of decades after independence. However, as organisational decay set in due to the imperatives of power and all the towering leaders were removed with the tide of time by the mid-1960s, the going got tough. The challenges by then were not merely from the secularist or socialist outfits coming out of it, but also from the Hindu nationalist BJS which got only more intense as democracy took deeper roots. Ghosh clearly brings out the challenges that forced the Congress to trip from the razor-edge balancing it had done to maintain the support of the Hindu society, including the dalits and minorities—Muslims, Christians and Sikhs. Once it tripped, it created space for the BJP, the reincarnation of the BJS.

The battle is not yet over. For, in order to maintain its hold, the BJP, which has yet to create an unchallenged sway in its favour in the heartland, is sticking to its strategy of consolidating the Hindu vote while making desperate attempts to win minorities too. A difficult task, because it is unable to rein in the lunatic fringe it has unleashed over the past decade, while the leadership too is unable to moderate its 'Hindu nationalism'. The Congress too finds the going tough because parts of its successful social coalition like the Muslims and the dalits have already been wooed by others.

While the battle continues, Ghosh puts a succinct question: whether the heartland would remain the epicentre of power in the near future. Coalition politics has given crucial space to the southern states at the Centre. Since the west and the south are at the centre of economic development too, they may dictate terms in the future.

The 'bi-nodal' thesis of the emerging party system advanced by Balveer Arora appears to attach low significance to the idea of the Third Front. Indeed, in the race for power in New Delhi a centrist secular alternative to the Congress has seemingly run itself out of the reckoning; having emerged as the first alternative to the Congress on two occasions, it is now looking at the 'third' space. The chapters by Bidyut Chakrabarty and Muchkund Dubey critically examine the phenomenon that emerged as a non-Congress coalition in the aftermath of the Emergency in 1977 under the banner of the Janata Party and became a victim of uninhibited soaring individual ambitions in 18 months and disintegrated within two years to offer back the space to the Congress on a silver platter. Its next opportunity came in 1989, again not as the Third Front, but as the second largest party in the Lok Sabha. The JD under the leadership of V.P. Singh met with the same fate in less than one year. It was back in power in 1996 for two years, this time as the Third Front because the BJP had emerged as the single largest party with 161 seats, followed by the Congress with 140 seats. While Janata Dal, the mainstay of the National Front in 1989 with 142 seats, had only 46 seats, the total strength of the United Front was not enough to form a government and it had to seek Congress support, the party it had stood against on two previous occasions. Indeed, the Front did not witness any major internal feud during its two-year stay in power; the Congress support did not prove stable. However, in the next two elections, in 1998 and 1999, the main constituents of the Front as well as the idea of the Front virtually disintegrated. Not only was the JD literally atomised, many of its leaders joined the BJP-led NDA, so did most of the regional parties supporting the Front.

Mapping the route to this disintegration of the Front, Chakrabarty locates the emergence and politics of the Third Front in the regionalisation of politics, shift in nature of contests from amongst parties to between parties and alliances and the emerging trend of coalition politics. However, the BJP could score over the Front in this strategy too because it could attract allies and leaders with its disciplined organisational core and keep dissidence to the minimum. He rightly concludes that despite its failure, the Third Front remains a potential contender for power at the Centre because as an idea and ideology, i.e., a non-Congress left of the centre alternative, it survives. Though small, the CPM provides organisational core to it without craving for power.

Muchkund Dubey reviews the Third Front, or the Third Force, as he prefers to call it, at the level of ideology. Basically, he attempts to review the ideological initiative of a 'ginger group' called the Initiative for National Renewal and Empowerment of the People (INREP), of which he himself was a member, for preparing a political platform and a minimum programme for a Third Force. Outlining a highly idealistic 'ideology', he concludes that '(a) strong genuine Third Force is not likely to emerge in the near future mainly because of the ills that have afflicted all the political parties, including those which can be expected to constitute the Third Force'.

The Regional Parties

Regionalisation of Indian party politics is a reality. No wonder all the contributions mentioned so far have emphasised it and analysed the Indian party system from that perspective. In fact, regions have always had a significant influence on Indian politics. The importance of regions was not lost to the leaders of the national movement, who at different stages took pains to accommodate regional aspirations and sentiments. This aspect comes out adequately in the chapter on historical development. In putting the discussion in the context of the notion of Indian nationhood, Pradeep Kumar too places the relationship between the region and the nation in terms of historical and socio-cultural processes. We have attempted to examine this relationship in the context of parties and the party systems at three levels. Of course, this is not to suggest that there could not be any other way of looking at it. We have looked at the regional parties from the perspective of the national parties, the regional party systems as they operate in their own political contexts and their approach towards the national parties and, finally, party systems in the small states. In the last category we focus on the northeast, basically due to its own complexities.

Pradeep Kumar has rightly emphasised the historical interlinkages of the Indian nation, as perceived and conceived in Indian thinking and philosophy, with the region, which persisted as India took shape into a nation in the western sense. As the Indian party politics went underway after independence, its importance was not lost despite the 'one party dominant system', because prominent and powerful regional leaders brought regions to the party and the forums of the national government. Even when some of them broke away during 1967–69, they attempted to project an identity of being regional chapters of the larger Congress political culture. Indira Gandhi dismantled the regional identities within the party only at her own peril, though it took nearly two decades for the monolith she had attempted to collapse. In fact, it created a series of problems for the polity that still fester. There was a brief resurgence of regionalism at the national level in 1977. However, regionalism became important from the perspective of national parties between 1989 and 1998. First, V.P. Singh and his National Front depended on regional parties. Then, it took deeper roots during the rule of Narasimha Rao as a countervailing force. The BJP realised the importance of regional parties after waiting in vain for them for 13 days. Their importance reached its peak in 1996–98 and the significance has only been strengthened in the following years.

However, Kumar's analysis shows that the continuing flux in the Indian party systems has made the dichotomy between the national and the regional rather misleading. He rightly says '(n)ot only are the former regional in their support bases, even the latter are sometimes non-regional in their "ideological" or programmatic make-up'. Second, many regional political expressions are 'social' in content and 'regional' only in the electoral catchment area. Finally, the trend of the national parties seeking out the 'regional' will continue, but the nature and shape of coalitions will remain in flux.

Suhas Palshikar's paper situates the regional parties within the broader framework of India's political process. His paper attempts to map the geographical and ideological space occupied by these parties and tries to conjecture about the nature of social support enjoyed by the regional parties. Palshikar's comprehensive, complex, but competent analysis reveals that 'anti-Congressism and a state-specific caste equation combined to produce separate state-level politics in many parts of the country in the post-1990 period. In a sense, the post-Congress polity is witnessing a fundamental contestation over the middle ground.' The resultant churning has put even the 'middle ground' in the process of being redefined, at times many times over. Hence, not only are the regional parties attempting to capture national space, they at times attempt to capture regional space after making their presence felt at the national stage. This not only results in national-regional or regional-national tie ups, it also results in the 'regionalisation of national parties'. That the entire process is linked to increasing democratisation, or the 'second democratic upsurge' in the country, goes without saying. Like Kumar, Palshikar also feels that despite change in the nature of democratic discourse, it is too early to predict the nature of the emerging polity, certainly too early to predict a 'weak Centre'.

Sajal Nag rightly describes party politics in the northeast as a 'contest for marginal space'. However, it is a crucial marginal space. The northeast has unfortunately figured on national politics in a rather negative fashion, though it has not hesitated to link itself to national politics while maintaining its distinctive identity. Assam was prominently into the national movement and it had an active unit of the Indian National Congress. However, the politics of Assam and the region had its own complexity. Naturally, the Congress was historically compelled to regionalism, because it was competing with regional forces. In the process, it not only acted parochially, it gave into parochial forces. The history of the region for the past two-and-a-half decades bears ample testimony to it. However, that must not give the impression that the going has been easy for the regional parties. Lacking in resources, many have at times joined the national parties *en bloc*. The socio-cultural texture and tradition of conflict has made dissension, defection and coalescence (within the region) permanent features of the political process. Of course, the sub-nationalist feelings and politics have made the regional parties important, but the limitations imposed by local socio-cultural factors and the compulsions of the national parties for a presence in the region have also produced national-regional coalitions.

Party Structures and New Challenges

Politics is about meeting 'new' unanticipated challenges all the time. Indeed, whatever we have outlined and discussed so far would be considered as emerging challenges by the parties. However, the challenges emerging out of economic reforms and statutory institutionalisation of local democracies are new to the extent that they impact the party politics in a way they have never done since Indian democracy got institutionalised and stabilised.

The change in state-market relations in the wake of the twin processes of liberalisation and globalisation has also changed the process of political discourse. The Bangalore resolution of the Congress in July 1951 not only created a particular economic structure, it also in course of time became the basis of a political rhetoric which looked at the market rather negatively. The same Congress Party had to dismantle that structure in 1991. However, the Chennai declaration of the BJP (27–29 December 1999), by deploring the 'phenomenal expansion of the state and commits the party to new market-orientation by converting the state', controller to facilitator. The party system is adapting itself to the new reality of the state's 'retreat' from vast areas of public endeavour, as old issues and rhetoric are giving way to new, despite the fact that new constituencies have not obliterated the old ones. Harish Khare captures this political tension between democracy and the market faced by the party system in India.

Sandeep Shastri explores another fascinating new challenge that is emerging for the party system in India—the local self-government. The history of the party system–local self-government interface in India is curious. Though the party system gained roots through participation of the leaders of the nationalist movement in urban local bodies, most of them were not in favour of according constitutional status to local self-government, particularly in the rural context. Naturally, not only did the Panchayati Raj have a chequered history, urban bodies too suffered. Parties and leaders neither at the national, nor at the state levels were favourably inclined to the Panchayati Raj Institutions (PRIs). Not surprisingly, when the constitutionally sanctioned PRIs began to be institutionalised, people showed greater faith in the PRIs than in the parties. Political parties, according to Shastri, have not been able to take advantage of the empowerment of the local level. Whether this empowerment would force any change on the 'culture of centralisation' in the party system, remains to be seen.

Future Trends

Can we speculate future trends in the party system in India depending on analyses in the forgoing chapters? The framework based on the change in the core structure of the party system suggested by Gordon Smith guides us in putting the discussion in perspective. Smith has used four parameters— temporary fluctuations, restricted change, general change and transformation—to determine the change in the 'core structure' of party systems. While 'temporary fluctuations' refer to short term variation in support bases, etc., transformation involves radical changes in the core structure of the party system. Smith did not clarify the crucial difference between 'restricted change' and 'general change'. However, his description of the stable vote share of the Social Democrats in Denmark despite being out of the government during the 1980s as 'restricted change', indicates what he means by the term. Obviously, 'general change' is change short of transformation.[43]

The analyses presented in the volume appear to create a little confusion on this parameter. For, while the first change does not capture the extent of power shift in Indian politics and the party system, the last two indicate a degree of change, which is quite far reaching. In reality, despite unseating of the Congress from the portal of power at the Centre and several States, transformation of the 'core structure' of the party systems in India has not taken place. What, actually has happened is that the essential party system has undergone temporary fluctuations. There are changes in the support bases of 'historic parties', an increase in factionalism in the established parties, an increase in the number of splinter parties, an increase in the number of 'relevant parties', and so on. It may, therefore, be appropriate to conclude that there has only been a 'restricted change' in the party systems in India.

The chapters in the volume in any case indicate unmistakable and distinct changes not only in the party system, but also in the electoral behaviour. The impact of these changes on the Indian polity too is indelible, changes that can only be outstripped by significant changes of greater far reaching consequence, but cannot be written off. Two notable changes impacting the party system and the polity are 'upsurge from below' and the processes of 'federalisation' in the party politics. The do not only indicate a power shift,

---

[43] Gordon Smith, 'Core Persistence: Systems Change and the "People's Party"', *West European Politics*, 12(4) pp. 157–68.

but also assertions of a federal society over a centralised polity. The party system is indeed responding to these changes, will the polity and political institutions also respond? Further, whether these changes are just 'unfreezing and thaw', or they are precursors to a 'general change' leading to a 'transformation', deserves more debate in the light of facts and analysis presented by contributors to this volume. I am sure; the volume will succeed in its modest objective of sparking this debate.

2

HISTORICAL DEVELOPMENT OF
THE PARTY SYSTEMS IN INDIA

Ajay K. Mehra

Theoretical studies on modern party systems, because of their Eurocentric focus, do not enlighten us sufficiently regarding the evolution of political parties and party systems in post-colonial societies. Neither the theories attributing emergence and growth of political parties to aristocratic cliques, plebiscitarian democracy and the initiation of mass politics, nor the ones linking it to parliamentary politics, adequately explain the factors that led to the sprouting of parties and party systems in post-colonial societies. In fact, Eurocentric theories also do not shed sufficient light on the various stresses and strains on the party system in such societies. For, due to society-specific peculiarities, anti-colonial movements did not follow similar routes in all cases. Their impact on colonial rule, as well as their responses to repression and political moves by the colonial rulers varied due to local situations as well as the strength of the leadership and the extent of mass participation in the movement. Equally important in sustaining the party system in these societies was social resilience to the emerging political scenario, which was at variance with the traditional primordial form of political institutions and their style of governance. Political parties could sustain themselves and evolve into a well-knit system only where primordial social institutions could transcend organisational and deep-rooted social cleavages, adapt to modern democratic politics and create sustainable political institutions. In societies where traditional village economy was transformed due to the impact of colonialism, a sustainable fusion of traditional social realm into modern political forms and institutions proved crucial in the long run for creating a dynamic and robust party system.

In India, for example, transformation of the self-sufficient village economy with the impact of colonialism, which introduced capitalism in the feudal economy of India, resulted in the economic unification of India, something which had not taken place ever before.[1] Consequently, the mass social awakening that eventually crystallised into the framework of a party system was initiated by the twin factors of socio-religious reforms and political reaction to colonialism. The factors may vary from one local context to another, however, a combination of the spread of western liberal ideas among the emerging middle-class urban intelligentsia, the indigenous reaction against prevailing social evils and consequent reform movements combined with the emerging culture of protest against the exploitative colonial regime culminating in demands for greater space (social, political and economic) within the existing colonial institutional structure, and popular participation and representation, set in motion political events that not only fuelled anti-colonial nationalist movements, but also sowed the seeds of evolution of party systems in these countries. The events, reform movements, the demands for representation of Indians in civil service and decision-making bodies as well as protests against the policies of the colonial government at various stages were led by powerful, committed and self-less leaders. Obviously, the emergence of committed leadership at different stages of the reform, protest and anti-colonial movements played a crucial role in the emergence of democratic political culture that not only led to the emergence of a party system in the country, but also to its sustenance and institutionalisation in the critical years after decolonisation.

In the Indian context, 28 December 1885, the day 72 gentlemen, representing 27 districts (out of 250) of British India met in the hall of the Gokuldas Tejpal Sanskrit College and Boarding House in Bombay (now Mumbai) to attend the inaugural session of what was originally called the Indian National Union (INU), can easily be identified as the day when not merely a political party, but a composite party system, took birth in the country.[2] Later renamed as the INC, it first became synonymous with the Indian national movement and later with the party system in the country. The founding of the INC deserves to be regarded as the birth of a party system in India because it set in motion processes that, on the one hand, were signal to a number of ideas to bloom, on the other hand, in the process of its evolution and growth, rules of

---

[1] A.R. Desai observes that the growth of capitalism during the British period 'destroyed the village self-sufficient economy and made village economy an integral part of a single unified Indian economy. It was this economic unification of India which became the objective material basis for the steady amalgamation of the disunited Indian people into a unified nation, for the growth of national sentiment and consciousness among them and for the rise and development of an all-India national movement for their political freedom, and social and cultural progress.' A.R. Desai, *Social Background of Indian Nationalism*, Bombay: Popular Prakashan, 1976 (fifth edition), p. 36.

[2] See N.R. Ray, Ravinder Kumar and M.N. Das, *Concise History of the Indian National Congress, 1885–1947*, issued under the auspices of the Congress Centenary (1985) Celebration Committee, New Delhi: Vikas Publishing House Pvt. Ltd., 1985.

political mobilisation and competition were written. Throughout this process, it remained the pivot on which the party system hinged before and after independence; of course, the context and processes differed in the two respective periods.

Though the founding of the INC was the most important benchmark in the evolution of political parties and the party system in India; it would be unfair to the reform movements that emerged during the 19th century in different parts of the country that created a spirit of association as well as social transformation in the country and mobilised the masses, if their contribution is not recognised in this important political development. In fact, even though the objectives and purposes of many of the reform movements and social organisations would hardly be in conformity with what the Congress professed to stand for in later years, the INC has accepted these movements as precursors to the founding of the party in its official chronicle, the five-volume centenary history of the organisation released in 1985.[3]

As stated earlier, both the 19th century reform movements and the INC were guided in their endeavour by important leaders. In fact, each initiative was a result of the crusading zeal of either an individual leader, or a group of them, who were dissatisfied with the existing state of affairs, or decay in social or political affairs. They took upon themselves the responsibility of campaigning for reform, or civic rights. Not surprisingly, the growth, strategising, success and failure, of the movements as well the organisations promoted for the purpose, were dependent upon these leaders at different stages of their development. Constraint of space does not permit a detailed analysis of their contribution separately in this essay. We would, therefore, evaluate the contributions made by these leaders in the evolution and growth of the party system in the country along with those of the movements.

The Early Stirrings

The emergence and growth of political parties in India is obviously related to the rise of nationalism in the country. However, the rise of nationalism in India was preceded by a fairly long period of gestation which witnessed the evolution of national consciousness in India. The stirrings visible in Indian society in the early decades of the 19th century, that is, even before the rule of the East India Company ended following the revolt of 1857 and the reins of power were formally taken over by Queen-in-Parliament in 1858, were precipitated only partly by British imperialism; they were largely the result of the existing social conditions. However, it is equally important that for over almost five decades after Warren Hastings selected Calcutta (now Kolkata)

---

[3] See B.N. Pande (general editor), *A Centenary History of the Indian National Congress*, in five volumes, New Delhi: All India Congress Committee (I) and Vikas Publishing House, 1985.

as capital of British India in 1773, 'a congenial atmosphere had been created for the diffusion of ideas from Europe, along with an institutional structure and technological means to facilitate Indian accommodation to modern thought from the West'.[4] Raja Ram Mohun Roy and his group had virtually laid the foundation for western education by supporting Macaulay and his compeers. He submitted a memorandum to the governor general in 1823 urging the government to 'promote a more liberal and enlightened system of instruction, embracing mathematics, natural philosophy, chemistry, anatomy, with other useful sciences'.[5] However, the net impact of this development was that stirrings were visible in the social arena, which witnessed the sprouting of educational institutions using European methods of instruction and textbooks as well as associations preaching and motivating initiatives for social reforms.[6] Politically, the stirrings found expression in rebellion against economic exploitation, and the East India Company had to employ considerable effort to suppress them.[7]

No wonder, Anil Seal does not regard the nationalist movements in India as the creation of imperialism, which however, did sharpen the conditions for their growth. According to Seal, the sprouting and mushrooming of Indian nationalism in the early 19th century was crucial for its growth as a stubborn tree later. In fact, the 1870s and 1880s were crucial due to the 'beginnings of a mutation in Indian politics which was to convert many of the western-educated from collaborators into critics of the regime'. Yet, during the 1880s they were groping for some form of all-India organisation, as their haggling for demands with the colonial administration was edging quite a few of them towards detachment from the British purposes. In studying this phenomenon,

---

[4] David Kopf, 'Precursors of the Indian National Congress', in Paul R. Brass and Francis Robinson (eds), *Indian National Congress and Indian Society, 1885–1985: Ideology, Social Structure, and Political Dominance*, Delhi: Chanakya Publications, 1987, p. 63.

[5] The Liberal school in Indian politics, which evolved later, followed the Raja's attitude in idealising western education. However, other nationalist groups (Pal, Ghose, Gandhi and others) criticised this attitude later for depreciating Indian culture. Desai, *Social Background of Indian Nationalism*, p. 146.

[6] Lord Bentinck, the governor general of India, endorsed this education policy and in 1835 the government's resolution stated that 'the great object of the British Government ought to be the promotion of European literature and science among natives of India, and that all the funds appropriated for the purpose of education would be best employed on English education alone ...', and further, 'that all the funds be henceforth employed in imparting to the native population a knowledge of English literature and sciences through the medium of the English language'. Ibid., p. 147.

[7] For example, the Sanyasi rebellion in Bengal, the Wahabi and Faraizi movements in northern India (crushed in the 1870s), the Moplah uprising in the south (1849–55), the Santhal rebellion in Chhotanagpur (1855–56), and the Indigo agitation (1859–60), each had politico-economic content. Amitabha Mukherjee, 'Genesis of the Indian National Congress', in N.R. Ray (ed.), *A Centenary History of the Indian National Congress, 1885–1919*, Vol. I, Delhi: Indian National Congress and Vikas Publishing House Pvt. Ltd., 1985, p. 81.

Seal begins from associations initiated by the western-educated intelligentsia concentrated in the Presidencies and he emphasises that these 'new
educated classes must be related to the religious, the caste, the linguistic and
the economic situations in which they lived'. He also analyses the 'multifarious systems of local politics ... from the point when they turned to the technique of association until they achieved a nominal all-India unity'.[8]

Expectedly, the social stirrings began in Presidency capitals—Calcutta,
Bombay and Madras (now Chennai). The citizens of these colonial cities were
first exposed to western education and life style.[9] The exposure, particularly
to western education, had given a new rationale and idiom to the traditional
zeal for association and social awareness. The founding of the Young Bengal by students of Hindu College (founded in 1817) in 1828, who, aside from
discussing free-will, fate, truth, virtue and idolatry, mocked at orthodox Hindu
practices was beginning of a new awakening. Inspired by Henry Derozio
and David Hare, while they mistook externalities of western civilisation as
modernisation, they also demanded free and compulsory education for all.
The alumni of Hindu College produced half-a-dozen journals between 1828
and 1943.[10] Despite its skewed perception of modernity, the movement created
a national awakening of sorts.

A decade later the Society for the Acquisition of General Knowledge was
formed, which enlisted 200 eminent members within five years, many of
whom became leading lights of the Bengal politics of that era. The Society
did considerable original research on statistical and historical surveys of
India. It also developed an association with the British India Society, which
had its headquarters in London. In 1843, its member George Thomson visited India. The objective of the Society was 'the collection and dissemination
of information relating to the actual condition of the people of British India
and the laws and institutions and resources of the country, and to employ
such other means of a peaceable and lawful character, to secure the welfare,
and extend the interests of all classes of our fellow subjects'.[11] Though the

---

[8] Anil Seal, *The Emergence of Indian Nationalism: Competition and Collaboration in the Later
Nineteenth Century*, Cambridge: Cambridge University Press, 1971, pp. 22–24.
[9] In Bombay there were supporters of vernaculars as the medium of instruction on the
Board of Education—Framjee Cawasjee, M. I. Mackba and Jagannath Shankarseth. A
positive impact of Shankerseth's forceful argument that 'the vernacular languages possess advantages superior to English' was that though English as the exclusive medium of
instruction was adopted at the collegiate stage, the use of the vernaculars was retained at
the secondary stage. The impact of this policy in downward filtration of modern ideas
cannot be underestimated. For a detailed discussion on the role of modern education in
shaping Indian nationalist ideas and by default creating conditions for the evolution of the
party system, see Desai, *Social Background of Indian Nationalism*, pp. 135–65.
[10] Seal, *The Emergence of Indian Nationalism*, pp. 195–96.
[11] Quoted by Kopf, 'Precursors of the Indian National Congress', pp. 65–66.

lessons learnt from the interaction with the British India Society were limited to raising political consciousness and the value of constitutional agitation, it did create preconditions that helped later political activity, including the Indian National Congress.

The establishment of the Brahmo Sabha in 1829 by Raja Ram Mohun Roy with the help of Dwarkanath Tagore proved a pioneering effort. The Tatvabodhini Sabha was organised in 1839 as an educational club by Debendranath Tagore, Dwarkanath's son, to reform as well as defend Hinduism from the 'Christian crusade' of the 1830s. It later attracted several members from the Young India movement. The Brahmo Samaj, established in 1843 was another initiative from Debendranath, which took over both the functions of the Brahmo Sabha and the Tatvabodhini Sabha. It began a trend in the organised assertion of the traditional viewpoint of Indian nationalism that Raja Ram Mohun Roy had initiated. In fact, looking at the number of issues on which the Raja, despite his firm belief in constructive collaboration with the British Raj, protested, petitioned the government and mobilised opinion, he can rightly be called the father of modern political agitation in India.[12] Raja Ram Mohun Roy, for example, was among the leading personalities of Bengal, who along with some 800 petitioners, rose against the abolition of *sati* in 1829 by Lord Bentinck; not because they condoned this inhuman act, but because they viewed it as an interference with the religion and customs of the Hindus.[13]

The establishment of the British Indian Association in 1851 was part of the same trend. While the Brahmo Samaj, despite several schisms within it that led to the proliferation of groups and societies, carried on the task of mass awakening in Bengal, for 25 years the Association championed the rights of Indian subjects of the British empire in the form of grievances submitted to the government in countless petitions.

Even though developments in Bombay were not as rapid and as 'radical' as in Bengal, the founding of the Elphinston Institution in 1827, which was

---

[12] In 1823 Raja Ram Mohun Roy protested against the censorship measures of the government, championing the liberty of the press; in 1827 he petitioned against a racist Jury Act; in 1830 he protested against the resumption by the government of all rent-free tenures; in 1833 (on the eve of the renewal of the East India Company's Charter) he demanded the abolition of the Company's trading rights and the removal of heavy export duties on Indian manufacturers. Appearing before a Parliamentary Committee in England in 1831, he suggested administrative reforms such as Indianisation of the army, introduction of trial by jury, separation of the offices of judge and magistrate, codification of criminal laws and substitution of English for Persian as the language of the law courts. He, thus, laid down the tradition of constitutional public protest in India, which was not only followed for the next couple of decades after his death, but became the mainstay of the politics of the INC against the Raj. Mukherjee, 'Genesis of the Indian National Congress', pp. 82–83.

[13] Kopf, 'Precursors of the Indian National Congress', pp. 63–64.

modelled on Hindu College, began a trend that came to fruition in the establishment of a college in 1834. The Students' Literary and Scientific Society established in 1848 brought together Parsis, Gujaratis and Maharashtrians. *Rast Goftar*, the fortnightly newspaper started in 1851, had a great influence on public opinion in Bombay in later years. These associations and several others influenced many politicians who were in the forefront of political activities in the Bombay Presidency in the 1870s. Dadabhai Naoroji describes the political and social zeal of Bombay citizens during the late 1940s and the first half of the 1950s, covering a whole gamut of areas and social activities, thus:

> The six or seven years before I eventually came to England in 1855 ... were full of all sorts of reforms, social, educational, political, religious, etc.... Female Education, Free Association of Women with Men at public, social and other gatherings, Infant Schools, Students' Literary and Scientific Society, Societies for the Diffusion of Useful Knowledge in the Vernacular, Parsi Reform, Abolition of Child Marriages, Re-marriage of Widows among Hindus, and Parsi Religious Reform Society, were some of the problems tackled, movements set on foot, and institutions inaugurated by a band of young men fresh from college.... Such were the fruits of the English education given at Elphinston College.[14]

The rising political consciousness of the intelligentsia in the three Presidencies by the middle of the 19th century is reflected in the birth of three associations in Calcutta, Bombay and Madras, as the East India Company's charter came up for renewal by the British Parliament in 1853. The three associations that dominated the politics in the Presidencies for the next quarter-of-a-century came into existence to petition Westminster regarding the system of government and improvement in the local administration. The British Indian Association in Bengal (1851) literally took over from the Landholders' Society, which represented the zamindars and the Bengal British India Society, representing upper-middle-class intelligentsia; and attracted members of both the societies. The Bombay Association was founded on 25 August 1852, consisting of the varied population of the city. Beginning as a branch of the British Indian Association, an independent Madras Native Association came into existence in the same year. Each of these associations petitioned the British Parliament seeking improvement in the state of government and representation of Indians in administration.[15]

Even though political consciousness had developed only among a miniscule minority of the citizens in the metropolises leading to a rather limited and subdued level of political activity, these associations as well as their predecessors were indeed precursors to the organised political organisation

---

[14] Quoted by Seal, *The Emergence of Indian Nationalism*, p. 197.
[15] Ibid., pp. 197–202.

and action represented by the Congress. For it was no mean achievement for these associations to demand reform of the Legislative Councils, a greater share of public office for Indians and a deliberative body possessing all the requisites of 'constitutional legislature' during the 1850s, preceding the revolt in 1857. Even soon after the revolt the associations were in search of a forum to give space to the 'voice of the people ... their views, their wishes, and their wants'. Indeed, the quest continued throughout the 1860s, leading to greater organisation amongst them.

The urge for associations and organisations grew along with the educated middle class during the 1870s. Though many of the societies established during the decade were short-lived, they proliferated in a wide variety of areas and activities. In fact, a government report on the Bengal administration in 1876 could see the linkage between the proliferating societies and education:

> Another result of education has been the formation of societies and associations, greater and lesser, in all parts of the country; they are about 60 in number, and they have about 2,000 members in all. Their chief objects are somewhat undefined perhaps, but pertain chiefly to educational and social matters, relating to political affairs only in representing to the British authorities the wishes and interests of the people ... they indicate a stir of thought and movement in the national mind.[16]

Obviously, most of these were bunched in Bengal. Yet, they created a consciousness of coming together for communitarian activities, which significantly spilled over into the low voltage political activity of 'representing to the British authorities the wishes and interests of the people'. In fact, as the relations between the ryots and zamindars worsened, both sides showed a proclivity to agitate, which was a significant development of a mindset that led to organised political activity. The emergence of rival associations to the British Indian Association meant that people were gearing up even to get into the oppositional mode, particularly as the associations claimed to go beyond the middle classes 'to the masses also; to "stimulate the sense of nationalism among the people"; and to encourage political education'.[17] Thus, when the Indian League was superseded by the Indian Association, younger, well-educated citizens of the Bengal Presidency found political space. Indeed, some of the members of the British Indian Association also found a place in its executive committee. The impact of these activities became visible in growing inter-religious empathy. However, one of the most significant developments during the decade, which drew the students into organised political activity, was the formation of the students' association in 1875.[18] The

---

[16] Quoted in ibid., p. 205.
[17] Ibid., pp. 210–13.
[18] Ibid., pp. 214–17.

Indian Association moved beyond Calcutta as the decade was coming to a close. First, it appealed to district towns to join the Association and expanded its agenda to local self-government in towns. Second, it took a daring step in including in its programme the issue of peasant rights. In fact, this was the main issue that caused a breach with the British Indian Association.[19]

The formation of associations displayed the will and determination to come together for common objectives. The proliferation of associations in Presidency towns clearly meant that citizens as well as the associations were also prepared to get into the opposition mode, a mindset which was important not only for the evolution and growth of the party system, but also for the gradual sprouting of anti-colonial sentiments. However, it was the growth of the 'politics of union' simultaneously with the 'politics of associations' that played a crucial role in initially organising a party structure in India. It began with the idea 'that Indians should take up a common political stance'. No wonder, from its inception in 1851 the British Indian Association made efforts to enlist the support of influential sections of Madras and Bombay with the belief that a concerted action from across the country had a greater chance of getting their demands conceded and it met with reasonable success as well.[20] Between then and 1884, when the Indian Union, an organisation consisting mainly of Hindu lawyers but containing a few Muslims, was formed in Calcutta, several efforts were made in all the three Presidencies to draw together various organisations and streams of politics. By 1885 the Madras Presidency had nearly 100 local associations. The Indian Association in the Bengal Presidency controlled some 80 branches by 1885. Thus, the second National Conference in 1885 in Calcutta (said to be the inspiration behind the National Congress in Bombay) as well as the first Indian National Congress in Bombay were the results of the joint efforts of the Indians, the British Indian and the National Mahommedan Associations.[21] It is equally important to record here that when the Indian nationalists lobbied with Robert Osborne, an English Member of Parliament, to present Indian aspirations in the British Parliament, he gave two advices in a letter to Pherozeshah Mehta on 18 April 1884. First, the Indian case must first be presented in India, and second, it must be articulated in unison. He said:

> If you succeed in establishing a permanent organisation, the first thing you ought to do is to draw up a programme of political reform, and if possible, obtain for this programme the approval of the educated classes in all three Presidencies. This, I apprehend, might be easily done through the various associations. Nothing would more strengthen the hands of your friends in

---

[19] Ibid., pp. 221–22.
[20] Ibid., p. 245.
[21] Ibid., pp. 252–64.

this country than to have some authoritative statement which would show
to all the world exactly what the people of India want ... to set the constituencies in motion will not be difficult, as soon as they know for certain what the
people of India wish for.[22]

The impact of this advice on the leading Indians in the three Presidencies cannot
be underestimated. Indeed, the activities of associations and the intelligentsia behind their activities during the closing years of the 1880s concretised
the foundation of the party system laid in the country by earlier associations.

The decade of the 1880s was important from another point of view. The
social reform movements, and their successor nationalist movements of a
more focused, aggressive and militant variety, are important as anti-colonial
platforms and organisational bases for the party system in a nascent nation;
their maturity, however, emerges from the participation of the leaders and the
intelligentsia in governance. Thus, when Ripon endorsed on 30 April 1881
the suggestion of the Finance Department to encourage 'the independence and
real self-government of municipalities, and to restrict direct administrative
interference ... as much as possible', he had unwittingly set in motion a
process of giving concrete basis to the foundation of the party system in
India.[23] As evident from autobiographies of several leaders of the national
movement, the urban local self-government bodies indeed were nurseries
that nurtured and refined their political and governance skills.[24] The foundation got firmer as the Indian intelligentsia got the opportunity to participate
in provincial councils in later decades. These may appear to be unconnected
events, but if coming together to organise associations, institutionalising
them on sustainable organisational principles, turning them into instruments of political recruitment and mobilisation, petitioning and negotiating
with a powerful colonial government, were initial exercises of modern politics, entering into the portals of government, even if through local self-government,
was indeed the beginning of the modern political process that leads to the
organisation of modern political parties and party systems.

The contribution of both the forms of socio-political activity cannot be
underestimated in the growth of later nationalism that shaped the historic
Indian National Congress and other forms of political protests in colonial
India. In fact, the model for the meeting in December 1885 in Bombay that
laid the foundation of the Indian National Congress was provided by the

[22] Quoted in Ibid., pp. 262–63.
[23] He was convinced that if municipalities and district boards were 'to be of any use for the
purpose of training the natives to manage their own affairs, they must not be overshadowed by the constant presence of the *Burra Sahib*'. Ibid., p. 154.
[24] For a discussion on this aspect of urban local bodies, see Ajay K. Mehra, *The Politics of
Urban Redevelopment: A Study of Old Delhi*, New Delhi: Sage Publications, 1991.

National Conference organised by the Indian Association in Calcutta from 28 to 30 December 1883. As Kopf rightly points out, 'Before the Congress, the Indian Association carried constitutionalism to its highest point. Their reformist role was a crucial contribution to the political process in modern India. Not nationalism, but the parliamentary system, I would argue, or representation and the accommodation of conflicting interest, was India's legacy from the liberals.'[25]

Anil Seal concurs that the associations of the 19th century were indeed precursors of modern politics in India, for they created the superstructure for party system in the country:

> Associations brought nineteenth-century India across the threshold of modern politics. Sometimes religious zeal, some times caste solidarity encouraged the propensity towards associations, but during the course of the century more of the associations in India were brought into being by groups of men united by secular interests. What now held them together were common skills and functions, a common education, and common aspirations and resentments against the policies of the Raj, not simply the bonds of joint family, caste and district. There was a time when these would have been the only points of union; but now that this was no longer so, Indians were converging on modern politics.[26]

And, the studies by Seal and Kopf clearly show that not merely their political interactions with the British, but also the interactions amongst themselves gave modern associations and modern politics an impetus.

The Indian National Congress

While existing and new associations[27] as well as social reform movements and nationalist movements during the early 19th century provided political background for the emergence of the party system in India, till the founding of the INC there was no organisational axis for party building. Though few will challenge the centrality of the Congress in the emergence of the party system in India, it is necessary to clarify at the outset of this discussion, that INC's pivotal position is being taken up here not only to highlight its own

---

[25] Kopf, 'Precursors of the Indian National Congress', p. 74.
We would like to underline 'the parliamentary system ... or representation and the accommodation of conflicting interest' in this observation by Kopf as crucial to the emergence of the party system.
[26] Seal, *The Emergence of the Indian National Congress*, p. 194.
[27] The role of associations in the reform movements that sprouted during the early 19th century, discussed in the previous section of this essay, has been highlighted and acknowledged in the official history of the Congress as well. See Ray et al., *Concise History of the Indian National Congress*, n. 2, p. 15.

role in the freedom movement, or for that matter in participation in the government during the colonial rule and for two decades in the post-independence period, but also in creating a basis for a multi-party system in the country. For one, the Congress itself was an umbrella party, encompassing within itself a number of strands, for another, its politics and policies too spawned several other movements and parties. The Muslim League was the most prominent among them. Further, the Congress itself emerged as a composite party system in the way it handled its own internal matters as well as the nationalist movement and negotiations with the British government.

The first session of the Indian National Union that later came to be known as the Indian National Congress was indeed a historic moment. What circumstances led to the convening of this historic session and which individuals and associations were instrumental in it are important historical events. Aside from the prominent associations in the three Presidencies, some other organisations and individuals played an important role in concretising the formation of the Indian National Congress. The Theosophical Society, founded in 1875 by the spiritualist Madame Blavatsky and Colonel Olcott, a veteran of the American Civil War, won many supporters in India when it reached the country in 1879. The society's Anglo-Indian branch was organised in Simla with Allan Octavian Hume as its president, which created hope of European support for Indian aspirations. Though some Theosophists claim it to be the precursor of the Indian National Congress, accounts of Annie Besant and Bipin Chandra Pal suggest that annual conventions of the Theosophists encouraged some Indian leaders to attempt an Indian political Congress. Hume's own experiences with and organisational failures in the Society played a crucial role in his efforts to organise the first Indian National Congress.[28]

The closing months of 1885, in fact, proved quite crucial for the founding of the Congress and institutionalisation of party system in the country because more than one conclave was being held in different parts of the country. In his speech to the second national conference of the Indian Association in Calcutta in December 1885, Surendranath Banerjea appropriately summed up the spirit, 'Indeed all India seems at the present moment to have met in solemn conclave to think out the great problem of national advancement'.[29] However, the organising of the various conventions also reflected the beginning of party politics. Surendranath Banerjea, for example, who was among the most prominent figures in the politics of associations as well as in articulating the desires and demands of the educated Indians, was deliberately kept out of the plans for the National Congress to be organised in Bombay because some people disliked him for a variety of reasons. Consequently, the

[28] Seal, *The Emergence of the Indian National Congress*, pp. 250–52.
[29] Quoted in ibid., p. 266.

Congress was attended only by three Calcuttans. It is a different matter that these issues were resolved by the time the second Congress was held in Calcutta the next year and the Indian Association merged with the Indian National Congress.[30] Anil Seal aptly sums up the political dynamics:

> The National Congress and the National Conference were organised 'on almost the same lines'. Both passed resolutions on the need to reconstitute the Legislative Councils, both demanded simultaneous examinations for the civil service, with a change in the age limit, both called for cuts in civil expenditure and condemned the proposed increase in military charges. Moreover, their plans for their own future were much the same: an annual convention meeting in the main cities of India in rotation. Where there was so much in common, the obvious outcome was union, and in fact in December 1886 the National Conference was to merge with the Congress when the latter met in Calcutta. Neither body was conspicuously stronger than the other, and it was merely the play of personalities and circumstances which decided that the Indian National Congress rather than the National Conference should become the matrix of the later national movement.[31]

Indeed, each of the individuals involved in the politics of associations and each of the associations aspiring for a better deal for the Indians under the colonial rule was responsible for the founding of the INC. Yet, Mr Allan Octavian Hume finds a special mention as the founder of the organisation that became the bedrock of the party system in independent India. Regarded as an able but eccentric civilian, Hume had inherited a bias in favour of India from his father. Having witnessed the 'Mutiny', he was of firm belief that unless the Raj was sympathetic to public opinion and Indian aspirations, it would collapse and he never hesitated to give unsolicited advice to the Viceroy or his civilian colleagues, most of whom did not relish it. After his retirement in 1882, Hume turned his undivided attention to the cause that was dear to him, creating and, if possible, representing a political India. In 1883 Hume appealed to the young men of Bengal to form an 'Indian National Union', which was set up with a number of local committees and planned to hold a conference in Poona (now Pune); the venue was later changed to Bombay. He already had support among the Indian leaders; his stature got a further boost due to Viceroy Lord Ripon's faith in him. After Ripon's departure in December 1884, Hume stayed on in Bombay to raise support for his ideas. In March he was in Calcutta stirring local opinion for the conference. Back in Bombay in July *en route* to England, he again met the Bombay Presidency Association, which was set up in January 1885 by Pherozeshah Mehta,

---

[30] Banerjea wrote later, 'The two Conferences met about the same time, discussed similar views and voiced the same grievances and aspirations.... Henceforth those who worked with us joined the Congress and heartily co-operated with it.' Quoted in ibid., p. 267.
[31] Ibid., pp. 266–67.

K.T. Telang and Badruddin Tayabji, three prominent leaders of Bombay.[32] He returned back in December, just in time for the first Indian National Congress. Thus, Hume may have been regarded as eccentric and impracticable in government circles, but he worked relentlessly to establish a trend towards national political organisation. The Indian National Congress eventually became both an icon and a catalyst in the endeavour.[33]

B. Pattabhi Sitaramayya aptly sums up the developments in the official history of the Congress:

> Whatever the origin and whoever the originator of the idea, we come to this conclusion that the idea was in the air that the need of such an organisation was being felt, that Mr Allan Octavian Hume took the initiative and that it was in March 1885, when the first notice was issued convening the first Indian National Union to meet at Poona in the following December, that what had been a vague idea floating generally in the air and influencing simultaneously the thoughts of thoughtful Indians in the North and the South, the East and the West assumed a definite shape and became a practical programme of action.[34]

Subramania Aiyar, the delegate who moved the first resolution of the first meeting of the Indian National Congress in Bombay on that historic 28th day of December in 1885, said:

> This assemblage in Bombay of my chosen countrymen from Calcutta and Lahore, from Madras and Sind, from places wide apart and difficult of inter-communication, indicates the beginning of a national political life, destined to produce a profound change in the immediate future. From today forward we can with greater propriety than heretofore speak of an Indian nation, of national opinion and national aspirations.[35]

As wished by Subramania Aiyar the Congress did not 'produce a profound change in the immediate future'. It was unlikely to, because most leaders in the first Congress, including its president W.C. Bonnerjee, 'almost were concerned with insisting on their loyalty and the blessings of British rule than

---

[32] The association had established close relations from the outset with the Poona Sarvajanik Sabha, the Mahajan Sabha of Madras and the Indian Association of Calcutta. Not only did it take up the project for a National Telegraph Union in April 1885, it also sent a joint delegation to England to present India's case before the British electorate. It was around this time that Hume had also gone to England. See Mukherjee, 'Genesis of the Indian National Congress', p. 92.

[33] Seal, *The Emergence of the Indian National Congress*, pp. 268–77.

[34] Pattabhi Sitaramayya, *The History of the Indian National Congress, 1885–1935*, vol. I, New Delhi: S. Chand, 1969, pp. 16–17.

[35] Quoted by Francis Robinson and Paul R. Brass, 'Introduction: The Development of the Indian National Congress', in Brass and Robinson (eds), *Indian National Congress and Indian Society*, p. 1.

calling for progress and reforms'.[36] However, building upon past efforts, it did create the feeling of 'an Indian nation, of national opinion and national aspirations'. Despite its modest beginning, over the years it quickened the growth of political consciousness of the Indian people, with the Congress becoming 'a visible symbol of their growing unity as a nation'.[37]

In any case, during the three broad stages in its development in the pre-independence period, it not only grew as a movement and political party, it also developed the Indian party system. During its first stage, from 1885 to 1905, it remained an elite debating society, petitioning the government for extra privileges for the few, in a manner that has been described as the 'politics of mendicancy'.[38] However, even at this stage, the national leaders wanted the Congress to be 'no isolated demonstration, but the beginning of a movement'.[39]

The second stage, spanning a little over a decade (1905–16), is crucial, as in this period, the great debate between the moderates and the extremists over strategy led to initial loss for the latter and they could return to the fold again only in 1916, but laid the foundation for change later. However, the most important political development brought about by the debate and con-sequent vertical split in the organisation was the dynamics of political sup-port and opposition, and beyond political strategy, the gradual evolution of political ideologies that not only provide direction to a political party, but also lead to the crystallisation of a party system. As the 19th century was drawing to a close, schisms between the old guard of the Congress, which still had faith in their strategy of petitions and appeals as well as good sense of the British, and the new crop of leaders, which was for a more aggressive strategy for pressing their demands, sharpened. Curzon's unpopular measures, including the partition of Bengal, though did not lead to the 'peaceful demise' of the Congress, as he had planned, definitely further eroded the credibility of the moderate leaders of the party. Lal (Lala Lajpat Rai), Bal (Bal Gangadhar Tilak) and Pal (Bipin Chandra Pal), might have been from three different parts (the Punjab, Bombay and Calcutta) of the country, but each extolled the 'glorious' past of India, particularly its militant dimensions, to raise popular self-confidence. Tilak's statement, 'Political rights will have to be fought for. The moderates think that these can be won by persuasion. We think that they

---

[36] Percival Spear, quoted by Mukherjee, 'Genesis of the Indian National Congress', p. 103.
[37] Ibid., p. 108.
Pattabhi Sitaramayya, the first official historian of the Congress, has rightly observed, 'Great institutions have always had small beginnings, even as the great rivers of the world start as thin streams.... It [the Congress] had to cut its way through mighty obstacles and therefore entertained modest ideals.... From an attitude of prayerfulness and importunity, it developed self-consciousness and self-assertion.' Pattabhi Sitaramayya, op. cit., p. 19.
[38] Robinson and Brass, op. cit., p. 3.
[39] S.R. Mehrotra, The Emergence of the Indian National Congress, New Delhi: Vikas Publishing House, 1971, p. 414.

can only be got by strong pressure', summed up contrasting approaches of two different generations, as well as the chasm between the two.

As it protested against the partition of Bengal and led the *swadeshi* movement, the 'Congress had begun to possess political power as well as power of persuasion'.[40] The growing differences between the two factions had significant political implication. Though they cooperated in the *swadeshi* and the boycott movements as well as protests against the partition of Bengal, and the moderates led by Dadabhai Naoroji supported and adopted *swaraj* or self-rule as the aim of the Congress movement in the 1906 session of the Congress, the two squabbling sections of the party finally split in the Surat Congress in 1907. The split that underlined sharp differences over strategy continued for the next one decade. Both the groups worked separately till they again came together in 1916.[41]

Viewed from the perspective of the emergence of the party system, this phase of development of the Congress is important in several respects. First, the dissenting groups learnt the lessons of political cohabitation in the face of differences. The moderates and the extremists did not split to begin with because they worked together on issues of agreement.[42] Second, it led to the crystallisation of the process of democratic dissent, debates on ideology and political strategy within the party. Before they split, the two factions carried on their differences within the party forums, sometimes opposing each other vigorously. Finally, their split and eventual coalescence after a decade are indicative of growing processes of democratic politics, leading to political organisation that is the basis of party system in any democracy. The struggle between the moderate and extremist factions for more aggressive political tactics, continuing with two contrasting strategies within the party till they split, carrying on with different strategies till they came together, not only reflect maturing of a political party, the developments clearly demonstrate the beginning of the process of evolution of a party system.

The third stage, beginning 1916, when the Congress took shape as a mass movement, came to an end in 1946 with the formation of the Interim Government. This is a crucial period in several respects, not only for the Congress, but also for the party system in the country. For, it was during this period that the rules of the game for the operation of the party system were defined, as from within the Congress and around it, rival groups developed. In the process, not only the Congress, but all of them, learnt the game of politics through collaboration with and in opposition to each other. As the Congress and the Muslim League

[40] Percival Spear, *A History of India*, 2, Harmondworth, Middlesex, England: Penguin Books, 1977 (A reprint of the 1970 edition with epilogue), p. 177.
[41] See S.R. Singh, 'Moderates and Extremists: The Congress Till the Surat Split', in Pande (general editor), *A Centenary History of the Indian National Congress, Volume I: 1885–1919*, pp. 154–71.
[42] Spear, *A History of India*, p. 172.

pressed hard to achieve their objectives with and away from each other, the British government played the role of the rival axis. In the process there were agreements and dissent, there was coalescence and there were splits.

The Lucknow Pact between the Congress and the Muslim League in 1916 was a fine example of this process. Largely the result of the efforts of Tilak, under the Pact, the Congress accepted the demand of the Muslim League for a separate electorate for the Muslims (and for the minorities), implemented since 1906 and provided for in the Act of 1909, in the Provincial Legislative Councils and the Imperial Legislative Council.[43] Of course, the pact had the negative impact of legitimising the claims of separateness made by the Muslim League for the Indian Muslims. It was, however, important from the perspective of the party system. Under this situation, there were two major political groups negotiating political space with each other and aligning together to bargain for greater political space from a common adversary.[44]

Just before the moderate and extremist factions of the INC reunited, Mohandas Karamchand Gandhi returned to India in 1915 after waging his epic struggle against racial bigotry in South Africa. Having gone there as a young lawyer, he had devised in South Africa a novel method of political agitation, which took protest against injustice to a higher plane, without resorting to violence; thus eventually exercising moral pressure on the government. His joining the nationalist struggle as much transformed the movement, as it had a lasting impact on the emerging party system and the discourse and strategies of party politics in the country. As he toured the country on the advice of Gopal Krishna Gokhale and acquainted himself with nationalist

---

[43] The Pact suggested, 'Adequate provision should be made for the representation of important minorities by election, and the Mohammedans should be represented through special electorates on the Provincial Legislative Councils ...' It further asserted: 'Provided that no Mohammedan shall participate in any of the other elections to the Imperial or Provincial Legislative Councils, save and except those by electorates representing social interests ...' For the Imperial Legislative Council it proposed, 'One-third of the Indian elected members should be Mohammedans elected by separate Mohammedan electorates in the several Provinces, in the proportion, as nearly as may be, in which they are represented in the Provincial Legislative Councils by separate Mohammedan electorates ...' See B. Shiva Rao, *The Framing of India's Constitution: Select Documents, Vol. I*, New Delhi: IIPA, 1966, pp. 26–28.

[44] Tilak's statement on the resolution brought out the emerging process of coalescence, 'It has been said by some that we Hindus have yielded too much to our Mohammadan brothers. I am sure I express the feelings of the Hindu community all over India when I say that we could not have yielded too much. I would not care if the rights of self-government are granted to the Mohammadan community only. When we have a fight against a third party, we stand on this platform united; united in race, united in religion, united as regards all different shades of political creed. That is the most important event of the day.' Quoted by B.N. Pande, 'Trends in Muslim Indian Politics, 1857–1918: The Role of Aligarh and Deoband', in Pande (general editor), *A Centenary History of the Indian National Congress, Volume I: 1885–1919*, p. 317.

66 Ajay K. Mehra

politics through discussions with the intelligentsia, he sought to redefine nationalist struggle and Indian politics with *ahimsa* and *satyagraha*. Jawaharlal Nehru's succinct observation—'He did not descend from the top; he seemed to emerge from the millions of India, speaking their language and incessantly drawing attention to them and their appalling condition'—summed up the new direction Mahatma Gandhi gave to Indian politics. The Congress obviously was bound to change under his impact. About the change he brought to the Congress, Nehru says:

> Gandhi for the first time entered the Congress organization and immediately brought about a complete change in the constitution. He made it democratic and a mass organization. Democratic it had been previously also but it had so far been limited in franchise and restricted to the upper classes. Now the peasants rolled in and, in its new garb, it began to assume the look of a vast agrarian organization with a strong sprinkling of the middle classes. This agrarian character was to grow. Industrial workers also came in but as individuals and not in their separate organized capacity.[45]

The transition in the strategy and social base of the Congress, from petitioning to mass politics, from the intelligentsia to mass base, by the end of the second decade was crucial for the development of the party system in India. The nature of the party organisation as well as its strategy changed significantly after Mahtma Gandhi emerged as the undisputed leader of the national movement and the Congress. Mahatma Gandhi understood the need to destroy the legitimacy of colonial authority by transforming the passive consent of the people into defiance of the British by broad-based political recruitment, which not only changed the social base of the nationalist movement and the party, but also created an unprecedented anti-British sentiment. He also successfully galvanised the Congress workers to rally all social classes behind the Congress. With the opening of the membership of the organisation to masses with each stage of civil disobedience movement launched by Gandhi, the organisation penetrated every district of British India. It also led to the setting up of nationalist organisations even in princely states. The most significant development during the 1920s and 1930s, however, was that, as Gandhi spearheaded movements against the payment of land taxes, land reforms in the rural areas of Bihar, Gujarat, Andhra and Uttar Pradesh, the base of the nationalist cadres as well as of the leadership widened to include persons from small towns and rural areas.[46] As Robinson and Brass rightly

---

[45] Jawaharlal Nehru, *The Discovery of India*, New Delhi: Jawaharlal Nehru Memorial Fund, 14th Impression, 1994, p. 360.
[46] Myron Weiner, *Party Building in a New Nation: The Indian National Congress*, Chicago: The University of Chicago Press, 1967, pp. 30–31. Stanley A. Kochanek, *The Congress Party of India*, Princeton, NJ: Princeton University Press, 1968, p. xxi.

point out: 'There were times of intense nationalist pressure which coincided with the devolution of power and the changing of the ground rules of politics: 1917–23, 1927–34 and 1939–46.'[47]

Despite differences, a highpoint of the Gandhian politics was successfully rallying together contrasting views and opinions both in organisation and in action. As the decade of the 1920s set in, Mahatma Gandhi was firmly settled in national politics as well as in the Congress and he consciously followed this strategy. The Rowlatt *satyagraha* and the Khilafat movement had more than proved the effectiveness of Gandhi's political strategy. Mahatma Gandhi remained important during the mass movement of non-cooperation (1920–22) and of civil disobedience (1931–32), but by 1942, i.e., at the high point of the 'Quit India' movement the control passed on to the young socialists. In any case, the *Purna Swaraj* resolution passed in the Lahore session of the Congress in December 1929 had indicated this transition, despite affirmations on Gandhi's leadership. The important outcome of these movements nonetheless was expansion of the base of the Congress phase by phase, streamlining of its organisational structure as a political party and political culture of protest.

These were important developments from the point of view of the growth of the Congress as a party. However, 1923 and 1937, when some of the Congress members worked within the political framework emerging out of their negotiations with the colonial administration, were more important from the point of view of the emergence of the party system. Their entrance into the legislative councils in 1923, or forming governments in seven out of 11 provinces after the elections of 1937, was crucial not only as a learning process for the party and its leaders, giving them lessons in the ground rules of electoral battle, it was also crucial for the party system as the British government very shrewdly tackled political rivals, in this case the Congress and the Muslim League, to their advantage.

The transformation of the Congress from an elite club of upper-class urban intelligentsia petitioning the colonial government as loyal subjects of the British Crown, to an unparalleled nationalist movement challenging the might of the British Raj with an unprecedented mass base despite colossal poverty and illiteracy, to a political party with features of an elaborate party system, and its sustenance (despite the decline) for over half-a-century, has been an unprecedented historical development in modern democracy. It is significant that the day before his assassination in 1948, Gandhi prepared a proposal, which was to be presented before the Working Committee, observing that Congress 'as a propaganda vehicle and parliamentary machine has outlived its use' and that 'it must be kept out of unhealthy competition with political parties'. He was in favour of the Congress becoming a non-political,

---

[47] Robinson and Brass, op. cit., p. 4.

non-governmental social service society concerned with rural development.[48] It is a matter of conjecture as to what would have happened had the Mahatma not been assassinated and had the Congress accepted his proposal. For, the Indian experience, as well as many others around the world, shows that political parties, particularly in a traditional and stratified society like India, sustain themselves if they evolve over a period of time. The parties that are created either in a hurry, or out of political exigencies and expediency, are unable to sustain themselves in the long run. Significantly, as Kochanek rightly observes: 'Before the transfer of power, the Congress was functioning more or less as a parallel government with an organization extending into almost every part of India.'[49]

The fourth stage (1946–51), which spills over to the post-independence period, is no less important, for during this period the Congress obtained the reins of power of the country. Also, it was in this process that the Congress was transformed from an all-embracing national movement into one dominant political party among several.

Swaraj Party

The formation of the Swaraj Party after the 1922 Gaya session of the Congress only reasserted the nature of the Congress as an umbrella party containing many strands of thoughts and beliefs. Differing with the Congress leadership over participation in the provincial assemblies, C.R. Das announced his resignation from the presidentship of the Congress, announcing that he was convinced 'that there are at least two schools of thought with fundamental differences. I cannot associate myself with most of the resolutions passed in the last session of the Congress ...'[50] After returning from the Gaya Congress, Motilal Nehru concurred with Das, 'I think the inevitable has happened. The two schools of thought which you now see sharply divided on certain points, have existed from the very commencement of N.C.O. movement ...'[51] Although the assertion of the Congress to keep away from the provincial assemblies was described as a triumph of Gandhi, who remained convinced that entering assemblies was an 'utter waste of time', he was not for coming in their way:

I am therefore engaged in surrendering to the utmost of my capacity to the Swarajists.... We must not hinder the Swarajists in their very difficult task. Wherever No-changers cannot have a majority without a bitter struggle,

[48] Weiner, *Party Building in a New Nation*, p. 39.
[49] Kochanek, *The Congress Party of India*, p. xxi.
[50] Quoted by S.R. Bakshi, *Swaraj Party and the Indian National Congress*, New Delhi: Vikas Publishing House, 1985, p. 36.
[51] Ibid., p. 38.

they must gladly and willingly and gracefully yield to the Swarajists, Liberal and all others.[52]

Mahatma Gandhi's remarkably tolerant attitude towards this strong expression of disagreement from the party strengthened the culture of dissent and created an atmosphere of tolerance. Though the Swarajists never snapped their ties with the Congress, neither did the Congress ever abandon them. By raising their disagreement to the extent of going against the professed party line and creating a new political outfit, they created a political atmosphere which was conducive to the growth of various shades of political opinion. Further, before their return to the Congress fold within five years, the Swarajists had given the British a taste of constitutional opposition within legislatures. Of course, they did not succeed in their ultimate objective of wrecking the constitution of 1919 from within; they ended up embarrassing the government with adverse publicity in India and Britain.[53]

From the perspective of the evolution of the party system in India, the Swarajist interlude is important in three respects. First, despite strong opposition from the entire Congress Party, the Swarajists stuck to their guns and took democratic dissent within the party to a new pitch. Second, the Swarajists had to devise their strategies within the legislatures, where they did not have a cakewalk in achieving their objectives. In legislatures elected on limited franchise, the landlord lobby was a strong stumbling block. However, they too learnt the lessons in constitutional opposition, which came in handy when they entered the legislatures again in 1937. Finally, they maintained their links with the Congress and returned back to the party after the experiment was over. It was undoubtedly the consolidation of the process that had begun with the split and convergence of the moderates and extremists, i.e., ideology-based splits and convergence.

The Congress Socialist Party

The formation of the Congress Socialist Party (CSP) in 1934 was a culmination of consultations amongst Congress leaders of socialist and Marxist hues in jails during 1930–31, where discussions on Marxism and contemporary trends in socialist thought made them skeptical of the strategies of the Indian national movement. Many of them who were active in the youth movements

---

[52] Ibid., p. 49.

[53] In his book, *The Dilemma in India*, Sir Reginald Caddock, a retired Governor, referred to the Legislative Assembly as an arena where the Government of India was 'perpetually humiliated and its spokesmen compelled to pretend that the men who indulge in these burlesques of reason are really the chosen representatives of the people'. Quoted by B.R. Nanda, 'The Swarajist Interlude', in Pande, *A Centenary History of the Indian National Congress, Volume II: 1919–1935*, p. 152.

in the 1920s were dissatisfied with Gandhian strategy and tactics. The Gandhi-Irwin Pact (1931) had totally disillusioned them. Many of them even opposed the pact at the Karachi session of the Congress. Yet they considered the Congress the primary body carrying on the national struggle for freedom. Looking for an alternative to Gandhism and liberal nationalism, they did not find themselves in agreement with the current political line of the Communist Party of India. Therefore, they were very clear that they must work within the nationalist movement led by the Congress. Acharya Narendra Dev, the Principal of the Kashi Vidyapeeth who was one of the key figures in founding the CSP, said emphatically, 'it would be suicidal for us to cut ourselves off from the national movement that the Congress undoubtedly represents'. They were determined to give the Congress and the national movement a socialist direction and to achieve this objective they wanted to organise the workers and peasants in their class organisations, transforming them into the social base of the anti-imperialist struggle.[54]

The contribution of the CSP within the Congress in nurturing values that developed a national party system in India deserves an assessment for a variety of reasons. First, it represented paradoxical acceptance of the organisation and the movement despite disagreement over objectives and strategies. Second, it introduced a new political philosophy in the party which the predominant leadership of the party was not in conformity with. Third, the CSP remained a stream within the party without being able to influence its overall philosophy. In fact, an influential section of the party, which eventually compelled it out, remained opposed to the socialists throughout. Finally, the socialists emerged as a significant political force in post-independence Indian politics despite the dominance of the Congress. Though they squandered political opportunity due to internal political contradictions, they have been in the political forefront in providing an alternative to the Congress. In fact, to date, splinters of socialists orbiting the Indian political firmament remain the components on which the consolidation of a third front is envisioned.

The socialists had received qualified support from Gandhi, who welcomed the formation of the party but disagreed with its programme. Having developed the idea of 'trusteeship', he could not reconcile to the Marxist idea of class struggle.[55] The founders of the CSP too differed on the character of the

---

[54] Bipan Chandra, 'Foreword', in Girija Shankar, *Socialist Trends in Indian National Movement*, Meerut: Twenty-First Century Publishers, 1987, p. vii.

[55] In a note prepared to answer questions raised by Minoo Masani, a prominent leader of the Congress Socialists, Gandhi stated:

I welcome the rise of the Socialist Party in the Congress. But I can't say that I like the programme as it appears in the printed pamphlet. It appears to ignore Indian conditions and I do not like the assumption underlying many of its propositions which go to show that there is necessarily antagonism between the classes and the

Congress. Some perceived it as a bourgeois organisation, others as a broader mass organisation with bourgeois or petty bourgeois leadership. They, however, were in agreement that having failed to develop a radical economic programme; the Congress was incapable of leading the masses to higher forms and stages of anti-imperialist struggle. It, therefore, sought to introduce the process of ideological and programmatic transformation of the party. Aware of the difficulties involved in the process, Jayaprakash Narayan told his followers in 1934, 'We are placing before the Congress a programme and we want the Congress to accept it. If the Congress does not accept it, we do not say we are going out of the Congress. If today we fail, tomorrow we will try and if tomorrow we fail, we will try again.'[56]

That indeed was the strategy that the socialists followed. However, though they sought to strengthen the left-oriented leadership in the Congress, they shied away when it came to forcing the issue. The notion of alternate leadership came up twice for realisation in the Tripuri Congress in 1939 and the Ramgarh Congress in 1940, but without much success. Though they successfully supported Subhash Chandra Bose to be elected Congress president, they shied away from forcing issue in the party for a left-wing leadership, as they feared a split. Jayaprakash Narayan said after the Tripuri Congress, 'We Socialists do not want to create factions in the Congress and to establish rival leadership. We are only concerned with the policy and programme of the Congress. We only want to influence the Congress decisions. Whatever our differences with the old leaders, we do not want to quarrel with them. We all want to march shoulder to shoulder to our common fight against imperialism.'[57]

Obviously, the emergence and existence of CSP within the Congress signified the evolution of a multi-stream and multi-ideology party. Though after a prolonged disagreement with the Patel group the socialists felt compelled to leave the Congress in 1945, the existence of the CSP for a decade-and-a-half and its politics contained the seeds of an emerging party system. This is signified by the importance of the socialists, despite numerous splits and coalescence within, in Indian politics for over three decades after independence. Not only did they remain a prominent vocal opposition, whatever their size in the Lok Sabha and legislatures, they played a critical role in coalition politics in 1967–72 and 1977–80 as a group and continue to remain

---

masses or between the labourers and the capitalists such as that they can never work for mutual good. My own experience covering a fairly long period is to the contrary. What is necessary is that labourers and workers should know their rights and should also know how to assert them.

'Observations on Masani's Socialistic Programme', *Collected Works of Mahatma Gandhi*, Vol. 58, New Delhi: The Publications Division, Ministry of Information and Broadcasting, Government of India, 1974, pp. 36–37.

[56] Chandra, 'Foreword', p. viii.
[57] Ibid., p. ix.

in current Indian politics individually. Some of them were even coopted by
Mrs Indira Gandhi during 1971–74 when she was wearing a socialist mask
to take on the old guard of the Congress.

The All India Forward Bloc

The formation of the All India Forward Bloc on 9 July 1939 by Subhash
Chandra Bose, which over six decades later continues to be a tiny political
outfit, represented the trend of existence of the seeds of a party system within
the Congress. Bose was elected president of the Congress in Haripura in
1938. He was reelected in the 1939 Tripuri Congress defeating Gandhi's
nominee Pattabhi Sitaramayya. However, he was compelled to relinquish the
presidency of the party by the Pant resolution, which sought to compel him
to choose his Working Committee in accordance with the wishes of Gandhi.

The formation of the Forward Bloc was his protest against the undemocratic politics of the Congress. Though he was disqualified from holding any
elective office of the Congress for a period of three years from August 1939, the
Bloc under his leadership organised the Anti-Compromise Conference at
Ramgarh in March 1940 at the same time when the Congress was in session
there. He sought to unite and lead all the 'left wing' anti-imperialist forces in the
country. However, he left the country, never to return again, before he could
shape a definite ideology for the Forward Bloc.[58] The formation of the Forward
Bloc nonetheless has to be seen within the larger political trend being highlighted here, whereby as part of the ongoing political process the Congress
became the foundation for the emergence of a party system in the country.

Muslim Indian Politics and the Party System

The trends in Muslim politics are very crucial for the evolution of the party
system in India. For, a sense of distinct identity, if not separateness, which
grew amongst the Muslim intelligentsia in the latter half of the 19th century
led several of them eventually to the formation of the Muslim League. Indeed,
in a multi-cultural society religion is among the important bases for political
organisation. It is, therefore, not surprising that as associations centred on
social reforms were coming up in the three metropolises, stirrings became
visible among the Muslim community as well. It is also not surprising that as
socio-cultural associations transcended into a political association with the
formation of the INC, the desire for a similar political organisation was felt
amongst the Muslim intelligentsia as well. That the need for a separate political

[58] S.N. Sadasivan, *Party and Democracy in India*, New Delhi: Tata McGraw-Hill Publishing
Company Limited, 1977, pp. 85–88.

organisation crystallised amongst the Muslim intelligentsia despite the efforts of the organisers of the INC to make it as broad-based as possible, indicates in retrospect that the seeds of separateness were contained in its formation. The Muslim League was formed 21 years after the Congress even as the number of Muslim delegates in the INC swelled from two in the first (Bombay) Congress in 1885 to 222 in the fourth (Allahabad) Congress in 1888[59] to several thousand in subsequent years.

The Muslim intelligentsia was gripped with a sense of political eclipse, as it were, in the aftermath of the 1857 revolt. Indeed, there was victimisation of the Muslims for a few years thereafter as they were perceived to be the main conspirators of the revolt by the British, but their social prominence continued. As the main beneficiary of education (imparted mainly in Persian and Urdu) and social privileges during the Mughal rule, they held a high proportion of posts in administration and public service, which were conducted in Urdu and Persian. Since the language of administration continued to be Urdu even under the new British dispensation, they retained their important place in the public services.[60] However, they had lost the official patronage enjoyed by them during the Mughal rule. Moreover, while they rued the loss and looked at English and western education with suspicion, other communities, including the Hindus, began taking advantage of this. Social and political ferment amongst the Muslims also took a little time to organise because 'In none of the three most westernised provinces was there a large elite of educated Muslims who could be drawn into the politics of the associations or later of the Congress'.[61]

However, the desire for associations was not absent among the Muslims. Since the Muslim zamindars in Bengal shared the interests of their Hindu counterparts, they joined them in the British Indian Association to defend the rights of the landlords. The Muhammadan Literary and Scientific Society of Calcutta was established in 1863. The National Mohammadan Association was launched in 1878. The Society and the Association were scrupulously averse to any confrontation with the British. Abdul Latif and Amir Ali, the persons behind these organisational efforts, were conscious of the need for government help in reviving Muslim fortunes. Aware of the fact that any representative system either in public services or in local bodies would reduce the Muslims to an invisible minority and without much say, they pressed for separate representation for the community. Syed Ahmed Khan made efforts to restore credibility of his community by denying that the mutiny was a Muslim conspiracy. Expression of loyalty to the British and education for his community were his strategies for reconciliation and revival of the

---

[59] Seal, *The Emergence of the Indian National Congress*, p. 329.
[60] Ibid., pp. 303–5.
[61] Ibid., p. 308.

community's fortunes. He succeeded in establishing the Muslim Anglo-Oriental College in Aligarh in 1875. He was against joining the Congress because he thought that in a representative system demanded by the Congress, Muslims would be 'in a permanent minority'. Obviously, the religion-based contestation for a greater share of the economic cake available under the colonial rule and for a larger political space began before the turn of the 19th century, even before the Congress was launched. However, with the launch of the Congress a contestatious politics was set in motion that carried seeds of competitive party politics. On the one hand the Congress was making an intensive effort to enlist larger Muslim support to present before the British a nationalist cause, on the other, Syed Ahmed Khan was carrying on a vigorous campaign against the Congress, exhorting the Muslims to remain loyal to the British and keep away from the Congress.[62] Competitive politics unleashed in the process had had a long-term impact on party politics as well as the party system in the country.

Thus the formation of the All-India Muslim League on 30 December 1906 was an extension of the quest of the Muslim intelligentsia and wealthy elite for a place under the Raj. It led them to contest the nationalist politics of the Congress and affirmations of loyalty to the Crown. The British took advantage of the trend when they found the Congress getting out of hand. Whether it was the partition of Bengal or the question of a separate electorate, the British took special care to see to it that the embers of separate identity existing among the Muslim elite were kept smouldering and were fanned into a raging flame at each appropriate opportunity. Despite the reconciliatory and accommodating attitude of the Congress, there were contradictory trends and forces within, which encouraged conflictual and communal politics.

In fact, even before the Muslim League came into existence, the Congress never succeeded in drawing a large number of Muslims to its fold. Muslims formed only less than 6.5 per cent of the yearly Congress sessions between 1892 and 1909. Their involvement peaked during the Khilafat-non-cooperation movements to nearly 11 per cent in the Ahmedabad session. By 1923 the Muslim attendance in Congress did not exceed 3.5 per cent.[63] Robinson cites interesting reasons from C.A. Bayly[64] for the inability of the Congress to enlist Muslim support in large numbers:

[62] Badruddin Tyabji reminded Hume, 'The prime object of the Congress was to unite the different communities and provinces into one and thus promote harmony. As it is, however, not only have the Mohammedans been divided from the Hindus in a manner they have never been before, but the Mohammedans themselves have been split into two factions, the gulf between whom is becoming wider every day.' Ibid., p. 337.
[63] Francis Robinson, 'The Congress and the Muslims', in Brass and Robinson (eds), *Indian National Congress and Indian Society*, p. 166.
[64] Robinson quotes from C.A. Bayly, *Rulers, Townsmen and Bazaars: North Indian Society in the Age of British Expansion, 1770–1870*, Cambridge: Cambridge University Press.

In explaining the ways in which the ideologies and institutions of the pre-colonial period contributed to the social formations of the colonial and post-colonial periods Bayly has shown how the commercialisation of royal power in the seventeenth and eighteenth centuries helped to bring about the development of a rooted Islamic service gentry and a unified merchant class. These were distinct social formations, expressing themselves in different cultural idioms and operating in sharply differentiated economic contexts—the one was to become increasingly the sustainer of an Islamic high culture, the other of a Hindu high culture; they were, Bayly declares, the most significant social formations to emerge from the decline of the Mughal empire.[65]

This shows the emerging socio-economic contradictions that shaped the politics of that time. Obviously, these contradictions left their impact on the emerging party politics as well. For, it was not possible for the Congress to change the established social texture; it was merely trying to draw support from the existing one.

From its formation in 1906 till it made a demand for a separate state of Pakistan for the Muslims, the Muslim League remained part of the pre-independence Indian party system.[66] Its discords, rivalry and collaborations with the Congress as well as with the British government to gain an upper edge, revealed strategies that are visible even today. Five occasions are significant from this point of view.

First, the Lucknow Pact of 1916 was an attempt in coalescence in which the League received acceptance from the Congress of its demand for separate electorates and extra seats over and above their proportion of the population in those provinces where Muslims formed a minority of the population. This

---

[65] Robinson, 'The Congress and the Muslims', p. 167.

[66] On 30 December 1906 a group of Muslim leaders joined together in Dacca (now Dhaka, capital of Bangladesh) and founded the Muslim League. Its aims and objectives were enunciated as follows:

Resolved that this meeting composed of Musalmans from all parts of India assembled at Dacca decide that a Political Association be formed, and styled All-Indian Muslim League, for the furtherance of the following objects:

(a) To promote, among the Musalmans of India, feelings of loyalty to the British Government and to remove any misconception that may arise as to the intention of Government with regard to any of the measures.

(b) To protect and advance the political rights and interests of the Musalmans of India and to respectfully present their need and aspirations to the Government.

(c) To prevent the rise among the Musalmans of India of any feelings of hostility towards other communities without prejudice to the other aforementioned objects of the League.

Craig Baxter, The Jana Sangh: A Biography of an Indian Political Party, Philadelphia: University of Pennsylvania Press, 1969, pp. 6–7.

arrangement came into effect in the Montagu-Chelmsford reform embodied in the Government of India Act, 1919.

Second, the politics of the early 1920s became significant as a consequence of the Act of 1919. On the one hand, from 1920 to 1922 the Congress coordinated the non-cooperation movement in harmony with the Muslims, on the other, separate electorates and the substantial Muslim interest groups they came to embrace, enabled the government to work a system of political control which in large part could ignore the Congress.

Third, the period from 1927 to 1929 witnessed the Congress opposing any power sharing arrangement with the Muslim League which accepted the principle of separate electorates. This again provided leverage to the British to impose a settlement. Obviously, the Muslim League was the gainer.

Fourth, the tussle between the Congress and the Muslim League over a coalition government in UP after the 1937 Provincial Assembly elections demonstrated stresses and strains inherent in an emerging party system in which two major communities were involved in bargaining and struggling for an influential space within the colonial state and a possible post-colonial polity. It is also significant that the Muslim League's stubbornness about the partition of India became stronger as it fared badly in the 1937 Provincial Assembly poll.

Finally, the tussle between the Congress and the League in June and July 1946 over a coalition Interim Government after the Muslim League had accepted the Cabinet Mission Plan for the constitution of an independent India demonstrated that the spirit of party system had come to stay in the emerging Indian polity. Though the Congress was offered leadership of the Interim Government as the single largest party, the two contested each other over portfolio and central space. Indeed, British India was to be partitioned in the subsequent year, but despite the partition the spirit of multi-cultural party politics stayed and was further nurtured through competitive politics.

The Communist Party of India

The Communist Party of India did not play any significant role in the Indian national movement. However, we cannot evaluate the origin of the Indian party system without including it in the analysis. It was first formed as an émigré group by the end of 1920 by M.N. Roy, who despatched several Indian communists trained in Russia to organise a communist movement in India. Even before they could coordinate their efforts, several of them were arrested by the British government in connection with the Cawnpore (now Kanpur) Conspiracy case in 1924. Yet, the foundation of the Indian Communist Party (ICP) was formally laid in Kanpur on 1 September 1924 by the UP communist group led by Satya Bhakta. Its first national conference was held on 26 December 1925. The important aspects of its role in developing the Indian party system are the contribution in the Trade Union movement, its strategy of infiltrating the Congress in the wake of repression and the beginning of the Telangana struggle.

However, even before the communists arrived to spread the message of revolution in the country, the embryo of 'leftism' had already sprouted in India. The end of the war had witnessed a spurt in trade unionism in India. About 125 unions were affiliated to the All India Trade Union Congress between 1918 and 1920. Trade union militancy became visible since January 1919, as in the following period a wave of strikes in India paralysed the whole industrial structure. Though there was neither 'leftist' consciousness, nor Marxist rhetoric, the Trade Unions pushed for demands for higher wages, dearness allowance, bonus and shorter hours of work, intensifying class consciousness and class solidarity in the process.[67] It indeed created a political base for the communists to work on.

Beginning with the formal establishment of the party in 1924, the ICP had its first national conference on 26 December 1925. However, Moscow exercised considerable influence over its growth at that stage. It asked Rajani Palme Dutt of the Communist Party of Great Britain to take over the direction of communist activities in India, who sent a mission to consolidate communism in the subcontinent. Since the colonial government had banned the ICP, workers' and peasants' parties were formed in Bengal, Bombay, UP and Punjab during 1926 and 1928 as legal cover for the banned communist party. The four were united in 1928 as the All India Workers' and Peasants' Party (AIWPP). Soon after its first Congress in Calcutta on 21–24 December 1928, the AIWPP was reconstituted as the Communist Party of India. The very next year the government discovered the Meerut Conspiracy and arrested 31 top leaders of the party and sentenced them to varying terms of imprisonment.

From its very inception the communist movement had inherent contradictions as far as its location in Indian politics was concerned. Since it came into existence during a colonial regime and at a time when the nationalist movement was in full swing it needed to locate the party in the existing triangular political continuum of alien government, nationalist movement and the people. However, the communists' rigid application of Marxism to the Indian situation at that historical juncture made them apply the same yardstick to both the government and the Congress. As a result, they went into oppositional mode vis-à-vis both from the very outset. Seeking to unite workers of India with the workers of the world, they perceived the Congress

---

[67] J.C. Jha, 'The Struggle for Swaraj', in Pande, (general editor), A *Centenary History of the Indian National Congress, Volume II: 1919–1935*, pp. 52–53.

and the nationalist movement as much as the colonial government as part of world capitalism.[68]

The 1930s and 1940s brought out the communists' dilemma in placing themselves in the Indian context further. At the height of the *swadeshi* movement they sported suits made of British cloth to express solidarity with the British workers and burnt the nationalist Indian flag on Chowpatty in Bombay. They declared the civil disobedience movement of the Congress as a bourgeois manoeuvre and dissociated themselves from it. However, when the government turned the heat on the party in 1934, the communists sought asylum in the Congress using their sympathisers within the CSP. A similar contradiction became visible during the Second World War which remained a 'fascist-imperialist war' till Hitler invaded Russia on 22 June 1941 and transformed it into a 'people's war'. The CPI received the recognition of the government in July 1942. Since it supported the British-Indian war-time home policy, the Quit India movement launched by 'the bourgeois Congress' and 'the reactionary reformist' CSP was dubbed as anti-people. Naturally, the Congress decided to banish the communists from the party in 1945. By 1946 the communists were convinced of armed insurrection. So a series of insurrections were carried out in the Varli areas of Maharashtra, Vayalar and Punnapra in Travancore, in Bengal, in Malabar and in Telangana during 1946–50.[69] The most intense and sustained armed struggle, however, was in Telangana in the erstwhile Hyderabad state which began in 1946 and was withdrawn on Soviet directive in 1951.[70]

Even though the CPI joined the electoral politics in independent India the dilemmas and paradoxes of the communist movement continued. However, despite the paradoxes, the emergence of the communists at a time when party politics was taking shape in India through the nationalist movement and its politics only laid a sound basis for a party system in the country.

The Rashtriya Swayamsevak Sangh and the Hindu Right

When the RSS was established in 1925 'as a kind of educational body whose objective was to train a group of Hindu men who, on the basis of their

[68] The Comintern in 1928 had resolved: 'The communists must unmask the national reformism of the Indian National Congress and oppose all the phrases of the Swarajists, Gandhists, etc., about passive resistance.' Quoted by M.R. Masani, *The Communist Party of India: A Short History*, London: Derek Vershoyle (in association with the Institute of Pacific Relations), 1954, p. 42.

[69] For details, see Masani, *The Communist Party of India*, and Sadasivan, *Party and Democracy in India*.

[70] For details, see Ajay K. Mehra, 'Naxalism and Militant Peasant Movement in India', in

character-building experience in the RSS, would work to unite the Hindu community so that India could again become an independent country and a creative society',[71] it was difficult to imagine that three-quarters of a century later it would be part of a political pivot that would rule India.[72] Its role deserves analysis primarily because while its approach has been non-confrontational towards authority, it remained at the centre of controversy since independence. Even though RSS had no direct role in the founding of the Bharatiya Jan Sangh, the ideas it preached certainly had a prominent role in the emergence of the Hindu right as a force at the centre stage of Indian politics, as, keen on involvement in active politics, its members in their individual capacity played a crucial role in founding the party and became its key leaders in the initial years.

The history of the Hindu right, however, precedes the RSS. An organised RSS in fact should be considered an extension of the existence of the Hindu right. As an immediate reaction to the founding of the Muslim League, the United Bengal Hindu Movement was formed. The Punjab Hindu Sabha founded in the same year set in motion a process that culminated in the establishment of the Akhil Bharatiya Hindu Mahasabha. It was later joined by many Arya Samajists. The same people were also active supporters of the Congress. Not surprisingly, the annual sessions of the Mahasabha were generally held at the same time and place as the Congress. Many of these leaders, who presided over both the Congress and the Mahasabha (e.g., Lala Lajpat Rai and Pt. Madan Mohan Malaviya) at some point of time or the other, were a unique combination of conservatism and progressive ideas. However, they did create a conservative, if not communal, bastion within the Congress. In the late 1920s, more particularly after the death of Lala Lajpat Rai in 1928, the separation of the Mahasabhites with the Congress was complete. But the new crop of the Mahasabha leaders like Vinayak Damodar Savarkar remained in active politics. So did Syama Prasad Mookerjee, the leader from Bengal who became a prominent Congress leader, and after his split from Nehru founded the BJS.[73]

K.M. de Silva (ed.), *Conflict and Violence in South Asia: Bangladesh, India, Pakistan and Sri Lanka*, Kandy, Sri Lanka: International Centre for Ethnic Studies, 2000, pp. 235–79.

[71] Walter K. Anderson and Shridhar D. Damle, *The Brotherhood in Saffron: The Rashtriya Swayamsevak Sangh and Hindu Revivalism*, New Delhi: Vistaar Publications, 1987, p. 2.

[72] The Bharatiya Jana Sangh, which took a new *avatar* in 1980 as the Bharatiya Janata Party following a brief honeymoon with centrist politics as a part of the Janata Party, was founded on 21 October 1951. Though it is BJS/BJP which has been in active electoral politics, the linkages within the Sangh Parivar have played crucial role in shaping their political strategies and politics. Since the present essay focuses only on the pre-independence period, we will confine ourselves to trends in the politics of the Hindu right as represented by the RSS.

[73] Baxter, *The Jan Sangh*, pp. 6–30.

The RSS was founded by a medical doctor, Keshav Baliram Hedgewar in 1925 along with four trusted friends in Nagpur. An active Congressman from 1916 to 1924, he was once general secretary of the Nagpur PCC. However, Islamic 'fundamentalism' in the 1920s across the country led him to believe in the importance of organising Hindu society, particularly the youth, to obviate the possibility of 'Muslim domination'. So intensive and disciplined was his effort that by the time he died in 1940 at an early age of 50, the RSS was a 1,00,000 strong body.

The Hedgewar period of the RSS was devoted to organising and expanding, which is evident in its growth from five persons in Nagpur in 1925 to an all-India body of 1,00,000 in 1940. However, its stance on the Hindu-Muslim question and its activities influenced by that stance had a political tilt.[74] Its decision to stay away from the 1942 Quit India movement was also political:

> The Sangh viewed the movement sympathetically but did not participate in it on the organisational level. It was felt that it was the time to organise and strengthen the people, and not to land ourselves in jail and remain immobilised for years.... All the same quite a few RSS workers participated in the 1942 movement in their individual capacity.[75]

It is true that Hedgewar had consciously not allowed the RSS to become a political prop for the Savarkar-led Hindu Mahasabha, but as admitted by Golwalkar in the above statement in the context of the 1942 movement, individual *swayamsevak*s were engaged in political activities through other affiliations. No wonder, its organisational record has not convinced anyone regarding its non-political nature. Myron Weiner observed: 'It was non-political only in one sense: it did not take part in elections nor was it organised for electoral purposes.'[76]

Despite its disclaimers on politics the RSS has been looked at with suspicion and has been banned more than once in the post-independence period. It has been perhaps perceived as a potential political challenge due to its high degree of organisation. And, its footloose politically ambitious members aligning with various political parties and organisations in their 'individual' capacity always remained its strong link with politics. In fact, soon after independence, once in the absence of Nehru, even the Congress decided to admit RSS members.[77]

---

[74] The RSS's own admission of its role as the saviour of the Hindus in the post-partition violence and official reports, including statements and notes of Sardar Patel, clearly highlight the role of the RSS in planning to violently change demographic composition in certain areas in Punjab and Jammu. Ibid., pp. 37–39.

[75] Golwalkar quoted in ibid., p. 37.

[76] Myron Weiner, *Party Politics in India*, Princeton: Princeton University Press, 1957, pp. 182–83.

[77] Anderson and Damle, *The Brotherhood in Saffron*.

Therefore, when Syama Prasad Mookerjee quit Nehru's cabinet in 1950 in protest against its lenient attitude towards Pakistan and decided to organise a political party, the RSS found a political base it could use. It was also the time when several senior RSS members were restive for active political role in the emerging polity. After all, the first general elections under the new Constitution were approaching. Mookerjee was sympathetic towards the Hindu Mahasabha and he remained in touch with the RSS. He was reportedly approached by some RSS members and assured support. In any case, Mookerjee and the BJS received full support of the RSS cadre and leaders; several of the RSS leadership emerged as senior leaders of the party, obviously with all the ideological baggage they had developed during their 25 years of existence. Thus, the founding of the RSS indeed became an important component of the evolving party system of India.[78]

Conclusion

The party system in India, thus, originated from the desire and zeal of the western-educated intelligentsia in the late 19th century to form associations for social reforms. The INC was a result of this zeal, as some prominent individuals in the three Presidencies felt the need for an organisation that approached the government on behalf of the people to make them aware of their requirements. However, in course of time, it was transformed into a movement representing the length and breadth as well as social heterogeneity of the country. It also brought together different points of view and ideologies and in the process functioned as a composite party system.

The emergence of the Muslim League and religion-based nationalism gave firm foundation to the spirit of party system in the country. Whether and where the Congress went wrong in tackling the politics of the League and whether or not it was possible to prevent the partition of the subcontinent is a contentious question. However, it is absolutely clear that in the triangular politics of colonial India, as the British discovered the Muslim League as a perfect foil to the Congress, the processes of laying the foundation of the party system in the country were set in motion.

The emergence of the entire spectrum of political ideologies also created a firm base for the party system in the country. From the right (the Muslim as well as the Hindu) to the left (even ultra-left, as the CPI transformed itself in revolutionary mode for five years from 1946 to 1951) each point on the ideological scale was fully represented. The Congress itself represented political beliefs from the right of the centre to the left of the centre. Organisationally

---

[78] Baxter, *The Jan Sangh*, p. 37.

too, the parties had begun relating to each other as they do in a mature democracy. True, India remained a one party dominant system for over four decades of its post-independence history, but seeds of a complex party system were sown during pre-independence politics.

3

FEDERALISATION OF INDIA'S PARTY SYSTEM

Balveer Arora

The last decade has witnessed far-reaching changes in both the structuring of the party system and the political practices that have emerged.[1] If party systems are defined, following Eckstein, as 'competitive interaction patterns among parties'[2] or, in Duverger's terms, as 'the forms and modes of their coexistence',[3] then the degree of competition is clearly a crucial variable. It also follows that 'non-competitive parties', i.e., those which are so minor that they hardly influence the outcome of the competition, can be considered marginal to the national party system.[4]

While we focus here on party systems, it is obvious that the distinctive features of the parties themselves, i.e., their social bases, internal organisations, and ideologies remain critical elements in understanding this interaction or coexistence. Furthermore, this process of interaction is conditioned by these characteristics, and participation in the system does not leave the parties themselves unchanged either.

In the sections that follow, we first look at the dimensions and contours of the party system before taking up a few concepts which may provide us with a framework for analysis. Foremost among them is federalisation, which helps us explain in the third section the linkages between political parties

---

[1] In the finalisation of this paper for publication, I have benefited from Douglas Verney's insistence that I make myself clearer on some points. K.K. Kailash, doctoral student at the Centre for Political Studies, Jawaharlal Nehru University, filled in data gaps and posed useful questions.

[2] Harry Eckstein, 'Party System', in *International Encyclopaedia of Social Sciences*, Vol. 11, (New York: Macmillan & Free Press, 1968, p. 436.

[3] Maurice Duverger, *Political Parties: Their Organisation and Activity in the Modern State* (third edition), New York: Harper & Row, 1964, p. 203.

[4] It is evident that parties which are non-competitive in the Lok Sabha are not ipso facto insignificant in the state electoral arena. Not only are they represented in state legislatures, but they also frequently influence electoral outcomes in Lok Sabha constituencies. In exceptional circumstances of wafer-thin majorities, such small parties can also influence outcomes in the Lok Sabha.

and institutions. Thereafter, we look into the ways in which parties can and are renewing themselves before concluding, in the final section, with some tentative observations on the perspectives opened up by federal coalitions and systemic reforms.

I

The movement of the party system at the national level during the 1990s has been clearly away from the 'dominance' pattern to a competitive multi-party system that can perhaps best be described as 'bi-nodal', a node being typically a 'centering point of component parts' or a 'central point in a system'.[5] We need, however, to specify who are the other participants in this bi-nodal system, which has clearly grown in both size and complexity. This is all the more important because recent trends have given rise to anxieties and apprehensions concerning an apparently uncontrollable fission process in the party system, leading to fears of instability and disorder. If we restrict ourselves to the parties which succeeded in winning at least one seat in the Lok Sabha during the 1990s, the picture that emerges is depicted in Table 3.1.

While the number of successful parties having obtained at least one seat in the Lok Sabha rose sharply after 1996, if we shift the focus to those which managed to cross the threshold of 0.5 per cent of the seats, i.e., three in a House of 543 elected members, the trend appears less startling. It is also interesting to note that 21 parties joined or supported the ruling alliance in 1998, and 18 in 1999.[6]

Table 3.1: Number of Parties Successful in Lok Sabha Elections (1991–99)

Parties	Elections			
	1991	1996	1998	1999
National parties (including two nodal parties)	07	07	07	07
State parties and registered parties	20	23	34	31
Total	27	30	41	38
No. of parties with over three seats	12	18	24	20

Source: Compiled from Election Commission (EC) data at http://www.eci.gov.in. Amongst the registered parties, the Election Commission recognises some as state parties. A few among them are given the national label.

---

[5] It remains to be seen whether the Communist Party of India (Marxist) (CPM) has the capacity to transform it into a trinodal system, after its decision at the Thiruvananthapuram special conference to participate in governance at the Centre and to work towards regrouping a non-Congress, non-BJP alternative. *The Hindu*, 24 October 2000.
[6] These alliance partners are identified in Tables 3.5 and 3.6. The Janata Dal (United) (JD [U]) briefly included the Samata Party, but they later applied for and obtained recognition

Let us now try to bring the contours of our universe of analysis into sharper focus by concentrating on the 20 parties which crossed the three-seat threshold in the 1999 general elections and are represented in the 13th Lok Sabha.

While Table 3.2 clarifies the number of players and the existence of at least two nodal parties with coalition-making capabilities, it still leaves us with the task of elucidating the process through which this transformation has taken place.

II

The factors responsible for fragmentation are obviously complex and varied in a multi-tiered system of governance. Speaking of a 'democracy of castes' in the context of caste and communal competition and conflict, Francine Frankel says:

> The increased participation in electoral politics of groups long considered peripheral, has ratcheted up pressure on the cohesion of national and even state political parties in the wake of voter fragmentation along regional, religious and caste lines.[7]

Fragmentation is first and foremost a term descriptive of empirical reality. It is also in many ways an emotive term, evoking the spectre of disintegration in a country which was born under traumatic conditions, scarred by the violence and migration of partition. Moreover, the term is, in our view, inadequately heuristic, inasmuch as it does not give us a handle on the possible reasons for the proliferation of parties. We argue here that federalisation as an analytical concept may prove more helpful in explaining the direction in which the party system has moved in the post-Congress dominance era.[8]

---

as separate entities in the Lok Sabha. The fear of an uncontrollable fragmentation of parties has led former President Venkataraman to suggest a gradual reduction in their number by what can only be called the 'musical chairs' method: the lowest scorer is eliminated at each successive election. See S.C. Kashyap, D.D. Khanna and G.W. Kueck (eds), *Reviewing the Constitution*, New Delhi: Shipra, 2000.

[7] See her introductory chapter, 'Contextual Democracy': Intersections of Society, Culture and Politics in India, in Francine R. Frankel, Zoya Hasan, Rajeev Bhargava and Balveer Arora (eds), *Transforming India: Socio-Political Dynamics of Democracy*, New Delhi: Oxford University Press, 2000, p. 12. Yogendra Yadav ('Understanding the Second Democratic Upsurge', in Frankel et al., *Transforming India*) shows that the participation of women, Sheduled Castes and Scheduled Tribes now equals male and general category participation.

[8] This is not to minimise the importance of purely caste-based multi-state parties such as the Bahujan Samaj Party (BSP), which do not inject the defence of states' interests into their electoral appeal. Most of the other multistate parties which have fragmented voter preferences by appealing to specific castes and communities are generally restricted to a

Table 3.2: Twenty Principal Parties in 13th Lok Sabha (1999)

Parties	Seats	% vote	States represented
BJP	182	23.75	All except Kerala and seven northeastern states. Ruling in Gujarat, member of ruling alliance in UP, Himachal, Punjab, Haryana, Goa, Meghalaya.
Congress	114	28.31	All except Haryana, Himachal, J&K, Delhi, Goa and four northeastern states. Ruling in MP, Rajasthan, Karnataka and Delhi, member of ruling alliance in Maharashtra, Bihar, Arunachal, Nagaland
CPM	33	5.41	West Bengal*, Kerala, Tripura*, Bihar, Tamil Nadu
Telugu Desam	29	3.65	Andhra Pradesh*
Samajwadi Party	26	3.74	Uttar Pradesh
Janata Dal (U)	21	3.10	Bihar and Karnataka
Shiv Sena	15	1.56	Maharashtra
BSP	14	4.15	Uttar Pradesh
DMK	12	1.73	Tamil Nadu*
ADMK	10	1.94	Tamil Nadu
Biju Janata Dal	10	1.20	Orissa*
National Congress Party	08	2.27	Maharashtra* and Meghalaya*
Trinamool Congress	08	2.57	West Bengal
Rashtriya Janata Dal	07	2.79	Bihar*
PMK	05	0.65	Tamil Nadu*
Indian National Lok Dal	05	0.55	Haryana*
CPI	04	1.48	West Bengal* and Punjab
J&K National Conference	04	0.12	Jammu & Kashmir*
MDMK	04	0.44	Tamil Nadu*
RSP	03	0.41	West Bengal*
Total Seats	514	89.82	94.7 % of the seats

Sources: Compiled from Election Commission data for 1996–99 at http://www.eci.gov.in supplemented by media reports on alliances and state government incumbency, as on 12 November 2000. (*) denotes ruling party/ruling coalition in the state.

Notes: 1. Members/supporters of the National Democratic Alliance (NDA) are indicated in italics.
2. Apart from the 11 NDA parties indicated here (12 if Samata is counted out of JD[U]) the six others are: S. Akali Dal (Punjab*), Loktantrik Cong (UP*), Himachal Vikas Cong (HP*), SDF (Sikkim*), MGR ADMK (TN*), MSCP (Manipur*).
3. Of the six seats held by independents, three are with the NDA. Apart from a few ruling parties in states having one or two seats, the only major party which gets left out in this tabulation is the Assam Gana Parishad,* which got 0.32 per cent of the votes, but no seats.

Insights from comparative studies of party systems using the concepts of dominance and exclusion suggest that some of the trends in the development of our parties and the ways in which they relate to each other can be traced to

single state; for example, the efforts of the Indian National Lok Dal and the Samajwadi Party to expand across state lines have been largely unsuccessful.

the erosion of the 'Congress System'. Duverger's description of dominance is still worth recalling today: 'A party is dominant when it is identified with an epoch; when its doctrines, ideas, methods, its style, so to speak, coincide with those of the epoch.'[9]

Particularly instructive in this context is a study by Ariel Levite and Sidney Tarrow comparing the stages and processes through which two delegitimated and excluded parties in two dominant party systems, Italy and Israel, managed to gain entry into power-sharing processes.[10]

Table 3.3 shows how the Bharatiya Janata Party (BJP), which was practically swamped by the electoral wave of 1984 after it emerged as a distinct entity from the short-lived Janata coalition, steadily clawed its way back into the political process from which it had been effectively excluded. Today Vajpayee heads a parliamentary majority comprising 305 members, to which the BJP itself contributes 182. This majority can be compared with the first non-Congress coalition at the Centre of 1977, when the Janata Party had 298 seats.

Table 3.3: Lok Sabha Seats of Five Main National Parties (1977–99)

Parties	Election Year							
	1977	1980	1984	1989	1991	1996	1998	1999
Total no. of seats*	542	529	542	529	511	543	543	543
Indian National Congress	154	353	415	197	227	140	141	114
Bharatiya Janata Party	@	@	02	85	119	161	182	182
Janata Party/Janata Dal	298	31	10	143	56	46	06	21**
Communist Party Marxist	22	36	22	33	35	32	32	33
Communist Party of India	07	11	06	12	13	12	09	04
Total five national parties	481	431	455	470	450	391	370	354
% of total seats	88.8	81.5	84.0	88.9	88.1	72.0	68.1	65.2

Sources: 1. Election Commission Data for 1996–99 available at http://www.eci.gov.in.
2. For the 1977–91 results, Subrata K. Mitra and James Chiriyankandath (eds), *Electoral Politics in India*, New Delhi: Segment, 1992; and *Election Commission of India Reports* for 1996–99.

Notes: @ The BJP was a constituent of the Janata Party in these elections.
* The total number of elective seats rose from 542 to 543 in 1987. Where a lesser total is indicated, it means that elections were not held for the remaining seats in the general elections due to compelling circumstances.
** The Janata Dal (United) included Samata Party (Bihar) and Lok Shakti (Karnataka).

---

[9] Duverger, *Political Parties*. p. 308. The classic statement on dominance in India is of course by Rajni Kothari, 'The Congress System in India', *Asian Survey*, 4(12), December 1964.
[10] Ariel Levite and Sidney Tarrow, 'The Legitimation of Excluded Parties in Dominant Party Systems', *Comparative Politics*, April 1983, pp. 295–326. They deal with the integration of two 'pariah' parties from opposite ends of the ideological spectrum, the Communist Party in Italy and the Herut\Likud in Israel. This study builds on an earlier one of the same two party countries by Alan Arian and Samuel H. Barnes ('The Dominant Party System: A Neglected Model of Democratic Stability', *Journal of Politics*, 36, August 1974, pp. 592–614), who analysed the processes of exclusion in dominant party systems.

While the share of the two main polity-wide nodal parties in terms of notes has risen from 49.1 per cent to 52.1 per cent, their relative share in terms of seats has undergone a marked decline, with the Congress dipping to an all-time low. Single and multi-state parties have registered a corresponding increase. As Table 3.4 shows, they now contribute over 45 per cent of the seats in the 13th Lok Sabha. It is from this group of parties that federal coalitions are forged.

The Congress nurtured and relied upon certain values and beliefs in order to sustain its dominance. In its electoral rhetoric, it steadily denounced parties based on three 'evils' that it said constituted threats to national unity: casteism, regionalism and communalism. In reality, while opposing such parties, it skilfully balanced within itself the requirements of different constituents derived from all three categories. Linked to this strategy was an effort to delegitimise and isolate parties which overtly appealed to and championed interests based on these categories. It drew a line akin to a *cordon sanitaire*, a quarantine imposed to limit contagion from infectious diseases, around such parties. This line was first breached in a significant way by parties advocating states' rights and interests.[11]

The secular–communal cleavage proved to be the most durable, and was still intact in 1996, when Vajpayee waited in vain for 13 days for other parties to join him in forming a government. They balked at crossing this Rubicon, and most state parties, which had incidentally carved their political spaces at the expense of the Congress preferred to look around for a non-BJP alternative rather

Table 3.4: Seats and Votes (%) won by Categories of Parties in the Lok Sabha, 1996–99

Parties	Election Year					
	1996		1998		1999	
	Seats	Votes	Seats	Votes	Seats	Votes
Congress	25.8	28.8	26.0	25.8	21.0	28.3
BJP	29.6	20.3	33.5	25.6	33.5	23.8
Sub-total	**55.4**	**49.1**	**59.5**	**51.4**	**54.5**	**52.1**
Multi-state parties*	18.8	20.0	11.8	16.6	13.3	15.0
State parties & Independents	25.8	30.9	28.7	32.0	32.2	32.9
Sub-total	**44.6**	**50.9**	**40.5**	**48.6**	**45.5**	**47.9**

Source: As for Table 3.1. N = 543 seats.
Notes: * Classified as national parties, they were as follows:
      1996 = CPM, CPI, Samata, Janata Dal, AIIC (Tiwari) and Janata Party.
      1998 = CPM, CPI, Samata, Janata Dal and BSP.
      1999 = CPM, CPI, Janata Dal (United) and BSP.

---

[11] Caste-based parties such as Ambedkar's Republican Party existed but were unable to build successful pan-Indian coalitions. The first serious challenge to Congress hegemony came from state parties who followed in the wake of the Dravida Munnetra Kazhagam (DMK). The 16th Constitutional Amendment (1963) was aimed at curbing such 'fissiparous tendencies' but the DMK readily adapted to the new rules of the game.

than cast their lot with a party which had been 'ghettoised' and effectively delegitimised for so long.

It is true that a slight shift occurred in 1977 when the Jana Sangh was included in the ruling coalition, but as L.K. Advani recently recalled, the BJP was born when the Janata Party 'wanted us to disassociate from the RSS'.[12] A further step was taken during the National Front–Left Front experiment of 1989–91, but as soon as the BJP proclaimed its intention to aggressively pursue its communal agenda, it was again isolated and a parting of the ways swiftly followed.

It was, however, the bitter experience of the rapid demise of two successive United Front governments (1996–98), composed largely of state-based parties, which dealt a death blow to the long-standing delegitimised status of the BJP that had effectively curbed its power and influence in national politics for over two decades. With the accretion to its own strength in the Lok Sabha being merely 21 seats in the 12th Lok Sabha, it was catapulted across the crumbling line which had hitherto demarcated secular and communal parties. A series of 'historical blunders' committed by major players in the secular camp no doubt contributed to this outcome. What was in the beginning a hesitant trickle was gradually developing into a torrent as the secular cement gave way.

While looking at the all-India party system, it is important not to lose sight of the fact that almost all the single and multi-state parties represented in Parliament are simultaneously members of fairly stable two or three party systems which produce full-term majorities at the state level in most cases.[13] As one analyst observed when the 1999 results came in: 'The BJP talks as if India were a single entity but it understands that India's polity is a network of states in which castes, communities, classes and parties co-operate and compete for the benefits conferred by political power. The BJP wins because it surfs this web better than any other party.'[14] Tables 3.5 and 3.6 map the growth of the Vajpayee majority, which began in 1998 as a jumble of pre-electoral pacts and post-electoral adhesions.

This process of insertion may be profitably compared with that of hitherto excluded parties elsewhere. 'The history of excluded parties shows that they

---

[12] Describing the relationship with the Rashtriya Swayamsewak Sangh (RSS) as historical and its influence 'moral', Advani reaffirmed the indestructible ties that bind the BJP to it. *The Hindu*, 18 October 2000. Two other events which tarnished the Congress secular credentials and secured allies for the BJP were the events at Amritsar and Delhi (1984) and Ayodhya and Bombay (1992–93).

[13] James Manor, 'Regional Parties in Federal Systems', in Balveer Arora and Douglas V. Verney (eds), Multiple Identities in a Single State, New Delhi: CPR-CASI/Konark, 1995. Goa is obviously an exception to this, and seems to be bucking the trend towards fewer defections in the states.

[14] 'How India Voted', *The Economist*, 16 October 1999, p. 33.

Table 3.5: State-wise Distribution of Seats between Parties in the 12th Lok Sabha, 1998

Zones/States	Seats	INC	BJP	Other	Details of Other Parties
Zone I: 245 Seats: North and North-West [8 States + Delhi NCT + Chandigarh UT].					
Uttar Pradesh	85	00	57	28	Samajwadi P 20\BSP 04\Samata* 02\SJPR 01 (CShekhar)\ Ind. 01(Maneka)*
Bihar	54	05	20	29	RJD 17\Samata* 10\JD 01\RJP 01
Madhya Pradesh	40	10	30	00	00
Rajasthan	25	18	05	02	AIIC(S) 01(Ola)\Ind. 01 (Buta Singh)*
Punjab + Chandigarh	14	00	04	10	S.Akali Dal*08\JD1(Gujral)\ Ind1(Kainth)*
Haryana	10	03	01	06	H LokDal 04\H Vikas P* 01\BSP 01
Delhi NCT	07	01	06	00	00
Jammu & Kashmir	06	01	02	03	J&K National Conference 03
Himachal Pradesh	04	01	03	00	00
Total North N-West	**245**	**39**	**128**	**78**	
Zonal Percentage	**100**	**15.9**	**52.3**	**31.8**	
Zone II: 88 Seats: East and North-East [10 States]					
West Bengal	42	01	01	40	CPM 24\Trinamool Cong* 07\RSP 04\CPI 03\Forward Bloc 02
Orissa	21	05	07	09	Biju Janata Dal* 09
Assam	14	10	01	03	ASDC 01\UMF 01\Ind.-Bodo SMC 01
Six North-Eastern States + Sikkim	11	03	00	08	CPM 2\Arunachal C 2\CPI 1\Manipur S Cong 1\ Mizo Citizens CF 1\Sikkim DF 1
Total East North-East	**88**	**19**	**09**	**60**	
Zonal Percentage	**100**	**21.6**	**10.2**	**68.2**	
Zone III: 78 Seats: West: [3 States + 2 UTs]					
Maharashtra	48	33	04	11	Shiv Sena* 06\RPI 04\PWP 01
Gujarat+D&D, D&NH	28	07	21	00	00
Goa	02	02	00	00	00
Total West	**78**	**42**	**25**	**11**	
Zonal Percentage	**100**	**53.9**	**32.0**	**14.1**	
Zone IV: 132 Seats: South: [4 States + 3 UTs]					
Andhra Pradesh	42	22	04	16	TDP 12\CPI 2\JD 01\MIM 01
Tamil Nadu + Pondicherry	40	00	03	37	ADMK* 18\PMK* 04\MDMK* 03\ TRC* 01 (V.Ramamurthy)\JP 01 (S.Swamy)* DMK 06\TMC 03\CPI 01
Karnataka	28	09	13	06	Lok Shakti *03\Janata Dal 03
Kerala	20	08	00	12	CPM 06\CPI 02\Muslim League 02\Kerala Cong (M) 01\RSP 01
Lakshadweep + Andaman and Nicobar	02	02	00	00	
Total South	**132**	**41**	**20**	**71**	
Zonal Percentage	**100**	**31.1**	**15.1**	**53.8**	
Total Seats	543	141	182	220	
Total Percentage	100	26.0	33.5	40.5	

Source: Compiled from Election Commission data on http://www.eci.gov.in, supplemented by media reports for information on alliances and support. Adapted from Balveer Arora, 'Negotiating Differences: Federal Coalitions and National Cohesion', in Frankel et al. (eds), *Transforming India*.

Note: Parties which ultimately joined the BJP-led majority in Parliament are underlined. Those with which the BJP had pre-electoral arrangements are marked* in addition.

Table 3.6: Parties and Alliances in the 13th Lok Sabha, 1999

Zones/States	Seats	INC	BJP	Other	Details of Other Parties
Zone I: 245 Seats: North and North-West [8 States + Delhi NCT + Chandigarh UT]					
Uttar Pradesh	85	10	29	46	Samajwadi P 26\BSP 14\RLokDal 02\Loktantrik Cong. 02\Ind 01 (Maneka Gandhi)\SJPR 01 (Chandra Shekhar)
Bihar	54	04	23	27	JD (U) 18\RJD 07\CPM 01\Ind 01
Madhya Pradesh	40	11	29	00	00
Rajasthan	25	09	16	00	00
Punjab + Chandigarh	14	09	01	04	S Akali Dal 02\CPI 01\SAD (Mann) 01
Haryana	10	00	05	05	IN Lok Dal 05
Delhi NCT	07	00	07	00	00
Jammu & Kashmir	06	00	02	04	J&K National Conference 04
Himachal Pradesh	04	00	03	01	Himachal Vikas Cong. 01
Total North N-West	**245**	**43**	**115**	**87**	NDA Members & Allies 34
Zonal Percentage	**100**	**17.6**	**46.9**	**35.5**	NDA Members & Allies 13.9%
Zone II: 88 Seats: East and North-East [10 States]					
West Bengal	42	03	02	37	CPM 21\CPI 03\RSP 03\FB 02\Trinamool Congress 08
Orissa	21	02	09	10	Biju Janata Dal 10
Assam	14	10	02	02	CPI(ML) 01\Bodo SMC 01 (Indep.)
Six North-Eastern States + Sikkim	11	04	00	07	CPM 02\NCP 02\MSCP 01\SDF 01\Ind.01
Total East North-East	**88**	**19**	**13**	**56**	NDA Members & Allies 21
Zonal Percentage	**100**	**21.6**	**14.8**	**63.6**	NDA Members & Allies 23.9%
Zone III: 78 Seats: West: [3 States + 2 UTs]					
Maharashtra	48	10	13	25	Shiv Sena 15\NCP 06\PWP 01\JDS 01\BBM 01\Indep. 01
Gujarat +D&D, D&NH	28	07	20	01	Indep. 01
Goa	02	00	02	00	00
Total West	**78**	**17**	**35**	**26**	NDA Members & Allies 15
Zonal Percentage	**100**	**21.8**	**44.9**	**33.3**	NDA Members & Allies 19.2%
Zone IV: 132 Seats: South: [4 States + 3 UT]					
Andhra Pradesh	42	05	07	30	TDP 29\MIM 01
Tamil Nadu + Pondicherry	40	03	04	33	DMK 12\PMK 05\MDMK 03\MGR ADMK 01\ADMK 11\CPM 01
Karnataka	28	18	07	03	Janata Dal (United) 03
Kerala	20	08	00	12	CPM 08\Muslim 02\KEC(M) 01\KEC 01
Lakshadweep + Andaman and Nicobar	02	01	01	00	00
Total South	**132**	**35**	**19**	**78**	NDA Members & Allies 53
Zonal Percentage	**100**	**26.5**	**14.4**	**59.1**	NDA Members & Allies 40.2%
Cumulative Totals					
Total Seats	543	114	182	247	NDA Members & Allies 123
Total Percentage	100	21.0	33.5	45.5	NDA Members & Allies 22.7%

Source: Compiled from Election Commission data available at http://www.eci.gov.in, supplemented by media reports for information on alliances and support. Adapted from Balveer Arora, 'Political Parties and the Party System: The Emergence of New Coalitions', in Kashyap et al. *Reviewing the Constitution.*

Notes: Members of the NDA and its allies, totalling 17 parties and three independents, are underlined.
The Janata Dal (U) pre-election merger agreement was not ratified by the Samata party and the parliamentary party consequently split into Samata 12 (including one independent) and JD (U) 10 members.

illustrate great strategic flexibility—although not always a proportional degree of wisdom—in varying these kinds and degrees of adaptation to their delegitimized status.'[15] The federalisation of the party system was crying out for an integrating arrangement that would enable state-based parties to continue to exercise if not the power, at least the influence they had gained at the national level after a protracted struggle. The Congress party was both unwilling and ill-prepared to assume this role, entrapped as it was in its centralist and dynastic legacies.

III

It is perhaps stating the obvious to say that there is a dialectical relationship between political institutions and processes, the latter being principally animated by political parties. While the impact of parties on institutions is extensively discussed in the literature, especially in the context of the decline of institutions debate, the reverse arrow is generally given scant attention. We would like to emphasise here the influence of governmental, and particularly federal structures and institutions on political parties, their organisational structures and practices.[16]

The impact of federal structures and institutions on the federalisation of the party system should not be minimised. The logic of federal democracy, with multiple levels of government, points to the primacy of state parties and the integrative role of 'national' parties. So long as the Congress was able to internalise this imperative, it was able to contain the challenge from parties wedded to the defence and promotion of states' rights.

Federalism introduces the territorial dimension in classical modes of power-sharing. Alliances based on the territorial demarcation of spheres of power and influence are in essence federal coalitions. Under such an arrangement, the geographical deficits of a party with nation-wide aspirations are bridged by electoral pacts with state parties whereby these parties are left in control of their sphere of influence in an elaborate scheme of power-sharing encompassing both levels of the federal system. The BJP has developed this strategy to great effect. Accepting the coalition era as a 'natural phenomenon', the BJP now promises a 'positive evolution of coalition politics by ensuring that

---

[15] Levite and Tarrow, *The Legitimation of Excluded Parties*, p. 298. They also argue that 'the delegitimation of the opposition helps prevent the ideological dispersion, the loss of will, and the opportunism that so often attend the exercise of power; delegitimation can preserve the unity and the purpose essential to the effective implementation of a political strategy'.
[16] For an earlier statement of this problem, see Balveer Arora, 'Party System and Federal Structures in India: Linkages and Issues', in T.C. Bose (ed.), *Indian Federalism: Problems and Issues*, Calcutta: K.P. Bagchi, 1987.

regional and sectional aspirations are properly harmonised with national imperatives'.[17]

Understanding this development enables us to better answer the question: How do institutionalised territorial cleavages impact the party system? There is a fair amount of literature on the integrative role of parties in federal systems. It is, however, axiomatic that the existence of sub-national governments creates political spaces for parties whose appeal and constituencies are, by their very nature, territorially restricted. The challenge for integrative parties is correspondingly greater and they have been known to falter in many parliamentary federations.[18] Federal coalitions provide the only viable alternative in such situations.

Clearly, the BJP took note of its geographical deficits and proceeded to bridge them. While the V(ajpayee)-Factor was undoubtedly important and largely responsible for the breakthrough, it was backed by a skilful alliance policy. Comparative studies suggest that once an excluded party has broken the legitimation barrier, its ejection from the power-sharing process on the earlier grounds becomes problematic.[19]

There is, however, more to the transformation of the party system in recent years than merely the politics of alliances. Interpreting the 1999 election results, a Centre for the Study of Developing Societies (CSDS) study points out that 'Just 281 of the 537 seats contested remained with the party that won the constituency in the election of 1998. Parties opposed to the BJP alliance took 88 of its seats away, and nearly half the alliance's seats came from its rivals.'[20] This points to another significant feature of the party system, which is the high degree of volatility among the floating segment of voters and their willingness to discard candidates who do not deliver the results expected. These are frequently very basic needs like drinking water, roads, health centres or schools.

There are two distinct approaches to the question of the relationship between decentralisation of parties and decentralised institutions. On the one hand, it is argued that decentralised parties preserve the pluralistic dimensions of the polity and promote decentralised government, countering centralising pressures. On the other hand, it is also possible to maintain that decentralised parties exist largely because of the constitutional structure of elective offices in a federal system, i.e., the structuring of electoral incentives and rewards.[21]

---

[17] Bharatiya Janata Party, *Chennai Declaration*, January 2000, p. 4.

[18] The fluctuating fortunes of 'national' parties in Canada are a good example. See Arora and Verney (eds), *Multiple Identities in a Single State*.

[19] 'Although accession to power does not automatically follow legitimation, once the latter has occurred it is extremely difficult for a once excluded party to be delegitimated again.' Ibid., p. 296. Unless of course it retreats totally and as a whole to its initial position.

[20] 'How India Voted', *The Economist*, p. 33.

[21] Elazar refers to the Diamond–Grodzins exchange in this connection. See Daniel J. Elasar, *Exploring Federalism* (Trescaloosa: Alabama University Press, 1987), p. 99.

In reality, these two approaches are not mutually exclusive: the relationship being, as we noted earlier, dialectical. In the Indian context, the disjunction between increased federalisation of the polity and increased centralisation of the Congress party was responsible in no small measure for factionalism in many of its state units. Where they were not defeated, they defected.

IV

Establishing a link between intra-party democracy, fragmentation and renewal, Pratap Bhanu Mehta argues, 'The more discretionary power is vested with leaders, the more a political party will depend solely on its leaders for renewal.... If there are no formal mechanisms to challenge entrenched party hierarchies and regulate conflict within, parties are more likely to fragment.... Our fragmented party system may, therefore, be as much an artefact of the institutional incoherence of parties as anything else.' [22]

The risk of obsolescence that confronts a centralist national party like the Congress as the party system becomes more federalised underscores the need to develop new integrative strategies. It is a truism to state that all national parties are influenced by regional imperative while all regional parties aspire to shape national policies. The extent of federalisation can best be measured by the autonomy of action states enjoy in their allocated spheres of jurisdiction, and can ultimately extend to the exercise of influence, by states, in spheres reserved for the national government. What is often overlooked, however, is that strong state parties are a distinctive feature of most federal systems, even if they integrate themselves with polity-wide organisations to make a bid for power and influence at the national level. Renewal efforts of parties aspiring to this integrative role must necessarily confront the imperatives of our federalised party system.

Let us now turn our attention to some of the areas in which the party system has sought to be reformed by addressing major infirmities. The shortcomings and lacunae of the Anti-Defection Act are too well known to bear repetition. It is perhaps time to ask whether all defections should be barred, without exception and without regard to numbers. The conscience vote would obviously be a casualty and more power would accrue to party organisations, which could be partially be offset by insisting on inner-party democracy. [23] Interestingly, the Election Commission has in recent years

---

[22] He adds: 'Poorly institutionalised intra-party democracy produces more factions.... The incapacity of many of our political parties, especially the Congress, to renew themselves, is evidence of this.' 'Reform Parties First', *The Hindu*, 31 October 2000.

[23] The EC began mentioning the party affiliation of each elected member in its notification constituting the Lok Sabha only in March 1998. In its efforts to reduce the number of

emerged as a significant force in pressing for reform, while introducing measures which go beyond its simple role of an arbiter ensuring 'free and fair elections'. It has begun insisting on the holding of organisational elections within parties. It has also decided, in the case of splits in recognised parties, to withhold recognition from splinter groups till they have proved themselves electorally, while allotting them symbols in the interim.[24]

However, its decisions regarding recognition of parties under the Election Symbols (Reservation and Allotment) Order, 1968, verge on the bizarre if not the absurd at times. Armed with its criteria of recognition, based on electoral results, it reviews the situation after each general elections and proceeds to reshuffle classifications. Thus, the number of national parties has now been reduced to five, with both the JD factions being eliminated, as well as the CPM with 33 Lok Sabha seats. Interestingly, the Nationalist Congress Party with eight Members of Parliament (MPs) from four states gains recognition.[25]

The taxonomy of the Symbols Order is not value-neutral, as 'national' is a term charged with history and emotion. After having been discontinued for the 1962 and 1967 elections, the 'national party' certificate from the Election Commission was reintroduced in 1971 and all multi-state parties were automatically re-designated national parties. The Congress (I), keen to emphasise its national character, obviously stood to gain by demarcating itself from various splinter groups and other challengers. In our view, no useful public purpose is served by retaining this distinction between national and state parties. The requirements of symbol allocation to multi-state parties can easily be met by simply specifying the states in which they are entitled to a reserved symbol for multi-state parties. In practical terms, it would make no difference to the electoral process if one single unified category of recognised parties were adopted by reverting to the practice in vogue for the 1962 and 1967 elections.[26]

---

frivolous candidates, the EC raised the security deposit to Rs 10,000 for Lok Sabha and Rs 5,000 for Assembly elections, from Rs 500 and Rs 250, respectively. Election Commission, *Elections in India: Major Events and New Initiatives, 1996–2000*, New Delhi: Nirvacahan Sadan, 2000, p. 43.

[24] This policy change was implemented in the 1998 elections, though almost all the parties qualified for recognition subsequently. In 1997 the Commission raised the valid votes polled criterion for recognition as a state party from 4 to 6 per cent, now including votes of all party candidates without exception. Ibid., pp. 352–53.

[25] Para 7 (1) of the Symbols Order, 1968, which provides for two categories of recognised parties merely states, 'If a political party is treated as a recognised political party in accordance with paragraph 6 in four or more States, it shall be known as, and shall have and enjoy the status of, a "National party" throughout the whole of India...'

[26] David Butler Ashok Lahiri, Prannoy Roy, *India Decides: Election 1952–1995* (3rd edition) (New Delhi: Books and Things, 1995, pp 20–21). The 1957 election saw four national parties (plus 12 state parties) and then the concept itself was abandoned. Among the parties which have been recently derecognised are Bansi Lal's Haryana Vikas Party, R. K. Hegde's

No discussion of renewal would, however, be complete without giving due weight to the role played by the Election Commission and the judiciary in carrying out essential reforms which would restore the credibility of the party system and the political class as a whole. This brings us to the second major area of concern which is the entry of criminal elements as direct participants in the electoral process. One survey prior to the 1998 general elections listed six different categories of persons that it considered unfit to contest and the names of as many as 72 candidates charged or convicted of various offences under various laws of the land.[27] The existing provisions of Section 8 of the Representation of the People Act, 1951, are manifestly insufficient, despite the fact that the Election Commission instructed returning officers in August 1997 to disqualify candidates convicted for offences listed therein, even those on bail or with an appeal pending.[28] More recently, the Delhi High Court instructed the Election Commission to inform voters of candidates who are 'accused of offences punishable with life imprisonment'.[29]

V

The fear of coalitions as harbingers of disorderly governance is frequently articulated and is in our view exaggerated in a needlessly alarmist manner. Announcing the 'bad news' after the 1999 elections, Swaminathan Aiyer bemoaned: 'Notwithstanding Vajpayee's victory, India remains very much in a coalition era, and this will be a hurdle to bold, decisive governance.'[30]

Lok Shakti (Karnataka) and Subramaniam Swamy's Janata Party. The fascination with the national status label obviously continues, as even the CPM has vowed to get the criteria modified to re-enter this exclusive club.

[27] *Outlook*, 23 February 1998. The majority of them were contesting from Bihar and Uttar Pradesh. Speaking of the links between crime syndicates (mafias) and political personalities, the Vohra Committee observes: 'some political leaders become the leaders of these gangs\armed senas and, over the years, get themselves elected to local bodies, state assemblies and the national Parliament', Home Affairs, India, *Vohra Committee Report* (as tabled in Parliament on 1 August 1995).

[28] Election Commission, *Elections in India*, p. 327. A format was prescribed requiring candidates to provide information regarding convictions with their nomination papers, supported by an affidavit. Data on how many nominations were actually rejected as a result of this directive is not available. The threshold for disqualification suggested by the Law Commission in its 170th Report is framing of a chargesheet by a court whereas the EC is in favour of setting aside only those convicted.

[29] 'PIL of Association for Democratic Reforms', *The Hindu*, 3 November 2000.

[30] 'Coalition Politics is Still Here', *The Economic Times*, 13 October 1999. K.K. Katyal explains the rise to prominence and power of state parties by their advocacy of 'defending state interests against a predatory Centre acting at the behest of other larger interests and forces'. 'Regional Issues Hold Sway', *The Hindu*, 13 September 1999.

The examples most often cited are the roll-back of proclaimed policies under the pressure of constituents, concessions often extracted in full media view.

It is possible to argue that political deals struck in earlier periods of single party majority rule were hidden from the public gaze and hence not seen to exist. Such deals are an inherent part of democratic decision-making and the public interest is arguably served by having them out in the open. The political class is engaged in a continuous process of adjustment and accommodation, which includes offers of various types of rewards, notably public offices. Only those that are clandestine, such as the arrangement arrived at between the Congress and the Jharkhand Mukti Morcha (JMM) under P. V. Narasimha Rao, are considered tainted by corruption.

What the Congress and the BJP both yearn for is single party majority, and it would be unnatural for them not to do so. What does set them apart however, are the strategies they are adopting to reach this goal, which may still prove, in the final analysis, to be elusive, even chimerical. Is it then the end of the road for pan-Indian 'national' parties as we have known them, of the type that gained prominence under Indira Gandhi and dominated the political scene for two decades (1969–89)? We have argued here that federal coalitions are a defining feature of the party system as it has developed over the last decade. Further, it can be argued that no multi-state (national) party will in the foreseeable future be able to encompass the entire polity without resorting to electoral alliances and understandings with state parties.

The changed economic policy context also lends support to this trend. One of the arguments in favour of any state party is its ability to influence decision-making at the Centre, particularly since many of them have a crucial bearing on states' interests. State units of the Congress skilfully exploited this electoral asset in the heydays of dominance. They derived their strength from the powerful central decision-making entity known as the Government of India. As decentralisation proceeds apace and more and more issues are left to be decided at the state level without constant reference to the Centre, this particular argument loses its gloss and old-style 'national' parties, some of their raison d'être. State parties in federal coalitions are able to flaunt this very same asset in the expectation of electoral advantage.

This in no way minimises the importance of structures capable of scaffolding and sustaining pan-Indian coalitions. The Congress Party retains such a scaffolding, a beehive-like structure which remains intact even when inactive. These structures alternately lie dormant or, when reactivated, buzz with energy.[31]

---

[31] The Congress obtained 28.31 per cent of the popular vote as compared to the BJP's tally of 23.75 per cent in 1999, but scored far fewer seats. It must, however, be pointed out that the BJP contested 471 seats in 1996 but has, after adopting an aggressive coalition building strategy, steadily contested fewer seats on its own: 388 in 1998 and 339 in 1999.

Party renewal takes place at two levels. The first is the renewal of cadres which, under the right conditions of intra-party democracy, can lead to a renewal of leadership. The second level is that of ideology, but innovative political strategies are often passed off by tactically mature party leaderships as pragmatic responses not incompatible with ideological consistency. As Levite and Tarrow point out, among the ways in which excluded parties react and adapt to their delegitimation, 'is to attempt to extend the party's influence among new groups of the population (and/or) ally with legitimate participants (and/or) accept the institutional rules of the game of politics while preserving the substantive values around which the excluded group was initially organised'.[32]

The BJP's renewal strategies are a good example of this phenomenon. The Chennai Declaration affirms: 'Although the ideals are constant, the policies and their interpretation in the light of the changing needs of new situations and challenges have to be renewed from time to time. This quality of principle-centred flexibility, adaptability, and self-renewal, while being true to one's essential nature and purpose, is the hallmark of any living organisation.'[33]

While there is some evidence to indicate that the BJP is steadily attracting more members directly rather than through the RSS channel, it still relies heavily on structures borrowed from the Sangh Parivar for its electoral machinery. Its moves to woo the very same groups—dalits and Muslims—that constituted the core of the Congress strategy is a part of its efforts to don the mantle that it considers to be rightfully devolving to it. It asserts: 'We are now well on our way to becoming India's natural party of governance, a distinction that the Congress party once enjoyed but which it lost due to its poor record of governance, corruption, factionalism, abandoning of internal democracy and servile surrender to dynastic leadership.'[34]

This description of the present state of the Congress will undoubtedly be contested and rejected by it, but little has emerged from its decision-making bodies in terms of strategic rethinking since the last elections. At the tactical level, it finally agreed to participate in a state government as a minority partner for the first time in Bihar after the March 2000 elections. The results of this experiment on the basis of a common minimum programme are at best mixed and it does not as yet represent a clear policy. At the Bangalore session (17–18 March 2001) the Congress declared itself 'prepared to forge electoral or coalition arrangements with secular parties' and play a pro-active role in restoring secular governance in the country'.[35]

---

[32] Levite and Tarrow, *The Legitimation of Excluded Parties*, p. 298.

[33] Bharatiya Janata Party, *Chennai Declaration*, January 2000, p. 5.

[34] Ibid.

[35] *The Indian Express*, 19 March 2001. The earlier insistence on single party rule is significantly downplayed as it moves away from its earlier anti-coalition stance.

Despite the size and complexities of the party system, it is arguably under-developed in terms of its capabilities for grappling with complex issues of national concern. There is a worrisome divorce of economics and politics, leading to an impoverishment of the political in its most profound sense. The best example of this tendency is the passage of the 1999–2000 Union Budget by Parliament by a voice vote without any discussion, while parties were engaged in an intense struggle for 'political' power, or more appropriately, political office.

Finally, we must consider the impact of the establishment of a third tier of elective offices, the Panchayats, on renewal processes in the party system. The forces set in motion by the 73rd Amendment could act as a powerful impetus to renewal and reform. Innovations such as reservation of seats for women and the need for party cadres to campaign and contest in third tier elections are factors which would gradually impact party organisations at all levels. They impart a new dimension to federal democracy by vastly increasing the number of elective offices on offer. In the long run they can act as agents of renewal of parties through the induction of more active members in party organisations. However, this outcome would depend greatly on the extent to which intra-party democracy is allowed to develop and flourish. The track record of most parties is extremely patchy in this regard.

In sum, beyond fragmentation there is federalisation. As federalisation progresses, polity-wide parties which do not adapt to the federal imperative get progressively weaponed and marginalised. As our political system has become more democratic, it has also become more federal. The future of this federal democracy will depend in large measure on how the party system is able to reshape state and local institutions to meet the very simple and basic demands of an electorate whose patience is wearing thin. As accountability mechanisms function vigorously and the frustration of voters brings swift retribution in its wake, the political class is under pressure to deliver on essentials.

4

THE PARTY SYSTEM IN GERMANY AND PARTY FRAGMENTATION IN THE EUROPEAN UNION

Karl-Rudolf Korte

I

The Role of Political Parties and the Legal Context

Political parties play a highly significant role in the political system of the Federal Republic of Germany. Indeed, critics have recently alleged that they play too great a role. The type of democratic system that the Federal Republic enjoys has been called 'party government' by some experts, a concept which includes the ideas that parties give coherence and direction to government through their policy programmes, that governments depend upon popular election (and, in many cases, on the inter-party bargaining that goes on prior to the formation of governing coalitions) and that parties take responsibility for the successes or failures of policy.[1]

This responsible role of parties in the political system is relatively new in Germany, and certainly was not found prior to the Second World War. In the Second Empire parties were secondary to powerful interest groups in terms of influencing and shaping policy. In the Weimar Republic parties remained too ideologically confined—each too concerned with the sectional interests of its clientele—to assume government responsibility or the task of policy development in the way in which parties in the Bonn Republic have done. Of course, the provisions of the Weimar constitution, especially the emergency powers of the president of the Republic, acted as a constraint on political parties, inhibiting the development of 'party government'. The Nazi period then did provide a 'party government', but of an absolutely non-democratic, totalitarian type.

So when after the Second World War the time came to allow a degree of self-government to re-emerge in occupied West Germany, parties were seen

---

[1] See G. Roberts, *Party Politics in the New Germany*, London: Kluwer Academic, 1997.

to be a key feature. Because of their potential to contribute to the development of democracy, they were allowed to form very soon after the commencement of the occupation regime. On the other hand, because of their potential to obstruct or pervert democracy—as experience in the inter-war period had so clearly shown—it was decided by the allies that political parties had to be licensed by the occupation authorities. When it came to the drafting of a temporary constitution for the Federal Republic of Germany in 1948–49, the role of parties in the political system was addressed and this role was later given explicit expression in Article 21 of the Basic Law, the German constitution, which also imposed responsibilities and restrictions on the parties. This inclusion of the role of political parties in a democratic constitution was extremely new, mainly because many other democratic constitutions pre-dated the modern democratic activity of parties.

Article 21 (Political Parties) of the Basic Law reads as follows:[2]

1. Parties shall participate in the formation of the political will of the people. They may be freely established. Their internal organisation must conform to democratic principles. They must publicly account for their assets and for the sources and use of their funds.
2. Parties that by reason of their aims or the behaviour of their adherents, seek to undermine or abolish the free democratic basic order or to endanger the existence of the Federal Republic of Germany shall be unconstitutional. The Federal Constitutional Court shall rule on the question of unconstitutionality.
3. Details shall be regulated by federal laws.

Section (2) of Article 21 of the Basic Law which states that non-democratic parties can be condemned as unconstitutional was twice the basis of cases in the Constitutional Court which resulted in bans being imposed on political parties. The extreme right-wing Socialist Reich Party (Sozialistische Reichspartei [SRP]) was banned in 1952, and the Communist Party of Germany (Kommunistische Partei Deutschlands [KPD]) in 1956, on the grounds that they did not conform to the requirements of Article 21 that political parties should not be hostile to the democratic constitutional system.

The production of legislation to fulfil the requirement of Paragraph 3 of Article 21 did not occur for several years. In the early years of the Federal Republic there seemed to be more pressing priorities than designing rules for political parties in order to implement the requirement in Article 21 of the Basic Law that a law should be produced to provide detailed regulation of

---

[2] See Basic Law for the Federal Republic of Germany, promulgated by the Parliamentary Council on 23 May 1949 as amended up to July 1998, published by the Press and Information Office of the Federal Government, Bonn, 1998, pp. 40–50.

political parties. However, once the political parties found that their finances were threatened by the absence of such legislation they quickly drew up a Political Party Act which was passed by the *Bundestag*, the first chamber of the German parliament, and the *Bundesrat* (Federal Council, the second chamber of the German parliament) in 1967.

This act elaborated on the status and role of political parties in relation to their constitutional responsibility defined in Article 21 of participating in the formation of the political will of the people. It set out the defining characteristics of political parties for purposes of the law, including the requirement of regular contests of *Bundestag* and *Land* (federal state) elections. It provided a framework for party structures and procedures, and for the protection of the rights of party members, standards with which parties had to comply and implement in their own statutes. It regulated the financial relationship between parties and the state by making available subsidies to the costs of election campaigning based on the relative shares of the vote which parties received at the election.

Together, Article 21 and the Political Party Act of 1967 provide an unusually explicit legal context within which German political parties must shape their activities. Few other West European democracies possess either such constitutional or legal regulation of parties. This context conveys privileges. However, it also conveys responsibilities and, in doing so, reinforces 'party government' in Germany since parties can point to this legal context and claim that, alongside the *Bundestag* and *Bundesrat*, the chancellor, the federal president, the Constitutional Court, and the federal system are organs of the state and not just a set of extra-constitutional voluntary organisations.

The Structure of the Party System

The party system of the Federal Republic in 1990, prior to reunification, consisted of five parties with representation in the *Bundestag*: the Christian Democratic Union (Christlich Demokratische Union [CDU], executing activities in all federal states with the exception of Bavaria) and the Christian Social Union (Christlich Soziale Union [CSU], the Bavarian sister party of the CDU with activities restricted to the Free State of Bavaria), the Social Democratic Party of Germany (Sozialdemokratische Partei Deutschlands [SPD]), the Free Democratic Party (Freie Demokratische Partei [FDP], the Liberals), and the Greens (Die Grünen). Since 1990, the Party of Socialist Democracy (Partei des Demokratischen Sozialismus [PDS])—which evolved after reunification in the re-established Eastern *Laender* (federal states) as a successor of the former communist Socialist Unity Party of Germany (Sozialistische Einheitspartei Deutschlands [SED]), the ruling party in the former German Democratic Republic—was represented in the *Bundestag* as well, on the basis of having achieved three direct mandates. In addition, a number of smaller parties existed and still do, few of which were ever of any significance at the federal level.

The West German party system had, in the early years of the Federal Republic, consisted of a much larger number of parties, but several factors contributed to a swift reduction, so that from 1961 until the entry of the Greens into the *Bundestag* in 1983, most of the time only three parties were represented in it.

This reduction in the number of parties by 1961 was produced partly by the structures of the electoral system resulting from revisions in 1953 and 1956. The need to obtain 5 per cent of list votes calculated for the whole of the Federal Republic (or three direct mandates) not only made it more difficult for small parties to retain *Bundestag* representation, it also made it difficult for new parties to break through and win seats, as the National-Democratic Party of Germany (National-Demokratische Partei Deutschlands [NPD]) experienced in 1969 and as the Greens found in 1980.

A second factor was the transformation of the two largest parties, the combined CDU-CSU and the SPD, into 'catch-all parties' (*Volksparteien*), enabling them to appeal to voters beyond the confines of their traditional church-related or working-class environments. This made it easier for them to attract voters who otherwise might have voted for alternative parties, such as the Catholic Centre Party which had been so strong in the Second Empire and Weimar Republic periods and which had survived chiefly in parts of the federal state of Northrhine-Westphalia after the Second World War, but which soon found competition from the CDU-CSU too strong.

Third, the rulings of the Constitutional Court in 1952 and 1956 which banned the extreme right-wing SRP and the KPD were important. These verdicts did not so much have an effect by eliminating those two parties themselves; after all, in terms of national politics they had become of negligible importance and neither had seats in the *Bundestag* when the ban was imposed. Rather, they emphasised that the government and the Constitutional Court were prepared to invoke the provisions of the Basic Law which required parties to be democratic, and this may have deterred other extremist parties from forming at all or, if they did form, from contesting elections.

Fourth, the success of Konrad Adenauer's Christian Democratic government in providing stability, security and prosperity for West Germany meant that more and more voters were prepared to support that government. It also meant that the Christian Democrats were successful in 'taking-over' politicians and supporters of other parties with which they had been allied, such as the German Party (Deutsche Partei [DP]). Only the liberal FDP resisted this gravitational pull of the Christian Democrats successfully, despite Adenauer's attempt to debilitate that party in 1956.

Only one new party succeeded in winning seats in the *Bundestag* between 1961 and the reunification of Germany in 1990. The Greens were successful in the 1983 *Bundestag* election, having built up strength in several of the *Laender* and after having contested the 1980 *Bundestag* election without success. They managed to overcome the obstacles and constraints of the electoral system by drawing upon what had become a widespread environmentalist movement and which coincided with an upsurge in support for the peace movement in the Federal Republic. This in turn reflected a new political mood among some sections of the population concerned with 'new politics' issues while disapproving of the orthodox parties and their procedures.

Reunification had a relatively minor impact on the party system. A fifth party, the PDS, entered the *Bundestag* and for one legislative period (1990–94) the West German Greens lost their *Bundestag* representation. Beyond that, and despite quite considerable West German–East German differences in levels of party support, the broad framework of the party system so far remains fundamentally unchanged.

The party systems of the *Laender* have tended to reflect those of the Federal Republic. In the early post-war years a number of parties developed locally: the Bavarian Party (Bayern Partei [BP]) and conservative Protestant or nationalist parties in northern Germany, for instance, but since the 1960s they have tended to disappear or decline into irrelevance. The party representing the Danish cultural minority in the federal state of Schleswig-Holstein—which has protected rights of representation in the Schleswig-Holstein *Land* parliament (local assembly) under the constitution of this *Land*—still exists as a factor in *Land* politics. Radical right-wing parties won seats from time to time in *Land* parliaments: the NPD in the 1960s; the Republicans (Die Republikaner) in South Germany and the German People's Union (Deutsche Volksunion [DVU]) in North Germany more recently. The STATT-Party, formed by discontented CDU members in Hamburg, sensationally won seats in the Hamburg *Land* parliament in 1993 but, though drawn into the *Land* government as the junior partner to the SPD, suffered from internal quarrels and decline in support and failed to win any seats in the 1998 Hamburg *Land* election.

Of course, the relative weight of the parties in each *Land* varies very considerably. The PDS is strong in all the East German *Laender* but in none of the West German *Laender*. The SPD has its strongholds in Bremen, Hamburg, Schleswig-Holstein and Northrhine-Westphalia, and more recently also in Brandenburg and Mecklenburg-Western Pommerania as well as in Saxony-Anhalt, for instance. The Christian Democrats are especially strong in Baden-Württemberg, Hessen, Saxony and Thuringia, the CSU traditionally is the dominating party in Bavaria. The FDP has been relatively strong, e.g., in Baden-Württemberg, but otherwise finds that its support can fluctuate considerably in every *Land*, though it is extremely weak in East Germany and since 1994 has not been represented in the parliaments of any of the 'new *Laender*'. The Greens have built up support especially in Hamburg, Hessen and Baden-Württemberg, but even though they merged with the East German citizen rights-movement party the 'Alliance '90', they are also, like the FDP, relatively weak in the 'new *Laender*'.

Identity of the Main Political Parties

The 'Union Parties': The CDU and CSU

The CDU is leading among Catholic and liberal-conservative voters. It also has traditional roots in large segments of the rural farming population, among the self-employed, the entrepreneurs, as well as the business community and all Catholics including a number of blue-collar workers with ties to the church. At the same time it is able to integrate national-conservative circles and, last but not least, has scored election successes with the newly emergent middle classes.

The SPD: The Social Democratic Party

Core voters of the SPD are mainly industrial workers with trade union affiliations. By means of the Godesberg Reform in 1959 it has managed to reach the Protestant traditional middle class and has been successful in winning over important segments of the new urban reform-minded classes.

The FDP: The Free Democratic Party

This party has never overcome its minority status, it also lacks any significant base of loyal voters. It draws many of its votes from those in self-employment, and members of the professions such as accountants, pharmacists or dentists. Paradoxically, despite being a weak party from the electoral point of view, constantly having to be anxious about retaining its representation in the *Bundestag*, it has been a member of federal coalitions for more years than either the Christian Democrats or the SPD. However, its pivotal role in the party system has been weakened by its relegation to fourth place behind the Greens in 1994 and 1998 and the presence of the PDS in the *Bundestag* also reduces the possibility of the FDP again being able to determine which of the two large parties will lead the government.

The Greens

The Greens (since 1993 officially named 'Alliance '90/The Greens') was formed as a party in the Federal Republic in 1980. Local citizen initiative groups concerned about environmental issues had, in some *Laender*, contested *Land* elections and had won significant electoral support, though not enough to win seats. Though the Greens failed to win seats in the 1980 *Bundestag* elections with only 1.5 per cent of the vote, they did enter the *Bundestag* in 1983 and 1987. They also won seats in most of the *Laender* parliaments and participated in governing coalitions in several *Laender*. Partly because of the party's originally hostile attitude to German reunification, partly because it was internally split by conflicts between its more radical 'fundamentalist' wing (the 'Fundis') and its more pragmatic 'realist' wing (the 'Realos') concerning policy and strategy, the Greens narrowly failed to secure the required 5 per cent in the 1990 *Bundestag* elections and thus did not win seats. In the 1994 *Bundestag* elections, the Greens not only easily overcame the 5 per cent hurdle, they also managed for the first time to win more votes than the FDP and in 1998 they won 6.7 per cent of list votes.

The PDS: The Party of Democratic Socialism

In December 1989, the ruling party of the German Democratic Republic—the SED—decided to undergo a thorough and radical reform of its structures and of some aspects of its ideology and programme. The result was the transformation in stages of the SED into the PDS which sees itself as a left-wing and socialist party. The party managed to do fairly well in the elections of 1990, including successes in the *Bundestag* elections that year. In Eastern Germany, in the 1998 *Bundestag* elections the PDS won 21.6 per cent of the vote. It has seats in all five of the East German *Land* parliaments as well as in the Berlin *Land* local assembly and, since the 1999 election, in the European Parliament. In 1997 the PDS had 1,00,000 members, of which only 2,600 resided in West Germany.

The Effects of the Electoral System on the Party System, the Government and the 1998 Parliamentary Election (*Bundestagswahl*)

The electoral system, though a system based on proportional representation, has certainly not produced a multi-party system. We see a bloc-type post-war party system traditionally dominated by two major parties (CDU or SPD) which succeed each other in government and opposition on relatively rare occasions at the federal or *Laender* level. The three-party system (CDU/SPD/FDP), unchanged for 20 years, expanded into a four-party system after 1983 (new: the Greens) and into a five-party system (new: PDS) after 1990.

The electoral system affects the type of government which the Federal Republic possesses. On the one hand, because the system is one of proportional representation of parties which makes it difficult for one party by itself to win an overall majority of seats, invariably there is a coalition government and, for the past 40 years, a coalition government consisting of only two parties. On the other hand, the restrictions imposed by the 5 per cent qualification for list seats has, for much of the period prior to reunification, limited the number of parties in the *Bundestag* to three or four. Such coalitions tend to be very stable.

The 1998 elections to the German parliament (*Bundestag*) stand out as one of the few examples in post-war German electoral history of *Machtwechsel* (change in government)[3] precipitated by the electorate rather than changes in the coalition behaviour of the parties. Yet the drama of the 1998 elections does not in itself mean dramatic party system change. The alternation of parties in government is one of the defining properties of liberal democracy and takes place in the most stable party systems. *Machtwechsel* is not, therefore, the main focus of this paper. Instead we are concerned with what the elections reveal about underlying party systems trends. On every recognised dimension of analysis, it will be argued, the evidence of the 1998 elections points towards the increasing complexity, fluidity and openness of the party landscape.[4]

The elections were remarkable in a number of ways. They brought to a close 16 years of Christian Democratic-Liberal government under Helmut Kohl, the longest serving chancellor in the history of the Federal Republic. Defeat resulted in Kohl's resignation as CDU leader, with Theodor Waigel standing down as leader of the CSU. For the first time in the electoral history of the Federal Republic, a change in government resulted directly from the incumbent's defeat at the polls rather than changes in the parties' coalition choices. For only the second time in the Federal Republic (after 1972), the Social Democratic Party became the strongest party in the *Bundestag*. The magnitude of the SPD's lead over the Christian Democrats was unprecedented, polling 5.8 per cent more than the CDU/CSU. After relatively speedy negotiations, a coalition between the SPD and the Greens was formed for the first time at the national level.

Unlike the period before 1969, the FDP is not in government. Changes in Germany's 'electoral geography' produced a majority of the left (SPD, Greens and PDS) which has no precedent in the Federal Republic's history. At the same time the aggregate vote of the German People's Union (DVU), Republikaner and the National-Democratic Party at some 3.3 per cent amounted to the highest share for the extreme right since 1969. Beyond these simple facts, however, lie many unanswered questions about political life after Kohl. Does it point towards new orientations within the parties or a

---

[3] See Karl-Rudolf Korte, 'Der Anfang vom Ende. Konjunkturen des Machtwechsels in Vergleich' (The Beginning of the End. Trends in the Change of Power in comparison), *Zeitschrift für Parlamentsfragen* (Journal of Parliamentary Affairs), 4/2000, pp. 833–57.
[4] See Karl-Rudolf Korte, *Wahlen in Deutschland* (Elections in Germany), Bonn: Bundeszentrale für politische Bildung (Federal Centre for Political Education), 2000.

reconfiguration of the party system? Can we expect it to signal significant changes in policy, or in the character and style of government and politics?[5]

The 'Party State' in Germany and the Crisis of the *Volksparteien*

Many commentators have described the political system of the Federal Republic as a 'party state'. But the gap is widening between the control of the party state and the basis for their legitimacy in society.

After many years of unchallenged domination the traditional party system dominated by CDU and SPD entered a decidedly critical phase. It was swamped by a wave of dissatisfaction, anti-party sentiment and criticism by intellectuals. There is a confidence crisis and extreme loss of public support. Aggregation provides a measure of the concentration of the party system around the large parties. *Volkspartei* domination has been one of the defining characteristics of the post-war party system, reaching its height in 1976 when the SPD and CDU/CSU collectively polled 91.2 per cent of the vote. In the 1998 elections this fell to 76.1 per cent. There is an unmistakable parallel between the loss of votes and the constant loss of members of both *Volksparteien*.[6]

The Erosion of the Electoral Base

The results of the *Bundestag* and *Landtag* elections of the 1990s including the most recent *Laender* election cycle of 1995–97 show that it is hardly possible to say that the trend has turned in favour of the major parties. At least the thesis on stabilisation and regeneration expressed after the election year of 1994 and still current, turns out to have been a hasty conclusion.

The fact that the major parties are still declining is mainly evident in the continuing loss of votes. Since the early 1980s, the aggregate share of votes for the two major parties has shown a downward tendency both for *Bundestag* and *Landtag* elections. The share of electoral support for the CDU/CSU and the SPD has dropped to 78.0 from 87.4 per cent in the five elections to the *Bundestag* held between 1980 and 1994. A synchronous trend can be observed for the *Landtag* elections.

[5] See Stephan Padgett, *The Boundaries of Stability: The Party System Before and After the 1998 Bundestagswahl*. For an overview, see Stephan Padgett and Thomas Saalfeld (eds), *Bundestagswahl 1998* (German Elections to the *Bundestag*), *German Politics*, 2/2000, pp. 88–107.
[6] See Elmar Wiesendahl, 'The Present State and Future Prospects of the German *Volksparteien*', *German Politics*, 2, 1998, pp. 151–75.

Membership Erosion

There is an unmistakable parallel between the loss of votes just described and the constant loss of members of both the CDU and the SPD which affects their self-image as *Volksparteien* based on mass membership. The *Volkspartei* system therefore is not only changing with regard to the voters but it also suffers increasingly from problems caused by organisational shortcomings and numerical weakening.

Reasons for the Decline of the *Volksparteien*

The decline of the *Volksparteien* in Germany must be seen in the context of a whole complex of interconnected causes. For example, Scarrow attributes the phenomena of erosion to an exaggerated intellectual criticism of the parties and the discontent in the form of 'mass anti-party sentiments' which it engendered.[7] Surely, it is also the problems resulting from German reunification which account for the turbulence the major parties are experiencing. But the phenomena of decline go back so far into the 1980s that for this reason alone a much broader background is needed to explain the negative development.

It should be pointed out that the partisan identification of the German electorate has decreased from 80 to some 50 per cent from the early 1970s to today. To be more specific, the share of party supporters with strong or very strong party affiliations has diminished from approximately one-half to one-quarter of the voters during the same period. On the whole, voters have become more independent, more mobile, more selective, and less predictable. As can easily be seen, however, the long-term weakening of party loyalties and the increasing volatility and fluctuation of voters in themselves call for an explanation. The surface phenomena may well have to be interpreted in the context of the deeper rooted causes of change in society.

Thus, the trend of decline of the major parties may be attributed to the shrinking, and partly even disappearing, environment of workers with ties to labour unions and Catholics faithful to their church, in which the SPD and the CDU/CSU, respectively, have their respective roots. These former core groups have been supplanted by new unaffiliated middle classes whose members hold jobs in the services sector and live in an urban environment. Moreover, other factors of social change such as secularisation and individualisation, cognitive mobilisation and participatory revolution, changing values, the pluralisation and segmentation of living conditions, and the greater diversification of lifestyle groups as well as, not least, an increasing abandonment of the principle of solidarity, have changed the electoral scene

---

[7] Susan E. Scarrow, 'Politicians Against Parties', *European Journal of Political Research*, Yearbook 1996, Oxford: Blockwell Publications, pp. 298–309.

so profoundly that these factors could well be used to explain voters' greater volatility and loss of party affiliation.

Such explanatory approaches based on sociological findings and theories of societal change, popular among election researchers, are quite appealing. However, one must not disregard other social forces that persist and give rise to tensions because of the non-correspondence between a modernising society on the one hand and social backwardness and unaffected traditionalism on the other. Owing to their comprehensive, all-inclusive approach to the electorate this has far-reaching consequences for the *Volksparteien* as they cannot avoid trying to reconcile and express irreconcilable tensions and opposing tendencies. They do so by using tactical freedom as well as alternative options of strategy in order to achieve results that appear advantageous in the changed conditions of the world around them.

Today, the *Volksparteien*, now open to the mobile middle classes, find themselves caught in some kind of modernisation trap. On the one hand they can no longer rely on the support of their regular voters whose loyalty they have strained too much. On the other hand they are not gaining sufficient support from the new middle classes to compensate for the losses they sustained among their core supporters. Consequently, the *Volksparteien* have reached the limits of integration. They lack a unifying force that would allow them to represent credibly and hold together both the frustrated traditional segment of voters and the middle-class segment that is unwilling to make a firm commitment.

If we now direct our view to the parliamentary representation level of the *Volksparteien*, the comments on their condition—which so far have been rather gloomy—reflect a much brighter situation. It is obvious here that the phenomena of decline and weakness can hardly harm them at the parliamentary and governmental level. The *Volksparteien*, as much as their societal grounding may be crumbling, are still the principal parties on the political stage. This statement may seem odd as they are transforming into 'medium-sized parties' because of their shrinking voter bases and, after dropping below the 40 per cent level, are heading for 30 per cent in terms of voter support and, even more, the number of mandates. However, the major parties are still relatively large and the small parties comparatively small, even if the gap between them is narrowing.

Admittedly, their habitual parliamentary and governmental supremacy is left untouched by these changed relations. Both *Volksparteien* retain their character as 'core parties'. Above all, their strategic majority-building position remains, for it is not possible to organise parliamentary majorities against them or to exclude one of the two. This does not mean, though, that the conditions for forming coalition governments would not be more difficult now for the major parties.

The fact that—in spite of the electoral weakening of the major parties—there are no indications 'that the parties have become marginalised in the political process', as Padgett stated quite correctly, is substantiated by their undiminished privileges conferred on the parties by the state at the governmental and administrative level. As powerful 'public office holders', the CDU/CSU and the SPD provide the heads of government everywhere at the federal and *Laender* level and the doors to state resources and sinecures are wide open to them.

If at all, one can speak of a critical destabilisation of major party rule in Germany only with a view to its eroding social base. In contrast, the party system represented at the parliamentary level—excluding the East German conditions—may well be said to have proven immune against any profound changes so far. Nevertheless this judgement does not go far enough since it is based on just a segment of the party reality in Germany which overall has indeed changed. The disturbed relations with society and the problems of uprooting have so far failed to affect the power balance in the parliaments which are still stable. Thus, there is a widening discrepancy between the loss of status in society and the unbroken parliamentary-governmental domination and central position of the (reduced) major parties.

This contradictory situation does not merely reflect 'critical shifts at the margin'. Rather, the view of Peter Mair regarding 'the essential contradiction between an apparent weakening of the role of parties as representative agents on the one hand and an apparent strengthening of their role as public-office holders on the other'[8] may be confirmed. The rule of *Volksparteien* in Germany is eroding from its social base without loss of stability or power at the party-state level. In other words, party democracy and party state in Germany are in the process of detaching themselves from each other and going separate ways at different times. What is particularly critical in this development is the fact that this undermines the broad foundation in society and the party-democratic basis of legitimacy of the major parties that dominate the party state.

An Example: The Reaction of the CDU

The CDU is still reeling under the repercussions of the party funds scandal.[9] Irrespective of this aspect however, the Christian Democrats view themselves as a classic *Volkspartei* confronted with modern day challenges. How can and should the party react to the social and political consequences of modernisation in terms of party policy and structure? The traditional model of the Bonn Republic provides no guidance with regard either to policy programmes or strategic action. This article will attempt to analyse the possibilities of constructive adjustment to a changed and complex electoral clientele using the CDU as an example.

---

[8] Peter Mair, 'Political Parties. Popular Legitimacy and Public Privilege', *Western European Politics*, vol. 3, No. 18, 1995, pp. 40–57..

[9] See Clay Clemens, 'A Legacy Reassessed', *German Politics*, 2, 2000; Ludger Helms, 'Is There Life after Kohl?', *Government and Opposition*, No. 35/2000, pp. 419–38.

Emerging Issues

Identifying issues is of critical importance, first and foremost in terms of electoral strategy. Elections can be won only if the electorate perceives a party as being competent on important issues, the most important of which continue to be labour market and economic policy. However, issues also play an important role in power politics. Political affinities must form the nucleus of solidarity and mobilisation within the CDU. Political debates on issues and agendas tend to promote cohesion. In the recent past, given its special role as ruling party in a coalition, this unifying function tended to be concentrated in an individual. However, when power is no longer the binding factor, political affinities must ensure integration. Such affinities emerge out of—often controversial—debates on providing the party with a new direction. Finally, issues are also important from a leadership perspective. The top leadership must be suited to the issues. At this stage the CDU needs personalities who can chart a course—for a limited period, if necessary. They must possess the ability to moderate where required while steadfastly focusing on the primary issues and be relied upon to steer towards core positions in turbulent times.

Bundestag elections can be successfully contested only by winning over the political centre.[10] Till the early 1990s favourable conditions prevailed for the middle class-conservative camp. Staunch anti-communism and the widespread Catholic climate in the regions along the Rhine led a majority of the centre to place their political allegiance in the Christian Democrats. The ending of the East-West conflict led to a dealignment of the party system in several European countries. In Germany, however, unification, which was the special German path adopted after the collapse of socialism, slowed down the disintegration of the middle-class conservative camp, without actually halting it altogether. To that extent, with the electoral loss of 1998 and the necessary process of renewal, the CDU now finds itself in the same boat as numerous sister parties in Europe were some years ago.

The party funds scandal acted as the catalyst for this renewal. The distinction between the left and the right on principal domestic and foreign policy issues has become obsolete. It is becoming increasingly difficult to clearly distinguish between the policies of the Social Democrats and those of the Christian Democrats as both seek to appropriate for themselves what is referred to as the 'new centre'. An additional problem for the CDU is that as Christianity takes a back seat leading to a 'de-christianisation' of society, the

---

[10] Confirmed among others by Hans-Dieter Klingemann and Max Kaase (eds), *Wahlen und Wöhler* (Elections and Voters) Westdeutscher Verlag, Wiesbaden 2001. This comprehensive publication has appeared for each *Bundestagswahl* since the 1980s.

party is losing many of its reliable and core voters.[11] The security of loyal vote banks thus no longer exists.[12] However, in this respect at least the CDU finds itself in good company since the SPD faces a similar predicament.

Structural dealignment, decreasing identification with a particular party and the concomitant higher voter fluctuation between ruling and opposition parties[13] have had an impact on all the *Volksparteien*. The response of the CDU to these changed manifestations of electoral will must also touch upon the issue of redefining conservatism in the 21st century. The CDU's reaction will have to be in tune with the political and cultural realities in Germany as also the broad trends. However, any programmatic modernisation at the political and cultural level that does not satisfy the widespread but equally ambivalent desire for peace and reform, consensual and democratic pragmatism as well as stability and security, is doomed to failure.

The CDU's successes in the last year were largely due to a general disenchantment with the policies of the Red-Green coalition.[14] The old CDU was able to win seats in the local and *Laender* elections primarily because by focusing its campaign on immigrants in Hessen, and by concentrating on the pensions issue in the Saarland, it managed to tap into the existing insecurities of the populace. Of course, since the fear of change is likely to increase, the CDU need not worry about its clientele in this respect.

However, the parties' strategic positioning must also be designed to appeal to new electoral groups—the floating voters. Thus parties need to formulate their position on major trends,[15] such as globalisation, Europeanisation, greying societies, virtual networking, creation of a knowledge society. What is needed is a party that is able to retain core supporters while managing to woo new sets of voters.

The general disorientation in society can be correlated to the pre-modern desire for leadership. Given this sentiment, the challenge would lie in the ability to translate the inevitable departure from old beliefs and values into a credible political message. The focus, however should not lie on the

---

[11] Franz Walter and Tobias Dürr, *Die Heimatlosigkeit der Macht. Wie Politik in Deutschland ihren Boden verlor* (Homelessness of Power: How Politics in Germany Lost its Ground), Berlin: Aufbau Verlga, 2000, pp. 123–55.

[12] Richard Herziger, 'Aufbruch ins Nirgendwo' (Emergence into Nowhere), in *Die Zeit*, 23 March 2000. For the political and cultural context, see Werner Weidenfeld and Karl-Rudolf Korte, *Die Deutschen: Profil einer Nation* (The Germans: Profile of a Nation), Stuttgart: Klett Cotta, 1991.

[13] For a discussion on the basic concepts, see Angus Campbell Warren Miller, Phillip Converse, *The American Voter*, New York: Ayred A. Konopf, 1960.

[14] *Landtag* elections also have an 'anti-governmental' sentiment—initially against 'Bonn' and now 'Berlin'. Karl-Rudolf Korte, *Wahlen in der Bundesrepublik Deutschland* (Elections in the Federal Republic of Germany), Bonn: Bundeszentrale für politische Bildung, 2000.

[15] Hypo Vereinsbank, Trend-Book 2000, Munich: Fink Verlag, 2000.

'packaging'.[16] Rather, a successful party is one that possesses the collective and organisational strength to politically articulate significant social cleavages.[17]

It is up to the party leadership to chart out the course and provide answers to the following questions:[18] Do the people understand the social and political environment in which they live and interact? Do people feel secure and sheltered? Is there a general feeling that fairplay and justice prevail? Are people able to contribute, participate or develop themselves?

There is no point in expecting prevailing trends to provide the answers to these questions. If one were to go by trend scouts, not a single of the major domestic and foreign policy decisions in the history of the Federal Republic would have been taken in the form it was. Neither re-militarisation nor the introduction of the euro could claim majority support. And had the populace of the old *Laender* been aware of the transformation costs they would presumably have rejected reunification.

The question that arises is how much scope political parties have and what range of action is feasible in a negotiating state. Appealing to new electoral groups as a strategic response to the erosion of voter constituencies can be extended through a policy-related reaction.[19] The catch-all approach should be extended to specific sectors, where possible, in order to bind even ad hoc issue-based alliances to the party. Based on its tradition of conservative, liberal and Christian social values, the party, as a *Neue Union* (Manuel Fröhlich), could focus on key political areas without having to make any ideological adjustments. In her inaugural speech at the national party convention in Essen, new chairperson Angela Merkel articulated the core issues of the future without getting into specifics. 'Market with a human face' is the new rallying slogan.

Party of the Regions

The response to what is frequently perceived as the threat of globalisation could lie in emphasising regional identities and in promoting subsidiarity

[16] For a discussion on these political styles, see Karl-Rudolf Korte und Gerhard Hirscher (eds), *Darstellungspolitik oder Entscheidungspolitik? Über den Wandel von Politikstilen in westlichen Demokratien* (Policy of Description or Policy of Decision? About the Pattern of Politics in Western Democracies), Munich: Hanns Seidel Stiftung, 2000.
[17] Walter and Dürr, *Die Heimatlosigkeit der Macht*, p. 216; Ulrich Eith and Gerd Mielke, 'Die soziale Frage als neue Konfliktlinie? Einstellungen zum Wohlfahrtsstaat und zur sozialen Gerechtigkeit' (The Social Question as a New Trend of Conflicts? Attitudes towards the Welfare State and to Social Justice), in Hans Rattinger, Edeltraud Roller & Jan Seth (eds), *Die Republik auf dem Weg zur Normalität* (The Republic on the Road to Normality), Opladen: Westdeutscher Verlag, 2000.
[18] Warnfried Dettling, *Politik und Lebenswelt. Vom Wohlfahrtsstaat zur Wohlfahrtsgesellschaft* (Politics and the World of Living. From Welfare State to Welfare Society), Gütersloh: Bertelsmann Verlag, 1999, p. 17.
[19] For more information, see Albrecht Müller, *Von der Parteiendemokratie zur Mediendemokratie* (From Party Democracy to Media Democracy), Opladen: Westdeutscher Verlag, 1994.

and de-acceleration. Globalisation would then become synonymous with the revitalisation of local regions and the awareness thereof. In terms of routine identity management what is required is someone comfortable in the shrinking world of global networking, global finance and share transfers, representing at the same time strong local ties, permanence and intense pursuit of leisure activities.

The new conflict scenario[20] that has emerged has transnational organisations and institutions on the one side with local and regional networks promoting identity building on the other—the globalisation divide.

The CDU could attempt to give direction to this diversity through a project that would offer solutions to the problems sans ideology. Competence in governance means to direct political developments in agreement with other players.

Party of Social Market Economy

The reforms necessary for restructuring the welfare state should be based on the concept of social market economy, which comprises both regulatory and social policy. The state continued to be responsible for the regulation of the basic economic policy framework. While the FDP favours a neo-liberal approach (less state intervention), the SPD favours social investments (more state intervention). By going back to Eucken and Müller-Armack, the founding fathers of social market economy, the Union parties could offer a path[21] which would also serve the interests of the losers of modernism. The key word here is generational justice.

It is only by adopting the social market economy model that the CDU can hope to complement what the SPD is trying to achieve through civil society and to place its concept of generational justice alongside the SPD's plank of equitable distribution.

Party for Promoting Acceptance of European Integration

There is a functional logic to European integration that exerts an inexorable gravitational pull. Governing at the nation state level has become an anachronism in view of the agenda for the 21st century. Yet it is precisely for this reason that resistance to giving up the nation state is increasing. The integration

---

[20] Scott Flanagan and Russel J. Dalton, 'Parties Under Stress: Realignment and Dealignment in Advanced Industrial Societies', *West European Politics*, 7 (January 1984), pp. 7–23.

[21] See Uwe Andersen & Dieter Grosser, *Der Staat in der Wirtschaft der Bundesrepublik* (State and Economy in the Federal Republic), Leverkusen: UTB-Verlag, 1985, for a further discussion on this issue.

process is viewed with mistrust, especially as regards the expansion towards the east.

These circumstances call for a party that favours a further reduction in sovereignty but is not prepared to make concessions as regards national and regional identities. Achieving this would require that the speed of integration is made verifiably compatible with acceptance by the citizens. This does not mean that demoscopic findings alone should be relied upon. Rather, the question relates to the pace of policies which would allow time to articulate and debate future steps towards integration in public. This is the only way in which policy makers will remain in touch with ground realities. It is also the only way to effectively meet the challenge of right-wing populism.[22]

Party for Internal Security

Security issues have always enjoyed a high priority. Nothing has changed in this regard, on the contrary, the widespread disorientation in society has fed growing fears. Thus practical and financially viable concepts to improve internal security will always meet with a positive response.

Party of Future Opportunities

The significance of 'social capital'[23] has increased in the wake of social transformation. The individual contribution towards the common good laid the foundations of democracy. In areas where the state steps back, the network society comes up. It is this development that needs to be given direction.

This can be achieved either by focusing on conservative values, e.g., adherence to the social state as a societal commitment or by more strongly focusing on family policy in terms of Christian and social values. Moreover, why does the *Neue Union* not attack the Red-Green tax reform package from a Christian perspective as a deliberate weakening of church finances?

However, even liberal approaches can be employed, e.g., through concepts on integration and immigration, promotion of education as the future capital of the coming e-generation and the knowledge society.

---

[22] A distinction between populism and the *Volksparteien* is made by Frank Böckelmann, 'Stellen Sie sich vor, jemand nennt sie "Faschist"' (Imagine, Somebody Calls You a 'Fascist'), in *Frankfurter Allegemeine Zeitung* (*FAZ*), 1 April 2000.

[23] Robert D. Putnam (ed.), *Gesellschaft und Gemeinsinn. Sozialkapital im internationalen Vergleich* (Society and Public Spirit. Social Capital in International Comparison), Gütersloh: Bertelsmann, 2000.

Impact of the Party Funds Scandal

It was the party funds scandal that brought the CDU face to face with the harsh reality of having lost power at the federal level. In fact, it was only after this scandal that the party really ended up where the electorate had sent it: in the opposition. However, the Christian Democrats would be wrong to see in this crisis the beginnings of the party's revival. This is being mouthed only as a consolation in the hope perhaps that it will have an auto-suggestive effect. Instead, the opportunity lies in being able to come to terms with the role of a competent opposition capable of providing a credible alternative. In opposition it is possible to have a much more versatile party programme than when in government. There is greater freedom from coalition compulsions and the public does not scrutinise each position and proposal for internal consistency.

One party chairperson has already fallen by the wayside in the CDU's process of general renewal. The party wanted a successor who would lead the party on the road to rehabilitation and recovery while simultaneously donning the mantle of innovation. The only problem is that rehabilitation is normally a process of winding up, of stabilising and clearing up in order to move on to the next problem. Rehabilitation and policy innovation do not usually go hand in hand. The process of renewal may thus take a heavy toll of personalities as happened between 1971 and 1973 (Kiesinger, Barzel, Kohl).

As regards finances, the system of organised irresponsibility needs to be addressed through a fresh financial statute. The delegates at the Essen party convention have already voted for a modification of existing practices. A system needs to be worked out that clearly allocates responsibility in the case of irregularities and promotes transparency and supervision in general.

Clarification is also required on why the financial requirements of the party have risen so dramatically in the last 20 years and how these will develop in the future. Do election campaigns really require a full-fledged organisation with thousands of permanent employees? The Americanisation of German parties has so far been evident only in the increased role of personality, event staging and professional campaign management. Modern cadre parties[24] should concentrate more on services, more on recruitment of elite membership and governing in parliament rather than just on campaign management. Small, lean organisations will always be able to perform better.

Angela Merkel is the first CDU chairperson who was not 'invented' in meetings of the party executive. The grassroots democratic process resulting in her appointment points to a future dynamism that should not be frittered

---

[24] Ruud Koole, 'The Vulnerability of the Modern Cadre Party in the Netherlands', in R.S. Katz and Peter Mair (eds), *How Parties Organize*, London: Sage Publications, etc. 1994, pp. 278–304. See also Peter Mair et al. (eds), *Parteien auf komplexen Wählermärkten* (Parties on Complex Voter Markets), Vienna: Schöningh Verlag, 1999.

away. She seems to satisfy the German yearning for political romanticism and instead of strategic manoeuvring and machinations in seedy backrooms, she represents credible answers to comprehensible problems. Despite having been elected party chairperson by a convincing margin she must now laboriously consolidate her position within the party by building up and nurturing informal networks rather than by exercising power in the classic sense. In an ideal scenario, Angela Merkel would combine two aspects: a culture of open debate not curtailed by compulsions of loyalty which would also go towards promoting party integration through a process of arriving at informal preliminary decisions. Her inaugural speech at Essen was illuminating in this regard. To a disoriented and leaderless party she offered a new feeling of solidarity. With the deliberate shift in the pronouns 'I', 'you' and 'we' she created a dynamically charged atmosphere without having to go into specifics.

What is finally required is organisational reform, and the question of centralised or decentralised power sharing will be critical. Ever since Kohl's confessions in November 1999, the party presidium has been revived as a committee with collective responsibility with specific areas assigned to individual members. Although this may appear attractive at first sight since it places less burden on the chairperson, it also qualifies his or her leadership role. In terms of power politics, a way out of the dilemma of routine decision-making would lie in a more clearly defined role for the triumvirate comprising the chairpersons of the CDU and CSU and the leader of the combined parliamentary group, rather than projecting the presidium as the leadership team.[25]

In this scenario the party units in the *Laender* could play a greater role than so far in providing creative inputs. At their level the principles of local identity and regional solutions have already been realised. The same holds true for other diverse associations of the CDU. Ideally, this would result in the formation of a think tank in which the central party leadership, the party units in the *Laender*, the *Bundestag* and *Landtag* factions and the party's foundations would compete to offer the best solutions.

Lessons from the 1970s

A comparable revitalisation of the party took place successfully after two decades in power (1949–69). There were several causes for this. First, after years of self-deception the CDU had to learn to admit that it had only itself to blame for the electoral losses in 1969. The party was no longer in touch with issues that would muster majority support. Making up for lost time, it then laboriously trimmed its domestic and foreign policy agenda towards reform

---

[25] For further information, see Karl-Rudolf Korte, *Kampagnen und Kompetenzen* (Campaigns and Competences), *Die politische Meinung*, No. 379 6/2001 pp. 19–23.

and détente. New, fresh faces managed to replace the old, worn leadership and were gradually able to regain lost confidence.

In addition, a strong desire for power needed to be rekindled. Half-hearted support for chancellor candidates and indecisive parliamentary debates gave voters the impression that the party was not yet ready to take on the responsibility of government.

The strength for renewal also resulted from the emancipation of the Christian Democrats from the Bavarian sister party. After 1971 Rainer Barzel held dual responsibility as party chairman and leader of the parliamentary group and was directly dependent on Franz-Josef Strauß. At the beginning of its term in opposition, the image of the Union was shaped almost exclusively by the activities of the parliamentary group, where the CSU had opportunities for direct political intervention. The federal party on the other hand had been rendered virtually silent after the Social Democrats assumed office, unwilling to ruthlessly analyse its own mistakes.

A change in leadership altered this configuration. Helmut Kohl took over as party chairman in 1973, while Karl Carstens became chairman of the CDU/CSU parliamentary group in the *Bundestag*. The newcomer Carstens was then considered—as Friedrich Merz is today—to be unencumbered. He manoeuvred between the old guard, spoiled by having been in power, and the forces eager for reforms. As premier of Rhineland Palatinate, Kohl was able to defy the CSU. Since he was not directly involved in the parliamentary group he was in a position to attract like-minded people from within the party who also regarded it essential to form a counterbalance to the CSU. Over time the CDU parliamentary party evolved into a federal opposition party. It even had the self-confidence to hold out the threat of extending its activities to Bavaria in response to the CSU's Kreuther resolution demanding that it resign from the parliamentary group (1976).

Towards the end of the 1970s the CDU and the CSU once again worked together as equal sister parties. Both Christian parties and the joint parliamentary group in the *Bundestag* competed with one another—as was apparent to the electorate from the clearly personified conflicts and controversies—to offer traditional conservative, Christian-social and liberal policy concepts. It was not uniformity in party programmes that held the key to the revival of the Christian Democrats but conceptual diversity, which in turn had emerged from the process of introspection within the CDU.

The modernisation of the party was pushed forward by the party's then general secretary Kurt Biedenkopf. Between 1971 and 1977 membership doubled from 3,29,000 to 6,64,000. Biedenkopf transformed what had more or less been a club to elect chancellor candidates into a modern party machinery with mass membership. Communication between the party leadership and the party units in the states and districts was professionalised, while parallel political and policy-related activities were concentrated in the party headquarters. The basic structure of the party, however, was not touched. The CDU is not an oligarchic monolith. It is more comparable to a loosely bound polyarchy with many layers of power sharing.[26] In fact, this very structure made it so important for Kohl to establish a closely knit personal network to serve as a political early warning system.[27]

By using slogans such as 'Freedom or Socialism' the party was able to bring about a polarisation and project an alternative programme with regard to domestic and foreign policy. This was not just an election campaign strategy. By raising issues such as the 'New Social Question' the CDU was in fact able to carve out a distinct position for itself. Biedenkopf and Heiner Geißler, his successor as general secretary, were usually the ones to skilfully introduce such issues.

In fact, it does fall upon the general secretary to promote innovation in party policy. Putting forward political alternatives is the job of the leader of the parliamentary group. Both in tandem give direction to political revival. The chairperson, on the other hand—especially in a party like the CDU with its heterogeneous and extremely federal organisational structure—functions as a moderator balancing different interests. (Wolfgang Schäuble sacrificed his brilliance on issues the minute he also became party chairman.)

Time will show whether the typifications described above can be extended to Ruprecht Polenz. His appointment resulted primarily from the desire to check the influence of the Northrhine-Westphalian party unit. Merz, Rüttgers and Polenz will now be watching each other's moves. As far as Angela Merkel is concerned, they are likely to neutralise each other.

FDP as Role Model?

A stock taking of the CDU's initial period in opposition confirms that a no-holds-barred discussion on the electoral loss of 1998 is imperative, although it has still not taken place. (It will not suffice to merely point out that 'Kohl must go'.) Similarly, transformation into a modern cadre party is due. This

---

[26] Peter Haungs, 'Die CDU: Prototyp einer Volkspartei' (The CDU: Prototype of a *Volkspartei*), in Alf Mintzel and Heinrich Oberreuter (eds), *Parteien in der Bundesrepublik Deutschland* (Parties in the Federal Republic of Germany), Bonn: Bundeszentrale für politische Bildung, 1992, pp.172–216; Peter Lösche, 'Wirklich nur ein Kanzlerwahlverein?' (Just an Organisation to Elect the Chancellor?), in *FAZ*, 25 August 1998.

[27] Karl-Rudolf Korte, 'Kommt es auf die Person des Kanzlers an? Zum Regierungsstil von Helmut Kohl in der Kanzlerdemokratie des deutschen Parteienstaates' (Is it the Personality of the Chancellor What Matters? On Helmut Kohl's Way to Govern in the Frame of Chancellor-Democracy of the German Party State), *Zeitschrift für Parlamentsfragen*, 3/1998, pp. 387–401; Karl-Rudolf Korte, *Deutschlandpolitik in Helmut Kohls Kanzlerschaft. Regierungsstil und Entscheidungen* (Chancellor Helmut Kohl's Policy Towards Germany: Pattern of Governance and Decision-Making), Stuttgart: Deutsene Verlagsanstalt, 1998.

will result in radical changes, such as the development of the party into a 'media party' where the leadership communicates with its members via the media, into an 'electoral campaign party' with a highly professional approach to conceptualising and projecting inter-party competition, into a 'service party' in which fewer members initiate the management of ideas. Achieving this involves constant work on long-term objectives, irrespective of election schedules. Membership in the future will be determined less by social identification than by a joint furthering of shared convictions.[28] Here the FDP could serve as a role model from an organisational perspective: it is not bound by the compulsions of appealing to a mass base, it functions without expensive party machinery and is not bogged down by tradition as far as content is concerned.

There is need for long-term planning, beyond 2002, for a complete overhaul of the party platform to align traditional content with the new realities. No organisation can be expected to have a completely smooth change at the helm when the predecessor was in office for 25 years. Successors need time.

The 'Normalcy' of Parties

If we examine the basic problems of party democracy, there appears to be a shift in the parameters to assess the 'normalcy' of parties. The Greens wish to become a 'normal' party, to do away with the distinction between office and mandate and substitute grassroots democratic elements with more rights for the party leadership (The plan has got bogged down for the time being). In appointing its new chairperson the CDU went back to the grassroots. Collective responsibility in the presidium and the party executive are being openly discussed. This very aspect was recently eliminated by the SPD on assuming power. The general secretary has now replaced the traditionally strong deputy chairperson of the party in influence.[29]

The yardstick to assess the 'normalcy' of parties is clearly derived from the dualism between government and opposition. Governing is made easier for the chancellor if power is centralised. It is more difficult to govern with 'programmatic parties' or parties with a specific agenda. The approach of the opposition is distinguished by the versatility in party programmes. Proposals of the opposition are not always examined for their actual viability. A culture of open debate is thus not harmful for opposition parties. Although surveys suggest a bonus for parties presenting a united front, this pertains to

---

[28] Wilhelm P. Bürklin, 'Viola Neu and Hans-Joachim Veen: Die Mitglieder CDU' (The Members of the CDU). Internal Paper, Konrad Adenauer Foundation, St. Augustin, 148/1997.
[29] Karl-Rudolf Korte, 'Das System Schröder: Wie der Kanzler das Netzwerk seiner Macht knüpft' (The System of Schröder: How the Chancellor is Going to Mesh the Net of his Power), in FAZ, 25 October 1999.

the results of particular policies and not to the process of arriving at those policy decisions. When after possibly prolonged and controversial internal debates a decision is finally taken in the appropriate fora, it must be projected unanimously following the majority principle. Subsequent discordance does not go down well with voters.

This fact is also applicable to coalitions as was demonstrated in the *Landtag* elections in Northrhine-Westphalia.

II

Party Fragmentation in the European Union

European parties are federal organisations of national parties from several member states of the European Union whose ideologies and objectives coincide. Their sphere of activity is the political system of the Union and they are represented in the European Parliament through their respective parliamentary groups. Article 191 of the Treaty establishing the European Community ('Amsterdam Treaty', formerly Article 138a of the 'Maastricht Treaty') states: 'Political parties at European level are important as a factor for integration in the Union. They contribute to forming a European awareness and to expressing the political will of the citizens of the Union.' At present, only the traditional political groupings organised at the Union level, i.e., the Social Democrats, Christian Democrats and Liberal Democrats, qualify to be called European parties. They are transnational in their structure and mode of functioning as also their goals and sphere of activity. Their self-perception as well as their conduct have shown them to be important players in the political systems of the EU, for whose structuring and development they assume responsibility. The same, with some qualification, lately holds true even for the Green parties. All other political forces represented in the European Parliament—radicals, right wing, Gaullists, communists, etc.,—have till now not been in a position to organise themselves in this manner since they are generally fixated on domestic issues or because they may not desire transnational integration due to ideological and political compulsions.

Institutional factors are of great importance in determining the nature of party politics in the EU. The small degree of party integration that has been achieved so far owes more to choices in the design of EU institutions than to the decisions of party leaders or to the structures of European political parties themselves. Party politics in the EU have progressed *pari passu* with the institutional reform of the Union. They have taken a step forward with each institutional or procedural reform of the European Parliament (EP) that has been agreed between the governments and institutions of the Union, often in the almost total absence of party leaderships. The impulse to party integration given by the direct election of the EP and the decision procedures created by the Single Act and the Maastricht Treaty are cases in point. In short, the history of party integration in Europe has predominantly been situated inside rather than outside the EP even if this situation must be understood against the wider background of the peculiar characteristics of the EU as a political system.

The EU is a multi-level system which comprises the Union institutions themselves, the states, the regions and other intermediary and subsidiary political bodies. All these levels have specific institutional and political configurations but within and across the various levels there are several political discontinuities. As all of the levels are themselves theatres of party politics where party competition takes several forms[30]—the EP elections, the EP itself, the formation of national governments and relationships with interest groups—the party politics of the EU can also be said to be discontinuous.

Transnational Parties

By definition, transnational parties exist in order to promote a 'European awareness' in their member parties and to contribute towards European integration (see Article 138a, Maastricht Treaty on Political Union). The revival of these organisations in the past several years appears to be tied to an emerging consensus among party leaders, both left and right, that the European level of decision-making is not only beyond their singular grasp, but that the significance of the EU has grown to the point that they appear increasingly helpless within their own domestic spheres in terms of promoting any alternatives or imparting direction to the EU policy process. Consequently, in addition to the biannual party leaders summits which for both the Party of European Socialists (PESs) and the European People's Party (EPP) include relevant commissioners and officials such as the president of the EP and president of the respective party group, a number of working groups or parties also operate under the auspices of the PES and EPP. Thus the occasions for *collaboration* in small group working environments have proceeded apace, bringing at times prominent national party figures into more intimate contact with colleagues from other parties as well as Members of the European Parliament (MEPs).

Party-to-party

The parties themselves have used the increased organisational collaboration fostered by the transnational party secretariats and their activities to

---

[30] See Werner Weidenfeld and Wolfgang Wessels (eds), *Jahrbuch der Europäischen Integration 1980-2000* (Yearbook of European Integration), Bonn: Bundeszentrale für Politische Bildung, 1980ff.

hold joint meetings among themselves, usually focused on one or a few significant issues. The PES leaders have employed a 'conclave' style of meeting before significant European events, and party-to-party initiatives may be launched from the discussions as was the case in 1993 in which an Employment Initiative was developed, coinciding with the efforts of the Delors Commission in drawing up the White Paper on Growth, Competitiveness and Employment. Since the party-to-party meetings many times include the president of the respective EP group, co-ordination of the EP parliamentary positions with national party and government (depending upon the government/opposition role in national politics) is magnified for public and partisan consumption.

The Party System of the European Parliament

We can now consider the shape of the party system in the EP, for its imperfections contribute to the overall discontinuity of party politics in the European political system. Though European political parties are passing through important changes in their functions and organisations as well as in their role in state and society, the left-right axis continues to be a good instrument for studying party competition. The left-right axis is easily 'transposable' from one system to another as a basis for comparison and it is, therefore, a useful means of placing parties from different states into a single analytical framework.[31]

The Groups of the European Parliament represent eight political families. Seven of them can be placed in the following order from left to right: Communist, Socialist, Ecologist, Liberal-Radical, Christian, Liberal-Conservative, Nationalist. The position on the left-right axis of the eighth tradition, the regionalist and ethnic parties, is generally identifiable at the national level but not at the European level because of the extreme heterogeneity of the regional and ethnic lists present in the European Parliament, which means that some are left-leaning and some are right-leaning.

Group of the European People's Party

Founded as the Christian Democrat Group on 23 June 1953 as a faction in the Common Assembly of the European Coal and Steel Community, the Group changed its name to the 'Group of the European People's Party' (Christian-Democratic Group) in July 1979, just after the first direct elections to the European Parliament and to 'Group of the European People's Party (Christian Democrats) and European Democrats' (EPP-ED Group) in July 1999. It has always played a leading role in the construction of Europe. The 233

---

[31] See David Bell and Christopher Lord (eds), *Transnational Parties in the EU*, Aldershat: Europa-Union Verlag, 1998.

members of the EPP-ED Group come from all of the 15 member states of the European Union. The Group is currently the largest in Parliament.

The European Socialist Family

The Parliamentary Group of the Party of European Socialists represents 181 MEPs at present and is thus the second largest grouping in the European Parliament. This reflects the deep-rooted values underlying the Socialist and Social Democratic movements on the European continent. Around these common values, parties with specific traditions and temperaments have grown up in the various countries. There were already genuine links between these parties within the framework of the Socialist International, but the process of European integration has fostered still closer links between the Socialists and Social Democrats in the member states.

The Euro-parties of the European Parliament are, however, not genuine parties, if by this we mean organisations that span and control the electoral linkage.[32]

First, these new parties do not have an electorate. In elections for the European Parliament the voters within each nation vote for their own parties. Few, if any, voters care about 'The Rainbow Group', the 'European Democratic Alliance', or some of the other more or less stable groups within the Parliament in Strasbourg when they go to the poll station.

Second, these 'parties' do not have an internal organisation to carry out the policies of the leadership. There may be some kind of executive board that co-ordinates the work of the supranational group, but the emphasis is just on co-ordination, advice, and on the administration of the considerable funds and other perks provided for the activity by the EU itself.

Third, the cohesion of such groups is not comparable to the cohesion of most national parliamentary groups. Group-consciousness is not high, and the same is true for the stability of the group's structures. After each election to the European Parliament new groups have arisen and older ones have disappeared. Splits and mergers take place now and then and individual members frequently switch from one group to another.

The Present Pattern of Party Politics in the European Union

If it is hard to avoid the conclusion that some role for political parties will be needed for the further democratisation and integration of the Union, how far

---

[32] See Klaus Pöhle, 'Europäische Parteien—für wen und für was eigentlich?' (European Parties: For Whom and for What Really?), *Zeitschrift für Parlamentsfragen*, No. 3/2000, pp. 599–619.

can the Union already be said to have its own system of political parties? The EU does, indeed, have a party-political dimension that superficially mimics some of the principal features of national party politics. The main players have developed an organisational division of labour between parliamentary and extra-parliamentary parties.

It would, however, be a mistake to dismiss the federations and groups as mere agglomerations of national parties. A further sign of party-political development at the European level is that transnational parties are increasingly well-adapted—in their functions and composition—to the demands of the EU's own political arena. In the case of the EPP, two political families—the Christian Democrats and the Conservatives—have merged into a single parliamentary group in response to the Treaty rule that requires the Parliament to organise majorities of its membership and not just of those voting (absolute majority rule). While the EP has not developed the hierarchical parliamentary parties typical of national political systems in western Europe, it has evolved groups with remarkably sophisticated consensus-building mechanisms. Once again this is, arguably, entirely appropriate to the specific characteristics of the EU's political system, one of which is constraints on the majoritarian—as opposed to consensual—democratic method.

Future Perspectives

As the political landscape acquires an increasingly European character, especially within national and also regional systems, the tendency to underrate the potential of the European parties—both by the parties and the parliamentary factions—is sure to decrease. There are growing expectations that solutions to major problems pertaining to domestic and social policy issues within the member states can be found at the European level. This will undoubtedly lead to a reassessment of the role and significance of the institutions of the Union. This changed perception will then also extend to the European Parliament since it not only directly debates on and expresses the concerns of the citizens but is also in a position to put forward its views clearly and to arrive at decisions regarding concrete measures, unfettered by the constraints of diplomacy, since it functions on the majority principle.[33]

It is only jointly, i.e., within the framework of the political system and the instruments of the EU that adequate solutions can be found as regards unemployment, immigration pressure, environmental protection, organised crime or international drugs trafficking and other cross-border problems. Increased

---

[33] See Andreas Maurer, 'Der Wandel europapolitischer Grundorientierungen nationaler Parteien in der EU' (The Change of Political Basic Orientations Towards Europe of National Parties in the EU), in Mathius Jopp, Andreas Maurer & Heinrich Schnieder (eds), *Europäische Grundverständnisse im Wandel* (European Basic Understanding in Transition), Bonn: Europa-Union Verlag, 1998, p. 301ff.

awareness has led to a growing recognition of the role and significance of the European Parliament amongst the political class, especially the national parliaments and national parties in the member states, and ultimately also amongst the public at large. The 'Europeanisation' of the party system will proceed *pari passu* with the constitutional reform of the Union. Both the major camps, the social democrats and the Christian democrats, will continue to exert a considerable attraction on the forces ideologically close to them. The moderate left-to-centre forces will gradually be assimilated in the PES, while those with right to centre leanings will throw their lot in with the EPP. This is due to the compulsions of European politics which requires a broad-based, supranational consensus that can only be mustered by parties or parliamentary groups with mass social and cultural roots. However, it is also in the interest of the national parties whose voters fall within the areas of interest and positions represented by the EPP and PES. To achieve anything at the European level these parties must be part of a multinational, or better still, a supranational faction that is big enough to accomplish something.

This convergence at the centre, finally, is also in consonance with the new political realities. The age of ideology is over. The development of *Volksparteien* in a largely de-ideologised environment is on the cards. Party profile will no longer be determined by the ideological leanings of the party leadership but rather by the socio-economic interests and political and cultural aspirations of its voters. Left vs right, conservative vs progressive, Social Democrat vs Christian Democrat, liberal vs socialist; in the European dimension and under the new set of circumstances these contrapositions are losing their ideological edge. They are perceived as various political and cultural alternatives available on the market. From this point of view, the distinctions between the various gradations and orientations within the 'left cultural' and the 'right cultural' camp, e.g., between liberal and conservative or between socialist and communist, cease to exist. This also explains why the Social Democrats cannot avoid embracing post-communist and other forces with leftist traditions in their European organisations, and why the EPP has been promoting the integration of conservative, liberal and other 'middle class' forces.

Given this background it is understandable why a realignment in the sphere of influence of both large European parties led to further changes during the fourth legislative period of the European Parliament (1994–99). The first indication of developments towards consolidation was the merger of two groups who are candidates to join the EPP, namely the French-Irish 'Gaullist' faction and the mono-national Italian faction Forza Europa, to form the Union for Europe (UPE). The process was completed in the summer of 1995. In November 1996, the Portuguese Partido Democratico Social (PDS) switched alliance from the ELDR to the EPP. Gradually there is a growing consolidation of forces that fit together in the European context and under the new conditions of post-ideological politics.

Considerable additional changes in the political systems of the European Union are expected in the coming years following the introduction of a single currency and as a precondition for enlargement of the Union by a number of new member states. This would also result in more power and influence for the European Parliament and consequently, for the European parties. Although the Treaty of Amsterdam did not bring about any concrete progress with regard to the legal foundation and status of the European parties within the Union's political system, a number of the new regulations have been very pertinent as regards developments in this direction. For instance, by committing the Union to the principles of democracy, respect for human rights and fundamental freedoms and the rule of law, considerable progress has been made from a union of states to a union of citizens, as proposed by the Maastricht Treaty. Even the new regulations pertaining to the freedom of movement, right to asylum and immigration are steps in this direction. In conjunction with measures to ensure internal security within the Union, these regulations form a further and important element in realising the idea of citizenship of the Union.

The same could be said of the regulations (aiming at greater legislative powers for parliament), of the simplification of decision processes (promising greater transparency) and finally, the more precise definition (guaranteeing more subsidiarity) of regulations for allocating tasks and responsibility at various levels of the Union. A combination of all these elements will result in the debate within the Union becoming more politicised, implying at the same time greater democratisation and transnationalisation. Clearly, this will lead to a growing role for the European parties since the debate is dependent on the structures provided by the European parties.

5

SOCIAL, CULTURAL AND ECONOMIC DIMENSIONS OF THE PARTY SYSTEM

Amit Prakash

The Indian party system has been witness to a number of significant changes over the past decade. The celebrated 'Congress System', characterised by the dominance of the Congress Party (the INC) and often seen to be synonymous with the Indian party system, has witnessed a progressive and drastic decline. A multiplicity of political parties has emerged on the political horizon of the country, each one representing a limited social, economic, cultural or economic interest. These parties have a rather limited geographical expanse, mobilise support on a limited agenda and represent the interests of its main support groups. Consequently, the media as well as scholarly writings have devoted much energy lamenting the 'fragmentation of the polity' or the 'narrow sectarian lines of political mobilisation' by these newer political parties.

In this context, this chapter seeks to examine the socio-cultural and economic support bases of political parties in India. One argument of this chapter is that in view of the nature and trajectory of the nationalist thought and mobilisation as well as the nature of the rationalist post-colonial state in India, it is no surprise that regional socio-cultural or economic interests have been seeking to assert their political strength and carve out a political space for themselves. What indeed *is surprising* is that it took half-a-century for these groups to arrive at this stage.

Before this question is taken up in detail, attention must be devoted to the pattern of support for the main political parties in terms of various social and economic categories of the electorate. It is therefore, important to delineate and analyse the support patterns of the political parties seeking to carve out a political space for themselves based on various social/socio-cultural and economic criteria.

Section I deals with the pattern of support as expressed in the voting pattern of the electorate on various social and economic categories of the electorate while Section II examines the patterns of major socio-cultural political mobilisations in India. Section III analyses and elucidates the inter-linkages between the present party system, nationalist thought, and the apparent challenge to the party system from these emerging political interests and parties.

I

Electoral support for various political parties on lines of socio-cultural and economic background for the electorate has been a subject of study for a long time but empirical data in support of such formulations has been thin. Election Commission data does not give us much insight into these factors. Election studies conducted by the Centre for the Study of Developing Societies (CSDS), New Delhi are perhaps the only source for such data. Hence, the chapter depends heavily on the published data of the CSDS election studies for empirical data.[1]

An analysis of the available data for the national elections of 1996, 1998 and 1999 (Figures 5.1–5.16)[2] shows that there are significant differences in

---

[1] Most data about the socio-economic background of political parties has been taken from Subrata K. Mitra and V.B. Singh, *Democracy and Social Change in India: A Cross-Sectional Analysis of the National Electorate*, New Delhi: Sage Publications, 1999, pp. 134–35; and Yogendra Yadav and Sanjay Kumar, 'Interpreting the Mandate', *Frontline*, 16(22), 23 October–5 November 1999, pp. 120–25.

[2] In the data discussed in this chapter, the components of the political formations are as follows:

1996 Elections:

INC+	=	INC+AIADMK
BJP+	=	BJP + Samata + Shiv Sena + Haryana Vikas Party
NF	=	JD + Samajwadi Party
LF	=	CPM + CPI + RSP + FBL

In the 1998 Elections:

BJP+	=	BJP + Samata + Shiv Sena + Haryana Vikas Party + AIADMK + Akali Dal + Trinamool Congress + Lok Shakti + Biju Janata Dal + TDP (NTR)
UF	=	Janata Dal + SP (Mulayam) + TDP (N) + AGP + TMC + DMK + MGP + CPI + CPI (M) + RSP + FBL

In the 1999 Elections:

INC+	=	INC + RJD + AIADMK + Muslim League + Rashtriya Lok Dal + Kerala Congress (Mani)
BJP+	=	BJP + JD(U) + Trinamool Congress + TDP + BJD + Loktantrik Congress + Shiv Sena + Jantantrik Congress + DMK + PMK + MDMK + Lok Dal Rashtriya + Himachal Vikas Congress + Shiromani Akali Dal + Sikkim Democratic Front + Tamizhaga Rajiv Congress + Democratic Bahujan Samaj Morcha + MGR-ADMK + MGR-Kazhagam + Arunachal Congress + Manipur State Congress Party + Independent (Maneka Gandhi)

Some minor errors that have crept into this data cannot be eliminated since a detailed breakdown is not available.

the pattern of support for various political parties on social, economic and cultural lines. This section analyses these patterns with an aim to demonstrate the degree of variations in the support bases of political parties in India and the importance of regional parties therein.

Gender

Figure 5.1 depicts the voting behaviour of the electorate according to gender. Though gender can perhaps not be defined as a socio-economic or cultural category, gender perceptions and gender stereotypes rooted in the cultural milieu definitely affect the support for certain political parties and thus, the outcome of elections. As is clear in Figure 5.1, the support base of the INC+ in the 1996 elections was equally balanced as far as gender was concerned. Approximately 27 per cent of the men as well as women exercised their franchise in favour of the INC+. However, by the 1998 elections, the picture was changing when 28 per cent of the female voters chose to vote for the INC but the support amongst male voters declined by almost 1 per cent (Figure 5.2).

On the other hand, the support for the BJP and its allies (even though the composition of allies changed between these two elections) saw a rather steep rise in their vote share amongst the men as well as the women. While 23 per cent of the women voted for the BJP+ in 1996, by the 1998 elections,

Figure 5.1: Support for Main Political Parties in 1996 Elections According to Gender

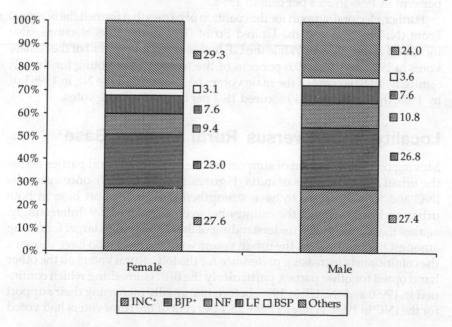

Figure 5.2: Support for Main Political Parties in 1998 Elections According to Gender

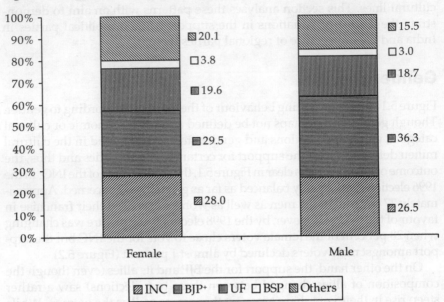

29.5 per cent of them were exercising their franchise in favour of the BJP⁺. Similarly, the support of the male electorate for the BJP⁺ rose steeply from 26.8 per cent in 1996 to 36.3 per cent in 1998.

Further, electoral support for the coalition of parties that formed the National Front (NF) in 1996 and the United Front (UF) in the 1998 elections, also increased rather steeply. While the NF had secured 9.4 per cent of the female votes in 1996, by 1998, 19.6 per cent of the women were voting for the UF. Similarly, 10.8 per cent of the male voters had supported the NF in 1996 but by 1998, the Left Front (LF) secured 18.7 per cent of the male votes.

Locality: Urban versus Rural Support Base

Moving on to distribution of support for the various political parties across the urban and rural areas of India (Figures. 5.3, 5.4 and 5.5), once again the INC and its allies seem to have strengthened their support base in both urban and rural areas of the country between 1996 and 1999. Interestingly, against that conventional understanding of the INC having a larger following amongst the rural voters, the urban voters were the ones who have shown a the continuously increasing preference for the INC. Rural voters on the other hand opted for other parties, particularly the BJP⁺ (something which continued in 1999) and the UF in 1998, before marginally increasing their support for the INC in 1999. While in 1996, 28.1 per cent of the rural voters had voted

Figure 5.3: Support for Main Political Parties in 1996 Elections According to Locality

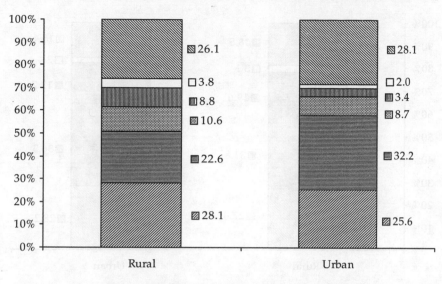

for the INC[+], the same declined to 27 per cent in 1998 but increased substantially to 34.30 per cent in the 1999 elections. On the other hand, 25.6 per cent of the urban voters had opted for the INC[+] in 1996 but by the 1998 elections, 28.2 per cent of these voters preferred to vote for the INC while by 1999, 30.8 per cent of the urban voters were voting for the party.

The support base of the BJP and its allies on the other hand, shows a continuous upward trend over the three elections (Figures 5.3, 5.4 and 5.5). Not only did the support for the BJP and its allies grow both in urban areas of the country, the rate of growth of this support far surpasses that of any other party. In 1996, 22.6 per cent of the rural voters opted for the BJP[+] while a much higher 32.2 per cent of the urban voters voted for the party. In 1998, the same figures had grown to 31.8 per cent and 36.3 per cent, respectively. This reflects a faster growth in the support for the BJP[+] in the rural areas, in addition to its traditional support amongst the middle-class urban voters. This trend of increasing rural support for the BJP[+] was accentuated in the voting patterns of the 1999 elections where 39.5 per cent of the rural voters opted for the BJP[+] while an even larger proportion of urban voters (43.7 per cent) along with 45.9 per cent of semi-rural voters voted for the BJP[+].[3]

---

[3] The available data for 1999 has an additional category of 'semi-rural voters' which is not available for the 1996 and 1998 elections.

Figure 5.4: Support for Main Political Parties in 1998 Elections According to Locality

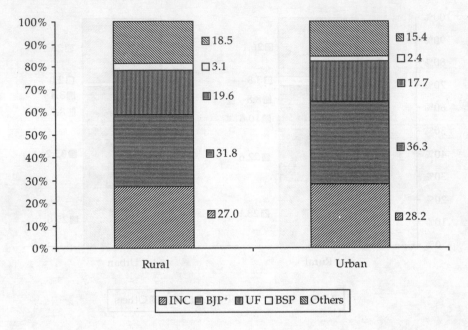

Here it must be noted that the electorate's apparently rising preference for the BJP+ in elections since 1996 is partially a product of its alliance with a wide variety of regional and socio-cultural parties in the 1998 and 1999 elections. This argument of a greater voter preference for regionally based socio-culturally located parties with mobilisation base in a distinct economic grouping in the society is bolstered by the rest of the data in Figures 5.3 and 5.4. The other figures also underline this formulation.

The political parties and groups that formed the NF in 1996 and the UF in 1998 were largely such socio-cultural parties with a regional base, representing the interests of a certain economic section of the society. As is represented in Figures 5.4 and 5.5, the electoral preference vote share of the NF/UF rose appreciably between the 1996 and 1998 elections. In the urban areas, 8.7 per cent of the voters preferred the NF in 1996, which rose to 17.7 per cent in 1998. However, in view of the fact that the parties and political groups which comprised the NF/UF, were representative of rural economic and socio-cultural interests, it is not surprising that the level of support for these parties in rural areas saw a larger rise. While 10.6 per cent of the rural electorate voted for the NF in 1996, in the 1998 elections the NF saw the support of 19.6 per cent of the rural electorate.

Similarly, despite the various components of the NF/UF representing the rural socio-economic interests, the Bahujan Samaj Party (BSP) as the party

Figure 5.5: Support for Main Political Parties in 1999 Elections According to Locality

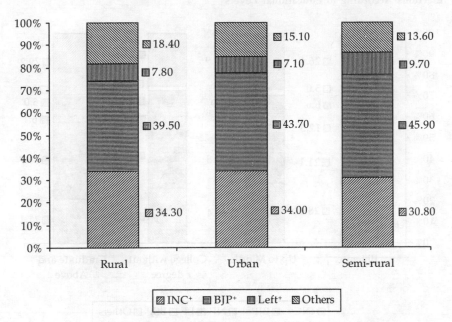

representing particular social and economic interests of the most backward voters continued to find increasing support amongst the rural as well as the urban voters. In the 1996 elections, 3.8 per cent of the rural and 2 per cent of the urban voters extended their support to the BSP while in 1998, 3.1 per cent of the rural and 2.4 per cent of the urban voters opted for the BSP.

Educational Levels of Voters

The voting pattern for various political parties and formations also differs according to the educational level of the voters. Figures 5.6 and 5.7 represent the level of electoral support for the various political parties according to the educational level of the voters.

The largest support for the INC was amongst the illiterate and poorly educated voters. While 28.6 per cent of the illiterate voters and 28.4 per cent of the voters educated up to middle school supported the INC+, the largest support for the BJP came from voters with higher education. Voters who have attended college with or without degree qualifications predominantly voted for the BJP in the 1996 elections (Figure 5.6). While 31.3 per cent of the voters who had attended college without acquiring a degree voted for the BJP, 36.7 per cent of the voters with degree qualifications supported it.

Figure 5.6: Support for Main Political Parties in 1996
Elections According to Educational Levels

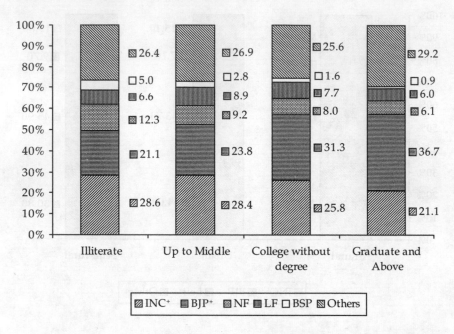

The pattern of the BJP's support base lying largely with the educated electorate was reinforced by the 1998 elections. In the 1998 elections, 34.3 per cent of the voters educated up to middle school voted for the BJP while 36.5 per cent of the voters who have attended college without degrees voted for the party. The voters possessing degree qualifications who voted for the BJP amounted to 42.5 per cent of the voters in this category. In addition to the educated voters, by the 1998 elections there was a swell in support for the BJP amongst the illiterate voters as well. While 21.1 per cent of the illiterate voters voted for the BJP in 1996, in the 1998 elections, 28.9 per cent of the illiterate voters supported the party.

Despite the rise in electoral support for the BJP, in the 1998 elections, the INC managed to retain most of its vote. Although the support for the coalition of parties that formed the NF/UF alliance in the 1996 and 1998 elections, respectively, increased substantially across all the educational categories, this did not eat into the INC votes but was a shift in support of the electorate from other parties. While in 1996, 12.3 per cent of the illiterate, 9.2 per cent of those with middle school education, 8 per cent of the voters who attended college without acquiring degrees and 6.1 per cent of the graduates and those with education levels above graduation supported the NF, the same figures for electoral support for the UF in the 1998 elections were 18.3 per

Figure 5.7: Support for Main Political Parties in 1998 Elections According to Educational Levels

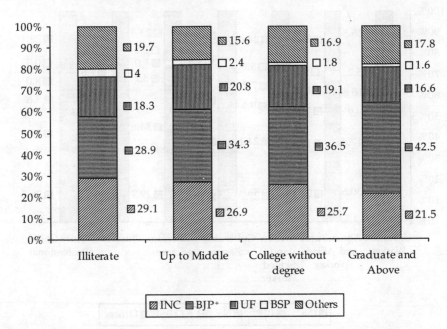

cent, 20.8 per cent, 19.1 per cent and 16.6 per cent, respectively. The Left Front, largely representing mobilisation on economic exploitation issues, lost support across all the educational categories on the other hand (Figures 5.6 and 5.7). Support for the BSP across educational categories remained largely unchanged.

Thus, electoral support was shifting gradually but surely in favour of political formations with a socio-cultural plank for political mobilisation across all educational categories of the electorate. The INC was not able to increase its vote share across any of the educational category, as it was unable to offer anything to counter the cultural nationalism plank of the BJP. Besides, the INC had no political solution to match the BJP's strategy of developing close relations with regional parties representing socio-cultural identities. The surge in the support for the parties of the NF/UF reflects the electorate's support for political formations premised on socio-cultural bases or representing particular economic identities.

Occupation

The correlation drawn in earlier elections that the BJP and its allies were essentially an urban-based middle class and traders party seems to break down

Figure 5.8: Support for Main Political Parties in 1996 Elections According to Occupation

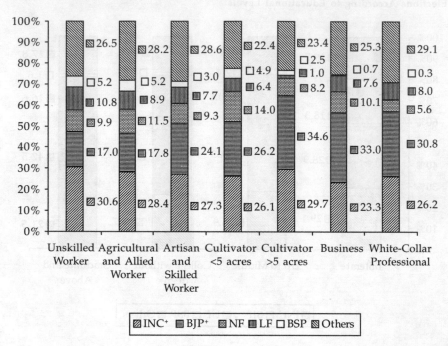

over the two elections for which data is available. In fact, no occupational interlinkages with political support can be witnessed in the available data.

While in the 1996 elections, 30.6 per cent of the unskilled workers supported the INC+, in the 1998 elections, 34.6 per cent of the unskilled workers voted for the party. The BJP was able to secure 17 per cent of the votes of the unskilled workers in 1996, rising to 23 per cent in 1998. The NF was chosen by 9.9 per cent of the unskilled workers in 1996 while the UF secured 21.4 per cent of the votes from unskilled workers in 1998.

Amongst agricultural and allied workers, the INC+ secured 28.4 per cent of the votes in 1996, which declined to 26.2 per cent in 1998 while the BJP's vote share amongst voters of this occupational category rose from 17.8 per cent to 26.2 per cent in 1998. The parties comprising the NF/UF were the main beneficiaries of this category as well. While 11.5 per cent of the agricultural and allied workers voted for the NF in the 1996 elections, 24.5 per cent of such workers voted for the UF in the 1998 elections. Electoral support for the BSP amongst the agricultural and allied workers declined from 5.2 per cent in the 1996 elections to 4.5 per cent in the 1998 elections.

Amongst the artisans and skilled workers, electoral support for the INC and its allies declined. While 27.3 per cent of the artisans and skilled workers voted for the INC+ in 1996, in the 1998 elections, 26.9 per cent voted for the INC. The BJP and its allies, on the other hand, increased their votes amongst this occupational category during the same period. While 24.1 per cent of the artisans and skilled workers voted for the BJP and its allies in 1996, in the 1998 elections, 30.6 per cent of such workers voted for the BJP.

Electoral support increased for the NF/UF coalition of parties in this occupational category, as well. While in 1996, the NF secured 9.3 per cent of the votes from the artisans and skilled workers, in the 1998 elections, 23.1 per cent of the votes of such workers fell in favour of the UF. Clearly, as in most other categories, the NF/UF parties were the greatest beneficiaries. The BSP's support amongst the skilled workers declined. While the 1996 elections had seen 3 per cent of these workers voting for the BSP, in the 1998 elections, the same figure fell to 2.1 per cent only (Figures 5.8 and 5.9).

Amongst cultivators having less than 5 acres of land, the support for the INC+ declined from 26.1 per cent to 21.7 per cent. The main beneficiaries of the changes in electoral support in this occupational category were the BJP and its allies along with the NF/UF parties.

While 26.2 per cent of the cultivators having less than 5 acres voted for the BJP and its allies in the 1996 elections, in the 1998 elections 32.8 per cent of these cultivators cast their vote for the BJP and allies. On the other hand, while the NF had secured 14 per cent of the votes of cultivators having less than 5 acres of land in 1996, in 1998, the UF secured 18.3 of such votes. The BSP's vote share amongst this occupational category declined from 4.9 per cent in 1996 to 3.1 in 1998.

Support for the INC, the BJP and the UF increased amongst cultivators having more than 5 acres of land. While 29.7 per cent of them voted for the INC in 1996, in 1998, 31.1 per cent voted for the INC. Similarly, the BJP and its allies secured a substantial increase in their electoral support amongst culti-vators having more than 5 acres of land. While 34.6 per cent of such cultiva-tors voted for the BJP and allies in 1996, 41.9 per cent of them voted for them in 1998.

A smaller though not insignificant hike was noticed for electoral support for the NF/UF parties in the same period amongst cultivators of more than 5 acres. While 8.2 per cent of this occupational category voted for the NF in 1996, in the 1998 elections, the UF secured 10.8 per cent of the votes amongst this occupational category. The BSP had poor support amongst cultivators of 5 acres or more in 1996 and continued to lose their electoral support in the 1998 elections (Figures 5.8 and 5.9).

As far as the electorate engaged in business is concerned, the INC, the BJP and their allies along with the NF/UF parties increased their support dur-ing 1996–98. While in 1996, the INC and its allies polled 23.3 per cent of the votes of the electorate engaged in business, in 1998, the same figure rose to 26.2 per cent. Similarly, support for the BJP and its allies rose from 33 per cent

Figure 5.9: Support for Main Political Parties in 1998 Elections According to Occupation

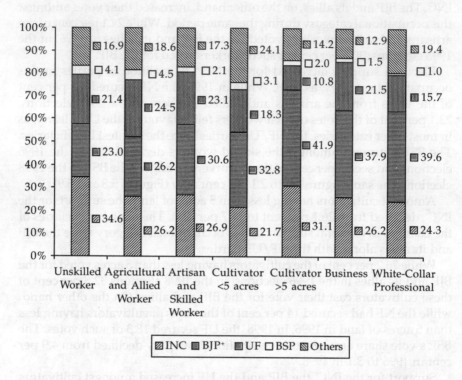

in 1996 to 37.9 per cent in 1998. The support for the NF/UF in this segment of the electorate also rose from 10.1 per cent in 1996 to 21.5 per cent in 1998.

White-collar professionals on the other hand, reduced their support for the INC and its allies in favour of the BJP and its allies and the NF/UF parties. Amongst the white-collar professionals, 26.2 per cent supported the INC and its allies in the 1996 elections while in the 1998 elections, only 24.3 per cent of them voted for the INC. On the other hand, while 30.8 per cent of white-collar professionals voted for the BJP and its allies in 1996, in the 1998 elections, 39.6 per cent of them voted for the BJP and its allies.

Support for the collection of parties that formed the NF in 1996 was at 5.6 per cent of the white-collared professionals' votes while the UF in 1998 polled triple of the proportion at 15.7 per cent. Clearly, the main gainers from the votes of this occupational category were the BJP and the parties comprising the UF.

Figure 5.10: Support for Main Political Parties in 1996 Elections According to Caste

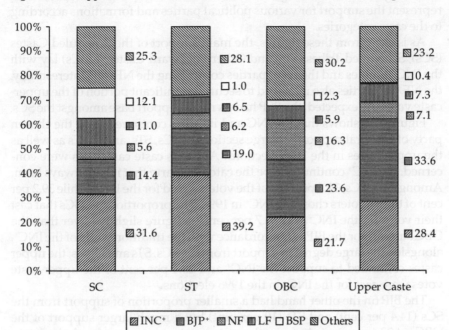

Caste[4]

Although caste-based political mobilisation has been a part of Indian political reality since at least independence,[5] it has acquired a greater salience during the paste decades. Although Indian polity has provided a special space for the backward castes by the mechanism of reserved seats since the first general elections, it is in the past 10 years or so that caste-based politically-relevant identities have crystallised and are now claiming separate political space rather than being a part of the larger national mainstream political parties. Hence, an analysis of the relative support for political parties

[4] In this analysis, ST has been listed as a caste category. While such a comparison is useful for the study of political dynamics, there is no effort to represent the STs as a caste of the Hindu fold. The chapter is conscious of the fact that there are significant differences in the political mobilisations based on caste lines and those on the basis of a shared tribal cultural heritage.

[5] Quite a large body of literature examines the caste-political mobilisation interlinkages. For instance, see Francine R. Frankel and M.S.A. Rao, (eds), *Dominance and State Power in Modern India*, 2 vols, Delhi: Oxford University Press, 1989/1990 and Zoya Hasan, *Dominance and Mobilisation: Rural Politics in Western Uttar Pradesh 1930–1980*, New Delhi: Sage Publications, 1989.

according to the caste categories is of salience. Figures 5.10, 5.11 and 5.12 represent the support for various political parties and formations according to the caste categories.

As is clear from these figures, the main support of the Scheduled Castes (SCs), Scheduled Tribes (STs) and Other Backward Castes (OBCs) lay with the INC, its allies and the set of parties comprising the NF/UF. Interestingly, the NF/UF parties also managed to secure a significant portion of the upper-caste votes. As expected, the BSP had its main support base amongst the SCs.

Figure 5.10 shows that the INC and its allies continued to be the chosen party of electoral support for large sections of SCs, STs, and OBCs as well as the upper castes in the 1996 elections. As far as caste categories were concerned, the INC⁺ continued to be the catch-all party that it had always been. Amongst the SCs, 31.6 per cent of the voters voted for the INC⁺ while 39.2 per cent of the ST voters chose the INC⁺ in 1996. The proportion of OBCs that cast their votes for the INC⁺ was 21.7 per cent—a figure slightly lower than the OBC support for the BJP⁺. In accordance with the traditional role of the INC⁺, alongside the large degree of support from the SCs, STs and OBCs, the upper castes continued to support the INC⁺ and 28.4 per cent of the upper-caste votes were cast for the INC⁺ in the 1996 elections.

The BJP on the other hand had a smaller proportion of support from the SCs (14.4 per cent) and STs (19 per cent) but a much larger support of the OBCs at 23.6 per cent. As far as the upper castes were concerned, the catch-all function of the INC notwithstanding, more than a third of them chose the BJP⁺ (Figure 5.10).

The NF secured a small degree of support in the SC votes (5.6 per cent), the ST votes (6.2 per cent) and the upper-caste votes (7.1 per cent) but a larger support amongst the OBCs at 16.3 per cent of the total OBC votes being cast for the NF. The BSP on the other hand, had a large degree of support amongst the SCs at 12.1 per cent of the SCs voting for the BSP but miniscule support in other caste categories.

In the 1998 elections, the SC support for the INC declined to 29.6 per cent, which increased for the BJP and the UF. In the 1998 elections, 20.9 per cent of the SC voters supported the BJP while 22.2 per cent voted for the UF. Support for the BSP amongst the SC voters declined marginally to 11.2 per cent. As far as the ST voters were concerned, 41.9 per cent voted for the INC, which was a little higher than 1996 but the support of ST voters for the BJP grew substantially to 25.6 per cent. The support of ST voters for the UF parties also grew to 11.6 per cent. The OBC voters marginally increased their support to the INC to 22.5 per cent but their support to the BJP grew drastically to 34.6 per cent. The UF parties also saw a larger support of the OBCs at 21 per cent. Upper castes' votes to the INC stayed at the 1996 level of 28 per cent but grew to 38.5 per cent for the BJP. Interestingly, the upper-caste votes for the UF parties also grew to 17.4 per cent in 1998.

Figure 5.11: Support for Main Political Parties in 1998 Elections According to Caste

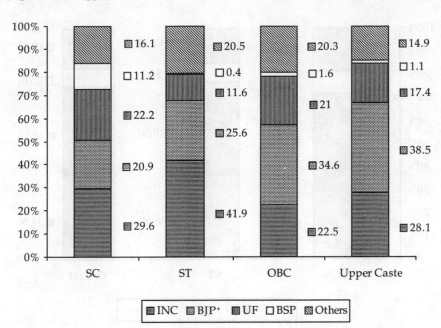

Scheduled Caste votes for the INC continued at the 29.6 per cent level in the 1999 elections but more than doubled to 42.2 per cent for the BJP. Similarly, while 36.8 per cent of the ST voters chose the INC in the 1999 elections, the same figure for the BJP was 40 per cent.

This substantial rise in the level of support for the BJP and its allies in the 1999 elections was a product of the large number of electoral alliances which the party had made in the run-up to the elections. It is noteworthy that most of the smaller parties that comprise the BJP-led National Democratic Alliance (NDA) are premised on socio-cultural and economic identities. In this sense, the data tabulated in Figures 5.11 and 5.12 underlines the formulation put forth earlier that the spectacular success of the BJP in recent years is a product of its alliances with parties with a regional socio-cultural or economic identity based political mobilisation.

Religion

In the half-century of post-colonial political history of India, not to mention the pre-partition political dynamics of the subcontinent, religion has played an important role in political identities' crystallisation and mobilisation. Religion as an important factor in the political life of the country, the secular

Figure 5.12: Support for Main Political Parties in 1999 Elections According to Caste

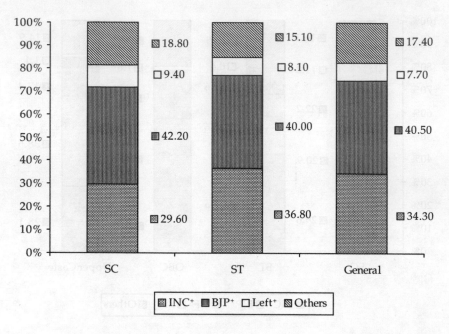

credentials of the formal state notwithstanding, continues till date. In light of this, it is crucial to focus attention on the support for the various political parties according to the religious affiliation of the voters. Figures 5.13 and 5.14 represent the pattern of support for the main political parties according to religion.

In the 1996 elections, Hindu voters had cast their votes mainly for the BJP while Muslims had divided their electoral support between the INC and the NF. However, this does not mean that Hindu voters had not supported the INC+. In fact, a little over a quarter (26.2 per cent) of the Hindu votes were cast for the INC and its allies. The BJP and its allies was chosen by 28.9 per cent of Hindu voters while the NF secured support from only 8.4 per cent of Hindu voters. The support for the INC amongst Hindu voters in the 1998 elections declined slightly to 25.6 per cent but increased for the BJP. In the 1998 elections, 37.4 per cent of the Hindu voters cast their votes for the BJP. The parties of the UF were also chosen by 17.4 per cent of the Hindu voters in this election.

As far as the Muslim voters in the 1996 elections were concerned, 35.3 per cent of them voted for the INC+ with a miniscule 3.1 per cent of them choosing the BJP+. However, the parties of the NF were voted for by 25.3 per cent of the Muslim voters. In the 1998 elections, the INC retained its support amongst

Figure 5.13: Support for Main Political Parties in 1996 Elections According to Religion

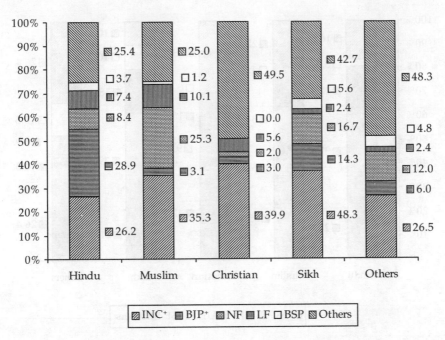

the Muslim voters with 35.1 per cent of them voting for the INC. The support for the BJP amongst the Muslim voters also increased to 6.8 per cent. However, the largest support of the Muslim voters was extended to the UF with 34.4 per cent of the Muslims voting for these parties. The BSP's share in the votes of the Muslim electorate stayed around 1.2 to 1.3 per cent.

Christian voters mainly voted for the INC or other parties. While in the 1996 elections, 39.9 per cent of the Christians voted for the INC+, the same percentage in the 1998 elections increased to 42.1 per cent. The support for the parties of the NF in the 1996 elections amongst the Christian voters was 2 per cent while in the 1998 elections, 18.6 per cent of them voted for the UF parties.

Sikh voters increased their support for the INC and the BJP as well as the NF/UF alliance over the two elections under discussion. While in 1996, 18.3 per cent of the Sikhs voted for the INC+, in the 1998 elections, 21.9 per cent of them chose the INC. However, the rise in their support for the BJP was larger. While in 1996, 14.3 per cent of the Sikh voters had chosen the BJP, in the 1998 elections, 39.8 per cent of them cast their votes for the party. The NF/UF parties also benefited from a larger support from the Sikh electorate. While in 1996, 16.7 per cent of the Sikhs voted for the NF, in the 1998 elections, 18 per cent of them chose the UF.

Figure 5.14: Support for Main Political Parties in 1998 Elections According to Religion

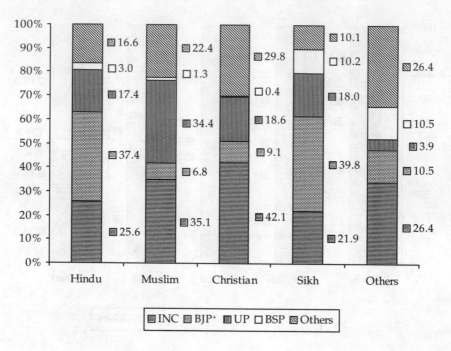

Economic Class

Apart from the socio-cultural factors, as noted earlier, economic class based identities have been a potent plank for political mobilisation. This is particularly true in cases of parties such as the BSP where socio-cultural factors have converged with economic factors to successfully mobilise a depressed class identity, which aggressively seeks political space and recognition, apart from social and economic empowerment. Hence, economic bases of support are crucial factors in the electoral support for the political parties. Left parties have been trying to forge a political mobilisation strategy on economic lines with intermittent and indifferent success, mainly due to the fact that economic determinism cannot be divorced from socio-cultural reality—a flexibility which some other parties attempting to mobilise the disadvantaged are rapidly recognising. This factor is also clear in an analysis of Figures 5.15 and 5.16, which represent the electoral support for the main political parties/formations according to the economic class of the voters.

Amongst the very poor voters, 29.6 per cent voted for the INC+ while 16 per cent opted for the BJP+ in the 1996 elections. The NF secured 10.7 per cent while the Left Front was the choice of 11.3 per cent of the voters in this

Figure 5.15: Support for Main Political Parties in 1996 Elections According to Economic Class

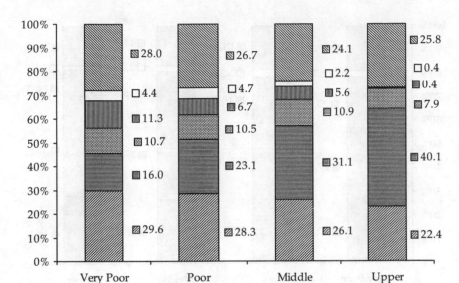

lowest economic category. The BSP polled 4.4 per cent of the votes of this section. In the 1998 elections, the traditional pro-poor posturing of the INC notwithstanding, it was able to secure only 27.3 per cent of the very poor votes. However, the BJP increased its vote share in this category to 27.1 per cent as did the parties of the UF at 23.7 per cent of the very poor votes. The BSP's claim of representing the most downtrodden notwithstanding, it was able to secure a lower share of the very poor votes at 2.7 per cent.

Amongst the poor voters also, the INC's popularity declined slightly from 28.3 per cent in 1996 to 27.4 per cent in 1998. However, the BJP and its allies were able to strengthen their position from 23.1 per cent of the poor votes in the 1996 elections to 31.8 per cent of the poor votes in the 1998 elections. The importance of socio-economic issues amongst the poor voters was reflected in the rising support for the NF/UF parties, many of whom combined socio-cultural identities with the economic identity plank for political mobilisation. While the NF secured 10.5 per cent of the poor votes in 1996, the UF polled a substantially larger 19 per cent of the poor votes in the 1998 elections.

The middle class is often seen as the least politically committed section of the electorate. Their votes perhaps, are the most important in causing 'swings' which can affect the final outcome of any election. However, the overall

Figure 5.16: Support for Main Political Parties in 1998 Elections According to Economic Class

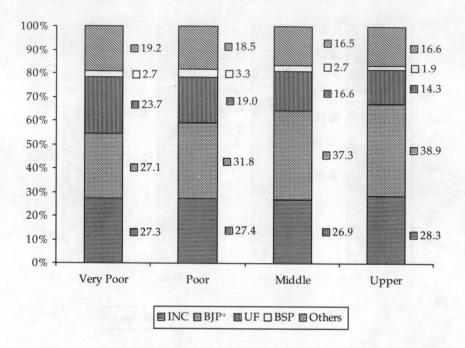

pattern of the very poor and poor voters was reflected in the choice of middle class voters as well. While the INC continued to get a little over a quarter of the votes of the middle class votes (26.1 per cent of such votes in the 1996 elections and 26.9 per cent in the 1998 elections), the BJP, along with the NF/ UF parties progressively found greater support amongst the middle class voters. While 31.1 per cent of the middle class votes were cast for the BJP in 1996, in the 1998 elections, 37.3 per cent of votes were cast for the BJP. Similarly, parties forming the NF had secured 10.9 per cent of the middle class votes in 1996 while in the 1998 elections, LF secured a substantially larger 16.6 per cent of the middle class votes.

In the pattern of support for various political parties and formations amongst the upper class, two significant differences exist. While support for the INC and its allies had remained at roughly the same level or had marginally declined in the other economic classes, there was a significant increase in the support for the INC amongst the upper class. While 22.4 per cent of the upper class voters voted for the INC+ in the 1996 elections, in the 1998 elections, 28.3 per cent of them supported the party.

Similarly, while electoral support for the BJP had increased among all other economic classes, upper class electoral preference for the BJP and its allies actually declined. While 40.1 per cent of the upper class voted for the BJP[+] in 1996, in 1998, 38.9 per cent of them opted for the BJP. Interestingly, despite the common perception of the parties of the NF/UF as parties of the poor voters, the upper class votes for these parties saw a noteworthy increase. While 7.9 per cent of the upper class voters chose the NF in the 1996 elections, in the 1998 elections, 14.3 per cent of them voted for the UF.

This analysis of the relative electoral support bases of political parties demonstrates that the support base of all political parties, including the national parties is fluid and is prone to change along the lines of socio-cultural and economic fractures in the society and polity.

Further, the analysis underlines that national elections are locally contested. Territorial constituencies ensure that regional socio-cultural and economic issues find a greater space in the local campaign of all parties. As discussed above, apart from a differentiation in the voting patterns on the lines of an urban–rural divide, factors such as caste, religion, occupational background, economic status, etc., also play a crucial role in the distribution of the electoral support for the political parties in the Indian political system. The political dynamics of these factors are local/regional and not national. Consequently, the regional parties will increasingly become more important than national ones.

The analysis of the electoral support has repeatedly underlined the fact that the political formations that have benefited the most over the past three elections are the BJP and the NF/UF parties. In fact, compared with the 1996 elections, the electoral support for the BJP in the 1999 elections was substantially larger. Both these patterns go on to stress the centrality of the regional socio-culturally and economically premised political parties. Many components of the NF/UF alliance were regional socio-cultural parties. On the other hand, the BJP, despite being a national party, had political alliances and seat-sharing arrangements with a large number of regional parties. Thus, the rising electoral support for the BJP apparent in the data discussed above is at least partially, the electoral support for these regional parties.

Hence, it must be stressed that the 'political life of a country is related to the socio-economic "substructure". Marxist and non-marxists seem to agree that some association exists.... If a nation has profound social cleavages based for instance on class, race, or religion, [the political system] will be concerned with these cleavages and ... the complexity of the political problems will be in some measure the consequence of the complexity of the social problem.'[6] The electoral support base of the political system examined above reflects these social cleavages in the highly plural society of India along the faultlines of caste, religion, locality, educational level and economic status of

---

[6] Jean Blondel, *An Introduction to Comparative Government*, London: Weidenfeld and Nicolson, 1969, p. 43.

the voters. The regional parties with their support bases premised on these socio-cultural and economic factors represent these cleavages in the society and therefore, play an increasingly larger role in the national political system.

II

The analysis in Section I elucidates that support for the major political formations amongst these socio-cultural and economic sections is becoming increasingly fluid with rising political assertion by political identities premised in these factors. Regional socio-cultural parties representing certain socio-cultural or economic identities are in a better position to represent these social cleavages leading to a greater support for these parties amongst the electorate. The rising electoral importance of these parties is underlined by the data presented in Table 5.1.

The national parties polled 69.8 per cent of the total votes cast in the 1996 elections, which means that 30.1 per cent of the votes were polled by regional parties (state parties and other registered parties, along with independents). Despite some electoral alliances and seat-sharing between the national and regional parties in the 1998 elections, the votes polled by the national parties in the 1998 elections declined to 63.1 per cent. Thus, regional political formations polled a substantial 36.9 per cent of the votes cast. Further, due to the large number of pre-poll alliances and arrangements by the BJP in the run-up to the 1999 elections, the total votes polled by the national parties rose to 67.11 per cent. However, 32.89 per cent of the votes were still cast for the regional parties. Besides, the votes polled by the national parties in the 1999 elections were lower than those polled by them in 1996. The political and electoral importance of the regional parties representing socio-cultural and economic social groups is thus evident.

Table 5.1: Vote Share Polled by National and Regional Political Parties/ Formations in the General Elections, 1996, 1998 and 1999

	1996	1998	1999
National Parties	69.8	63.1	67.11
State Parties	20.6	19.2	26.93
Registered Parties/Others	3.3	15.3	3.22
Independents	6.3	2.4	2.74

Sources: *Statistical Report on General Elections, 1999 to the Thirteenth Lok Sabha,* New Delhi: Election Commission of India, 2000; and Subrata K. Mitra and V.B. Singh, *Democracy and Social Change in India: A Cross-Sectional Analysis of the National Electorate,* New Delhi: Sage Publications, 1999.

The translation of social cleavages in the society into politically self-conscious identities is a complex process. Identities are either latent[7] or conscious. When an identity is latent, it continues to serve merely a descriptive purpose. Such an identity is not politically very significant (for instance, man, woman, Indian, Hindu, Bengali, Tamil, Goanese, etc.).[8] When an individual (or a group of individuals) consciously perceives a certain descriptive identity as indispensable to the definition of his/her (or their) personal identity and accepts that descriptive identity as predominant and paramount over other such descriptive identities and *seeks to acquire political resources on the basis of this identity*, that conscious identity becomes politically significant. When the individuals concerned translate this descriptive identity into a self-conscious political identity (by whatever process, premised on any attribute of the group), they emerge as an ethnic identity.

The regional socio-cultural political parties are manifestations of such an articulation amongst some social groups in India. The progressive articulation of politically pertinent socio-cultural identities in India over the past half-century has transformed the political system in a significant way, which has often been seen as 'fragmentation of the party system'.[9] While the emergence of multiple regional and state-level parties is a fact, it is doubtful if this 'fragmentation' of the party system is a new phenomenon. It may be recalled that the INC in its heydays of one party dominance was always a coalition of multiple interests and its decline can be correlated to the decline of this internal coalition and centralisation pursued by Mrs Indira Gandhi.

Once the national parties, most notably the INC, failed to offer enough political space to the multifarious socio-cultural and economic identities within the party, they started emerging as separate parties. One proof of this formulation is the fact that many of the leaders of the new regional parties were ex-INC workers. The process was also assisted by the participative political mobilisation under the universal adult franchise based general elections.

---

[7] Identities may be latent in the sense that although they may be seen as a distinct sociological category by outside observers, they are not self-conscious political identities.

[8] Each of these terms is a descriptive term to refer to the relevant individual. However, any of these terms have the potential to become a politically relevant identity. For instance, the term 'woman' may be used to distinguish between genders and remain a descriptive term. However, during the last few decades it has also acquired a certain degree of political currency and has emerged as a politically relevant identity. Similarly, the term 'Hindu' pertains to the relevant individuals belonging to a religious group in the society. However, the mobilisation of a large numbers of persons on the grounds of Hindutva in recent years by the Bharatiya Janata Party in India has led to its emergence as a politically significant identity.

[9] The media and the academia, both, have spent a lot of time and space commenting on this 'new' trend in the party system. For example, Pradeep Chhibber and Irfan Nooruddin, 'Party Competition and Fragmentation in Indian National Elections: 1957–1998', in Ramashray Roy and Paul Wallace (eds), *Indian Politics and the 1998 Elections: Regionalism, Hindutva and State Politics*, New Delhi: Sage Publications, 1999.

The articulation of socio-cultural and economic identities in India is generally premised on lingual, racial, ethnic, historical and geographical bases. Under the British colonial rule, 'these local and regional identities were accorded a position of dignity by the nationalist leaders within the broad church of the anti-colonial struggle'.[10] After the transfer of power into the hands of the national leaders, the sub-national imagined political communities[11] began to assert themselves in order to generate political power to give concrete expression to their political aspirations. Apart from the cultural factors, 'a feeling of deprivation, or neglect, resulting from the nature of national decision-making process ... provide the logic for mass movement in most cases'.[12] The feeling of neglect combines with the cultural factors to forge potent socio-cultural and economic sub-national political identities. The demands of these socio-cultural and economic identities range from greater autonomy to complete independence.[13]

Cultural factors combined with developmental issues and a feeling of alienation from the state and its policies, have led to the articulation of socio-cultural and economic identities in many parts of India. The socio-cultural identity articulation in the Gorkha regions of West Bengal under the political banner of the Gorkha National Liberation Front (GNLF) combines the underdevelopment of the population in the region with the lingual/cultural bases to demand political recognition.[14] Similar patterns can also be noticed in other parts of India such as the tribal autonomy and socio-religious movement amongst the Bhil, the Dang, the Dhodia, the Gamit, the Naik, the Kokna, the Warli and the Kathodi tribes in south Gujarat.[15] Instances of socio-cultural identity articulation can also be noticed amongst the 83 tribal groups in south India, which include the Koya, the Malayali, the Irula, and the Paniyan tribal groups. These sub-national identity articulations draw upon cultural and historical factors and include socio-economic considerations born out of imbalances in the development process as additional bases of mobilisation.[16]

---

[10] Subrata K. Mitra, 'Introduction', in Subrata K. Mitra and R. Alison Lewis (eds), *Subnational Movements in South Asia*, Oxford: Westview Press, 1996, p. 7.

[11] Identities are imagined in the sense of being adopted by those who see themselves as marginalised by the state.

[12] Madan P. Bezbaruah, 'Cultural Sub-Nationalism in India's North-east: An Overview', in Mitra and Lewis (eds), *Subnational Movements in South Asia*, p. 175.

[13] Ibid.

[14] See A.R. Das, 'The Language and Script Movement in the Darjeeling Himalayan Area', in, K.S. Singh (ed.), *Tribal Movement in India*, vol. I, New Delhi: Manohar, 1982, pp. 349–59.

[15] See I.P. Desai, 'The Tribal Autonomy Movement in South Gujarat' in Singh (ed.), *Tribal Movement in India*, pp. 243–60; and R.B. Lal, 'Socio-religious Movement Amongst the Tribals of South Gujarat', in ibid., pp. 285–308.

[16] P.K. Misra, 'Tribal Mobilisation in Southern India', in ibid., pp. 325-37.

Other examples of such sub-national identity articulation in India are the cases of Khalistani[17] identity in Punjab and Kashmiri identity in Jammu and Kashmir where religious and cultural factors have led to the powerful articulation of a regional socio-cultural identity. These socio-cultural and economic identities are demanding complete independence. As in other sub-national identity articulations in India, the socio-economic factors have also played a role in the articulation and character of these identities.

The fact that the sub-national identities in most parts of India draw upon socio-economic factors in addition to their cultural bases of mobilisation has also led to their inclination to adopt a radical leftist idiom of politics in some regions, particularly in the tribal regions of West Bengal and Bihar and in some parts of Andhra Pradesh. Such mobilisations have come to be known as 'Naxalite' politics, which advocate radical action such as execution of 'exploiters' after trial in 'people's courts', forcible harvest of fields alienated from the tribal peasants and violent overthrowing of the existing administration.[18]

Amongst the many instances of such sub-national assertions in India, the case of the northeast is perhaps most significant due to the number as well as intensity of sub-national/regional socio-cultural assertions.[19] This region includes seven states—Arunachal Pradesh, Assam, Manipur, Meghalaya, Mizoram, Nagaland and Tripura and has an extraordinary diversity of cultural identities. It contains 209 tribes[20] and the 'linguistic diversity of the area contributes to the complexity of the nationality problem in the region' where '420 languages and dialects are spoken'.[21] As the region is multi-ethnic, multi-lingual and multi-religious, language often provides the criterion for the articulation of these socio-cultural and economic identities.

The articulation of sub-national identities in the northeast can be classified into three broad categories. The first category includes those types of conflicts that arise out of a concept of distinct and separate identity leading to a secessionist movement and the inevitable clash with the Indian state.[22] Examples of this kind of sub-national identity articulation in the northeast

---

[17] See R. G. Fox, *Lions of Punjab: Culture in Making*, Los Angeles: University of California Press Ltd., 1985, for the dynamics of sub-national identity formation amongst Sikhs in Punjab.
[18] Edward Duyker, *Tribal Guerrillas: The Santhals of West Bengal and the Naxalite Movement*, Delhi: Oxford University Press, 1987. Also see Ashim Kumar Adhikary and Ranjit Kumar Bhattacharya, 'The Extremist Movement: An Appraisal of the Naxalite Movement with Special Reference to its Repercussion Among Tribes' in Singh (ed.), *Tribal Movement in India*, pp. 119–28.
[19] See N.K. Das, *Ethnic Identity, Ethnicity and Social Stratification in North-east India*, New Delhi, 1989, for a full discussion of the dynamics of sub-national politics in northeast India.
[20] Bezbaruah, 'Cultural Sub-nationalism in India's Nort-east', p. 172.
[21] Ibid.
[22] Ibid., p. 173.

are the Nagas,[23] some strands of the sub-national movement in Manipur and Tripura and the activities of the Mizo National Front.[24]

The second category of sub-national movement in the northeast is the demand of some groups for a distinct political identity, separate but within the broad framework of an existing one. Such sub-national movements in the northeast are often professedly democratic, directed mostly against the central government who have the authority to bring in constitutional changes to give political recognition to sub-nationality aspiration.[25] However, the disruption to law and order leads to their clash with the state government as well. One instance of such movements in the northeast is the Bodoland movement.[26]

The third strand of sub-national identity articulation in the northeast includes those groups who are neither numerically dominant nor live in geographically compact areas but nevertheless, are apprehensive of their identity being subsumed into the dominant political and cultural identity. Hence, they assert themselves to seek protection of their culture.[27]

In the Hindi heartland, socio-cultural and economic identities have become more assertive over the past decade. Bihar has seen Janata Dal (JD)/Rashtriya Janata Dal (RJD) mobilising support along caste lines on a plank of social justice while UP has the BSP and Samajwadi Party (SP) stressing similar issues. However, caste-based politics is not the only pattern of socio-cultural and economic mobilisation in this region. Jharkhand Mukti Morcha's (JMM) campaign for an autonomous state carved out of the southern districts of Bihar combined the socio-cultural and economic reasons to knit a powerful political identity.

South of the Vindhaya's, what started as lingual assertion in Tamil Nadu, Maharashtra, Andhra Pradesh and Karnataka has acquired full-blown regional identity proportions. The All India Anna Dravida Munnetra Kazhagam (AIADMK), Dravida Munnetra Kazhagam (DMK), Telugu Desam Party (TDP), amongst others, are premised in regional socio-cultural and economic identities but also play a significant role in national politics.

The rise of these socio-cultural and economic identities in the Indian political system has had profound affects on the party system. As has been pointed out in Section I, the electoral support for political parties premised on these identities has been rising over the past decade or more, leading to talks of 'fragmentation' or 'rise of centrifugal impulses' in the polity. Often, the reasons put forth to explain and understand such mobilisations are simplistic

---

[23] See N.K. Das, 'The Naga Movement', in Singh (ed.), *Tribal Movement in India*, pp. 39–52, for a discussion of sub-national identity articulation amongst the Nagas.
[24] Bezbaruah, 'Cultural Sub-nationalism in India's Nort-east'.
[25] Ibid.
[26] Ibid.
[27] Ibid.

and inadequate. Hence, Section III tries to examine the question: In a polity with a central bias and active efforts by the post-colonial state in India to assimilate and integrate the polity into one, why have the national political parties failed to consolidate their electoral support? In this effort, the discursive structures of the national movement, the post-colonial Indian state and the emergence and growth of regional socio-cultural and economic identities therein have been analysed and some formulations offered to understand the issue at hand.

III

In the introduction to this chapter, it was argued that it is not surprising that political parties premised on socio-cultural and economic identities are able to find a larger degree of electoral support. This section explains this formulation and argues that the successful creation of a national identity by the nationalist discourse in the cultural/spiritual domain during the anti-colonial movement carried within itself the seeds of the assertion of regional socio-cultural and economic identities in post-colonial India. Here it is not out of place to remark that perhaps, such assertions are desirable in a democratic polity so that popular participation in the country's political system increases and legitimacy of the state and regime can be sustained and strengthened.

In this context, this section argues that the rationalist-integrationist paradigm of the colonial discourse was carried into the political arrangements of post-colonial India. Hence, the political system's ability to intervene in socio-political movements is still informed by some of the fundamental assumptions of the colonial discourse, severely limiting the ability of the system to respond to the demands of the socio-cultural and economic identities.

Colonial Discourse and the Nationalists

There exists a marked continuity between the colonial discourse and the post-colonial political system towards marginalised societal groups and socio-cultural and economic identities due to the dependence of the nationalist discourse on the colonial discourse. Nationalist discourse in India emerged first as a reaction and later as an alternative to the colonial discourse and hence, a brief analysis of the colonial discourse in India is vital in this chapter.

The British colonial state in India comprised of a set of institutional structures as well as a set of discourses. The colonial enterprise of the generation of legitimacy for the colonial state and maintenance of political stability, which was essential for the colonial economic enterprise, was dependent on the success of this discourse. This discourse drew closely upon the discourse of Enlightenment. Both the functionaries as well as the critics of the colonial state believed that it drew its power from the 'grand theories of European rationalism—its theories, self-definitions, narratives, delusions and strategies ... [which it used] to define and describe itself, to negotiate and bring under control the alien social world'[28] it had come to administer. Those who had to deal with this colonial state, whether in a collaborative or contesting manner, recognised and respected the indivisibility and importance of the myth of invincibility of western rationality which was fundamental to understanding its institutions and logic of functioning. These persons adopted a number of avenues to deal with the myth of invincibility of western rationalism. While some tried to acquire western education in order to master the occult powers of invincible western rationality, others tried to adopt and adapt the ideals of English Utilitarianism into the figures of traditional Indian mythology. Still others tried to avoid it completely by turning towards the traditional discourse.

However, the reaction against colonial discourse was muted because the colonial state adopted multiple levels of dialogue for the three kinds of audience it had to address—British public opinion, Indian western-educated intelligentsia and middle class, and the masses of India—while still employing the essentials of western rationality. When addressing the British public opinion, it used the tone of reasonableness; that of education and legislation in its dealings with the Indian intelligentsia and the indigenous middle class; and that of force and power with respect to the large and distant masses of India. The language of discourse which the colonial state employed with the middle class and Indian intelligentsia was most significant in generating and maintaining political hegemony in India. It generated a new kind of discourse, which at once, consolidated the power of the colonial state, as well as undermined it in the years to come.[29]

The colonial state's projects of legislation and education led the Indian intelligentsia to view the colonial state, in contrast to the pre-colonial state, as one that defended the rule of law, gave security to life and property and provided an opportunity to acquire knowledge of European arts and sciences.

---

[28] Sudipta Kaviraj, 'On the Construction of Colonial Power: Structure, Discourse, Hegemony', in Dagmar Engels and Shula Marks (eds), *Contesting Colonial Hegemony: State and Society in Africa and India*, London: British Academic Press, 1994, p. 21.

[29] For a full discussion of the processes by which the nationalist discourse emerged, see K.N. Panikkar, *Culture, Ideology, Hegemony: Intellectual and Social Consciousness in Colonial India*, New Delhi: Tulika Publications, 1995; Kaviraj, 'On the Construction of Colonial Power'; Sudipta Kaviraj, 'The Imaginary Institution of India', in Partha Chatterjee and Gyanendra Pandey (eds.), *Subaltern Studies: Writings on South Asian History and Society*, vol. VII, Delhi: Oxford University Press, 1992, pp. 1–39; and Partha Chatterjee, *Nation and its Fragments: Colonial and Post-colonial Histories*, New Delhi: Zed Books (for United Nations University), 1995.

Furthermore, the vision of the political future as projected by the colonial state was even more attractive to these intellectuals. 'In their conception, England which held out the ideals of parliamentary democracy, civil liberties and modern economic development, would act as the instruments for their dispensation to other countries of the world. England was a "mirror of their own future...". British rule was, therefore, "welcomed as the chosen instrument"' to change the 'despotic conditions of pre-colonial India into a bourgeois-democratic system'.[30] Notwithstanding the sharp criticisms of the colonial rule, which were put forward by the intellectuals of the time, the belief that the transformation of India would occur within the colonial framework was clear.

A collaborative relationship developed amongst the colonial rulers and the colonised people in which the latter accepted the worldview, apparatus of knowledge, criteria of judgement and ideology of the former. One strand of this discourse was particularly important in reinforcing this relationship as it suited the hegemonic consensus. This view accepted the separateness of Indian history in spiritual/cultural matters but sought to retain British control over economic and political questions since in the latter the superiority of the British rationality was evident.

Apart from generating legitimacy for the colonial state, this project also went on to produce unintended and opposite results in the long run. 'By integrating society, introducing symmetric trends of social hierarchy, enumerating society, familiarising Indians with theory of public power and democracy, placing before them the universality of reason and the great narratives of European nation-formation and introducing the skills of forming associations, this imperial discourse had also taught the Indians how rationalism could be turned against colonisers themselves.'[31]

Some western-educated intellectuals, while employing the rationalist tools, which they had learnt from western education, began to put forward an alternative historical narration that contested Universalist imperial history. Thus, the nationalist view of history began by creating a dichotomy between the material and the spiritual domains as opposed to the dichotomy of public and private spheres offered by the colonial state.[32] In the opinion of the nationalists, in the material domain of economy, statecraft, technology and science, the west had proven its superiority and this superiority had to be acknowledged, studied and replicated.[33] However, the greater the success in

---

[30] Panikkar, *Culture, Ideology, Hegemony*, p. 22.

[31] Kaviraj, op. cit., p. 44.

[32] Chatterjee, *The Nation and its Fragments*, p. 6.

[33] Although some stands of nationalist discourse such as the Arya Samaj believed that classical Indian thought and practises were superior in the material realm too.

adopting and imitating the material imperialist domain, the greater was the need to preserve the distinctness of the cultural domain as the essentials of the identity existed there.

This is perhaps, fundamental to the trajectory of nationalism in India. It is reflected in the social reform efforts of the 20th century when the necessity of change in the social and cultural domain was acknowledged but intervention by the colonial state in the guise of legislation was sought to be excluded.[34] It was within this domain that nationalists contested the imperialist history of India with a history of their own which although used the universality of rationality as a tool, endeavoured to construct a modern national culture that was not western. The 'imagined community' of the nation came into being in this domain where it was already sovereign. The major areas where this transformation of a colonised culture into a nationalist culture took place were those of language, literature, mass media such as drama, art, nationalist educational institutions, family and religion. Indian nationalism started by asserting its autonomy and sovereignty in these areas and constructing the 'Indian' identity with its historical, cultural and symbolic appendages.

In the domain of the material, nationalism was unable to emphasise the difference, as it was able to in the spiritual and cultural domain.[35] Therefore, it began to assert itself in the public domain constituted by the modern/colonial state. Its main task was to challenge colonial hegemony over the middle class, i.e., to contest the 'rule of difference'. The growth of institutions in the country required that the 'rule of difference' be also institutionalised.[36] Nationalism, utilising the rationalist thought and humanism that it had learnt from the colonists, contested this difference between the rulers and the ruled with the result that it became a force in the public domain as well. The public area occupied by nationalism expanded as nationalist politics grew stronger.

The nationalists were thus successful in creating a dichotomy between the material and the spiritual/cultural, having earlier declared sovereignty in the latter realm. The rationalist colonial state on the other hand, operated within the distinction of public and private domains whereby it sought to ensure equality of all private domains (in terms of religion, caste, etc.). The nationalist discourse operated in a set of contradictory domains. On the one

---

[34] Unlike the earlier period when social legislation was desired by most reformers.

[35] Chatterjee, *The Nation and its Fragments*, discusses why the cultural domain was more amenable to the creation of the community than the material domain.

[36] The colonial discourse embodied the concept that there was an essential difference between the British rulers and the Indian subjects. This led to a 'rule of difference' that dwelt on the superiority of the European race and their cultural practises over the Indian population and their practises. Examples of this include barring of all Indians from certain areas of Indian cities and the outcry from the European population living in India over the Ilbert Bill whereby an Indian judge could try European offenders.

hand, in the cultural domain it was able to construct a new discourse that was premised on the difference from the colonial discourse and on the other hand, it accepted and revered the colonial model in the realm of the material.

Therefore, to some extent, parts of the public domain of the colonial state and the material domain of nationalism overlapped. Nationalist thought was not successful in constructing an alternate discourse in the material domain (partly because the nationalist leaders were convinced of the superiority of the western rationalist discourse within the material domain). Consequently, it also accepted the colonial model of economic and political development consisting of politico-economic and social integration and industrialisation.

The acceptance of the essentials of the material domain of the colonial discourse by the nationalists had an important impact on the political and discursive structures of the post-colonial state in India. There is a strong continuity of colonial discourse in the Constituent Assembly and hence, the Constitution.[37]

National Discourse and Socio-Cultural Identities

The nature and character of nationalist discourse that emerged also significantly affected the trajectory of ethnic identities' mobilisation and articulation in post-colonial India. The nationalist project had begun with an autonomous form of imagination of the community in the spiritual/cultural domain, which was not amenable to rationalist reductions. The nation was first imagined in this domain and declared sovereign. 'The result is that autonomous forms of imagination of the community were, and continue to be, overwhelmed and swamped by the history of the post-colonial state.... If the nation is an imagined community and if nations must also take the form of states, then our theoretical language must allow us to talk about community and the state at the same time....'[38]

Politically-relevant socio-cultural and economic identities premised on various cultural lines (for instance, the Oriya identity premised on a distinctive language in present-day Orissa, Jharkhandi identity premised on tribal heritage and culture, the caste identities of UP and Bihar premised on social and economic marginalisation, Tamil, Kannada, and other similar identities premised on linguistic as well cultural bases, and numerous identities premised on cultural factors in the northeast) also employed the autonomous method of imagination of community that the nationalists had used vis-à-vis the colonial state. The leaders in these societal groups were quick to learn

---

[37] See Amit Prakash, 'Contested Discourses: Politics of Ethnic Identity and Autonomy in the Jharkhand Region of India' *Alternatives: Social Transformation and Humane Governance*, 24(4), October–December 1999, pp. 461–96 for a full discussion of the subject.
[38] Chatterjee, *The Nation and its Fragments*, p. 11.

from the nationalist leaders. They began employing a version of local history, glorified incidents such as the tribal revolts and utilised the uniqueness of their respective social group to engender a process of such autonomous forms of imagination of the community that soon started to desire political recognition.

The nationalist leadership's endeavours at creating a national identity autonomous of the colonial discourse by utilising cultural appendages such as language, literature, mass media such as drama, art, nationalist educational institutions, family and religion, all offered ready-made fodder to the leadership of these socio-cultural and economic identities. All these cultural factors in the plural society of a country like India had be locally located in order to find mobilisation support amongst the people. To elucidate on this point further, attempts at construction of a national identity around the linguistic-cultural factors of Hindi would have hardly found support in most of peninsular India, not to mention all other areas, apart from the Hindi belt. The fact that most Indian languages and forms of cultural expression grew rapidly during the national movement attests to this formulation. Thus, the Indian identity construed by the nationalists was a collection of sub-identities premised on socio-cultural and economic factors.

After independence (and during the national movement), the 'sub-national' communities (emerging ethnic identities) employed the same avenues, which the nationalists had employed vis-à-vis British colonial rule to invent and declare their political identity in the spiritual/cultural realm. Once such a political identity has been articulated, it began to contest not only the colonial discourse but later, also the dominant nationalist discourse by mobilising the electorate in the form of regional political parties on a plank of socio-cultural and economic identity. It began to seek political recognition from first, the colonial state[39] and then, the post-colonial Indian state.[40] These 'ethnic', 'sub-national', 'socio-cultural' or 'regional' identities also shared with the nationalists a belief in rapid rationalist development.

As far as the mainstream political and party system dominated by the nationalist discourse is concerned, once the nationalist government had taken office, it sought to implement all the elements of colonial discourse that the nationalists saw as desirable. The creation of the nationalist state was

---

[39] For instance, proto-Jharkhandi identity was articulated in the late 1920s in a memorandum to the Simon Commission, 'Memorandum Submitted by the Chota Nagpur Improvement Society', *Report of the Indian Statutory Commission, Vol. XVI: Selections from the Memoranda and Oral Evidence by Non-Officials*, Part 1, London: HMSO, 1930.

[40] In the colonial state, the demand for greater political recognition took the form of a demand before the Simon Commission for greater democratic administration (including the demand for the Chota Nagpur region to be converted into a chief commissioner's or a governor's province) in the Excluded Areas. In the post-colonial state this demand crystallised into a demand for an autonomous federal state.

seen as the fulfilment of the national community and the Indian state was not left with much intellectual use for the autonomous community that had been imagined by the nationalists. The independent Indian state left this aspect of nationalist thought to the regional communities to experiment with and in some cases, achieve political recognition from the political system. For instance, the lingual reorganisation of Indian states in 1956 was an acceptance by the state that some degree of political recognition to 'sub-national' socio-cultural communities was required.

The various socio-cultural and economic identities now articulated as regional political parties, did not see the issue from the point of view of the mainstream political system and the autonomous forms of the creation of community continued in post-independent India. The lessons that the nationalists had learnt from the colonial discourse were also internalised by the smaller communities. These communities started using the same tools that the nationalists had used and began demanding political recognition and at times, autonomy, by mobilising on India's electoral scene. The social support for these demands is expressed in the form of rising electoral support for regional socio-cultural political parties and the decline of support for national parties.

Herein lies the root of the contemporary political instability and turmoil in the Indian party system. The discursive underpinnings of the Indian party system will have to evolve from a integrationist model to accept the 'salad bowl' reality of Indian political identity whereby all the regional/'sub-national' socio-cultural and economic identities are a part of the Indian identity and electoral support for the political parties will necessarily reflect this reality.

The 'fragmentation' of the party system over the past decade does not undermine of the party system or weaken it. It makes the party system more democratic which reflects the actual political reality of India. 'An open polity that is truly open is also a highly integrated polity.... It admits of self-articulation of the authentic "nationalities" and their genuine federalisation. If, on the other hand, they are kept suppressed ... violent movements for restructuring the territorial basis of population are bound to erupt.'[41]

---

[41] Rajni Kothari, *State Against Democracy: In Search of Humane Government*, New Delhi: Ajanta, 1988, p. 131.

6

HOW MANY PARTIES ARE TOO MANY?

Pran Chopra

In the mid-1940s, when it began to look like India would soon become independent, a debate started about India's future polity, and it quickly reached two conclusions. First, India would not disintegrate in chaos, despite the foreboding aroused by the impending breaking away of what was soon to become Pakistan. And second, what would then become India would be a democracy. But a presidential or parliamentary democracy? That question remained open for slightly longer but was answered in favour of the parliamentary system before the 1950s began.

However, that did not silence all doubts regarding the suitability of that system for a country of the size and diversity of India, and some of these doubts are still with us. Some notable public figures and commentators continue to advocate the presidential system. But more relevant to this paper are two doubts regarding the particular form of the parliamentary system that India adopted.

The first is whether we should have jumped straightaway into the deep end by adopting universal adult franchise at one go instead of starting with a more limited franchise first. Not as limited as we had until the very last election held before independence, in which only about 12 per cent of the people had the right to vote out of those who would have been entitled to it under universal adult franchise, but limited at least by some educational qualification, if not economic and gender qualifications as well. The second doubt, which is more basic and reinforces the first, is whether parliamentary democracy can function at all if each of the numerous pieces of each of the many Indian societal, economic, cultural, linguistic and other mosaics has the right to form a political party of its own, each jumping into the electoral fray with the full weight and force of all the adults who constitute it.

The persistence of these doubts, whether one shares them or not, is understandable because they are watered by many different streams of reasons. First, the intellectual climate of the times in which these doubts began to be raised. The effective political class of the 1950s, except the Gandhians among them, had a high proportion of those who were not only English educated but had a higher understanding of the English polity than of certain Indian political realities which, though somnolent at the time, were present all around them. They also had a high proportion of Anglophiles among them who believed that what was English was best. England had become an adult franchise democracy only by stages, and also had only two or three effectively contending political parties. Therefore, for this early generation of intellectuals of independent India, this was the direction that India needed to take.

Slightly later, intellectuals came under the influence of an alien political theory. As they prepared for the third wave of democracy—consisting of many Southeast Asian, African, and Latin American countries; the first wave being Western Europe and America and the second the teeming millions of South Asia—many schools of western political thought drew up a code for determining which countries had the endowments for parliamentary democracy and which did not. In fact this code was nothing more than a catalogue of the societal characteristics of the countries in which parliamentary democracy had succeeded. But the codifiers converted the catalogue into a political theory on the specious basis that the successful countries had certain characteristics and therefore no country which lacked them could succeed in practising parliamentary democracy.

India clearly lacked many of these characteristics, such as a homogenous population, high literacy and living standards, etc., and therefore could not be expected to succeed. But India also provides a significant example of the irrelevance of 'codes' which fail to take into account major differences between the life cycles of different countries. While the theorists were theorising India was going through a movement of mass political education which encompassed more millions than any other similar movement ever had, more millions than the total population of any country which had ever debated the democratic option so keenly as India was doing on the eve of becoming independent.

Mahatma Gandhi had launched his non-violent civil disobedience movement for independence in the early 1920s, which by the very nature of its strategy generated the active political participation of the bulk of India's population in one way or another. India did not win independence through a violent revolution or a military revolt, either of which would have involved a relatively small number of people, whether it succeeded or failed. It won independence through the daily preaching and practice of small acts of non-violent political protest by so many millions of people so often that it brought the colonial government to its knees while at the same time it awakened political consciousness throughout the country. This combination of poverty and politics was to result in a society about which *The Economist* of London was to say some decades later: 'Indians have more political sense per thousand calories than any other people.'

By the time India became independent its population had become a potential electorate, the leaders of the movement had become an elected government in the making, different strands of the movement in different regions of the country, each with its own societal and political characteristics, had become incipient parties of the future, whether within or already outside the main vehicle of the movement, the Congress Party. That is how it came to pass that within the first decade or so of gaining independence India acquired all the essential tools of a parliamentary democracy while still lacking many of the essential qualifications prescribed by the prevailing theory of it.

By the early 1960s India had an electorate of more than 25 crore, with a voter turn out of more than 50 per cent (now about 60 crore and more than 60 per cent). Proof of the freedom with which they voted lay in the fact that the ruling party never got even half the vote (and lately no one, except coalitions, has had more than a third). Anyone could form a party, and so many did that Parliament had more than two dozen parties in it apart from the many dozens who could not win a seat. On the floor was the whole range from extreme right to left, with a big cluster in the middle, and all with sufficiently stable and measurable constituencies for pollsters to be able to predict the outcome of an election with just about as much success as in democracies which have had more of the necessary 'qualifications' and for much longer.

In more recent years a number of new developments in the polity, all born of India's own experience, have made some sections of our society sceptical of our ever making a success of the adult franchise and free-for-all parliamentary democracy. The sceptics are not large in number but are very vocal, and wield disproportionate influence among the urban upper-middle classes, which in turn wield an even more disproportionate influence in our economy and the media and therefore also on the polity. Since their numbers are small, they cannot sway the outcome of elections as much as they can the economy and the media. This can—though it hasn't yet—limit their influence on legislatures in the first place, and in the second place on such policies, institutions of governance, and instruments of state which legislatures can control if they decide to do so.

The danger of this limitation makes the members of this sceptical class very ambivalent in their relations with India's mass based parliamentary system. On the one hand the majority of these people have a liberal and democratic outlook, and therefore, on the whole support democracy. They also have a more educated and developed understanding of the theory and practice of democracy and can be better than others at diagnosing the defects of our system and suggesting remedies. But on the other hand they also wish to protect their disproportionate stake in the economy and the media against the influence which the far more numerous but deprived sections of the population can exercise, if they try to, through the legislatures and on the agencies and policies of the state because of their numbers. Therefore, the skeptics focus much more on the defects and deformities of our parliamentary polity than on ways of reforming it without diminishing the power of the adult franchise electorate and the party system thrown up by it.

This is what accounts for the irony that the most deprived sections of Indian society are more zealous in exercising their right to vote than are the better off and more educated urban middle class. The former see their vote as their only means of reaching the levers of power through legislatures elected by them. The latter are more interested in reaching them, and are able to, through the market and the media in which they are predominant, and which they use zealously to curb the reach of the state and legislatures. Two specific examples of this are in the massive study of the Indian electorate by the Centre for the Study of Developing Societies, New Delhi, under its projects 'Election Studies' and the 'National Election Study, 1996'. The studies, based upon exit polls in recent elections, are so huge that some of their conclusions might be regarded as inadequately backed by data. But they are strongly enough backed by extensive and educated observation of public attitudes, biases, preferences, and by all indications the direction of the conclusions is correct.

The studies show, first, that though the rural population, often regarded as generally 'backward' compared with the urban equivalent, had a lower voter turn out in the earlier elections—partly due to deficiencies of the electoral apparatus in villages—it has not only caught up now with the urban population but its turnout has been more than 5 percentage points higher than that of the urban population in country-wide elections in recent years. It shows, second, that both in urban and rural India voters who are underprivileged in economic terms have a higher turnout than the better off ones. And it shows third that the turnout is higher in elections to State Assemblies, which are at the lower tiers of India's three-tier democratic system—the federal level at the top, the state level in the middle, and the town and village level at the bottom—than in elections to Parliament.

The studies recognise that the extent and number of elections at the lowest level, to town and village elective bodies, are not great enough as yet to warrant firm conclusions about them. It is only very recently that, through an amendment of India's Constitution, it was made mandatory for states to constitute elective bodies in towns and villages. But the principal analyst of the study, Yogendra Yadav, has filled an important detail into the second feature mentioned above, that the underprivileged have a higher turnout. He writes:

India is perhaps the only large democracy where the (voter) turn out of the lower orders of society is well above that of the most privileged groups.... The odds ratio for different economic strata in 1971 was quite like the rest of the world. The richer you were, the greater the likelihood that you would vote. By 1996 there was a neat reversal of this pattern. The data for 1998 show highest turn out for middle income groups, but the richest continue to be the lowest in turn out.... While the last two decades have witnessed a decline in the proportion of illiterates, they have also seen an increase in the propensity of the illiterates to vote.[1]

Yadav does not say so but it is worth recalling here that in leading the movement for independence Mahatma Gandhi laid at least as much stress on his movement for uplifting the most depressed classes. Where Gandhi left off upon his death, democracy took over. It is the first function of democracy, which it has performed well in India, to give a voice to those sections of society which would otherwise have lacked it, being disadvantaged in other respects as well. It is its second function to enable and urge all sections of society to throw up parties of their own as their advocates in the people's court. The advent of the parties of the depressed sections in the political arena, and with the force indicated by Yadav's analysis, shows that Gandhi's legacy and the logic of democracy continue to be at work, and have been most so in the decades of the 1980s and 1990s, which churned up politics as few earlier decades had done. This has relevance for the pros and cons of the proliferation of parties, as well as for a neglected theme of the future which is mentioned below.

This is the background against which one should consider the current discourse on three of the most conspicuous problems of the polity—corruption, the number and working of political parties, and the associated instability of governments—and also consider the lack of discourse on a fourth problem, which is more important than the other three: the incongruity between electoral equality for all on the one hand, and on the other hand, grave economic and social inequalities. This mismatch between the polity and the economy invites the most potent question about both: What will happen when the electorally equal begin to bring the full political weight of their numbers to bear upon the inequalities they have borne for so long?

Corruption and Political Parties

The problem which figures most in the current discourse is corruption in its many forms. Though at least as prevalent in business and commerce, it is political corruption which is debated most though its causes lie less in the parliamentary system, the number and structure of parties, or the polity as a whole, than in a general decline in the standards of public and social morality, leading to widespread tolerance of administrative and judicial laxity in investigating and prosecuting offences. Democracy as such has contributed

[1] Yogendra Yadav, 'Understanding the Second Democratic Upsurge: Trends of Bahujan Participation in Electoral Politics in the 1990s', in Francine R. Frankel, Zoya Hasan, Rajeev Bhargava and Balveer Arora, (eds), *Transforming India: Social and Political Dynamics of Democracy*, New Delhi: Oxford University Press, 2000, pp. 120–45.

such remedies as democracy can; for example, the necessary laws, backed by popular approval, which empower the appropriate investigating and prosecuting agencies to be more effective. If the remedies are not applied it is because society lacks the will, not the polity the means. But two of the causes of political corruption are directly related to the polity and call for discussion in the present context. The first causes the administrative laxity mentioned above; the other promotes proliferation of parties.

It is widely believed that if corrupt candidates were kept out of the electoral arena, they would not be able to rise on the democratic ladder to positions where they can protect the corrupt and thus cause the laxity. The fact that they do cause it, or at least are widely suspected to, degrades the moral authority of the parliamentary system, which in turn emboldens corruption in the electoral arena and thus sets up a vicious circle. The suspicion is understandable but not justified, because the problem lies elsewhere.

Provisions exist in electoral laws, and are often enforced, to bar or unseat candidates who are definable as 'corrupt' under these provisions. But the problem lies with the definition. It is often demanded that 'chargesheeted' candidates should be automatically debarred from seeking election. But there is no general agreement on what sort of 'charges' should invite the bar. That is, charges made by whom and for what sort of 'offences'. Laws are sometimes violated, or are alleged to be, by those opposing, for example, the citing of a nuclear plant or a dam or polluting industries, not to speak of a particular place of worship at a particular location. Such sorts of violation should of course also invite the sanctions of the law. But should they also invite externment from the electoral arena? At one time, prior to independence, anyone who had ever served a jail term for an offence committed in agitating for independence had proudly worn this fact as a badge of honour.

But as the first step each candidate should be required to reveal, along with anything he considers his positive credentials, whether any charges have been laid against him, by whom and for what offence. This would help in separating those charged with socially dishonourable offences from those who have only allowed their social conscience to drive them past the limits of the law. The former would then hesitate to run the gauntlet of public opinion, assuming of course that the forums of public opinion are in good health (which takes one back to the point made above that often what is wrong with the polity is only a symptom of what may be wrong with society).

Second, an investigating agency, whether the lowly police constable or the high profile Central Bureau of Investigation, has to lay charges in order to present the case to the court. Even assuming—an assumption not always justified—that the agency has laid the charges in all honesty, no one, not even the judicial system, knows till much later whether they are sustainable, let alone proven. It would be questionable to debar anyone from seeking an election or to require that he resign his seat merely because an unproven charge is pending against him. However, if proved in the trial court, the charges should remain a bar so long as they are not dropped by a higher court. But there needs to be much greater public consensus behind these issues for them to be enshrined in enforceable laws, and an even wider consensus for the laws to be invoked effectively. The cause of cleaner politics would gain if more energy went into evolving such a consensus and less into defaming democracy and political parties. Prime Minister Vajpayee invited a public debate on this issue during a discussion in Parliament on the Ayodhya controversy in the winter session of 2000. But there was not much response from political parties.

All this remains valid in spite of the fact that in the early months of 1996 public opinion did force a number of leading politicians (not all, alas) to step down when the smell of corruption became strong around them. But a second type of corruption which is directly related to the polity and in particular to the party system concerns the manner in which members elected on the ticket of one party split away from it to form another before the next election, and often do so more than once, creating four or more parties where there was only one. The anti-defection law has eased the problem but not eliminated it. A more stringent law would help. At the least it should provide that a split would be recognised only if at least half the members of a party, not one-third as now, broke away from it, signifying that the majority of the party members favoured a shift in its plank and desired to make it in time for the next election to give legitimacy to its new point of view. Ideally, any member who disowns the party on whose ticket he was elected should be required to seek re-election. This proposition was aired but not pursued during the debate on the anti-defection law. But surely he should be required to do so if he defects to a party which he had opposed in the preceding election, because in electing him his constituency had in effect rejected the party to which he chooses to lend his affection after the election. If his plea be that his constituency itself has changed its mind and he is only responding, he should let his constituency be the judge of that plea.

These suggestions require that every party should have inner party democracy, a constitution which provides for elected institutions at all levels, and regular elections to them, preferably overseen by an independent and public authority. Apart from being a good value in itself and confirmation of the party's commitment to democracy, such a structure is necessary if there is to be a recognised and competent authority for properly determining whether there has been a defection, for identifying the defector, and for instituting such action against him as may be required by the party's constitution as well as the country's. At present the anti-defection law is implemented only if a member of the party's legislative wing disobeys a whip issued by the leader of that wing. But this leaves room for dispute, for instance over the question whether the leader was appointed in accordance with the party's constitution, for then alone he would have the authority to issue a whip in the first place.

The present tendency in some parties to leave it to some top leader of the party to nominate all functionaries is undesirable on many counts. A party may *elect* anyone unopposed to any office, as a constituency may elect one to a legislature, but cannot *appoint* one, bypassing the prescribed electoral procedure. The country's largest single party, the Congress, decided at the end of the year 2000 that all members of its highest executive authority, the Working Committee, would be nominated by the party's current president, Mrs Sonia Gandhi, whereas the party's constitution provides for the election of half of them. Such a departure from the party's constitution can expose some future decisions of the Working Committee, such as expelling a 'defector' or a dissident, to challenge in court on the grounds that the Committee itself lacks the sanction of the party's constitution. As these lines are written, a court in Jammu has ordered the local unit of the Bharatiya Janata Party (BJP), the country's second largest party, to elect its president 'in accordance with its constitution'.

Similar is the case with other safeguards for the proper working of political parties. For instance, parties are required to submit audited statements of accounts to the Election Commission or else face withdrawal of their recognition by the Commission. This threat should be carried out more diligently. Laxity here can lead to laxity in another and more important respect. All parties are required to maintain proper accounts of the election expenses incurred by their candidates in order to make sure that these remain within the limits which have been prescribed by the Commission for curbing misuse of money for influencing the outcome of elections. Obviously, the limits can be enforced only if the party itself ensures compliance by the candidates, and the Commission ensures that the party's own funds are not surreptitiously diverted to the candidate. There is also need to put controls on what a party may spend on its own election campaign as a party, apart from what is spent by its candidates.

This proposition has not received enough attention because it raises the larger—and hitherto shirked—question of how parties and elections should be funded. State funding, at least partially, has been debated often but never conclusively. Private funding comes mostly, and sometimes under the counter, from the corporate sector, which is not keen to let go of this lever upon a party when it comes to power and forms the government.

Convenience versus Democracy

The case for such restrictions on parties and candidates as are only aimed at restricting the number that may enter the electoral fray is, however, weak. One too many is better than one too few. Too many may pose problems of management. But allowing too few would be undemocratic. In any case, by what criteria would any authority decide that one party (or a candidate) may contest but another, not otherwise disqualified, may not? Two restraints are in use and their enhancement has been proposed. A candidate has to deposit a security, which he forfeits if he fails to get a (prescribed) minimum share of the votes cast. A party is given the status (and campaign facilities) of a 'recognised' party only if in the preceding elections it has polled a prescribed minimum share of the vote. It has been suggested that both thresholds should be raised. But it would be unfair to raise the security amount in a country in which many contestants are as poor as the majority of the voters are. It would also be unfair to raise the threshold for the recognition of a party, because with more than 100 lakh voters in an average parliamentary constituency it takes a new party more than one election to reach even the presently prescribed threshold.

Exasperated reformers have argued that the country should junk the parliamentary system and adopt the presidential, so that there would be only one elective office to fill. This is counsel of despair, if not even surrender to an authoritarian bent. The foremost function of a democratic polity, whether presidential or parliamentary, is to elect a governing authority which reflects its people as faithfully as it can. Which procedure is more convenient for ensuring that is less important than which produces a more representative government. The parliamentary system crowns the polity with an apex which is more representative of the base, the electorate, than a one-man presidency can be. In India, for example, a Parliament consisting, as it does, of a directly elected Lok Sabha with more than 540 members, and a Rajya Sabha elected by the legislatures of all the federating members of the Union of India, reflects the totality of the Indian electorate much better than a one-man presidency can. In his own eyes perhaps, and more certainly in the eyes of many sections of the electorate, the president would be more identified with the community to which he belonged—be it regional, religious, linguistic, social, economic or any other community—than parliament in its totality can be. In that sense the parliamentary system is more democratic, and this is one of the reasons why it is preferred in India although electing a parliament is more cumbersome.

An excess of candidates or parties in an election can make the apex less representative of the electorate only if it so fragments the electorate that no candidate or party can claim to have been elected by the majority of the electorate. That has certainly become a serious defect in the Indian system. It has been further aggravated by the 'first-past-the-post' voting system, with a single non-transferable vote and single member constituencies, which India copied from Britain. It was argued that a 'proportional' or 'list' or any such alternative voting system would throw up too many parties. The reasoning was understandable but it backfired. In practice it has meant a distortion: A party can obtain a far higher share of seats than of votes, because any party can win a constituency with a minority share of the vote if no other party has polled one vote more. If a party wins many seats in this way it can have a much higher share of seats than of votes.

This is not a theoretical projection. For four decades the Congress often got huge majorities in Parliament without *ever* getting anywhere near half the votes in the country as a whole, because as the oldest party it could poll more votes in more constituencies than any other party. Since it often formed the government only as the largest single but *not* a majority party in Parliament, it meant that often the country had a government which represented only a minority in Parliament which itself represented an even smaller minority of the electorate. With a majority of the electorate not supporting the government, the latter's mandate lacked moral authority. This has become a serious problem of governance. But the remedies for that lie elsewhere, not in restricting numbers.

The concern over numbers of candidates and parties is both misplaced and misdirected. Misplaced in the sense that it exaggerates the problem. Misdirected in the sense that it seeks remedies in the wrong direction. It also misunderstands the problem, and in all these respects the British example of a two party system is not only irrelevant but misleading.

How Many Parties are too Many?

First, the exaggeration. The number of parties is undoubtedly too large. It has to be counted not in scores but in a few hundreds. All of them have some degree of recognition by the Election Commission. Therefore the number of candidates is also cumbersome. While the number of parliamentary seats at stake rose only from 489 in 1952 to 543 at present, the number of candidates contesting them rose from just under 1,900 to almost 14,000 in 1996. But apart from the fact that much of this increase in the number of parties and candidates is due to causes which, as will be explained later, are supportive of democracy, and that the number has declined from that peak, the increase is more on paper than on the ground. It has added enormously to the labours of the election staff. But its impact on the outcome of elections is little. Had it caused a corresponding fragmentation of the electorate and of legislatures the problem would have been serious. But it has not, and to the extent it has it is remediable by means which are quite practicable, are perfectly compatible with democracy, would in fact enhance it, and are gaining support. More about them later. But first about the extent of fragmentation, and the extent of its seriousness.

For the first four decades or so of India's adult franchise democracy, the number of parties which actually entered the fray in a parliamentary election remained below 30. More important, around three-quarters of the total vote was harvested by less than half-a-dozen parties, and they were strung out on the spectrum usual in a democracy, that is, from the extreme left to the extreme right, with the ideologically middle-of-the-road parties occupying much more than half the middle space, an architecture which also reflects India's Middle Path socio-philosophical bent. That the extreme left was more prominent than the extreme right in terms of economic ideology is the electoral reflection of India's socio-economic reality that though India is not a poor country most Indians are, and economic inequalities are great.

That the extreme left included the communists, both when they were a single party and when they split between pro-Soviet and pro-China parties, like the communist movements in many countries, is a plus point rather than a negative one. India became one of the first countries in which the communists became democratised enough to take part in elections, and probably the first in which, strictly through the ballot box, they also won enough seats in any legislature to form the government, which they did in the state of Kerala. Reflecting the reality of India's socio-political philosophy of secularism is the fact that although about 80 per cent of Indians are Hindus, parties espousing any extremist reaction of Hindu orthodoxy against secularism counted for very little for a very long time, and began to count for more only as they began to moderate such a reaction.

The nexus between the results of elections and the socio-political reality surrounding them is about as close in India as in the older and more established democracies. Hence it happens that, first, predictions by psephologists are just about as reliable in India as anywhere else; second, their direction and magnitudes do not vary much from educated guesses based upon the class topography of the electorate; and third, they also correspond substantially to the very detailed electoral analysis of Indian society which, as mentioned earlier, has been carried out by the Centre for the Study of Developing Societies.

Politicians in the field have experienced the power of this nexus in another way also. A party which is the predominant representative of one segment or strata of society may split in to two or more parties, either because of rivalry between factional leaders within a party (as happens more often in non-ideological parties) or divergence in points of view (more frequent with ideological parties). But while a party may split at the top and its socio-economic support base may also split accordingly, the base does not shift its support to another socio-economic segment, to a very different segment of the electorate or to a party which predominantly represents a different segment. Such shifts may take place between segments which are geographical or ideological neighbours, but not between those which are distant in both respects. Governments and party alliances may be unstable, but not the social and political profile of the electorate.

One mentions all these facts only to show that the large number of parties or candidates did not seriously fragment the electorate or the polity. Such fragmentation is a burden which is better avoided. But not by constricting anyone's right to form a party, or a party's or an individual's right to contest. Similarly, though illiteracy and inexperience are no qualifications for an electorate, they have not prevented India's adult franchise electorate from adequately performing the first task of a parliamentary system: that it should elect a parliament which faithfully reflects the society which elects it. In fact, the increase in their numbers, gradually during the 1960s and 1970s and more rapidly during and since the 1980s, happened because the polity was evolving out of a less democratic nature into a more democratic one. This, and the rise in voter turnout, are also the reason why the number of parties and candidates has increased over the years, and in ways which are wholly consistent with and supportive of democracy and its purposes; more segments of society and numbers of people take elections seriously as a way of expressing their interests and mobilising support for them.

Commentaries on India's upper and middle urban circles look back on Indian elections of the 1950s with nostalgia as being neat and tidy. That they were, but less because we knew democracy better then than since but because at that time India had practically a one party Lok Sabha, the lower house and the real seat of democracy. The dominant party, the Congress, indeed had many parties within it, and was once described as a congress of parties, and it was run much more democratically than later. But a single group and its platform was dominant. The electorate willingly gave it the dominance it enjoyed. But it still was an urban middle class dominance in a country which was predominantly rural and poor. In 1952 the Congress had 364 seats in a house of 489 and in 1957 it had 371 out of 493 (with a vote share of a little under 45 and 48 per cent, respectively). The next largest party had only about 10 per cent of the vote and 12 seats in 1952 and 19 in 1957.

In the next 20 years and through many ups and downs (during which the Congress also reached its highest spike, in 1984, with 415 seats out of 542, and a vote share of 48.1 per cent, in a sympathy wave aroused for the Congress by the assassination of Mrs Indira Gandhi only two months earlier), India gradually became a more genuinely multi-party democracy. Till 1977, when it suffered its first major setback since independence, the Congress had only one weak moment, in 1967, even then it could win only 40.8 per cent votes and 54.4 per cent (283 out of 520) of the total seats in the Lok Sabha. The 1977 loss of the Congress at the hustings was a result of a mix of factors—Mrs Gandhi's unseating from the Lok Sabha by an Allahabad High Court ruling at the height of growing popular dissatisfaction against her government and major protests in Gujarat and Bihar and the imposition of a constitutional Emergency in June 1975, which blocked the parliamentary elections which were due less than a year later, and which she was widely expected to lose. But as disapproval mounted at home and abroad she was obliged to restore elections. The electorate retaliated, and for the first time ever India had a non-Congress government at the national level though there had been some much earlier in some of the states.

But more significant in the long run was the fact that India entered an era of coalitional politics, with interludes of single party rule by the Congress. The first non-Congress government, of 1977, was in fact a coalition though its members had hastily merged to form a single party. Eversince then a single party, hitherto only the Congress, has only once had a majority of the seats, and that too slender, slippery and questionable. The Congress share in the Lok Sabha fell to 140 seats in 1996, 141 in 1998, and only 114 in 1999, or about a quarter of the peak it reached in 1984. Its vote share has declined less steeply, but even then from the mid-40 per cent in most earlier elections and near-50 per cent in 1985 to 28 per cent in 1999. On the other hand its principal rival, the BJP, had a 24 per cent vote share and 182 seats in the elections in 1999 but it had to take the help of a dozen other parties and an independent to form the government.

Such figures make a jig saw puzzle, not a neat and tidy picture. But that is not the issue before the country, because no one wants what would make the tidiest picture of all, that is, one-man rule without the encumbrance of a jumbo parliament. The real issue is how and why this change has happened, what has this done to democracy, and has more democracy meant less governance?

Diversity, Democracy, Governance

The Congress did not become dominant by undemocratic means. It had become so for three reasons, all of them democratic, as also are all the reasons why it has ceased to be dominant. It became dominant because, first, it was the prime platform of a cause, independence, which had the support of all sections of the people, including those who were later to form Pakistan but also saw independence as a pre-requisite for that as well. And since, second, everyone supported the cause, the Congress was able to bring just about everyone under its flag, whatever his religion, caste, language, or any other community or economic status. Third, though Indian society was as fissured then by these distinctions as it is now, the electorate, unexposed yet to the processes—call them defining or dividing—by which political parties mobilise support in all democracies, was as yet an amorphous mass, able to be united across these dividing lines by a cause which had a sufficiently comprehensive appeal. Fourth, it had the inestimable advantage of the leadership, for the country as a whole of course but also for the party, of two of the most remarkable personalities of the post-colonial world, Mahatma Gandhi and Pandit Nehru. Nor is the fifth to be underestimated, the country's resilience in the face of a really serious crisis, which was demonstrated four or five times in the first decade of independence.

But also demonstrated within this decade was the power of these dividing lines to start defining the electorate internally into the multi-party polity the country was to acquire soon. A demand had been building up in the early years of the decade that the internal boundaries of independent India should no longer remain what they had been till then, a product of the convenience and exigencies of the expansion of British rule over India. As more and more of India was conquered by the colonial power, its internal borders were redrawn according to what was administratively or politically convenient. As one conquered province became too large it was divided into two. If one part surrendered more willingly it was merged with another, if yet another proved more recalcitrant it was appeased with a separate or special status, or territories were added to it.

But now cultural and national sentiments began to require that the units of the Union which had come into being as a federation should be given boundaries which respected historical identities, particularly linguistic. This sentiment had a powerful appeal for many areas of the country, each a large territory inhabited by several million people, each with a distinct linguistic and cultural personality, that is, each with the dimensions of a nation—and each, or so the misgiving was, able to aspire to be a nation one day. This misgiving misled many into resisting the demand, including Nehru, but the more it was resisted the more it posed a challenge to the survival of India in one piece. But what prevailed instead was, first, the even more historical, overarching, civilisational unity of India; second, Nehru's own vision of the future, which he summed up in one of the most telling phrases about India, its 'unity in diversity'; third, a combination of the accommodative spirits of democracy and federalism; the innate patriotism of most of the people of most of the units; and the safe as well as mutually satisfying compromise found between those who desired a rigidly unitarian polity and those suspected of separatism.

Over the years this amalgam matured into what is today one of the more prominent features of India's multi-party parliamentary system, the score or so of regional parties, forming the government in their respective states of the Union, and many of them very powerful members of coalition governments at the federal level. At one time they were prominent entities within the Congress but in power only in their respective states, or at the most were the power behind the governments formed in the name of the Congress. Today they rule these states in their own names, often in opposition to the state-level branches of the Congress or other national-level parties; and yet they are in coalitional partnership with the governments formed by these very national parties at the national level in New Delhi. There has never been such a wide nor such a dense web of criss-crossing linkages within the multi-party system as India has had for the past decade or so.

While parties were multiplying at one level for these justifiable reasons of regional identities, they were also multiplying at another level for equally justifiable socio-economic reasons, which were particularly compelling in the India of the 1960s and 1970s. This process began around the mid-1950s. The Congress began to put land ceilings on a system of huge landholdings of largely absentee and non-cultivating landlords. The system had existed in pre-British India too but the British expanded and reinforced it as a convenient tool of indirect rule, which made it even more oppressive than it had been because the hereditary landlords were left free to use and treat their (non-owning) cultivators and (landless) labour pretty much as they willed so long they paid the revenues for which the lands were (permanently) settled upon them. It was an achievement for the Congress that this reform was carried through by more or less democratic and mostly non-violent means, and fairly fast. But because of the influence petty landlords had in it, the Congress stopped short of transferring the surplus land to the landless and instead used it to let non-owning tenants-at-will become permanent tenants.

This is the mould in which parties multiplied and grew in large parts of northern India, where the old system had persisted, while over much of the rest of India cultivators had become owners over a longer and more natural process, with no dead hand of a 'permanent settlement' holding them down. The landlords also tried to form parties of their own but failed, because they did not have the numbers. The new breed of owner-cultivators, gaining prosperity because of their hereditary skills and new pride of ownership, formed powerful parties because they had the numbers and now the means as well. The landless, who had the numbers but not the means, drifted for a time, joined radical left parties next or the even more radical and violent underground movements, and only over the past decade or so have built up parties of their own.

The landless and the owner-cultivators of small holdings have also become a check upon communal parties of Hindu orthodoxy, particularly in northern India. This has happened because of the strong nexus between India's modern parliamentary polity and one of the world's most ancient social organisations which is deeply rooted in India, the caste system. Its intricacies are mind boggling, but in an oversimplification it can be called rural India's version of what is more familiar elsewhere as the class system, because the lowest castes, the bulk of them landless, are also the bulk of the Indian poor; the middle castes, both in rural and urban India, are the growing and increasingly rich middle class; while the bulk of the higher castes are among the traditionally large landowners in rural India and the professional classes in urban India.

This pattern is fading in daily life. But its imprint continues to be strong on the party system, particularly in rural India, and has been galvanised afresh by the currents of mobilisation upon which parties float. Their higher caste status has drawn the formerly large landowners into parties of Hindu orthodoxy of late, just as their once great influence in the village had once made them natural partners in power with the Congress. On the other hand the antagonism of the lower castes towards the high has alienated the low from the BJP, the prime parliamentary party of orthodoxy although, drawn by the need for numbers in elections, and witnessing the general decline of orthodoxy, the BJP has been trying to loosen its links with some specific agendas of many orthodox Hindus.

Problems and Answers

The relevance of all this to the present theme is that at various stages in India's social and political evolution in the past 50 years, strong urges have existed in the arena of parliamentary democracy which, whether one likes them or not, have caused hundreds of millions of voters to aggregate into one or another of the numerous parties which correspond to and are thrown up by what they see as their sectional interests. When the need arises, voters do subordinate their sectional interests to wider national interests. A good example is the speed with which the movement for linguistically defined states, once very strong and suspected as a form of separatism, disappeared once such states were formed. But often political leaders lack the skills, or the sincerity, or both, which are needed for projecting national interests as such. That is why such leaders are often suspected, whether rightly or not, of using national interests as cloaks for their sectional interests. Such suspicions make people cynical about politics. Typical of this phenomenon is the suspicion with which parties with a centrist bias have viewed the rapid emergence of regional parties, and the mirror of reciprocal suspicion the latter show to the national parties.

The increasing salience of regional parties on the national scene has understandably caused some anxiety about national unity. But on the whole, 'national' leaders have been wise in building them into credible 'national' purposes instead of making the mistake of treating them in a colonial context in post-colonial India. Such a mistake would have made regional entities suspect 'national integration' to be a device for 'absorbing' them into the national whole to the extent of wiping them out of existence. The dangers of such a misunderstanding have been very well discussed by Amit Prakash in his chapter 'Socio-cultural and Economic Dimensions of the Party System' (Chapter 5). As he explains, it can be a part of a colonial agenda to over-ride native identities, but it cannot be a part of independent India's national agenda. In addition, Suhas Palshikar's chapter on 'Regional Parties and Democracy' (Chapter 13) makes a very valid distinction between regional and regionalist parties. Most of the state-level parties which are in power in their respective states are regional in the sense that they are confined to one state or at most are prominent in one region. But few are regionalist in the sense that even in critical situations they would place their state-level interests above national needs where they see a conflict between the two.

But that apart, considering the deep and diverse roots from which many parties have sprung, it is idle to expect that India can do with three or four parties. On the contrary it is surprising and creditworthy that India really has only about half-a-dozen 'national' parties of consequence. The rest are either regional parties, of great relevance to their respective regions, of which many are as large as most countries are, or are inconsequential fragments which flit in and out of existence. But even this much proliferation of parties raises problems which need answers, beginning with what the emergence of only 30 or 40 active parties on the electoral scene has done to the chances of any single party exercising anything like the hegemony the Congress exercised all over the country for many years.

In the days when competing parties were in any case few, the Congress had the advantage that neither its own character nor the electorate's had been even differentiated, let alone segmented, by competing interests. Both were amorphous, and the Congress could have, or pretend to have, something for everyone, and attract all without offending anyone. This ceased to be so during and after the 1960s, beginning with the political impact of land ceilings in northern India. As more parties came into being outside the Congress and developed their own agendas, each began to arouse and attract one or another out of the numerous pieces of India's social and economic mosaics which till then had hibernated within the folds of the Congress. The Muslims and the lowest castes were the first to seek other pastures, and then others followed.

While the Congress still retained more bits of more of them than any other party, it soon had fewer people left from each segment than the parties formed especially by and for each of these segments. The Congress remained more spread out throughout the polity than any other party, but more thinly in particular parts of it than the various parties which were clearly identified with those parts. Thus it still had more Muslims than many other parties, but less than those parties which had been formed or favoured by Muslim organisations. This aggravated the problem noted earlier, that while the Congress got more seats in Parliament than justified by its share of the vote, most other parties got less, and the government in Delhi became less and less representative of the majority of the electorate, especially when the government was formed by a minority of the house and was sustained only by the failure of opposing parties to come together to vote it out. The Congress governments thus fell foul of the first and foremost obligation of a government in a democracy, to represent the people, or at least the majority. But this is probably going to be the fate of all umbrella parties and the governments formed by them. The problems this might create for governance are obvious.

The most serious among them, next only to the reduced representativeness of governments, is their instability, and of policies too as a consequence. Single parties are less and less likely to be able to form governments, and even less able to sustain themselves because, as stability declines and interparty rivalries grow, parties will come together more readily, despite the incompatibilities between them, to join in bringing down the government of the day just to get their backs on it. The anti-defection law has helped up to a point and it remains essential. But it has not been sufficient and will not be, because it does not come in the way of a party as a whole, or a substantial part of it, changing sides without sufficient cause.

But the number of parties is less to blame for these problems than the systems we have for electing legislatures and governments, and on the whole the bigger parties have been more responsible for instability than the smaller ones. The Congress, using its manipulative skills and during long tenures in Delhi, destablised or even dismissed more governments at the Centre and in the states than all other parties put together. The BJP followed suit when it got the chance. So did some other parties. They brought down governments either by cajoling, pressurising, inducing one small party or another to quit a coalition and reduce it to a minority, or by refusing to share power in a coalition even when a coalition was the only way to have a majority for forming a government, or by promising support to a coalition without joining it and then suddenly withdrawing the support without any convincing and sufficient reason except that they found a ripe opportunity. Small parties do not have the weight to destabilise a government by shifting their positions unless several of them combine just for that purpose, or are shifted about by a major party in its own interests.

But these problems have answers, and all of them are within the domain of parliamentary democracy. They would make the government more representative, more stable, without depriving any government, party, segment of the electorate, of any democratic rights which are legitimate. Their rights would not be less in any way than the rights they have at present, and their existing rights would be preserved better than they might be for long if the existing problems continued to be neglected much longer.

The first answer is that a candidate should be declared elected only when he has polled at least half the votes cast in his constituency, plus at least one more to make it a majority. This might require two rounds of election in any constituency which does not elect any candidate by majority in the first round. The second round would be open only to the leader and runner-up in the first round, and the second round would be considered valid only if the total votes cast in it were not less than half the votes cast in the first round. The second round would be held within less than 10 days of the first round, so that no drastic changes intervened between the two rounds. This would ensure that the legislature was representative of at least half the votes cast by the electorate, because each member would have been elected by at least half the votes cast in one or the other round.

The second answer is that the government should be formed only by a person who, after having been invited by the head of the state to form it, has been endorsed by at least half the total number of members of the concerned legislature, in a contest which is open to all members. If no one secures a majority, there should be a second round, open only to the leader and runner-up in the first round. It should then be mandatory for the head of state to invite the winner of the second round to form the government. This would preserve a role for the head of state but make it ultimately subordinate to the will of the legislature, as it should be, and at the same time would ensure that no one forms a government who does not have the demonstrated approval of half the legislature which itself has the approval of at least half the voters who had cast their votes in electing the legislature.

The third answer is that the incumbent government should remain in office till the end of its term unless the legislature, by the same two-round procedure as mentioned earlier, invites anyone else by a majority vote to form another government. In other words, there should always be a government in office which has been formed by a person who has been approved by a majority vote in the legislature. This would prevent rule by minority governments chosen by minority legislatures. It would also discourage parties which have mutually antagonistic constituencies from coming together only for the negative job of bringing down the government, because they would know they might have to cooperate in electing the next. In other words, it would encourage some ideological cohesion in the composition and policies of the government, and some clarity in the answer to a troubling question: When someone complains that governance has deteriorated he should also answer the question, who is supposed to be governing whom for whose benefit. Sometimes the loudest complaint that a new government is giving bad governance comes from those who feel the new government's priorities are different from their own or from what the priorities of the preceding government were.

It is inevitable that any policy of any government benefits some and disappoints others, and it is legitimate that a government should seek to benefit more than it disappoints. This is sometimes dismissed as populism. But what can be properly called populism—pleasing a section of the electorate in the short-term at the expense of the long-term interests of the total electorate—does not pay in genuinely elective politics. It soon dies a natural death because the favoured few cannot re-elect a populist government which has disappointed the many. Similarly, it is only an illusion that policies which are beneficial to more in the long-term can bring down a government because they are unpopular with a few in the short-term. The illusion becomes a reality only if the government, carried away by the noise of a small number of losers, fails to enlighten and mobilise the gainers, whose number should be much larger if the policies have been perceived correctly and carried out efficiently. Only then will the political equality conferred on all by universal adult franchise survive the economic inequalities which some might have to suffer until policies for lifting them up produce their results.

However, none of this can stop criticism of a democracy, whether of the parliamentary or any other kind, which is misdirected in the sense that it lays at the door of the polity blame which may more properly be placed at the door of society. If the society has warts, they will certainly show up in a democracy, more than they might in a non-democratic polity, and they will show up all the more clearly the more genuinely democratic the polity is. It is the function of a democratic polity to reflect the electorate as faithfully as it can, warts and all. The responsibilities of the democrat may need the support of the social reformer. But he cannot be blamed for the failures of the latter.

7

THE ELECTORAL FRAMEWORK, PROCESS AND POLITICAL PARTIES

Madhav Godbole

Introduction

It may be worthwhile to note some significant details regarding the mammoth election exercise in India.[1] The number of voters has gone up from 17.32 crore in 1952 to 60.23 crore in 1998. During the same period, the number of polling stations has gone up from 1.96 lakh to 7.65 lakh. As many as 8,50,000 to 9,00,000 polling booths had to be erected in the general elections in 1999. For managing the booths, 45 to 50 lakh personnel had to be deployed. This is in addition to the police, home guards, National Cadet Corps (NCC) cadets and paramilitary personnel deployed on security duties.

The government expenditure on holding elections has gone up steeply from just Rs 11 crore in the 1952 elections to Rs 626 crore in 1998 and a staggering figure of Rs 900 crore in 1999. With the increasing problems of lawlessness and violence, paramilitary forces have to be moved from one part of the country to the other. Their presence is insisted upon in some states by the candidates themselves due to the fears of politicisation of the local police and home guards. This has meant holding the elections to the Lok Sabha and the Legislative Assemblies in a staggered manner in five phases spread over a period of five to six weeks.

Due to the weakening of national political parties on the one hand and the emergence of regional parties and splinter groups on the other, political stability has been seriously compromised in the states as also at the Centre. The 1999 elections to the Lok Sabha were the fourth in less than five years. The last Uttar Pradesh (UP) Legislative Assembly elections too were the fourth in six years. The increasing frequency of elections has serious long-term implications which cannot be lost sight of.

---

[1] This chapter is based on the author's forthcoming book: *Public Accountability and Transparency—Imperatives of Good Governance*.

The composition of candidates contesting elections is undergoing a perceptible change. The typical *khadi*-clad Congress politicians donning white *khadi* caps are giving way to more diversified political representation from particularly the lower social and economic strata of society. Now, the *khadi* cap is a rare sight among Members of Parliament (MPs). Criminals and persons from the business world too have made in-roads in politics, though the strides by the former group are much greater than the latter. But politics is still largely the preserve of professional politicians. Hardly any professionals, technocrats, or grassroot social workers dare to enter this field.

Neglect of Electoral Reforms

Though India takes pride in declaring that it is the world's largest democracy, the subject of electoral reforms has been consistently and consciously neglected by all political parties during the last five decades since independence. It is interesting to see that a joint committee on amendments to the election law submitted its 121-page report to Parliament as far back as 1972. Among its members were Somnath Chatterjee, Atal Behari Vajpayee and L.K. Advani who continue to call the tune in Parliament even today. Nearly three decades have elapsed since then and these venerable members have gone places in their political careers but the electoral reforms have remained where they were! The Goswami Committee on Electoral Reforms (1990) had rightly underlined that 'electoral reforms are correctly understood to be a continuous process. But the attempts so far made in this area did not touch even the fringe of the problem.'

Time and again, political parties have talked about the imperative need of undertaking electoral reforms in their election manifestos but these promises have remained on paper. In the last decade, each in-coming government assured the public that it would introduce a comprehensive bill for electoral reforms in Parliament but it has never been translated in practice. The only serious effort made in this direction was during the tenure of the V.P. Singh government in 1989–90 but since the government lost majority in the House, this initiative too was a non-starter.[2] Even the special session of Parliament called during the term of the P.V. Narasimha Rao government failed to arrive at any consensus on the outstanding issues relating to electoral reforms. Now, once again, the Bharatiya Janata Party (BJP)-led coalition government headed by Atal Behari Vajpayee has, in the president's address to the joint session of Parliament in October 1999, announced that a comprehensive electoral reforms bill, to cleanse the poll process and introduce proxy voting

---

[2] Ministry of Law and Justice, Legislative Department, Government of India, New Delhi, *Report of the Committee on Electoral Reforms* (*Goswami Committee on Electoral Reforms*), May 1990.

for defence and security forces, will be brought up in Parliament. It is to be seen how far and when it gets translated into reality.

Though the Election Commission (EC) came into prominence and caught the imagination of the people during and after the tenure of T.N. Seshan as chief election commissioner (CEC), the previous CECs too had worked silently and diligently on the subject of electoral reforms and had submitted to the central government, from time to time, detailed and highly sensible proposals for electoral reforms. Unfortunately, these did not receive any attention in the government. As S.L. Shakdhar, the then CEC had lamented, 'Despite a wide measure of agreement on the subject, the question of electoral reforms generally seems to come up only on the eve of a general election when the stock answer is that it is too late and that such ideas had better be postponed until "next time". That "next time" has not arrived.'

A Framework for Electoral Reforms

For want of space, it may not be possible to deal with all issues relating to electoral reforms in this paper. In the following paragraphs, an effort is made to bring out some of the more important and critical issues which can make a significant difference to cleansing the electoral and political party system in the country.

Election Commission of India

The question of inherent powers of the Commission needs to be reviewed afresh in the light of the problems being encountered in holding peaceful, orderly and fair elections in the country. The history of electoral reforms has shown that political parties will never agree to any significant and fundamental changes to rid the system of several ills and malpractices. It is a distressing fact that violence continues to mar the election process in a number of states. Booth-capturing, intimidation and impersonation of voters, and similar other serious electoral malpractices are still rampant. It was not, therefore surprising that in the 1999 elections, even two ministers of the Bihar government had to be arrested for electoral malpractices. The EC had to order the chief minister of Haryana, Om Prakash Chautala, to leave Bhiwani district from where his son was contesting the elections.[3] On an all-India basis, the election process has had to be extended to an exasperatingly and frustratingly long period of nearly six weeks to ensure holding of orderly elections. A number of these problems were not foreseen by the Founding Fathers of the Constitution. If India is to survive as a democracy, the question

---

[3] *The Indian Express*, 25 September 1999.

of the inherent powers doctrine is no less important in the case of EC than it is in the case of higher judiciary.

Against this background, it is imperative to give, by effecting a suitable amendment in the Constitution, wide powers to the EC to conduct elections in the best manner possible so as to enhance the integrity, fairness and purity of the process. Now that the Commission has been made into a multi-member body, there need be no hesitation in giving such wide and, in a sense, undefined powers to the EC. It is necessary to remember that the EC's actions will always be subject to review by the higher judiciary. While undertaking such an amendment in the Constitution, the following points may also be incorporated therein:

(i) The maximum number of members in the Commission should be specified as three, so as to ensure that, in future, the government does not try to pack the Commission with its own nominees, as the Rajiv Gandhi government tried to do in 1989. Till then, the EC consisted of only the CEC. When the government found CEC Peri Sastry inconvenient, the government added two members to the commission. It was only when the V.P. Singh government came to power in December 1989 that the two additional members were removed. There are again news reports that the Atal Behari Vajpayee government is planning to expand the EC to five members.[4] It is time such pressure tactics are put to rest, once and for all, by making a requisite change in the Constitution to fix the strength of the EC at three members.

(ii) The selection of the CEC and the other members may be done by a committee comprising the prime minister (PM), vice president, speaker, chief justice of India and the leader of opposition and, in his absence, the leader of the largest opposition party in the Lok Sabha. In the case of members of EC, the CEC should also be consulted.

(iii) All members of the Commission should enjoy the same terms and conditions of service and privileges and immunity as the CEC.

(iv) The CEC and the members of EC should be made ineligible not only for any appointment under the government but also to any office, including the office of governor, appointment to which is made by the president.[5]

(v) The protection of salary and other allied matters relating to the CEC and the election commissioners should be provided for in the Constitution itself on the analogy of the provisions in respect of the chief justice and judges of the Supreme Court.[6]

---

[4] *The Times Of India*, 25 November 1999.

[5] Ministry of Law and Justice, *Report of the Committee on Electoral Reforms*.

[6] Ibid.

(vi) The provision regarding appointment of regional commissioners should be scrapped.

(vii) At present, the Model Code of Conduct (MCC) issued by the EC does not have any legal sanction. It is imperative that the MCC is recognised as having been issued in pursuance of the inherent powers of the EC and should have constitutional sanction. If for any reasons this is not considered feasible, a separate legislation may be passed for the purpose. In addition, to give some teeth to the legislation, as suggested by the Goswami Committee, the violations of these provisions should be made an electoral offence and not just a corrupt practice.

(viii) Section 77 (3) of the Representation of the People Act (RPA) should be amended so as to empower the EC to revise the ceilings for election expenses, from time to time, and powers in this regard need not vest in the government.

(ix) Any ambiguity in respect of the powers of the EC to suspend or withdraw recognition of a national or a state party and allot symbols to political parties, which fail to hold organisational elections at regular intervals, keep regular accounts, have them audited, file income tax returns, file an annual return to the EC confirming compliance of all these and any other requirements, and fail to comply with the MCC, should be removed.

Political Parties

As in some other countries, there must be a parliamentary law pertaining to the registration, structure and functioning of political parties in India, whether at the state or the national level. Unless a party is registered under such a law, it must not qualify for recognition by the EC, allotment of a symbol and state funding in the elections.

Such a law must ensure internal democracy in each party. The elections of all political parties must be held under the supervision of the persons to be nominated by the EC in a transparent manner. This may be considered odd by some but looking to the state of affairs of most political parties, there is no escape from taking such an extreme step. One could understand a Fascist party like the Shiv Sena resisting the demand for holding organisational elections but even the Congress Party has tried to put off its organisational elections time and again. It is meaningless to talk of democracy if the political parties which are its bulwark are to be permitted to be run as personal fiefdoms or dynastic outfits.

The related question is whether any special efforts need to be made to bring about polarisation of the political process in the country. The Law Commission of India has made certain recommendations in this regard with a view to arresting and reversing the process of proliferation and splintering of political parties. The aim of the Law Commission is to reduce the number of political parties or pre-election political fronts to three or four parties/fronts. The Commission has, *inter alia*, recommended that any political party, whether recognised or not, which obtains less than 5 per cent of the total valid votes cast in an election to the House of the People shall not be entitled to any seat in that House. Any constituency which has elected the candidate of a political party which is deprived of a seat in the House of the People or in the Legislative Assembly shall be represented by the candidate of a political party which has obtained the next highest votes provided that his political party obtains 5 per cent of the total valid votes cast in that election and that he has not lost the security deposit.[7]

The recommendations of the Commission are clearly short-sighted. Political polarisation cannot be brought about in any country by a fiat or a mere constitutional amendment. And this is particularly true in a country as diverse linguistically, culturally, socially and religion-wise as India. It is bound to take a long time to achieve political polarisation. Enough time will have to be given patiently for this purpose. It will also have to be noted that the splintering of political parties and the emergence of regional parties has come about, in no small measure, due to the weakening of national parties, lack of any ideology or principles in political parties and parties becoming fiefdoms of certain families and individuals. It is only by learning from experience that the smaller political parties at the margin will shed their individual identities and merge themselves in a larger entity. It must also be borne in mind that a number of small parties represent the minorities or special interest groups. Their separate identity as political parties is important not only for safeguarding their interests but also for giving them a sense of security against majoritarianism and other hostile elements. Forcibly erasing their identity will lead to social and political tensions as in Punjab or Jammu and Kashmir. The Law Commission's recommendation in this regard is therefore not only ill-conceived but against the larger national interest of fostering a united and strong India.

Electoral Funding

Money and muscle power have dominated the elections in India for the last five decades. Muscle power itself is largely dependent on the monetary clout of a candidate. Thus, the root cause of a large number of ills can be traced to money power or 'moneyfestos' as picturesquely described by V.P. Singh. S.L. Shakdhar, former CEC, had also highlighted the danger of 'captive politics' on the analogy of the saying 'he who pays the piper, calls the tune'.[8]

---

[7] Law Commission of India, *Reform of the Electoral Laws*, One Hundred Seventieth Report, Government of India, New Delhi, May 1999, pp. 184–85.
[8] The Voters' Council and Citizens for Democracy, Delhi, 'Electoral Reforms in India', address by S.L. Shakdhar, Chief Election Commissioner, 26 September 1980, pp. 1 and 7.

The nexus between black money and election spending has been established at least since the early 1970s, if not even earlier. One of the recommendations of the Direct Taxes Enquiry Committee (Wanchoo Committee) Report, received in 1971, was the demonetisation of high value currency notes. When the then Union Finance Minister, Y.B. Chavan, went to Prime Minister Indira Gandhi to seek her approval for implementing the recommendation, she asked Chavan only one question: 'Chavanji, are no more elections to be fought by the Congress Party?' Chavan got the message and the recommendation was shelved.[9]

Some years later, M. C. Chagla said that elected members do not represent the people; they represent money power. Raj Krishna, eminent economist, was right when he said Indian politics was becoming increasingly capital intensive.

S.L. Shakdhar, the then CEC had underlined, 'There is an atmosphere, too thick for anyone to ignore, that elections are tainted with money illegally obtained. This creates a doubt as to whether elections are indeed free, fair and pure.'[10] The National Institute of Public Finance and Policy, in its report, *Aspects of Black Money in India*, has shown the influence and role of black money in the Indian political system.[11]

The ridiculously low ceilings on maximum permissible expenditure by a candidate, laid down from time to time (currently Rs 15 lakh for Parliament and Rs 6 lakh for an Assembly election), are observed more in the breach. A newly elected legislator begins his tenure by knowingly and wilfully filing a false affidavit that the expenditure incurred by him does not exceed the ceiling laid down by law. In its judgement in *Gadak Y.K. vs Balasaheb Vikhe Patil* in November 1993, the Supreme Court observed that the 'prescription of ceiling on expenditure by a candidate is a mere eyewash and there is no practical check on election expenses for which it was enacted to attain a meaningful democracy.... This provision has ceased to be even a fig leaf to hide the reality.' There is no ceiling on the expenditure which a party may incur on its candidates.

Huge unaccounted expenditure by candidates is perhaps the most serious issue in any programme of electoral reforms. The estimates of such expenditure vary from constituency to constituency. A great deal depends on the candidates contesting the election and the prestige attached to winning the seat. But, leaving aside these exceptional cases, the average expenditure of a serious candidate for a Parliament election in 1999 was estimated at Rs 2–3 crore. According to another estimate, it was Rs 1.3 crore in the 1998 elections.

---

[9] Madhav Godbole, *Unfinished Innings—Recollections and Reflections of a Civil Servant*, New Delhi: Orient Longman, 1996, pp. 87–88.
[10] The Voters' Council, 'Electoral Reforms in India', p. 7.
[11] Acharya, Shankar N. et al., *Aspects of the Black Economy in India*, New Delhi: National Institute of Public Finance and Policy, 1986.

Where does this money come from? Partly, it comes from the candidate, his friends, supporters and well-wishers. But, a big chunk of it comes from the political party which sponsors him. Therefore, it is necessary to go into the question of financing of not only the candidates but more importantly, of the political parties.

Let us first take the question of foreign money. The issue was first raised in Parliament as far back as 1968. Chitta Basu, in a discussion during the question hour in Rajya Sabha, had referred to a news item from *The New York Times* published in *The Economic Times* of 14 June 1967 that the US Central Intelligence Agency had given substantial sums of money to right wing parties and candidates. The government had admitted that the Intelligence Bureau (IB) had been asked to prepare a report on the use of foreign money in the general elections held in 1967.

The question of foreign money came up again on 12 April 1979 when Kanwar Lal Gupta raised the matter 'regarding reported disclosure made by former US Ambassador about Indira Gandhi having received US money'. The matter came up for detailed discussion in the House in May 1979.[12] The reference was to certain disclosures by Moynihan in his book *A Dangerous Place*.

A reference must be made to an Unstarred Question No. 1523 tabled by Jyotirmoy Bosu in Lok Sabha regarding the statement of former Prime Minister, Charan Singh, on withdrawal of huge sums by Prime Minister Indira Gandhi from a Swiss bank for elections in 1980. As was to be expected, the then Finance Minister, R. Venkataraman, denied the allegation. However, the remaining part of his written reply was more significant. He said: 'The policy of the present government is not to collect any information about expenses incurred by any of the political parties for contesting elections or sources from which they have financed such expenditure.' It can be seen how far the Indira Gandhi government had travelled between 1968 and 1980 on the funding of elections in the country. The government had decided to close its eyes to the problem and had become totally oblivious to the hazardous legacy it was leaving behind for the country.

It was shocking to see that the same nonchalant attitude to this grave problem continued in the I.K. Gujral government in the case pertaining to the donation of Rs 3.75 crore received by the Congress Party from abroad, during the term of Sitaram Kesri as the party treasurer, between 1993 and 1995. Additional solicitor general of India, Abhishek Manu Sanghvi, told the Delhi High Court, in a public interest litigation (PIL), that the central government had not taken any final decision on the applicability of the Foreign Contribution Regulation Act (FCRA) in this case.[13] This was in spite of the explicit

[12] 'Alleged Payment of Foreign Money for Elections in India by American Government', *Lok Sabha Debates*, Lok Sabha Secretariat, 7 May 1979.
[13] *The Indian Express*, 30 July 1997.

provision in Section 4 (i) of FCRA. In fact, later, in the affidavit filed by the government it asserted that donations received by the Congress Party from abroad were legal. What is surprising is the 'opinion' of three former chief justices of India. All three say these donations do not fall under the FCRA.[14] The much touted FCRA has been a dead letter in so far as funding of political parties from abroad is concerned. This weapon of FCRA has been used almost exclusively by the Centre against academic institutions and NGOs in the name of their compromising the independence and integrity of the country!

It may be relevant in this context to refer to what S.P. Hinduja, one of the richest Indian businessmen in the world, had to say on this subject. He has 'disclosed that Indian politicians collecting money abroad, ostensibly for party funds, were stashing away large portions of it in foreign banks for their personal use ... even way back in the early 1970s, the economy had to be drained of as much as Rs 250 crore to provide just one-tenth of that amount for the elections. Almost 25 years later, perhaps, even our richest businessmen are finding it difficult to generate enough black money to feed the insatiable hunger of our politicians.'[15] It is not surprising that successive governments at the Centre, belonging to almost all major political parties, are reluctant to go deeper into the funding of elections. Even way back in 1972, the joint committee on amendments to electoral law had come to the conclusion: 'The committee have also considered the recommendations made by the EC in their reports to the effect that the political parties might also be called upon to account for the expenses incurred by them for the election campaign of their candidates. After careful scrutiny, the committee have come to the conclusion that due to various practical difficulties, it is not possible to pursue such a course.'[16]

At the heart of the matter is the maintenance and audit of accounts of the political parties. The present situation in almost all parties is best described by a popular saying concerning the Congress Party during the long tenure of Sitaram Kesri as its treasurer. It used to be said, *'Na khata na bahi, jo Kesri kahe wahi sahi'* (there is neither any ledger nor any notebook, what Kesri says alone is true).

It is interesting to see that in spite of explicit provisions of the Indian Income Tax Act, the Income Tax Department did not take any action against political parties for the infringement of the provisions of the Act. Finally, Common Cause, an NGO in Delhi, filed a PIL in the Supreme Court. As it came to light in the context of this writ petition, the Income Tax Department had noted on the relevant file on 31 March 1993 that, 'it is hereby assumed that they [the political parties] do not have any income to declare; accordingly the proceedings are hereby dropped'!

---

[14] T.V.R. Shenoy, 'While We Looked Away—Congress Foreign Receipts', edit page article in *The Indian Express*, 2 August 1997.

[15] 'Bet On This', *The Economic Times*, the editorial, 8 February 1996.

[16] The only minute of dissent was by Mahavir Tyagi. See Lok Sabha Secretariat, New Delhi, *Joint Committee on Amendments to Electoral Law, Report, Part I*, January 1972, p. 65.

Fortunately, the Supreme Court decision on the above PIL was a major step forward in the crusade for a clean public life. The Court, *inter alia*, decided as under:

1. That the political parties are under a statutory obligation to file return of income in respect of each assessment year in accordance with the provisions of the Income Tax Act. The political parties ... who have not been filing returns of income for several years have *prima facie* violated the statutory provisions of the Income Tax Act.
2. That the income tax authorities have been wholly remiss in the performance of their statutory duties under law. The said authorities have for a long period failed to take appropriate action against the defaulter political parties.
3. A political party which is not maintaining audited and authenticated accounts and has not filed the return of income for the relevant period, cannot, ordinarily, be permitted to say that it has incurred or authorised expenditure in connection with the election of its candidates in terms of Explanation 1 to Section 77 of the RPA.

Such is the state of governance in the country, so insensitive are the political parties to public opinion and such is the utter disregard for the explicit orders of the highest court that Common Cause had to file yet another petition in the Supreme Court to get the previous orders of the Court on maintenance of accounts by political parties implemented expeditiously. During the hearing of this petition it came to light that, 'except one party, all others had declared "nil" return. They were seeking to convince the court that without any income they were able to manage the party affairs. Not a small achievement!'[17]

At long last, the Central Board of Direct Taxes (CBDT), more out of fear of being hauled up before the court for contempt action than any genuine respect for law, has issued orders for compulsory scrutiny of all pending and forthcoming returns filed by political parties. It has also decided that assessments should be made only after an in-depth study of returns under Section 143 (3).[18] It remains to be seen how effective the implementation of these orders is.

Funding of political parties by business and industry has always been a hush hush affair. Almost all such transactions are in black money and cash. Against this background, it is interesting to note the proposal of Tata Sons to set up an electoral fund for donations to political parties. The objective is to make political contributions in a manner that is transparent, non-discriminatory and non-discretionary in order to create a climate where business and industry can be carried on more economically and efficiently. The money would be

---

[17] Rakesh Bhatnagar, 'Law Commission Report on Key Electoral Reforms Gathers Dust', *The Times of India*, 12 January 1999.
[18] *The Economic Times*, 27 August 1999.

distributed in two phases. In the first phase to parties (no individual contributions) which hold more than 5 per cent of seats at the start of elections. In the second phase, to parties which secure more than 5 per cent seats. Up to 5 per cent of each company's average net profits during the preceding three previous years will be disbursed in this manner.

Understandably, while larger parties broadly supported the proposal, the small parties and communist parties scoffed at the idea. The Communist Party of India (Marxist) (CPM), in fact, returned the donation sent by the Tata Electoral Trust. Most other industries and business houses were cool to the suggestion.

Against this background, the main question which arises for consideration is whether the present system of funding of elections should continue or whether it be replaced by state funding of elections. The joint committee on amendment to electoral laws had recommended as far back as 1972 that, 'a process should be initiated whereby the burden of legitimate election expenses should be progressively shifted to the State'.[19] Very limited state funding of elections was also recommended by the Goswami Committee on Electoral Reforms in 1990. The Committee on State Funding of Elections (Indrajit Gupta Committee), which submitted its report in December 1998, has, *inter alia*, recommended that:

(*i*) State funding of elections is fully justified—constitutionally, legally and also in the larger public interest.
(*ii*) State funding should be confined only to the parties recognised as national or state parties by the EC, and to the candidates set up by such parties.
(*iii*) Given the budgetary constraints and the present financial stringency, only part of the financial burden of political parties may be shifted to the state, for the time being.
(*iv*) Any state funding should be in kind, and not in cash.[20]

It can be seen that the recommendation is half-hearted and makes only a token gesture to the proposal of state funding. In that sense, it is no better than the view propounded by the joint committee of Parliament in 1972. The committee has also not made any recommendation regarding the manner in which financial resources should be raised by the government for this purpose.

The Law Commission Report on Reform of the Electoral Laws, submitted in May 1999, too recommends that, 'in the present circumstances only partial State funding could be contemplated more as a first step towards total State funding but it is absolutely essential that before the idea of State funding (whether partial or total) is resorted to, the provisions suggested ... relating to political parties (including the provisions ensuring internal democracy, internal

---

[19] Lok Sabha Secretariat, *op. cit.*, p. 64.
[20] Government of India, New Delhi, Ministry of Law, Justice and Company Affairs, Legislative Department, *Committee on State Funding of Elections, Report*, December 1998, pp. 57–58.

structures) and maintenance of accounts, their auditing and submission to EC are implemented.... The State funding, even if partial, should never be resorted to unless the other provisions mentioned aforesaid are implemented lest the very idea may prove counter-productive and may defeat the very object underlying the idea of State funding of elections.'[21] It is disappointing to see that even the Law Commission has failed to do any justice to the subject and has remained satisfied by making only a token gesture.

The successive reports on this critical issue during the last three decades have failed to grasp that what is at stake is not just the purity and integrity of elections, but, more importantly, combating the evil of black money, improving the credibility of democracy and cleansing public life of the cancer of corruption. To achieve these objectives, no price should be considered high enough. In fact, state funding of elections is the 'least cost solution' to these formidable and intractable problems. Further, it should be easily possible to find the financial resources of over Rs 2,000 crore each year by discontinuing the Members of Parliament Local Area Development Scheme (MPLADS) and similar other on-going schemes for Members of Legislative Assembly (MLAs), and municipal corporators/councillors, zilla parishad members and others. Even if some additional money has to be found, it will be well worth finding it by curtailing other low priority expenditure.

From the foregoing discussion, some major points arise for consideration.

- **First**, Section 77 of the RPA which allows the political parties to spend any amount on its candidates should be amended so as to include such expenditure in the ceiling on total expenditure prescribed for a candidate.
- **Second**, it is time the Income Tax Act is amended to make it obligatory on the income tax authorities to give wide publicity to the returns filed by political parties and the assessment orders passed thereon. This will be the best way to ensure that the provisions of the Act are implemented faithfully.
- **Third,** the expenditure statements filed by each candidate before the EC should also be made public for scrutiny by the people and their watch-dog organisations.
- **Fourth**, a scheme should be evolved for providing entire funding of election expenditure of candidates from the public exchequer.

    Once the scheme is fully implemented, it would, among other things, mean that:

    (i) There would be complete ban on donations by companies and the relevant law would need to be amended accordingly. The law should also be tightened to remove any scope for clandestine contributions to political parties.

---

[21] Law Commission of India, *One Hundred Seventieth Report on Reform of the Electoral Law*, May 1999, pp. 118–19.

(*ii*) All accounts of political parties must be maintained in the prescribed forms and must be duly audited.

(*iii*) Once such funding is provided, the political parties will be barred
from raising any funds for elections.

(*iv*) Political parties will not be permitted to spend any amount on
their candidates. If a party is found to have incurred any expenditure on a candidate, it will be treated as the expenditure incurred
by the candidate himself. Thus, the ceiling on election expenses
will include expenses incurred by a political party on behalf of a
candidate. The RPA should be amended to restore the position
existing before 1975, in conformity with the Supreme Court decision in the Amarnath Chawla case (which was nullified by the
1975 amendment of the Act). This will also apply to the expenditure incurred by the friends and well-wishers of a candidate.

(*v*) The candidates themselves will not be permitted to spend anything over and above what is provided by the state.

(*vi*) State funding will be available only to the candidates of political
parties recognised by the EC and in proportion to the total number
of votes polled by a party.

(*vii*) Independent candidates will not be eligible for any financing under the scheme.

Decriminalising Indian Politics

Criminalisation of politics and politicisation of criminals has become a shocking reality of national life. Criminals are no longer satisfied with supporting
certain candidates in elections. They now aspire to occupy the seats of power
themselves. Some have even floated their own political parties. Thus, for
example, Arun Gawli, a dreaded crime lord, has floated his own political
party by the name of Akhil Bharatiya Sena.

Criminals have also made in-roads in all political parties, whether at the
national or regional level. In the 1996 Lok Sabha elections, more than 1,500
candidates had a criminal background. It is interesting to see that these
candidates belonged to almost all states. A citizens' panel comprising former
Supreme Court judge, Kuldeep Singh, social activist Swami Agnivesh and
this author, which was set up by the weekly magazine *Outlook*, had compiled a list of 72 candidates contesting elections to the Lok Sabha in the 1998
elections against whom criminal proceedings were pending. Within the short
time which was available between the filing of the nominations and the
holding of elections, the panel could compile and scrutinise the data in
respect of only 500 of the 4,693 candidates in the fray. G.V.G. Krishnamurthy,
the then election commissioner, had observed that thanks to the role played
by the media, the number of Lok Sabha candidates with criminal records

had reduced from 1,500 in 1996 to around 150 in the 1998 elections.[22] It was, however, disconcerting that in the elections to the Bihar Assembly in February 2000, more than 12 notorious criminals were elected as MLAs and both the coalitions of parties were vying with each other to seek their support to form the ministry.

'Winnability' has become the sole criterion for selection of candidates by political parties.[23] Such is the level of cynicism on this subject that Bal Thackeray, Shiv Sena chief, when asked by news reporters about a large number of criminals getting Shiv Sena tickets in the elections, had the temerity to say that these persons were political activists and if they were to be called criminals then Gandhi and Nehru would also have to be called criminals.[24] A Karnataka MLA is facing charges of rape and extortion. He had contested the 1999 State Assembly elections from prison.[25]

In 1997, one out of every 14 MPs and as many as 700 MLAs had a criminal background.[26] Though consolidated data in respect of the 1999 Lok Sabha and Assembly polls is yet to become available, from UP alone, at least seven MPs with criminal background have been elected. Of them, two belong to BJP, three to SP and two to the BSP which brings out once again that all political parties are equally guilty in this behalf.[27]

But, it will be wrong to blame only the political parties. Criminals have often fought elections as independent candidates and people have voted for them with open eyes. Pappu Yadav, who is facing a murder charge, fought the Lok Sabha poll in 1999, as an independent candidate, from Purnia jail and managed to get 66.3 per cent votes which was the highest in the state of Bihar.[28] The fact that Yadav was elected with a lead of over 2 lakh votes shows that the influence of caste continues to dominate in Bihar, as in several other parts of the country. For once, Bal Thackeray is right when he says, 'In India, people don't cast their vote, they vote their caste'.[29] Pappu Kalani, a noted criminal in Maharashtra, who won as an independent candidate in the Assembly polls held in 1999, has been detained in the Yeravada jail and seems to be enjoying five-star facilities.

According to the provisions of the RPA, only a person convicted in a criminal case is barred from contesting elections for a period of six years. The

[22] *The Indian Express*, 9 August 1999.
[23] Madhav Godbole, 'Crime and Blandishment: My Thug Is Better Than Yours', *The Times of India*, 18 April 1997; *The Changing Times: A Commentary on Current Affairs*, New Delhi: Orient Longman, 2000, p. 50.
[24] *Sakal*, 20 February 1997.
[25] *Loksatta*, 7 November 1999.
[26] 'Editorial', *Loksatta*, 23 August 1997.
[27] *The Maharashtra Times*, 13 October 1999.
[28] *The Times of India*, 6 November 1999.
[29] *Outlook*, 8 November 1999.

EC, by its order in August 1997, has decided that a person will not be eligible to contest an election if he is convicted by a court and his appeal against such conviction is pending in the higher court. The EC has also made it compulsory for each candidate to give necessary information in this behalf while filing his nomination. The legality of this order is yet to be tested in the courts but, it must be admitted that this was a long overdue step.

The Law Commission has recommended that a person against whom a charge has been framed under certain sections of the Indian Penal Code (IPC), the Unlawful Activities (Prevention) Act, 1967, the Narcotic Drugs and Psychotropic Substances Act, 1985, or any other offence punishable with imprisonment for life or death under any law, 'shall be disqualified for a period of five years from the date of framing the charge, provided he is not acquitted of the said charge before the date of scrutiny notified under Section 36 of this Act'.[30] While this may be fine as far as it goes, the question still remains whether this is adequate to meet the requirements of the situation. The time limit of five years, from the date of framing of charges, proposed by the Law Commission for disqualification of a candidate will hardly serve any purpose looking at the inordinate delays in deciding criminal cases. There is also no reason why the disqualification may be restricted to charges framed only under certain sections of certain criminal laws.

Ideally, no law-breaker should be a law-maker. With this objective in view, the citizens' panel established by *Outlook* magazine had laid down, in February 1998, the following criteria for identifying candidates of criminal background and making an appeal to the voters to reject them:

(i) Person who has been convicted by a criminal court regardless of whether an appeal is pending with a higher court.

(ii) Person who has been chargesheeted by a judicial court in a criminal case.

(iii) Person against whom there are *prima facie* findings by an investigating agency on the basis of which a challan has been filed in a court.

(iv) Person who is absconding from law, although he may not have been challaned.

(v) Person who is in jail, under preventive laws, on economic or criminal grounds, after approval by the advisory board

(vi) Person who has a long crime history in his area and who has been in and out of the police net several times.

In drafting a law to keep criminals away from legislatures and other forums of governance, it is necessary that these principles are adopted. After all, contesting an election is not a fundamental right. A set of reasonable restrictions can

---

[30] Law Commission of India, *Reform of the Electoral Laws*, pp. 133–34.

and should be laid down to ensure the purity and integrity of the system. In doing so, one should err on the stricter side rather than being liberal as otherwise it can undercut the very credibility of the system and the confidence of the common man in the institutions of democratic governance.

Reducing the Number of Non-Serious Candidates

Looking to the rapidly increasing cost of holding elections, it is necessary to lay down some reasonable restrictions on non-serious candidates contesting the elections. In the elections in 1980, in one constituency, there were as many as 39 candidates. Most constituencies had 25 to 30 candidates. In some constituencies in Karnataka and Tamil Nadu, elections had to be postponed to make special arrangements for the printing of ballot papers of the size and thickness of notebooks and larger numbers of bigger size ballot boxes for casting these notebooks! This situation has improved to some extent over the years but still the number of candidates in some constituencies is a matter of concern. Most of these are independent candidates. The number of candidates contesting the elections has come down sharply from the elections in 1998 after the deposit required to be paid by a candidate was increased.

The percentage of independent candidates forfeiting their deposits has gone up steeply from 51.27 per cent in the 1957 elections to 99.70 per cent in 1996 and 99.11 per cent in 1998.

In spite of the declining number of independent candidates getting elected in each election, the presence of independents has complicated the question of stability of governments at the Centre and the states. Horse-trading in respect of independent candidates has become a matter of serious concern. Often such independent candidates supporting a government have to be provided with ministerial births. In the long run, the country must move towards a two party or at least a multi-party system, rather than having to cope with the problem of managing independents.

A reference may be made in this context to the judgement of the Division Bench of the Bombay High Court in March 1997 by which the court has held that independent candidates cannot come together after elections to form a new grouping or give up the platform on which they had contested the election. In a case pertaining to Mahabaleshwar Giristhan Nagar Parishad, the High Court has disqualified the concerned councillors for non-adherence to this principle under the anti-defection law and has cancelled their election. Their appeal is now pending in the Supreme Court. A final decision in this case will be of considerable significance to the future of independent candidates and their role in India's increasingly fractious polity.

It is often suggested that there should be a total ban on contesting elections by independent candidates. In the Law Commission's view, the time is now ripe for debarring independent candidates from contesting Lok Sabha and Legislative Assembly elections.[31] This will be an unreasonable restriction, particularly when, in the typically Indian party system, persons who are not professional politicians hardly ever get an opportunity to contest elections as party candidates. It cannot be denied that there is a need for induction of eminent persons from various fields in the politics of the country. It should also be noted that after the state funding scheme is introduced, the fact that such funding will not be available to the independent candidates will itself be a factor which will discourage such candidates from contesting elections. Against this background, there need be no explicit bar to independents contesting the elections. However, to reduce the number of non-serious candidates still further, the deposit payable by candidates should be further increased. Yet another safeguard may be introduced by way of a stipulation that any independent candidate getting less than 1/4th of the total votes polled in a constituency should be disqualified from contesting the election again for a certain number of years, say, 10 years.

Bar on Contesting from more than One Constituency

In 1980, one candidate stood for election from 13 parliamentary constituencies and several others from three to four constituencies. Finally, in 1996, the RPA was amended so that a person could contest at the most from two constituencies. Even stalwarts such as Indira Gandhi, L.K. Advani, Mulayam Singh Yadav and Sonia Gandhi have contested from more than one constituency at a time. There have been cases where a candidate has been elected from more than one constituency. In such a case, he has to resign from one of the constituencies, leading to fresh elections therein. Though the number of such cases has gone down over the years, it is still an avoidable public expenditure which the country can ill afford. It is high time the electoral law is amended to prohibit a candidate from contesting an election from more than one parliamentary/Assembly constituency or simultaneously from a parliamentary and an Assembly constituency.

Punishment for Electoral Offences

As emphasised by the Law Commission, there is an urgent need to enhance the punishment for various electoral offences mentioned in the RPA as well as in the IPC. All of them are electoral offences and seriously interfere with a fair electoral process. The punishments at present provided are totally inadequate and are ridiculously low.[32]

---

[31] Ibid., p.186.
[32] Ibid., p. 134.

A reference must be made in this context to the punishment of disqualification and defranchising imposed by the president of India on Shiv Sena chief Bal Thackeray. Of particular concern is the punishment which bars Thackeray from casting his vote in any election for a period of six years up to 10 December 2001. The punishment was announced a full 11 years after he committed the electoral malpractice. Rather than being considered a deterrent, the punishment brought public ridicule to the electoral law and its implementation.

It is for the first time that such a punishment has been imposed on any one, and that too on the chief of a political party. The wisdom of such a course of action can be seriously challenged. The ends of justice could have been met by disqualifying Thackeray from contesting any election for a certain period. But how can anyone be divested of his right to vote? In a democracy, it makes no sense to deprive anyone of his right to vote. If a more stringent punishment than mere disqualification had to be imposed, the political party of which he was and continues to be the chief (for a life-time, according to his own public statements), could have been derecognised so long as he continues to head the party. Clearly, the existing provisions of law in this regard deserve to be looked into afresh.

Caretaker Government in the Period Leading to Elections

M.S. Gill, CEC, has suggested that chief ministers should demit office six months before elections are held in their states. While the sentiment behind this suggestion will be universally shared, it is doubtful if the suggestion itself can be implemented.

At the outset, it has to be accepted that the governments, both in the states and the Centre, have been remiss in observing ethical proprieties in the period preceding the polls. Even after five decades of democracy, political parties in power have been conducting themselves irresponsibly. The fact that the words 'caretaker government' have not been mentioned in the Constitution has been made much of in this debate. The media is also responsible, in no small measure, in encouraging the governments to take all decisions during this period as if they are firmly in the saddle. This 'business as usual' literally becomes 'business' most unusual. It is needless to say that the conventions, guidelines, norms and proprieties in a democracy are as important, if not more important, than the written word of the Constitution, particularly where ethical standards are involved. Successive governments at the Centre have thrown all responsibility to the winds in taking decisions to appease one section of the voters or the other. The same is true of the governments in the states.

But the question is whether imposition of president's rule is the answer to the problem.

- **First**, there is no provision in the Constitution for imposition of president's rule at the Centre. This would mean treating the Centre differently than the states. This can hardly be justified.
- **Second**, president's rule will mean rule by the central government. It is quite likely that the Centre will be as partisan, if not more partisan in its dealings, particularly if the political party in power at the Centre is different than that at the state.
- **Third**, president's rule implies putting the governor in charge of the state. Looking to the manner in which active party functionaries belonging to the political party in power at the Centre are being appointed as governors, this again will mean rule of the Centre by the back door.

A more reasonable solution will, therefore, lie in the president of India/ governor keeping a close watch on the decisions of the government at the Centre and state, respectively, in the period preceding the elections. Whenever any undue favours are shown to any person, industrial house or a section of society with an eye on elections, the president/governor should direct the government not to implement the said decision till after the incoming government is consulted. Second, the media must play its role in vigilantly giving publicity to such uncalled for and partisan decisions. Third, as a matter of normal practice, the in-coming government should review all decisions taken by the earlier government six months before the elections. Once everyone knows that all decisions will be reviewed in this manner, both the officers as also the politicians will be more careful in taking decisions. The concerned parties will also not be keen on getting decisions which may create controversy or be reversed by the new government.

Size of Legislatures and Redrawing of Constituencies

The Constitution (42nd Amendment) Act, 1976, froze the boundaries of constituencies demarcated on the basis of the 1971 Census and deferred further delimitation and statewise reallocation of seats until after the census scheduled for the year 2001. The first question for consideration is whether the size of the Lok Sabha and State Assemblies needs be increased further.

The same arguments for which the above Constitution amendment was passed in 1976 hold good even today and will continue to be relevant in the future. The rate of growth of population in the BIMARU states (Bihar, Madhya Pradesh, Rajasthan and Uttar Pradesh) is much higher than in the other states and they will, therefore, take that much longer to stabilise their population. To increase the number of seats in Parliament on the basis of revised figures of population would mean giving much larger representation to these states than at present. This is likely to create new tensions and anxieties in the country. Increasing the number of seats in Assemblies will also pose similar difficulties in respect to the election of the president of India, and the size and composition of the Rajya Sabha.

Though no leaders of political parties are prepared to accept it, India, with its population crossing the billion mark, is faced with the serious problem of population explosion. One wonders whether experts in this field, in which they have been proved wrong time and again, should be believed. But, according to some estimates, India's population is expected to continue to grow till at least it reaches the 15 crore mark. It is true that while parliamentarians in the US or Russia represent a population of about 30,000 to 50,000, in India each MP represents a population of about 3 lakh. Several constituencies are even larger. But, if the seats in the Parliament and State Assemblies are to be increased on the basis of population, the sessions of these bodies will have to be held in Olympic size in-door stadiums! We cannot afford to have such large, unwieldy and unmanageable forums. Conducting any meaningful business in such mass meetings will be impossible.

In this light, it is difficult to agree with the recommendations of the Law Commission of India to increase the size of the Lok Sabha and State Assemblies.[33] We will have to make do with the present number of seats in these forums. Their number thus should be frozen for all times to come. Fortunately, the population policy announced by the Centre in the year 2000 makes a categorical pronouncement to freeze the number of constituencies for a long time to come. The other alternative would be to increase the number of seats in the Lok Sabha to some extent while at the same time keeping the present proportion of the number of seats between the states the same. A national consensus will need to be evolved on this sensitive issue.

But, in any case, in view of the large and unjustifiable discrepancies in the size of the constituencies—the number of voters in some constituencies is more than twice that in some other constituencies—opportunity should be taken, after the population census in 2001, to redraw their boundaries. For example, while the Outer Delhi constituency has 20 lakh voters, Chandani Chowk has merely 3.75 lakh voters. It is imperative that in re-drawing the constituencies, as far as possible, their size, in terms of the number of voters, is brought on par, except in cases where the population is widely dispersed or geographical considerations militate against this.

Election Petitions

The delays in court decisions in election petitions has become a matter of serious concern. Thus, for example, the Supreme Court annulled the election of an Orissa Congress MLA from Bhanjanagar Assembly Constituency, held in 1995, only in September 1999 (*The Indian Express*, 23 September 1999).

---

[33] Law Commission of India, *Reform of the Electoral Laws*, pp. 167–69.

There are several cases in which election petitions have been finally decided long after the term of the House, to which a person was elected, had expired. The most shocking case of its kind was the punishment imposed in July 1999 on Bal Thackeray, referred to earlier, almost 11 years after the offence was committed. This should be an excellent case study for all students of political science, political analysts, thinkers and policy makers. Such inordinate delays make a mockery of the provisions of law.

It needs to be considered whether, by effecting an amendment to the Constitution, powers to decide such cases cannot be given to the EC. During the off-election period, the Commission has ample free time which can be conveniently devoted to deciding such petitions. Since the EC is now a multi-member body, full use must be made of its time and expertise. As the members of the Commission are of the rank of a Supreme Court judge, only one appeal may be provided against the decision of the EC and that too only to the Division Bench of the Supreme Court.

Minimum Educational Qualification for a Legislator

At its independence, India took a revolutionary step by accepting the concept of universal suffrage in its Constitution. In the Constituent Assembly, there was a demand that some minimum educational qualification may be prescribed as eligibility for contesting elections to the Lok Sabha and State Legislative Assembly. In retrospect, it has to be admitted that the Founding Fathers wisely decided against any such step at that time, considering the level of literacy in the country and the need for building up a united country and creating a sense of belonging and social cohesion in which all citizens are treated equal.

After 50 years of India's independence, it is, however, time to consider whether a minimum educational qualification may not be prescribed now. The educational profile of the legislators has been showing considerable improvement over the years. While it is possible to argue that democracy is much more than governance, looking to the complexity of issues of governance which come before legislatures, it is only appropriate that the legislators are able to comprehend the issues and contribute to the deliberations in the House. The same is true of legislative proposals which come before the Parliament and State Legislatures. In smaller forums such as committees, it is all the more necessary that MPs/MLAs understand the nitty-gritty of the subjects and are able to keep the government on its toes. Further, it is difficult to argue that while it is necessary to have a minimum educational qualification for the post of a peon or a messenger or a clerk, no such qualification need be prescribed for a legislator who is to be a law-giver of the land.

Against this background, it is necessary to lay down that a degree should be the minimum educational qualification for contesting an election as an

MP/MLA. There is no dearth of suitable persons with such qualifications even in tribal areas, leave aside other rural areas.

Number of Children—Another Qualification for a Legislator

In a democracy, rulers have to lay down the example for others to follow. Just as the moral tone of a society is set by its rulers, a lead in family planning too has to be provided by its leaders. It is, therefore, time a legislation is passed to lay down that an aspiring legislator will have to satisfy the condition of having not more than two children. Such a requirement can be considered as quite reasonable.

A Constitution amendment bill for this purpose has been languishing since 1992. This is in keeping with the general lack of seriousness on this subject among all political parties. The bill needs to be resurrected from cold storage and passed without any further loss of time.

First-Past-The-Post vs List System

The Law Commission has recommended that the House of People shall, in addition to its members as at present, consist of not more than 138 members chosen according to the list system in such manner as Parliament may by law provide. In the case of State Legislative Assemblies, according to the Commission, 25 per cent of the enlarged membership of the Assemblies shall be chosen according to the list system.

We have discussed earlier the inadvisability of increasing the strength of the legislatures. That apart, the list system will further increase the hold of the leadership of a political party on the organisation. Further, as has been seen from the experience of the Rajya Sabha, the list system is likely to lead to more professional politicians, who are not likely to get elected directly, being included in the lists of nominees by respective parties.

The insistence of the Commission that a person to be declared elected must get more than 50 per cent plus one vote of the total valid votes also seems to be unworkable in the Indian context where even without it, the election process is spread over a period of six to seven weeks. Repeating the election exercise till a victorious candidate emerges according to the new criterion will be exorbitantly expensive. Any further time spent thereon is also likely to be resented by the people and stretch their patience beyond reasonable limits.

Representation of Women in the Lok Sabha

The representation of women in the Lok Sabha continues to be dismal. The highest number of women members (44) was in the eighth Lok Sabha, followed by the 12th (43) and 11th Lok Sabha (40). As a percentage of the total number of seats, it has never exceeded 8.1, a far cry from the reservation of 33 per cent of seats for women which is being talked about more as a political propaganda by most parties. This is in stark contrast with 'Scandinavia where women's representation has been over 40 per cent. In the recent elections to the South African National Assembly there were 120 women out of a total strength of 400, crossing the 30 per cent threshold. The African National Congress alone has 97 women among its 226 members in the National Assembly constituting 36.47 per cent.'[34]

The female literacy in India is a mere 35 per cent, well below the 63.9 per cent for men. Female infanticide, child marriages and dowry deaths are rampant. We have referred earlier to the continuing high rate of growth of population in the country, particularly among the BIMARU states. Giving women a place in the sun will go a long way in hastening the overdue reforms and changes in these vital areas. One of the most important reforms pertains to reservation of seats for women in legislatures. Strictly speaking, considering their percentage in the total population, 50 per cent of seats must be earmarked for women. However, in view of the resistance to the reservation of 33 per cent of seats in one go, it is suggested that the reservation may be progressively stepped up starting with 15 per cent in the next Lok Sabha, and thereafter by 5 percentage points in each of the succeeding Lok Sabha elections till the reservation of 33 per cent is reached. It should be further provided that the reservation of 33 per cent would continue for 25 years, in the first instance.

Muslim Representation in Lok Sabha

As a country, we must be prepared to face the truth, howsoever unpalatable it may be, if future catastrophes are to be avoided. One of these relates to the miserably small representation of Muslims in Parliament and state legislatures. The maximum number of Muslim members (46) was in the seventh Lok Sabha, followed by the eighth Lok Sabha (41). The percentage in terms of total membership declined steeply from 7.27 in the first Lok Sabha and 8.5 in the seventh Lok Sabha to 4.99 in the 12th. As compared with the percentage of Muslims (13 per cent) in the total population, this is undeniably too low.

For the first time since independence, there are just two junior Muslim ministers in the Atal Behari Vajpayee Ministry formed after the 1999 elections. This kind of insensitivity and short-sightedness certainly sends a very wrong message to the Muslim community. It cannot be denied that, except for a few elite Muslim families, the common Muslim has remained outside the mainstream of national life. The levels of literacy among Muslims continue

---

[34] Sushila Ramaswamy, 'Women in Politics', *The Hindustan Times*, 14 September 1999.

to be much lower than the other sections of society. In a large measure, their primary and secondary education is restricted to religious institutions (*madrasas*), away from the liberal education stream. Their share in organised sector employment is miserably low. Their percentage in employment in the government and public sector is negligible. This is equally true of the police and security forces. No society which neglects a large section of its population in this manner can ever hope to make the grade. One crucial element in addressing these urgent problems is to give adequate representation to the minorities in the Lok Sabha and state legislatures. If this aspect continues to be neglected, India will, sooner than later, be faced with the demand for reservation of seats for Muslims. Such a demand will have large and unmistakable political overtones and will militate against the principle of secularism which is a part of the basic structure of the Constitution. It is high time all political parties hear and, more importantly, act upon this message.

Opinion and Exit Polls

The pre-election waters, preceding the 1999 Lok Sabha and Legislative Assembly polls, had become muddied due to a number of controversies. One of the more enduring of these was the one pertaining to the publication of the opinion and exit polls.

As has been underlined by M.S. Gill, CEC, this is also a topic of debate in other democracies. New Zealand made opinion polls an offence in 1993. In the US, an exit poll on the east coast is not allowed to be revealed until the last vote is cast on the west coast.[35]

The problem would have been much less intractable if the polling was to be held over a much shorter period of three days to one week as in the past. But now the polling process takes over five weeks to complete all over the country. Unless some dramatic amendments are made in the electoral laws and the punishment for electoral offences made much more stringent, it is unlikely that the election process will be smooth or even peaceful in the near future. This may therefore mean even a longer period in which polling is held in different states. This factor must be borne in mind in coming to any final view on the manner in which opinion and exit polls should be dealt with.

Equally relevant is the question of impartiality and credibility of the agencies conducting such surveys. It is no longer a secret that often the sponsors of these surveys have an axe to grind and a goal to achieve. It is not therefore surprising that the result of the poll can often be predicted on the basis of the political leanings of the sponsors of the polls and/or the agency conducting the polls. As Bhaskar Rao, founder chairman of Centre for Media Studies has observed,

---

[35] Interview with M.S. Gill, 'I Refuse to be a Thanedar', *Outlook*, 11 October 1999, p. 22.

The concerns about poll surveys today arise for different reasons. They include, proliferation of poll surveys by all kinds of known and unknown agencies often without transparency about the poll itself and the methodology used, use of such surveys by political parties in their campaign, the way the media itself has been using poll surveys, giving it authenticity and prominence; so much so that I came out with a paid advertisement two years ago cautioning the public that the results of my survey were not the accurate results.[36]

The debate as to whether such polls influence the voter is meaningless. If they do not, there is no reason why such polls need be conducted at such cost and their results published with so much fanfare. Clearly, such polls are sponsored and published because they influence the voter significantly but in a subtle manner. This is particularly true in respect of exit polls conducted in areas in which polling has been concluded. If the trend of voting is in favour of any party or a political front, the voters in other areas which are yet to go to polls are unlikely to go against the trend. The importance of these polls cannot therefore be minimised or overlooked.

There is no mechanism at present to do any rating of the agencies conducting the polls. It may be noted that the credit rating agencies which do the credit rating of companies and state governments have now to work under broad guidelines laid down by the Securities and Exchange Board of India (SEBI). It is time the agencies conducting opinion and exit polls are similarly brought under the overall supervision of the EC. The methodology adopted by these agencies to conduct the polls, the manner of selection of the sample, the nature of questions asked and so on are matters which need a closer look. It must be made mandatory on these agencies to publish all this information from time to time. The EC may appoint a standing panel of experts, whose impartiality and objectivity is beyond any doubt, to go into these and all other related matters and to advise the EC. The EC's findings thereon may be published from time to time so as to enable the people to evaluate the poll results.

It is interesting to note that the Press Council of India (PCI) too had issued guidelines that no newspapers should give publicity to the results of such polls before voting in all constituencies has been completed. The chairman of PCI had expressed an apprehension that if this is not done 'democracy may become mediacracy'.[37]

The orders issued by the EC banning the publication of the results of such polls were struck down by the Supreme Court on the preliminary ground that there was no mechanism for their enforcement. The Court is reported to have observed, 'Your [EC's] guideline will remain a guideline.... At the end of the day you (EC) may go home with a perception that you have far less

[36] Vrinda Gopinath, 'Polls, Pollsters and Politicians', *The Indian Express*, 25 September 1999.
[37] *Sakal*, 24 September 1999.

powers than the public perception of it.'[38] This is a far more damaging observation of the Court than the mere striking down of the ban orders.

The Supreme Court had not gone into the substantive issues pertaining to the merits of such polls or the implication of the ban on publication on the fundamental right of freedom of speech and expression guaranteed under Article 19 of the Constitution. These issues will no doubt be agitatedly discussed in the Supreme Court again at some point of time in the future. But, in the meanwhile, as discussed earlier in this section, it is necessary to empower the EC by a requisite constitutional amendment to put the question of his powers to conduct elections in a free, fair and credible manner, beyond any shade of doubt.

Some Issues Pertaining to Rajya Sabha Elections

Rajya Sabha was conceived as the House of Elders and was meant to be a sobering influence on the House of the People. Over a period of time, the complection of the Rajya Sabha has changed perceptibly. Now, there is nothing much to distinguish it from the Lower House. Rajya Sabha is as noisy a place as the Lok Sabha. It too boasts of its own 'shouting brigades'. It is the same House in which the then chairman, Shankar Dayal Sharma, was so mistreated and insulted that he had wept in the chair.

One issue which requires urgent consideration on the part of all political parties pertains to the criteria which may be applied for selection of candidates for contesting the Rajya Sabha elections. By and large, professional politicians, who are unsuccessful in Lok Sabha elections or lack public support to contest the Lok Sabha elections get nominated to the Rajya Sabha. Since the election to the Rajya Sabha is an indirect one, those who are lucky to be so selected are well provided for for a period of six years. It is very rarely that the political parties have adopted talented and accomplished persons from other fields as their candidates for the Rajya Sabha. As a result, the respect which the House of Elders should command has declined perceptibly. The only category of professionals which has been treated favourably is the journalists who enjoy a lot of clout among politicians due to their capacity to do considerable harm or good to them.

In some cases, candidates who had lost the Lok Sabha elections were immediately brought in, in the Rajya Sabha, thereby completely undoing the public mandate. This is making a mockery of democracy.

Rajya Sabha was also supposed to represent the states. This was the main justification for the second chamber. Though not explicitly stated anywhere, it was expected that the members representing a particular state would belong to that state. This is how the selection of candidates took place in the initial

---

[38] *The Indian Express*, 15 September 1999.

years. However, later, the Rajya Sabha was largely used by some political parties to accommodate the favourite candidates of the leadership of the parties, irrespective of the state to which they belonged. These persons had no qualms in knowingly giving incorrect information as to their place of residence, etc., in their nomination papers. The EC had ordered an inquiry in 25 of such cases among the sitting members of the Rajya Sabha during 1994–95. Manmohan Singh, former Union Finance Minister, was one of them. The actual number of such members may be considerably larger. The decision of the Supreme Court in the case of Manmohan Singh to quash the proceedings started by the CEC and the electoral registration officer, on purely technical grounds, was indeed unfortunate as the case involved a major constitutional issue.[39] It is imperative that the matter is pursued further through appropriate constitutional amendment.

There is no evidence to show that the Rajya Sabha has done anything notable to safeguard the interests of the states. It is therefore time to go into these issues and to examine seriously whether there is a need for such a second chamber at all. It does not seem to serve any purpose except to duplicate the discussions in the Lower House and to delay the transaction of business.

Another matter of some concern is the composition of the Rajya Sabha. Since one-third of its members retire every two years, it takes a long time for the Rajya Sabha to reflect the changed composition of the Lok Sabha. And, by that time, the composition of the Lok Sabha itself may undergo a change! This often means a dead-lock with one party or a political front enjoying a majority in the Lok Sabha and the parties in the opposition in the Lok Sabha having a majority in the Rajya Sabha. As the experience in the last few years has shown, this is becoming a hurdle in the speedy transaction of legislative business in Parliament as a whole. The country has often seen the sorry spectacle of parties in majority in the Rajya Sabha holding to ransom the government elected by a direct mandate of the people. The recent case of its kind was the threat given by the Congress Party that it will hold up important legislative bills for speeding up economic reforms if Rajiv Gandhi's name is not removed from the list of accused persons in the charge-sheet in the Bofors case. This situation was clearly not visualised by the Founding Fathers of the Constitution. It is time this issue also is addressed with some urgency. More importantly, there is a good case for the abolition of the Rajya Sabha itself. This will be a strong signal for the downsizing of the government and the legislature.

To sum up, it has to be accepted that the political party system in India has evolved the way it has primarily because the Founding Fathers of the Constitution did not provide for a proper and sustainable framework for political parties as in the case of the Basic Law in Germany. In a way, the political

---

[39] *The Hindu*, 2 December 1999.

parties can be said to have evolved so far in a purely *ad hoc* manner to suit the requirements of electioneering. Disintegration and degeneration of a major national party, namely, the Congress, gave rise to a number of splinter groups. The emergence of regional parties can, in no small measure, be traced to the collapse of the Congress Party and the desire of the people to fulfil certain regional aspirations. As one looks at the future, however, it is imperative that a proper constitutional and legislative framework is provided for the emergence and coherent and in-step development of the party system and electoral framework in India.

8

PARTIES, CIVIL SOCIETY AND THE STATE IN INDIA

S.K. Chaube

The Problem

'Someone should prove that there is rule of law', said Chhagan Bhujbal, deputy chief minister and home minister of Maharashtra, to *The Hindustan Times* (*HT*),[1] referring to the state government's decision to prosecute Bal Thackeray in July 2000. A few days earlier, a division bench of the Supreme Court, headed by Chief Justice A.S. Anand, asked, 'Is there something called collective responsibility?' referring to the statements of some Union ministers on the arrest of Bal Thackeray, the Shiv Sena chief, but without naming them. Ketan Tanna, *HT* correspondent, wrote:

> Meet the Bully No. 1 of Mumbai. As word got out last Saturday about the green signal given for prosecution of Bal Thackeray, tension gripped Mumbai. Mobs of Shiv Sainiks went around closing shops and other commercial establishments.[2]

As a consequence of this the then Union Law Minister, Ram Jethmalani, a distinguished criminal lawyer himself, lost his job but Bal Thackeray, his political patron, was released by a metropolitan court. At the background of this drama there lies the 1992–93 mayhem ignited by the demolition of the Babri Masjid and Thackeray's provocative articles in the Shiv Sena mouthpiece, *Samna*.[3] Chargesheets had been framed against the Bharatiya Janata Party (BJP) leaders, who were appointed ministers and administered oaths of office commanding them to 'bear true faith and allegiance to the Constitution'. Between the two events this 'party with a difference' (i.e., BJP) demanded the resignation of a leader (i.e., Laloo Yadav) of a party of 'social justice' (i.e., Janata Dal) from the state government of Bihar when he was chargesheeted

---

[1] 'He Must Respect the Law', *The Hindustan Times*, 23 July 2000.
[2] *The Hindustan Times*, 27 July 2000.
[3] *Samna* is edited by Bal Thackeray.

for corruption on the plea that political crime is above board while economic crime is not. Earlier, this same 'party with a difference' had declared that *Ram Janmabhumi* was a matter of faith and, therefore, beyond the jurisdiction of the court of law. Its predecessor ruling party at the Centre had vandalised the Constitution and law of the land during the dark days of the emergency and the saint-politician, Vinoba Bhave, had welcomed the Emergency as *anushesan parva*, a lesson in discipline. For half the period since independence the country's civil society and the state have been held hostage to party politics that paid scanty regard for the law of the land.

Parties in Political Theory

Relations between parties, civil society and the state have much wider ramifications than the misdemeanors of political leaders. Jennings was not quite right in stating that 'John Stuart Mill wrote a book on Representative Government without mentioning parties'.[4] Mill did mention the Tories and the Liberals.[5] But he did not dwell upon the intricacies of the party system. He treated the political divisions in his contemporary Britain in terms of class,[6] not in a Marxist sense but in the statistical sense of a group of similarly placed people.[7] One reason of this is that traditional political science treated parties as extra-constitutional bodies. J.G. Garner's textbook, *Political Science and Government*, written in 1938, had no place for political parties. It was in the writings of politicians, on the other hand, that parties appeared. As early as 1787, in 'The Federalist Number Ten', James Madison used 'parties' alternately with 'factions'.[8] In his 1798 farewell address George Washington expressed his 'serious concern' at 'characterising parties by geographical discrimination' and warned that 'one of the expedients of party to acquire influence, within particular districts, is to misrepresent the opinions and aims of other districts'.[9]

---

[4] Sir Ivor Jennings, *The British Constitution*, fourth edition, Cambridge: Cambridge University Press, 1961, p. 29.
[5] Mill's *Consideration on Representative Government* was published in 1861, two years after his death. In the chapter entitled 'Ought Pledges to be Required from Members of Parliament?' he wrote about the elections. 'The ablest member may be a Tory and the electors Liberals; or a Liberal and they may be Tories' (John Stuart Mill, *Utilitarianism, Liberty and Representative Government*, London: Everyman's Library, 1948, p. 318).
[6] Ibid., and elsewhere.
[7] For the different meanings of 'class', see Shibani Kinkar Chaube, 'Marxism and the Developing Countries', in Neera Chandhoke (ed.), *Understanding the Post-Colonial World*, New Delhi: Sterling Publishers, 1994, pp. 152–69, at p. 161.
[8] See Richard D. Heffner, *A Documentary History of the United States*, New York: Mentor Books, The New American Library of World Literature, 1960, pp. 41–47.
[9] 'Washington's Farewell Address', also reproduced in Heffner, op. cit., 60–70. The present quotation is from p. 63.

Throughout the 19th century the idea of a political party was rather vague. But certain conceptions were emerging. First, a party was a part and not the whole of the civil society. Second, it was formed on the basis of common/ shared opinions and aims. Third, a party concerned politics, that is, state power. Fourth, if there is one party, there must be at least another. In short, the state is larger than a party and the civil society is larger than the state. A party has to operate within the general normative structure of the state and the civil society. The state should not engross the civil society and the party should not engross the state. A party seeking to engross the civil society was out of the question. At the same time, a certain amount of political autonomy was allowed to the parties to conduct their own affairs.

Parties and Their Members

In 1938 Bertrand Russel wrote that 'Political parties were, until recently, very loose organizations which made only very slight attempts to control the activities of their members'.

> Throughout the nineteenth century, Members of Parliament frequently voted against their party leaders, with the consequence that the results of divisions were far more unpredictable than they are now. Walpole, North, and the younger Pitt controlled their supporters, to a certain extent, by means of corruption; but after the diminution of corruption, and while politics was still aristocratic, governments and party leaders had no way of bringing effective pressure to bear. Now, especially in the Labour Party, men are pledged to orthodoxy, and failure to keep the pledge usually involves both political extinction and financial loss.[10]

Analysts of British politics noted that the difference between the Conservative and the Liberal parties was not fundamental. It was the Labour party—'historically, an extra-parliamentary party'[11]—that started off from an oppositional position. Its rules were rigid. Yet Jennings observed that 'the Conservative or the Liberal party is an intra-parliamentary party with a large extra-parliamentary organization'. The result is 'much the same'.[12] He found more difference in disciplinary practice between the Houses of Parliament than between the parties and that

> there is more cross-voting in the House of Lords than in the House of Commons. In the latter House it is thought necessary that the whips should be put

[10] Bertrand Russel, *Power: A New Social Analysis*, 1938, London: George Allen & Unwin Ltd., 1960 edition. For a more detailed treatment of the party control mechanism see Jennings, *The British Constitution*, pp. 50–60.

[11] Jennings, *The British Constitution*, p. 50.

[12] Ibid.

212 S.K. Chaube

on, i.e., that members should vote according to the party in respect of almost every motion and that members should always obey the whip. The Labour party expressly and the other parties by implication allow a member with conscientious scruples—whatever that may mean—to abstain from voting on a particular issue. The whips are less fierce than they are commonly represented to be.... There is a sanction against a member who consistently disobeys the whip, but examples of its use are rare because the local party organizations are usually more orthodox than the whip and begin to ask question of their member long before the withdrawal of the whip is contemplated. More often, members themselves sometimes refuse the whip, especially in the early stages of a Parliament for most members become more orthodox as a general election approaches.[13]

Denial of renomination—rather than expulsion—is the key to conformity of a Member of Parliament (MP) with the wish of his/her party. It works because the party organisations are fairly effective at the local levels and the constituencies are stable. 'It is known', writes Jennings, 'that a very high proportion of electors, probably 80 per cent, vote in the same way in the successive elections'.[14] Even Winston Churchill, in the early 20th century, lost the election when he changed his party.

Here is a conflict between the individualistic norm of liberal democracies and the collectivistic norm of the party system. It is resolved by the conception of a contract. A voter votes for a candidate on the basis of his affiliation to a party. When a legislator, on his/her election, changes his political loyalty, he/she must take the voter into confidence and seek fresh election. The contract works on the basis of a civic norm. However, when the state formalises this contract through a statute, it clearly encroaches upon the domain of the civil society. Such encroachment assumes that the civil society is too weak to impose its norms upon a legislator or the losing party is too weak to persuade the civil society to punish a truant member. What parties fail to achieve politically they seek to achieve by law—because of their failure to convince the voters of the impropriety of the defection. This, in turn, may impart a kind of callousness to the civil society about the observance of the norm. Even Jennings observed that 'Actual cross-voting is more common in the Labour Party than in the Conservative Party', and explains it in terms of the Old Boys' attachment in the latter compared to the formal demands of discipline in the former.[15]

When a state institution like an election commission insists upon election of office bearers of a party this encroachment produces a comic effect as in the case of the Shiv Sena 'unanimously' electing Bal Thackeray its president

[13] Ibid., p. 51.
[14] Ibid., p. 65.
[15] Sir Ivor Jennings, *Parliament*, Cambridge: Cambridge University Press, 1957, p. 91.

a few years back. And when the state seeks to finance the parties' expenditures in general elections, there may be quite undesirable effects as were seen in Germany in the year 2000.

No individual adult citizen of India can be statutorily disenfranchised except on grounds of electoral offences and certain other disabilities laid down under Article 325 of the Constitution of India. Therefore, the greatest argument against ban on small parties is the individual. Right to vote includes the right to contest election sanctioned by the Indian Constitution. Though not a Fundamental Right in the strict judicial sense, the right to vote and contest election is integral to the republican parliamentary democracy of India and is a basic feature of the Constitution of India. A party, big or small, is a collection of individual voters or potential voters.

There are political parties in India representing microscopic ethnic groups. Debarring such parties from electoral contest will be an invitation to national disaster.

Parties and the Civil Society

'The powers of organization other than the State over their members depend upon the right of expulsion and are more or less severe according to the obloquy and financial hardship attached to expulsion', wrote Russel.[16] 'The powers of organizations over non-members are less easy to define', he added.[17] While the powers of the states over foreigners and other states ultimately depend upon war or the threat of war and upon less severe measures like tariff and immigration laws,

> the external powers of private organizations are apt to be regarded by the State with jealousy, and are therefore extra-legal. They depend mainly upon the boycott and other more extreme forms of intimidation. Such terroristic influence is usually a prelude to anarchy or revolution.... A State which cannot cope with this kind of illegality usually soon comes to grief.[18]

The tribal kind of 'consensual democracy' or the Rousseauvian concept of sovereignty of the 'general will' is inconsistent with liberal democracy that is based on the fundamental principle of the right to dissent. A political party in a liberal democracy is assumed to be capable of achieving power or influencing governmental decisions by mobilising public opinion through persuasion rather than coercion. It is the rules of bargain, which are standardised and respected by consensus. By the same token no party may be allowed

---

[16] Russel, *Power*, p. 122.
[17] Ibid., p. 123.
[18] Ibid.

to conscript members or exclude the existence of another party though the state can banish a political party on the grounds of law and order.

There are two consequences of this logic. First, compulsory voting is ruled out in a liberal democracy, for the right to dissent includes the right not to vote for *any* of the political parties in an electoral contest. Second, contest is a cardinal principle of election though uncontested elections are not impossible in rare cases. In short, the civil society must be completely free to choose its representatives to a state. Restriction of voting rights in any way may be compatible with an elitist system of government as in the 19th century west or in several post-colonial regimes today. Such regimes, however, have always been susceptible to violence, revolutions and protest.

There is a further demand of liberal democracy on the party system. Liberal democracies take individual citizenship as the basic unit of rights and rule out any tangible grouping of citizens along caste, class and communal lines. Therefore, they separate the church from the state, which is the sum and substance of secularism. They also disallow any kind of separate electorate or reservation of seats though some of them provide for proportional representation. On the other hand, caste, class and communities are realities of civil society. Political parties are hard put to resolve this contradiction. The solution is found in the formula that even if sectarian parties take part in the elections and get into the government, as far as state matters are concerned, they must abhor sectarianism. Banning political parties on ideological grounds is inadvisable for a democracy, as it would encourage clandestine activities.

Nor is it advisable to exclude any political party on the grounds of size because the formation of a political party is a part of the right to association under a liberal democratic constitution. The recent proposal for banning small parties from contest is thoroughly misconceived. The citation of the German model in support of this proposal is misplaced. The German system rules out the small parties not from contesting elections but from getting state funds in their election campaigns. Before the introduction of the rather questionable system of state funding of elections the question about the parties' size just does not arise.

Parties and Representation

Perhaps the greatest dilemma confronting the analyst of political parties is that between composition and representation. V.I. Lenin had been born to the middle class but he claimed to represent the working class. Jawaharlal Nehru was an aristocrat by birth and upbringing, but he spoke for the downtrodden and advocated democratic socialism of a variety close to Marxism. His daughter was denied by Jagjivan Ram, in 1977, the right to speak for the poor as she had been 'born with a silver spoon in her mouth' calling for a retort from Congressmen that he had made good his poverty at his birth through politics. Today the critics of Jawaharlal Nehru and Indira Gandhi are numerous as are the critics of Lenin who see in the Bolshevik revolution only a nasty coup that led to the foundation of the world's worst despotism.

In spite of a separate electorate, Mohammad Ali Jinnah and the Muslim League, which claimed to represent the Indian Muslims, could not win any provincial election except that of Bengal in 1946 and East Bengal (Pakistan) walked out of Pakistan in 1971. B.R. Ambedkar, the Scheduled Castes Federation leader and member of the Viceroy's Executive Council during the Second World War, was elected to the Constituent Assembly of India with the support of the Congress Party, which commanded an overwhelming majority of the Scheduled Caste members of the provincial Assemblies. The dominance of the Communist Party of India on the Indian working class movements ended in 1947 when the Indian National Trade Union Congress walked out of the All India Trade Union Congress. The Bharatiya Janata Party claimed to represent Hindutva, calling its opponents 'pseudo-secular' but it could never win the support of more than 25 per cent voters in a country where 82 per cent of the population is Hindu. The classic case of incoherence is the invitation by the National Commission of Minorities, in the first half of 2000, to the Vishwa Hindu Parishad (VHP) and the Bajrang Dal as representatives of the Hindus to have a dialogue with the representatives of the Christians on violence against the Indian Christians. In August 2000 several opposition MPs wrote to the United Nations (UN) secretary general protesting against the invitation to the VHP, as representatives of the Hindu religion, to the world religious summit on peace.

Liberal democracies, which gave birth to the modern party system defined parties as organised groups of people sharing common opinions. Lenin formed a revolutionary party on the basis of ideology and the two organising principles of secrecy and democratic centralism. The behavioural social scientists consider opinion as unstable and, in any case, a dependent variable and reject ideology as 'false consciousness'. They would rather see political parties as aggregates of 'interest groups' and confine their attention to composition of the parties (origin and background of the members). Operationally, however, liberal democracy insists upon abstraction of politics from the socio-economic background of political actors, and regards the election to government as the goal of open contest under norms of tolerance of opposition, neutrality of the bureaucracy and independence of the judiciary. Within these norms independence of the election machinery is a vital instrumentality and freedom to vote an article of faith.

Another fundamental dilemma of liberal democratic theory is that parties represent opinions/interests and are supposed to pursue them while the state is neutral. Can a political party, on securing the government, pursue its objectives without paying heed to the other interests? Can the election manifesto of a party be a source of power? The Construction of a Ram temple, for instance, was a part of the election manifesto of the BJP in the 1991 elections to the Uttar Pradesh (UP) State Assembly. Did the victory empower the BJP to demolish the Babri Masjid? The answer of liberal democracy is that a manifesto is an inventory of promises and responsibilities and not a pronouncement of power. In other words, it is a contract of a party with its voters binding the former and not the latter. It does not commit the state to the violation of the rights of any citizen. Nor does it absolve the state of its responsibility to maintain the rule of law. Ex-post facto 'regrets' by members of a government or a party are no compensation for such misdemeanours.

For, the contract makes the party *represent* the voter, not *advocate* his case. The difference lies in the fact that the advocate seeks justice for his/her client from a court, the legislator represents the voter within a body that distributes justice. The legislator is required to be impartial and free to exercise his power according to his conscience. The concept of a 'mandate' is a political one and has no place in liberal constitutionalism.

An interesting aspect of this dilemma is the BJP's discomfort in the National Democratic Alliance (NDA) most of the allies in which, do not approve of the BJP agenda on the Ram temple, Article 370 of the Constitution of India and a common civil code for the country. After the Staten Island speech of Mr Atal Behari Vajpeyee, where he declared himself as a *'swayamsevak* for life' the prime minister took great pains to explain that he had meant himself to be the *'swayamsevak* of the nation' (all *Rashtriya Swayamsevak*s are, by definition, *swayamsevak*s of the nation), that he had not said anything about Ayodhya there (even though the VHP members had raised the issue before his speech), that Ayodhya, like Article 370 and the common civil code, was not a part of the NDA agenda, and that the BJP could fulfil the dream of all Indians when it got a majority.[19] The prime minister, therefore, displayed a quadruple personality, as a *swayamsevak*, as a BJP leader, as an NDA leader and as the head of the government. He spoke nothing about the BJP agenda though some of his party colleagues have assured the nation that the Ram temple question was not on the BJP agenda 'now'. Nor would it find a place in the party's manifesto in the next UP Assembly elections.

The important point of these assertions is that the BJP is the nation. If any section of the population does not conform to its standard, it is not part of the nation. They are in this country of the Hindus because of some 'historic wrong'. All their contributions to this country's civilisation are out of place. A fine replication of the Rousseauvian theory of 'general will'!

Every political party naturally claims to represent the whole of its constituency. In 1885 the Congress was formed to speak for the nation. In 1932, Gandhi, at the Second Round Table Conference, claimed that the Indian

[19] See *The Times of India*, 13 September 2000.

National Congress represented the whole Indian nation. Subsquently, Jinnah claimed to be the sole spokesperson of the Muslims of India and even propounded the 'two-nation' theory. To validate their respective claims the Congress and the Muslim League tried to build the maximum consensus within their constituencies. Their difference lay in the fact that for the Congress the Indian nation was territorial and inclusive, for the League the Muslim nation was communal and exclusive.

The BJP's notion of the Indian nation is coloured by its notion of Hindutva. The Hindutva is cultural, if not explicitly religious. Faith in *Ram Janmabhoomi* is an essential part of Hindutva, not the whole of it. One who does not subscribe to Hindutva is not an Indian, far less is he/she entitled to the constitutional rights of the Indian citizens. The faith of the Hindus is above the 'pseudo-secular' Constitution of India. Moreover, while the Congress Party's 'Indian' and the Muslim League's 'Muslim' are deceptive categories, the BJP's 'Indian' is a prescriptive category. It will also not be correct to call it the Taliban of India for, while the Taliban wants to purify Islam and exclude the non-conformist believers, the BJP seeks to expand the horizons of Hindudom. The BJP's 'Hindu' is inclusive while its 'India' is exclusive.

The State and the Civil Society

Actual political parties in the western liberal democracies tread between the collectivistic and the individualistic norms. Thus, till the end of the 19th century the Liberal Party in Britain was patronised by the British trade unions along with the Whig bourgeoisie. In the early 20th century the trade unions shifted their loyalty and constituted the Labour Party. The Democratic Party in the United States of America (USA) has the backing of the trade unions and the blacks along with the middle strata of the US society. The Christian democratic and the socialist/communist parties in continental Europe have strong links with religion and class, respectively.

For historical reasons, in the west, race, religion and class have partly converged. Migration, caused by industrial capitalism, has substantially contributed to this convergence. Even there wholly or primarily Catholic parties like the Christian Democrats and the *Mouvement Républicain Populaire* operate on the secular plane. The key to such operation is a certain consensus that law and order, personal freedom, equality before the law and judicial independence are above all sectarian conflicts.

In India colonial modernisation politicised the religious, linguistic and ethnic divisions of India while stunted industrialisation has allowed only a limited growth of a working class. Post-independence land reform, on the other hand, diluted, if not wiped out, the traditional feudal class relation turning the Indian peasants, still constituting two-thirds of the population into the famous 'sack of potatoes'.[20] Technology has enriched a section of the new peasants simultaneously reducing the volume of hired labour. No organisation of agricultural labourers worth the name has come up. At the same time the rich peasants have failed to form economic cartels. They find it easier to reach the goal of profit enhancement by means of political pressure on the state through elections. Organised industrial labour never exceeded 10 per cent of the work force. Thanks to structural adjustment their proportion has sharply declined. There is more competition for securing 'permanent' jobs, which are available only in the government and public sector undertakings, than ever. Linkages of caste, community, language and locality are crucial to success in such competition. Reservation is a political means of institutionalising such linkages.

Political Parties in Colonial India

In colonial India political parties emerged as public fora and turned into movements. The Indian National Congress was born in 1885 through the union of Presidency associations[21] of middle- class professionals and was remarkably free from traditional aristocracy. It was not a bourgeois association as the Indian bourgeoisie did not open its purse strings to the Congress before the end of the First World War.[22] In the early period the Congress did not take up even the question of exploitation of the tea garden labour by the British planters, as it was a 'local issue'.[23] Until January 1999, when the All India Congress Committee announced that it was the most authentic repository of the spirit of Hinduism, the Congress never took a religious/communal stand. The Congress was not officially represented during the setting up of the All India Trade Union Congress in 1920. The peasants took part on a mass scale in the freedom movement in the 1930s. The All India Kisan Sabha was officially welcomed to the Congress venue only in 1936. It was thrown out in 1937. The party sponsored land reform only after transfer of power.[24]

Caste and communal organisations grew side by side with loyalist and anti-Congress trends. Sir Syed Ahmad exhorted the Muslims not to join the Congress and cooperate with the British government. While his pleadings had some impact in the north, in the south casteist organisations took the same role. None of these organisations/movements had a monolithic unity. The Khilafat movement split Sir Syed's legacy. In north India, on the other

---

[20] Karl Marx, 'The Eighteenth Brumair of Louis Bonaparte' in K. Marx and F. Engels, *Selected Works*, Vol. I., Moscow: Progress Publishers, 1971, p. 478.

[21] See Sumit Sarkar, *Modern India, 1885–1974*, Madras: Macmillan, 1983, p. 65.

[22] Ibid., p. 70.

[23] Ibid., p. 91.

[24] For a brief description of the Congress's relation with the peasants, see ibid., pp. 362–65.

hand, organisations like the Kayastha Mahasabha gradually moved towards the Congress. In the south caste movements remained powerful but, as Sumit Sarkar noted, in the 1930s, the less fortunate sections of the non-Brahmin castes in the south moved toward the Gandhian movement and, later, even toward the communist movement.[25] By the mid-1930s, as Bipan Chandra noted, casteism as a major political force was overcome except in Punjab.[26]

Parties in Independent India

Independent India adopted republican parliamentary democracy. Her party system, like the British Labour Party, was historically rooted in the opposi-tional position—legal and extra-legal. The Congress was transformed from a movement into a ruling party. It was at this stage that the party shifted its attention from political mobilisation to administrative consolidation except for the purpose of contesting elections. Social and economic issues like the Hindu Code, land reform, industrial relation, economic planning and removal of untouchability came to the fore. The Constitution of India granted universal adult franchise and laid down the Directive Principles of State Policy stimu-lating a massive penetration of the civil society by the state. The communal political parties eclipsed under the impact of the Gandhi murder though communal and casteist forces remained active manipulators of the electoral process. The Congress remained the predominant political party till the elec-tions of 1962 but was unable to meet the demands of the new social and economic forces during the fourth general elections (1967). Side by side with the leftist parties, caste and communal parties entered the domain of power. The new situation unleashed caste, class and communal conflicts on a much larger scale than what obtained until that time, caused a great deal of minis-terial instability at the state level and accentuated the politics of manipula-tion and corruption of the bureaucracy including the law-enforcing authorities.

Parties have used civil society institutions as much for moulding the civil society as to promote their own interest. Yet, when Jawaharlal Nehru piloted the Hindu Code Bill his whole party was not behind him. Hindu marriage and succession came to be regulated by the state. The Shiromani Akali Dal keeps its two legs in the government and the Sikh Gurudwara Prabandhak Committee. The Indian Union Muslim League dominates the Muslim Per-sonal Law Board that keeps control over the secular affairs of the Muslim society, according to the holy Quran. The BJP-Rashtriya Swayamsewak Sangh (RSS)-Vishwa Hindu Parishad axis tries to build a *Hindu Rashtra* with Ayodhya as the Vatican City. Yet the BJP and the Shiv Sena are the only two

---

[25] Ibid., pp. 55–58 and 244.
[26] Bipan Chandra, *Essays on Contemporary History*, New Delhi: Har Anand, 1993, p. 58.

parties which seek to 'order' the broad, national, civil society by prescribing whether a Muslim shall have one wife or four, whether the Indian Christians will have a *sarsanghachalak* or whether India should play cricket with Pakistan.

The two major happenings that severely damaged the political fabric of Indian democracy were the imposition of Emergency in 1975 and the demolition of the Babri Masjid in 1992. The former was an assault of the state on the political opposition, within as well as outside the ruling party, the latter an assault of an organised mob on the state. Both created a kind of hostage syndrome symbolised by the kidnappings of Rubaiya Sayeed and Dr Raj Kumar.[27] Nothing is impermissible, nothing is sacrosanct. The question is, how could this kind of situation arise?

A welfare state is not only expected to protect the life and liberty of the citizens equally. It is also a source of patronage. Consequently, there grows enormous competition among the citizens to secure such patronage. The trade unions, peasant organisations and pressure groups are the formally recognised agencies of advancing such claims. Racial/ethnic, communal, casteist and linguistic organisations take over their functions when they prove ineffective, as they often do in the third world countries including India. Slogans of sons of the soil, Hindutva and reservation emanate from such fora. If the state has overshadowed much of the civil society, the civil society has penetrated deep into the state.

It is possible to see such churning as the revolution of rising expectations. The Patna crowd that invaded the Rajdhani Express on the plea that they had got their own railway minister or the Member of Parliament who summoned the civil aviation minister to the Palam airport, over the impermissible cell phone, to demand the diversion of a flight, were just putting their civil linkages over the regulations of the state. The same attitude motivates a party supporter to run to his legislator or his minister for extra-legal assistance in civil and criminal cases or to put political pressure on the police and the investigating agencies. Thus a generalised political contract within the framework of rule of law turns into a patron-client relationship in which the parties move from accommodation of group interests to subordination to them.

---

[27] Dr Rubiya Sayeed, daughter of the then Union Home Minister Mufti Mohammad Sayeed, was kidnapped in Srinagar on 8 December 1989 by Kashmiri extremists and was later released in exchange for extremists in custody. This incident triggered extremist violence in Jammu and Kashmir, which is still unabated.

Dr Raj Kumar, a celebrated Kannada actor, was kidnapped by notorious forest brigand and sandalwood smuggler Veerappan on 30 July 2000. The incident showed the Karnataka and Tamil Nadu governments in bad light as neither of them could track down the brigand and secure the release of the thespian. The release could finally be achieved through the mediation of the editor of a Tamil weekly *Nakkeeran*, who had earlier met Veerappan, interviewed him and once even tried to secure his surrender by mediating between the government and Veerappan.

It is hoped that this is a passing phase. One of the heroes of the Mandal agitation has already gone on record that the reservation issue is becoming irrelevant in the days of privatisation.[28] When a political party grows up and reaches the corridors of power, larger needs of support persuade them to tame the groups that had originally sponsored/backed them. Hence the manoeuvres of the BJP today to rein in the VHP, the Hindu Jagaran Manch and the Bajrang Dal, and to seek the support of the Muslims. The same applies to the casteist parties like the Samajwadi Party and the Bahujan Samaj Party.

Until that happens the parties will be susceptible to extremist violence and vandalism if only to attract public attention. However, violence has become necessary for 'building the base', capturing booths or 'liberating' villages from 'enemy' holds. The BJP's activities in the early 1990s, naxalite activities since the 1970s, killings by secessionist groups in the northeast and the northwest of the country, constitute a range of threats to civil society. Violence is resorted to even to suppress dissidence within a political party or to express dissidence from a leadership. Such violence may not always be in-house. Often they involve innocent lives and property. Christian-bashing, for instance, may have been an effective method to embarrass the leadership of the Hindutva brigade trying to present a moderate face.

When intense class/sectarian conflict spreads over large areas, war-like situations obtain. The liberal state is often at a loss to determine whether such situations should be handled politically or as matters of law and order. The dilemma becomes poignant on account of the growth of the human rights movement in the recent period. A government may be forgiven when it fails to solve the dilemma. What cannot be forgiven is a government's refusal to act on the plea of such a dilemma as in the case of the Babri Masjid demolition and its consequences.

The Civil Society and the Constitution of India

Some provisions of the Indian Constitution have a direct bearing upon the civil society. The Constitution provides three kinds of rights. Some are available to all persons living in India (Articles 14, 20, 21, 22, 24, 25, 27, 28 and 34). Some are available to groups of citizens (Articles 26, 29 and 30), while some are available to individual citizens (Articles 15, 17, 19 and 23). The formation of political parties springs from the individuals' right to form associations. The 10th Schedule, however, seeks to regulate the functioning of the parties. The Law Commission has suggested the constructive vote of no-confidence, which seeks to impose certain restrictions on the functioning

---

[28] Ram Vilas Paswan reported in *The Times of India*, 5 July 2000.

of the parties. There are proposals for banning small parties and state funding of elections. One suspects that this kind of integration of the state, the civil society and the political parties will not be good for the health of the Indian democracy.

In India reservation of legislative seats as well as government services for members of the Scheduled Castes and Scheduled Tribes was provided for as ameliorative measures (Articles 330, 332, 334 and 335). The reservation in legislatures was expected to be of short duration, that is, until those disadvantaged people come up to a level field. Reservation of government services for any backward class of citizens, which, in the opinion of the state, was not adequately represented in the services under the states, was also permitted (Article 16, Clause 4), for an unspecified period. In the subsequent period reservation of government jobs for other backward classes (OBCs)—that is, classes other than the Scheduled Castes and Scheduled Tribes—has been enhanced. Reservation of legislative seats for members of the OBC is a contentious political issue involving several political parties. At the moment, it cross-cuts the demand for reservation of legislative seats for women. At the least, legislative reservation on such a large scale has the potential of fragmenting the polity.

Conclusion

Though Locke is credited with the original authorship of the concept of 'civil society' he did not clearly outline the contours of the term 'civil'. He explicitly regarded the civil society as contractual but admitted the pre-contractual society was 'civil'. Clearly, the contractual construction of 'civil society' carries a value while the literal meaning of civil society is generic. The desideratum of Locke's pre-contractual (civil) society is the state. Yet the contractual civil society of Locke was not the state. The state is a mere functionary of the civil society charged with the function of interpreting and applying law uniformly in terms of the contract. This requires the maintenance of autonomy of both the civil society and the state. The dictum became the guiding philosophy of liberal constitutionalism.

The conception of democracy by Rousseau sought to improve upon the anti-authoritarian content of Locke's social contract and produced the notion of a majoritarian democracy that cut at the root of freedom that Locke was fundamentally concerned with. Freedom is a goal while democracy is an institutional arrangement for its achievement. This freedom can be threatened not only by authoritarianism but also by the zealots of majoriatarian democracy.

When intense class/sectarian conflict spreads over large areas, war-like situations obtain. The liberal state is often at a loss to determine whether such situations should be handled politically or as matters of law and order. The dilemma becomes poignant on account of the growth of the human rights movement in the recent period. A government may be forgiven when it fails to solve the dilemma. What cannot be forgiven is a government's refusal to act on the plea of such a dilemma as in the cases of the Babri Masjid demolition and Christian bashing on the question of religious conversion or political violence in northeast India.

9

THE CONGRESS AND THE BJP

STRUGGLE FOR THE HEARTLAND

Partha S. Ghosh

Introduction

It is commonly believed that whosoever controls the heartland of India controls
the political power in the country. This heartland concept is not new. Throughout Indian history, the nucleus of pan-Indianism was centred in this region.
Starting with the Mauryas, through the Guptas, the Sultanate, the Mughals,
and lastly the British, it remained so. The British began by setting up the
capital of the Raj in Calcutta (now Kolkata), but ended up shifting the capital
to Delhi in the early 20th century. The only challenge to this north India
based pan-Indianism came from the Vijayanagara Empire and the Marathas
but they failed to emerge as pan-Indian political forces. The Chola Empire
was anyway more eastward looking (beyond south India, into Sri Lanka
and South East Asia) without having any pan-Indian outlook.

In the current political parlance this heartland connotes the nine Hindi-
speaking states, namely, Bihar, Chhattisgarh, Haryana, Himachal Pradesh
(HP), Jharkhand, Madhya Pradesh (MP), Rajasthan, Uttaranchal and Uttar
Pradesh (UP). Collectively they are also referred to, particularly in Western
literature, as the Cow Belt, meaning thereby that the majority Hindu factor
there influences the thrust of national politics. Although after the creation of
Chhattisgarh and Jharkhand, this Hindu factor is somewhat diluted because politics in these states is going to be dictated by the tribal populations,
a majority of whom are Christian, essentially it still remains Hindu and
Hindi-centric. Barring Morarji Desai, P.V. Narasimha Rao and H.D. Deve
Gowda, who together accounted for only nine years in power, all the prime
ministers of India since independence have belonged to this region. The
debacle of the Congress in 1996, even after Narasimha Rao's five years of
fairly good performance, can be attributed to its neglect of this heartland and
the corresponding filling-up of the gap by its rival, the Bharatiya Janata
Party (BJP). This chapter attempts an assessment of the relative strengths

and weaknesses of the Congress and the BJP to control this politically important region during the last five decades, and makes speculations about the shape of things to come in India's national politics.

Historical Background

When the Bharatiya Jan Sangh (BJS), BJP's forerunner, was established in 1951, the Congress was in its 66th year. Though both parties entered the electoral fray in independent India's first general elections held in 1952, the Congress had already developed a long tradition of seeking vote and support, most conspicuously from the elections of 1937 onwards, from the Indian masses irrespective of caste or religion. Unlike the Congress, the BJS was new and it had no electoral experience. But its ideology was not new and during the previous half-a-century or more, it had carved out for itself a sizable support base, though largely dormant. According to this ideology Indian nationalism and Hindu nationalism were one and the same thing and whosoever tried to distinguish between the two was working against the interest of India's nation building. In that sense, BJP's origin can be traced to the 18th century Bengal renaissance itself. The latter, which is considered to be the cradle of Indian nationalism, often confused the same with Hindu nationalism, though, probably, unwittingly. It has been the historical experience globally that nationalism finds its first expression in the religious and communal nationalism of the majority community. It is also the historical experience that this gives rise to minority suspicions that invariably drive a wedge in an otherwise composite nationalist movement. India followed this textbook model. The Congress had realised this danger and worked out its strategy in a way so as not to alienate the minorities while at the same time keeping intact its primary base amongst the majority Hindus. The Hindu nationalists too vied for the same base constituency without, however, bothering much for the minorities. On the contrary, they considered that their minority bashing would help them consolidate their base amongst the Hindus. The competition for power between the BJP and the Congress is the story of this antagonistic approach to politics and nation building.

One need not go into the details of this rivalry during the nationalist phase. Still, for the purposes of putting our discussion in perspective, its broad contours may be drawn. The Congress, under the leadership of Mahatma Gandhi, understood that India being socially plural, Hindu nationalism itself would not be enough to build the national movement upon. Moreover, because of the fact that the Hindus themselves were stratified on caste and sectoral lines the conceptualisation of Hindu nationalism itself was problematic. How to incorporate into the nationalist mainstream the huge mass of people who were still 'untouchable' was also one of the biggest challenges. Having identified the problem, the Congress decided to identify itself with all the communities and caste groups both individually and collectively so as to represent the cross-section of the Indian masses. In this strategy both the Hindu and Muslim 'traditionalists' found an equally important place under its canopy though they sometimes talked at cross-purposes. But at no point, it may be emphasised, was this strategy implemented at the cost of that ideology which had treated Indian and Hindu nationalism as one and the same thing. For example, the Hindu Mahasabha (meaning the Grand Congregation of the Hindus), which represented the Hindu nationalistic ideology, also found a place in Congress strategy, as Lala Lajpat Rai's prominence in the party demonstrated.

According to hard core Hindu nationalists, however, this all-comprehensive nationalist strategy of the Congress tended to dilute the Hindu thrust of Indian nationalism. In the initial stages, these people thought that the Hindu Mahasabha would rival the Congress claim of speaking on behalf of the Hindus. But in due course they realised that the Hindu Mahasabha would not sufficiently serve their purpose as it had shown the tendency of being co-opted by the Congress, particularly after Mahatma Gandhi had occupied the centre stage of Indian politics in the 1920s. Gandhi's deep devotion to Hindu religion and his determination to give the nationalist movement a strong moral content based on his Hindu upbringing confused these people. The establishment of the Rashtriya Swayamsevak Sangh (meaning National Volunteers Union), or the RSS, in 1925 was an effort to buttress their ideology through this more militant and ideologically clear-headed outfit. The central doctrine of the RSS was 'Hindutva', the concept that the BJP is so closely identified with.

The concept of Hindutva was first articulated by V.D. Savarkar of the Hindu Mahasabha in his book of the same title published in 1923. It encompassed the entire gamut of cultural, social, political and linguistic aspects of Hindu life. There was considerable confusion in the idea, though. For example, while on the one hand it tended to use the words Hindu and Indian interchangeably, on the other hand it differentiated one from the other so sharply that there was hardly any possibility of their ever merging into one single whole. A dissection of the ideology reveals that neither can a Muslim ever become a Hindu (read Indian) because his holy land is beyond the borders of India, nor can an American ever become an Indian citizen (read Hindu) through naturalisation because he does not carry Hindu blood in his veins. Logically, therefore, India should belong to only those whose forefathers were born in India and who had not embraced any faith whose origin could be traced beyond the borders of India. The religions that originated on Indian soil were Hinduism, Buddhism, Jainism and Sikhism. Only their adherents, therefore, were eligible to be called Hindu, read Indian.[1]

---

[1] For a detailed discussion of the concept, see Partha S. Ghosh, *BJP and the Evolution of Hindu Nationalism: From Periphery to Centre*, New Delhi: Manohar, 1999, pp. 64–71.

This theory was fine-tuned by M.S. Golwalkar, who became the head of the RSS in 1940. He gave the organisation a definite purpose and direction. He said: 'The idea contained in the word Nation is the compound of five distinct factors fused into one indissoluble whole: the famous five "Unities"—Geographical (country), Racial (race), Religious (religion), Cultural (culture), and Linguistic (language). India is the land of the Hindus and is the terra firma for the Hindu nation alone to flourish upon.... We must bear in mind that so far as the "nation" is concerned, all those who fall outside the five fold limits of that idea can have no place in the national life, unless they abandon their differences, and completely merge themselves in the National Race.' He added: 'There is a triangular fight. We Hindus are at war at once with the Muslims on the one hand and the British on the other.'[2]

Although the RSS and the Hindu Mahasabha had certain views about nation building based on the preeminence of Hinduism they did not have a clear notion about how to translate it into a politically achievable goal. The RSS anyway was not a political organisation by definition and as such had no defined political agenda. The British did not take much time to understand this reality and increasingly looked upon the Congress to be the representative of the Hindu interests and the Muslim League to be the representative of the Muslim interests. The ostensible idea of course was to divide the nationalist movement vertically on communal lines. To a large extent they also succeeded, as the partition of India proved. There were people in the Congress who did not find the RSS ideology an anathema to their own. For example, during the partition riots when the RSS provided significant humanitarian assistance to Hindu and Sikh refugees it drew praise from no less eminent a Congressman than Sardar Vallabhbhai Patel, the first home minister of independent India. He was so much impressed by the RSS volunteers that he even implored his party to win them over 'with love' and make them join the Congress.

From the above discussion two things emerge. First, despite its emphasis on secularism and composite Indian nationalism the British treated the Congress Party as if it alone represented the Hindu interests. Second, there were important elements in the Congress who did not find it pathologically wrong to have any truck with the Hindu nationalists including the RSS. The situation to come, therefore, was complex. Both the Congress and the BJP were to compete for the same constituency with more or less the same political tools.

Preeminence of the Congress

During the five general elections held in 1952, 1957, 1962, 1967 and 1971, the Congress virtually controlled the politics of the country although in the

---

[2] M. S. Golwalkar, *We and Our Nationhood Defined*, Nagpur: Bharat Publications, 1945, pp. 26, 32, 50–51, 53–56.

Table 9.1: Performance of BJS in Parliamentary Elections (1952–71)

Year	Seats fought	Seats won	Per cent vote
1952	94	3	3.1
1957	130	4	5.9
1962	196	14	6.4
1967	251	35	9.4
1971	157	22	7.4

Source: Subrata Kumar Mitra and Mike Enskat, 'Parties and the People: India's Changing
Party System and the Resilience of Democracy', *Democracy* (Essex), 6(1), Spring
1999, p. 131; and *The Hindu* (New Delhi), 9 April 2000.

elections of 1967 there were straws in the wind pointing to difficult times
ahead for the party. Compared to the Congress, the performance of the BJS
was lacklustre (Table 9.1). This calls for some explanation. Although the
partition of the country and the communal riots that came in its wake had
made the Hindus a natural constituency for the BJS, it could not cash upon
the temper. This was particularly true with the Bengali refugees. But since
they do not fall within the purview of this paper we will not discuss that
dimension here.[3] So far as the Punjabi refugees were concerned, since the
Hindu Mahasabha had already had a strong base in Punjab, the initial constituency of the BJS became these refugees. But that alone was not enough.
The party needed a wider base in the Hindi belt to be of any consequence.
This did not seem to be simple because the Congress tended to appropriate
the BJS platform.

In the Hindi belt the BJS platform included a ban on cow slaughter and an
effort to make Hindi the official language with its anti-Urdu slant, both of
which were projected as parts of the Congress agenda as well, particularly at
the district level.[4] While this was the situation in the 1950s and 1960s, in the
1970s, under the leadership of Indira Gandhi this championing of the Hindu
cause became a wider phenomenon, though under different idioms. The BJS
had to adjust itself to this new challenge. This was evident in its participation in the Janata experiment.

The Janata Experiment

During the 1970s, particularly after the Bangladesh war of 1971 and the First
Oil Shock of 1972, when the economic hardships of the people mounted

[3] See Partha S. Ghosh, 'The Bharatiya Janata Party: Hindu Nationalism versus Compulsions of Pluralism', in Subrata K. Mitra, Mike Enskat and Clamens Spiess (eds), *Political
Parties in South Asia*, Westport, CT: Praeger, 2003.
[4] B.D. Graham, *Hindu Nationalism and Indian Politics: The Origins and Development of the
Bharatiya Jana Sangh*, Cambridge: Cambridge University Press, 1990, p. 256.

severely causing civic protests of various varieties, the Congress found itself more and more cornered. The JP movement (named after its leader Jaya Prakash Narayan, a Gandhian), in which the BJS/RSS activists played an important role, looked like the nemesis for the Congress. To thwart this challenge Indira Gandhi aligned herself with the ideology of Hindu nationalism to bolster her mass appeal. She started making publicised visits to Hindu temples and talking of the rights and fears of the majority community as never before.[5] But before this strategy could fully blossom as it did in the early 1980s she was dislodged from power in the elections of 1977, following 18 months of Emergency rule. This miracle was performed by the Janata Party, a motley group of ideologically diverse political formations in which the BJS, the socialists, former Congress members and others rubbed shoulders. It is not possible to say as to what exact contribution the BJS made in the elections that the Janata Party won with 295 parliamentary seats and 41.3 per cent of the votes. What the experiment, however, proved was that neither was the BJS untouchable as many tended to project nor was the Congress an epitome of secularism as it itself trumpeted. The Muslims totally deserted the Congress for its forcible family planning drive, which at many places was directed particularly towards them.

The Critical Decade of the 1980s

In the race for the heartland, the 1980s was the most critical decade. By the end of 1979 the Janata experiment had collapsed because of its inherent contradictions. The Congress once again seemed to be on the ascendance. Within the erstwhile Janata Party the only faction that seemed to be in a position to take on the Congress was the former BJS. But the situation warranted some change in strategy. One of the causes of the Janata Party's collapse was the controversy over the split loyalty of the BJS faction. The point of contention was whether a Janata Party member could simultaneously remain loyal to the RSS. Following the 1980 elections in which the Congress made a comeback under the leadership of Indira Gandhi, the BJS was revived in April 1980 under a new banner called the Bharatiya Janata Party. Significantly, it allowed its members to retain their RSS tag but did not insist that all its members must owe their loyalty to the RSS. In order to enlarge its mass appeal the party emphasised the Gandhian concept of development. According to the party constitution, BJP was 'committed to nationalism and national integration, democracy, Gandhian Socialism, Positive Secularism, that is, *"Sarva Dharma Samabhav"* [equal respect for all religions] and value based politics'. One may argue that in a society where the numerical strength of

---

[5] Achin Vanaik, 'Communalism and Our Foreign Policy', *Seminar*, 374, October 1990, p. 18.

different religions varies so much the phrase 'equal respect for all religions' effectively meant the negation of minority rights and the promotion of majoritarianism by other means.[6] Still, since the BJP constitution also talked about its 'true faith and allegiance to the Constitution of India as by law established and to the principles of socialism, secularism and democracy', it ipso facto subscribed to the theory of minority rights as enshrined in the Indian Constitution. That way it looked like any other secular party in the country.

Clearly, the political situation was uncertain. Here was a secularist Congress that was showing tendencies to appropriate the advantages of Hindu nationalism while on the other hand there was this Hindu chauvinistic BJP that was increasingly identifying itself with Gandhism thereby diluting its own commitment to the Hindu cause. From this point onwards how the BJP returns to its Hindutva fold in the 1990s is an important story for it tells the efficacy of the 'Hindu vote' for controlling the heartland. But it also exposes the limits of the strategy.

The ascendancy of the Congress during the 1980s was largely attributable to the growing importance of religion in Indian politics. Several events on the national and international scene contributed to this development. With the Iranian revolution in the late 1970s, the most publicised aspect of which was the hostage crisis, there was a resurgence of international Islam. The fallout of this phenomenon was the politicisation of religion all over the world. India was no exception. The Khalistan movement with its thrust on Sikhism and with active support from Pakistan, the Assam agitation behind which was the issue of unauthorised Muslim settlers from Bangladesh, the use of the Hindu card by the Congress in the Jammu and Kashmir elections, the controversy over the Meenakshipuram conversions, the massive Ekatmata Yagna, the assassination of Indira Gandhi by her Sikh bodyguards and the resultant anti-Sikh riots in Delhi, all these happenings in the first half of the 1980s were clear indications of this trend. The massive victory of the Congress in the elections of 1984 demonstrated how the Hindus felt concerned about 'their' nation's territorial integrity which seemed to be endangered by the non-Hindus whether they were the Sikhs of Punjab, the Muslims of Kashmir, the Christians of the northeast, or the Muslim settlers in Assam. Notably, all these regions were in the bordering areas of the country.

The BJP did not take much time to realise that the illusory 'Hindu vote' that it unsuccessfully chased for decades had ultimately materialised. But when it actually did, the Congress grabbed it. Its own strategy of broad basing its support with an emphasis on Gandhian *anytodaya* failed miserably as the results of the 1984 parliamentary elections demonstrated. It captured

---

[6] See Neera Chandhoke, *Beyond Secularism: The Rights of Religious Minorities*, New Delhi: Oxford University Press, 1999. See also her 'The Illusions of Formal Equality', *The Hindu*, 2 May 2000.

only two seats with 7.68 per cent votes. The party looked for a new idiom which its president L.K. Advani provided as soon as he took charge of the party in 1986. He said: 'If anyone were to ask me which is the most distinctive trait of BJP's personality, I would say that BJP is the voice of unalloyed nationalism. Ours is a "Nation-First" party. It aspires to be the heartbeat of India.'[7] He denounced cow slaughter and the destruction of as many as 45 Hindu temples in Kasmir although it was not wholly true. He declared that 'for many politicians, and political parties, secularism has become only a euphemism for political appeasement of minority sections, which tend to vote *en bloc*. These politicians unabashedly propound the thesis that there is no such thing as minority communalism.'[8] It was obvious that his target of attack was none other than the Congress.

In the race for the 'Hindu vote', the Congress could not have matched the BJP rhetoric. It had two handicaps. In the earlier decades it could play with two balls simultaneously taking advantage from both. On the one hand, at the macro level, it projected its image as a secularist party, which effectively meant equi-proximity with the traditionalist elements of all religions. This was reflected, for example, in its decision to go slow on implementing a Uniform Civil Code. On the other hand, at the micro level, it talked about banning cow slaughter and preventing Urdu from assuming comparative importance with Hindi, as we have mentioned earlier. But this dual strategy was now under threat from the BJP. So far as the macro strategy was concerned, the BJP onslaught against its 'pseudo secularism' was increasingly receiving mass support. The Congress was in a dilemma. If it went whole hog in favour of the Hindus it might alienate the minorities which had traditionally supported the party. If it did not do so, the BJP was waiting in the wings to take advantage of the situation by making further inroads into the Hindu vote bank. At the micro level also the party could not match the BJP. While the latter had an in-built cadre base amongst such Hindu chauvinistic outfits as the RSS, the VHP and the Bajrang Dal, the Congress had virtually no cadre. Its over dependence upon central leaders, particularly from the days of Indira Gandhi in the early 1970s, had destroyed the organisation almost totally at the grassroot level.

It was against this background that two controversies came in handy for the BJP, one was the Babri mosque issue and the other was the Shah Bano case. By the end of the 1980s, the Hindutva forces had become confident that the Babri controversy would split all parties vertically. It was the claim of the VHP that 'we have now decided to create a strong [Hindu] vote bank on our seven point demand'. It challenged all parties by saying that those who

[7] Manini Chatterjee, 'Seeds of Fascism', *Seminar*, 399, November 1992, p. 20.
[8] Yogendra K. Malik and V. B. Singh, *Hindu Nationalists in India: The Rise of the Bharatiya Janata Party*, New Delhi: Vistaar, 1994, p. 76.

would support and work for these demands would get these votes. The BJP indeed was the most serious contender. In its National Executive meeting held in June 1989, the party officially demanded that the temple controversy should be decided in favour of the Hindus. Earlier, in April 1989, while addressing a mammoth RSS meeting in Mumbai, Vajpayee asked to hand over the mosque site to the Hindus.[9] Similarly, on the Shah Bano case also, the BJP was able to project the decision of the Rajiv Gandhi government to undo the Supreme Court verdict in favour of the traditionalist Muslims as a retrograde step to appease the Muslims. It took the opportunity to harp on the necessity of a Uniform Civil Code as a progressive move for the social integration of the nation.

That BJP's accent on Hindutva paid its dividends at the cost of the Congress was visible in the electoral results. From two parliamentary seats and 7.5 per cent votes in 1984, it improved its performance to 86 seats and 11.5 per cent votes in 1989. Correspondingly, the Congress tally fell from 415 seats and 48 per cent votes to 197 seats and 39.5 per cent votes, respectively.

Consolidation Drive

Following the 1989 elections, a coalition government was set up with V.P. Singh as the prime minister. The BJP was a partner in the coalition but decided to support the government without participating in it. Seemingly, its ambition was to buy time to consolidate its gains. The opportunity as well as the stimulus came when the V.P. Singh government decided in 1990 to implement the decade-old Mandal Commission Report to provide reservations in jobs to the Other Backward Classes (OBCs). Since the plan had the potential of dividing the Hindu community vertically between the upper and lower castes which was going to destroy the BJP's hard-earned Hindu vote-bank the party saw an inherent danger in the Mandalisation of Indian politics. To counter the political threat, in August 1990, L.K. Advani decided to launch his so-called *rath yatra*,[10] a march from Somnath in Gujarat to Ayodhya in UP,[11]

---

[9] Dagmar Markova, 'Babar's Mosque versus Ram's Birthplace: A Case Study of Misuse of Religion', *Archiv Orientalni* (Prague), 59(3), 1991, pp. 271–73.

[10] *Yatra*, a Sanskrit word, means journey. Prefixed with *teertha* it means pilgrimage. The use of *yatra* in this context was symbolic and evocative, since in popular parlance it evokes the pious memory of pilgrimage.

[11] The political significance of the two places and the sites must be underlined here. Somnath is the site of an ancient temple of Lord Shiva. The temple was plundered and ravaged several times by Mahmud of Ghazni during his campaigns on India in the 11th century. Sardar Vallabhbhai Patel, first deputy prime minister of independent India took it upon himself to rebuild the temple and restore its glory. The BJP had used the case of Somnath to plead its case for Ram temple in Ayodhya; arguing that as the Somnath temple was rebuilt at the initiative of the deputy prime minister of India, so should the construction of the Ram temple be permitted by the Government of India. The carefully

through 10 states, in a Japanese jeep improvised to look like an ancient Indian chariot used in battle. The march was supposed to reach Ayodhya on 30 October 1990 to start the construction work for the Ram temple at the Babri mosque site. Although the march was aborted as Advani was arrested in Bihar, his followers continued with the march. Ultimately, there was police firing on the marchers and the event ended with several casualties. Following this the BJP withdrew its support to the V.P. Singh government as a result of which the government fell on 16 November 1990.

While the BJP was consolidating its Hindu votebank, the Congress was in search of its base which was constantly in the process of eroding. The Bofors scandal, which had contributed in a big way to the debacle of the party in the 1989 elections, still cast its shadow on its fortunes. On the Mandal issue too on which every party was taking a clear position thereby consolidating its support base, the Congress appeared to be ambivalent. So much was the disarray that had it not been the assassination of its popular leader Rajiv Gandhi during the course of the 1991 elections it would have fared very badly. As almost half the number of constituencies went to the polls after the tragedy the sympathy wave made some significant difference in favour of the party. Still, in terms of overall result, it lost further ground. In 1989 it had polled 39.5 per cent votes but in 1991 it polled only 36.6 per cent. But in a strange quirk of multi-party democracy it raised its tally from 197 to 244. Compared to this, BJP's growing strength was noticeable. From 86 parliamentary seats and 11.5 per cent votes in the 1989 elections it improved its position to 120 seats and 20.1 per cent votes in 1991. Barring Himachal Pradesh, its gain was in the entire Hindi heartland (Table 9.2). There was hardly any doubt that this gain was largely on account of the Ram temple

Table 9.2: Vote Share of BJP in Hindi States (1989 and 1991 elections)

State	1989	1991
Bihar	11.7	16.0
Haryana	8.3	10.2
Himachal Pradesh	45.3	42.8
Madhya Pradesh	39.7	41.9
Rajasthan	29.6	40.9
Uttar Pradesh	7.6	32.8
Delhi	26.2	40.2

Source: David Butler, Ashok Lahiri and Prannay Roy, *India Decides: Elections, 1952–91*, New Delhi: Living Media, 1991; *Report on the Tenth General Election, 1991*, New Delhi: Election Commission, 1991.

crafted *yatra*, or the political pilgrimage, of L.K. Advani, therefore, was symbolic in more than one sense. By craftily mixing several layers of past into the present, the party had attempted a political mix that was conveying several messages to the voter.

agitation and the tirade against the so-called 'minorityism'. Opinion polls conducted in early 1991 showed that 42 to 54 per cent of Hindus in northern and eastern India endorsed Advani's indictment of 'minorityism' and his party's stand on the Ayodhya dispute.[12]

The Decisive Push

Following the elections a Congress government headed by P.V. Narasimha Rao was installed in Delhi but a major part of the heartland went to its rival. Bharatiya Janata Party governments were formed in Himachal Pradesh, MP, Rajasthan and UP. The last mentioned was particularly important being the most crucial state in Indian politics. For the first time since independence, the governments at the Centre and UP belonged to competing parties. The situation was now ripe for the final encounter. Taking advantage of the situation that the BJP ruled UP, the party brought the temple controversy to a head on 6 December 1992 when the Babri mosque was demolished by a mob belonging to the Hindutva *parivar*, which included some top BJP leaders, most notably, Advani, Murli Manohar Joshi and Uma Bharati. The Rao government at the Centre, which had intelligence reports suggesting what was going to happen on that fateful day, did little to prevent it from happening. Later, it justified its inaction by arguing that the Central Reserve Police which was stationed some distance from the Babri mosque could have been requisitioned only by the order of the state government, which the latter did not do. Under the circumstances, there was nothing that could prevent the demolition.

A question that can be legitimately asked is whether the demolition really helped the BJP to better its electoral prospects in the heartland. If one goes by results of the Assembly polls that followed, one would agree that it did not. In November 1993, all the above mentioned four states plus the newly created Delhi semi-state went to elect their Assemblies. In Delhi the BJP won handsomely (49 seats out of 70), but in all the remaining states, its performance was below expectations. Barring Rajasthan, where it formed the government as a majority party but without winning half the number of seats, in all the remaining three states, where it had ruled prior to the polls, it lost out to the opposition. In UP it remained the majority party but the government was formed by a coalition of the Samajwadi Party (SP) and the Bahujan Samaj Party (BSP) which earned the support of almost all the non-BJP opposition including the Congress and the Janata Dal. In Himachal Pradesh and Madhya Pradesh, the Congress formed the government.

These results, however, did not reveal the whole truth. Apparently, BJP's Hindutva ideology did not work. But if one looks at the percentage of votes

---

[12] For details of these polls, see Swapan Dasgupta, 'Battle for Ram: Issue is the Denial of the Temple', *The Times of India* (New Delhi), 15 April 1991.

polled, one would see that the BJP gained further ground. Barring Himachal Pradesh where its percentage dropped, in the remaining three states and Delhi it gained. In all five states put together, it polled 36.18 per cent as against the Congress's 26.24 per cent. The fact that the BJP failed to make good in terms of Members of the Legislative Assembly (MLAs), was more due to tactical voting on the part of the minorities and not due to any loss of its popularity. The BJP, however, realised that while the Congress had lost its popularity amongst the Muslims and the lower-caste Hindus, the same had not come to its fold. The real gainers were the SP and the BSP. The BJP's strategy was, therefore, to woo these groups without of course causing any damage to its Hindutva base.[13] It was a difficult tightrope walk for the BJP because the Congress too vied for these very votes. The 1996 elections showed the direction of the political winds.

The Elections of 1996, 1998 and 1999

In three years between 1996 and 1999, three general elections were held, which showed the fragility of coalition governments in India and the shifting political loyalties of the parties. In the elections of 1996, no party won an absolute majority in Parliament. The BJP with its tally of 161 seats emerged as the single largest party. In terms of popular votes it registered a swing of 1.2 per cent in its favour compared to the 1991 elections. In 1991, it had received 20.1 per cent votes; in 1996 it got 21.34 per cent. In comparison, the performance of the Congress was worse compared to the 1991 elections. It won 140 seats and 28.8 per cent votes in 1996 as against 244 seats and 36.6 per cent in the 1991 elections. In the elections of 1998, the BJP won 182 seats and 25.6 per cent votes and the Congress 141 seats and 26.4 per cent votes. The Congress was systematically on the decline, while the BJP was on the ascendancy. This tendency was reinforced in the elections of 1999. While the BJP retained its position in Parliament with 182 seats the Congress figure fell to 114. One must not read too much into the fact that the BJP's percentage of votes fell from 25.6 in 1998 to 23.8 in 1999. It may be noted that under some electoral arrangements with other parties the BJP contested only 339 seats in 1999 as against 388 seats in 1998. So far as the Congress and its allies were concerned, they contested for 453 seats, won 114 seats and garnered 28.3 per cent votes in 1999, as against the Congress's earlier performance of 26.4 per cent votes in the 1998 elections. For the detailed break-up of the party position in the 1999 elections, see Table 9.3.

---

[13] For more on this point, see Ghosh, *BJP and the Evolution of Hindu Nationalism*, pp. 102–14.

Table 9.3: Tally of Seats by Political Parties and Alliances, 1999 Elections

BJP+	Seats	Congress+	Seats	Others	Seats
BJP	182	Congress	114	CPI (M)	33
Shiv Sena	15	RJD	7	CPI	4
JD (U)	21	AIADMK	10	AIFB	2
SAD	2	JMM	0	RSP	3
TDP	27	KC	1	CPIML (L)	1
Trinamool Congress	8	ML	2	NCP	8
BJD	10	RPI (P)	0	RPI (A)	0
NC	4	UMFA	0	JD (S)	1
PMK	5	Others	4	BSP	14
DMK	12	**Total**	**138**	HVC	1
MDMK	4			AGP	0
HVP	1			MNF	0
Lok Dal	5			SJP	1
Loktantric Congress	1			JP	0
Jantrantric BSP	0			SDF	1
AC (Apang)	0			SP	26
Others	4			TMC	0
Total	**301**			TUJS	0
				UDP	0
				Independents	5
				Others	4
				Total	**104**

Source: Yogesh Atal, *Mandate for Political Transition: Reemergence of Vajpayee*, Jaipur: Rawat, 2000, p. 237.

Social Base

What accounts for the BJP's rise and the Congress's decline in the heartland? The changing social identifications can provide some clue. Traditionally, the BJP in the form of its precursor BJS, was known as a 'baniya' party, connoting that it was the party of small traders and *petit* bourgeoisie. The popular base of the BJS consisted of this class that was mainly concentrated amongst the refugees from West Pakistan. In addition, there were also sections of the landed aristocracy of Punjab who owed their allegiance to the ideology of the Hindu Mahasabha. It was on account of this narrow base, in addition to the causes mentioned earlier, that the BJS could not perform well at the polls. This was in spite of the fact that the RSS had provided the necessary manpower required for the purposes of electioneering in a mass democracy like India.

The situation, however, has changed. The BJP's popular base is much wider now and it draws its support from almost all social groups of the country although in some regions it is still in the periphery. A national survey of the political mood conducted in the mid-1990s by the Delhi-based Centre for the Study of Developing Societies (CSDS) revealed that the BJP and its electoral allies had a sizable base in almost all social classes. Where it

Table 9.4: Social base of the BJP and allies (Samata Party, Shiv Sena and the Haryana Vikas Party) and the Congress and allies (AIADMK), 1996

	BJP	Congress
All India Average	24.8	27.4
Rural	22.7	28.1
Urban	32.0	25.2
Men	26.7	27.4
Women	23.0	27.6
Hindu	28.7	26.1
Muslim	3.1	35.1
Christian	3.7	42.9
Sikh	14.2	18.1
Scheduled Castes	14.4	31.6
Scheduled Tribes	20.3	40.1
OBCs	23.1	21.8
Upper Castes	33.2	27.2

Source: Subrata Kumar Mitra and Mike Enskat, 'Parties and the People: India's Changing Party System and the Resilience of Democracy', *Democracy* (Essex), 6(1), Spring 1999, p. 135.

failed miserably to make any dent were the Christians and the Muslims, and to some extent, even the Scheduled Castes (SCs). This would particularly make sense if one compares these figures with those of the Congress and the National Front (NF), the two other national parties or alliance systems in 1996. While the Congress had bases in all social groups the NF had visibly stronger bases amongst the Muslims and the OBCs. If one compares the BJP with these two forces it would be seen that the BJP certainly had a better claim to call itself a national party only next to the Congress (Table 9.4).

Limits of Hindutva

When the Congress dominated Indian politics, it did so by a clever mix of several ideologies and interest articulations which Rajni Kothari character-ised as the 'Congress system'. The decline of the Congress is attributable to the fact that from Indira Gandhi onwards this balance was destroyed. She concentrated all the powers in herself. Several leaders of group identities felt marginalised, which led to the formation of new parties with specific ethnic or group agendas. Some of her policies pursued in a highhanded manner, such as the family planning drive during the mid-1970s, alienated sections of the Muslims too. All this made a dent in the Congress's support base, which could not be compensated by its newly found strategy to woo Hindu senti-ments. The Hindu appeal has logic, and it works, but it has its limits too. Even the BJP has started realising this. There are visible indications that it is trying to augment its mass base amongst the Muslims and the SCs although so far there has not been any indication to do so in respect of the Christians.

238 Partha S. Ghosh

The reasons could be that Christians, in the first place, are small in number (2.34 per cent according to the 1991 Census), and two, they are mostly concentrated in the northeastern states and Kerala; in neither of the places does the BJP have much hope of making quick political inroads. On the contrary, the recent attacks on some of the religious leaders of the community by known or unknown Hindu zealots may make the task more difficult.

The BJP is trying hard to enlist the support of the SCs. In the Marathwada University renaming controversy of 1994, the party took a clear pro-SC stand even at the cost of its relationship with its ideological partner, the Shiv Sena. In the same year, it protested unequivocally against the Supreme Court judgement (November 1992) that stated that reservation for the SCs and Scheduled Tribes (STs) pertained only to their recruitment and not to their promotions. The BJP has reiterated this stand: 'The rules and regulations governing promotions for the SCs and STs would be further liberalised paving the way for quick and just promotions in Government jobs and merit would not be the only consideration. We should not forget that we are dealing with that section of society which has faced criminal neglect over the past five decades and now things have to be set right.'[14] The party's general secretary and one of the leading ideologues, K.N. Govindacharya, had even tried to conceptualise this pro-SC stand within the overall rubric of Hindutva. He argued that the awakening of the SCs was a positive sign in Indian politics and the BJP must change its outlook, character and temperament to take advantage of this phenomenon. He advised the party cadres to drive home the message that Hindutva did not mean the return to Brahmanical order, rather the opposite. 'In fact', he explained, 'the real life of an Indian citizen is to be governed by the Indian constitution and not by *Manusmriti* or any other religious text.' He said that 'the rise of the dalit [SCs] power will eventually merge with the larger entity of Hindutva for the well-being of the whole society'.[15] The making of Bangaru Laxman, a dalit, as the BJP president was a move in the same direction.

In respect of the Muslims, the BJP's efforts are subtle. To start with, the party promises the community 'genuine secularism' thereby meaning that their patron, the Congress, had given them only lip service in the name of secularism without doing anything tangible for their uplift. The hidden message is that once they came to the BJP fold their interests would be protected better. That the idea contradicts the party's allegation against the Congress of 'pampering the Muslims' seems to be of little consequence. On the eve of the 1996 elections, it created a Minorities Cell within the party which prepared a comprehensive package offering the Muslims *taaleem* (education), *tanzeem* (organisation) and *tijarat* (employment). It organised Muslim conventions at various places and

[14] *The Hindu* (New Delhi), 18 April 2000.
[15] *The Times of India* (New Delhi), 27 December 1993.

toned down its rhetoric about the re-conversion of mosques into temples. Evidently, nothing worked to register the support of the community, which even Atal Behari Vajpayee conceded.[16] The BJP's image as an anti-Muslim party is too deep to be obliterated by these sops and before any real change occurs, either of the following two things must happen. The party must change its ideological orientation, or, its record of governance must point in that direction. Neither of these is visible at the moment.

In the given scenario, to remain in power, therefore, the party would have to contend with its essentially urban and upper-caste Hindu base and depend on its regional allies. But even to do that it would have to make compromises on the Hindutva front. No ideology is sacrosanct. Compulsions of power seeking and power wielding are different. The same ideology that the BJP has used to come to power is increasingly becoming a liability for the party and the Vajpayee government is realising this. As a result, the undercurrents of conflict between the BJP as a party on the one hand, and the other constituents of the Hindutva family on the other, are increasingly surfacing. To understand this phenomenon two factors should be taken into account, one, BJP's dependence on other political parties as well as on all those leaders who have joined it of late, and two, its traditional connection with Hindutva. Both are important for the party and they need delicate balancing. An appeal to Hindu sentiments helps but for that the RSS, the VHP, etc., do not necessarily serve the purpose. On the contrary, the overt display of that sentiment as reflected in the anti-'Water' violence, the anti-Pope agitation, the killing of Father Staines and his children and the subsequent controversy over conversion, and so on, becomes a liability for the party. Given the plurality of the Hindu religion a pro-Hindutva understatement is more appealing to the masses than tom-toming it. If the backward caste movement is a permanent fixture in Indian politics ever since V.P. Singh has Mandalised it, so is the 'Hindu vote' a reality in Indian politics ever since BJP has given it political respectability. But that 'Hindu vote' alone, say, 25 per cent, is not sufficient to ensure that the BJP remains in power. More important is that crucial 25 per cent plus which is available only in the turf of other parties. If BJP identifies too much with the RSS-VHP variety of Hindutva it would not only alienate its partners in the National Democratic Alliance (NDA) but also those non-RSS BJP members for they would be reduced to second class members in the party. The danger is so real that it may rend, leave alone NDA, even the BJP, asunder. Even L.K. Advani and Murli Manohar Joshi, the two most important leaders after Vajpayee, and who are otherwise staunch Hindutva champions, seem to be adapting themselves to this hard reality. Vajpayee has done it already.

---

[16] *The Asian Age* (New Delhi), 15 April 1996.

Is Congress a Spent Force?

However one may think that the Congress's political prospects are finished forever, it is probably still premature to write it off. Two things might go in its favour. One, the continued misgovernance of the motley regime in power might make people think once again that probably the Congress was a better bet. Two, unlike many other parties, there is no leadership controversy in the Congress. Sonia Gandhi might be lacking in experience and leadership quality, she at least commands the unflinching loyalty of her party men as the contest for presidentship with Jitendra Prasada has shown. The fact that she has the tag of the Nehru-Gandhi family cannot be underestimated either. Over and above this, because of her foreign origin and Nehru-Gandhi mantle, she is above the caste squabbles of Indian politics giving her the advantage of not identifying with any social group thereby making her acceptable to many, cutting across all social divides. These advantages would come to the fore the moment the present regime makes some gross political mistake thereby giving the Congress an opportunity to make political capital out of it.

Party System in Perspective

It is elementary political science that a strong party system is the best warranty for a successful democracy. It is equally elementary that a strong party system must mean nationally based parties, and within each party, an inner party democracy. The party organisation should be federally structured, the lowest unit being the district. The process of succession should be orderly. The charisma of the party leader is important, but not everything. And last, but not the least, there must be a programme of action for development. To what extent do the BJP and the Congress qualify the test?

The credentials of BJP (read with BJS) as a national party are strong. It was as early as the first general elections of 1952 that the party was recognised as one along with the Congress, the Socialist Party, the Kisan Mazdoor Praja Party (KMPP), and the Communist Party of India (CPI). The criterion was that a party must secure 3 per cent votes; BJS secured 3.1 per cent. This share has grown over the years and now it is in the range of about 25 per cent. But there is an important element that should also be taken into account to brand a party as a national party, namely, a broad-based social and regional support. There are certain groups amongst which the BJP has virtually no base at all, viz., the Muslims and the Christians. Similarly, there are certain regions, such as the northeast, south, and, to some extent, east, where it has very limited support. If the party wants to become a national party in the true sense these gaps would have to be filled.

In terms of the above checklist, the Congress has a better claim to be called a national party. At the moment its chips are down but its social and regional spread is wide. In the heartland area it is facing the biggest challenge ever, as caste alignments have left it in the lurch. But the contours might change. Still, in all probability, it cannot make it to power all by itself. Only as a leading coalition partner can it do so.

So far as inner party democracy is concerned BJP has reason to boast of having one. Organisational elections are held regularly and there is no dynastic contagion that has afflicted the Congress. The regular change of guard ever since the formation of the BJS proves the point. But here a caveat has to be entered. It has been seen that all the BJP presidents have owed their loyalty to the RSS. Now that a large number of members have joined the party without any explicit allegiance to the RSS it is to be seen whether the same criterion would continue to apply. If it does, then one would have to reconsider one's premises about the party's commitment to inner party democracy. So far as the Congress is concerned, its inner party democracy is a sham. But strangely, the party has lived with it for more than a hundred years and it still does not mind it. What is generally noticeable is that all parties, including the Congress and the BJP, are increasingly behaving like bureaucracies the underlying characteristic of which is hierarchy in which the high command decides everything including the state leadership questions. The latest example is the way the Congress handled the Chattisgarh chief-ministerial issue and the BJP those of Jharkhand and Uttaranchal.

With regard to the leadership criterion, the record of the Congress is well known. Its dependence on the Nehru-Gandhi family is total and the rise of Narasimha Rao was an exception that proved the rule. The record of the BJP on this count is mixed. It passes the test well so far as smooth leadership transition is concerned. In the last 50 years of its existence (read with the BJS), it has seen as many as 14 faces at the helm. Moreover, so far, there have been only four leaders who have held the office of the president for more than one term. But there is an unhealthy trend as well, and that is BJP's over-dependence on Vajpayee. He has not only held the presidency for as many as 10 years but he has been projected as the prime ministerial candidate during all the last three elections—1996, 1998 and 1999—purely for the purposes of vote gathering and matching the Congress's leadership charisma trump. But, as one scholar notes, 'experience round the world shows that charisma succeeds over substance and good policies only to a limited extent and for a limited period'.[17] The BJP better take note of this.

A related desirability is that the prime minister should avoid becoming the party boss as well. That has a tendency to breed centralisation of power within the party as was the case with the Congress. Such a centralising tendency can ensure the stability of the government by bringing the party

[17] Ajay K. Mehra, 'Political Parties and Party System in India', in D.D. Khanna and Gert W. Kueck (eds), *Principles, Power and Politics*, New Delhi: Macmillan, 1999, p. 246.

and the government in harmony, but an inevitable fall-out of the process is the growth of factionalism. Each faction tries to be in the good books of the 'high command' for favour and influence, which starts with the distribution of party tickets to contest elections. The BJP's record in this regard is better but how long it will remain so is a moot point. Like any other Indian party it too has factions and that is despite the fact that the party president and the prime minister are two different people. Newspapers are rife with stories of factionalism in the party units of Gujarat, Madhya Pradesh, Rajasthan and Uttar Pradesh.

So far as the national programme is concerned, the Congress is more accommodative whereas the BJP is more particularistic with clear notions about nation building and national security. Most of the programmes of the BJP such as the question of a Uniform Civil Code or the abolition of Article 370 and complete absorption of Jammu and Kashmir are nationalistic in their orientation, but there is an inherent divisive element in them. Earlier, it stood for certain divisive policies, such as, building the Ram temple at the Babri mosque site, making Hindi the national language, and banning cow slaughter. Lately, however, these are being down played so as not to prick the sensitivities of certain sections of the population. Compulsions of power are increasingly drawing the party to a more universally acceptable agenda even at the cost of certain ideas the party held so dearly all these years. What would happen to that agenda if the party comes to power all by itself without depending upon its partners in the NDA is a situation to be watched.

Conclusion

The BJP has created a niche for itself in the heartland largely at the cost of the Congress. The segments that it has failed to penetrate into because of its sectional base, it is trying to compensate through its NDA partners. From that sense, if the NDA in some form or the other remains in existence with BJP as the leading partner, it would not be surprising if in due course it becomes the 'NDA system' of the 'Congress system' vintage. It is, therefore, possible to visualise Indian polity essentially in a two-party framework—one consisting of the Congress and its allies and the other consisting of the BJP and its allies. The chances of a third front to succeed are dim, at least in the near future. At the moment the only problem seems to be BJP's narrowly focused nation-building strategy. But it may be surmised that its living together with the NDA partners would increasingly mellow that outlook in favour of a broad-based strategy. In any case, Hindu nationalism, because of the very structure of Hinduism, has its limits and the BJP has realised this. This is reflected in its growing efforts to woo the Muslims, dalits and the OBCs. What was bound to happen has happened, and, therefore, that day is not far when the BJP would accomplish the historic mission of emerging as an alternative to the Congress. In India, that seems to be the only model that could work.[18]

The Congress should not at all be written off. Since its social and regional bases are still much broader than the BJP, it has the potential to provide the nucleus for an anti-BJP front. Too much importance should not be attached to the issue of inner party democracy, for almost all the Indian political parties are hierarchical bureaucracies with one dominant leader who matters the most. The BJP, therefore, may underestimate the Sonia factor to its own peril. She has two distinct political advantages, namely, one, her non-casteist image, and two, her non-communal image. Both have their base in her Nehru pedigree.

But the larger question is whether the heartland would remain the epicentre of power or not. The way technology is moving and the way other parts of India, most notably the south and the west, are taking advantage of it, thereby occupying the centre stage of development, that time is not far when the Hindi heartland would lose its shine. What impact it would have on Indian politics is difficult to predict. Already there are straws in the wind pointing to a regional divide. Tamil Nadu has forced the prime minister to order a freeze on the delimitation of parliamentary constituencies as the differential family planning record of the south and north is going to lead to a mismatch of political and economic development in the nation. The creation of several new states within the heartland also may adversely affect the political power that the area hitherto enjoyed.

[18] I have elaborated this point in 'Election 1999: Whither Indian Polity?', *Economic and Political Weekly* (Mumbai), 34(48), 27 November 1999, pp. 3340–42.

10

THE THIRD FRONT OR THE THIRD FORCE

A POLITICAL MAZE OR AN IDEOLOGICAL OASIS?

Bidyut Chakrabarty

The Third Front, also referred to as the Third Force, defines itself as an ideological alternative (sic) to the two contemporary major political formations in Indian politics, represented by the two major political parties, the Indian National Congress (INC) and the Bharatiya Janata Party (BJP).[1] Both these nomenclatures are used interchangeably to describe the conglomeration that owes its birth and sustenance to a perceived political space different from what the Congress and the BJP presently occupy.

The history of what is today known as the Third Front goes back to the formation of the Janata Party in 1977, the quickfix party formed soon after Mrs Indira Gandhi dissolved the fifth Lok Sabha and announced the sixth general elections. To put the discussion in appropriate politico-historical context, it deserves to be recalled that many of the political formations and actors both within the BJP-led National Democratic Alliance (NDA), including the BJP's forerunner Bharatiya Jan Sangh, and those with the proposed Third Front, were a part of it. The Communist Party of India (Marxist) (CPI [M]) supported it from outside. The same set of formations and actors supported

---

[1] In recent times, the idea of a third alternative was mooted by the four former premiers—V.P. Singh, Chandrashekhar, H.D. Deve Gowda and I.K. Gujral—who, in April 2000, proposed the formation of a front of 'secular' forces to combat both the Congress and the BJP. What was immediately necessary, as Deve Gowda suggested in an interview with the author (in August 2000), was a third front because of 'the failure of the recognised opposition, viz., the Congress, to contain the communal BJP'. In other words, what is needed now is to create 'a political forum' of those forces which are opposed to the Congress and the BJP. Similar feelings were expressed by the CPI (M) in its recently concluded Thiruvananthapuram plenum (October 2000). According to the octogenarian CPI (M) leader Jyoti Basu, the third left democratic alternative to the BJP-led National Democratic Alliance was 'the only option to save India's secular-democratic fabric'. Ideologically, the CPI (M) wants, adds Basu, 'to form a Front sans the BJP and the Congress'. Jyoti Basu's press statement in *The Times of India*, 23 October 2000.

V.P. Singh's Janata Dal (JD) in the 1989 general elections, including the left parties and the BJP, which proved its nemesis 11 months later. While the BJP went alone in these elections, which witnessed the INC losing power for the second time at the Centre since independence, the alternative Centre led by JD and the left parties formed the National Front (NF), which Rajiv Gandhi arrogantly described as national affront. However, till then it was only politics of anti-Congressism, to which the left, the centre (JD et al.) and the right (BJP) alike subscribed. The 13th general elections in 1996 changed the political arithmetic as the BJP emerged as a political force ready to challenge the Congress. As it lost the crucial opportunity to remain united as the United Front (UF) during 1996–98 after the 11th general elections and hold on to power, and the Congress lost the crucial chance twice to forge a new political future by supporting the centre-left political space, these political formations have been desperately trying to create and consolidate the political space they have gifted away. The task has been made difficult by the fact that many of the ardent supporters of the centre-left political space have grabbed the political opportunity to join the political bandwagon of the BJP.[2]

Although the label 'front' may not be conceptually apt to describe the Third Front experiments in India given its amorphous character due largely to diametrically opposite predilections of the constituents, the description is nonetheless a broad indicator of the political character of those 'forces' seeking to capture and consolidate the 'third space' of an 'alternative' other than the Congress and BJP. That the political outfits experimenting with political convergence clearly remained amorphous 'forces' rather than a compositely organised front is evident in their quick disintegration over 'trivial' issues which could easily have been amicably sorted out had there been broad ideological agreement among the constituents. The failure of those parties— which sought to form an alternative on the basis of a negative agenda of anti-Congressism and anti-BJPism—to rise above the parochial considerations of caste and region largely accounted for its failure to take off more than once as a challenging political force. In a highly competitive democratic environment, where the hitherto neglected socio-economic groups have acquired political salience, but have not been represented in the prevailing party system adequately due to paradoxical political compulsions, the Third Force claims a natural political space. Presumably because it has brought those issues to the surface which both the Congress and the BJP have perennially neglected, probably to avoid a major shake-up either in the prevailing socio-economic set up, or in their ideological vision.

Drawing upon the sentiments opposing both the major parties, this conglomeration appears to be the best possible way of organising disparate socio-political

---

[2] This political band includes such luminaries as R.K. Hegde, Sharad Yadav, Ram Vilas Paswan, etc.

forums with a broad ideological affinity among them. Although what brings them together and sustains their 'unity' is their opposition to both the Congress and BJP, the emergence of the Front is nonetheless a significant political intervention highlighting those intricate socio-economic and political processes in which the hitherto peripheral segments of society figure prominently. Notwithstanding the growing importance of the Third Force in Indian politics in recent years, it has, so far, failed to emerge as a stable political formation due to reasons connected with its composition and the circumstances exposing its fragility as a structure that is neither ideologically homogeneous nor united with a common agenda. Nonetheless, the experiment is refreshing and intellectually stimulating for having drawn our attention away from the stereotypical assumptions regarding Indian politics to those factors and considerations highlighting the slow but steady changes at the grassroots. Both the Congress and the BJP appear to be inadequate in articulating, leave alone representing, the demands of the 'new' social groups presumably because of their conventionally projected ideological tilt in favour of 'partisan' interests.

The Third Force is not a mere conglomeration of parties, it is rather a search for a political platform, seemingly left out by the Congress and the BJP. Equally, it appears to be a quest for a space that has been time and again abdicated by the players who are seeking it. Although its past record may not be impressive, the Third Force is nonetheless a potentially challenging structure especially in view of its well-directed effort at organising the marginalised socio-economic groups. One has, however, to be careful in making this statement since not all the constituents of the Third Force have an equal acceptability among the target groups. For instance, the success of the Samajwadi Party in Uttar Pradesh (UP) or that of the CPI (M) in West Bengal may not correspond with the track record of other partners. Despite being confined to specific regions, both the CPI (M) and the Samajwadi Party appear to have provided the necessary ideological back-up striving to unite those with essentially anti-Congress and anti-BJP stances. Not only is the Third Force theoretically challenging, it is also a viable alternative structure drawing sustenance from the dissenting voices against the so-called stable ideological formations, articulated by the Congress and the BJP. The aim of this chapter is therefore twofold: first, there will be an attempt to grasp the phenomenon in its historical context, and second, to assess its potential within the available explanatory tools of analysis.

The context and its historical role

Politics in India is undergoing a dramatic metamorphosis. Indian democracy is acquiring a vibrant mass character as the hitherto marginalised and underprivileged groups seek a space in the political process through active participation. At the same time, old political equations are rapidly changing, shaking the party system from its roots. Not surprisingly, a new era of coalition politics has begun.[3] What appears to be crucial in this process is not the 'ideological purity' but 'the exigency of the situation'. Parties with a clearly defined ideology seem inclined to form a coalition with the avowed object of challenging, if not resisting, a worse political 'foe'. Significant in this configuration is the formidable presence of the regional parties which hold, on occasions, the key to the very survival of the coalition.[4]

The beginning of the decline of the old parties effectively coincided with the beginning of the historic decline of the 'Congress system'[5] from the late

---

[3] This new trend began with the 1967 elections in which the Congress lost power in a majority of Indian provinces. The transition from Congress hegemony to 'multipartyism' has made coalition government inevitable. See N.C.B. Ray Chaudhury, 'The Politics of India's Coalitions', The Political Quarterly, 40(3), July–September 1969, pp. 296–306; Ajay K. Mehra, 'Coalition-making in India—Imperatives, Disincentives and Pitfalls', in Lakshmi Krishnamurthi, R. Hariharan and Gert W. Kueck (eds), Making Success of Coalitions, Chennai: East West Books (Madras) Ltd., 2000, pp. 77–94; and Ajay Mehra, 'Functioning of Coalition Cabinets: Pressures, Constraints and Compulsions', in M.P. Singh and Rekha Saxena (eds), Ideologies and Institutions in Indian Politics, New Delhi: Deep and Deep Publications, 1998, pp. 286–303.
[4] Aditya Nigam has, for instance, elaborated this point in his study of the 1996 national elections. See Aditya Nigam, 'India After the 1996 Elections: Nation, Locality and Representation', Asian Survey, 36(12), December 1996, pp. 1157–69.
[5] Rajni Kothari described the Congress system as a huge, hierarchically structured party, broadly rooted throughout the countryside, apparently providing mechanisms whereby a plurality of elites, sub-elites and groups could both voice their claims and attempt to realise them. The old Nehruvian order had also provided a unique model of integration based on a coalition of diverse interests that the Congress Party had represented in the decades following independence. At the same time, the Congress could adequately mediate and settle these multiple and often conflicting claims. If necessary, the Congress High Command could intervene to seal the final bargain. Within this system, the range of social groups represented in the ruling party was considered its most positive feature, making it possible for the opposition parties to forge links with like-minded Congress factions. Furthermore, two factors that appeared to have strengthened the system were (a) the practice of intra-party democracy, and (b) socially rooted party and political leaders at the state and district levels. Rajni Kothari, 'The Congress System in India', Asian Survey, 4(12), December 1964, pp. 812–28.
While reviewing his model in 1974, Kothari reiterated his faith in the Congress system as the most effective means of countering 'the challenges that the country faces'. Hence, his suggestion included: 'rebuild the Congress Party and its regional infrastructure that has become so weak of late, reinvest the electoral process with legitimacy, restore to the opposition parties their due role in parliamentary politics and at regional levels, and restructure the communication linkage between government, party units and the people, so that the system becomes more responsive and has to rely less on coercion.' See Rajni Kothari, 'The Congress System Revisited: A Decennial Review', Asian Survey, 14(11), December 1974, pp. 1052–53.
Over a period of time, the situation however has changed radically and the Congress system has largely lost its grip over the Indian reality. In the words of Kothari, '[b]uilt as it was around a system of one party dominance the Congress system while allowing a

1960s and early 1970s. The Congress system collapsed due largely to its internal weaknesses that gradually loomed large. Both the 1998 and 1999 national polls clearly suggest that the prospects for any single party to address itself to the task of building a more broad-based coalition of interests appear to be absolutely marginal. Although there hardly exists a pattern, voters seem to have preferred a coalition government endorsing the multiplicity of interests that can seldom be articulated by a single party. A stable coalition, based on a democratic combination of compatible parties, is what is being projected as most suitable for a multi-cultural India. This has set in motion a process by which the regional parties have become formidable partners in the national coalition. The emergence of coalitional arrangements at the Centre both in 1998 and 1999 reconfirms the growing 'regionalisation' of Indian politics even at the national level. So what began in the provinces in the post-1967 era with the capture of power by the state-based political parties has become a well-entrenched trend, exemplified by the major coalitions of parties, brought in under one umbrella where ideology does not appear to be as significant as it is generally construed. In other words, the poll outcomes unequivocally endorse the increasing importance of the multi-party system as integral to India's democratic governance and contestation.

Furthermore, the 1998 and 1999 poll outcomes have radically altered the socio-political map of India. Three changes are immediately evident: (a) the regionalisation of politics; (b) the growth of new social constituencies; and (c) the changing terms of political discourse. All three have contributed to important structural changes in the political realm. In south and northeast India, these changes are articulated in regional terms; in West Bengal and Kerala, they are sometimes represented in explicit class terms. In north India, especially in the Hindi heartland (particularly, Bihar and UP), new social constituencies find expression along caste lines. The conspicuous factor in all these is a desire for greater voice in public policy and political processes, processes that excluded aspiring socio-political groups from the centralised power structure fashioned by the Congress since the early 1970s. The propensity

---

great deal of internal flexibility and a long period of stable democratic functioning, nonetheless produced a centralised, bureaucratic apparatus that was lacking in effective distributive policies and any sound philosophy of justice, it eventually ended up in a neoliberal, marketised doctrine (popularly described as liberalisation and globalisation) that led to consequences which produced a sharp reaction from the people at large. An electoral democracy...broadened its social base and shown special regard for diverse types of minorities and hence gained so much legitimacy got eroded over time and forced the political managers to compromise with and ultimate become party to monied and "mafia" interests, in the process undermining the autonomy of the state and the political system.' See Rajni Kothari, 'The Democratic Experience', in Partha Chatterjee, *Wages of Freedom*, Delhi: Oxford University Press, 1998, pp. 27–28.

towards such politics is linked to the retreat of the state and its failure to engender radical changes in the conditions of social existence.

Building upon the politicisation of social cleavages and the diminishing appeal of the Congress, the formation of non-Congress governments in UP, Bihar, Rajasthan, Maharashtra, Karnataka and Andhra Pradesh, after the 1993–95 State Legislative Assembly elections, brought to an end the Congress system which had dominated Indian politics during the first three decades after independence.[6] The decline of the highly centralised Congress Party has resulted in the decentring of politics and has shifted its centre of gravity from New Delhi to the states. This has generated considerable interest in post-Congress politics in the states and in the larger social and economic conditions and political processes responsible for these transitions.[7]

Three national elections in quick succession during the period between 1996 and 1999 have set a new trend with the installation of coalition governments at the Centre. The drive of the all-India parties to solicit the cooperation of the regional parties is another significant development reinforcing the importance of coalition as the only device to consolidate the apparently disparate groups. Whether the National Democratic Alliance, led by the Bharatiya Janata Party (BJP) shall survive is difficult to predict since the prevalent political scenario is both fluid and highly volatile.[8] The net result of the last national poll is, however, that the Indian variety of coalition provides a rather 'moderate' form of government in which large national parties have been forced to accept the need for alliances and accommodations with a variety of new and old parties, including the regional parties. In view of the

---

[6] No longer is the Indian party system characterised by a dominant party embodying a centrist consensus, with rightist and leftist parties on the margins. Each state within the Union now has a genuine two-party system even though the picture is not uniform throughout the country. The Congress has a toehold in most states, but it barely exists in the key northern states of UP and Bihar. The BJP has a substantial presence in the north and west, but its success in the south is marginal. The CPI (M) is confined to West Bengal, Tripura and the southern state of Kerala. The Janata Dal, while it has allies among other regional parties, has its hold in Karnataka and marginally in Bihar and Orissa. See for details, Pratap B. Mehta 'India: Fragmentation Amid Consensus', *Journal of Democracy*, 8(1), January 1997, pp. 56–69.

[7] In her study of the decline of the Congress and its impact in Uttar Pradesh, Zoya Hasan explores the growth of the oppositional politics of farmers, Other Backward Classes and Hindutva that contributed to the collapse of the Congress Party and the disintegration of the Congress system. Zoya Hasan, *Quest for Power: Oppositional Movements and Post-Congress Politics in Uttar Pradesh*, Delhi: Oxford University Press, 1998.

[8] Atul Kohli expresses doubt because the BJP-led coalition 'does not command a parliamentary majority, the partners are disparate, and, more fundamentally, the BJP itself is trapped between its Hindu-nationalist core and the moderation that it must assume (whether sincerely or not) to govern peacefully and effectively'. See his 'Enduring Another Election', *Journal of Democracy*, 9(3), July 1998, p. 11.

short duration of the two successive coalition governments at the Centre, it is probably inappropriate to comment on the viability of coalition[9] at the national level though there are clear indications in that direction.

The recent elections in India, particularly the 12th and 13th general elections, reveal a significant shift in the nature of electoral battle. From being contests between parties the elections are increasingly being contested between fronts and alliances. Obviously, coalition politics has achieved a deeper penetration. What is new in this pattern is the formation of an alliance of the parties holding uniform views vis-à-vis some major electoral issues. For instance, none of the partners in the BJP-led National Democratic Alliance has endorsed the 'Hindutva' of the BJP and yet they are united under a single platform presumably because of their explicit opposition to the Congress. The anti-Congress stance is only a cementing factor in view of the mind-boggling contradictions in their ideological approaches, programmatic diversities and regional alignments. The other striking characteristic of these emerging coalitions is reflected in its growing dependence on the regional parties. As evident in 1999, both the NDA and the Congress-led fronts were region-based and did not hold beyond its boundaries.

A significant trend emerging out of political alignments and realignments is irrelevance, if not the demise, of ideology in coalition making. Both the Congress and the NDA have demonstrated this. As the tendency cuts across party lines, the Third Front constituents too are part of this trend. The CPI (M), for instance, had an alliance with the Congress in Tamil Nadu, Punjab and Bihar in the 1999 national poll but was opposed to it in Kerala, West Bengal and Maharastra. Attributing the decision to its ideological battle against the 'communal' BJP, the CPI (M) preferred to ally with the Congress in areas where its presence was not significant.[10] What ultimately emerged were 'haphazard, non-ideological fronts almost entirely oriented to the single purpose of seeking and securing political power'.[11] Whatever the political dividends, the equivocal support to the Congress elsewhere appeared to have caused dissension among the CPI (M) grassroots activists who found it

---

[9] The coalition government that came into existence in the wake of the 1996 national elections did not last long probably because of the inability of the coalition partners to rise above 'petty' interests apart from 'personality clashes' that manifested in an ugly form following the resignation of H.D. Deve Gowda as prime minister. While writing about the nature of coalition in the context of India, E. Sridharan draws our attention to some of these features likely to plague the coalition. See his, 'Coalition Politics', *Seminar*, 437, January 1996, pp. 18–22.

[10] The CPI (M) ideologue Sitaram Yechuri candidly made this point in his press statement of 17 June 1999. *The Telegraph*, 18 June 1999.

[11] Nagindas Sanghavi and Usha Thakkar, 'Regionalisation of Indian Politics', *Economic and Political Weekly*, 35(3), 12 February 2000, p. 515.

difficult to defend such 'an opportunistic' alliance in terms of what Marxism taught them.[12]

Given the multiplicity of India's socio-political character and the failure of a single party to provide a stable structure of governance for obvious reasons, the Third Force representing a coalition of parties with an identical political goal of keeping the Congress and BJP out of power is potentially the most challenging alternative to these parties. There is, therefore, a broad unanimity among the constituents of the Third Force. Unlike the BJP-led coalition that collapsed within a year of its formation in 1999 due to internicine feud[13] the Third Force seems to have projected, at least theoretically, an alternative, since the constituents were united under one political platform seeking to provide a stable government without the BJP and its *bete noire*, the Congress. So, ideology may not be as effective as it would seem and what has brought the Third Front constituents together is their opposition to both the Congress and the BJP.

The Third Front and its Manifestation

Considering that a tri-nodal party system began taking shape after the 9th general elections, the Third Front began its journey with the formation of the National Front in 1989 under the leadership of V.P. Singh. Although the non-Congress government that came into being in the aftermath of the 1975–77 Emergency had among its constituents parties that later on became two nodes of political alternatives to the Congress, the Morarji Desai-led Janata Party government was said to have initiated a new trend in Indian politics that was governed by a rainbow centrist ideological preference for non-Congress parties. Of course, it had no aversion to splinters from the Congress. Two important issues however made the 1989 elections a significant one: the Congress was ousted from power for the second time since the 1952 elections; and for the first time a minority government was sworn in in India representing those political parties, which are currently striving for a Third Front with 'outside support' of two contrasting parties. The dramatic decline in Congress's parliamentary seats was illustrative of a shift from a majority Congress to a minority non-Congress national government. It was possible probably because of the changing nature of non-Congress parties, manifested in their willingness to work together concertedly to strategies their electoral plans against the formidable Congress. However, for the first time

---

[12] In informal interviews conducted by the author, before and during the 1999 national poll, a large number of the CPI (M) local and district committee members in Calcutta have characterised this decision as 'strategically wrong' and 'politically inappropriate'.

[13] What led to the collapse of the Vajpayee government in 1999 was the withdrawal of the Jayalalitha-led AIADMK from his government.

since independence a triangular political scene seemed to be emerging in a political system that has variously been described as a one party dominant system and multi-party system, as the BJP emerged as the third major party with 88 seats in the Lok Sabha.

Mobilised primarily around issues of corruption in high places, rising prices and the ineffective leadership of Rajiv Gandhi, the National Front posed a threat to the Congress hegemony. What was striking was the projected image of the Front as a united forum bringing together forces opposed to the Congress. In the 1989 elections, the Congress suffered a setback because most of the significant opposition parties reached a prior electoral agreement. As a result, an arrangement was made to fight the Congress Party in every constituency with one candidate. Since the Congress won, as history shows, with less than 50 per cent votes, a single candidate in every constituency was certain to 'play havoc with Congress's electoral fortunes'. This is what happened. There was 'a small but significant decline in Congress's normal level of support, and the opposition cashed in on the situation by fielding one-on-one contests across much of India'.[14] The Congress lost its majority in the 9th general elections, held in November 1989, resulting in the formation of a minority government by the National Front. Led by the Janata Dal with 141 Lok Sabha seats, the Front comprised the Telugu Desam Party (two seats), the Dravida Munnetra Kazhagam (DMK) (no seat) and the Congress (S) with a single parliamentary seat. The key to its survival, however, was held by the BJP (88 seats) and the Left Front with 55 seats (CPI [M] 32, Communist Party of India [CPI] 12 and others 11)—which provided the crucial 'outside support'. An ascendant BJP, though in third place behind the Congress and the JD, was neither willing to join the alliance, nor unconditional about the support. The BJP President L.K. Advani's commitment only of 'critical support' to the NF clearly meant that the party would use the first opportunity to embarrass the NF for its own aggrandisement. With the Advani-led BJP already having discovered the Hindutva formula for electoral success, the possibility of that potent weapon being used against the NF at the first available opportunity was always there.

The coming together of disparate political parties under the National Front was, by itself, a significant development both electorally and politically. Apart from the political sentiments against the Congress, what largely accounted for consolidation of the Front was probably the emergence of V.P. Singh as an acceptable leader despite minor differences among the major Front partners regarding his selection. It caused resentment too because to a significant section of the Janata Party, Chandrashekhar was the natural choice for the leadership for his relentless crusade against the authoritarianism of

[14] Atul Kohli, 'India's Democracy Under Rajiv Gandhi (1985–1989)', in Atul Kohli (ed.), *India's Democracy: An Analysis of Changing State-Society Relations*, New Delhi: Orient Longman, 1991, p. 332.

Indira Gandhi during the 1975–77 Emergency. Since V.P. Singh, a junior minister in Mrs Gandhi's council of ministers before and during the Emergency, was identified as a close associate of Sanjay Gandhi, he was identified with those who were instrumental in imposing a dictatorial regime in the country.[15] So, the Front seemed to have begun its first innings with an internal feud over leadership that gradually became the Achilles heel for the National Front government.

It is important here to briefly sketch the formation of the JD and the NF to understand the dispute over leadership that eventually became the nemesis of this brief experiment. V.P. Singh, who held important finance and defence portfolios in the Rajiv Gandhi government (1984–89), fell out with him over the issue of corruption in high places and resigned. He left the Congress and created a platform, Jan Morcha (People's Front), to campaign against corruption in high places and for a long time he insisted that the Morcha was a non-political front with no political or electoral ambitions. As his campaign struck roots in Bihar, UP and some other northern states, non-Congress parties and leaders joined him in his campaign. It was almost on the eve of the 1989 elections that the Janata Party of 1977 vintage and some others decided to join hands with the Jan Morcha to form Janata Dal. Though in the eyes of some since the new non-Congress space had been consolidated by V.P. Singh's relentless campaign against corruption in high places, it gave him an unquestioned claim over the leadership of the new political formation, there were unsatisfied leadership desires within the Janata Dal and National Front. Chandrashekhar, the 'Young Turk' of the 1970s, had kept the Janata Party flag flying under adverse circumstances as its first president since 1977 and nursed prime ministerial ambitions. Devi Lal, the 'heavyweight' from Haryana, had played a crucial role in the realignment of JD and considered that seniority should go in favour of his leadership claim. As V.P. Singh had fudged the issue of political recruitment by leaning on old leadership of various parties, he manipulated the leadership issue as well with Devi Lal.[16] The seed for political discontent was thus sown at the very outset.[17]

---

[15] V.P. Singh's selection as UP chief minister after the 1980 Legislative Assembly elections was said to have been at Sanjay Gandhi's behest.

[16] Since Chandrashekhar was bent upon election for the post of leadership of the National Front parliamentary party, a sleight of hand was planned to tackle this issue. Devi Lal's name was proposed and seconded for leadership and prime ministership. Devi Lal got up and announced that persons of his age in Haryana were known as *Tau* (elederly uncle) and generally people seek their advice. He would retain that status for himself and offer the leadership of the Janata Dal (and National Front) parliamentary party to V.P. Singh. However, the status of *Tau* did not prevent him from accepting the chair of deputy prime minister. This angered Chandrashekhar.

[17] For a discussion, see Ajay K. Mehra, 'Political Parties and Party System in India', in D.D. Khanna and Gert W. Kueck (eds), *Principles, Power and Politics*, New Delhi: Macmillan, 1999, p. 259.

Thus, the Front constituents—many of whom were associated with the first non-Congress Janata government during 1977–79—appeared to have agreed to submerge the internal differences among themselves mainly to politically combat the Congress. In other words, the non-Congress parties were convinced of the rewards of working together in circumstances where the Congress had lost its appeal. The changing political situation in the second half of the 1980s when several regional parties captured power in the states, therefore appeared to have created a wave supporting a non-Congress victory. The 1989 poll results were an ambiguous judgement against dynastic rule since the Indian voters did not give the National Front a comfortable majority in the Lok Sabha. Better known as 'the crutch government', the Front also brought the two diametrically opposite political forces, viz., the BJP and the left, under a broad coalition of parties to keep the Congress at bay by any means. For the BJP and the left, the decision to support the government 'from outside' was strategically governed since it gave them an opportunity to remain in 'the mainstream' of Indian politics. None of them was keen to join the V.P. Singh government simply because it would have been disastrous to their images. They agreed to provide support in Parliament to pre-empt a Congress government at the Centre. So, the Front came into being and consolidated, at least at the outset, its existence as a viable political alternative on the basis of its opposition to the Congress.

The crisis that dramatically altered the fate of the National Front government was both internal and external.[18] Internally, the principal difficulty arose from the political camp of Devi Lal, the deputy prime minister, whose son, the Haryana Chief Minister, Om Prakash Chautala, was forced to resign twice, the second time conclusively, for his alleged involvement in violence and rigging in his own election from the Meham Legislative Assembly constituency in Haryana.[19] Unable to swallow this, Lal resigned from the cabinet on

---

[18] Initially, it was clear that the danger to its stability lay not where minority governments usually floundered—the uncertain support of the allied parties outside the government. Rather this government was most likely to be endangered from within. For details, see Partha Chatterjee, *A Possible India: Essays in Political Criticism*, Delhi: Oxford University Press, 1997, pp. 200–205.

[19] Om Prakash Chautala, the eldest son of Devi Lal, became chief minister of Haryana on 2 December 1989 following the victory of Janata Dal in the Assembly elections. He was then an MP (Rajya Sabha). He contested election from Meham for the Legislative Assembly in March 1990. There was violence during the polling and rigging was alleged. He was compelled to resign under tremendous political and public pressure on 2 May 1990. Banarsi Das Gupta, a close associate of Devi Lal was made 'interim' CM, till Chautala was elected to the Assembly, which he was on 27 May from Darba Kalan. He again became CM on 12 July. However, there were protests from within the NF at his reinstallation, led by Arun Nehru, Arif Mohammad Khan and Satyapal Malik, who resigned from the Cabinet on 13 July. To avert the crisis Chautala was finally compelled to resign as Haryana CM on 17 July and his confidante Hukum Singh, who was deputy chief minister

16 March 1990, but on persuasion took back his resignation three days later. However, as mentioned earlier, the Chautala incident refused to blow over despite unprecedented political drama. There was political rift between Ajit Singh, who annoyed Devi Lal by visiting Meham, and Devi Lal. Finally, Chautala had to quit as CM despite being elected to the Assembly. Stung by this 'personal' affront to him and his family, he struck back by forwarding a forged letter to the president, allegedly written by V.P. Singh in 1987 implicating Arun Nehru in the Bofors deal and making accusations of financial misdemeanour against Arun Nehru and Arif Mohammad Khan and also making derogatory remarks against the prime minister. He was dropped from the cabinet on 1 August 1990. He stayed in the Janata Dal till Chandrashekhar and Devi Lal along with 25 members were expelled from the party and declared unattached by the speaker. This was a serious blow to the government.

The external crisis that finally sealed the fate of the Front built over the confrontation with the BJP that had agreed to provide the required numerical strength in the Lok Sabha to keep it going. The withdrawal of the 'ouside support' by the BJP immediately after L.K. Advani's well-publicised *rath yatra*, a well-crafted design to garner support for Hindutva,[20] the contentious ideology that became BJP's mainstay later, was stopped and Advani incarcerated by Laloo Yadav, then Bihar chief minister. The V.P. Singh government was finally voted out on 7 November 1990.

Two issues that brought about radical changes in India's political arithmetic were articulated during the period when the National Front government was at the Centre. The first one, structured around Hindutva, has drawn upon the logic of majoritarianism.[21] Seeking to protect the interests of the majority community, the Hindus, the arguments in favour of Hindutva had created a constituency for the BJP which, so far, remained with a centrist party like the Congress.

The second issue is concerned with protective discrimination for the 'other backward castes' (OBCs) in government jobs on the lines of reservation for the Scheduled Castes and Tribes, as suggested by the Mandal Commission in 1980. The NF government's announcement in August 1990 to implement the Mandal Commission's recommendations provoked violent protests by upper-caste students and youth in Delhi and in many cities all over India; even leading to attempted self-immolation by some of them.[22] The anti-Mandal

---

in the Banarsi Das Gupta government, was made CM. The whole incident, however, left the seeds of destruction of the Janata Dal/National Front government.

[20] The *rath yatra* is a remarkable event in India's post-colonial history. See my *Whither India's Democracy*, Calcutta: K.P. Bagchi, 1993, especially the introduction, pp. 1–28.

[21] See my 'Roots of Indian Nationalism: The Contemporary Agenda', *Encounter*, 1(3), September–October 1998, pp. 29–50.

[22] According to Partha Chatterjee, when the interests of dominant minorities are threatened, the reactions are always the same. For instance, when the demand was made to

agitation and self-immolation of upper-caste students in north India in 1990 were illustrative of the uncertainty of 'an established middle class, haunted by fears of what was seen as a "plebeian" threat to its hitherto complacent way of life and social position'.[23] The Mandal issue also played a crucial role in articulating the resentment among upper-caste and middle-class groups (both rural and urban) against the growing assertiveness of lower caste and less educated communities. The Mandal issue contributed to an OBC identity while the Mandir issue became a reference point for mobilising the Hindus as against the 'others' as a homogeneous community. Not only did these two issues gain salience politically as soon as they were crystallised, they continue to remain as formidable as they were before in contemporary India presumably because none of the parties can afford to ignore these issues which remain crucial in garnering support in elections.

The third crucial stage in the crystallisation of the platform for the Third Front came at the formation of the United Front government, which in its two incarnations during 1996–98 owed its birth and continuity to the Congress which agreed to extend support, once the UF jigsaw acquired some identifiable political shape, to contain the BJP in the aftermath of the 1996 national poll. The 'Janata' experience, which has been the basis of experimentations with a non-Congress centrist alternative, has continued with its habit of splintering in both its 'Party' (1977–79) and 'Dal' (1989–) variants in a period that has spanned a crucial quarter-of-a-century of Indian democracy. Its quest for a third space began in 1996 because the political formation that registered a decisive victory against Indira Gandhi's Congress in 1977 (298 seats to Congress's 154) could muster only 31 and 10 seats in the next two elections; in 1980 without Charan Singh's faction but with the current BJP component, and in 1984 without the BJP too, which got only two seats. Having shown signs of revival with V.P. Singh's resurgent campaign in 1989, when it returned with 143 Lok Sabha seats to become the basis of a non-Congress alternative, it slid to 56 and 46 seats in 1991 and 1996. Bickerings, splits and splintering were its bane during this period too. Hence, when it vociferously claimed to be the axis of another non-Congress government in 1996, this time with Congress support (sic), it had only 46 Lok Sabha seats. The BJP, i.e., the political ideology represented by it, for the first time in the

enable the Indians to sit for the ICS examination, the British civil servants were aghast. Similarly, those who lost their property and other privileges following the zamindari abolition in the 1950s were critical of the government for violation of universal property rights. The arguments made in the provincial legislatures of Bengal, Bihar and UP were tuned to protect the rights of the privileged who traditionally remained the 'natural' social leaders due to ingrained socio-political structure where their hegemony was never undermined. Chatterjee, *A Possible India*, pp. 205–10.

[23] Thomas Blom Hansen, *The Saffron Wave: Democracy and Hindu Nationalism in Modern India*, New Delhi: Oxford University Press, 1999, p. 145.

history of Indian politics emerged as the single largest party with 161 seats in the Lok Sabha, to get the presidential invitation to form the government. Thus, from being the second political force, the alternative centrist formation began a new quest for a political space as the Third Force, ironically with the support of the Congress!

A hurriedly put together political outfit, the United Front, comprised an informal alliance between the Janata Dal, the Samajwadi Party of Mulayam Singh Yadav (a former stalwart of JD and UP chief minister in 1989) in Uttar Pradesh and the Left Front of CPI (M) and CPI and other smaller left parties. After the poll, several regional parties, like the Telugu Desam Party (TDP) in Andhra Pradesh, the DMK in Tamil Nadu and the Tamil Manila Congress (TMC) which broke away from the Congress, as well as the Asom Gana Parishad (AGP) in Assam, joined the UF. It indeed appeared creditable at that stage, from the point of view of the secular political tradition of India, that none of these parties were lured by the offer of offfice and political power during the 13-day tenure of the first BJP government. The H.D. Deve Gowda-led United Front had to rely on the Congress for survival because it lacked adequate majority to defend its existence in Parliament. The UF tally was 136 in which the Janata Dal and the CPI accounted for 46 and 12 Lok Sabha seats, respectively.[24] However, the leadership issue, both in terms of claims-counter claims and the manner in which it was sorted out, proved to be the Achilles heel for the UF. It was a hattrick of leadership crisis.

It was partly an ideological compulsion that led the Congress to extend support to the Front. Hence, according to Jaipal Reddy, the Front spokesperson, 'the credit must be given to the Congress'[25] for having strengthened the campaign against Hindutva. Based on its principled distance from both the BJP and the Congress, the United Front was governed by the following ideological traits—(a) laying greater emphasis on the federal character of the Indian polity, (b) strengthening the secular character of Indian society, (c) protecting the rights of those classes and castes which have been hitherto neglected, (d) adopting a pragmatic economic approach to keep pace with

---

[24] In the 1996 Lok Sabha poll, the seats of the Janata Dal were reduced drastically in comparison with its share of 56 in the 1991 elections. The Left Front as a whole got 53 as compared with 55 seats in the 10th Lok Sabha. They have virtually remained stagnant and have failed to make inroads in the Hindi heartland. The real gainers from the space, evacuated by the Congress (and the BJP) were the various regional parties which had no pretensions of playing a major role beyond the states in which they operated. For details, see Achin Vanaik, *Communalism Contested: Religion, Modernity and Secularism*, New Delhi: Vistaar, 1997, pp. 342–53. Also see Balveer Arora, 'Political Parties and the Party System', in Subhash C. Kashyap, D.D. Khanna and Gert W. Kueck (eds), *Reviewing the Constitution*, New Delhi: Shipra, 2000, pp. 261–89.

[25] Jaipal Reddy's interview in the *Seminar*, 454, June 1997, p. 55.

world development.[26] In an elaboration of the ideology, it was emphasised that the United Front was not 'opposed to Congress ideology and [was] for the restoration of the official ideology of the Congress party (sic)'.[27] That its existence was dependent on Congress support was evident when Sitaram Kesri, the Congress president, dictated the choice of the Front leader by categorically expressing his reluctance to support the incumbent Prime Minister, H.D. Deve Gowda. What exposed the fragility of the Front was the selection of I.K. Gujral as the leader of the Front due to Kesri's insistence on choosing anybody except Deve Gowda.

The second crisis for the idea of the UF came from Bihar, the state represented in the Rajya Sabha by Prime Minister Gujral. Bihar Chief Minister Laloo Yadav was chargesheeted in the infamous fodder scam and the prime minister, having earlier been obliged with a Rajya Sabha seat by Yadav, could not take a decision against him. Eventually, Laloo Yadav split the JD to form his own Rashtriya Janata Dal, for his own support base was intact in Bihar.

The Third Front: Its Significance as a Political Force

The idea of a Third Front—variously called the third alternative or the Third Force—was conceived when the polity was polarised between the Congress and the BJP. The left and those who became its allies sought to create a space for themselves by trying to remove the Congress (I) and prevent the BJP from taking its place. Its emergence as an alternative is significant in two fundamental ways: first, most of those who constitute the Front are at best state-based or regional parties with support bases in one or two states other than the state in which it has formidable presence. Illustrative here is the CPI (M). The rise of the state parties has changed the nature of political alternatives. Parties like the Samajwadi Party, Samata Party, and Trinamool Congress are not cast in the same mould as the classical regional parties like the Akalis or the DMK or even the TDP. Their political presence is 'state specific but their political vision is not'.[28] Second, apart from the left, it is arguably difficult to suggest that the Front is a stable political combination presumably because its constituents are not ideologically as well-knit as they seem to project. By supporting the present BJP government, the TDP and some of the erstwhile Janata Dal constituents—which spearheaded the movement for an alternative to the Congress and the BJP—have, for instance, clearly shown the fragility

---

[26] In his interview in *Seminar*, Jaipal Reddy, the then spokesperson of the United Front (he later joined the Congress), dealt with the ideological dimensions of the Front that maintained an equal distance from both the BJP and the Congress. See ibid., p. 53.

[27] Ibid., p. 55.

[28] Aditya Nigam and Yogendra Yadav, 'Electoral Politics in Indian States, 1989–99, *Economic and Political Weekly*, 34(34 and 35), 21–28 August, 1999, p. 2395.

of the bond that the Front aspires to establish. This probably indicates the weaknesses of a formation in which ideology does not appear to be as significant as it indicates. While its failure to consolidate into an all-India formation has greatly reduced its say in national politics, this failure has also kept open a diversity of political choices within the mainstream of national politics.

Despite its eclipse as a substantial political force in Parliament especially after the 1999 national elections, the Third Front as a model continues to remain viable simply because the political space, structured around the opposition to the BJP and the Congress, exists. Despite its short tenures at the national level, its achievement is also significant. With the acceptance of the Mandal recommendations,[29] submitted to the Government of India in 1980, the V.P. Singh-led National Front brought about radical changes in India's social fabric. The three volumes of the Mandal Report gathered dust on government shelves till they were retrieved and dusted up by the V.P. Singh government, which was keen to consolidate the 52 per cent OBC votes for the National Front. Although the Mandal formula ensuring 27 per cent reservations in central jobs for the OBCs appears revolutionary, the Front decision was probably prompted by the following factors showing the extent to which political expediency conditioned the decision:

(a) populist vote catching device as the OBCs constituted the majority of Indian population;
(b) a move to upstage the Haryana leader, Devi Lal who was threatening the V.P. Singh-led coalition with rural-urban polarisation;

---

[29] 'Protective discrimination' for the 'backward castes', as suggested by the B. P. Mandal Commission, has a long history in India. Considered to have been suffering from disabilities due to social discrimination and exploitation for centuries, the Scheduled Castes and Scheduled Tribes were given statutory guarantee of 'protective discrimination' for their social and economic advancement. Since government jobs were considered to be the most important and preferred avenue of employment, in highly stratified society of India such demands were made from other sections as well. As demands for reservation for the 'backward castes' were made since the 1950s. Kaka Kalelkar Commission was set up by the central government in 1953 with the task that the Mandal Commission was entrusted with in 1978. The Kalelkar Commission report, submitted in 1955, identified 2,399 castes as backward, but failed to recommend a fool proof formula for reservation; naturally the report was shelved. In 1977–78, the then Bihar Chief Minister Karpoori Thakur introduced 26 per cent reservation for the OBCs. The formula which took into account the economic backwardness as a criterion for reservation provoked violent outbursts in the state in which 118 people were reported to have been killed. The Madhya Pradesh government raised the reservation from 28 per cent to 32 per cent in 1985 which sparked off violent riots and arson. So widespread and alarming was the trouble that the government was forced to withdraw the decision. Gujarat shared the same fate in 1985 when the Madhavsinh Solanki government fell following the introduction of reservation in promotions in medical colleges. These illustrations draw out the fact that north India has not had a consensus regarding reservations for the OBCs.

(c) to shift the focus from the *Ram Janmabhoomi* issue that singularly created a solid vote bank for the BJP especially after the L.K. Advani-led 1990 October *rath yatra*;

(d) the realisation that it was an issue on which none of the allies of the Front would be able to openly oppose the government, if presented with a *fait accompli*.[30]

Whatever advantages the Mandal formula may have held for the NF, reservations for the backward castes and for the religious minorities were directed towards maintaining a balance of power in India's caste-ridden and highly stratified social structure. As a scheme striving to strike a balance between the privileged upper castes and the hitherto neglected OBCs, the Mandal recommendations deserve appreciation. In reality, however, the better-off sections of the OBCs reap the benefit at the cost of the more deserving sections within these castes. The caste dynamics in north India is illustrative here. Till the 1950s, the domination was enjoyed in the rural areas by a combination, better known as AJGAR comprising four caste groups, the Ahirs, Jats, Gujars and Rajputs.[31] They gained remarkably in material terms after the green revolution [32] and all of them moved well and truly into the modern sector. The intermediate castes like Kurmis, Koeris and Lodhas also benefited but not uniformly. So there is, therefore, a considerable social and economic heterogeneity in each of these castes. Hence, the Mandal definition of 'backwardness' itself is problematic in view of its implicit tendency in homogenising the OBCs. Furthermore, the hegemonic domination of the relatively better-off sections within the OBCs leads to a situation in which 'the rhetoric of reservation is addressed to the mass of underprivileged, but their rewards are reserved for the waferthin affluent upper crust of the OBC society'.[33]

---

[30] A commentator thus commented, '[n]o report has united the elite as much as this one. Yet, no report has unwittingly exposed it as much as this one. It has questioned our radical and academic pretensions, our models of social change, our involvement in social justice. It has shown us what we are, nervous, pretentious, deeply intolerant, mouthing radicalisms as long they are gloriously abstract and romantic.' Shiv Visvanathan, 'Democracy, Plurality and Indian University', *Economic and Political Weekly*, 35(40), 30 September 2000, p. 3602.

[31] Chandan Mitra, 'Moulded in Caste: Electoral Patterns in North India', in Bidyut Chakrabarty (ed.) *Whither India's Democracy*, Calcutta: K.P. Bagchi & Co., 1993, pp. 135–43.

[32] It has been well-documented in the available literature. See for details, Francine R. Frankel, *India's Political Economy, 1947–77: The Gradual Revolution*, Princeton: Princeton University Press, 1978; Pranab Bhardhan, *The Political Economy of Development in India*, Delhi: Oxford University Press, 1984; Atul Kohli, *The State and Poverty in India: The Politics of Reform*, Cambridge: Cambridge University Press, 1987; Francine R. Frankel and M.S.A. Rao (eds), *Dominance and State Power in India: Decline of a Social Order*, Vols. I & II, Delhi: Oxford University Press, 1990.

[33] Ashok Guha, 'Reservation in Myth and Reality', *Economic and Political Weekly*, 15 December 1990, p. 2716. Since most of the benefits are likely to be appropriated by the upper crust within the OBC in view of the prevalent socio-economic structure in India, M.N.

The political imperatives behind reservations are thus apparent. What prompted the Front to accept the Mandal recommendations was probably a well-calculated design of mobilising the support of the OBC elites. By virtue of its unique status in the OBC society, its wealth, its relatively high educational level and its hegemony in a majority of caste councils, the OBC upper crust was viewed as the significant power brokers in the Hindi heartland. So, the Mandal formula, addressed to social justice, was actually a scheme for creating and sustaining a secure vote bank for the National Front.

The Front decision to implement the Mandal formula was also characterised as an effort to effectively draw on caste sentiments for victory in elections. The Mandal Commission was thus described as 'a caste commission' that was seen 'as a passport to power'.[34] It is not therefore strange that elections are conducted on caste calculations, the candidates are nominated on caste considerations, and as a consequence, patronage (sic) is likely to be distributed on caste basis and public policies are also tilted in favour of the caste support base. Apart from polarising the political forces more sharply than before, the implementation of the Mandal scheme indicated further the disintegration in north India of 'long established patterns of vertical mobilization, and placed in relief the outline of a new basis of horizontal cooperation of the disadvantaged social groups'.[35] The Third Force therefore seems to have steered the class-caste conundrum in a direction hitherto unknown in India's political history.

India's social fabric was radically altered with the introduction of the reservation scheme, as suggested by the Mandal Commission. On the economic front, the new industrial policy, adopted by the V.P. Singh-led National Front, contained the seeds of globalisation that was to grip India soon. The new policy with less emphasis on the public sector was, argued V.P. Singh's bete noire and later Prime Minister, Chandrashekhar, designed to 'please the World Bank and the multinationals'. It would not 'ease the foreign currency situation at all, but exacerbate it'. It would bring in 'wasteful and unhealthy investment by the multinationals in the luxury sector'.[36] Both the CPI and CPI (M) supported these arguments. Even the BJP seemed to echo his sentiments about the undesirable entry of multinationals.

Srinivas thus suggested, 'when a certain caste has political clout, it should be excluded from the backward caste list; otherwise, the richer members of the higher groups among the backward classes ... will hog the benefits which should have gone to the genuinely deserving backward classes'. M.N. Srinivas, 'End of the Egalitarian Dream', *The Sunday Observer*, New Delhi, 12 August 1990.

[34] C. P. Bhambri, 'The Politics of Caste Alliances', *The Telegraph*, Calcutta, 23 May 1991.
[35] Francine R. Frankel, 'Decline of a Social Order', in Frankel and Rao (eds), *Dominance and State Power in Modern India*, p. 513.
[36] Chandrashekhar's interview published in *The Times of India*, New Delhi, 14 July 1990.

What was initiated in the new industrial policy under the Front became an overarching concern of the Congress government that captured power in 1991. It was probably difficult to reverse the well-entrenched economic trends when the United Front administration took over power during 1996–97. Although there was a change of leadership, the economic policy of the UF continued to remain more or less the same. Like its predecessor, the UF accepted liberalisation with conditionalities. Some of the steps undertaken by the UF were significant in fine-tuning the structural adjustment programme. For instance, the decision to eliminate 'licensing requirements' for trade and storage was calculated to augment investment in India. Similarly, the phasing out of the public sector procurement, abolition of the remaining controls on imports and exports of many agricultural items and the licensing of agro-processing industries, were certain major decisions upholding the policy prescriptions of the International Monetary Fund (IMF)/World Bank/World Trade Organisation (WTO).[37]

The Third Front and its Electoral Viability

Despite changes in the composition of the Third Front, its electoral presence is remarkable. A perusal of the poll results since 1989 clearly shows its growing importance at the national level. Its constituents, primarily regional parties with firm roots in specific provinces, have largely failed to emerge as a national alternative like the Congress and the BJP. Even the CPI (M), which has remained a recognised national party since its inception, was stripped of its national status by the Election Commission of India in 2000 on the basis of its performance in the 1999 national poll. Of course, the status was later restored to it. However, as pointed out earlier, since its inception in 1989 when it polled nearly 18 per cent national votes and captured 142 seats in the Lok Sabha, the Janata Dal has gradually lost its popular support base as well as strength in Parliament. The main factor why it has lost its presence on India's electoral map is that with self-perpetuating leaders, it always seemed to have been imbued with a death wish. Naturally, a significant force in 1989, the Janata Party has suffered considerably in the last Lok Sabha poll. However, several of its leaders, with new, and in many cases, single leader outfits, have not only managed to win a few seats from particular regions or states, they allied after the 1999 Lok Sabha elections with the BJP and are part of the NDA. As Table 10.1 illustrates, even other constituents of the Front, including the left parties, have experienced reversals in polls since 1989.

---

[37] A commentator thus characterised the UF economic policy as nothing but a blatant surrender to these transnational agencies. See BM, 'UF Government Emerging in True Colours', *Economic and Political weekly*, 31(25), 22 June 1996, pp. 1568–69.

Table 10.1: Electoral Performances of the Third Front: 1989, 1991, 1996, 1998 and 1999[38]

Parties	1989	1991	1996	1998	1999
Janata Dal	142 (17.8)	52 (11.6)	46 (10.7)	06 (1.1)	00
CPI (M)	33 (6.5)	35 (6.6)	32 (6.6)	32 (6.7)	33 (6.5)
CPI	12 (2.6)	12 (2.4)	12 (2.4)	09 (2.8)	04 (2.3)
Other Left Parties	07 (1.1)	07 (1.4)	07 (1.3)	07 (1.3)	05 (1.2)
DMK	00	00	17 (5.3)	06 (5.2)	00
Samajwadi	00	00	17 (5.2)	20 (6.1)	26 (6.8)
Janata Dal (S)	00	00	00	00	1 (1.1)

Sources: • Statistical Report on General Elections, 1989, Vol. 1, Election Commission of India, New Delhi, 1989.
   • Statistical Report on General Elections, 1996, Vol. 1, Election Commission of India, New Delhi, 1996 (this volume contains data for the General Elections of 1991 as well).
   • Statistical Report on General Elections, 1998, Vol. 1, Election Commission of India, New Delhi 1998.
   • Statistical Report on General Elections, 1999, Vol. 1, Election Commission of India, New Delhi, 1999.
Note: Figures in the parenthesis show the percentage of votes captured by the parties.

Not only is the table illustrative of a dramatic decline of the Third Front within a span of 10 years, it is also indicative of the extent to which the Front is volatile as an electoral force. Apart from the consistent performance of the cadre-based CPI (M), other constituents of the Front suffered miserably in these elections. One of the basic reasons appears to be the failure of the Front to muster enough support to form a government on its own. It owed its survival to outside support. In 1989, it was the BJP and in 1996 and 1998, it was the Congress that pledged to support the Front to contain the BJP. Obviously, a major factor in its failure has been its inability to situate itself positively in the highly volatile and transient political arena. If it sought out the BJP in 1989 to keep the Congress out of power, it sought out the Congress to keep the BJP out of power in 1996 and 1998. Apart from its endeavour not to antagonise the party whose support was crucial for its continuity, the Front was, as its records in power show, mostly engaged in sorting out intra-party differences and internal differences among its partners. Interestingly, the internal contradictions among the Front partners were not responsible for the fall of the two Front governments during 1996–98 led respectively by

---

[38] In the 1989 and 1991 elections, the Telugu Desam Party was a part of the United Front, while in the 1998 and 1999 elections, Tamil Nadu based Tamil Manila Congress contested the elections as a constituent of the Front. Further, neither the Janata Dal (United) which captured 21 seats with 6.3 per cent popular votes nor the DMK which won 12 seats with 5.8 per cent popular votes in the 1999 Lok Sabha poll was aligned with the Third Front. Ironically, the H.D. Deve Gowda-led Janata Dal (Socialist) is a Third Front constituent with no seat in the 13th Lok Sabha.

H.D. Deve Gowda and I.K. Gujral; both these governments collapsed due to the withdrawal of Congress support.

An Assessment

Though historically a broad centrist alliance encompassing the ideological spectrum from far left to far right emerged in order to provide an alternative to the Congress in its route to the contemporary Third Front, this political configuration has developed into a region-dictated political phenomenon.[39] In order to combat both the Congress and the BJP, several regional political parties with an identical aim to capture the political space occupied by the Congress and the BJP, have been striving to come together to form a coalition. Even in the ruling NDA, the regional parties appear to have a significant say in its consolidation and continuity at the Centre. The rise of the regional parties as a combined force staking their claim to power at the national level is possibly due to five factors.

First, the decline of the Congress as an institutionalised party representing a variety of, and at times conflicting, socio-economic interests, created a political vacuum. It lost its hegemony due, *inter alia*, to the departure of the nationalist generation, demise of internal democracy and the emergence of personalised mass appeal of the top leadership.[40] No longer did the Congress remain a party capable of accommodating conflicting social interests and fulfilling the individual ambitions of those involved in its expansion at the provincial and local levels.

Second, with successive elections, new social groups and strata have been introduced to the political processes. Since the entrenched groups in the dominant party tended to impede their entry to the political processes, these new entrants found it easier to make their debut through non-Congress parties or occasionally even founded new parties. So, the emergence of new parties outside the BJP and Congress fold to articulate hitherto neglected socio-political interests seems to be a major factor that contributed to the consolidation of a coalition with a seemingly different ideological perspective.

Third, the judiciary also played no less significant a role in upholding the importance of regions in national politics. The judicial verdict in the famous

---

[39] For an evaluation of this historical trend and of its sources, see Achin Vanaik, *The Painful Transition: Bourgeois Democracy in India*, London: Verso, 1990, pp. 273–78.

[40] This trend is best exemplified during the period when Indira Gandhi held power. By her capacity to directly communicate with the electorate, Mrs Gandhi could afford to ignore the party organisation that gradually became dependent on her charisma for its viability. Sudipta Kaviraj has graphically illustrated the process that ultimately contributed to the decline of the Congress as an institutionalised party with its organisational tentacles spread all over India due to historical reasons. Sudipta Kaviraj, 'A Critique of Passive Revolution', *Economic and Political Weekly*, 23(45–47), pp. 2429–44.

S.R. Bommai case (1994) is illustrative here. Although the Supreme Court upheld the dismissal of the four BJP state governments on 15 December 1992 under the Article 356 of the Constitution it nonetheless defended that the presidential authority in this regard is subject to judicial review. In this changed environment, even the instruments of governance, like the president, governors, the Election Commission and various inter-governmental agencies, that so far tended to behave in a rather 'highhanded' manner have displayed a greater sensitivity towards issues and demands, couched in regional terms.

Fourth, a perusal of the history of the Third Front reveals the extent to which the conglomeration owes its birth and consolidation to individual personalities. In other words, the Front draws upon the Laswellian sense of 'who gets what, when and how' and the dominant section is built and consolidated around the seemingly most capable personality under the circumstances. What caused irreparable damage to the National Front was the non-cooperation of the group clustered initially around Chandrashekhar and later Devi Lal. The Front was largely personality-based and its so-called ideological goal was conveniently sacrificed if personal/political interests of those constituting the Front were impaired. Except the ideologically governed left, what brought the Front constituents together was personalities with a relatively stable support base in regions and states. So, individual personality provided the Front with the required political capital that adequately streamlined its activities at least at the outset when the desire to hold the Congress appeared to be the only guiding principle. As regards the United Front, the personality factor acted in two different directions: on the one hand, the United Front agreed on a personality not because of his strong political base but because of his acceptability to the constituents. The selection of Deve Gowda as the Front leader was guided largely by the fact that he was less controversial and thus acceptable to even those jockeying for the highest seats of power. He was never considered a threat politically probably because he had neither a strong base in his state Karnataka nor a national image. I.K. Gujral became the leader by default because the Congress that extended the necessary parliamentary support to the Front for survival was reluctant to accept anybody except him. And, the Front had no alternative but to endorse the Congress dictation and Gujral was chosen for the highest post in the United Front government.

Finally, what appeared to have plagued the Front in its different incarnations was certainly the lack of an ideological bond among the major partners, except the left parties. It is the left which, with all its failings, stood as the core component of the Front. Of the left parties, CPI (M) has taken the lead to see that a third alternative is constituted. What has irked its supporters at the grassroots is the relatively soft attitude of the CPI (M) towards the Congress. This is justified, according to a CPI (M) source, 'as a short-term "tactical" strategy to keep the BJP out of power'.[41] What brought and kept most of the Front partners together was this short-term strategy. But this in itself does not express any deep-rooted commitment to abiding hostility to the BJP and the Sangh Parivar. Herein lies probably the reason as to why some of the prominent Front partners switched their loyalty later to the BJP-led NDA government.

A perusal of the Third Front's track record reveals that without a social alliance at the grassroots, durable coalitions are bound to remain a pipe-dream, no matter how frequently they may be put in Delhi, cemented by the exigencies of a hung parliament and power lust. In other words, the longevity of a political arrangement in whatever form depends on the strength of social coalitions at the grassroots. Given that most political parties represent certain well-defined class/caste interests, it is important that a social coalition is forged at the grassroots which eventually translates into a political arrangement. Illustrative here are examples from West Bengal and Kerala. The Left Front in West Bengal owed its continuity to a successful mobilisation of 'the marginals' along class lines. Kerala provides a more interesting example because both the Congress and Left Front are simultaneously engaged in forging parallel caste/class alliances with stable partnership arrangements to combat each other electorally. The other side of the coin can be illustrated by examples from Uttar Pradesh. An electoral alliance between the Bahujan Samaj Party and the Samajwadi Party led to the formation of a Mulayam Singh Yadav-led government in Uttar Pradesh. The fragility of the alliance was soon exposed because the historic contradiction is 'too deep-rooted to be resolved by a mere electoral alliance between a Yadav-dominated Samajwadi Party and an exclusive dalit formation, the Bahujan Samaj Party'.[42] It is therefore plausible to argue that the stability of a political arrangement is proportionally linked with the strength of the social coalitions, forged at the grassroots. Underlying this argument lies a significant clue as to why the Third Front—that came into being in 1989 and 1996—was never as strong as it appeared at the outset largely because of the failure to create a stable social base for itself. That its constituents, except CPI (M) and Samajwadi Party, had not had a solid social base was evident in the 1999 poll outcome.

Conclusion

Gone are the days of the dominant parties and the Third Front/Third Force is a real possibility. What is constantly changing are its constituents which are united neither in terms of an ideology nor in terms of an attitude that prominently governed the formation of the National Front in 1989. Except

---

[41] Sitaram Yechuri's press statement, *The Hindu*, 17 October 1998.
[42] Chandan Mitra, 'Unholy Alliances', *Seminar*, 454, June, 1997, p. 16.

the ideologically well-knit CPI (M), none of the partners seem to be as committed as the CPI (M) in their opposition to the Congress and BJP. For instance, to some of the leading members of the Front, like the DMK, TDP and the newly created Janata Dal (U), the BJP does not appear to be as formidable a foe as it was before primarily because it has watered down its ideological goal due to electoral compulsion. Not only are they part of the BJP-led NDA, they seem also to have found an ideological affinity (sic) with the BJP holding diametrically opposite views of what constitutes the nation in India.

In view of its fluid composition, the Third Front appears to be a situational force and its locus is highly dispersed. The erstwhile United Front constituents are divided in their attitude towards the Congress which will hamper the Third Front's revival.[43] Even the CPI (M) which is capable of providing an ideological leadership is not very categorical in its attitude towards the Congress. The party has, on a number of occasions, expressed its willingness to combine with the Congress, even if that causes a dilution to its basic ideological preferences, to combat the 'communal' BJP. This also indicates that there is no centre of gravity as regards the Front and its partners decide their stance vis-à-vis the Congress and BJP according to what is politically most appropriate under particular circumstances. In other words, the governing principle may not be the same with regard to those who are keen to combine forces in opposition to what the BJP and Congress uphold. So what the National Front and later United Front sought to define was a unique political trend that no longer remains a mere conceptual category but has become a viable alternative at the Centre given the volatile nature of the BJP-led NDA government.

Despite their short tenure and controversial track records, both the National Front and United Front governments are indicative of regionalisation of Indian polity even at the national level. The locus of power has shifted from the Centre to the periphery. Regional parties with their formidable presence in the respective states have carved out a significant space for themselves and

---

[43] In its October 2000 plenum at Thiurvananthapuram, the CPI (M) resolved to bring together the former United Front constituents on the basis of what it perceives to be growing resentment against the NDA government's pro-reform economic policies. However, the Third Front's revival is unlikely to be easy given that several constituents of the United Front like the DMK and the TDP, are now, as part of the NDA, on the opposite side of the political spectrum. Besides, the proposed Third Front has already been crippled by the decision of the Mulayum Singh-led Samajwadi Party not to align with the CPI (M) and the Laloo Prasad-led Rashtriya Janata Dal for their willingness to prop up a Sonia Gandhi-led Congress government in the aftermath of the fall of the Vajpayee government in 1999. The Rashtriya Janata Dal has its compulsions—the Congress is its ally in the Rabri Devi ministry in Bihar. Given the strong aversion of Mulayum Singh Yadav to the Congress, it is unlikely that the Samajwadi Party will come under the same political platform with parties having links with the Congress.

emerged as a major stakeholder at the Centre.[44] Similarly, due to their failure to emerge as a party with a comfortable majority in Parliament, both the Congress and BJP seem to have conceptualised their role as a major, if not leading, partner in an alliance comprising regional parties that is ideologically less rigid and politically expedient under particular circumstances. So, in an age of alliance and fronts, the Third Front is just another endeavour seeking to unite those parties, opposed to the coalition, led by either the Congress or BJP. What probably differentiates the Third Front from the rest is the presence of the ideologically coherent left parties, particularly the CPI (M) that has succeeded in sustaining a Left Front government in West Bengal for more than two decades, though this experiment cannot be replicated at the national level due to the obvious complex socio-economic and politico-cultural texture of the nation as a whole.

Along with the Congress and BJP, the Third Front is therefore a potential contender for power at the Centre as well. By bringing together those forces striving to flourish outside the Congress and BJP fold, the Front has sought to translate into practice the ideology of the periphery. The trend that was articulated first at the state level in 1967 with the assumption of power by the regional parties became a reality with the formation of the National Front in 1989 and the United Front in 1996. Although both the Front governments failed to realise the full potential of a third alternative due to their disintegration within a relatively short span of their presence at the Centre[45] they nonetheless added a completely new chapter in India's political history since independence. As they were a coalition of regional parties there were serious endeavours at the behest of both the National Front and United Front governments to revive and revamp those national agencies underlining India's federal character. Given the soft, if not fragile, core and the heterogeneous base, it was not possible for the Front leadership to bypass the political institutions which became absolutely peripheral under the highly centralised and personalised leadership of the previous regimes. The restoration of political

---

[44] There is a serious danger here. Once the regional parties are crucial stakeholders in power at the Centre, their *raison d'etre* is to maximise their state's interests. Hence there is a possibility that the disputes involving more than one states cannot be properly resolved in the absence of any group or individual who towers over petty regional interests to take a dispassionate view of such complex matters. Illustrative here are the Alamati and Cauvery disputes in which none of the United Front prime ministers found an acceptable solution. So, regionalism cannot be the basis of a stable coalition because, as a commentator agues, 'there is a limit to how long conflicting state interests can be pushed under the carpet'. Mitra, 'Unholy Alliances', p. 17.

[45] The National Front minority coalition headed by V.P. Singh lasted for less than a year (4 December 1989–10 November 1990) with external support from the Left Front and the BJP. The United Front government, led by H.D. Deve Gowda and later I.K. Gujral had continued a little longer than its predecessor (1 June 1996–28 November 1997).

power to the designated institutional structures—that reflects today in a growing assertiveness of the various agencies, including the CBI, in the executive, the higher profile of judicial activism and wider process of political consultation between the Centre and states—would not have been possible without the intervention of the Front governments in the last decade. Neither of the Front governments was, however, a perfect example of a Third Front due to ingrained weaknesses that led to their collapse. What they strove to articulate was the possibility of a third alternative in contrast with the major political parties, viz., the Congress and the BJP.

11

THE THIRD FORCE

AS AN IDEOLOGY AND AS A REALITY

Muchkund Dubey

The Third Force in contemporary Indian politics refers to the political coalition offering an alternative to the two major political parties of India, i.e., the Congress and the Bharatiya Janata Party (BJP). In essense, it is a coalition of the left, secular and democratic forces in Indian politics. Therefore, its core components have been the traditional leftist parties, like the Communist Party of India (Marxist) (CPI [M]) and the Communist Party of India (CPI), and the recently emerged left-leaning formations like the Janata Dal (JD) (including its various factions), the Samajwadi Party, and the Samata Party. In addition, the Third Force has leaned heavily on regional parties which reflect regional aspirations and demands and whose political support is confined to particular regions.[1]

The Third Force rejects the Congress because of the way it has compromised secularism, its pronounced lurch towards right-wing economic policies of liberalisation and globalisation, its dynastical tradition and its image as a party symbolising misgovernance and corruption. The Congress's compromise with communal forces started from the time of Indira Gandhi. It was taken many notches higher by Rajiv Gandhi's compromises on the Shah Banu Case and on the Ayodhya Ram Mandir issue. Then came the demolition of the Babri Masjid in 1992 during the Narasimha Rao government at the Centre. This shook the very foundations of secularism in India and made the entire Muslim community feel insecure as never before. The Congress is seen as steeped in corruption. Its last two prime ministers are presumed to have been personally involved in cases of corruption.

---

[1] The term 'regional party', as used in this chapter, means political formations which have been set up specifically to champion regional causes and work for the realisation of regional aspirations. It does not include parties like the Rashtriya Janata Dal (RJD), Samata Party, and Samajwadi Party, which call themselves all-India parties even though their electoral support is confined to particular regions.

The most important reason why the Third Force is opposed to the BJP is its communal origin and character and its proclivity, as demonstrated in the demolition of the Babri Masjid, to resort to Fascist means to impose its Hindu majoritarian views. The Third Force is opposed to BJP's refusal to recognise other religious and cultural identities unless they are prepared to regard themselves as a part of the culture of Hindutva. The Third Force believes that all the members of the Sangh Parivar, i.e., the Vishva Hindu Parishad, Bajrang Dal, Swadeshi Jagaran Manch, Rashtriya Swayamsewak Sangh (RSS) and the BJP are unitedly working to the purpose of bringing about the ultimate triumph of the Hindutva ideology. This is the surest recipe for pushing India into a civil war and destroying its unity and cohesion. The BJP has only one face and that is a communalistic one. If a different moderate face is sought to be projected, it is only for tactical purposes.

In spite of its basic rationale being an alternative to the Congress and the BJP, the Third Force need not be seen as a mere negation of these two political formations. It has a positive ideology of its own and hence a distinct space in the Indian political spectrum.

On the two occasions when a Third Force government was in power, first in 1989 and second in 1996–98, it had to seek the support of one or the other of the two major political formations. In 1989, the National Front government received BJP's support from outside and remained in power only as long as this support was available. The United Front government in 1996–98 was totally dependent on the Congress for remaining in power. The dependence on any of these two major parties cannot but dilute the ideological character of the Third Force. But the very fact that there was in power at the Centre, a government other than that of the Congress and BJP, having its own ideology and programme and occupying its own space, had the potential of making a difference to the economic, social and political situation in the country.

Though the V.P. Singh (1989–91) government can be regarded as a Third Force government, the most determined effort to prepare an agenda for a Third Force and bring it to power was made before the 1996 general elections. In its compromise on secularism and in corruption, the then Congress government had sunk to the lowest imaginable level. In one area where the government had ostensibly done well, i.e., on the economic front, large sections of the population had either been adversely affected or had started feeling concerned about some of the fall-outs of the liberalisation policy and of the Uruguay Round agreements. This inspired hope in the Janata Dal to repeat the performance of its predecessor, the Janata Party, in the 1989 elections when it had captured 142 Lok Sabha seats. From the beginning of 1995, the political parties constituting the core of the Third Force, i.e., the CPI (M), CPI and the Janata Dal started consultations with a view to forging a united front of the Third Force.

This coincided with the initiative by a group of Delhi-based individuals who, towards the end of 1994, formed themselves into a ginger group called the Initiative for National Renewal and Empowerment of the People (INREP)[2] and started working on a political platform and a minimum programme for a Third Force. Their draft was ready by March 1995 and over the next two months it was discussed with each of the political parties constituting the core group of the Third Force (henceforward referred to as the constituent political parties) with the exception of the Samajwadi Party with whom, because of some logistical reasons it did not become possible to arrange a discussion. The draft was then discussed in a joint meeting of these political parties under the chairmanship of V.P. Singh and with the participation of top leaders of these parties. INREP's objective was to get these and some other like-minded political formations committed in advance to the political platform and the minimum programme so that they could enter the next general elections as a united front with an agreed platform. Most of the political parties were prepared to follow such a course of action, but the CPI (M) had reservations. Their view was that in order to form a winning coalition to form a government it might become necessary to forge post-election alliances. Commitment to an agreed platform before the election would, by binding the hands of the constituent political parties, come in the way of forming a winning coalition after the elections. In the CPI (M), there was a difference of opinion between Shri Jyoti Basu who was in favour of a pre-election agreed platform and some others who would have liked to have flexibility in this regard. The issue was debated in the highest policy-making forum of the party and those who did not want the party to commit itself to a platform before the elections, ultimately prevailed. INREP was advised by the CPI (M) to release the document drafted by it in a public function in which the CPI (M) would participate along with the other constituent political parties, and endorse it. Accordingly, INREP released the document in a public function in the Press Club of India in October 1995. Top leaders of most of the constituent political parties attended this function and publicly endorsed the political platform and the minimum programme[3] (henceforward referred to as the Agenda). This is the closest that the Third Force ever came to having a common ideological and programmatic platform before entering a general election. Such an exercise has not been repeated since then partly because of the continuing deterioration in the prospect of a Third Force. Since then, there has been a general disarray in the ranks of the individual constituent parties.

---

[2] The original members of the INREP were Praful Bidwai, Anuradha Chenoy, Kamal Mitra Chenoy, Muchkund Dubey, Seema Mustafa, Deepak Nayyar, Kamala Prasad, S.P. Shukla and Achin Vanaik.

[3] This was subsequently published as a book under the title *Towards a New Politics: Agenda for Third Force*, New Delhi: New Age International, 1996.

The leaders who were present at the release function included V.P. Singh, I.K. Gujral and Surendra Mohan of the Janata Dal, Har Kishan Singh Surjit and Prakash Karat of the CPI (M), and Indrajit Gupta of the CPI.

Mulayam Singh Yadav walked out of Janata Dal with his supporters soon after the fall of the V.P. Singh government in 1990 to form the Samajwadi Party. Before the 1996 elections, a faction of the Janata Dal in Bihar split from the party and formed the Samata Party, aligning itself with the BJP. Thereafter, the remaining Janata Dal split into two, the Rashtriya Janata Dal (RJD) and the Janata Dal (United) (JD [U]). The Janata Dal's performance in the 1996 general elections was poorer than even in the 1991 elections. It won only 46 seats as compared to 52 in the 1991 elections. In spite of this, a Third Force United Front government was formed after the election and remained in power, with a change of prime minister in between, for about two years, with the support of the Congress.

Though because of its internal feud and its abdication of almost everything it stood for, the Third Force has lost its credibility, it is still surviving as an idea. Even after the BJP's emergence as the largest political group in the Lok Sabha and its coming to power in 1998, the constituent parties have sought to revive the Third Force from time to time. Prominent political leaders who had earlier led the Third Force movement and its government at the Centre, are trying to stage a comeback in Indian politics by reviving the Third Force. At its Thiruvananthapuram Special Conference in October, the CPI (M) took a decision 'to participate in governance at the Centre and work towards regrouping a non-Congress and non-BJP alternative'.[4] The CPI has also made a public commitment to this effect. However, in the context of the forthcoming Assembly elections in Tamil Nadu, both the parties are thinking of an alliance with the Congress and the All India Anna Dravida Munnetra Kazhagam (AIADMK) to ensure their political survival in the state. They are justifying their stand on the grounds of the need to preserve the unity of secular forces in order to defeat the Dravida Munnetra Kazhagam (DMK)/BJP formation. And as regards the Third Force, national secretary of the CPI, Mr D. Raja recently stated that 'even if a Third Front came into existence neither it would be effective nor would it decisively influence the course of events in the absence of a major formation leading it'.[5]

Third Force as an Ideology[6]

The INREP publication, *Towards a New Politics: Agenda for Third Force* seeks to define the Third Force as an ideology. This ideology does not, and by its very nature cannot, claim to be an ideal political platform for India. In fact no political formation is entitled to have such a pretension regarding its political

---

[4] *The Hindu*, 20 October 2000.
[5] *The Hindu*, 12 February 2001.
[6] The ideology includes the political philosophy of a Third Force and a minimum programme for it.

platform. This ideology sets the Third Force apart from the two main political formations of the country, i.e., the Congress and the BJP and delineates its space in the Indian political spectrum. The following are the main elements of the ideology of the Third Force.[7]

The Old Politics practised by the Congress was a centrist consensus which tried to reconcile the interests of an emergent Indian bourgeoise and a rising middle class with the aspirations of the poor. This came to be known as Congress socialism. It failed because it was not a socialism in any genuine sense of the term, but a state-driven capitalism. It failed to safeguard the interests of the depressed and deprived groups. State capitalism also gave rise to massive inefficiency and rampant corruption.

The degeneration of the Old Politics coincided with the beginning of the decline of the Congress starting from the late 1960s and the early 1970s. The main reasons for the decline of the Congress were:

(a) Rise of rich farmers looking for political expression outside the Congress.
(b) Growth and consolidation of an industrial elite lacking in commitment to the development of an indigenous industrial base and strong technological self-reliance.
(c) Shift within the grand Congress coalition, with these rising elites becoming more powerful and more successful in imposing their strategic vision, thereby further enlarging the distance between the Congress and the downtrodden masses.
(d) Support extended to this elite by a crucial section of the bureaucracy.
(e) Rise of a criminalised lumpen business class linked with black money and tax evasion; at the same time the lumpenisation of the polity with the consequent rise of a lumpen political elite.
(f) Rising expectations and increasing electoral volatility of the core minorities.
(g) The increasing lopsidedness of the economy and its inability to meet the basic needs of the poor.
(h) The growing federalist pressures leading to the formation of non-Congress regional parties, often by the disgruntled ambitious leaders of the Congress Party itself.
(i) And, above all, the emergence of new social groups and strata in Indian politics which the dominant parties were neither capable of nor willing to accommodate.

Indian politics has remained in flux ever since the beginning of the decline of the Congress. With the rise of numerous political formations reflecting regional aspirations and those of the newly rising social forces, the base of the Congress has been getting narrower and narrower. The BJP has tried to fill the

---

[7] What follows in this section is basically a summary of the Agenda.

vacuum from the right, responding to the growing craving in the upper castes for order and discipline threatened by the rise of hitherto neglected social classes. Subsequently, the BJP has tried to broaden its social base by securing the support of the rising social classes also and it has succeeded in this effort to some extent. But because of its rightist leanings and communal ideology, there are absolute limits to its making further progress in this direction. Therefore, the prospects of a single party addressing itself to the task of building a broad-based coalition of interests are not bright. The results of the general elections since 1977 suggest that the emergence of any kind of stable two-party system at the Centre is highly unlikely. This leaves a big space for alternative political coalitions.

The two principal crises facing the country are: assault on secularism, and the dramatic lurch of the economy towards neo-classical economic policies. After the 1991 balance-of-payments crisis, the Congress government went in for such policies as though there was no different way of linking with the global economy.

There is, therefore, a need to launch a new political movement which can bring this prolonged instability in Indian politics to an end. This movement can be best spearheaded by a Third Force comprising the coalition of parties united on a platform which provides an idealogical alternative to both the BJP and the Congress.

In the realm of economic policies, it is imperative to continue with measures to reform the Indian economy in order to remove excessive controls and allow market forces to play a greater role. Given the role of private foreign capital in the global economy, steps need to be taken to attract foreign private capital. The state should gradually withdraw from economic activities other than in the social, strategic and infrastructural fields. There should be selective linking with the global economy. However, a development strategy based entirely on the neo-classical liberal economic doctrine should be categorically rejected, principally because it ignores some of the basic features of the Indian economy, i.e., its mass poverty, the vast sections of its population being outside the market place, its long tradition of community ownership and management of resources and of living in harmony with nature.

The context and quality of growth is as important as its quantum and the emulation of the consumption pattern and standards of the West is morally unacceptable and ecologically untenable. The following are the main features of the alternative development strategy advocated by the Third Force:

(a) The principal objective should be to meet the basic needs of the people in an ecologically sustainable way.

(b) An employment oriented development strategy: employment generation, particularly off-farm rural employment, should be at the very heart of the economic policy.

(c) Poverty reduction is a function of economic policy and not of growth. A strong comprehensive anti-poverty programme should be implemented.

(d) The trend of falling investment in agriculture should be reversed and land reform measures should be vigorously implemented.

(e) Domestic savings rate should be further raised. India should not depend on foreign investment for its development.

(f) The tax system should be revamped to shift the burden from indirect taxes to direct taxes, to expand the tax base and to control evasion.

(g) There should be massive reductions in public expenditure and a conscious demonstration and inculcation, by way of personal examples of leaders as well as by policy measures, of the spirit of austerity and renunciation.

(h) There should be no unthinking resort to privatisation. Instead, the public sector enterprises should be made truly public and efficient, particularly by liberating them from excessive bureaucratisation and political privileges. The soft option of divesting public sector equities to finance the government's deficits should not be resorted to.

(i) The state should retain the strategic control and direction of the economy. It should raise substantially the capital expenditure in infrastructure.

(j) There should be a new policy on science and technology, geared specifically to the promotion of need-based and indigenous resource-based technologies.

(k) A deliberate policy of delinking from the forces of global capitalism should be followed in selected sectors, particularly in food security, health care, energy, and space and other selected areas of frontier technology.

(l) Economic policies should be geared to making India free from foreign debt within a time-bound period.

(m) Foreign investment should be welcome but on a selective basis and on terms that strengthen India's potential for self-reliance and technological advance.

(n) Excessive and indiscriminate imports should be restricted and vigorous effort should be made to promote exports.

Priority should be accorded to investments in the social sector. Human development should be the highest social responsibility of the state. A conscious policy should be adopted to reduce substantially inter-personal, inter-class and inter-regional inequities. Conditions should be created for the active participation of the marginalised groups, particularly dalits, tribals and women, in the process of development. The state's responsibility in this regard should go beyond emancipation through legal means and welfarism, and should be aimed at their empowerment.

There is a strong need for targeted affirmative action in favour of the underprivileged and dispossessed. To that end, loopholes in the existing schemes of reservations should be plugged. In addition, positive promotional actions, particularly in the field of education, should be taken to enable the underprivileged classes to take advantage of the reservations in their favour and generally to raise their social and economic status.

The excessive consumptionist model of growth is rejected. Steps should be taken to preserve and enhance bio-diversity and to ensure the access of the poor to natural resources. Projects involving large-scale displacement of people should generally be shunned. In case such projects have to be undertaken on compelling economic grounds, then every effort should be made to ensure that they cause minimum displacement, and they are made subject to the scrutiny and approval of those to be displaced.

A fundamentally new orientation should be given to Indian federalism. There should be a radical devolution of power, including of finances, from the Centre to the states. On Jammu and Kashmir, the letter and spirit of Article 370 must be observed and under it maximum possible autonomy should be granted to the state.

Political and financial powers should be devolved not only from the Centre to the states but also from the state to the Panchayat level. The Panchayats should receive resources from the state and also directly from the Centre, as provided in the 73rd and 74th Amendments to the Constitution.

There is no scope for any compromise on the objective of secularism. The principle of a fundamental separation of the state from religious influence and power should be accepted. The state should stand above religion, but it should not be anti-religion. The Third Force rejects the definition of secularism as *sarva dharma samabhava*, i.e., 'equal treatment to all religions'. For, it is the duty of the state to protect the religious practices and places and cultural identities of the minorities. Laws to prevent the use of religion as a basis for winning political support should be enacted.

Above all, there is need for the progressive secularisation of the Indian society. The inculcation and spread of an ideology of secularism must be promoted by the Indian state. What is called for is a refurbishing of the concept of secularism and the launching of a movement to inculcate the values of secularism among the masses, particularly children and the youth. A conscious and vigorous effort should be made to promote a rational scientific and modern notion of secularism, as well as the humane values of all religions. These must be incorporated in school curricula and public education programmes and inform the conduct of state functionaries.

A New Politics in India will not be credible unless it confronts headlong the prevailing malaise of deepening corruption and unaccountability of governance which has reached unprecedented proportions. Every citizen feels insecure and has lost faith in institutions which are expected to enforce fundamental rights and the rule of law. In the situation of an all-pervasive erosion of democratic institutions, it is the poorest who are suffering the most. There is also an increasing resort to violence by state agencies against the poor and in favour of their social exploiters. Therefore, giving India a semblance of accountable government should be a matter of the highest priority. Nothing will be more conducive to combat the evil of corruption than the personal examples of those who are at the helm. This would mean evolving a new style of leadership moving away from the charismatic one, and maintaining a distinction between the party leader and the government leader. The creation of unaccountable centres of unacceptable power should be firmly opposed.

It will be necessary to promote genuine transparency in decision making. Right to information should be recognised as a fundamental right. And major policy issues should be subjected to parliamentary scrutiny and debate.

Specific measures for fighting corruption should include: declaration of assets by all legislators and public servants; expeditious enactment of the Lok Pal and Lok Ayukta bills, no immunity of elected representatives and public servants from prosecution for corruption; top priority to be given to electoral reforms aimed at eliminating the role of money and muscle power from the electoral process; a specific rule to disallow communal propaganda in elections; and the decriminalisation and democratisation of the political party system.

On foreign policy, the highest priority is attached to improving relations with neighbours and pursuing the goal of a 'common security' in South Asia. For this purpose, it will not be desirable to allow any hiatus to be created in the continuing dialogue, including at the summit level, with all South Asian countries. An uninterrupted and determined effort should be made to resolve India's bilateral problems with its neighbours.

And India should 'take unilateral initiatives and make non-reciprocal concessions, particularly in trade and other economic areas, in keeping with its much superior economic and technological capabilities'.[8]

India should pursue a new kind of Non-aligned Movement (NAM) appropriate to the post-Cold War era. The following should be some of the important areas of common struggle under the banner of NAM:

(a) Arresting the erosion of national sovereignty.
(b) Opposing economic exploitation and technology exclusion.
(c) Resisting ecological and cultural imperialism.
(d) Preventing the introduction by the North of new forms of protectionism through non-tariff barriers, discriminatory application of sanitary and phyto-sanitary measures and the insertion of social and environmental clauses in the international trading system.

---

[8] *Towards a New Politics: Agenda for Third Force*, p. 27.

This principle was later given the nomenclature of the Gujral Doctrine and implemented to a limited extent in India's relations with some of its neighbouring countries. It helped in creating a generally favourable climate of cooperation in the region. But in substance it did not amount to much.

The United Nations forum should be used for waging this common struggle. India should continue to use the chosen instrumentalities of G-77 and G-15 for the conduct of India's multilateral diplomacy. It should also network with like-minded non-government organisations (NGOs), both national and international, for pursuing these objectives. It should work for arresting the trend of the decline of the United Nations and restoring to it its over-arching and holistic functions provided in the Charter.

In the area of security and disarmament, efforts should continue to seek the complete elimination of nuclear weapons within an agreed time sched-ule. India is not necessarily opposed to the Comprehensive Test Ban Treaty (CTBT), but thinks that CTBT, a treaty for fissile material freeze and the Non-Proliferation Treaty (NPT) make sense only in the context of a decision to move towards a nuclear weapon-free world. India should retain its nuclear weapon capability and should, therefore, continue to oppose NPT. However, it should give a pledge of no-first-use of nuclear capability against Pakistan. India should also oppose ad hoc discriminatory regimes like the Australia Club, London Club, Missile Transfer Control Regime (MTCR), etc., for pre-venting the transfer of material, substances and technologies which can be used for the production of weapons of mass destruction.

Third Force as a Reality

There is thus a space for a Third Force in Indian politics, based on a distinc-tive and viable ideology. However, in reality, the constituent political parties of the Third Force are seldom able to forge a cohesive alliance and agree on a platform before going to an election. There is considerable divergence in the separate manifestos they adopt for an election. They are not generally seri-ous about the commitments they make in their manifestos. And if they happen to come to power, they keep on making all kinds of compromises on the pledges given by them, in order to stay in power as long as possible. An analysis of the 1996 general election manifestos of the constituent political parties brings out their divergence from the ideology of the Third Force summarised in the above section.[9]

In their criticism of the neo-liberal economic policies, the CPI (M), CPI and the Samajwadi parties were closest to the Agenda. They believed that the economic policies followed by the Congress led to a path that mortgaged India's economic sovereignty and systematically dismantled the self-reliant basis of development. The CPI (M) called for a reversal of the policies of

---

[9] The 1996 election manifestos analysed in this section are those of the CPI (M), CPI, Janata Dal, Samajwadi Party and Samata Party. Out of these, the Samajwadi Party's manifesto was the shortest. As the Samata Party was still trying to emerge as a political force at the time of the 1996 elections, its manifesto cannot be given the same weightage as that given to the manifestos of the other constituent parties.

unbridled liberalisation and stopping the privatisation of the public sector. The CPI was more circumspect in its criticism of the policy of liberalisation. It accepted the need for reforms. It was not against privatisation, but only against the 'wholesale attack' of privatisation. Similarly it was not against divestment, but against divestment 'below par'. The Samajwadi Party was almost as much, if not more, strident in its criticism of the liberalisation policy and in its determination to scrap it, as was the CPI (M). It blamed the Congress for taking the country to economic slavery and expressed its determination to frustrate these efforts. It promised to 'cancel the document of new economic policy' and 'take India out of [the World Trade Organisation] WTO'.

The Janata Dal was the most circumspect in its criticism of the policy of liberalisation. It referred to the Congress government's pursuit of 'so-called' liberalisation, as 'faulty' privatisation and an 'improper manner' of globalisation. This means it was not against liberalisation, privatisation and globalisation per se.

The Janata Dal came closest to accepting the various elements of the alternative economic policy outlined in the Agenda. The CPI came next in adopting these recipes. The CPI (M) confined itself to some of its well-known doctrinnaire approaches. Both CPI (M) and CPI laid particular stress on land reform. The Janata Dal preferred to adopt a cautious attitude on land reform. It promised to 'review and revise the existing land reform laws to plug the loopholes...'. All the constituent parties included in their programmes the enforcement of the 'right to work'.

In the field of social development, promises made by the parties were common and well-known, like allocation of 6 per cent of the gross national product (GNP) for education, increased allocation of resources for basic health and sanitation, health care for all, etc. It is, however, difficult to take these general pledges too seriously.

On federalism, all the parties accepted the suggestion in the Agenda of restructuring Centre-state relations with a view to devolving more powers, including finances, to the states. The Agenda had favoured the creation, where necessary, of more states and had particularly mentioned Uttarakhand and Jharkhand. But bearing in mind the problem faced by some of these parties in the states which they either ruled or where they had major stakes, they suggested the establishment of a State Reorganisation Commission to make recommendations on this subject.[10] On Kashmir, CPI (M), CPI and JD reiterated the policy outlined in the Agenda.

All these parties expressed themselves strongly in favour of devolution of power to the Panchayat level. The Samajwadi Party promised that it would empower the Panchayats, Development Block Councils and Zila Parishads. The CPI (M) made it a point to assert that financial assistance to Panchayats should flow through the state government.

[10] See the manifestos of CPI (M), Samajwadi Party and the Samata Party.

Given the importance of the votes of the backward classes, all these parties pronounced themselves unreservedly in favour of reservations. In fact, even the Congress and BJP did not want to be left behind in this race and in their manifestos generally supported reservations. Some of the constituent parties went further. The CPI and JD wanted to extend reservations to the private sector. The JD wanted it also to be extended to the judicial services. The CPI (M) wanted to bring Christians, converted from scheduled classes, within the ambit of reservations.

The exploitation of reservations for particular OBCs in Bihar had brought the state to the brink of a caste war. The Samata Party showed an awareness of it in its manifesto which stated that 'reservations alone are not enough to struggle against the evil of feudal system'. It also said that reservation without positive action is not of much significance. Finally it expressed concern about 'the toiling and disadvantaged poor of the upper class'. The Janata Dal also showed sensitivity to this issue and promised to bring 'a Constitutional amendment to provide reservation for the economically backward among the forward castes'. The CPI (M) said that with reservations for the Other Backward Castes (OBCs), the creamy layer principle should be implemented. However, the JD, apparently under the influence of its prominent backward class leaders, did not want the creamy layer to be removed until the reservation quotas were filled.

All the constituent parties paid their obeisance to secularism. They all, with the exception of the Samata Party, recognised the danger posed to secularism by the rise of the BJP and castigated the Congress for its compromise on secularism. The Samata Party's stand was less polemical and conciliatory.

None of the constituent parties, except the JD, paid much attention to the suggestion in the Agenda for a pro-active positive programme for promoting and inculcating secularism. The Janata Dal was the only one to make some commitment in this regard, but it was rather vague and general. It said: 'the need for a strong, vibrant and people-based reform movement inspired by the teachings of our philosopher saints, sufis and social reformers to promote religious tolerance and intellectual dissent, cannot be over-emphasised.'

All these parties expressed their concern at the alarming increase in corruption. Their manifestos referred to broadly the same measures to combat this evil, i.e., declaration of assets, adoption of the Lok Pal bill, electoral reforms, etc. The Samajwadi Party promised to 'eliminate corruption from every level'. And the JD talked about state funding of elections.

On foreign policy, all the constituent parties emphasised the need for South Asian cooperation and active cooperation with neighbours. The Samajwadi Party included in its manifesto its longstanding but ill-advised proposal establishing a confederation of India, Pakistan and Bangladesh. It is unfortunate that this party is not able to understand that such a proposal is bound to be taken by Pakistan and Bangladesh as India's refusal to get reconciled to their status as sovereign states and, hence an assault on their sovereignty. The CPI (M) and CPI manifestos had pronounced anti-American salience. The CPI (M) promised to 'strengthen international anti-imperialistic solidarity' and offer 'firm resistance against the US imperialistic attempt to impose its New World Order'. Both CPI (M) and CPI wanted India to cancel what they called the 'military cooperation pact' with the United States. Moreover, as expected, the manifestos of these two parties highlighted the importance of India's non-aligned foreign policy and of South-South cooperation.

The Janata Dal manifesto reproduced verbatim the section of the Agenda on foreign policy with the difference that it specifically declared its opposition to CTBT, describing it 'as an adjunct to NPT'. The JD manifesto also promised to 'establish a National Security Council as a matter of highest priority'.

On security matters, all the constituent parties wanted to keep open the nuclear option of India. All of them were, therefore, against India signing the NPT. The CPI (M) and JD were also against signing CTBT.

The 1996–98 Third Force Government

The Third Force government did not have any significant achievement to its credit when it was in power in 1996–98. With the exception of the signing of the Farakka Agreement, it did not do anything which would mark it out as a government with a difference. It devoted most of its tenure to ensuring its survival as long as possible. In most major respects, it continued the policy of the previous government. It not only continued with the policy of liberalisation but also fine-tuned it and took several steps to impart further momentum to the process. These included further liberalisation of licencing procedures, abolition of controls and phasing out of public sector activities. It resorted to even worse forms of profligacy than the Congress. The phenomenal hike in the salaries of government servants which triggered a chain of such hikes all around and the forgiveness of a huge amount of loans owed by a state government are just a few examples of such profligacy. Some of its constituents openly allied themselves with criminal elements in politics. A good percentage of its elected members had criminal records. It remained in power with the help of political formations which have become the symbol of corruption in the country. Far from setting personal examples of austerity and renunciation, its leaders had an opulent life style.

The propensity of its constituents to compromise even on secularism was demonstrated after the 1998 general elections when the Samata Party and a number of very important regional formations made an alliance with the BJP to form the government at the Centre. This makes it difficult to take the secular credentials of these parties at their face value.

The government took no initiatives for redeeming some of the important pledges made in the manifestos of the constituent parties. These included launching a pro-active programme for promoting secularism, devolution of power to the states and the Panchayats, initiating a broad-based dialogue for strengthening Article 370 and granting maximum autonomy to the state of Jammu and Kashmir and carrying out some of the promised reforms to contain corruption. The Lok Pal bill could not make much headway as, among others, it got bogged down in a controversy as to whether the prime minister should come within its ambit. This was in spite of the fact that the manifestos of almost all constituent political parties had pledged that the prime minister would be covered by this piece of legislation.

The Farakka Agreement was a major achievement because it is doubtful whether any other government at the Centre would have been able to sign this agreement. For, an agreement on this issue would have been possible only with the full cooperation of the state of West Bengal which is the principally affected party. The fact that the ruling party in West Bengal, i.e., the CPI (M) was a constituent of the Third Force which was in power at the Centre, was the main reason for the successful conclusion of the agreement.

The basic constraint of the second Third Force government was its dependence on the Congress support to remain in power. It had to look over its shoulder all the time in a bid to ensure that this support was not withdrawn. And ultimately it collapsed because of the withdrawal of the Congress support. The other major constraint was the opportunistic alliances it had to make with all kinds of undesirable political forces to ascend to and remain in power. The concessions it had to grant to these political forces made a nonsense of its ideological stance.

The Future of the Third Force

In spite of the declared intention of some political parties and leaders to revive the Third Force, the prospects for it do not appear to be promising. In the context of the forthcoming state elections, the CPI (M) and CPI, which are committed to the Third Force idea, have already given it a back seat in their desperate bid to retain their political influence in these states. This is in keeping with the past experience of opportunistic and shifting alliances formed by the constituents of the Third Force. The ideology becomes the first casualty of opportunistic alliances. Personality factors, caste and community considerations and even money play an important role. The over-riding objective is to ensure political survival. For the same general elections, alliances have been made with a major party in some states and against that party in some other states. Alliances have been made with political parties and leaders steeped in corruption and deeply involved in criminal activities. Such alliances are often called secular alliances. But this is a mere slogan. For, it has been seen that the same political formations which had earlier joined a secular front had no hesitation in deserting that front and walking away with BJP in order to ensure their political survival at the state level and share power in the central government. Besides, can a political leader (or his party) be trusted to have any basic value, including that of secularism, when he habitually violates all other basic values or norms of social and public behaviour, like flouting the rule of law, resorting to violence as a means of conducting politics, looting public funds, etc.? Unfortunately, there is increasing evidence recently of the criminalisation of the party machinery of even the CPI (M).

Some political leaders who had in the past led Third Force governments have started movements which may appear to have the potential of reviving the Third Force.[11] These movements are around the theme of the adverse effects of liberalisation and globalisation, impact of the WTO Agreement on Agriculture on Indian farmers, the problem of the settlement of those who live in urban slums, and the problems created by the relocation of polluting industrial units outside urban centres. These essentially single-point issues are designed to serve as an entry point for launching a full-fledged political movement for reviving the Third Force. These single-point issues are not necessarily in keeping with the Agenda for the Third Force. For relaunching the Third Force movement, what is required is an integrated programme containing all the major elements of the Third Force Agenda.

Besides, opposition to liberalisation and globalisation per se, is unlikely to become a basis for reviving the Third Force. Single-point issues relating to an agreement to which India is a party or an issue which affects different sections of the population differently also have no future. Movements launched by these political leaders are, therefore, seen as opportunistic. Moreover, it is believed that these leaders themselves would not be able to adhere to these platforms once they ascend to power.

Economic reforms by themselves have not very much influenced the outcome of elections in India recently. In spite of the turn-around in the economy brought about by the economic reforms during the Congress rule in 1991–96, the Congress has gone on losing ground starting from the 1996 elections. Similarly, political formations like the CPI (M) and CPI which made opposition to liberalisation a principal plank of their political platform have also lost ground and, in any case, have not improved their positions. The reasons for electoral reversal or success, therefore, do not lie in the stand taken on economic reform but elsewhere, in broader economic, social and moral domains. While opposing economic reforms when out of power, no political party has tried to upset the apple cart of reforms after it has come to wield or share power. So the process of reform has been moving apace without interruption, though at the typical Indian pace and with typical Indian compromises. Every political party when it came to power, adopted additional measures to

---

[11] These leaders are former Prime Ministers V.P. Singh, Chandrashekhar and Deve Gowda.

keep the process of liberalisation going. At the same time, they have all buttressed and strengthened the government's anti-poverty programmes. There is also a consensus among the political parties not to give up control which will block avenues for making money or dispensing with patronages which are regarded as essential for remaining in politics.

Though there is no prospect for an early revival of the Third Force, there are compelling reasons why the Third Force will survive as an idea in the foreseeable future. This is mainly because neither the Congress nor the BJP can emerge as a political party with an absolute majority of seats in the Parliament. Even though the BJP is projecting a liberal non-communalist image and has, by virtue of this and other factors, somewhat succeeded in widening the base of its political support, it remains fixated in the public mind as a Hindu party. It has not, therefore, made much of a dent into the minority vote banks. Moreover, the BJP's support base remains confined to northern, central and western India. It has not made much headway either in the south or in eastern India. Its share of the dalit, tribal and OBC votes is still small. It has come to and remains in power mainly by virtue of regional and other parties which command a larger share of these vote banks. If the BJP really changes its face in order to lure away voters from these groups, there is a danger of its losing its huge vote bank of the believers in Hindutva, which has expanded phenomenally in recent years. Thus there is a self-operating limit on the extent to which the BJP can expand its support base.

The Congress has ceased to be a party of consensus combining in it all the mainstreams of Indian politics. Now many independent streams have been formed by factions splitting away from the Congress. It is impossible to bring them back into the Congress. At best, it can seek their cooperation. But then there are other contenders. Besides, they also have their own ambitions. The continuing dynastical rule in the Congress, its rampant practice of cronyism and its lack of internal party democracy, should rule out the prospect of its being revived as a party with a broader and stronger support base.

Both the BJP and the Congress remain severely compromised on some of the burning issues in the country, such as, secularism, combating corruption, the role of the Indian state in bringing about social transformation and effective transfer of power to the grassroot level. It is futile to expect from these parties anything different from the *status quo* on these matters. On the other hand, changing the *status quo* in these areas is the defining characteristic of the Third Force.

Some Conditions for Reviving the Third Force

The revival of the Third Force can be facilitated if it is led by a single large formation as in the case of the Janata Party in 1989, with broad-based national support. The formation should be totally wedded to the ideology of the Third

Force and should be led by leaders of unimpeachable integrity. The chances of electoral success of a Third Force will improve materially if its constituent parties can forge an agreed platform before going to an election.

In spite of their recent errant behaviour and serious distortions in the CPI (M) party mechanism, the leftist parties will have to be in the vanguard of the movement for reviving the Third Force. They are the only ones who are uncompromisingly wedded to the core of the Third Force ideology. They have also considerably moderated their earlier extremist positions on some aspects of economic reforms and globalisation. Once in government, they have demonstrated their capacity to act in broad national interest, leaving aside their ideological baggage.

It would be absolutely essential to seek the support of regional parties. The task of mobilising this support will be difficult, but not impossible. There are many reasons why regional parties should be natural components of a Third Force. The Third Force is in favour of the federalisation of Indian politics. This also happens to be the *raison d'etre* of the regional parties. It is widely recognised that the Indian polity has gone too far in the direction of centralisation. This imbalance needs to be corrected by appropriate devolution of power to the states. However, there would continue to be a need for a strong central government in India. This will be needed not only for the protection of the sovereignty and territorial integrity of the country, but also for the creation and maintenance of a single integrated national market, which is the *sine qua non* for acquiring economic efficiency and competitiveness and for taking the fullest possible advantage of the process of liberalisation and globalisation. Even the Chinese central government which, as a part of the economic reform, devolved a large measure of decision-making authority to the local level, has come to realise that things have gone rather too far in one direction, and is now working to achieve a degree of uniformity in the rules, regulations and policies governing economic activities and transactions. The participation of the regional parties in the government at the Centre will itself make them realise that the balance cannot be tilted too far in the direction of federalisation and that they have a stake in a strong central government.

With the exception of the Shiv Sena, no regional party has demonstrated any pronounced communal leaning. Most of them also reflect the aspirations of the rising social strata, particularly the deprived sections of the population. They have also demonstrated that they have a pragmatic and balanced approach to the issues of liberalisation and globalisation. These stances are perfectly in harmony with the ideology of the Third Force. What is needed is a pro-active programme to mobilise the support of the regional parties and a continuing dialogue between these parties and other components of the Third Force as a part of a mutually reinforcing process of secularisation and radicalisation.

In order to forge alliances, there will no doubt be a need for some flexibility in ideology. But the core ideology must remain intact. Any compromise on it will destroy the very basis of the Third Force. This core will consist of:

- No compromise with forces of communalism.
- Consciously working for the welfare and empowerment of the minorities, and marginalised sections of the population, that is, the dalits, tribals, other backward classes and women.
- Offering a clear-cut alternative to the policy of unbridled liberalisation and globalisation: Among others, offering an employment-oriented and people-centred development strategy.
- No compromise with forces of corruption and crime.
- Providing a clean government which works and delivers what it promises.
- The practice of internal democracy in each of its constituent parties.

A strong genuine Third Force is not likely to emerge in the near future mainly because of the ills that have afflicted all the political parties, including those which can be expected to constitute the Third Force. But the Third Force must be kept alive as an ideology, as a mirror to all political parties to enable them and the people at large to see their true face, and as a reminder of the direction in which the Indian economy and polity should move. There is also a need for a ginger group which keeps on working on the ideology of the Third Force and mobilising support for it. For all one knows, the Third Force may suddenly emerge as a major force on the Indian political scene once, on account of the continuing crises of the Indian polity and economy, things start sharply deteriorating, the unity of the nation is jeopardised, the economy starts stagnating and the current disregard for law and order and resort to violence assumes endemic proportions.

12

THE NATIONAL PARTIES AND THE REGIONAL ALLIES
A STUDY IN THE SOCIO-POLITICAL DYNAMICS

Pradeep Kumar

I

Institutions do not exist in a vacuum and therefore, cannot be studied in isolation.[1] They are always in interface with several other institutions, an interaction which eventually determines their nature. In fact it is not the institutions that so much affect the society, as it is the latter that actually determines the real nature of the institutions by making them operate in its social, cultural and political milieu. In his study of federalism, W.S. Livingston observed several decades ago that the real determinant of federal institutions is not a federal constitution, but the federal nature of that society. Even if the legal constitutional framework does not provide for a genuine federal system, the latter would be established as a consequence of the operational dynamics of that society, provided that the society is federal in nature. Federal government is thus only a device by which the federal qualities of a society are articulated and protected.[2]

This emphasis on the social determinants of institutions is particularly significant in the modern context in those societies where democratic institutions have been introduced over a period of time. It is only through the operation of the democratic principle that the real underlying tendencies can manifest themselves through the process of unfoldment. Needless to say, this does not happen in a short span of time, but may take several decades if the society is exposed to the democratic institutions for the first time, and the people are yet to come to terms with the working of these democratic bodies.

India combines antiquity with continuity which has made the Indian society excessively diverse. This diversity is not merely linguistic as goes the general

---

[1] This article broadly concerns itself with an analysis of the national-regional interaction, and leaves out the details of data, assuming these are well known.

[2] W.S. Livingston, *Federalism and Constitutional Change*, Oxford: Clarendon Press, 1956, p. 2.

impression in view of the creation of the linguistic states, but extends to other domains of life, such as, culture, religion and caste as well. More than this, the 'antiquity' of the Indian civilisation, as perceived by its people, has led to a historiography which has helped in the construction of several territorially organised cultural peoples. They perceive themselves to be cultural entities with their own histories, cultures, literatures, religions and linguistic traditions, and have a 'glorious' past to fall back upon, when face-to-face with the existential realities of political and economic deprivations. Unlike the American society where centuries of rapid industrialisation have levelled the social ground by bulldozing the social and economic 'unevenness' to a great extent, the essentially agrarian nature of the Indian economy has retained these diversities. The latter have only been reinforced by the retarded and uneven growth of capitalism during the colonial and the post-colonial periods.[3]

India has in fact been termed a 'continent of many communities united through shared experience but powerfully motivated by parochial and regional considerations'.[4] It is this existence of culturally distinct regions or sub-regions in India (not necessarily coinciding with the political units, called states) which tends to counteract the attempts at centralisation. It is these cultural regions which have, over the years, strengthened and helped the process of the manifestation of the centrifugal forces operating in an extremely diverse society like that of India.

No centrifugal force, however, can really be strong enough to exercise any tangible impact on a system unless it is reasonably strong and organised. The organisation becomes possible through mobilisation, and it is through mobilisation that some kind of a regional identity can be constructed which is so essential to exert pressure on the Centre in a federal system. This role is generally played by the regional parties which provide to these regional forces an opportunity to articulate their interests through the mechanism of their party apparatus. It is important to note here that regional parties do not merely provide a platform to regional forces to organise and manifest themselves, but at the same time they also strengthen regional sentiments. This means that while drawing support from regional sentiments, these parties also lend strength and support to them. It is largely through the operation of such parties that the regional interests really come to influence the balance of power in a federation.

A federal government is usually placed in an advantageous position to deal with various kinds of regional and sub-regional tendencies, as it provides them with a forum to enjoy some degree of autonomy. But the federal

---

[3] Pradeep Kumar, 'Centrifugalism in the Indian Federation: A Sociological Study', in Rasheeduddin Khan (ed.), *Rethinking Indian Federalism*, Shimla: Indian Institute for Advanced Studies, 1997, pp. 103–23.
[4] Lewis P. Fickett, 'The Politics of Regionalism in India', *Pacific Affairs*, 44(2), Summer, 1971, p. 193.

government by its very nature provides a congenial political environment for the growth and strengthening of such feelings in the first place. A federal system in fact aims at maintaining some kind of a balance between these regional pulls and the sentiments for cohesive nationalism.

It may be important here to mention a few lines about the very notion of nationalism in India. Ravinder Kumar[5] has called it a civilisational state preferring this word over nation state. Similarly, yet another scholar has used the word 'nationism' to denote the Indian variety of nationalism, thereby meaning a more subtle and abstract desire of the Indian people to be together, without actually underplaying the various diversities and variegated identities which demand cultural and political space to flourish and enrich their sense of common living.[6] Thus, 'from the very outset, the notion of a nation-state was difficult to reconcile with the wide range of regional cultures and local solidarities which went into the making of Indian civilisation.... The crystallisation of democratic politics in our society, since the attainment of independence, has created a heightened consciousness of local and regional identities. [Consequently] the very use of the term Nation sends tremors of alarm through wide swathes of the Indian people.'[7]

The nature or content of Indian nationalism is obviously not the same as that of the European nations which have been, by and large, linguistically and culturally homogeneous small entities, evolved over centuries of conflict and strife. The Indian concept of *rashtra* which has been translated as 'nation', is, on the contrary, a geographically and culturally[8] loose entity which has 'felt' united through its history and culture, which in turn, have been diverse but have held some basic tenets in common. These common tenets cannot actually be codified, and this is precisely the reason that when someone asks an Indian statesman to define the concept of 'composite culture', one is asking

---

[5] Ravinder Kumar, *The Emergence of Modern India: Retrospect and Prospect*, Shimla: Indian Institute for Advanced Study, 1990.

[6] S.L. Verma, *Federal Authority in the Indian Political System*, Jaipur: RBSA Publishers, 1987, pp. 165–66.

[7] Kumar, *The Emergence of Modern India*, p. 39.

[8] The definition of the Indian *rashtra* in the Puranic literature has been essentially geographical. Thus the Vishnu Purana defines India as:

Uttarany at Samudrasya, Himadreshchaiva Dakshinam,
Varsha Tad Bharat, Naam Bharati Yatra Santatih.
(North of the oceans and south of the snows, lies the land of Bharat whose children are Bharatis.)

Also V.D. Savarkar gave a somewhat similar definition in his Hindutva:

Aa Sindhu Sindhu Paryantah, Yasya Bharata Bhoomika,
Pitribhu Punyabhuschaiva Sa Vai Hinduriti Smritah.
(From the river Indus to the Indian ocean, lies the land of Bharat, which is the father land as well as the sacred land for the Hindus.)

for a problematic task, both conceptually as well as descriptively. It is naturally not as cohesive and cemented a nation, as are most nations of Europe.

It is this essential difference between the two contextual settings that makes it necessary to further distinguish the European and the American 'policies' of 'multi-culturalism' from the basic cultural and traditional 'philosophy' of 'unity in diversity' in India. In the west, multi-culturalism was adopted as a political policy of accommodating the 'other' cultures which came face-to-face with the indigenous cultures of these countries as a result of the influx of migrants from various Asian and African societies. To negotiate and re-negotiate the political equations and the social relationships with these 'alien' cultures, was the political compulsion of these western nations. In a way it was making virtue out of necessity that the concept of multi-culturalism became a part of the political ideology of even a country like the USA where the nation had been a 'melting pot' of various diverse cultures, which were to gradually lose their Hispanic, Red Indian, Eskimo or Ukrainian roots, to get melted in the White Anglo Saxon Protestant (WASP) 'mega melting pot'.

What happened in the Indian subcontinent was much different. The diverse cultures did not come from any 'alien' lands, they had inhabited the land for several thousand years, and their antiquity was the subject of controversies and debates for the historians but not for themselves. (The reference is to diverse cultures, and not necessarily to religions, some of which did origi-nate outside India.) The principle of 'unity in diversity' may have been part of the 'political policy' of the government, but it was in a way also embedded in Indian culture and psyche for centuries, not as a 'policy' but as a cultural idiom, where diverse cultures co-existed without much hostility on this account. The Shaivites, the Vaishnavites and several other sectarian saints did move around the length and the breadth of the *jambu dweep*, interacting with the fol-lowers of different schools of philosophy in the north and the south. The Bhakti saints of the south and of Maharashtra inspired the movement in the north. Thus, tremendous cultural and sectarian diversity co-existed within a broad geographical land mass, without being necessarily co-terminus with any political boundaries. This made the Indian *rashtra* quite distinct from the western notion of a nation.

II

The somewhat lengthy discussion on the content of Indian nationalism is helpful in understanding the nature of regional pulls. These have been affected as a result of a politicisation process which began with the advent of democ-racy in the colonial period itself when it was introduced in small doses. Later, with the dawn of independence, it became the guiding principle of the polity, and still later in the post-Emergency period, this regional diversity was more fully reflected in the political realm when the electoral democracy broadened its base, and the masses were drawn into it in a big way.

The regional pulls were inevitable in the wake of the marriage of tremendous territorially organised diversity with the process of politicisation which gradually extended further, and enveloped every section of the polity with the massification and 'grass rootisation' of the electoral democracy. One may divide this process of gradual emergence and strengthening of the regional pulls into broadly four time spans.

In the first period that lasted between 1950 and 1967, the pulls were (i) not fully operative in the absence of a fully grown democratic system necessary to strengthen such regional sentiments in the first place, and (ii) were severely handicapped and felt constrained in the wake of the working of a dominant party system which subsumed most regional feelings. The latter had very little scope for articulation in the political realm outside the Congress system which nearly monopolised the political space in the first two decades of the post-independence period.

Much of the pressure that was exerted on the Congress Centre in this period, actually came from the regional satraps from within the loose Banyan tree-like heterogeneous structure of the Congress Party. This popularly came to be known as the era of strong chief ministers[9] which eventually culminated in what came to be popularly called the 'federalisation' of the Congress Party.[10] Many regional leaders who were Pradesh Congress Committee (PCC) chiefs in many states (locally called state Congress presidents) were known for exerting pressure on the party. This made some of them replace the Congress chief ministers of their respective states. Many scholars writing about the developments of the 1960s, actually analysed these pressures from the regions as an inevitable consequence of the working of democracy in a one-party dominant system. Yet others described this as the working of a 'system' that the Congress had turned itself into to cope with the large number of regional and other diversities.

[9] M.M. Rahman catalogues some of these leaders as K. Kamaraj of Tamil Nadu, S.K. Patil of Bombay, N. Sanjiva Reddy of Andhra Pradesh, S. Nijalingappa of Mysore. He describes the emergence of this group of state leaders as the third area of power that emerged in the Congress Party after the death of Nehru, the other two being dominated by Indira Gandhi and Morarji Desai. M.M. Rahman, *The Congress Crisis*, Delhi: Associated Publishing House, 1970.

Myron Weiner calculates the strength of the chief ministers on the basis of their duration as chief ministers and classifies Ghulam Mohammad Bakshi (1953–64), K. Kamaraj (1954–65), Partap Singh Kairon (1956–64), B.C. Roy (1948–62), and Govind Ballabh Pant (1946–55), as strong chief ministers. Myron Weiner (ed.), *State Politics in India*, New Jersey: Princeton University Press, 1967, p. 49.

[10] Pradeep Kumar, *Studies in Indian Federalism*, Delhi: Deep and Deep Publications, 1988, pp. 194–210.

In a way, the regional pulls were so much in operation that the Congress in the 1960s had to work like a federal organisation whose state/regional units were at times behaving like the regional parties, putting all kinds of pressures to force the central ruling leadership to succumb to their demands. The non-implementation of the Official Language Act and the Three-language Formula, the tardy implementation of land reforms in most states, the non-compliance of the West Bengal and Bihar governments on the Damodar Valley Corporation project,[11] the strong sentiments on the linguistic states issue, were some such examples which showed the areas of serious conflict between the Centre and the regional units of the Congress Party in the 1950s/1960s. This was a very interesting case of an embryonic development of a model where a 'national party' had to negotiate its terms with its 'regional allies', all of course, within the political space provided by the Congress Party, which, needless to say, was severely restricted, constrained and therefore, limited.

The second phase began in the aftermath of the fourth general elections in 1967, and continued for a decade or so, only to end in the post-Emergency democratic upsurge. The elections in fact only manifested the hidden tensions that the Congress system had already developed. While it is true that the loose organisation of the Congress Party accommodated the regional pulls to a great extent, it should be conceded that there is a limit beyond which no party worth its salt can give space to the dissenting groups. It was in that sense that the fourth general elections were nothing but a manifestation of some kind of a political revolt that symbolised the growing assertion of the 'regional allies' within the Congress system. It was not the emergence of these regional satraps, but the ease with which they opted out of the Congress Party, that was more significant than any other development.

It is interesting to observe that the breaking of the umbilical cord with the (parent) national party was not entirely complete, and this was indicated in the nomenclature of most of these newly emergent political parties. The latter were actually only regional outfits which had earlier been representing the strong regional forces within the Congress system. These newly formed parties took such Congress-sounding names as the Kerala Congress, the Bang Congress, the Jana Congress and the Utkal Congress, as if they were only the regional organisational units of the parent Congress Party. An attempt was thus made to tread the middle path by keeping the national image intact with its Congress suffix, but at the same time identifying with the regional support base by using the state name as its prefix.

This was in a way a beautiful linguistic expression to identify the transitional phase that characterised the gradual opening up of the national political space for the regional political formations. It is, however, true that this experience

[11] Marcus Franda, *West Bengal and the Federalising Process in India*, New Jersey: Princeton University Press, 1968, p. 105.

was relatively short lived, and soon thereafter the mid-term elections were forced on several states in 1969, which only further reinforced the fluid nature of this transitory politics. The re-emergence of the dominant party system in the 1971 and 1972 Lok Sabha and Vidhan Sabha elections, respectively, was more in form than in reality. The restoration of the system, as analysed by several scholars, did not result in the accommodation of political dissent, as had been the case earlier. It only further narrowed and restricted the space for the dissenting groups, many of which were the regional satraps. The shrinking space within the Congress Party gave rise to an ironical situation where increased electoral presence of the Congress Party in the Lok Sabha actually meant growing power of the regional political outfits. The crude and brutal way in which the central leadership of the Congress Party resorted to the pulling down of its own governments in the states, and the unceremonious ways in which the Congress chief ministers were removed, further reflected the narrowing political space.

More than the non-Congress chief ministers, it was the Congress chief ministers on whose heads the Democle's sword actually hung. This meant more 'revolts' in the regions, both within as well as outside the Congress Party. The regional pulls were so strong that the attempts to suppress them by the mighty Congress Party soon undermined the strength of the party, resulting in the imposition of Emergency. Paradoxically, the frequent imposition of president's rule under Article 356 of the Indian Constitution, symbolised not a powerful Centre but a 'pathology' of federalism resulting from the powerlessness of the Centre.[12]

A logical consequence of this development was the third phase which marked the eventual emergence of these regional groups as independent political forces at the level of the states. In many states these became the ruling parties, either on their own or in coalition with some other regional outfits. In some other states, some of these regional parties were in a position to compel the Congress Party to coalesce with the regionally dominant party. The latter was in a position to call the shots, and the Congress had no choice but to acquiesce in this arrangement, alternative to which was ouster from political power in the state. Thus the period between 1980 and 1996 broadly characterised this kind of politics. In the 1980s, two types of two-party systems emerged, 'those in which regional parties formed the principal opposition to the Congress, and those in which the principal opposition was from all-India parties'.[13] Thus, in very many states the regional parties became either

---

[12] Paul R. Brass, *Ethnicity and Nationalism: Theory and Comparison*, New Delhi: Sage Publications, 1991, pp. 148, 152–53.

[13] Sudha Pai, 'From One-Party Dominance to Multi-Partyism: Regionalising Trends in the Development of the Indian Multi-Party System', in S. Bhatnagar and Pradeep Kumar (eds), *Some Issues in Contemporary Indian Politics*, Delhi: Ess Ess Publications, 1997, pp. 172–73.

the dominant coalition partners or even the sole ruling parties. In some others, they continued to be the sole ruling parties-in-waiting.

And finally, in the period following the eclipse of the Congress Party in the 1996 elections, the regional formations came to share the political power, not merely in the states, but became indispensable at the Centre as well. In a way, the rapid withdrawal of the Congress Party from the political scene in the 1990s was co-terminus with the rise of the regional parties which were literally stepping in to fill up the space created by the gradual but steady decline of the Congress throughout the 1980s. Ironically, the 1980 and the 1984 Lok Sabha elections which the Congress won with comfortable majorities (it won in 1984 with an unprecedented majority) had also marked the decline of the party. It has been maintained that the party continuously gave way to the regional forces, and neither of these two elections restored the Congress dominance.[14]

In a way, the 1996 Lok Sabha elections only marked the arrival of the regional political formations on the national scene. In the 1980s, and also on most earlier occasions, the national parties had faced a challenge from these regional groups/parties/formations, largely at the state level. And when the non-Congress coalitions were formed at the Centre, as in 1977 and 1989, it was always some national party that had been in the dominant position. In fact, the 1977 coalition of the Janata government broadly comprised Congress for Democracy (CFD), Bharatiya Lok Dal, Congress (O), Jana Sangh and the socialists, all of whom in fact had an all-India ideological plank, and though restricted in their electoral bases, were not regionalists in their programmatic mobilisation. The CFD was in fact only a group of Congress men who had left their party on the eve of the sixth Lok Sabha poll, Jana Sangh was a strong 'nationalist' party with an all-India ideological constituency. The socialists and the Bharatiya Lok Dal were, however, confined to certain states in the north, and had not till then emerged as players in national politics.

In any case, more important than this was the fact that the very circumstances that virtually forced these parties to come together concerned the national issues of civil liberty, and restoration of the democratic institutions after the 19-month period of Emergency. In other words, even if the constituents of the Janata Party could be treated as regional formations in view of their narrow regional electoral bases, the issues on which they mobilised votes during the electoral campaigns were certainly pan-Indian. In fact the regional issues were then put into the background in the wake of the larger issue of political survival. It was this important reason that made these parties not only coalesce but also merge their identities into a single political entity, called the Janata Party.

Contrary to this, in 1989, the regional groups that challenged the Congress Party rather successfully, did not like to lose their identities, and all that they

---

[14] Pai, ibid., p. 168.

conceded to each other was the National Front. This was symbolic of the
desire of these parties to join each other only on a 'front' to fight the Congress,
something they had all been doing separately in their respective states
throughout the previous decades, mobilising the anti-Congress vote. It was,
however, still the National Front where the dominant leadership, both in
qualitative and quantitative terms, largely came from the Janata Dal (JD)
which was the principal political party to have mobilised the anti-Congress
vote, mainly on the Bofors issue, thereby giving an all-India call against
corruption in high levels of governance. The major supporters of this Janata
Dal-led National Front government, namely the Left Front and the Bharatiya
Janata Party (BJP), were in no way 'regionalist' in their ideological predilections, and some 'regional' constituents of this Front, like the Telugu Desam
Party (TDP) in Andhra Pradesh, the Congress (S) in Kerala, and the Dravida
Munnetra Kazhagam (DMK) in Tamil Nadu, had actually failed to perform
very well in terms of electoral gains.

The real assertion of the regional parties, however, became possible in
1996 when the National Front government, formed in the aftermath of the
resignation of the 13-day-old BJP government, was essentially a coalition of
various regional parties. Important to note is that unlike on the previous
occasions (1977 and 1989), this was not entirely a pre-election alliance. There
was actually no mobilisation under any national stalwart like Morarji Desai
(1977) or V.P. Singh (1989). This was very clearly evident in the making of the
prime minister in H.D. Deve Gowda, a small regional leader whose politics
had till then remained confined to his home state of Karnataka. Most people
in fact could not have even speculated his name among the prime ministerial
candidates.[15] The 13-odd parties which merged their differences to rally
against the two national parties, the BJP and the Congress, did not merge
their identities. Even a feeble attempt in this direction was not made.

It was truly a coalition of several region-based parties, many with their
own regional agendas, something which actually disturbed the metropolitan
'nationalist' voters who anticipated instability, 'regional parochialism', and
the consequent neglect of national interest.

The defeat of the BJP-led government within 13 days in office in 1996,
really forced it to do some rethinking on the issue of coalitional partners. The
party, with its national, all-India political ambitions, had till then carefully

---

[15] It is interesting to mention that in an interview schedule, prepared at the Centre for the
Study of Developing Societies, Delhi, to conduct an all-India survey of the general elections in 1996, with which this author was also associated, Deve Gowda's name did not
figure among several options given to the voters to identify the choice of their future prime
minister. This is significant in view of the fact that this list was quite exhaustive and
included such names as those of Mayawati, Kanshi Ram, V.P. Singh, Chandrashekhar,
Mulayam Singh Yadav, Laloo Yadav, and perhaps every conceivable name. Also see,
'Cover Story', *India Today*, 31 August 1996.

avoided regional alliances, and had in a way denounced regionalism. Its alliance with the Shiv Sena in Maharashtra was more in tune with its Hindutva plank than an arrangement with a regional party. The BJP had even viewed regionalism as something antithetical to nationalism, which had earlier made it denounce the idea of small states. It was only in the late 1980s that it compromised on the issue in the wake of the growing sentiments for separate states in Uttarakhand (Uttar Pradesh [UP]) and Jharkhand (Bihar), and included these demands in its party manifestoes for the subsequent elections.

It was the realisation of the impossibility of forming a government on its own that gradually forced the BJP to enter into active alliances with regional political parties. It was this dawning of political wisdom which made it a dominant partner in the 1998 government, something which the Congress Party consistently ignored. The downfall of the BJP-led coalition in 1999 and the subsequent elections, only further underlined the need for the BJP to broaden its base by not merely accommodating, but giving space to the regional political parties. This made some partners of the National Front, like the DMK and the TDP, swing their loyalties to the BJP-led coalition government. Even a faction of the Janata Dal, another constituent of the Front, eventually came over to this national coalition of the regional political parties. This government in fact became a coalition of the largest number of regional parties that ever came together to form a government in India.

The decline of the Congress was not so much in terms of its own base, which had in fact improved in some states at least, as it was in terms of its total neglect of the need to see the writing on the wall. The party kept on insisting on fighting elections alone, and indeed decried the coalition arrangements as unworkable and unstable.[16] The Jayalalitha factor in 1999, and the Chandrababu Naidu or the Mamata factor in the contemporary scenario, only indicate the growing power of the regional satraps of the parties that have emerged in the last one decade, as powers to be reckoned with.

III

A brief analysis of the factors that might have been responsible for this gradual but steady shift from national to regional politics may be in order here. This will help us in understanding the nature of the regional allies that have come to affect the balance of power at the Centre. Let us begin with the study of the process of democratisation that has characterised Indian politics in

---

[16] Balveer Arora, 'Regional Aspirations and National Cohesion: Federal Coalitions in the 1998 Lok Sabha Elections', *West Bengal Political Science Review*, Vol. 1, Nos 1 & 2 Inaugural issue, January–December, 1998, pp. 69–70.

the post-independence period. It may look quite rhetorical, particularly to the dominant sections of our middle class, that the survey data collected on the eve of various general elections held in the 1990s,[17] clearly reveals that there has been a massive churning of the electorate in these years. Not only has the total turnout gone up and stabilised around 60 per cent, but even the nature of this massive electorate has considerably changed.

The periodic elections based on universal adult franchise have ensured some kind of an 'electoral socialism'[18] whereby everyone has got a chance to exercise one's vote. While there may have been cases of intimidation with regard to the weaker sections, and also those of violence, booth capturing and rigging, these have not over the years seriously or materially affected the outcome of the elections held on such a massive scale. Even the much maligned 'vote banks' are no longer the 'frozen' vote banks which could permanently ensure any party's victory or defeat. These have actually materially changed in their content.

The various vote banks have changed strategies and supported different political formations in different elections, thereby determining decisively the fortunes of various political actors. Thus, to take an example, if the dalits and the Muslims constituted the vote banks of the Congress Party before the 1977 elections when they voted en bloc for it, in the last two decades they have not stuck to any one political formation. In UP the Muslims have generally favoured the Samajwadi Party, but elsewhere they have voted for other parties, including the Congress. Once again attempts are being made by the Congress in UP to woo back the Muslim voter, and even with some success. Similarly, the dalits in UP have switched over to the BSP, but this also in no way is final, and the Congress or even the BJP may partly succeed in winning over at least some sections of the dalits in UP. Similarly, if a section of the Other Backward Castes (OBCs) (like the Kurmis or the Koeris) supports the BJP in UP, another powerful section (the Yadavs) aligns with the SP.

It is this fluid nature of the erstwhile frozen vote banks that has made some analysts use other terms such as cluster voting[19] or bloc voting[20] for the conventional term used for these voting patterns. This has largely become possible due to the trickling down of democracy to almost all sections of the society, something which was greatly facilitated by the operation of the political process through periodically held elections. Politicisation has cut across all sections of the society, drawing massively all communities, including the

---

[17] CSDS, 'Participatory Upsurge of the Oppressed', *Frontline*, 26 November 1999, p. 48.
[18] Pradeep Kumar, 'Massification of Electoral Democracy and Political Fluidity', *Mainstream*, XXXVI(8) 7 February 1998, p. 19.
[19] Ibid.
[20] Gail Omvedt, 'Dalit Politics', *The Hindu*, 1 April 1998.

illiterates, within its fold.[21] Survey data shows that ironically, the illiterates, the poor, the backwards, the dalits, the other lower castes, the ruralites, the weaker sections, etc., have shown greater tendency to vote than those who are relatively better off, educated, urban, upper castes.[22] This has also been evident from the greater enthusiasm shown by the rural voters in terms of their turnout in election meetings and rallies.

All this however did not happen in one go. In the initial years of the Republic, politics remained largely confined to the educated, upper caste, upper class, urban elitist sections of the population, and the 'subaltern' masses found themselves only at the tail end of the political process. It is the churning of the massive electorate over the decades that entirely changed the political scene, first in the states, and later at the Centre. This 'grassrootisation' of democracy, and excessive politicisation led to the massification of the electoral politics in India. This of course was not accompanied by any major opening up of the employment sector in the wake of the retarded growth of industrialisation. Agriculture, however, was modernised in many states by introducing the new techniques of the green revolution. This was actually preceded by the zamindari abolition acts and the land ceiling and other related land reform laws.

All this gradually created a class of small landholding farmers, many of whom constituted the dominant castes in their respective regions or states. It was this combination of the rising agrarian class and the deepening of politicisation which gradually but steadily marginalised the hitherto dominant elitist sections of the society, which somehow continued to dominate the bureaucracy and the economy but were peripheralised in the electoral politics in many states. The lack of any break neck rapid speed of industrialisation hindered the process of 'ground leveling' of the social diversities. The latter were in fact further reinforced through greater politicisation, and in the process graduated from the private or social domain to the public or political domain.

It is this intense politicisation of each and every small social diversity over the years that eventually made the one party dominant model unworkable. As discussed before, there is a limit beyond which this model could not have withstood the strains and pressures exerted by these divergent groups. This was possible in the initial decades largely on account of the managerial skills of the charismatic upper-class and upper-caste nationalist leadership, and the corresponding lack of politicisation of many subaltern groups.

---

[21] Survey data related to the 1996 Lok Sabha elections reveals the following facts about political participation.

Above national average: Very poor (+) 2.9, Men (+) 2.4, Dalit (+) 1.9, Rural (+) 1.1

Below national average: Muslim (–) 0.8, Upper castes (–) 1.6, Women (–) 2.2, Urban (–) 3.0, Graduates (–) 4.5. See, 'Cover Story', *India Today*, 31 August 1996, pp. 36–53.

[22] CSDS, 'Participatory Upsurge of the Oppressed', p. 48.

The leadership of the early decades by its very nature was drawing support from across all regions of the country. The social groups down the ladder were not politically powerful or articulate enough to challenge this dominance. The coming up of the agrarian bourgeoisie and the politicisation of the masses, gradually made these groups assert vis-à-vis this central leadership. This made the rainbow coalitions break up, which were replaced in some states by the dominant caste leaders whose support bases were concentrated in some regions or regional pockets. This was unlike that of their predecessors who had enjoyed a scattered social base.

The rise of regional political formations in a way, coincided with this social and economic development. Thus, the breakdown of Congress dominance as manifested in the outcome of the fourth general elections in 1967, also marked the rise of the Jats in UP, symbolised by the exit of Chaudhary Charan Singh from the Congress Party. Similarly, many powerful chief ministers of the 1960s came from the dominant caste groups of the Congress Party itself. Thus the Marathas in Maharashtra, the Jats in Punjab and Haryana, the Lingayats and the Vokkaligas in Karnataka, the Reddys in Andhra Pradesh, the Patels or the Pattidars in Gujarat, dominated the legislatures of their respective states on most occasions.

The logic of the deepening of the political consciousness did not stop at these peasant castes which had earlier replaced the upper (twice-born) castes. This process in fact went further, and many backward castes challenged this growing political power of the dominant peasant castes. Thus, in the 1970s and the 1980s in many states, it were these backward castes, or their coalitions with other smaller groups, that came to stake claims to power. In Gujarat, the Pattidars'/Patels' dominance was challenged by the KHAM (Kshatriya, Harijan, Adivasi and Muslim) alliance, in Maharashtra a Vanjara (backward caste) became the chief minister, and in Karnataka and Andhra Pradesh the Vokkaligas/Lingayats and the Reddys had to face a challenge from many backward castes. In fact, Dev Raj Urs had done this in Karnataka much earlier in the late 1970s.

It was the third stage of mobilisation which strengthened the regional political formations, both within as well as outside the Congress Party. The gradual decline of the Congress in the 1980s can in fact be analysed in terms of the corresponding rise in the political strength of these more numerous backward castes, many of whom were no longer content with the Congress Party, and consequently had thrown their weight behind the non-Congress (regional) political formations.

The last phase that began somewhere in the 1990s, was the culmination of this process of politicisation which eventually brought the various hitherto marginalised and peripheralised weaker sections to the political arena. This churning resulted in the politicisation of every single social group, thereby giving rise to several political parties, many of which were actually quite distant from the conventional rainbow coalitions which had earlier dominated the political scene by mobilising not one but several coalitions of social and economic groups. Thus the rise of the Bahujan Samaj Party (BSP) and the Samajwadi Party (SP) in UP, the Pattal Makkal Katchi (PMK) and the Pudiya Tamizhagam (PT) in Tamil Nadu, Samata Party and the Rashtriya Janata Dal (RJD) in Bihar, and the JD in Karnataka, in the 1990s, symbolised this process of exclusivist political formations, catering respectively to the dalits, the Yadavs (and the Muslims), the Vanniyars, the dalits, the Kurmis, the Yadavs and the Vokkaligas. Most of these have been exclusivist in the sense that their electoral support, at least in the 1990s, has remained confined largely to particular caste groups, that too in certain states only.

The distinction between the 'national' and the 'regional' parties may at times be misleading in this context. It is only for the purposes of reservation of the election symbols that the Election Commission of India classifies political parties as regional or national on a technical condition of securing a particular percentage of votes in certain number of states. For all practical purposes, some of these national parties are either confined to just one state, or sometimes to a group of two or more states. In the latter case too, these states do not share this party in common, but the various state units in these states may actually be, more or less, independent parties joined only through a loose coalition at the all-India level. Thus, while the BSP has become a national party as per its recognition by the Commission, its base is largely confined to certain sections of the dalits in UP. Similarly, the JD for a long time has been a loose coalition of its Karnataka, Orissa, UP and Bihar units, which of course have now split into independent parties, namely, Biju Janata Dal (BJD) in Orissa, SP in UP, RJD in Bihar and JD (Secular) in Karnataka. The rump of the old JD has now finally been de-recognised by the Election Commission in September 2000 as a national party, and instead, its two factions, JD (S) of H.D. Dewe Gowda, and JD (United) of Sharad Yadav, have been accorded the status of regional parties in Karnataka and Bihar/Karnataka, respectively. Even the Communist Party of India (Marxist) (CPI [M]) has now lost its recognition as a national party precisely on account of its shrinking base in states other than West Bengal, Tripura and Kerala. The Samata Party and the Communist Party of India (CPI) are also severely restricted in their electoral spread to the states of Bihar and West Bengal/Kerala, respectively.

In a way this dichotomy between the national and the regional parties is misleading in yet another way. Not only are the former regional in their support bases, even the latter are sometimes non-regional in their 'ideological' or programmatic make-up. Thus a party like the Shiv Sena in the 1990s is no longer a party that stands for Maharashtra only, but using its Hindutva plank, aims to mould the broad policy framework of the national government. Similarly, the two TMCs, namely the Trinamool Congress and the Tamil Manila Congress, have broken out of the same parental national party, the

Congress Party, and therefore may not be entirely regionalist in their political agenda. This may also be true of Sharad Pawar's Nationalist Congress Party, which mobilised dissension in the parent Congress Party, not on any regional issue, but on a national issue of the citizenship of Sonia Gandhi. Even if it remains confined in its electoral base to some states only, its agenda cannot entirely be identified with those states, like one does in the cases of the TDP, the DMK, the AIADMK or the Asom Gana Parishad (AGP), etc. One may use a different nomenclature to cover these parties, and may call them 'trans-regional' or 'cross-state' parties, instead of using the conventional national/regional dichotomy.[23]

IV

The politicisation of social reality has changed the nature of the Indian federal system. In the 1950s and the 1960s, it was largely linguistic nationalism that was actually struggling for greater cultural space vis-à-vis the larger mainstream nationalism represented by the Centre. It was never, however, a cartographic federalism that has characterised the states of USA, where straight geometrical boundaries divide the administrative units called states. In India, federalism or regionalism was never about the struggle for better revenue distribution or efficient administration, or even about the share in the Rupee raised by way of taxation by the central agencies. It was rather an assertion for 'home lands', for 'self-respect', for 'cultural nationalism'.[24]

The advent of the mass-based politics of the 1990s, and the intense politicisation of the numerous socio-cultural groups have changed the federal scene further. The regional formations that have emerged in the electoral arena are not the political parties in the western sense of the term, where they tend to represent the interests of a broad spectrum of the electorate, and owe allegiance from a certain set of this electorate which may also enroll itself as the party members. On the contrary, in India the membership of most political parties, more particularly of the smaller regional formations, is not formal, and in fact represents not the individuals but whole communities. This

---

[23] Paul R. Brass raises an interesting issue on this point, namely, whether or not the 'national' parties that exist in more than one state, share much beyond a common name and a national executive committee. He argues that the Congress itself was a 'national' party only in limited respects. Brass, *Ethnicity and Nationalism*, pp. 140, 164–65.

Also see, K.R. Bombwall, 'Regional Parties in Indian Politics: A Preview', in S. Bhatnagar and Pradeep Kumar (eds), *Regional Political Parties in India*, Delhi: Ess Ess Publications, 1988, pp. 1–16.

[24] Pradeep Kumar, 'Indian Federalism: Issues and Challenges in the Context of Demands for New States', in Kausar J. Azam (ed.), *Federalism and Good Governance*, Delhi: South Asia Publishers, 1998.

has led to the growth of small and very small parties, whose own size depends precisely on the numerical size of these communities.

Many a time, what is seen as 'regional' is therefore 'social', and tends to be regional only in terms of its electoral catchment area. Sometimes this may not even be confined to a state, but only to a sub- or sub-sub-region in that state. It is this nature of political formations that has resulted not merely in coalition governments at the Centre which may be seen as coalitions of various regional parties under the umbrella of a national party, but also the coalition governments in the states. In the latter case, the sub-regional groups (which may indeed be politically mobilised sub-regional caste groups) may come together to form the state government.

The support bases of these regional parties are therefore not necessarily co-terminus with the political boundaries of the states, as is generally assumed, but may actually be confined to some sub-regions, or sub-sub-regions, or even only to certain communities. One may cite such cases as those of the BSP and SP (UP), RJD and Samata Party (Bihar), PMK, Marumalarchi Dravida Munnetra Kazhagam (MDMK) and TMC (Tamil Nadu), Shiv Sena (Maharashtra), and Akali Dal (Punjab).

It may be relevant here to make a reference to the Akali Dal and the BSP. These two are considered regional and national parties, respectively. If one looks at their ideological base, it is a different story. The Akali Dal is regional only to the extent its Sikh voters are concentrated in Punjab. In fact, in one of its representations before the then governor of Punjab, B.D. Pande, its leaders maintained that their demand for the enactment of an all-India Gurudwara act to bring all the Gurudwaras within the purview of the Shiromani Gurudwara Prabandhak Committee (SGPC), was actually aimed at greater integration with the nation, and did not represent the regionalist sentiment to that extent (interview with B.D. Pande at his residence at Almora, on 10 October 1997). Similarly, the BSP has a clearly defined political agenda aimed at the political empowerment of the dalits and some Most Backward Castes in UP and some neighbouring states. It is not national in the pan-Indian sense, or even in terms of its ideological or political agenda or programme.

V

What are then the prospects for the national parties and the regional allies to work together in a coalition? The western theories of such alliances perhaps will not work in the Indian context in view of the political infrastructural realities of these alliances. It is generally expected by the observers of the Indian scene that stable coalitions would emerge at the central and the state levels, which may then alternate, exactly in a fashion in which the two-party system is expected to operate. The successful alternative coalition governments

Table 12.1: 'Do You Feel Close to Any Political Party?'

Responses	Lok Sabha Polls 1971	Lok Sabha Polls 1996
Yes	37%	31%
No	63%	69%

in Kerala, and the structured stable coalition government in West Bengal have given credence to such expectations. Even at the Centre, it is sometimes hoped that another coalition of the regional parties under the Congress may successfully challenge the BJP-led coalition government in the near future.

While projections into the future may be more in the realm of speculation than analysis, it appears that the making of the national-regional coalitions may not follow a unilinear trajectory. The continuous churning of the political ocean may lead to construction, de-construction and re-construction of many such coalition groups, depending on the reconciliation of their antagonistic and non-antagonistic differences in the social, economic and the political arenas. It has been observed that over the years, there has been a declining trend of party identification. This became clear in a survey conducted by the Centre for the Study of Developing Societies, Delhi, after the general elections to the Lok Sabha in 1971 and 1996.[25] Obviously, compared to the 1971 Lok Sabha poll, fewer people felt closer to any single political party at the time of the 1996 Lok Sabha poll.

The developing political scenario therefore may not in the near future result in any 'frozen' or stable coalitions, but instead may keep the pot boiling for some time more, till such arrangements are evolved where the national and the regional partners do not cut into each other's electoral base, and in fact devise a political mechanism to exist in a symbiotic relationship.

Thus newer and newer regional and sub-regional groups may continue to emerge, and may continue to forge newer coalitions with fresh partners. Over the years there has been a clearly distinct trend towards the non-national parties (see Table 12.2). It is very likely that the social bases of these parties will determine which of these would be considered 'national' and which would end up as 'regional'. The electoral base rather than the policy programme, may compel these national and regional parties to look for coalition allies, both at the central and state levels. Two scenarios seem possible; one, a pan-Indian party, catering to the various religious and caste minority groups, scattered all over the country, emerging as the pivot, rallying several regional parties, with state or sub-state level electoral support, around it; two, the

---

[25] This author was associated with the 1996 survey. ('Congress' [party] in this article stands for the Indian National Congress, and its dominant factions under Indira Gandhi, namely Congress (R) and Congress [I].) For details of the survey by the CSDS, see 'Cover Story', *India Today*, 31 August 1996, pp. 36–53.

Table 12.2: Lok Sabha Elections: Votes Polled in Percentages[28]

Parties	Year					
	1980	1984	1989	1991	1996	1998
National Parties	85	80	79	77	69	68
State Parties & other groups	15	21	20	23	30	32

Note: Percentages have been rounded off to the nearest figures and are indicative only, and therefore not very exact.

various powerful regional parties themselves coalescing at the all-India level with some other cross-regional parties governing from the Centre with the help of their smaller regional allies who may be operative only in some states or even in various regional pockets of these states. The increasing trend among the voters to show more loyalty to their region, and greater interest in the state governments than the central government, has also led to the greater acceptance of the idea of coalitions than before.[26] It may be interesting to know that unlike in the 1970s and the 1980s when the people voted in the State Assembly elections as if they were electing a prime minister, in the 1990s people voted in the parliamentary elections as if they were choosing a state government.[27]

Thus, the unfolding of the hidden complex social reality has been made possible by the operation of the democratic system, resulting in the remoulding of the federal institutions via new political arrangements. Not the legal but the political system, has ensured the working of a federal arrangement in India, in which the difference between the national and the regional is somewhat blurred, and the regional allies increasingly call the shots. This is something that had been unfortunately denied in the original spirit of the Constitution, but something that was more than discernible in the spirit of the debates of the Constituent Assembly of India.

[26] Yogendra Yadav, et al., 'Election Analysis: Issues and the Verdict', *Frontline*, 26 November 1999, p. 45.
[27] Yogendra Yadav, 'The Third Electoral System', *Seminar*, 480, August 1999, p. 18.
[28] Compiled from Douglas Verney, 'A More Federal India', *Seminar*, 459, November 1997; and Arora, 'Regional Aspirations and National Cohesion'.

13

THE REGIONAL PARTIES AND DEMOCRACY

ROMANTIC RENDEZVOUS OR LOCALISED LEGITIMATION?

Suhas Palshikar[1]

Ever since the decline of the Congress became apparent, two features of Indian politics have attracted the attention of students of the Indian political process. One is the coalition-based structure of party politics and the other is the rise of many smaller and regional parties to prominence in national level politics. Even a casual observer will not miss these features which emerged in the 1990s. What is remarkable about these features is that the Congress was not/is not being replaced by any single party. Thus, a wide range of regional formations has become the centerpiece of the emerging party system. The present chapter summarises the electoral performance of regional parties since the mid-1990s. It also attempts to map the geographical and ideological space occupied by these parties. Third, the chapter tries to conjecture about the nature of social support enjoyed by the regional parties. Finally, we shall try to situate the regional parties within a broader framework of India's political process.

I

Often, a party is easily identified as a 'regional' party if it propagates the ideology of regionalism or thrives on invocation of regional pride. Parties like Asom Gana Parishad (AGP) or the Telugu Desam Party (TDP) or Dravida Munnetra Kazhagam (DMK) are quickly recognised as regional parties. However, yet another type of party needs to be incorporated in the category of regional parties. These are parties which enjoy considerable support only in one state of the Indian union. Such parties may not emphasise their regionalist

[1] The author wishes to gratefully acknowledge the help of Sanjay Kumar and CSDS Data Unit for the data used in this chapter.

outlook. They have, in fact, an all-India perspective but only a regional reach. The Forward Block (FB) and Revolutionary Socialist Party (RSP) in West Bengal or the Peasants' and Workers' Party (PWP) in Maharashtra may be cited as examples. The 1990s have witnessed the rise of such parties in Bihar and Uttar Pradesh. In fact, together with the 'regionalist' parties, these parties are also playing an important role in the political developments that unfolded in the 1990s.

Yet another point deserves mention. Observers of Indian politics often accept, even though grudgingly, that 'regional' parties and their leaders have a somewhat legitimate claim over power structures at the local and state level. But these leaders are not supposed to stake claims to power at the all-India level. This power seems to be reserved for leaders with a non-parochial (meaning non-regional) background. The mention of state leaders aspiring for national level power is frequently made with a pinch of cynical censure. Words like local *subedar*s, regional satraps, etc., are found not only in journalistic vocabulary but also in the lexicon of scholarly political analyses. This betrays a bias against regional parties and regional leaders.

We shall proceed with the simple test of popular-electoral support. When a party is practically confined to only one state, it may be treated as a regional party even if its leaders nurse all-India ambitions or its nomenclature declares the party to be of all-India standing. Thus understood, the Trinamool Congress (TC), Samajwadi Party (SP), Rashtriya Janata Dal (RJD), Samata Party, would be treated as regional parties along with self-proclaimed regionalist parties. Alternatively, these parties have been referred to as state-based parties[2] and single-state parties.[3] (In a lighter vein, one could add to this a category of single-individual parties like those of Chandrashekhar, Subramanyam Swamy, and so on!)

We shall exclude from our discussion of regional parties, the two communist parties and the Bahujan Samaj Party (BSP). It is often pointed out that the Communist Party of India (Marxist) (CPI [M]) has been confined only to West Bengal and Kerala and the Communist Party of India (CPI) is, in any case, a small party now. But CPI (M) has a presence in Assam, Tripura, Andhra Pradesh (AP) and Tamil Nadu (TN) while CPI also has some base in AP, Bihar, Punjab and TN. In the case of BSP, its base in Jammu and Kashmir (J&K) (4.8 per cent in 1999), Madhya Pradesh (MP), Punjab, and Rajasthan, justifies our exclusion of this party from the category of regional parties.

---

[2] Pradeep Chhibber and Irfan Nooruddin, 'Party Competition and Fragmentation in Indian Elections: 1957–1998', in Ramashray Roy and Paul Wallace (eds), *Indian Politics and the 1998 Elections*, New Delhi: Sage Publications, 1999, p. 37.

[3] Paul Wallace, 'General Elections 1996: Regional Parties Dominant in Punjab and Haryana', *Economic and Political Weekly*, Vol. 32, No. 46, 15 November 1997, p. 19.

Rise of Regional Parties

The existence of regional parties is nothing new. Their entry into national-level politics is, however, a new phenomenon. In 1977, the Akali Dal and DMK were partners in the Janata Party government, although, the Janata Party had a clear majority (295 seats) on its own. This was the first time that regional parties shared power at the national level. There were 51 members belonging to various regional parties in 1977. In 1980, regional parties lost their newly found moment of glory when the Congress returned to power. The DMK managed to win 16 seats but the Akalis were reduced to one seat and the total tally of regional parties including the smaller left parties of West Bengal remained only 36 in the seventh Lok Sabha. The elections to the eighth Lok Sabha were held in the backdrop of Indira Gandhi's assassination. But in 1984, regional parties increased their share in the Lok Sabha. There were 76 members belonging to different regional parties in the eighth Lok Sabha. The rise of Telugu Desam in Andhra and Asom Gana Parishad in Assam were the main factors responsible for this performance of the regional parties. However, with the Congress having 415 seats in the Lok Sabha, the role of regional parties was bound to be insignificant in national politics.

Non-Congressism brought many regional parties together in the National Front (NF) formed in 1988. These included the TDP, DMK, AGP and Congress (S), apart from the newly formed Janata Dal. But in the elections in 1989, these regional parties did not meet with success. In the ninth Lok Sabha, 45 members belonged to regional parties but the regional allies of NF had only two seats (won by TDP). In spite of their disastrous performance, these regional parties became partners in the NF-led government of 1989. In 1991, the strength of regional parties in the Lok Sabha was at 56 but this time around TDP had a fair share (13 seats). The All India Anna Dravida Munnetra Kazhagam (AIADMK), Janata Dal (G), Indian Union Muslim League (IUML), Sikkim Sangram Parishad (SSP) and Kerala Congress supported the Congress government of Narsimha Rao. However, these parties were not part of the government. In any case, both in 1989 and 1991, regional parties were playing a crucial role at the national level in making or unmaking the central government. Thus, the 1977 elections not only speeded up the demise of the Congress system but also inaugurated a new era of partnership between all-India parties and regional parties; something which had never happened in the pre-1977 period.

Since 1996, regional parties have become indispensable in the formation of the government at the national level. They have been important partners in the coalitions that came to power after 1996. Besides, the numerical strength of the regional parties has considerably increased, with a sizable vote share being captured by regional parties. Finally, regional parties have emerged in a large number of states. The experiment of the United Front (UF) government first underscored the centrality of regional parties to national politics. In the 1996 Lok Sabha, 137 Members of Parliament (MPs) belonged to various regional parties. At that time, it appeared that most regional parties were gravitating against the Bharatiya Janata Party (BJP). Thus, 95 of the 137 MPs belonging to regional parties were part of the UF coalition. This gave rise to the impression that regional parties were occupying the 'third' space—outside of the Congress and the BJP. Soon, this picture disappeared almost as quickly as a rainbow disappears. And the UF was actually described as a rainbow coalition. Rainbows are ephemeral. They make for a good view but do not last long. The United Front proved to be similarly short lived although its supporters drew satisfaction from the fact that a large number of parties agreed to block a communal party from coming to power.

The regional forces—at least some of them—quickly switched over to the BJP-led National Democratic Alliance (NDA) in 1998. The Lok Sabha in 1998 included 161 MPs belonging to regional parties; 92 of these were part of the NDA. The TDP, which was one of the leading parties of the UF, chose to join the NDA, which proved crucial for the survival of the government. Another regional party, AIADMK, played a decisive role in defeating the NDA government. The 13th Lok Sabha (1999) has 168 MPs (188 if JD factions are considered as regional parties) who belong to regional parties. The NDA includes 109 MPs from different regional parties. In all, 32 regional parties are represented in the 13th Lok Sabha of which 15 are part of NDA, four are constituents of the Left Front (six MPs), six are Congress allies (23 MPs) and seven parties have not joined any front or alliance (38 MPs) (see Tables 13.1–13.3). It may be noted that the above discussion of the 1999 elections does not treat the Janata Dal (United) (JD [U]) as a regional party although this party consists of four regional groups—the Samata Party of Bihar, JD of Bihar, Lok Shakti of Karnataka and one JD faction from Karnataka. There is little coordination between the Karnataka unit and the Bihar unit of JD. Also, relations between the Samata faction and the JD faction in Bihar are only nominal. The JD (U) won 17 seats in Bihar and three seats in Karnataka.

It can be observed that since 1996, the BJP and Congress together get a little over 50 per cent of the share of the total votes. The communist parties, BSP and JD were the three other non-regional parties. Together, they had not more than 20 per cent votes. Thus, at least one-fourth of the electorate voted for regional or state-level parties. In 1999, the share of votes polled by regional parties shows an increase. While BJP polled 23.5 per cent votes, its regional allies polled 18 per cent votes. The regional allies of the Congress polled 5 per cent votes. Other regional parties polled more than 15 per cent votes. Thus, if we look at the votes polled by all-India parties and state-level parties, their vote share is almost 60:40. The rise in the vote share of regional and state-level parties is mainly due to the broad range of alliances forged by the BJP with various parties since 1998. In 1998 the BJP had allied with 15 regional parties, while in 1999 it allied with 19 regional parties. This also

Table 13.1: Regional Parties in the Lok Sabha: 1952–71

Party	1952	1957	1962	1967	1972
NC	–	–	1	–	–
AD/P	4	–	2	3	1
RRP	3	–	–	–	–
VHP	–	–	–	–	1
HLS	–	–	1	–	–
MGP	–	–	1	–	–
PWP	2	4	–	–	–
SCF/RPI	2	6	3	1	1
UG(S)	–	–	–	1	1
FB	1	3	1	2	2
RSP	2	1	2	1	3
KC	–	–	–	–	3
ML	–	–	–	–	2
MML	1	–	–	–	–
TNT	1	–	–	–	–
CW	3	–	–	–	–
TTC	1	–	–	–	–
DMK	–	2	–	25	22
PDF	7	–	–	–	–
TPS	–	–	–	–	10
GP	–	7	–	–	–
UC	–	–	–	–	1
JKP/D	3	7	1	–	1
CSJ	–	3	–	–	–
BC	–	–	–	–	1
AGP	5	–	–	–	–
APHLC	–	–	1	1	1
EITU	–	1	–	–	–
UFN	–	–	–	–	1
NNO	–	–	–	1	–
Total	35	34	13	36	51

Source: Compiled from V.B. Singh, *Elections in India: Data Handbook on Lok Sabha Elections: 1986–1991*, New Delhi: Sage Publications, 1994, pp. 197–279.

indicates that since 1998 most regional parties have been gravitating towards BJP in contrast to the situation in 1996.

Areas of Influence

Let us look at the areas in which regional parties are predominant. In the states of Rajasthan, Gujarat and MP regional parties do not have much presence. Gujarat had two small breakaway groups originating in the splits in Janata Dal and BJP. But both were short-lived and finally gave way to a bipolar contest between the Congress and the BJP. Karnataka has a potential for regionalised politics since the two JD factions together garner a quarter of the votes. Finally, politics in Kerala is neatly divided between the two fronts,

Table 13.2: Regional Parties in the Lok Sabha, 1977–89

Party	1977	1980	1984	1989
NC	2	3	3	3
AD	9	1	7	6
PWP	5	–	1	–
SS	–	–	–	4
RPI	2	–	–	–
MGP	1	1	–	1
CS	–	–	3	1
IUML	2	3	2	2
KC	2	1	2	1
RSP	4	4	3	4
DMK	1	16	2	–
AIADMK	19	2	12	11
TDP	–	–	30	2
MIM	–	–	1	1
JKP	1	–	–	–
JMM	–	–	–	3
CJ	–	1	1	–
IPF	–	–	–	1
GNLF	–	–	–	1
FB	3	3	2	3
SKJP	–	1	–	–
SSP	–	–	–	1
AGP	–	–	7	–
Total	51	36	76	45

Source: Compiled from V.B. Singh, *Elections in India: Data Handbook on Lok Sabha Elections: 1986–1991*, New Delhi: Sage Publications, 1994.

the Left Front and the United Democratic Front. In both these alliances smaller state-level parties are important partners but the Congress and the communist parties dominate politics.

In terms of seat share, regional parties dominate nine states since half of the MPs from these states belong to regional parties. These include the smaller states of Manipur, Meghalaya and Sikkim. Besides these, other states in this category are Andhra Pradesh, Tamil Nadu, Orissa, Maharashtra, Haryana and Jammu and Kashmir. Another test of the prominence of regional parties would be their vote share. In 13 states, regional parties had 30 per cent or more share of the votes in the 1999 elections. They include the smaller states mentioned above. In Manipur and Sikkim, regional parties polled 67 and 95 per cent votes, respectively. Other states where regional parties polled around 30 per cent or more votes are J&K, Haryana, Punjab, Maharashtra, AP, Tamil Nadu, Orissa, West Bengal, Bihar and Uttar Pradesh. In Tamil Nadu, various regional parties together polled 75 per cent votes. In Maharashtra and Andhra, regional parties polled 44 and 42 per cent votes, respectively. The vote share of regional parties in West Bengal, Punjab, Orissa and Haryana

Table 13.3: Regional Parties in the Lok Sabha, 1991–99

Party	1991	1996	1998	1999
NC	–	3	2	4
HVC	–	–	1	1
AD*	–	8	9	3
HVP	1	3	1	–
INLD/HLD	–	–	4	5
JDG	1	–	–	–
SS	4	15	6	15
PWP	–	–	1	1
RPI*	–	–	4	2
NCP	–	–	–	7
MGP	–	1	–	–
UGDP	–	1	–	–
LS	–	–	3	3 (JDU)
KCP	–	1	–	–
IUML	2	2	2	2
KC*	1	1	1	2
RSP	3	5	5	3
CS	1	–	–	–
DMK	–	17	6	12
AIADMK	11	–	18	10
TMC	–	20	3	–
PMK	–	–	4	5
MDMK	–	–	3	4
TRC	–	–	1	–
JP	–	–	1	–
MADMK	–	–	–	1
MGRK	–	–	–	1
TDP	13	16	12	29
MIM	1	1	1	1
BJD	–	–	9	10
MPVC	–	2	–	–
SP	–	17	20	26
SJP	5	–	–	–
CT	–	4	–	–
LC	–	–	–	2
LD	–	–	–	2
RJD	–	–	17	7
SMP	–	8	12	17 (JDU)
JMM	5	1	–	–
TC	–	–	7	8
FB	4	3	2	2
SDF	–	–	–	1
AGP	1	5	–	–
ASDC	1	1	–	–
UMF	–	–	–	–
MSC	1	–	1	1
AC	–	–	–	–
NPC	1	–	–	–
Total	56	137	161	188

Source: Compiled from V.B. Singh, *Elections in India: Data Handbook on Lok Sabha Elections: 1986–1991*, New Delhi: Sage Publications, 1994; *India Today*, 31 May 1996; *Frontline*, 3 April 1998; *Frontline*, 5 November 1999.

was between 33 and 35 per cent in the 1999 elections while in other states regional parties polled between 29 and 31 per cent votes. Considering the multipolarity of electoral contests, this performance is certainly impressive.

Even before the rise of regional parties during the 1990s, regional parties dominated state-level politics in many states. Apart from the states of the northeast, politics in J&K, Punjab, Tamil Nadu and Orissa had witnessed the rise of regional parties at the state level. The National Conference has been central to politics in J&K. In Punjab, the role of the Akali Dal was limited till 1966. Since then, however, Punjab politics has revolved around Akali politics. The Akalis established themselves politically by winning 43 of 104 seats in the legislative elections of 1969. Similarly, DMK rose to prominence in the 1962 Assembly elections winning 50 seats. It came to power in 1967 with 138 seats. The AIADMK replaced the DMK in 1977. Thus, Tamil politics has been regionalised since 1962. Although Orissa has now joined the group of states dominated by regional politics, regional political parties between 1952 and 1975 earlier dominated the state. The Ganatantra Parishad won 31, 51 and 36 seats in the 1952, 1957 and 1961 Assembly elections, respectively. Later, the Jan Congress won 26 seats in 1967, Utkal Congress won 33 seats in 1971 and 35 in 1974. The two regional parties, Maharashtrawadi Gomantak Party (MGP) and United Goan Party (UGP), too, dominated Goan politics. Local parties of Karnataka had captured 41 seats along with independents in the state legislature in 1967 while local parties of AP won 70 seats along with independents. The Forward Block and RSP together won 22, 13 and 33 seats in the West Bengal Assembly in 1962, 1967 and 1969, respectively. The 1980s saw the rise of the AGP in Assam and TDP in Andhra. To sum up, regional parties dominated state-level politics in many states in the pre-1990 period.

Ideological Positions

A variety of regionalist and/or non-regional ideological positions are taken by the regionalist and state-based parties. Many such parties are personalistic and centred around one leader. Yet, formation of a party requires an ideological location even if it is only like a fig leaf as far as legitimisation of the party's existence is concerned. Besides, the compulsions of electoral politics force a party into presenting some arguments. The regional parties frequently combine the regionalist and non-regional arguments in order to explain their raison d'être to the electorate.

Regional parties extend a broad range of regionalist arguments. These surround invocation of regional pride and marks of regional identity. Regional arguments involve demands pertaining to regional culture, history and language. The demands for formation of a state or inclusion of certain territories into a state are potent weapons of mobilisation. Yet another aspect of regional ideology is the demand for more autonomy to the state. Such demands are posed as opposition to the role of the governor, to Article 356, etc. Finally, the regionalist ideological position takes the form of demands for the state's development. Such regionalism deals less with issues of identity and more with issues of backwardness, investment and industrial progress. Regional parties variously use these arguments—identity, statehood, autonomy and development. The National Conference, Akali Dal, DMK, often combine identity and autonomy arguments. Parties like Biju Janata Dal (BJD) or TC emphasise the development arguments. The TDP emerged on the basis of the identity argument but Chandrababu Naidu has led the party quietly to the development argument. Many parties originate in the demand for statehood. The Jharkhand Mukti Morcha, Chhattisgarh Mukti Morcha, Vishal Haryana Parishad, are examples of parties demanding statehood. Most parties of the northeast continue to combine the identity issue with autonomy or statehood demands. By invoking regionalist arguments, a regional party can easily identify with the different sections in the regional society. Its language of identity appeals to the intelligentsia and the masses alike. Besides, identity discourse also benefits the materially dominant sections of the society.

However, it is not always necessary that a regional party would confine itself only to regionalist arguments. Many times regional parties cover non-regionalist ideological ground. While the Akalis tend to define regional identity in terms of religion, the Shiv Sena uses the two ideologies of regionalism and religious communalism according to the exigencies of electoral politics. Regional parties also rely on caste for their ideological formulations. Thus, the DMK originally combined Dravidian identity with non-Brahminism. By employing anti-caste ideological resources, the DMK strengthened its claims pertaining to a separate Dravida identity vis-à-vis the Aryans. More recently, the PMK in Tamil Nadu has also combined the regional rhetoric with an anti-caste social position on behalf of the Other Backward Cates (OBCs). Such ideological formulations should not be seen cynically only as marriages of convenience. There is also a broader implication involved in such formulations. They tend to restate the meaning of 'regional' identity. Thus, the Akali claim implies that the Punjabi identity is not merely a territorial and linguistic identity. Being a Punjabi is implicitly equated with being a Sikh also. Similarly, the Shiv Sena keeps on shifting its rhetoric from Maharashtrian pride to Hindu pride. It believes that there is no contradiction between these two identities. On the other hand, the latter is the extension of the former. The symbol of Shivaji employed by the Shiv Sena embodies both these ideological assertions. Shivaji—a 17th century Maratha chief—is portrayed both as the savior of 'Marathi' pride and the protector of Hindutva. The Dravida parties—particularly the DMK, originally—also defined the regional identity in the context of two factors. First, the regional identity was defined in terms of the juxtaposition between outsider-aggressor vs indigenous pride; i.e., the Aryans vs Dravidas. Second, it was claimed that Dravida identity belongs to the masses—the non-Brahmans. Thus, regionalist ideology disinherited the Brahmans from Dravidian legacy. If regionalism is exclusionary in the sense that it excludes persons belonging to other regions, then, some regionalist formulations involve a double exclusion: of outsiders and exclusion of certain (religious, social or caste) communities (and by implication, inclusion of insiders and certain communities).

Some state-based parties employ only the second variety of exclusion/inclusion. There are parties which seldom explicitly rely on regionalist exclusion. Instead, the primary locus of exclusion/inclusion is caste/community/tribe. Second, because the principle of exclusion/inclusion has a regionally specified political salience, the party becomes a single state party. Although examples of such parties are more prominent in the late 1980s and 1990s, regional parties did exist earlier also which did not rely on regionalist ideology. The Republican Party of India was conceived as an all-India party. But it operated in the framework of exclusion/inclusion on the basis of caste. In the late 1950s, dalit mobilisation on such basis could take place only in Maharashtra. So the party became confined to Maharashtra. This same constraint impinges the growth of BSP outside the typical context of UP. More recently, in 1993, the Bahujan Mahasangh (BMS) has emerged in Maharashtra as a party of OBCs favouring dalit–OBC cooperation and unity. But the more dramatic examples of this type of parties are those of the SP and RJD. Both aspire to be national, i.e., all-India parties. Both are non-regionalist in their ideology. They have reached the regional station through the caste-route of exclusion/inclusion. In principle, the ideology of OBC uplift can have all-India applicability. But these parties have defined their ideological positions in the specific context of their respective states. As a result, their ideology is translated into the ideology of the upwardly mobile OBC communities. The rhetoric of protecting the minorities too, does not attract people outside of UP; nor does Laloo's rhetoric about Advani's ignorance about milking the cow appeal to OBCs outside of Bihar! In other words, the meaning of pro-OBC ideology becomes state-specific in the case of the Bahujan Mahasangh of Maharashtra, Samajwadi Party of UP or RJD of Bihar. Yet it is undeniable that these parties cover a very significant ideological terrain. Caste and tribe exist both at the all-India level and at the state level. An ideology based on those factors may claim all-India status but such an ideology becomes relevant and meaningful only in specific contexts. Discussion of peasantry castes has to pin down whether we are talking about middle castes like Jats, Marathas, etc., or if we are talking about peasant OBCs like Yadavs or Malis, etc. This peculiarity often forces anti-caste parties into state-specific or regionalised positions. Perhaps, this characteristic of anti-caste ideology may continue until the gap between caste-specific identity and supra-caste mega-identities (like dalits, OBCs, Bahujans) is filled or overcome. Till then, caste ideology will keep on regionalising the forces claiming anti-caste space.

II

Social Bases of Regional Parties

We noted earlier that initially, after the rise of regional parties in 1996, politics appeared to be becoming triangular. Since the Congress and BJP entered into a competition in many states, observers felt that a bipolar situation was about to emerge.[4] The growth of regional parties also upset the established patterns of voter preferences. Not only were new segments of voters ushered into the electoral arena but traditional loyalties too were put under strain. The regional parties succeeded in mobilising a greater share of votes. The Congress was the obvious loser in most states; notably in Andhra, Assam, Kerala, Punjab, Tamil Nadu and West Bengal. While this description is factually accurate, it captures only one aspect of the reality. The other aspect is the fragmentation of non-Congress and non-BJP votes. This has happened in Bihar, Karnataka and UP where the so-called Janata Dal was divided into regional fragments.

The third aspect of the political reality was readiness of regional parties to enter into alliances with the BJP rather than with the Congress. Since most of the regional parties had a tradition of anti-Congressism and a social base which was mobilised on a non-Congress ideological basis, these parties were constrained in choosing electoral allies. This electoral arithmetic produced two results. First, by aligning with BJP, these regional parties made it possible for the BJP to take over state power. Second and more importantly, an alliance with BJP signalled new social equations. For instance, Lok Shakti practically facilitated the entry of BJP into Karnataka in 1998 by breaking the Lingayat and Vokkaliga axis. It isolated the Vokkaligas and turned the Lingayats towards BJP.[5] The Samata Party in the case of Bihar accomplished almost a similar task. In Maharashtra, the NCP went ahead with the consolidation of Marathas in 1999 and facilitated the efforts of the BJP-Shiv Sena to garner OBC votes.[6] In this background, it becomes interesting to locate the exact social territory occupied by different regional parties in their respective states. Below, we present a summary of the social base of the major regional parties based on the National Election Study (NES), 1999 conducted by the Centre for the Study of Developing Societies (CSDS). The trends presented here are from a post-election survey.

[4] Sudha Pai, 'The Indian Party System Under Transformation: Lok Sabha Elections 1998', *Asian Survey*, Vol. 38, no. 9, September 1998, p. 845.
[5] Harold Gould, 'The 12th General Election in Karnataka: The BJP Achieves Its Southern Beachhead', in Roy and Wallace, *Indian Politics and the 1998 Elections*, pp. 183–209.
[6] Suhas Palshikar and Nitin Birmal, 'Fragmented Marathas Retain Formal Power', in Paul Wallace and Ramashray Roy (eds), *Lok Sabha Election: 1999*, New Delhi: Sage Publications, 2003, pp. 206–232.

Table 13.4: Social Profile of Voters of Akali Dal (1999) (all figures in percentages)

		Share Among Akali Voters	Share in Sample
Age:	Up to 25 yrs.	12.3	14.4
	26–35 yrs.	27.7	32.3
	36–45 yrs.	29.2	21.4
	46–55 yrs.	15.4	15.3
	56 & above	15.4	16.6
Education:	Illiterate	24.6	37.6
	Up to primary	27.7	24.9
	Up to matric	30.8	22.7
	College & above	16.9	14.8
Community:	Upper caste	13.8	20.1
	OBC	20.0	13.1
	SC	12.3	16.7
	Muslim	–	1.7
	Others	53.8	28.4
Gender:	Male	46.2	46.3
	Female	53.8	53.7
Locality:	Urban	27.7	48.9
	Rural	72.3	51.9

Source: National Election Survey, 1999 conducted by the CSDS, Delhi, CSDS Data Unit.

Akali Dal

Active and central to the Punjab political scene since the mid-1960s, the Akali Dal has forged a social base of rural peasantry in Punjab. Almost three-fourths of its supporters come from the rural population. The party draws support from diverse sections in terms of caste and community. However, more than half of its votes are from the Sikh community. A sizable proportion (43 per cent) of OBCs support the Akali Dal accounting for 20 per cent of its votes. The social base of the Akali Dal is marked by weak support from the dalits. The party draws equal support from men and women. Since the Akali Dal is a well-established regional party of Punjab, it has a slight edge among middle aged (36–45 years) voters but the party is not exactly popular among young voters (up to 35 years of age). It may be conjectured that being part of the establishment, the party is not popular both among the young as well as the elderly voters. Another interesting feature of the Akali support base is that it has weak support both among illiterates and those with higher education. The bulk of its support comes from the primary and matric educated voters (see Table 13.4).

AIADMK and DMK

Politics in Tamil Nadu has been exclusively region-based since the mid-1960s. From 1989 the Dravida parties have realised that they can make and unmake national governments. This has changed their perception entirely. Now the two Dravida parties simultaneously adopt a nationalistic and all-India stance as well as revert to shrill regionalist rhetoric. The former is necessary to assert an all-India role while the latter is required to prove that they have not lost sight of their original ideological position. In the case of DMK, observers have noted a drift towards pan-Indian nationalism. As a balancing act, the DMK also initiated Tamil prayers (*archanas*) in temples in the place of Sanskrit prayers. This move has helped in the Hinduisation of Tamil culture. Not surprisingly, this move by the DMK was supported by the non-Brahman Saivites who are staunch Hindus.[7] The AIADMK has generally been silent on the question of the non-Brahman legacy of the Dravida movement. During AIADMK rule, Tamil Nadu witnessed the spread of the Vinayak cult.

In this sense both the DMK and AIADMK traverse an identical ideological space. It appears from survey data that both parties have a weak base among the younger voters (see Table 13.5). But in most other respects the parties are dissimilar. The DMK has equal support among men and women while AIADMK is more popular among the women voters. The DMK has a strong base in urban sections and educated voters while AIADMK is popular among

Table 13.5: Social Profile of Voters of DMK and AIADMK (1999) (all figures in percentage)

		Share Among DMK Voters	Share Among AIADMK Voters	Share in Sample
Age:	Up to 25 yrs.	18.2	12.8	12.1
	26–35 yrs.	29.5	35.8	30.4
	36–45 yrs.	22.7	25.7	24.7
	46–55 yrs.	13.6	12.2	15.1
	56 & above	15.9	13.5	17.8
Education:	Illiterate	15.9	30.4	28.7
	Up to primary	9.1	36.5	30.4
	Up to matric	45.5	27.0	27.0
	College & above	29.5	6.1	13.9
Community:	Upper caste	22.7	1.4	4.6
	OBC	56.8	64.2	59.4
	SC	4.5	25.0	26.8
	Muslims	6.8	6.8	3.7
	Others	9.1	2.7	5.6
Gender:	Male	50.0	45.9	51.6
	Female	50.0	54.1	48.4
Locality:	Urban	95.5	40.5	29.5
	Rural	4.5	59.5	70.5

Source: NES '99: CSDS Data Unit.

---

[7] M.S.S. Pandian, 'Tamil Friendly Hindutva', *Economic and Political Weekly*, Vol. 35, no. 20–21, 27 May 2000, pp. 1805–6.

rural and less educated voters. Two-thirds of AIADMK voters are either educated up to the primary level or not literate at all. Interestingly, a large chunk of DMK support comes from upper castes and OBCs, while AIADMK is dependent on OBCs and the Scheduled Castes (SCs). Thus, the two parties appear to be leading two different social coalitions in Tamil Nadu.

Biju Janata Dal

Non-Congress politics in Orissa has often been based around localised forces. Although the Swatantra party played an important role in state politics between 1967 and 1972, the formulation of a government depended upon the Gan Congress (1967–71) and Utkal Congress and Jharkhand Party (1971–72).[8] It has been argued that the middle class-upper caste nature of the Oriya political elites has contributed to the consolidation of region-based politics in Orissa.[9] Even when Nandini Satpathy or Biju Patnaik chose to participate in non-Congress politics at the all-India level, their state-level politics continued to be anchored in a regional discourse. The Janata Dal unit of Orissa under Biju Patnaik always functioned independently. It remained within the confines of the all-India party primarily in order to pave the way for the regional leader to enter the national political arena. The JD unit in the state quickly disintegrated after the death of Biju Patnaik and gave way to the formation of a state-level party under the leadership of Navin Patnaik who promptly aligned with the BJP. This decision was based on two considerations. One was the logic of anti-Congressism which drove Navin Patnaik towards the BJP. The other was an aspiration to play a role at the all-India level. With the demise of the United Front, a regional party could gain access to the national centre of power only by aligning with the BJP. Navin Patnaik has thus consolidated anti-Congress politics in the state with himself (his party) as the main nucleus of anti-Congressism. However, it is suggested by observers that in the long run, the BJP might undermine the position of BJD as the locus of anti-Congress politics in Orissa.[10]

In order to appreciate the type of social base which the BJD enjoys, it may be repeated that the party speaks less of regional pride. Instead, BJD places emphasis on Orissa's backwardness. At the same time, the party posed itself as opposed to Congress misrule and corruption. Its theme of anti-Congressism combined with the state's progress must have been appealing to the middle-class voters. While maintaining an overall gender balance, BJD successfully

[8] Bishnu Mohapatra, 'Politics in Post-Cyclone Orissa', *Economic and Political Weekly*, Vol. 35, no. 16, 15 April 2000; p. 1354.
[9] Bishnu Mohapatra, 'Elections and Everyday Politics', *Economic and Political Weekly*, Vol. 35, no. 4, 22 January 2000, p. 173.
[10] Mohapatra, 'Politics in Post-Cyclone Orissa'.

Table 13.6: Social Profile of Voters of BJD (1999) (all figures in percentage)

		Share Among BJD Voters	Share in Sample
Age:	Up to 25 yrs.	16.4	16.4
	26–35 yrs.	27.9	30.1
	36–45 yrs.	27.1	23.8
	46–55 yrs.	10.0	11.2
	56 & above	18.6	18.4
Education:	Illiterate	37.1	34.5
	Up to primary	29.3	33.4
	Up to matric	18.6	22.7
	College & above	14.3	8.2
Community:	Upper caste	53.6	34.8
	OBC	25.7	18.6
	SC	18.6	28.2
	ST	0.7	16.2
	Others	1.4	1.6
Gender:	Male	48.6	47.9
	Female	51.4	52.1
Locality:	Urban	8.6	7.7
	Rural	91.4	92.3

Source: National Election Survey, 1999, conducted by the CSDS, Delhi, CSDS Data Unit

attracts slightly more women than men. The party has greater support among the middle-age (36–45) voters compared to other age groups. But, on the whole, the party draws balanced support from voters of all age groups. The BJD has good support among urban voters (43 per cent). Its supporters comprise large sections of illiterates and well-educated voters. This combination is perhaps well explained by the caste composition of BJD voters. More than half of its voters come from upper castes and a quarter come from the OBCs. In contrast, BJD has a weak base among SCs (25 per cent SCs support BJD) and a non-existent base among Orissa's tribal population (see Table 13.6).

RJD and Samata

Both the Rashtriya Janata Dal and the Samata Party are Bihar-based parties. Both had a common origin in the Janata Dal. While RJD has been a strong exponent of the advancement of OBCs, the Samata Party relied heavily on an anti-Laloo campaign which talked of good governance. It also opposed corruption. The Samata Party was one of the earliest allies of BJP (barring Shiv Sena) since 1996 onwards. It is well known that the party enjoys the support of Bihar's peasant OBC community, the Kurmis. Laloo Prasad's RJD came into being in 1998, but even before that, the Bihar unit of the Janata Dal was practically autonomous. In 1999, RJD had an alliance with the Congress. But the Bihar state unit of the Congress was not very enthusiastic about this

SCs of Bihar. However, he and the RJD have not been able to concretise the alliance. Laloo Prasad forged an invincible coalition of OBCs, Muslims and support of the OBCs. The leadership of Laloo Prasad has been identified with a disproportionate rise of the Yadav community. The RJD is seen as primarily a Yadav party with the support of Yadavs who account for around 11 per cent of the state's population.

The 1990s have been generally seen as the decade of political upheavals marked by a shifting political base. Very few parties were able in this period to retain a steady share of the electorate. The RJD has successfully retained the core of its base during this period. The charges of being an exclusively Yadav party notwithstanding, its support base has been fairly diverse. For instance, in the 1999 elections, RJD drew balanced support from voters of different age groups and educational groups. It received only relatively higher support from voters in the age groups of 46 years and above, and less from younger voters. Also, contrary to the general impression, the RJD receives larger support from the educated voters than it receives from the illiterate. Less women vote for RJD compared to its male supporters and its support among urban voters is higher than among rural voters: While almost 17 per cent rural voters supported the RJD in 1999, 32 per cent urban voters voted for the party. In terms of community, the RJD's base comprises Yadavs, Muslims, low OBCs and SCs. Although some erosion did take place in the support base of RJD across various social sections, survey data for the 1998 elections also shows a similar pattern of OBC, Muslim and SC support to RJD.[11] It may be further noted that almost one-third of RJD voters still come from the lower OBC community (see Table 13.7).

The Samata Party, on the other hand, seems to have benefited from its alliance with the BJP. Voters of the Samata Party constitute a combination of Rajputs and upper castes (who together account for 30 per cent of Samata votes) apart from lower OBCs (one third of Samata votes). Thus, it is a combination of upper and lower castes. Interestingly, 65 per cent Rajputs and almost 40 per cent upper caste voters vote for the Samata Party. In terms of political identification, this means that voters of upper castes do not perceive the Samata Party as an OBC party like Laloo's RJD. The Samata Party draws more support from rural voters than urban voters. Yet, like RJD, Samata Party, too, is slightly more popular among male voters. Its voters come mainly from the age group of 26 years to 45 years. In terms of education, the Samata Party's base is fairly spread across different groups. It draws somewhat more support from the voters having education up to the matric level; over 33 per cent voters from this category vote for the Samata Party. All these

---

[11] Sanjay Kumar, 'New Phase of Backward Caste Politics in Bihar', *Economic and Political Weekly*, Vol. 34, no. 34–35, 21–28 August 1999, pp. 2477–78.

Table 13.7: Social Profile of Voters of RJD (1999) (all figures in percentage)

		Share Among RJD Voters	Share in Sample
Age:	Up to 25 yrs.	22.5	22.2
	26–35 yrs.	25.0	24.7
	36–45 yrs.	19.4	24.5
	46–55 yrs.	13.1	12.0
	56 & above	20.0	16.5
Education:	Illiterate	56.9	58.7
	Up to primary	15.0	13.7
	Up to matric	18.1	18.8
	College & above	8.1	7.2
Community:	Rajput	0.6	7.8
	Upper caste	0.6	9.5
	Yadav	25.0	14.1
	Kurmi	3.1	6.7
	Low OBC	31.9	31.1
	SC	16.9	14.6
	Muslims	20.0	9.1
	Others	1.9	0.7
Gender:	Male	58.1	51.5
	Female	41.9	48.5
Locality:	Urban	16.3	9.3
	Rural	83.8	90.7

Source: NES '99: CSDS Data Unit.

features of the support base of Samata Party have remained stable over a period of time since the same findings were noted in 1995 also.[12]

Samajwadi Party

Like RJD, the Samajwadi Party originated from the Janata Dal. Since its base could not expand beyond UP, this party has been identified as a state-based party. The SP has made efforts to carve out a base for itself in Maharashtra relying upon the Hindi-speaking population of Mumbai and the Muslims in Mumbai. This party has played a significant role in the politics of Mumbai city in the 1990s. In Uttar Pradesh, the Samajwadi Party is seen as a party of Yadavs and Muslims. Since the BSP captures a large section of UP's dalit votes, the expansion of SP has been halted. However, like the RJD, the success of the Samajwadi Party lies in the fact that in UP's turbulent political waters, this party has more or less retained its base during the 1990s. Just as there has been a keen tussle between BSP and SP for UP's dalit voters, the BJP and

[12] V.B. Singh, 'Support Bases of Political Parties: A Study of Bihar Elections 1995', paper presented at a seminar on State Assembly Elections, ICSSR, New Delhi, 1995.

Table 13.8: Social Profile of Voters of Samajwadi Party (1999) (all figures in percentage)

		Share Among SP Voters	Share in Sample
Age:	Up to 25 yrs.	22.9	19.2
	26–35 yrs.	28.6	29.4
	36–45 yrs.	23.3	20.5
	46–55 yrs.	12.9	14.2
	56 & above	12.4	16.7
Education:	Illiterate	44.8	45.0
	Up to primary	20.5	15.3
	Up to matric	21.9	23.1
	College & above	11.9	16.1
Community:	Brahmin	2.4	7.3
	Rajput	2.4	9.7
	Yadav	31.0	7.8
	OBC	37.6	33.1
	SC	5.1	20.8
	Muslims	21.0	9.1
Gender:	Male	61.4	56.0
	Female	38.6	44.0
Locality:	Urban	28.1	25.0
	Rural	71.9	75.0

Source: National Election Survey, 1999, conducted by the CSDS, Delhi, CSDS Data Unit.

SP are engaged in a battle for OBC votes in Uttar Pradesh. The BJP has been trying to forge an alliance of upper castes and lower OBCs in UP. Mulayam Singh on the other hand, seeks to unite the OBCs under Yadav leadership. The Samajwadi Party gets more support among the young voters below 25 years and among voters of the 36–45 years age group. Over 60 per cent of its voters are men. Moderately educated voters (with only primary education) support the SP more than both illiterates and voters with higher education. The Samajwadi Party is more popular among urban voters compared to rural voters. Its voters comprise Yadavs, OBCs and Muslims. Almost two-thirds Yadav voters support the SP, while 37 per cent Muslims and 18 per cent OBCs support this party (see Table 13.8). Thus, the SP has a very strong Yadav association. Both in the case of SP and RJD, there is room to conjecture that they are supported by those sections of the backward communities who have now become upwardly mobile.

Shiv Sena and NCP

For long, politics in Maharashtra was dominated by the Congress. Regional parties like Peasants' and Workers' Party (PWP), Republican Party of India (RPI) and even Shiv Sena did not matter much. Ironically, Shiv Sena shot into prominence after it underplayed its regionalism and projected itself as a Hindu party. Yet, Shiv Sena identifies itself with 'Marathi' people in the

Mumbai-Thane-Konkan region. Outside this region, this party does not invoke regionalism. In the 1990s, Shiv Sena emerged as a militant Hindu party of moderately educated youth from both the Maratha caste and the OBCs. In 1995, when Shiv Sena came to power in the state along with BJP, it had the support of 17 per cent voters from the Maratha-Kunbi caste cluster. The party has consolidated this base over a period of time and added to it a valuable section of OBC voters. In 1998, the party had almost 30 per cent support among the OBCs. All through this period, the base of Shiv Sena consists of illiterates and less educated voters.[13] Some slight changes were observed in the survey of 1999. There is a gender balance among the Sena's supporters. Similarly, the Shiv Sena draws a balanced support from rural and urban voters. Young voters (up to 25 years of age) and voters in the 46–55 age group constitute the main supporters of the Sena. Second, matriculate and college educated voters dominate the Sena's supporters. Over the last five years the Shiv Sena continued to receive support from Marathas (25 per cent), Kunbis (20 per cent) and OBCs (34 per cent).

The Nationalist Congress Party (NCP) has a strong base in Maharashtra. The social composition of NCP's base is somewhat comparable to that of Shiv Sena (Table 13.9). Although the NCP was formed with a view to dividing the Congress all over the country, Sharad Pawar succeeded in only dividing the Congress in Maharashtra. Pawar was already a leader of the breakaway Congress Party in Maharashtra between 1980 and 1986. It appears that he has retained his following. In 1999, NCP received balanced support from voters of various age groups. The party was supported more by women, rural voters and illiterates. In terms of caste, there was a keen competition between NCP and the Shiv Sena for Maratha, Kunbi and OBC votes. Almost one-third of the NCP voters were Marathas. The main difference between NCP and Shiv Sena was that the former got a sizable support from SCs and Muslims. More than 20 per cent dalits and 30 per cent Muslims voted for NCP. Since 47 per cent of NCP voters are from the Maratha-Kunbi community, the party can be identified as a party of the Maratha-Kunbis of Maharashtra. Like Lok Shakti in Karnataka, NCP seems to have played an important role in formalising the fragmentation of the Maratha-Kunbi vote bloc in Maharashtra.

Telugu Desam Party

It may not be an exaggeration to say that TDP marks the beginning of the present era of prominence of regional parties. The TDP has successfully polarised Andhra politics between itself and the Congress. In the 1990s the party assumed a significant role at the all-India level. In order to retain that

[13] Suhas Palshikar, 'Shiv Sena: An Assessment', Occasional Paper II:3, Department of Politics and Public Administration, University of Pune, Pune, 1999, pp. 19–20.

Table 13.9: Social Profile of Voters of Shiv Sena and NCP (1999) (all figures in percentage)

		Share Among Shiv Sena	Share Among NCP	Share in Sample
Age:	Up to 25 yrs.	18.5	14.2	16.3
	26–35 yrs.	25.0	17.3	27.0
	36–45 yrs.	20.5	21.0	21.7
	46–55 yrs.	19.5	18.9	15.9
	56 & above	16.5	28.3	19.0
Education:	Illiterate	35.5	50.7	38.4
	Up to primary	25.0	25.6	26.4
	Up to matric	25.0	15.1	23.2
	College & above	14.0	8.2	11.6
Community:	Upper caste	9.5	7.8	11.2
	Maratha	30.5	31.5	23.6
	Kunbi	20.0	16.0	12.8
	OBC	34.0	20.1	27.2
	SC	3.0	8.2	8.3
	ST	2.0	4.1	6.5
	Muslims	0.5	11.9	8.3
	Others	0.5	0.5	2.1
Gender:	Male	51.0	47.9	49.5
	Female	49.0	52.1	50.5
Locality:	Urban	32.0	23.7	33.3
	Rural	68.0	76.3	66.7

Source: National Election Survey, 1999, conducted by the CSDS, Delhi, CSDS Data Unit.

position, Chandrababu Naidu swiftly switched over to the National Democratic Alliance from the United Front. The TDP, right from its inception, has proved to be a rallying point for Andhra's peasant OBCs although it does not invoke the ideology of OBC uplift. As a result of N.T. Rama Rao's (NTR) charismatic appeal and populist policies, TDP earned popularity among the poor, rural voters, especially among women. It was also supported by SCs and OBCs.[14] It has been further observed that the original social coalition forged by NTR incorporated middle peasants and the middle class from backward castes; but by 1998, while the party electorally assuaged the backward castes, some poor and backward caste voters shifted to the BJP.[15] The alienation of OBCs from the Congress since the early 1980s has been observed by students of Andhra politics[16] and this has been accounted for by the

[14] K. Srinivasulu and Prakash Sarangi, 'Political Realignments in Post-NTR Andhra Pradesh', *Economic and Political Weekly*, Vol. 34, No. 34–35, 21–28 August 1999, p. 2457.
[15] Karli Srinivasulu, 'Regime Change and Shifting Power Bases: The Telugu Desam Party in the 12th General Elections', in Roy and Wallace, *Indian Politics and the 1998 Elecions*, pp. 218–24.
[16] F.D. Vakil, 'Congress Party in Andhra Pradesh: A Review', in George Mathew (ed.), *Shifts in Indian Politics: 1983 Elections in Andhra Pradesh and Karnataka*, New Delhi: Concept, p. 68.

pro-Harijan policies of the Congress.[17] However, TDP's strong regional developmentalist argument and the following it received, can be understood only in the context of the rise of the peasant OBCs—the Kammas. By 1980, this section had attained a crucial amount of economic power and control over the state's economy. That is why, in the first place, the appeal of regionalism worked with this section and in the second place, Chandrababu Naidu's technology-savvy policy also appealed to this section.

It is remarkable that the TDP has more or less retained the earlier composition of its social base in spite of the policy shift effected by Chandrababu Naidu. Its voters are evenly spread among different age groups. Although slightly more women voters vote for TDP than men, there is no gender imbalance in its base. Its base is predominantly rural. Less than 30 per cent urban voters support the TDP. Less educated and illiterate voters extend greater support to TDP than the well educated. As has been observed earlier, over 70 per cent Kamma voters support the TDP. However, the secret of TDP's success does not lie in this Kamma support alone. Substantial support among tribals and a very large support among peasant OBCs accounts for the electoral success of Telugu Desam. In fact, TDP would be more dependant upon OBC voters in general than on Kamma votes alone (see Table 13.10). There is room to surmise that the regionalist identity and a strong developmentalist policy appeals to the upwardly mobile rural sections that have acquired domination only recently. In comparison, the support of SCs has declined in 1999 in comparison to the NTR period.

Trinamool Congress

Since the Left Front has been the ruling front in West Bengal since the late 1970s, politics in the state revolves around left and anti-left poles. It has been further observed that the success of the Left Front is attributable to the typically Bengali identity acquired and nurtured by left parties. In this sense, politics in West Bengal had already become regionalised. Strident anti-left agitation by one section of the state Congress further contributed to this regionalisation. The Congress in West Bengal was divided between two factions, one trying to associate with the all-India perception of politics leading to the anti-BJP strategy (effectively meaning a soft approach to the Left Front) and another faction rooting its politics firmly in the trajectory of state-level politics which led to a tacit understanding with the BJP.[18] The Trinamool Congress emerged from this scenario in 1997. Although the new party did

[17] Atul Kohli, 'The NTR Phenomenon in Andhra Pradesh: Political Change in a South Indian State', *Asian Survey*, Vol. 36, no. 10, October 1998, p. 997.
[18] James Mayers, 'Transformation of Opposition Politics in West Bengal', *Economic and Political Weekly*, Vol. 33, no. 33–34, 15–22 August 1998, p. 2254.

Table 13.10: Social Profile of Voters of TDP (1999) (all figures in percentage)

		Share Among TDP Voters	Share in Sample
Age:	Up to 25 yrs.	16.9	16.9
	26–35 yrs.	26.8	27.6
	36–45 yrs.	22.5	22.3
	46–55 yrs.	12.7	15.0
	56 & above	21.1	18.3
Education:	Illiterate	57.5	53.4
	Up to primary	21.4	19.1
	Up to matric	12.4	14.2
	College & above	7.9	12.9
Community:	Upper caste	6.2	7.2
	Reddy	3.1	5.1
	Kamma	6.2	3.7
	Peasant OBC	22.0	16.5
	Maratha, etc.	10.1	8.6
	Lower OBC	20.6	20.8
	SC	5.4	7.4
	ST	13.8	13.7
	Muslims	8.7	13.0
	Others	3.9	4.1
Gender:	Male	47.0	47.4
	Female	53.0	52.6
Locality:	Urban	20.3	28.5
	Rural	79.7	71.5

Source: National Election Survey, 1999, conducted by the CSDS, Delhi, CSDS Data Unit.

not enter into an alliance with the BJP—it had only seat adjustment in 1998—the Trinamool Congress finally allied with the BJP in 1999. The Trinamool Congress draws heavily on Bengali nationalism but identifies itself with minorities and poorer sections of the state. It has been observed that in contrast to the Bhadralok politics of CPI (M), Trinamool's plebian politics attracts the voters on the social and economic fringe.[19] Survey data shows that more men vote for Trinamool than women (which is contradictory to the *didi* image of Mamata Banerjee among women). Second, the larger support to the party comes from voters in the age group of 26 to 35 years. In fact, Trinamool draws relatively less support from the middle-aged and elderly voters. The educational profile of its supporters is fairly balanced, though it has a slightly higher level of support in the group with education up to matriculation. In spite of reverses, which the Trinamool Congress handed out to the LF support in rural areas and in contrast to its plebian image, 44 per cent of its supporters come from upper castes. Although Trinamool has reasonably good support among SCs and OBCs, support among the Muslims is quite weak (Table 13.11).

---

[19] Dwaipayan Bhattacharya, 'Elections 1999: Ominous Outcome for Left in West Bengal', *Economic and Political Weekly*, Vol. 34, no. 46–47, 20 November, 1999, p. 3269.

Table 13.11: Social Profile of Voters of Trinmool Congress (1999) (all figures in percentage)

		Share Among TC Voters	Share in Sample
Age:	Up to 25 yrs.	20.8	21.2
	26–35 yrs.	34.1	30.9
	36–45 yrs.	20.2	22.8
	46–55 yrs.	12.1	12.8
	56 & above	12.7	12.2
Education:	Illiterate	22.0	22.9
	Up to primary	26.0	26.8
	Up to matric	34.7	29.1
	College & above	16.8	18.7
Community:	Upper caste	43.9	36.0
	OBC	11.6	11.5
	SC	24.9	28.4
	ST	1.2	2.7
	Muslims	8.7	13.1
	Others	9.8	8.4
Gender:	Male	59.0	53.7
	Female	41.0	46.3
Locality:	Urban	7.5	11.0
	Rural	92.5	89.0

Source: National Election Survey, 1999, conducted by the CSDS, Delhi, CSDS Data Unit.

III

The foregoing sections show that regional parties employ various ideological arguments and draw support from different sections in different states. The BJP's allies broadly receive support from a combination of upper castes and lower castes while most opponents of BJP have a strong base among upwardly mobile peasant castes (often peasant OBCs) and dalits. However, these differences are overshadowed by the crucial role played by regional parties during the 1990s. Regional parties existed earlier also. But they often confined their role to state politics. In contrast, the rise of regional parties in the post-1990 period is marked by their central role in national-level politics. So much so, that some regional parties first became active in all-India politics and then entered the arena of state politics. Lok Shakti, Biju Janata Dal, Trinamool Congress are examples of this pattern. Thus, it is the role of parties in national level politics that has been attracting comment. In one more respect, the regional parties of yesteryears are different from the post-1990 period. Earlier, most regional parties could be explained in terms of regional sentiments (linguistic state, etc.) and/or in terms of local splinter groups of national parties, notably the Congress. Whenever a local- or state-level faction got a raw deal in the party, that faction would start functioning as a separate regional party—till the time it was accommodated in some larger or national party. But the rise of regional parties in the 1990s has been on such a scale that the amalgamation of regional parties with national parties does not seem to be feasible. As a result, the political actors have been forced to develop coalition strategies whereby they enter into alliances with a view to retaining their respective existences separately. Besides, regional parties from different states, too, cannot forge a grand federal alliance. Such alliances appear attractive on paper and may even be workable at the national level but each state has different sets of political compulsions forcing regional parties to align with national parties rather than with each other. It is necessary, therefore, to situate the phenomenon of regional parties (and overall regionalisation of politics) in the context of changes in the electoral party system, the evolution of Indian democracy and the political economy in the post-Emergency period.

Competing Frameworks of Politics

Since the decline of the Congress system, at least two competing frameworks of politics have been trying the hold the middle ground that was hitherto occupied by the Congress Party. These are the framework of backward caste politics and the framework of majoritarian politics of Hindu communalism. This competition momentarily displaced the emphasis on anti-Congressism and gave way to the 'third space' discourse. From the neat division of politics into Congress and Opposition, political configuration became complex. The capital 'O' in opposition disappeared. Now, politics involved three options: anti-Congress, anti-BJP and opposition to both Congress and BJP. Besides, the politics of backward castes presented two possibilities. The backward castes could be accommodated in either the Congress or the BJP. Alternatively, the backward castes could remain autonomous and redefine the terms of politics. It is in this sense that the increase in the numerical choices available to voters[20] also implies a qualitative change. One qualitative change involved the availability of differentiated sets of alternatives, just as the anti-Congress alternative in the form of BJP was also available. Similarly, two OBC party alternatives in the form of Samata and RJD became available while a similar option existed in the case of anti-BJP politics also.

Another qualitative change is related to the nature of electoral mobilisations. The competition among the Congress framework, BJP framework and caste framework produced opportunities for sharply focused mobilisations. Mobilisation around a single issue, single social section, etc., became possible. Thus, a new space for mobilisation emerged in terms of exclusivist mobilisation.[21]

---

[20] Yogendra Yadav, 'Electoral Politics in Times of Change: India's Third Electoral System— 1989–99', *Economic and Political Weekly*, Vol. 34, no. 34–35, 21–28 August 1999, pp. 2394–95.
[21] Yogendra Yadav, 'Reconfiguration in Indian Politics: State Assembly Elections, 1993– 1995', *Economic and Political Weekly*, Vol. 31, no. 2–3, 13–20 January 1996, p. 100.

More importantly, this mobilisation entered the arena of national-level politics and became relevant there. One obvious implication of these developments was that the theatre for defining the boundaries of political contestations often turned out to be the state. Whether a party will be only anti-Congress or also anti-BJP depended upon the state-level configuration of forces rather than on national-level exigencies or ideological positions. Thus, both the Trinamool Congress and TDP have reasons to claim their secular credentials openly. And yet they cannot be part of the anti-communal front anymore. In the case of Trinamool, its anti-communalism is circumscribed by the fact that the Left Front holds the central position in the anti-communal politics in the state. Thus, while LF represents anti-communal Left politics, Trinamool represents anti-left secular politics in West Bengal. In Andhra, TDP hopes to occupy anti-Congress secular space while in UP, Mulayam Singh Yadav aspires to occupy secular, OBC and anti-Congress space. This situation constitutes the political background in which many regional and state-level parties have emerged in the 1990s.

Since the Congress held the middle ground in most states (except Tamil Nadu where it did not and West Bengal where it shared this space with the Left Front), state-level parties in almost all the states follow the anti-Congress frame of reference. Thus, anti-Congressism may be seen as a common feature of a majority of regional parties. Besides, the emerging framework of caste politics supplied additional strength to the anti-Congress stand. The claim of various peasant OBC castes in different states directly challenged the Congress because the latter was instrumental in retaining the political hold of the upper castes and rich peasant castes. However, the caste framework of politics could not generate one all-India vehicle since caste configurations have been state specific. Thus, anti-Congressism and state-specific caste equations combined to produce separate state-level politics in many parts of the country in the post-1990 period. In a sense, the post-Congress polity is witnessing a fundamental contestation over the middle ground. Students of Indian politics have already noted the difficulty involved in occupying the 'middle space' in national politics.[22] What needs to be emphasised, however, is the fact that the 'middle ground' is itself in the process of being redefined. Whereas the Congress system shaped the middle ground by constantly negotiating the various social cleavages, the caste framework as also the BJP framework sought to redefine what constitutes the middle space. The rise of dalits and OBCs has forced parties to claim that sharpening of social cleavages rather than their negotiation, constitutes the middle ground. This has further inspired exclusivist parties and focused on the states as theatres of politics. In other words, now there is no single 'middle' ground in Indian politics, there are multiple middle grounds specific to various states and they have been defined

---

[22] Ibid.

or invented in opposition to existing middle spaces in those respective states. The BJP in UP, for instance, has to follow the rules of game as dictated by the newly emergent 'middle space' and incorporate the large OBC contingent within its fold. The regionally understood 'middle space' thus, defines the politics in a state. The regional parties and the regionalisation of national parties represent this churning.

Democratisation

The rise of regional parties is seen by scholars as related to democratisation in three respects. It has been argued that politics in the 1990s is characterised by a democratic upsurge involving greater participation by women, tribals, dalits, lower castes and rural voters. Regional parties are seen as carriers of this democratic upsurge.[23] Second, the issue of regional parties is seen in the context of federal polity. It is argued that established opinion has always seen regional parties and regionalism with suspicion because the Congress system of politics placed heavy emphasis on the nation as the unit of political action rather than the states. However, both on grounds of plurality and democratic principle, the federalisation of the polity has been seen as a positive development.[24] It is further argued that although regional parties are not self-consciously working in the direction of rewriting Centre-state relations, this is precisely what will result from their attempts to diminish the Centre's powers over states.[25] The third dimension is related to the discourse shift taking place in Indian politics. It is said that the rise of regional parties suggests that established discourse on nation and nation building is being challenged. The idea of a homogenised nation and of politics sanitised by excluding the local elements is being effectively challenged by the rise of new localities around which much of contemporary politics is centred.[26] In essence, these arguments tend to posit the regional parties with a democratising potential and suggest that the rise of regional parties may indicate the possibility of further democratisation possible within a liberal democratic framework.

It is true that the decline of the Congress system has released a number of forces which contain democratic possibilities. Besides, expansion of the competitive arena opens up politics for new contestations which were hitherto muted. The rise of regional parties is associated with these developments.

---

[23] Ibid., pp. 96–100.
[24] K.R. Bombwall, 'Regional Parties in Indian Politics: A Preview', in S. Bhatnagar and Pradeep Kumar (eds), *Regional Political Parties in India*, New Delhi: Ess Ess Publications, 1988, pp. 2–12.
[25] Mahesh Rangarajan, 'One, Two, Many Indias?', *Seminar*, August 1999, pp. 28–29.
[26] Aditya Nigam, 'India After the 1996 Elections: Nation, Locality and Representation', *Asian Survey*, Vol. 36, No. 9, September 1996, pp. 1165–66.

On the other hand, it would be unrealistic to expect regional parties to fully or effectively transcend the characteristics of Indian polity. These characteristics constrain their democratic potentials. The rise of regional parties has effectively put an end to the plebiscitary character of elections based on charismatic leadership. This fact has been more than sufficiently underscored by Rajiv Gandhi's defeat, the failure of Sonia Gandhi to generate a wave and also the failure of the BJP in winning elections on the basis of Vajpayee's popularity. Yet, elections continue to be plebiscites regarding state-level leaders. Orissa, Andhra Pradesh, Tamil Nadu, Haryana, Bihar, are examples of this. In fact states where regional parties do not exist or are weak have shown a non-plebiscitary character. Most regional parties derive their electoral strength from the popularity of one leader and there is always an emotional bond between the leader and the electorate. Such a structure of politics allows the leader/party to claim mass support (mandate) *and yet to ignore the expectations in policy formulation.*

Second, while regional parties have certainly shifted the 'locale' of political discourse, it is too early to visualise a weak Centre. What appears to be possible is that the clout of regional parties will give states a counter to bargain with the Centre and wrest some concessions. But the fact that the majority of the regional parties are partners in central government also means that there will be limits to the anti-Centre demands of regional parties. Thus, 'interlocking' of the national system and state party systems[27] may work in both directions. It may push federalisation; it may as well restrict states' anti-Centre rhetoric. More importantly, almost all the regional parties not only want a share in central politics but also do not want to be identified as parochial. This forces them to be magnanimous in their approach to issues of federalism.

This situation warns us against the romanticisation of regional parties. In terms of the structure of politics, new localities have certainly been emerging in the sense suggested by Aditya Nigam.[28] These localities have changed the political idiom. But have they changed—sought to change—the essential characteristics of the political discourse? The dramatic consensus on issues of economic policy involving structural adjustments and on the issue of the nuclear option suggests that parties positioning themselves on different 'locales' from national parties, do not necessarily think and act differently. This suggests that parties across the board share a nationalist rhetoric, which makes the issue of locality somewhat weak. The transformation that is taking place lies not so much in the content of discourse but in the participants of that discourse. In a significant shift, newer sections seek to displace those who have thus far monopolised the political discourse.

[27] Pai, 'The Indian Party System', p. 851.
[28] Nigam, 'India After the 1996 Elections'.

Political Economy

How far this shift will affect the polity in the long-term will probably depend upon the nature of India's political economy. Already, the association between the rise of regional parties and economic changes has been noted by scholars. It is argued that as globalisation deepens, the role of 'localities' as the sites of political agency and of domination will become more important.[29] Further, it is noted that the shift in power and bargaining leverage from the Centre to the states is advanced by the programme of economic liberalisation.[30] More specifically, the policy of liberalisation has changed the competitive ability of states to attract fresh investments. Instead of credit flows in the direction of low-income states (as in the pre-reform period), the high-income states have been receiving credit flows since 1994.[31] This trend is going to (a) increase the gap between rich and poor states and (b) increase the clout of rich states in policy making. Thus, one can predicate the economic status of a state along with the decline of the Congress in order to measure the role of regional parties. The economic disparity, however, appears to be a non-factor in explaining the existence of regional parties. Just as better-off states like Andhra Pradesh, Maharashtra, Tamil Nadu, Punjab, Haryana, etc., have strong regional parties, low-income states like Bihar, UP, Orissa, too have their regional parties. Thus, instead of working as one 'bloc' of state-based parties, regional parties will be divided among themselves on the issue of federal structure and the content of liberalisation policy.

Within the overall context of contradiction thrown up by the process of liberalisation, one has to take note of the rise of new sections among the ruling classes and the response of ruling classes to the democratisation that has been taking place. Both these developments can be located in the post-Emergency period. Looking specifically at the example of Andhra Pradesh, Srinivasulu has argued that the emergence of a rich peasant class in the aftermath of the green revolution as the junior partner in the ruling class is a crucial development. This class is favourably disposed to the available ideological reserve contained in regionalist ideology.[32] The rise of this new section of ruling class is accompanied by the rise of OBCs as an electoral political force. The former assumed the role of political leadership of this new social force.

I have argued elsewhere that the moment of transformation is often, in the Indian experience, coupled with an aspirational coup by emergent sections

---

[29] Mohapatra, 'Elections and Everyday Politics', p. 171.
[30] Ramesh Thakur, 'A Changing of the Guard in India', *Asian Survey*, Vol. 38, no. 6, June 1998, p. 615.
[31] Rangarajan, 'One Two, Many Indians?'.
[32] Srinivasulu, 'Regime Change', pp. 216–17.

of ruling classes.[33] The rise of regional parties needs to be seen in this specific context. The 1980s and 1990s were definitely marked by the political assertion of the masses. The dalits and OBCs in terms of caste, but the disprivileged in general, were retaining their stakes in the political process. These democratic claims met with two responses from the political establishment. One, these claims were incorporated within the Hindutva rhetoric. Two, they were locally digested in the twin polemic of regional pride and regional development. Both these responses were effectively worked out by the new middle classes, which have placed themselves in the forefront of politics in the 1990s. The middle classes endorsed the Hindutva rhetoric and they also provided the rationale for regionalism. In this context we also need to note that the social composition of the middle classes is changing to include rural sections and OBCs. This is how the democratic upsurge can be usurped by the ruling classes through the middle class.

The processes of liberalisation and globalisation of the Indian economy have upset the balance within the ruling classes. While these processes have underscored the overall ascendance of capitalism, the new dispensation has brought into the picture at least three players. One is the metropolitan capital both in the form of multi-nationals and global financial companies. These have threatened the Indian bourgeoisie or reduced it to a secondary place. The other is enterprising sections among the rich peasants who are turning to capitalist farming and exports. This new section is vociferously pro-development in the sense of regional development. The third player within

Table 13.12: Performance of Some Regional Parties: 1995–1999

	1996		1998		1999		1994–1995		1996–1997		1999–2000	
	Seats	Votes (%)	Seats	Votes (%)	Seats	Votes (%)	Seats	Votes (%)	Seats	Votes (%)	Seats	Votes (%)
Akali	8	28.7	8	32.9	2	28.6	–	–	75	37.8	–	–
BJD	–	–	9	27.5	10	33.0	–	–	–	–	68	29.6
DMK	17	25.6	5	20.1	12	23.1	–	–	173	42.1	–	–
AIADMK	–	7.8	18	25.9	10	25.7	–	–	4	21.5	–	–
RJD	–	–	17	26.6	7	28.3	–	–	124	28.2	–	–
Samata	6	14.5	10	15.7	–	–	7	7.1	–	–	84	8.8
SP	16	20.8	20	28.7	26	24.1	–	–	110	21.8	–	–
SS	15	16.8	6	19.7	16	16.9	73	15.5	–	–	69	17.0
NCP	–	–	–	–	6	21.6	–	–	–	–	58	22.5
TC	–	–	7	24.4	8	26.0	–	–	–	–	–	–

Source: National Election Survey, 1999, conducted by the CSDS, Delhi, CSDS Data Unit.

---

[33] Suhas Palshikar, 'Democratic Practices and Hegemonic Project in India', paper presented at a seminar on Understanding Indian Politics, Deptartment of Politics and Public Administration, University of Pune, Pune, January 2000.

the ruling classes is the middle class. Its rural component has an excellent equation with the rich peasant class and the urban component has a favourable predisposition towards metropolitan capital.

Coupled with the decline of the Congress, this new set of the political economy presents the ruling classes with a fundamental problem. On the one hand, it is necessary to give a political share to the rich peasant and middle classes, and on the other hand, the economic policies need to be legitimated. This requires new political instrumentalities. With the BJP not yet being able to fulfil both the above tasks, regional parties will be expected to function as the mechanism routing new elites to places of power and shaping local mandates for the advance of economic restructuring. Paradoxical though it may seem, regional parties have been and are going to be both agencies of legitimising domination and sites of democratisation. The contradiction inherent in this duality of their roles is the defining factor in their careers.

14

THE CONTEST FOR THE MARGINAL SPACE
PARTIES AND POLITICS IN SMALL INDIAN STATES

Sajal Nag

The Indian Union comprises 35 federal units termed as states and Union Territories. Although these units are an integral part of the Union, each of them has a cultural identity and a distinct past. The empire-building process of the British and the distribution of provinces of British India was arbitrary and meant to meet the needs of the growth of the British power. Thus, in some cases, several cultural groups were often combined within one administrative unit while in other situations one cultural group was distributed among many provinces. Marathi lands, for example, were in the Bombay Presidency, Central Provinces, Hyderabad and the small principalities of the Deccan; the Telugus were in Madras as well as in Hyderabad; the Malayalis in Madras and Travancore-Cochin; the Oriyas in Madras, Bengal and the Central Provinces; the Bengalis in Bengal as well as in Assam. The dynamics that set the forces of the Indian national movement (pan-Indian) in motion were also responsible for the beginning of the formation of nationalities amongst cultural communities. Such a nationality-formation process had manifested itself in multiple ways: the growth of respective vernacular literature, the movement for establishing particular languages as official languages of the area, the struggle of backward or suppressed cultural communities to break away from the domination of the advanced ones, and the fight of communities categorised as tribals against the encroachment of exploitation by outsiders.[1]

The Indian National Congress as a national party had recognised the principle of linguistic provinces as the key to tackling and settling the nationality questions arising out of the ethno-cultural plurality of India, even as it led the national movement. It incorporated the principle in its organisational

---

[1] See Sajal Nag, *Nationalism, Separatism, Secessionism,* Jaipur: Rawat, 1999, pp. 120–59 for details.

structure and passed an official resolution on it in its Nagpur Congress (1920), wherein it drew up a comprehensive scheme of organising India into several provinces such as Madras, Karnataka, Andhra, Kerala, Punjab, North West Frontier Province, Delhi, Ajmer, Marwar and Rajasthan, Central Provinces, Berar, Bihar, Utkal, Bengal, Assam and Burma. The resolution was passed due to the pressure from its regional units, most of which represented a cultural area. But partition as well as the integration of the princely states into the Indian union and the arduous task of consolidating the newly achieved independence delayed the implementation of the commitment.

Although the Congress, the party in power, still adhered to the principle of linguistic states, it often vacillated when it came to realising the principle in full. Three States Reorganisation Commissions (SRCs) were appointed successively and several new states were created. But the clamour for new states continued to emerge, often violently. Thus, the Union, which intially organised itself into 14 states after the recommendations of the States Reorganisation Commission were implemented in 1956, had 25 states and seven Union Territories by the close of the 20th century.[2] Most of the new states created since 1956 were results of people's movements, or overwhelming popular desire, which were expressed either in terms of ethnic or linguistic identity, or regional underdevelopment due to discriminatory policies or both. Since India is a union of multiple identities, developed as well as dormant, federal units were created on the basis of cultural markers, of which the linguistic marker was the most prominent one. Naturally, the identities are not uniform either demographically, or territorially, hence the states varied in size. Thus, small and large states[3] were embedded in the very logic of the linguistic provinces.

However, this logic does not dilute some of the prominent features of federal India. The first six large-sized states (Sl. Nos 1 to 6 in Table 14.1) contained more than 50 per cent of the total land area (32,87,263 sq. km) as well as the total population (Table 14.2) of the country (48,0118,000 out of the total 84,6303,000 in 1991). As against this, 15 small states (Sl. Nos 18 to 32 in Table 14.2) made up only 8.9 per cent of the total area and 5.5 per cent of the total population. Although academics consider both area and population to characterise a state small or large, the Government of India uses only the population structure for this purpose.[4] For example, although Assam is much

---

[2] After the carving out of Uttaranchal, Chhattisgarh and Jharkhand from UP, MP and Bihar, respectively, in November 2000, the number of states has risen to 28. Still there are demands for elevating Delhi from a Union Territory to a state and movements for Vidarbha, Telengana, Harit Pradesh are simmering.

[3] In our discussion here all the 32 units (three new states were created after this chapter was finalised), even Union Territories, would be referred to as 'states' for convenience.

[4] *Bulletin Sample Registration System (SRS)*, 33(1), 1 April 2000, published by Registrar General of India, Vital Statistics Division, New Delhi.

smaller than Arunachal Pradesh, the former is considered a large state whereas the latter is categorised as small. Similarly, Jammu and Kashmir with a large territory is categorised as a small state. Again, states like Goa and Union Territories like Delhi, Chandigarh, Pondicherry and Dadra and Nagar Haveli are smaller than some of the northeastern states, but have less dependence on central aid. As against this, the northeastern states, including Sikkim, receive 90 per cent of their budget requirement from the Centre. Punjab, Haryana, Kerala are smaller than the small states of Arunachal Pradesh, Assam and Himachal Pradesh, but are among the most prosperous of Indian states, while the latter are deficit states run on assistance from the Centre.

Table 14.1: Order of States and Union Territories in terms of Area

State	Area (sq. km.)
Madhya Pradesh	4,43,446
Rajasthan	3,42,239
Maharashtra	3,07,690
Uttar Pradesh	2,94,411
Andhra Pradesh	2,75,068
Jammu and Kashmir	2,22,236
Gujarat	1,96,024
Karnataka	1,91,791
Bihar	1,73,877
Orissa	1,55,707
Tamil Nadu	1,30,058
West Bengal	88,752
Arunachal Pradesh	83,743
Assam	78,438
Himachal Pradesh	55,673
Punjab	50,362
Haryana	44,212
Kerala	38,863
Meghalaya	22,429
Manipur	22,327
Mizoram	21,087
Nagaland	16,579
Tripura	10,486
Andaman & Nicobar	8,249
Sikkim	7,026
Goa	3,702
Delhi	1,483
Pondicherry	492
Dadra and Nagar Haveli	491
Chandigarh	114
Daman & Diu	112
Lakshadweep	32
Total (India)	32,87,263

Source: *India 2000*, New Delhi: Publication Division, Ministry of I&B, Government of India, 2000.

Table 14.2: Order of States and Union Territories in terms of Population (1991 Census)

State	Population (in 000's, rounded)	Lok Sabha MPs
Uttar Pradesh	1,39,112	85
Bihar	86,374	54
Maharashtra	78,937	48
West Bengal	68,078	42
Andhra Pradesh	66,508	42
Madhya Pradesh	66,181	40
Tamil Nadu	55,859	39
Karnataka	44,977	28
Rajasthan	44,006	25
Gujarat	41,310	26
Orissa	31,660	21
Kerala	29,099	20
Assam	22,414	14
Punjab	20,282	13
Haryana	16,464	10
Delhi	9,421	7
Jammu and Kashmir	7,719	6
Himachal Pradesh	5,171	4
Tripura	2,757	2
Manipur	1,837	2
Meghalaya	1,775	2
Nagaland	1,210	1
Goa	1,170	2
Arunachal Pradesh	865	2
Pondicherry	808	1
Mizoram	690	1
Chandigarh	612	1
Sikkim	406	1
Andaman & Nicobar	281	1
Dadra and Nagar Haveli	138	1
Daman & Diu	102	1
Lakshadweep	52	1
(Nominated)		2
Total (India)	846,303	545

Source: *India 2000*, New Delhi: Publication Division, Ministry of I&B, Government of India, 2000.

The Indian federal structure also has an interesting cultural dimension. The large states like Uttar Pradesh, Madhya Pradesh, Rajasthan and Bihar are located in a predominantly Hindu, Hindi-speaking belt which has been identified as the core of the Indian mainstream.[5] These areas have been traditional supporters of the Congress. In terms of political power, 40 per

[5] A.C. Sinha, 'Managing the Social Consequence of Smallness: The Developmental Strategy of Small Indian Frontier States', in B.L. Abbi (ed.), *North East Region Problems and Prospects of Development*, Chandigarh: CRRID, 1984, pp. 111–26.

cent of the seats in the Indian Parliament are controlled by them. In the second category, there are states like Gujarat, Maharashtra, Karnataka, Kerala, Tamil Nadu, Andhra Pradesh, Orissa, Haryana, West Bengal and Assam which, though not Hindi-speaking, have a predominantly Hindu population subscribing to the Brahmanic ideology. This cultural political zone may be seen as an associated outer circle of the core or mainstream which controls 52 per cent of the seats in the Lok Sabha. These states have been the strongholds of national parties too. On the outer fringe of these two zones are states like Jammu and Kashmir, Punjab, Goa, Lakshadweep, the Andaman and Nicobar Islands, Mizoram, Nagaland, Meghalaya, Arunachal Pradesh, Tripura and Sikkim. These units are inhabited by predominantly non-Hindu, non-Hindi-speaking cultural communities and have a strong tradition of regional parties or state-based parties. They elect only 8 per cent of the Lok Sabha MPs.[6] It may be pointed out here that Jammu and Kashmir and Lakshadweep are the two Muslim majority units of India, Punjab is the only state with a majority Sikh population, Sikkim the only state with a predominantly Buddhist population. Nagaland, Mizoram, Meghalaya and Arunachal Pradesh have a predominantly Scheduled Tribe (ST) population. The first three states among them have a majority Christian population, while the last one has various forms of animism. As a broad generalisation most of the large states can be said to belong to the mainstream of the Indian state while the smaller states are located in the periphery.

Thus, when we talk of party politics in small states, we are basically talking of the political space provided by this 8 per cent representation. Since here we are concerned only with the eight northeastern states, this percentage comes down to a meagre 4.58 per cent which constitutes the marginal space of the national politics. This also explains why national politics or Lok Sabha elections are so unimportant to these states. In contrast, state politics at the provincial level assume much significance to the parties and people of these states.

This chapter concentrates mainly on the state-level scenario. We try to examine the implications of the geo-political locations of these small states and why smaller states are the strongholds of regional parties. We also try to understand what these regional parties are and why they are labelled so. Lastly, we study the function of the parties, whether national or regional, their compulsions and participation in electoral politics and the pattern of their mobilisation process when they function in small states, and conclude with the emerging patterns and feature. Although we concentrate on the northeastern states of India, occasional references will be made to other small states as well. When we talk of the northeastern states of India, we are talking

---

[6] S.K. Chaube, 'Cultural Frame and Dynamics of Federalism in India', *Social Science Probings*, 1(2), 1984, pp. 235–37.

about three former native states (Sikkim, Tripura and Manipur); three Excluded Areas (Nagaland, Mizoram and Arunachal Pradesh); one partially Excluded Area (Meghalaya) and a Chief Commissionerate which graduated to the status of a Governor's Province (Assam). Thus, except for Assam no other state was directly a part of the political developments that took place in the rest of India during the national movement.

The Roots

As stated earlier, the process of party formation cannot be isolated from the process of identity formation. Since both the processes began in India with the advent of British colonialism, the present political configuration cannot be understood without a reference to the colonial past. Political parties emerge from society to politically respond to the demands of the civil society. As most of the states in India generally demarcated a cultural or nationality area, where dynamics of nationality formation were set in motion by the advent of British capitalism in colonial form, parties and political organisations often emerged to represent the interest and aspirations of the emerging nationalities. Thus, at the national level the Indian National Congress emerged as the expression of rising Indian nationalism, at the regional level there were organisations and parties which articulated sub-national interests and aspirations. Thus, we had the Assam Association in Assam, the National Conference in Jammu and Kashmir, the Justice Party in Tamil Nadu, the Akali Dal in Punjab, the Andhra Mahashabha in Andhra, Karnataka Ekikaran Sangh in Karnataka, the Gujarat Sabha in Gujarat (1884), the Naga National Council (1946), Mizo Union (MU) (1946), Tripura Rajya Gana Parishad (1939), Tripura Mukti Parishad (1948), Jaintia Darbar (1900), Khasi National Darbar (1923), Nikhil Manipuri Mahashabha (1934), Sikkim State Congress (1947), and so on. While the Congress led the freedom struggle with a pan-Indian outlook, these organisations concentrated on the local crises, both of which rarely came into conflict with each other. Subsequently, some of these organisations crystallised into regional political parties while some others tenaciously continued their struggle for statehood till they attained it. Quite often some of these organisations merged with or transformed themselves into the local unit of the Congress. In Assam, the Assam Association (1882) likewise transformed into the Pradesh Congress.

The Congress, it must be remembered, was not an unchallenged party in Assam during the national movement. With substantial Bengali Muslim immigrants as well as tribal population, the Muslim League and prominent tribal political organisations made their presence felt. In fact, during the colonial period the Congress was in power only twice; once in 1938 for about a year through coalition and from 1946 onwards. During this entire period the Congress concentrated on tackling the crisis facing the Assamese nationality.

When Assam was constituted into a Commissionerate in 1874, three Bengali-speaking districts, Sylhet, Cachar and Goalpara were transferred into it from Bengal. Thus started the Bengali dominance in Assam which the emerging Assamese nationality contested.[7] The inflow of Muslim immigrants from Bengal districts, patronised by both the colonial state and the Muslim League ministry, threatened to reduce the indigenous Assamese into a minority. The Pakistan Resolution of the Muslim League contemplated the inclusion of Assam in the prospective state of Pakistan whereas the Cabinet Mission Plan schemed to tag Assam with Bengal. Both the proposals was perceived by the Assamese as a threat to obliterate the identity of Assam.[8] Since the Muslim League claimed to protect the interests of the Muslims alone, it was left to the Pradesh Congress to respond to the crisis the Assamese nationality was confronted with. The Assamese people looked up to the Congress as a national party and its pro-Hindu pro-Assamese leaders to guard it from this grave danger. When the Congress came to power in 1946 with an absolute majority in the Legislative Assembly, it immediately created a plan to evict the immigrants from the forest reserves of the Brahmaputra valley. The eviction operation started in November 1946 with the help of the army. But it precipitated another crisis and fuelled a communal riot.[9] However, the Gopinath Bordoloi government had to suspend the operation on the instructions of the high command.

However, even before Bordoloi could resolve the immigration crisis the Cabinet Mission Plan surfaced. It proposed a scheme of a three-tier federal government for India in which all the provinces would be grouped into three zones—A, B and C. The C group was to consist of Bengal and Assam. Such grouping would not only deny provincial status to Assam but also permanently place the Assamese under the socio-cultural and political hegemony of the Bengalis. The Assam Pradesh Congress Committee (APCC) immediately intimated 'the deep resentment of the people of Assam and their opposition to the Grouping Clause'.[10] A memorandum was submitted by Bordoloi to the Congress Working Committee which read 'if the Working Committee did not stand up to safeguard the Assamese against these sinister proposal, then Assam and her people will be compelled to think that the Working Committee in their anxiety to think of larger provinces have given this small province a go by. It will not be a surprise if many in Assam will consider it to be a great betrayal.'[11] A delegation from Assam met Mahatma Gandhi, who

[7] Ibid.
[8] Sajal Nag, *Roots of Ethnic Conflict: Nationality Questions in North East India*, New Delhi: Manohar, 1990, p. 97, for the details of the Assamese nationality questions.
[9] Ibid.
[10] Ibid., pp. 149–52.
[11] Memorandum by Gopinath Bordoloi to CWC, Delhi, 19 May, APCC papers, 1946, APCC office, Gauhati.

advised Assam to reject the plan. The APCC resolved that 'in no circum-stances APCC was agreeable to accept the grouping'.[12] Pressurised by the Assamese delegation Gandhi asked the Assamese not to allow 'that Bengal should dominate Assam in any way'.[13] But irritated by their persistence Gandhi eventually reacted, 'I cannot understand this panic on the part of the Assamese'.[14] In fact the fate of the Cabinet Mission Plan 'hang(ed) on Assam'.[15] The rejection of the Plan was a major victory for the Assamese. Once again the Pradesh Congress came to the rescue of the Assamese nation-ality defying the high command's position. The anti-grouping agitation ended with the announcement of a referendum in Sylhet. The Assamese welcomed the decision as with partition the artificial union of Sylhet and Assam would now be over. The transfer of Sylhet to Pakistan would reduce the strength of Bengalis as well as the Muslims in Assam. The League started a frantic mobilisation of the Muslims to vote in favour of Pakistan, the Congress remained passive. When there were vociferous allegations of large-scale rigging by the Muslim League, the Congress made no noise about it. 'The Assam leader-ship, too eager to get rid of Sylhet with a view to carve out a homogeneous province, arranged little protection for minorities of Sylhet in the free exer-cise of their limited franchise. When the result of the referendum was declared, there was a subdued sense of relief in the Assam Valley.'[16] The Assam Pradesh Congress unit had, thus, saved the Assamese from grave threats; not surpris-ingly the people paid their debt to the Congress by returning it to power uninterruptedly until 1978. In fact, in this sense, the Congress acted as a party of the Assamese tackling the problems only of the ethnic Assamese although Assam comprised a large number of tribals, Bengalis, Nepalis and a tea garden labour population. The sub-national concern of the Pradesh Congress was evident in its election leaflet of 1946: 'unless the province of Assam be organised on the basis of Assamese language and Assamese culture, the survival of the Assamese nationality and culture will become impossible. The inclusion of Bengali speaking Sylhet and Cachar and the immigration or importation of lacs of Bengali settlers on waste lands has been threatening to destroy the distinctiveness of Assam and has in practice caused massive disorders in its administration. For appropriate solution and redress of this big problem the Congress party should be installed as the majority party in the Assembly.'[17] It is interesting that on the basis of such appeals the party

[12] Amalendu Guha, *Planter Raj to Swaraj: Freedom Struggle and Electoral Politics in Assam*, New Delhi: ICHR, 1977, n. 24, p. 313.
[13] APCC papers, 1946, APCC office, Gauhati.
[14] Gandhi to M. Tayebullah in Taeybullah, *Between the Symbol and the Idol at Last*, New Delhi: Allied, 1964, n. 2, p. 203.
[15] Ibid., n. 2, p. 200.
[16] R. N. Aditya, *From the Corridors of Memory*, Karimganj: Author, 1970, pp. 35–36.
[17] Congress election leaflet, quoted in Guha, *Planter Raj to Swaraj*, pp. 302–3.

polled 48 per cent of the votes in that election. More significantly, it polled 78 per cent in the general constituencies where the Assamese were in a majority.[18] It is evident that the Assamese considered the Assam unit of the Congress as their own party committed to the protection of the Assamese identity, while they detested the unsympathetic attitude of the Congress high command, as reflected in the issue of restrictions on immigration, or the Cabinet Mission Plan. In this respect, the Pradesh Congress went along with regional organisations like Asom Jatiya Mahashabha—a pro-Hindu party. The only difference was that the Congress was in power while the other was not.

Similar questions of identity emerged in the Princely States of Manipur and Tripura as well, which resulted in the emergence of regional organisations in support of the regional or ethnic cause. The Nikhil Manipuri Mahashabha, for example, was established in Manipur in 1934 modelled on the Indian National Congress. The moderate sections of the Sabha merged with the state unit of the Congress in October 1946. Carrying the popular sentiment forward, the Congress demanded in 1948 a responsible government in Manipur. But the Congress started losing popularity as it supported the merger of Manipur with India and constitution of a Purbanchal Pradesh by merging Manipur, Cachar and Tripura. The popular sentiments were against both[19] and in favour of retaining the independent identity of Manipur at least for some time. The state Congress unit's manoeuvre to expedite the merger was seen by the people as an effort to 'sell the Manipuri praja to India without taking public opinion or by falsely alleging that it had the support of the people'.[20] The elected representatives in the Manipur Assembly passed a resolution saying 'if integration or merger is imposed on her (taking advantage) of our unfortunate helpless circumstances and violating the principles of Bapuji, without the consent of the people, the present moral submission of the Manipuris in India, which is most precious, may disappear.... If the people have been sinned and wronged, they have to be watched over across the frontier.'[21] No wonder when the merger was actually effected (21 September 1949) the Manipuri people were aghast and anguished. They blamed the Congress for the tragedy. While the state Congress rejoiced, a paper wrote, 'We are insulting the honour of our forefathers if the consequence of an independent India is going to be enslavement of Manipur'.[22] Another wrote,

[18] Ibid., p. 356.
[19] B.J. Deb and Dilip Lahiri, *Manipur: Culture and Politics*, Delhi: Mittal, 1987, p. 159. The text of the quotation is as given in the original.
[20] Ibid.
[21] Sajal Nag, *India and North East India: Mind, Politics and the Process of Integration*, New Delhi: Regency, 1999, n. 116, p. 106. The text within the quotes is as in the original resolution.
[22] Ibid., p. 112.

'About fifty years ago a British Chief Commissioner came to Manipur and he was killed here ... if an Indian Chief Commissioner arrives here it might be the case of history repeating itself and we are afraid Manipur may witness a miniscale war'.[23] With the Congress regarded as a betrayer, it was a foregone conclusion that only a party of the Meitheis would receive popular support in Manipur. However, the Congress had been in power in Manipur since then, not on the strength of Meithei votes, but on its Naga-Mizo-Kuki base and through a coalition with regional parties, as we shall see later.

The tiny state of Tripura was ruled by an autocratic monarchical regime whose subjects were Bengalised tribals. Although excluded from participation in Indian politics, Tripura was nevertheless influenced by the developments. Political organisations were born to introduce modern politics. The first political platform was the Tripura Rajya Gana Parishad (1939) which modelled itself on the Congress. It eventually transformed itself into the state unit of the Indian National Congress (1946).[24] The other such organisation, the Tripura Rajya Praja Mondol (1946), tried to 'unify all democratic forces ... to prepare the ground for emancipation for socio-economic and political exploitations'.[25] The impending withdrawal of the British and the growing revolutionary activities of the Praja Mondol made the Maharaja panic and express his desire for merger with India even before India was independent. However, the Indian government delayed the merger and effected it only on 9 September 1949.

Meanwhile, the partition of India changed the political scenario in Tripura. Suddenly the Tripurans found themselves surrounded by East Pakistan on three sides and virtually geographically isolated from mainland India. On the one hand, there was the shadow of an aborted conspiracy to transfer Tripura to Pakistan and on the other, an incessant inflow of Hindu refugees from East Pakistan created a difficult situation. It had lost a very fertile region of Chakla-Roshanabad to Pakistan due to the inertia of the Congress government. Under such a surcharged political atmosphere the Tripura Rajya Mukti Parishad was born in 1948. It fought for the rights and interests of the tribal population of Tripura and even trained them in guerrilla warfare against the administration. In 1949, some Mukti Parishad leaders formed the Communist Party in Tripura. Since the party was banned its activities were carried out under the banner of the Mukti Parishad, which attracted tribal masses in thousands, giving it a strong grassroots base. It took up the issues of refugee

---

[23] Ibid.

[24] See, for details, Ranjit Kumar De, *Socio Political Movements in India: A Historical Study of Tripura*, New Delhi: Mittal, 1998, pp. 151–216.

[25] Pradip Kumar Basu, *The Communist Movement in Tripura*, Calcutta: Progressive Publishers, 1996; and T.J. Nossier, *Marxist State Governments in India: Politics, Economics and Society*, London: Pinter, 1988, pp. 144–69.

rehabilitation, mobilisation of the Halams, writing off outstanding land revenues, providing land to the tillers and restoration of the democratic rights to the people.[26] Due to its campaign and mass mobilisation activities the Communist Party of India (CPI) grew in strength, specially among the tribals. The state Congress had a very tough time fighting for its survival. It waited for the states merger with India to start life afresh. When the merger was effected it lost no time in befriending the administration which found an ally in the Congress to wipe out the radical activities of the communists. Thus, while the administration increased its ruthless suppression of the tribals in the name of law and order, the Congress condemned the communist armed struggle as an anti-Bengali gesture or Bongal Kheda movement. It is to be mentioned here that the incessant inflow of Bengali refugees had substantially increased the number of Bengalis in Tripura whom the Congress adopted as its support base against the tribals who were the base of the communists. Since then the Congress emerged as the party of the Bengali refugees while tribals took to the CPI as their protector. The result of the polarisation was evident in the first general elections of 1952; the two Lok Sabha seats were convincingly won by the CPI.

Sikkim, a trans-Himalayan native state, was the traditional homeland of a Mongoloid tribe called the Lepchas. There were waves of migration of Tibetans locally called Bhutiyas, and Nepalis. During the tutelage of the British, the immigration of Nepalis was on such a massive scale that soon they outnumbered both Lepchas and Bhutiyas together. The Bhutiyas had emerged as the rulers of Sikkim in the 17th century and the Tibetan Lamas controlled the spiritual authority of the Lepchas. The ruling power was an autocratic regime based on feudal institutions. The Maharaja and his family had the largest and most fertile land of this land-scarce mountainous terrain as their personal estate. Of the total cultivable area of about 90,130 hectares, 15 private estates of the king accounted for about 12,740 hectares.[27] For these royal estates labour was extracted from the tillers under two feudal practices—*chakareys* and *pakhureys*. The king directly or through the revenue department collected revenue and taxes from the tenants of his land. The royal family members lived in huge palaces whose rental value was Rs 50,000 per month in the 1960s. The King had a share in cinema theatres, cooperative societies and had taken agencies of motor vehicles, petrol and spare parts. The royalty were also the sole agents of those essential commodities which were supplied by India under restricted quota. Even the Lamas flourished under the protection of the king. They had big monasteries which were granted large pieces of land. In fact, 50 feudal landlords controlled about

[26] Ibid.
[27] R.S. Chauhan, 'Sikkim: Politics of Immigrants', in Iqbal Narain (ed.), *State Politics in India*, Meerut: Meenakshi Prakashan, 1977, pp. 545–56.

26,700 hectares of land and six monasteries held 8,560 hectares of land. While the feudal landlords mercilessly exploited the tenants under the *adhiadar* and *kutdar* system, the Lamas had their land cultivated free of rent by the disciples of the monasteries.[28] This left the commoner with no avenue of business enterprise left for subsistence and absolutely dependent on agriculture on a rocky mountain terrain. Under such an oppressive regime there was simmering discontent brewing for centuries which generated anti-monarchical sentiment.

Under the influence of modern political development in neighbouring India, Sikkim too experienced winds of change. The first sign of this change was political party formation. The democratic forces rallied together to form the Sikkim State Congress. It was modelled on an ideology and programme similar to the Indian National Congress. Not a surprise, for its major leaders such as Tashi Tehering, Kazi Lendgup Dorzee, D.B. Gurung, D.S. Lepcha, Sonam Tshering were all admirers of the Indian National Congress. On inception, the Sikkim Congress created a stir by making radical demands like the abolition of landlordism, formation of a responsible government and merger with India. The party had a popular base specially among the Nepali migrants who were discriminated against in Sikkim.[29] To counter the growing influence of the Congress, the palace floated another party called the Sikkim National Party which promised to protect feudal relations, championed the cause of the Bhutiya-Lepcha minority in the name of indigenous people and started an anti-India propaganda. When the democratic process was introduced in Sikkim the Congress came to power with an absolute majority (1974). It took the opportunity to frame a constitution for Sikkim whose basic features were (*a*) due representation to the people on the basis of one man one vote, (*b*) it stripped the Maharaja, now called Chogyal, of his absolute power and (*c*) vested India with larger responsibility in the administration of this protectorate. The angry royalty and the feudal elements who ran the bureaucracy paralysed the administrative apparatus and incited communal violence between the Nepalis and the Lepcha-Bhutiyas. This violence and disorder compelled the Chogyal to sign the merger agreement with India which was subsequently ratified by a referendum.

Meanwhile, in the hills, the Naga and Mizo people were facing an epistemological crisis. Not sure of their identity or security, they debated whether or not to merge with India.[30] The struggle of these two communities and their consequent politicisation were led by their newly born parties, the Naga National Council and the Mizo Union. The Nagas toyed with the idea of remaining independent, but later they decided to try the option of joining

---

[28] Ibid.
[29] N. Sengupta, *State Government and Politics in Sikkim*, New Delhi: Sterling, 1985, p. 20.
[30] For details, see footnote 19.

India for a period of 10 years and signed an agreement with the Government of India to that effect. However, the interpretation of the 'period' clause led to disagreement. The Mizos also considered merging with India or Burma or remaining independent. But the prospect of getting rid of the oppressive institution of chieftainship under a republican Indian regime made them opt for merger with India. Naturally, these two regional parties remained the undisputed representatives of the two ethnic groups for some time to come.

The 25 Khasi chiefs merged with India. The Congress had made some inroads into the Khasi hills before independence as J.J.M. Nichols Roy and McDonald Kharkongor joined the party. However, personality clashes among leaders led to the formation of several smaller parties, e.g., the Khasi Jaintia Federated, the State National Conference centring around the personality of Nichols Roy, the Khasi Sate People Union led by G.G. Swell, R.R. Thomas and Mrs Dunn, and the Hills Union led by Kharkongor. None of these were wholly representative of the Khasis, and this trend was visible even in the later period.

The trend of party formation and the themes of politics continued to remain the same even in the subsequent period when northeast India was reorganised into seven small states.

Parties and Politics in the Period of Parliamentary Democracy

The partition of India on 15 August 1947 was a momentous event in the history of the region. It reduced the northeast to a land-locked region surrounded by three hostile neighbours, China, Pakistan and Burma, leaving only a 22 km chicken's neck corridor to link it to the rest of India. Added to these factors, the influx of refugees from East Pakistan (now Bangladesh) complicated the demography and political development of the region in the long run. In Assam, however, the Congress was well entrenched. The transfer of Sylhet to Pakistan had reduced the Bengali Muslim population in Assam substantially, thereby reducing the threat perception to the Assamese identity. In fact, the Simon Commission Report had shown that the Bengalis were the majority in Assam in 1927; out of a total of 65 lakh, 35 lakh were Bengalis and 17.5 lakh were Assamese, which shattered the Assamese dream of converting Assam into a unilingual province. But the census of 1931 recorded 31.4 per cent Assamese and 26.8 per cent Bengalis and by 1951 56.7 per cent were Assamese and 15.8 per cent were Bengalis. This was no 'biological miracle'. Apart from the transfer of Sylhet, the assimilation of Bengali Muslim immigrants and ex-tea garden labourers had prevented the Assamese from being reduced to a minority in their own state. The Assam unit of the Indian National Congress realised that its consolidation remained in appropriating regional issues of the state. It took up issues relating to the Assamese identity for implementation. The first step was the introduction of the Official Language Bill of 1960, which sought to make Assamese the official language of poly-cultural Assam. Naturally, it sparked opposition, protest riots and violence throughout the state. A demand for a hill state to be carved out of Assam had already been submitted to the States Reorganisation Commission in 1954. After the Official Language bill all the tribal leaders, who were made mem-bers of the Eastern India Tribal Union, met to organise the All Party Hill Leaders Conference (APHLC) (1960), a political party formed not only to resist the imposition of Assamese language but also to demand a hill state separate from Assam. Subsequently, even some District Congress Commit-tees joined the demand.

But the APCC continued its function as a party committed to the interests of the Assamese rather than as a national party. Under a growing noise about a large number of Pakistani illegal immigrants in Assam, the Congress government launched an operation to evict and expel the infiltrators giving June 1965 as the target date.[31] The police became active and hundreds of infiltrators were expelled. It fuelled protests and complaints by the Muslim leaders that on the pretext of foreign nationals, Assamese Muslims were being harassed. A few Muslim leaders under the leadership of Umaruddin threatened to resign if the harassment continued.[32] The government had to withdraw the operation due to growing communal tension, but the Muslims became indifferent to the Congress. Along with the APHLC's demand for a hill state, demands for a Kamata state in Goalpara and an Ahom homeland in Sibsagar and Lakhimpur also surfaced. Added to this was the mishandling of the food crisis of 1966 by the Congress government which the communist parties never failed to politically exploit. Thus, from the second general elec-tions itself the Congress was losing its base.[33] The entry of APHLC into the election battle gave a serious blow to the Congress Party network in the hill areas. The APCC was totally against the demand for a hill state. In fact, it was taking steps for the merger of the North East Frontier Agency (NEFA) region into Assam on the pretext of integration of the region.

The Congress, however, kept on bungling on the tribal issues. It was blamed for the mishandling of the Mizo Famine of 1958 which gave rise to another ground for insurgency in the region under the leadership of the Mizo National Front (MNF). It tried to placate its dwindling support base by raising the slogan of central apathy.[34] In fact, although the CPI and Praja Socialist Party (PSP) had launched the movement for a second refinery in Assam, the Congress

---

[31] K.M. Deka, 'Assam: The Challenge of Political Integration and Congress Leadership', in Iqbal Narain, *State Politics in India*, Meerut: Meenakshi Prakashan, 1977, p. 34.
[32] Ibid.
[33] Ibid.
[34] Ibid.

hijacked the movement and led the agitation to reinforce its image as the party committed to the cause of the Assamese.[35] It expressed its opposition to Nehru's Scottish Plan and Indira Gandhi's plan for a hill state of Meghalaya.[36] Failing to convince the central leadership about the essentiality of preserving the integrity of the state, the APCC out of frustration and largely as a face-saving device associated itself with public agitation against plans and criticised the central leaders publicly.[37] They also highlighted the economic negligence of Assam. Even the most moderate Congress leaders like Chaliha and Bhagwati shared this view. In fact, Chaliha once remarked that the Congress president and the Government of India were so preoccupied with other problems that they had no time for the problems of Assam.[38] Chaliha, actually, made the remark 'Assam for Assamese' which he subsequently had to clarify.[39] Such rhetoric not only alienated the non-Assamese component of the state, the Assamese themselves were not convinced any more about the strength of the Congress in taking care of their specific problems. The 1978 election results returned the Congress as minority. The next few years were a period of instability as no political party had absolute majority. A number of coalition governments headed by the newly formed Janata Party had been experimented with. The Foreign National Movement launched by the All Assam Students' Union (AASU) and Assam Gana Sangram Parishad (AGSP) in 1979 created another period of turmoil. The six-year long movement demanding the detection and deportation of the illegal Bangladeshi nationals ended with the Assam Accord in 1985. In 1983, there was an imposed election in Assam in which a Congress (I) government managed to capture power. But with the Assam Accord, roads were paved for the emergence of another regional party, which was expected to be stronger and cleaner than the existing shades of politicians and which was expected to deliver. When the former AASU and AGSP leaders with their record of leading a six-year long movement on issues on which depended the survival of the Assamese nationality, the courage of defying the state power and the image of unshaken young men, came to form the Asom Gana Parishad (AGP), it was a foregone conclusion that it would be in power immediately.

In fact, as the anti-foreigner movement picked up momentum, the movement leaders increasingly felt the need for a regional party capable of focusing on the aspirations and sentiments of the Assamese middle class. Although there were already some regional parties like the Asom Jatiyatabadi Dal (AJD) and the Purbanchal Lok Parishad (PLP), they failed to embrace all

[35] Ibid.
[36] Ibid.
[37] Ibid.
[38] Ibid.
[39] Ibid.

sections of people. As a first step towards this direction, the AASU organised a national political convention of like-minded organisations and Assamese people at Jorhat on 10–11 January 1984. In that convention, there emerged a consensus over the formation of 'a strong regional party to capture power in the state'. The resolution of the convention stressed the necessity of a broad-based programme for the 'construction of the greater Assamese society, politically, economically and ethnically'. At an emergent meeting called by the AASU on 7 February 1984, it was resolved to unite all the regional parties of Assam so that the people of Assam could be politically organised on a common platform. But a series of conventions yielded no results. In view of the failure of the regional parties, particularly the PLP and AJD, to unify themselves in spite of the wishes of the people, they were left with no alternative but to form a new regional party. In the Golaghat convention held on 12–14 October 1985, a new regional party named Asom Gono Parishad was born with former Assam Movement leaders in which eventually both the AJD and PLP also merged. The AGP pledged to work for a free and progressive society based on secularism, democracy and socialism 'and promised to establish a "Sonar Asom". Its sole agenda was the implementation of Assam Accord in letter and spirit.'[40] The AGP was voted to power in the general elections of 1985 entirely on the belief that the lakhs of foreigners who were supposed to have been living in Assam illegally would be expelled by the AGP. However, during the entire five years of their rule, the AGP government could detect only 3,000 odd foreign nationals in the state. Chief Minister Mohanta blamed the central government and the Illegal Migrant Detection Tribunal (IMDT) Act, 1983 as the stumbling block in the detection and deportation of foreign nationals. Interestingly, however, the AGP government did not make any attempt to abrogate the Act, rather, it adopted a non-official resolution requesting the central government to amend certain provisions of the IMDT Act, 1983.[41] To top it all, the party even went on to deny the existence of any foreign national in the state, when its president Thaneswar Bodo on 8 May 1991 declared in a press conference at Guwahati Press Club that foreign nationals do not remain foreign nationals for ever.[42]

The AGP's sole social base was among the Assamese. The rise of the United Liberation Front of Assam (ULFA), prolonged movements for separate states from the Bodos, Karbis and Dimasas, created a turmoil in the state. Growing unemployment in the state created resentment among the people, which was further aggravated by the lavish life styles of the young ministers,

[40] Girin Phukan, *Politics of Regionalism in North East India*, New Delhi: Spectrum, 1996, pp. 44–60.
[41] H. Srikanth, 'Communalising Assam: AGP's Loss is BJP's Gain', *Economic and Political Weekly*, 34(49), 4–10 December 1999, pp. 3412–14.
[42] Ibid.

even as reports of corruption tarnished the clean image of once adored former student leaders. The Muslims too broke away by forming a party called United Minority Front in November 1985. The results of the Assembly elections of 1991 were a foregone conclusion. The AGP could secure 19 out of 119 seats. But the authoritarian and corrupt rule of the Congress (I) government led by Hiteswar Saikia brought regional and leftist parties together on the eve of the general elections of 1996. The AGP leaders, who had by then become more pragmatic, entered into an electoral alliance with the CPI and CPI (M) which they had earlier branded as Bengali parties. Understanding the significance of minority votes, they wooed the Muslim community too and won the support of the United People's Party of Assam (UPPA). These political adjustments brought the AGP back to power in the Assembly elections of 1996. Once in power for the second time, despite AASU's demand for the repeal of the IMDT Act, the AGP avoided taking action fearing a Muslim backlash. Naturally, it began losing electoral support again.

The loss of electoral and social base by the AGP became the Bharatiya Janata Party's (BJP) gain. Although the BJP was a rising power elsewhere in India, it failed to have a foothold in Assam until 1991. This despite the fact that the caste-Hindu Assamese were living under constant fear of being reduced to a minority due to illegal Muslim immigration. The breakthrough for the BJP came in the 1998 parliamentary elections when in its manifesto it promised to repeal the IMDT and strengthen the immigration laws. It talked of the National Register and identity cards for legal citizens. All these went down well with the middle-class Assamese Hindus. Although the BJP could win only one seat from Silchar, its overall vote share increased to 24.5 per cent. After the BJP came to power in New Delhi, Prime Minister Atal Behari Vajpayee and Home Minister L.K. Advani visited Assam and promised measures against illegal migration. The new governor, Lt. Gen. (Retd.) S.K. Sinha, sent a 42-page report to the home minister mentioning that the illegal immigration had changed the demographic profile of the state and posed a grave threat to the Assamese and recommended the repeal of the IMDT (Act). There were indications that the BJP was consolidating the Assamese Hindu votes in the state.

It worried the AGP when the parliamentary elections were announced in 1999. The AGP realised that since it could not succeed in getting minority votes it had to stop further erosion of its traditional Hindu Assamese votes. Therefore, it followed the BJP path of projecting itself as an anti-Muslim party. In a press conference the chief minister talked of the threats to Assam posed by the ISI. He alleged that the *madrasas* were playing host in recruiting the Muslim youths for ISI-sponsored organisations. These statements were taken by the public as a duplication of the age-old BJP propaganda and therefore, strengthened the BJP's base rather than the AGP's. In the next election AGP could not win a single seat for the second consequent time while the BJP increased its share of votes to 30 per cent within a span of less than a year.[43] Of course, due to a shift in minority votes the BJP lost its Silchar seat to the Congress (I). Even the CPI and CPI (M) who had aligned themselves with the AGP had alienated themselves from the masses.

Although born of regional movements with a regional agenda the AGP failed to deliver. The Assamese masses had turned from the Congress to the AGP with a lot of hope but lost no time in looking for viable alternatives. The BJP fit the bill. It was in power at the Centre. It was pro-Hindu and it promised to check illegal immigration and declare Bangladeshis as stateless citizens. All these points appealed to the Assamese middle classes. Once they realised that secessionist politics did not benefit them (the enthusiasm for ULFA was lost and recently the people were defying the ULFA dictate) they turned to the BJP whose pro-Hindu agenda suits the regionalist demands of the Assamese identity. With the majority of Bengali and Assamese caste-Hindus turning to the BJP and Muslims as well as other minorities favouring the Congress, the Assamese electorate was polarised on the eve of the State Assembly elections scheduled in 2001. They were looking up to political parties, either national or regional, who would address the issues concerning Assam. But the BJP's alliance with the ruling AGP on the eve of the elections proved disastrous for both. The electorate in Assam rejected the alliance and opted for the Congress. The Congress became victorious mainly on a negative vote.

Tripura was another state adversely affected by partition, particularly because of its tiny size. Had the area of the state been large enough to absorb the influx of refugee population, the adverse impact of partition would have been less. When the first census was taken in 1872, the tribal population was an overwhelming 64 per cent. By the turn of the century, it was down to 52 per cent. In 1941 it was 40 per cent and by 1951 the tribals were already a minority at 35 per cent. In 1981 it came down to as low as 28 per cent and 15 per cent by 1987. This altered the political developments and party alignments in the state. We have already seen that CPI had emerged as a champion of the tribals and the Congress of the Bengali non-tribals. The Congress was confined to urban areas, while the communist base was in the interiors. Since 1952, the electoral contest has been essentially bi-polar. When the CPI split in 1964, the entire CPI in Tripura switched over to CPI (M) and although there have been minor defections since, the CPI (M) has remained more or less united. Interventions by third forces of national origin such as the erstwhile Bharatiya Jana Sangh or the Praja Socialist Party have only briefly disturbed the pattern, without any long-term impact.

When the States Reorganisation Commission (1955) recommended the merger of Tripura with Assam, it evoked sharp reactions from the communists, who organised massive movements against the 'conspirational scheme'

---

[43] Ibid.

directed at the destruction of Tripura's identity. Under such pressure, the SRC modified its recommendation and provided for a Union Territory status for Tripura (States Reorganisation Act, 1956). Realising that the tribal population formed the social base of the communists, the Congress turned its attention to the refugees. Sukhomoy Sengupta, the Congressman in charge of the election campaign undertook hectic tours among the refugees and carried the message that if the communists returned to power in the next election the refugees would have to pack their bags and return to East Pakistan.[44] The result of the 1957 elections showed the shift in the balance of power. In the next contest each of the opponents captured one Lok Sabha seat and 14 each for the Tripura Territorial Council. But the Congress, despite winning the votes of the refugees, was unconcerned about their systematic rehabilitation. The communists, on the other hand, instead of meddling with the refugee rehabilitation schemes, demanded adequate safeguards for the tribals who had been reduced to a minority in the state. At the same time, they also supported the struggles of the refugees for proper resettlement, thereby making forays into the Congress domain. They also commenced a movement for the introduction of parliamentary democracy in the state. The 1962 general elections showed the success of the communist campaign. They won both the Lok Sabha seats.

The Land Revenue and Land Reform Act of 1960 had prohibited transfer of tribal land to the non-tribals, but the Act was implemented more in breach than by compliance. In fact, illegal transfer of lands went on with grim regularity. The areas once densely populated by the tribals were fragmented in the name of rehabilitation of Bengali refugees in a calculated manner. The communists' demand for the implementation of the Fifth Schedule of the Constitution for protection of tribal interests was not heeded. Instead, a fear was generated in the minds of Bengalis about its post-implementation scenario. Tripura Upajati Juba Samiti (TUJS) was born under these circumstances in June 1967. The Congress encouraged its emergence on the calculation that the tribal loyalties would be divided, making a dent in the CPI (M)'s electoral base. The CPI (M) intensified its opposition to the government on food policy, forest conservation, the Fifth Schedule and anti-democratic repressive measures. The results of the 1971 elections turned those of 1967 upside down. The CPI (M) proved to be the natural heir to the communist movement in the state bagging both the Lok Sabha seats. It captured 45.2 per cent and 42 per cent of votes in the east and west constituencies. The defeat generated internecine squabbles within the Congress Party; the CPI (M), on the other hand, enthused by its success, stepped up its campaign against the misdeeds of the government. The Gana Mukti Parishad (GMP), its tribal wing, launched a struggle demanding autonomous councils in tribal dominated areas. Its peasant

[44] Basu, *The Communist Movement in Tripura*.

wing, the State Committee of All India Kisan Sabha initiated a movement on a 10-point charter of demands which included protection of rights of the landless Jhumias, replacement of the existing laws for the preservation of forests, distribution of usable and extra-ceiling lands among the landless peasants and writing off the outstanding agricultural debts.

The North East Reorganisation Bill, 1972, upgraded Tripura to a state. Elections for the new Legislative Assembly were held in the aftermath of the Bangladesh war, which had soared Indira Gandhi's popularity. Naturally, the Congress swept the poll, bagging as many as 41 seats, leaving 19 to CPI (M) (CPI–1). During 1972–75 the CPI (M) agitated against the grabbing of the tribal land by the non-tribals. The Congress piloted the Land Revenue and Land Revenue Bill, 1960 instead, amending provisions for the abolition of the tribal reserve. The tribals agitated against the proposed amendment under the leadership of the communists. Amidst state-wide discontent, the GMP demanded the introduction of the Sixth Schedule of the Constitution, which existed in some northeastern states, as it realised that the formation of the Tribal Advisory Council under the Fifth Schedule would not be able to deliver justice to the tribals. It wanted the restoration of 'Tribal Reserves' and pressed for the return of tribal lands transferred since 1961 to the original owners. It also demanded the introduction of 'Kok Borok' as the medium of instruction at the primary level. Still insensitive, the Sengputa ministry (Congress) issued a decree called the Tripura Land Revenue and Land Revenue (second amendment), 1974, adversely affecting the interests of the tribals. The CPI (M) flayed what it described as 'the naked vengeance' against the impoverished and backward tribal peasantry and the TUJS termed the ordinance as 'a challenge to the very existence of the tribals in the state'. The CPI (M) intensified its campaign, but did not gain electorally in the 1977 elections. It failed to retain either of the Lok Sabha seats. In this election, following the national trend, two new all-India political parties, Janata Party and Congress for Democracy had been born in Tripura too.

The 1977 Assembly elections were held amidst political turmoil, chaos and confusion. The Congress was already a divided house. Its votes were shared by the Congress for Democracy, Janata, TUJS and the independents. Only the leftists could form a grand coalition to avoid the division of their votes. Thus, as expected, the results were an astounding victory for the leftists. They captured 53 seats out of 60. The remaining seven seats were shared by TUJS (four), Revolutionary Socialist Party (RSP) (two) and independents (one). In January 1978 Nripen Chakraborty became the CPI (M) chief minister of Tripura and completed his full five-year term. As soon as it came to power the CPI (M) government passed the Tribal Areas Autonomous District Council Act (TAADC), 1979 which provoked a bloody Bengali backlash. While the Congress was unscrupulous in fomenting communal tensions, the CPI (M) was struggling to maintain a semblance of secularism in Tripura politics.

Since the tribals were the original support base of the communists, they focused on the question of tribal identity as a distinct issue of urgent concern. The TAADC Act was an attempt in this direction. Following the elections in January 1982, an Autonomous District Council (ADC) covering 68 per cent of the state and a population of 31 per cent, of which 76 per cent were tribal, was established. Subjects such as education, land, industry and tribal welfare were devolved upon it. An amendment in 1986 gave more powers to the ADC to frame by-laws in agrarian matters, levy taxes, market and other fees and retain a share of forest and mining royalties. Although the available funds were limited and powers finite, the ADC was successful in reducing the gap between the advanced and the backward sections of the population. However, it was not easy to persuade the majority Bengali community to accept the claims of the tribals for the return of land alienated in dubious circumstances. It is this failure which contributed to the support base of the TUJS and Tripura National Volunteers (TNV), which emerged as a secessionist outfit notorious for its Mandai Massacre (1985).

The CPI (M) recognised the claim of the Kok Borok language and introduced it at the primary level and restored alienated land to the extent possible. The CPI (M)'s own report had listed the following: (a) reduction of the burden of taxation and debt on weaker section, (b) introduction of free education at all levels, (c) enhancement of agricultural and other labourers' wage rate, (d) introduction of (Centre funded) food for work programme, (e) free midday meal for primary students and (f) attacks on moneylenders and contractors through the establishment of cooperatives. Amidst growing insurgency and communal carnage plaguing the state, the party pledged that 'struggle for the conservation of tribal rights is a struggle of the whole party' for the CPI (M). The support of the tribal cause in the midst of communal bloodbath, turned the refugee masses to the Congress in the hope of succour. But a divided Congress could not reap the fruit of this hope. Hence, the CPI (M) came back to power, albeit with reduced strength in the 1983 elections. It captured 37 seats followed by the Congress (12) and TUJS (six). But the 1988 elections saw the CPI (M) dwindling. It won only 26 seats although it polled more than the Congress in terms of percentage. The Congress-TUJS coalition formed the ministry under the chief ministership of Sudhir Ranjan Mazumder. But the next two elections in 1993 and 1998 saw the return of CPI (M).

In Tripura, therefore, right from the beginning it was a straight contest between two national parties both inside the legislature and outside. But like the Congress in Assam, CPI (M) was more concerned about the rights and aspirations of the indigenous people. In this sense there was nothing national about it. Its agenda programme and modus operandi was state specific. Hence, it was a foregone conclusion that the tribals would vote for it. But the continuous immigration and the Congress championing their causes challenged the communist hegemony. Even the Congress, a national party, secular and representative of all people at the national level, acted partisan, pro-majority and even communal in Tripura. Thus, the national character of the Congress had been eroded in Tripura.

The first general elections in Sikkim were held in 1979. But by then the political situation in this 22nd state had changed. The desire for merger with India was actually confined to the middle class. The majority of Sikkimese, either Nepali or Lepcha-Bhutiya, had cherished the emerging 'Sikkimese' identity and were for maintaining the status quo. They wanted Indian intervention only to end the oppressive Chogyal regime. But when the realisation came that merger with India meant absorption of the unique Sikkimese identity, there was resistance. Immediately after the merger there was discontent and debate over the ramifications of the merger. Moreover, the manner in which the Indian state effected the merger generated resentment. This growing sentiment was whipped up by a firebrand anti-merger leader Nar Bahadur Bandari. Bhandari formed a new political party, the Sikkim Janta Parishad which eclipsed the Sikkim Congress in the elections. The promise of 'giving the Sikkimese people back their self respect and sense of dignity'[45] brought Bhandari to power with a thumping victory. On assumption of power, Bhandari in a surprise move joined the Congress (I) *en bloc*. This was a clever ploy to camouflage his anti-Indian image and attract central favours. But the honeymoon was over soon. On the recommendation of the governor that the chief minister 'ceased to command his pleasure' the ministry was dismissed vide Article 164 (1) of the Constitution.[46] In reality, it was due to his continued anti-India activities. In disgust Bhandari left the Congress (I) and formed the Sikkim Sangram Parishad. Bhandari's popularity had not waned. The dismissal made a martyr of him. In the next elections he came back to power with virtually no opposition and continued to rule Sikkim for the next 14 years. But undiminished base and absolute power made Bhandari corrupt. There were allegations of widespread corruption and nepotism against him. He promoted a Bawun (Brahmin)–Chetri nexus and bestowed favour on them, neglecting the lower castes. This alienated the majority of Tamang-Gurung-Rai lower castes as well as the Lepchas. There were indications of rebellion within the party. His one-time lieutenant Pawan Kumar Chamling—a Rai himself—led the lower-caste rebellion, left the party and formed the Sikkim Democratic Front. The mobilisation on the basis of caste had borne immediate results. The Democratic Front was returned to power in the next elections routing both Bhandari and the Sangram Parishad.

Under different circumstances, Sikkim was the stronghold of two regional parties. One had been wiped out by the rise of the other. The Sikkim Congress

---

[45] K.R. Chakravarty, 'Government and Politics in Sikkim', in Mahendra P. Lama (ed.), *Sikkim: Society, Polity, Economics, Environment*, New Delhi: Indus, 1994.
[46] Ibid.

succeeded because of its struggle against the ruling regime and leading the state to the path of democracy as well as ridding it of oppressive feudal relations. But its eclipse was due to the emergence of a strong Sikkimese identity vis-à-vis the Indian identity. The Democratic Front consisted of elements from the Sangram Parishad itself due to a polarisation on caste lines. Right from the time of merger there were a number of national parties who entered the fray in Sikkim but were hardly able to make a dent in the base of regional parties. The rise as well as the decline of certain regional parties in Sikkim was due to their own contradictions and not because of any challenge from the national parties.

The Hill States

The North Eastern Reorganisation Act (1971) led to the birth of Meghalaya. By its very composition Meghalaya was a conglomerate state with three major tribes—Khasi, Jaintia and Garos—constituting it who had not much communication among themselves. Although the Khasis were the most advanced among them, they had no individual leadership except the acceptable J.J.M. Nichols Roy. As the trend in party formation in the British period showed, despite the early establishment of the Khasi National Darbar, there was no single Khasi party. A number of splinter groups around individual personalities were formed. In fact, it was a Garo, Williamson Sangma who took over Khasi leadership after the demise of Nichols Roy. Since the All Party Hill Leaders conference led by Sangma was the main architect of the state of Meghalaya, it was certain to capture power in the state after the general elections in 1972. But the Congress was already entrenched in the Garo hills. In fact, while the APHLC was stronger in the Khasi Jaintia hills, the Congress was the familiar organisation among the Garos. The APHLC bagged 39 seats followed by the Congress. Despite the pre-poll alliance between them, the APHLC had formed the ministry all by itself. But APHLC as a party had lost its relevance after the formation of the Meghalaya state. It appeared that its agenda was the creation of a hill state and once that had been achieved, its purpose was over. It neither had a clear-cut ideology, nor a substantive programme to attract the tribals. At the Mendipathar conference (16 November 1976) the party split and the group led by Captain Sangma merged with the Congress. It meant that the APHLC ministry in Meghalaya was transformed into a Congress ministry. The other group led by B.B. Lyngdoh sat in the opposition. In the 1978 elections to the Legislative Assembly the Congress bagged 20 seats. The APHLC won 16 seats, the Hill State Peoples Democratic Party (HSPDP) 14 and the independents 10. Thus, the first coalition ministry was formed in the state. In fact, since then the state continuously had coalition governments, led by the Congress with different combinations of regional or local parties.

Despite the unpopularity of the Congress in the Khasi hills, the Congress had always managed to survive and in spite of the local pressure groups' (like the Khasi Students' Union) urge to have a regional party in power, no strong regional party of the Khasis could emerge. Although there are a number of them like the APHLC, HSPDP, Public Demand and Implementation Convention (PDIC), and their combinations like the Hills People Union in the Khasi Janitia hills, one single party reflecting the Khasi aspirations failed to emerge. This despite the fact that a willing social base is ready to support such a party. This has happened because the tribal political elite eager to become MLAs and ministers has no ideological inclination nor any intention or agenda for the development of their region. What the Congress did for the Assamese or CPI (M) for the Tripura tribals was strangely absent. In the absence of such an inclination neither a regionalist ideology nor a regional party was born. Personal ambitions and minister making were the interplay that shaped the politics of this tiny state.[47]

Nagaland too has had a similar story. To conciliate the secessionist movement in the Naga Hills District of Assam, it was granted statehood on 1 December 1963 and the first Assembly elections were held in January 1964. The Naga National Council, which was still leading the Naga struggle for 'independence', had gone underground. Nagaland began with a two party system consisting of regional parties. The Naga National Organisation (NNO), a party of moderate Nagas, born out of the Naga Peoples' Convention (NPC) that had spearheaded the cause for the Nagaland state, came to power with an absolute majority (34 seats) in the 46-member Legislative Assembly. The Democratic Party of Nagaland (DPN) was the other party (11 seats).

But soon there was an internal split in the party and the P. Shilu Ao ministry was voted out by his own party and T.N. Angami formed the government in 1966. The NNO was challenged by a new party, the United Front of Nagaland, in the second Assembly elections in 1969. The NNO with 20 seats in the 52-member Assembly could still form the government under the leadership of Hokishe Sema with the help of 12 MLAs indirectly elected by the Tuensang Regional Council. In the third general elections in 1974, United Democratic Party (UDF) secured 25 seats and NNO 23 seats in the 60-member Assembly. Vizol formed an NNO-UDF coalition ministry when 14 NNO MLAs joined him, but he became the victim of the same politics of defection that had helped him form the government. The state experienced president's rule for the first time since it came into existence. Interestingly, during this period the NNO transformed itself into the state unit of the Congress. Thus, a national party could make its presence felt only by political manoeuvres that instilled uncertainty in a vulnerable political party. Yet the Congress could form its first ministry in Nagaland in 1982 only in coalition. Though

---

[47] B, Pakem, *Coalition Politics in North East India*, Shillong: ICSSR, 1999, pp. 96–107.

the Congress (I) formed the government again after the 1987 elections, defections from the party led to its fall soon after. However, it came back to power in 1989 for a short while, till fragmentation and defection brought the Nagaland People's Council, a new party, to power. In the 1993 elections the Congress (I) came back to power with 35 seats leaving 18 to the NPC. Due to the boycott call by the National Socialist Council of Nagaland (NSCN) (IM), 34 Congress (I) candidates were elected unopposed and formed the government.

Thus, in the over three-and-a-half-decade-old history of electoral politics, Nagaland has had 12 governments, including three coalitions—Vizol (1974), Jasokie (1977) and Vamuzo (1990). Another landmark in Nagaland politics is that ethnic composition of the state consisting of the Angami, Ao and Sema tribes necessitates coalition politics; at times, even intra-party coalition. This was demonstrated when the P. Shilu Ao government was voted out by his own party. Since practically all Naga tribes are divided into sub-tribes, whose loyalty to their respective tribes is virtually sacrosanct, such intra-party coalitions were normal. What, however, is baffling is that the Naga hills, which gave rise to organisations like the NNC and NSCN (IM), largely representing all the Naga tribes, were not able to throw up a regional party representing larger Naga interests.[48]

The state of Arunachal Pradesh is a category by itself. Composed of about 101 listed tribes, it came to the political spectrum very late. In January 1972, it was made into a Union Territory and upgraded to statehood in 1987. Right from the beginning of party formation in Arunachal Pradesh, the trend was of alignment between the party in power at the Centre with a regional party. Thus, a few of the local political elite formed the state Congress Party unit, while others declared themselves to be a part of the Janata Party. These formations at the state level were legitimised by blessings from the respective party headquarters. Thus, in the first general elections (1978) as a Union Territory, there were two political rivals, the Janata Party and the People's Party of Arunachal, in which the former won an absolute majority. The disease of defection, however, set in soon and resulted in the inevitable president's rule causing the next elections in 1980. Though both the Congress and PPA secured 13 seats each, the Congress resorted to defection to form the ministry again. However, since the 1980 elections the Congress Party has been able to retain its dominance in the state. The dominance of the Congress Party was further strengthened by 'a strong tendency in the state on the part of the opposition MLAs to join the ruling party in the state as soon as election is over, irrespective of their previous party affiliations'.[49] In the wake of the Chakma issue, and the party's differences with the high command, the state Congress (I) unit (and the government) transformed itself into a regional party, the

---

[48] Ibid., pp. 114–22.
[49] Ibid., pp. 62–67.

Arunachal Congress. Again in a classic display of solidarity with the local issues, the ruling Congress government sided with the student union in demanding expulsions of the Chakma refugees and opposition to the grant of citizenship to them.

In Manipur, the Congress was never a strong force. Although its rivals were the individual communists, they failed to organise a strong communist party. Thus, despite the tarnished image of the Congress Party in Manipur due to its role in the merger issue, people had no alternative party to vote for. In 1967, certain leaders of the ruling Congress left the party, formed the United Left Front (ULF) and wrested power from the Congress. When this too collapsed, the need for a party of the Meitheis was felt. The former ULF members thus formed the Manipur People's Party (MPP) in December 1968. Its announced objective was to 'espouse the cause of Manipur'. In the first general elections to the State Legislative Assembly in 1972, the party secured 15 seats while the Congress won 17 seats and 19 members were independent. The MPP was thus able to form a coalition government with non-Congress parties. In the mid-term poll of 1974 the MPP secured 20 seats. The election 'brought into existence the era of coalition and counter coalition'. In the 1980 general elections too no party could secure a majority. While national parties like the Congress and Janata won 13 and 10 seats, respectively, the CPI, the Congress (U) secured five and six seats, respectively, while independents secured a majority of 19 seats. Such political instability has been the unique feature of Manipur politics. Like the rest of India, the Congress (I) swept the 1984 elections securing 30 seats while MPP had only three seats. But in the 1990 elections the Congress bagged only 26 seats while the Janata Dal and the MPP won 10 seats each. The political instability brought president's rule in the state which lasted a massive 346 days beginning from 31 December 1993. The 1994 elections saw a Congress (I)-led coalition ministry. But the instability and lack of absolute majority for any party existed even after the 1995 elections. In fact, Manipur 'is perhaps the only state in NE India where political instability is the rule rather than an exception.... Till today no one can really know for sure which way the ruling and opposition members in the Manipur Assembly would behave. This kind of political behaviour on the part of the elected representatives of Manipur indicates the political configuration of the state—the hill politics versus valley politics as well as ethnic politics both in the hill areas and in the valley. The strategic position of the state in the periphery of a big country from the point of views of insurgency movements and the sense of *irredentism* on the part of the people of the state are also contributing factors to continuing political instability....'[50]

---

[50] Ibid., p. 96.

This leaves us with Mizoram. The Mizo Union had the strongest popular base in the state. Thus, in the first general elections (1972) it gained 21 of the 36 seats. But like many other parties in the region MU seemed to have lost its purpose after effecting the merger with India and the abolition of chieftainship (1955). A weak MU saw merit in unifying with the Congress in May 1974. The disappearance of MU, the only ethnic party, paved the way for another, the Peoples' Conference (PC). The party was born out of the anguish of the people, oppressed and tortured under the Military operations launched to counter the insurgency led by the Mizo National Front. The 1978 elections saw the PC capture power under Brigadier Sailo. But personal ambition for ministership brought factionalism and defection in PC. The resignation of PC followed by its return to power in the mid-term elections of 1979. The 1984 elections saw the emergence of Congress (I) riding on the Congress wave. But the Mizo Accord of 1986 saw the transformation of MNF from a banned secessionist outfit to a political party. At the same time Mizoram was also granted statehood. The first general elections in the state (1987) returned MNF to power. But a defection game saw the eclipse of this 19-month-old government. Political instability was followed by president's rule. When the next elections were held in 1989, they saw the return of the Congress with an absolute majority. Due to a pre-poll alliance between the Congress and Janata Dal (formed by the former PC) the elections saw the wresting of power by the Congress (I) again in 1993. It was only in the 1998 elections that MNF and its alliance partner the Mizoram People's Conference (MPC) were able to capture government. In the last seven general elections since 1972, there were ups and downs in the fortunes of regional parties as well as the Congress Party. For 12 years (1972–84) the regional parties under the MU and PC had an edge over the Congress Party. The Congress captured power eventually in 1984, only to be replaced due to political compulsions (Mizo Accord, 1986) by the MNF, another regional party. According to the provisions of the Accord, the Congress had to abdicate power in favour of the MNF, which would form the interim government till the elections. The MNF came to power in the 1987 Assembly elections, but within 19 months dissidence led to defection and the Laldanga ministry fell. The Congress returned to power after a brief period of president's rule and won the subsequent elections in 1989. For the next nine years the Congress (I) commanded the confidence of the people of Mizoram; obviously the regional parties failed to group together and pose a threat to it. However, in the 1998 elections the MNF in alliance with the Mizoram People's Conference, another regional party, could highlight the failures of the Congress rule and win back power.[51]

---

[51] Ibid., pp. 107–14.

Emerging Features and Patterns

The foregoing analysis suggests that state boundaries also demarcate areas with ethnic, linguistic and other identities. Large states often combine a number of cultural areas with different identities, invariably dominated by one visible prominent identity. Small states naturally have more clearly defined structures of identities. Since national parties have a pan-Indian ideology, programme and agenda, their bases are generally in states where people's identities are pan-Indian, generic or even undefined in terms of nationality as in Uttar Pradesh, Madhya Pradesh, Rajasthan and Bihar. In contrast, the regional parties are based on sub-national identities, and therefore, their strongholds are small states. Regional parties acquire a foothold by championing the interests and aspirations of these nationalities and often the small states are actually the result of the struggle of these parties. In this sense these parties are sub-national parties rather than regional or minor parties. These are not regional because their influence does not cover the entire region of their operation, but only those portions where their nationality is preponderant; nor are they minor parties because although in central politics they have a marginal role in a single party dominance system, within its frontier they are major parties. But it does not become a rule that only regional parties are relevant to small states. National parties also have often acquired a deep-rooted stronghold in such states when they picked up micro issues of the area and ensured grassroot mobilisation as in the case of the communists in West Bengal, Kerala and Tripura or the Congress in Assam. From this perspective the state units of CPI (M) in West Bengal, Kerala[52] and Tripura, and the Congress in Assam, were more a regional party.

The tasks of regional parties in small states, as our analysis suggests, are not easy. They have had to ensure grassroot mobilisation and compete with the national parties which wield immense power, resources and a country-wide network. Unlike the regional parties, national parties in the northeast have often just superimposed themselves on some pre-existing organisational network, rather than creating their own political space. Sometimes compulsions of sheer survival and politico-economic considerations lead regional parties to merge with a national party in power *en bloc*, as seen in the cases of Sikkim, Mizoram and Arunachal Pradesh. These regional parties are perpetually haunted by the threat of dissension and defection. Not surprisingly, defections in the regional parties are at the insistance of national parties, for they have invariably, if not always, been the beneficiaries. Most of the regional parties in northeast India are conglomerations of people belonging to different

---

[52] The state units of CPI (M) in Kerala and West Bengal have been viewed as regional parties only. See Paul Brass, *The Politics of India Since Independence*, Delhi: Oxford University Press, 1990, reprint, 1995, p. 94.

tribes and sub-tribes, whose tribal loyalties supersede the party ideology when the political crunch comes. Hence, they always remain vulnerable to defection.[53] Thus, defection, dissension, coalition and early collapse have always been characteristics of regional parties in the northeast.

A national party could neutralise such dissension by satisfying the personal ambition of leaders by offering them appointments in governmental apparatus as governor, ambassador or a high party functionary. No leader from the northeast has so far been able to emerge as a leader of national importance unless supported by a national party. Thus Purno Sangma could reach the position of national eminence mainly because he belonged to a national party and a personality like G. G. Swell could not do so since he belonged to a regional party. In fact his candidature for the high office of president was frustrated by the reluctance of the national parties (except the Bharatiya Janata Party) to patronise him even though the consensus was in favour of a Scheduled Caste or Scheduled Tribe candidate.

The other threat the regional parties face in reaching the portals of power has been the invocation of Article 356. In fact, a survey shows that president's rule had been imposed on states on 10 occasions between 1950 and 1966, 26 times between 1967 and 1974 and 54 times between 1975 and 1993. During the period 1980–90 there was a fivefold increase in the propensity to invoke Article 356. What is relevant for our purpose is that most of the time it was a regional party which suffered by such acts of dismissal and a national party at the Centre was responsible.[54]

The rise of regional parties in India has been coeval with the emergence of sub-national movements. It is now accepted that India experienced two simultaneous processes of political development—national and sub-national. While the former was based on pan-Indian identity and stimulated the freedom struggle, the latter was based on regional cultural identity leading to self-assertion of sub-national identity. Although during the freedom struggle the sub-national movements either remained under the shadow of the national movements, or ran parallel to it, independence gave them a new political context to surface independently. In fact, sub-national movements took place in India in two phases. The first phase began from the 1950s, subsiding by the 1970s; the second phase beginning in the 1980s is still on. The first phase witnessed demands, at times violently expressed, for the reorganisation of cultural areas, movements for statehood and autonomy and unification of divided nationality groups. The regions affected were Andhra, Gujarat, Maharashtra, Punjab, Karnataka. Besides these there were disturbances in

[53] B. C. Bhuyan, 'Regional Political Parties and State Politics in North East India', in his *Political Development in North East India*, vol. 1, New Delhi: Omsons, 1989, p. 32.
[54] *The Statesman* (Calcutta), 7 March 1994. Also, J.R. Siwach, *Politics of President's Rule in India*, Shimla: IIAS, 1979, passim.

Jammu and Kashmir due to alleged subversive activities. The crisis reached its peak when Hindi was sought to be made the official language of India. There were protests and violence throughout the country and in some parts there were 'veiled threats of secessionism'. Selig Harrison immortalised this crisis period by terming it as the 'Dangerous Decades'. As a result of this crisis the Congress lost its legitimacy as a national party as it played partisan to the Hindi-Hindu-Hindustan axis and several regional parties came to power in Punjab, Tamil Nadu, Jammu and Kashmir. It is also significant that most of them suffered dismissal by the Centre. The successive reorganisation and creation of states seemed to have pacified the upsurge.

The second phase began with the launching of the foreign national movement in Assam. This was immediately followed by the revival of demand for statehood in Jharkand, the autonomy movement in Punjab on the basis of the Anandpur Sahib Resolution, rise of insurgency in Kashmir, followed by statehood demands for Gorkhaland, Bodoland and Chhattisgarh. This was also the phase when national parties with a regional orientation like the CPI (M) came to power in West Bengal and Tripura. A state-oriented party like the Telugu Desam replaced the Congress in Andhra Pradesh and certain declining parties like the DMK in Tamil Nadu and Shiv Sena in Maharashtra had a resurgence. Even in large states like Uttar Pradesh the rising Samajwadi and Bahujan Samaj Parties uprooted the Congress from its traditional stronghold. The remains of the Janata Dal made its appearance as the Rashtriya Janata Dal in Bihar and captured power. The CPI (M) is threatened by Trinamool Congress in West Bengal. Asom Gono Parishad came to power in Assam. Thus, in this phase even the large states could not escape the impact of the sub-national upsurge.

The sub-nationalist upsurge is not just responsible for the rise of regional parties but also the decline of the national parties which lost their traditional domain to the former. This paved the way for coalition politics at the Centre. Coalition politics is not new for the small states and regional parties. But this was the first time regional parties got to ally with the national power at the Centre as an equal partner. In this alliance the regional parties supported the national parties in tackling the macro issue concerning the country and in turn the national parties had the obligation of backing the regional parties in tackling the micro issues at the provincial level. This has been the theoretical principle on which the politics of coalition in this phase was based. A closer look would reveal that such principled coalition has been the pattern already in small states long before it was experimented with at the national level. Although the regional parties played a marginal role in national politics earlier, due to their increasing numerical strength (as large states also returned regional parties) these parties now had more say in policy decisions. But one difference remained, although regional parties from large states could strike a bargain with national parties, such parties from small states continue to be a mere tangent in national politics.

15

MEDIATING ECONOMIC REFORMS

PARTY POLITICS FROM BANGALORE TO CHENNAI

Harish Khare

This chapter makes an attempt to understand how the twin processes of globalisation abroad and liberalisation at home have combined to change, if at all, the nature and content of political contest in India, and how the political parties find themselves having to cope with the new demands that are being made over the collective resources, all in the name of globalisation/liberalisation.

The party system in India has traditionally been called upon to address four minimum functions, to enable its state system to perform the primary task of imposing a political order. These functions are: (*a*) To generate and sustain democratic legitimacy for the governing arrangement of the state order. This the political parties do by initiating a public discourse that taps the society's traditional concerns and values in the aid of the government arrangement; this means claiming and cranking up acceptability, respect, consent and agreement for the leaders and their policies; (*b*) To provide governmental elite(s) at various levels. In the context of parliamentary democracy in a federal level, this means essentially putting up candidates in the electoral arena, and working for their victory; (*c*) To calibrate and modulate the inevitable competition over allocation of societal resources—social prestige, economic gains and opportunities, political office and influence; and (*d*) To provide reasonable hope about individual and group mobility, from fringe to centre, from the periphery to the Centre. This means ensuring credible rules of games—formal and informal—in which dissent, dissatisfaction, disputes, distrust, disagreements and differences would get addressed.[1]

---

[1] See the argument in Harish Khare, 'The Indian National Congress: Problems of Survival and Re-invention', a paper read at the International Workshop on 'Political Parties in South Asia: Asianization of a Western Model?', University of Nottingham, UK, March–April 2001.

The argument here is that the political parties in India have found themselves constrained to rework these functions in the context of the demands imposed on the state order in the era of economic liberalisation and globalisation.

Globalisation Cometh

Without getting much bogged down in the debate on the meaning and content of globalisation, we need to note that globalisation does impinge on the nation-state and its executive agency, the state.

In its most extreme and most eager version, the new orthodoxy of globalisation insists that we are entering a new phase of cross-border flows in goods and services, investments, finances and technology; all these flows are creating a seamless world market. In other words, we are witnessing the gradual demise of the nation-state as a power actor. This perhaps is too radical a view; nonetheless, there is a new realisation that strong globalisation does lead to considerable erosion in state power.[2]

Liberalisation has come to mean that the markets be allowed to have their own logic, that the bureaucracy should get out of the way of economic entrepreneurs, that the political leaders and parties recognise the inevitability of fiscal reforms and fiscal discipline. Above all it means an acknowledgement that there are very definite limits to what the state can do and should be allowed to do.

The globalisation/liberalisation process seeks to redefine three relationships: (a) state-to-state, (b) state and the super market, and (c) state and individuals.

It follows, as a corollary to the twin process:

(a) the state is no longer able to enjoy a monopoly over information and increasingly over coercion;

(b) the state remains the highest—if no longer the sole—depository of legitimacy;

(c) if the nature and contents of what the state can do, what the state cannot and should not do, then the functions of the state institutions change, and the space available for political contest will necessarily shrink; and

(d) at the same time, the state remains indispensable as a requirement if an enforceable political order based on legitimacy and democratic consent has to be achieved.

---

[2] Linda Weiss, *The Myth of the Powerless State: Governing the Economy in a Global Era*, Cambridge: Polity Press, 1998; Kenichi Ohmae, *The Borderless World*, New York: Collins, 1990; Robert B. Reich, *The Work of Nations*, New York: Vintage, 1992; M. Horsman and A. Marshall, *After The Nation-State*, London: Harper-Collins, 1994.

The Indian State Redefines its Mandate

Let us take a very brief overview of the Indian state, from Bangalore, circa 1951 to Chennai, 1999, with a brief stopover in New Delhi in November 1996.

BANGALORE: The raison d'etre of the Indian state was politically spelled out by the Congress leadership in Bangalore in July 1951, on the eve of the first general elections. For two days, 13 July and 14 July, the All India Congress Committee debated a draft document, 'The Congress Election Manifesto'; Jawaharlal Nehru, who repeatedly intervened during the debate, moved the document. His utterances at Bangalore constitute the most coherent vision of what the Indian republic ought to be striving for, and the subsequent refashioning of the various institutions of the Indian state can be traced back to this vision.[3]

At Bangalore, Nehru spelled out various themes:

(*a*) An egalitarian social order: 'freedom of the masses from exploitation and want ... a cooperative commonwealth based on equality of opportunity and of political, economic and social rights.'

(*b*) Democratic approach: method is one of cooperation and the avoidance, as far as possible, of competition and conflict. 'We do believe in the essence of democracy and therefore, even at the cost of some apparent slowness in the progress, we stick to democratic methods.'

(*c*) A secular state: 'in which every individual has equal rights and opportunities, and the removal of barriers of caste, class or region. Every citizen has the same duties, rights, privileges and obligations as any other. He has full freedom to profess and practise his religion.'

(*d*) Role for the state in planned development: method of planned development is essential for progress and must be continued. Stress must be on uniform progress, special attention to backward areas, especially those 'who have suffered neglect in the past and this must be made good'.

(*e*) Rejection of the unadulterated market forces: 'it is not possible to pursue a policy of laissez faire in industry ... this peculiarly unsuited to present-day conditions in India. It has long been the Congress policy that basic industries should be owned and controlled by the State. This policy holds and must be progressively given effect to.'

(*f*) Popular legitimacy: 'Ours is democratic State. If we had been an authoritarian State then a decree can be issued from the top and the people will have to obey whether they suffer or not. We have to get the people to agree ... we have to have in a very large measure not only public

---

[3] *Selected Works of Nehru*, Vol. 2, Second Series, Volume Sixteen, Part II (published by Jawaharlal Nehru Memorial Fund, Teen Murti Bhavan, New Delhi; distributed by Oxford University Press, New Delhi, 1994), pp. 13–30.

approval but support and co-operation ... it is very difficult for the Government to impose something unless there is a consent and agreement.'

What is remarkable is that Nehru, in his characteristic manner, went about the country during the first general elections, explaining to the people, garnering their silent support and eventually reaping democratic and electoral legitimacy for his vision of a new Indian state.

This mandate has been generally categorised as a welfare state, probably with unmistakable Fabian imprints. Almost all the constitutional institutions gradually readjusted—or were made to readjust—to this mandate of a maximalist, interventionist and caring state.[4]

Since the Congress Party occupied such a huge space in the polity—both at the Centre and in the states—these Nehruvian notions and themes became the basic parameters of political debate, discourse and disputes.

NEW DELHI (a stopover): The revised mandate of the Indian state was spelled out by Dr Manmohan Singh on 13 November 1996, just a few months after he relinquished the office as finance minister, during the course of the 28th Jawaharlal Nehru Memorial Lecture, entitled 'India: The Unfinished Agenda of Economic Reforms'.[5]

Dr Manmohan Singh referred to the grave economic crisis of 1991–92 that accelerated a process of rethinking leading to 'far-reaching changes (have been) made in our economic policies during the last five years so as to align them with contemporary realities'. He noted a kind of elite pact, 'a broad national consensus about the basic design of our economic policies', and stressed the delinking of the economic policies from the need for popular endorsement. 'Economic policies have been considerably depoliticised. Indeed one can say now with some justification that the stand a political party takes on economic reforms depends more on which side of the Lok Sabha its members sit than on preconceived ideological convictions. It promises continuity of basic economic policies even when Governments change.'

Unlike the Nehruvian dream of the state directing the economy from its commanding heights, Manmohan Singh seeks to redefine the relationship between the state and the market. The argument is that the Indian state needs

---

[4] Flush with respectability and adoration, the post-independence leadership was using the triumphant nationalism to (a) integrate the polity; (b) mass mobilisation for change, and (c) use state power for social engineering. See Rasheeduddin Khan, 'The Total State: The Concept and its Manifestation in the Indian Political System', in Zoya Hasan and Rasheeduddin Khan (eds), *The State, Political Processes and Identity*, New Delhi: Sage Publications, 1989, pp. 33–72. Also, Sudipta Kaviraj, 'The Modern State in India', in Zoya Hasan (ed.), *Politics and the State In India*, New Delhi: Sage Publications, 2000, pp. 37–63.

[5] 'India: the Unfinished Agenda of Economic Reforms', 28th Jawaharlal Nehru Memorial Lecture (November 13, 1996). Monograph, published by Jawaharlal Nehru Memorial Fund, New Delhi, 1996.

to be modernised for 'enhanced governance capacity'. Accordingly, there is need for a 'reorientation of the role of the State to enhance its capacity for governance and thereby to maximise its developmental impact'.

In the post-1991 paradigm shift, the state has to largely give up its role as an entrepreneur, must redefine its role as a regulator, and should become a facilitator of economic growth through the market place and forces.

The argument is that Nehruvian politics, as practised largely by the Congress governments, has failed to live up to its promise. Manmohan Singh talks of 'excessive political interference' and laments that 'political power in our country is now passing into the hands of groups who do not willingly accept limits to their intervention or interference in the affairs of the public sector'.

In the new economic order decision-making has to be rescued from the politicians and their compulsions and cravings. Says the former finance minister, somewhat sternly:

> There is too little appreciation of the fact that sustained development is not like going to a free dinner party and that, in the final analysis, standard of living is a matter of high productivity and there are no short-cuts to it. Within the Government, it is only the Finance Minister who worries about fiscal imbalances. However, the correction of these imbalances is not a simple technical exercise. It requires hard political decisions for which a broad based consensus is essential, particularly since the fiscal correction has to be brought about without a cut in public investment and social spending. Fiscal deficits basically are a reflection of destructive populism, increasing political instability and widespread social indiscipline that prevail today. The challenge ahead is to develop a political consensus, uniting our people in a common national endeavour supportive of high rates of savings, investment and growth as part of a grand design to get rid of chronic poverty and to make India a major global player in the world economy. An alert public opinion and the strong support of the civil society alone can ensure that political processes move in the right direction.

CHENNAI (1999): The journey that began in Bangalore has ended up, for now, in Chennai.

The Chennai Declaration (CD) was adopted at the Bharatiya Janata Party's (BJP) National Council meeting in Chennai on 27–29 December 1999, and it sets out the BJP's thinking on how to make the 21st century India's century. The document spells out significant themes, reflective of the BJP's adaptation to the new market orientation.[6]

The BJP re-commits itself to an overall goal of a 'proud and prosperous India', a commitment it made, along with its allies in the National Democratic Alliance (NDA), at the time of the 1999 elections. True, the party does not say it

---

[6] BJP, Chennai Declaration, December 1999.

was in any way less committed to the cause of the poor than the Congress ever was. 'The BJP has been consistent in our approach that the focal point of all economic policies and programmes should be the Daridra (the poor) in whom is manifested "Narayan" (divinity). We believe that this is indeed possible to be achieved by adopting the three-point economic strategy—maximisation of production, equity in distribution and restraint in consumption.'

The Declaration deplores the 'phenomenal expansion of the State: This "unbridled expansion" had "stifled the creative endeavours of the people and created excessive dependencies on the State".' Second, 'the ability of the State to deliver results has been seriously compromised by its sheer size and innate efficiency. India is over-governed without being effectively governed. The State is doing too much of what it should not be doing and doing too little in what it should be doing.'

Like Dr Manmohan Singh, the CD contends that 'the BJP believes that the role of the State has to be transformed from a controller to a facilitator'.

What follows, then, is a commitment to extensive de-regulation and de-bureaucratisation: 'restrict governmental role as only a policy-maker and facilitator of development in all areas of development except strategic sectors such as defence and nuclear. All unnecessary controls and procedural hurdles in the path of Indian industry, especially small industry must go.'

Accordingly, there will be large-scale disinvestment (from the public sector), though avoiding private monopolies or foreign dominance. Also, the trend will be to 'rationalise' subsidies since 'fiscal discipline is the need of the hour', though 'an effective Indian State has an obligation to the weakest'.

The CD calls for an elite pact on how to deal with the demands of globalisation. 'Initiate a national consensus in the political, business and social establishments on India's strategy for globalization.'

And, then, refashion the institutions to meet these lowered vision and strategic objectives of the Indian state. 'Implement a broad agenda of bold reforms to complement and supplement the economic reforms presently under way. This agenda should include Constitutional reforms, electoral reforms, administrative reforms, and judicial reforms and police reforms. Urgent action should be taken to scrap all the outdated and inessential laws, regulations and procedures that hinder growth and cause harassment to the citizens.'

The CD calls upon the BJP leadership to develop a national consensus for achieving these goals. 'It is high time all the political parties developed a common approach to these national issues to achieve speedy national progress.'

At Chennai the BJP patted itself on the back for having 'replaced the Congress as the principal pole of Indian politics' and asserted that it was 'conscious of its responsibility to give India a new political culture. Ours is a party with a difference—both in ideology and in political conduct ... we must realise we have on us the onerous responsibility of overhauling the content and culture of the Indian politics.'

The Chennai Declaration reflects the adjustment that a dominant section of the political community has made in terms of perceptions about its role in re-casting the state-economy relationship.

Markets Get Going

A fundamental change can be discerned in ties between the state and the market in India. The earlier distrust, which at times degenerated into open hostility, between the government and the business community is now only an unhappy memory. From Nehru's disdain for the '*bania*' to Indira Gandhi's calculated affront to the industrial class to Rajiv Gandhi's instinctive fondness for the rich and the affluent, to P.V. Narasimha Rao's deliberate bow in the direction of corporate India, it is the ups and downs in this relationship that have defined the political economy of India all these years. The political class—ruling politicians at the Centre and in the state, functionaries in various political parties—as well as the bureaucracy have come to look upon the business and corporate classes with respect, if not awe. There is now an attitude of reliance and partnership with the business classes.

For example, let us listen to one representative voice of this new, confident and demanding attitude of the market: 'Issues on the global agenda have become more numerous, more complex and more inter-dependent. Dealing with all these pressing issues has become an overwhelming task for the society. The role of civil society, including the business sector, has expanded tremendously. Governments have lost ground for the reason that their structures and operating procedures are often inappropriate to anticipate and resolve such multiple, complex and systemic problems, let alone manage them from a global and long-term perspective. Neither business nor government nor civil society alone can meet the challenges of the global economy in the 21st century. They have to act in partnership.'[7]

The business community, in particular the corporate sector, has, on its part, acquired a new confidence to deal with the state and its functional organs—politicians and the bureaucracy. This change in confidence can be traced to a number of developments:

(a) Decline of the Congress monolith; especially the feeling of helplessness that the entire polity had when the Nehru-Gandhi dynasty seemed so immovable, so erratic and so arrogant that everyone else in the political arena had to deal with the Congress/dynasty from a position of intrinsic weakness.

---

[7] Rahul Bajaj, 'Building a Globally Competitive India: The Challenge and the Way Ahead', The 14th CSIR Foundation Day Lecture, 26 September 2000, New Delhi.

(b) The state's self-induced retreat from the commanding heights; and, what is more, this retreat was accompanied by an intellectual concession that the way the political class and the bureaucracy had operated the state, the Nehruvian raison d'etre of the Indian state has been squandered away.

(c) The seeming inadequacies of the Indian state became all the more glaring as the Mandir-Masjid-Mandal-oriented political disputes could not be sorted out amicably; the widespread disorder and instability created an objective desire for order and stability; what was more, for the first time the middle classes began to get alienated from the grand egalitarian design of the Indian state.

(d) Corporate India discovered the usefulness of exploiting its sway over the media to tap the middle classes' growing scepticism, and began developing a tentative constituency for liberalisation, economic reforms, and the related paradigm shift.

There was another reason for putting the state-market relationship on a different basis. The demands in terms of policy concessions that outsiders made on the Indian state in the name of globalisation forced a kind of closing of ranks between the Indian government and corporate India. At one level the traditional approach prompted the governmental decision-making establishment to promote and protect 'Indian' interests—a call that comes naturally to the Indian bureaucracy, especially the foreign service crowd—in international organisations and forums; P.V. Narasimha Rao became the first prime minister to travel to Davos (in Switzerland) to attend the World Economic Forum, a platform that aggressively asserts that the agenda of growth and development can only be efficaciously pursued by the corporate community, and the governments' only job is to make the corporate community's job easier by changing laws and lowering barriers of all kinds to global trading.

It is to be noted that since 1991, corporate organisations have emerged as the most self-confident interest group, demanding a say—and having a say—in the way the Indian state went about its business. The three main bodies—the Confederation of Indian Industry, the ASSOCHAM and the FICCI now think of themselves as equal partners with the government in directing the economy; successive governments, whether of the Congress, the United Front or the National Democratic Alliance, have found it expedient to 'energise' this relationship.

This new *jugalbandi* is best on display every year when the World Economic Forum organises an India Economic Summit, generally in the first half of December. This occasion witnesses the entire Government of India, from the prime minister downward, to all 'economic' ministers and chief ministers, and seniormost bureaucrats interacting with the business community, Indian and foreign. The word 'interaction' essentially means the corporate voices telling the Indian policy makers what policy or legal changes, encouragement and incentives they need from the Indian state. The tone is set by the keynote address by Mr Claude Smadja, who is the managing director of the World Economic Forum. In his last such exercise, on 6 December 1999, Mr Smadja talked down to the Indian gathering. Three aspects need to be noted.

First, Mr Smadja patted the Indians on the back for willing to change their ways of thinking and doing things: 'There are clear indications that this is exactly the mindset of the top government officials, but also the perspective of corporate India becoming more and more outward-looking, as it continues to go through the dramatic restructuring process started in the mid-nineties.' Second, he plainly told the Indian audience that globalisation was in India's own interests. 'It is only through this second generation of reforms that India can truly be able to ensure its economic take-off and align itself with the global economy. Here, one has to be very clear: joining the global economy, aligning itself with the trends which are shaping this economy is not something "imposed" upon India as some circles in this country still seem to think. It is not either a "favour" that India is doing to the rest of the world. It is quite simply recognition of the inescapable reality. The irreversibility of globalization is beyond doubt.' And, third, that 'there is a generational change inside corporate India ... which will continue and accelerate. A first generation of entrepreneurs is contributing to reshape the corporate landscape; and a fledgling middle-class keeps emerging, boosted also by the growing impact of the new knowledge-based activities taking hold in the country...this middle-class is beginning to become sufficiently noticeable to start having an impact on the mindset in this country.'[8]

Mr Smadja's overbearingness notwithstanding, it is possible to argue that there is a perceptible change in the attitudes of the governing class—politicians and bureaucrats—towards corporate India. According to India's seniormost economic policy maker, Mr N.K. Singh, the then secretary to the prime minister, and generally regarded as the economic czar: 'Today's smart politician understands that power does not mean an exercise of discretion in favour of this or that business house or corporate entity; he knows the real power means changing the policies in a manner that would encourage economic activity, which in turn will generate employment and revenue.'[9]

This change in politicians' attitude is reflected in the way bureaucracy has reoriented itself: 'A senior IAS officer knows that the political bosses want to do things differently; unlike in the earlier times, an IAS babu dare not carry a personal or ideological animus against an industrial house because he knows we can go in for appeal to the higher ups, and that the higher ups

---

[8] Claude Smadja, 'The Second Generation of Reforms: Meeting the Requirements for India's Take-Off', New Delhi: World Economic Forum, December 1999.
[9] Interview with N.K. Singh, 6 November 2000.

would over-rule the IAS *babu*. There is no more a stigma to be seen in working in tandem with the businessmen; this or that IAS officer may not like my face, and may pass the burden of decision-making to yet another senior officer, but he cannot hold me up indefinitely or deny to me what is legitimately due to me and my company.'[10]

In other words, the governing class has internalised the new demands of globalisation and liberalisation. For instance, a few days ago, Capt. Kanwaljit Singh, the finance minister of Punjab, was representing his state at a conference on 'Dynamic North: Global Competitiveness through Partnership', organised by the Punjab, Haryana and Delhi Chambers of Commerce and Industry (PHDCCI). This Punjab minister's speech is full of themes that underline the new *jugalbandi* between business and the government:[11]

(*a*) 'The State has well knit infrastructure and we have made much headway to facilitate private sector participation in infrastructure development. Requisite legislative framework for this purpose has been laid down and Punjab Infrastructure Development Board which will play the role of "Credit Enhancer & Development Financier" has been set up.'

(*b*) 'The industry is looking upon the State Governments to provide the requisite support and direction. The State initiatives have, therefore, to be focused towards enhancing the international competitiveness of industrial units. State Government has set up an Expert Committee to prepare a status paper on the impact of WTO.'

(*c*) 'We have simplified and streamlined procedures so that an entrepreneur can devote his energy and resources in capacity building of the unit.'

(*d*) 'State government has taken a major initiative to introduce computer education in the schools and colleges of Punjab which will ensure that the boys and girls are computer literate when they pass out. We have also involved the Private Sector in reorienting the syllabi of ITI and polytechnics to match the availability of technical manpower with the needs of the Industry.'

(*e*) 'The State government is fully committed to bring about the necessary Administrative Reforms in the State for better public services through use of IT-enabled services.'

(*f*) '...the Government of Punjab initiated a series of dialogues with the Chamber on the subject (of changing labour legislation) with the objective of giving concessions to Trade and Industry, under the Labour Laws.'

The ultimate tribute to the market and its growing clout was grudgingly paid when in September 2000 six chief ministers travelled to New Delhi to have a collective audience with the Microsoft king, Mr Bill Gates.

---

[10] Interviews with top executives of leading industrial house, November 2000.
[11] Punjab, Haryana and Delhi Chambers of Commerce, 10 November 2000.

Recasting Party Politics in the age of Reforms

Let us begin with an observation an external analyst made about how the Indian party system was negotiating the painfulness of the transition to the market reforms and to the state-market partnership:

> Beginning under the late Prime Minister Rajiv Gandhi in the 1980s and accelerating under the current Prime Minister, P. V. Narasimha Rao and Finance Minister Manmohan Singh, the Indian economy has undergone a renaisscance. The elimination of many of the restrictions, controls and licences has freed Indian businesses to stand or fall on their own. The resulting gains in efficiency and economic growth, which has averaged nearly five percent a year since the beginning of the reforms under Gandhi, have stoked the growth of a pro-democratic middle class and built up support for the Congress Party as a reform-oriented party of the future.[12]

That was a judgement made in the early 1990s. However, the agenda of economic reforms has not exactly brought spectacular political dividends for the Congress Party. The process of economic reforms and globalisation is generally conceded to be disruptive of existing social contracts.

This leads us to the larger theme of the role of the political parties and the party system in facilitating transition to economic reforms, liberalisation and globalisation.

The process of market-oriented reforms and globalisation is now generally conceded to be disruptive of existing social contracts, creating fear and deprivation among the entrenched groups, generating resentment among those support groups that benefited from the rent-seeking activities in the 'socialist era'. What, then, is the role of political parties in managing and calibrating 'the tension between the egalitarian logic of democracy and economic systems based on private property and initiative that imply inequality of both income and wealth'?[13]

---

[12] John D. Sullivan, 'Democratisation and Business Interests', in Larry Diamond and Marc F. Plattner (eds), *Economic Reforms and Democracy*, Baltimore: Johns Hopkins University Press, 1995, p. 187.

[13] Stephen Haggard and Robert R. Kaufman, *The Political Economy of Democratic Transition*, Princeton: Princeton University Press, 1995, p. 377.

The process of globalisation has been deemed to be disruptive even in the developed polities. 'The process that has come to be called "globalization" is exposing a deep fault line between groups who have the skills and mobility to flourish in global markets and those who don't either have these advantages or perceive the expansion of unregulated markets as inimical to social stability and deeply held norms. The result is severe tension between the market and social groups such as workers, pensioners and environmentalists, with governments stuck in the middle.' See Dani Rodrik, *Has Globalisation Gone Too Far?* Washington, D.C.: Institute for International Economics, 1997, p. 2.

Unlike Latin America and Europe, the losers in the 'market transition' in India are not entrenched economic interests (with the exception of organised white-collar trade unions) but the unorganised masses, or at least those who are believed to be not so well organised. If the vast masses (which is also the largest segment of the national electorate) get a feeling of being deliberately short-changed or neglected, then do political parties (at least the ruling ones) invite electoral backlash? It may be worth noting that in the 1999 Lok Sabha elections, two of the most pro-economic reforms candidates (Dr Manmohan Singh and Mr Murli S. Deora) from two of the most middle-class dominated constituencies (South Delhi and South Mumbai, respectively) lost out.

It is recognised that 'managing distributive conflict requires either the resources to effectively compensate losers—resources that are typically in short supply during economic crises—or the political capacity to override their objections'.[14] How are political parties in India being helpful in providing the 'political capacity' to deal with the resentment, anger, alienation of the losers?

The closest the Indian polity comes in this matter is the Latin American experience, where the traditional state-interventionist parties had to come to terms with the task of providing 'political capacity' to pursue a course of reforms that often penalised important constituents of these parties, at least in the short term. In fact, the problem is most acute in the case of a ruling party. Three approaches have been deployed in Latin America in refashioning the government-executive and ruling party. First, party neglecting: the executive goes ahead with the agenda of reforms, without bothering to consult and humour the ruling party. Second, party yielding: the executive cedes to the demands of the party, and in effect abandons the rigorous pursuit of the reforms agenda. Finally, party accommodation: the executive negotiates some compromises with the party, granting political concessions in return for the party's consent to implement reforms.[15]

The party system in India curiously and effortlessly settled for a mixture of the party-neglecting and party-accommodation approach. This was possible because of a long tradition—dating back to the first days of the Nehru regime after Independence—of the party organisation deferring to the superior wisdom of the prime minister/government. Even the BJP, a party that took pride in its organisational culture and identity, happily played second fiddle to the government in the matter of economic reforms. For instance, meeting after its finance minister had presented a 'dream budget' (read pro-business and corporate interests), the new president, Mr K. Jana Krishnamurthy, gushed forth: 'The government has gone in for second generation reforms. The budget has, contrary to expectations, been welcomed by all. There is bound to be some

---

[14] Haggard and Kaufman, *The Political Economy of Democratic Transition*, p. 158.
[15] John Corrales, 'Presidents, Ruling Parties, and Party Rules: A Theory of the Politics of Economic Reforms in Latin America', *Comparative Politics*, 32(2), January 2000.

criticism from some quarters or other. This is natural, as no budget is a perfect budget. Every budget has to take into account the ground realities of the year and the short-term and long-term needs of the country. For the first time an attempt has been made to keep the long-term needs of the country in mind while framing the budget. We congratulate the government and the finance minister for his bold approach.'[16]

Tools of Mediation

First the Congress (1991–96), then the United Front (1996–98), and now the National Democratic Alliance (1998–till now) have attended to the following identifiable chores, which helped create the requisite 'political capacity' to pursue the economic reforms agenda. As the NDA Prime Minister, Mr Vajpayee has asserted there was no longer any need to question the direction of the economic reforms.[17]

A number of tasks have been undertaken by the political parties. First, in a limited way, selling the idea of reforms; at least, create a public awareness for the changing of the ways of running the state, government and the economy.

Second, absorbing social and political costs of dislocations; each ruling party sought to change the vocabulary of public discourse in a manner that those who were opposing the reforms came out as 'populist', 'irresponsible', etc. At the same time, because of the fear of a perception or of a criticism that the government was 'anti-poor', voices within the ruling party would insist on a demonstrative commitment of resources for poverty alleviation, etc. This insistence would ensure that the dominant political discourse would keep paying obeisance to the welfare of the largest section of the electorate; this took care of the need 'to help groups express their interests while allowing governments to govern'.[18]

Third, by mediating between the government and the various organised and unorganised interests, the political parties helped in garnering a semblance of democratic consent for 'hard decisions' and reinforced the political system's legitimacy. The involvement of political parties, in selling and opposing the

---

[16] Speech at National Executive, 24 March 2001, New Delhi: BJP.

[17] 'After all, our Government has been in office only for the past three years. The process of economic reforms was initiated by a Congress Government. It was later carried forward by two United Front Governments. In different ways, State Governments rules by various political parties are also pursuing economic reforms on their own. Thus, there is a broad consensus on the need for reforms for achieving faster and more balanced growth ... there is no need for questioning the basic direction of our reforms process.' Vajpayee's speech at the golden jubilee seminar of the National Sample Survey, 12 May 2001, text: New Delhi, Press Information Bureau.

[18] Scott Mainwaring and Timothy Scully, *Building Democratic Institutions: Party Systems in Latin America*, Stanford: Stanford University Press, 1995, p. 22–23.

economic reform process, helped ensure that the 'democratic rules of the game' were observed, at least in form but not in spirit.

For example, the BJP's National Executive passed, on 24–25 March 2001, a resolution on the central budget, presented a few weeks earlier by its Finance Minister, Mr Yashwant Sinha. The resolution is a classic instance of a party using its consent-garnering licence to sell reforms-oriented policies as being pro-poor and pro-public interest. 'Proposal to end monopoly of Food Corporation of India in handling procurement, storages, etc., would lead to efficient and cost-effective handling of foodgrains to the benefit of consumers.... The proposed labour laws reforms would ultimately result in better returns to workers and enhanced job opportunities.... The procedure for privatisation of public sector enterprises has now been considerably streamlined. To maximise returns, approach of the government has shifted from disinvestment of small lots of shares to strategic sales of blocks of share to strategic investors.'[19]

Let us look at the techniques used by the ruling party of the day in pushing the agenda of economic reforms.

First, by pretending that nothing has changed. Narasimha Rao coined the phrase, 'continuity with change'.

Second, to suggest that the commitment to the poor remained unchanged. For instance, addressing the centenary celebrations of the CII at Calcutta on 4 January 1995, Mr Narasimha Rao noted: 'It has been said that the new policies have not benefited the poorer sections. Coming from a rural background and having had the experience of one meal a day during my studies for the degree course, my concern for the poor happens to be quite genuine.'[20]

Third, argue that the change was for the benefit of the poor. In his last address to the nation from the Red Fort, 15 August 1995, Narasimha Rao observed, 'We have invested a lot of money in poverty alleviation programmes and we are doing so since 1992. All our programmes are to remove poverty. We have not given any money to the rich and on the other hand, we have made them invest their money in industry. Whatever money we saved from their investment, we spent it on the poor.... This means that whatever resources the Government has were utilised for the poor.'[21] It is of course a different matter that Narasimha Rao and the Congress did not cut much ice with the electorate.

Fourth, chant the mantra of 'consensus'; Narasimha Rao did it to secure the non-confrontation, if not cooperation, of the non-Congress parties in the reform process. The 'consensus' mantra was also bandied about to secure the acquiescence of the elites—bureaucratic, business, media—behind the economic reforms; the elites in turn were able to insist that the political parties

---

[19] 'Resolution on the Central Budget: 2001–02', National Executive, BJP, March 2001.
[20] P.V. Narasimha Rao, 'Economic Reforms: For People's Ultimate Benefit', New Delhi: Ministry of Information and Broadcasting, 1995.
[21] Text published by Government of India, August 1995.

were free to carry on their feuds and vendettas as long as they did not derail the economic reforms agenda.

This 'consensus' mantra came in handy when the United Front ruled with Congress support from the outside; the parties which were partners in the United Front, that had all been critical, even opposed, to the Narasimha Rao-Manmohan Singh agenda, were now overnight agreeable to carry forward the 'consensus' on reforms.

During the National Democratic Alliance regime, from 1998 onward, the 'consensus' technique has been used to rope in parties that were otherwise not enamoured of the reforms process. In its economic resolution, the AICC Bangalore session (17–18 March 2001) 'notes that all governments that have come to power at the Centre since May 1996 when the Congress left office have claimed to follow the essential approach to economic policy pioneered by the Congress during 1991–96. To some extent, this is true. Political parties that opposed us when they were in the Opposition changed their views completely when in power.'[22]

Indeed, now we see the interesting phenomenon of 'populist' ministers like Ram Vilas Paswan and Sharad Yadav being made to preside over the process of privatisation, corporatisation and disinvestment in the ministries under their charge. There has been a discernible willingness to concede political space to otherwise intractable political actors while securing their support for 'harsh' economic measures.

Thanks to the self-hypnotising powers of this 'consensus' mantra, the only charge the Congress has been able to make against the NDA government is that it is not following as vigorously and as transparently the agenda of economic reforms as is ideally required. (However, in recent days the Congress has been caught in an internal debate over the direction of economic reforms, though the party has been extending critical and crucial support to the NDA government to push through WTO-related legislation.)[23]

On its part, as a ruling party, the BJP has been faithfully endorsing the government's agenda of economic reforms, though arguing that it would be more mindful of 'national interest' in taking the path of globalisation. In 1999, the NDA became the first political entity to use the word 'privatisation' in an election manifesto. In its last major conclave, the National Council at Nagpur (August 2000), the BJP's political resolution displayed extraordinary aggression in taking on its opponents who were nitpicking about the reform agenda. 'No less deplorable is the Congress turnaround on economic issues. After pursuing economic reforms and market economics while in

---

[22] *Economic Policy Resolution*, Indian National Congress, 81st Plenary Session, 17–18 March 2001, Bangalore.

[23] Interview with Mr P.R. Chavan, convenor of the Congress Party's Policy and Programme Group, 16 November 2000.

power, the Congress now wants India to go back in time to the days of Licence-Permit-Quota Raj. After following a policy of disinvestment in public sector units and supporting the United Front Government on this issue, the party now wants to reverse the reform process. The BJP is fully committed to unshackling the energies of the Indian people and utilising their potential for the utmost advantage of the Indian nation.'[24]

The fifth development that has proven rather crucial is the federalisation of the Indian party system. The growth of regional sentiment, regional parties and regional business interests has been a parallel phenomenon, and the last few years have witnessed a convergence between these regional forces. Regional businesses have used their alliance with regional parties to crow-bar their way into areas of policy breaks which otherwise used to be usurped by the big businesses, and, second, have used their clout in the national coalition regime to strike working networks with the international business community. The regional parties and dominant regional businesses have as much stake in globalisation as anyone else does.[25]

It has also helped that a political party may be in power in a state where its government undertakes harsh fiscal measures and therefore finds it difficult to oppose a similar harsh policy package at the Centre being put in place by another political party. The Telugu Desam, for example, has initiated very harsh reforms in the power sector; and, therefore, beyond a token resistance, it cannot oppose the Vajpayee government's measures aimed at cutting subsidies, etc. On the other hand, there has been a willingness to be flexible and mollify entrenched interests. For instance, thanks to the Akali Dal's clout in the national coalition, the Punjab farmers have got too many unreasonable breaks, and, other regional parties are also demanding similar breaks.

Overview

The party system has shown remarkable adaptability and innovation in coping with the demands of globalisation and liberalisation. Like the parties in Europe in the 1970s, and in Latin America in the 1980s, the Indian political

---

[24] *Nagpur Message*, BJP, New Delhi, September 2000.

[25] In an excellent analysis, Sanjay Baru has argued that 'it became clear to regional business groups that any system which increased the leverage of the state governments over the central government would increase their relative strength vis-à-vis national big business'. 'Economic Policy and the Development of Capitalism in India: The Role of Regional Capitalists and Political Parties', in Francine R. Frankel, Zoya Hasan, Rejeev Bhargava, Balveer Arora (eds), *Transforming India: Social and Political Dynamics of a Democracy* (New Delhi: Oxford University Press, 2000), pp. 207–30. The theme is taken further by Lloyd I. Rudolph and Susanne Hoeber Rudolph, 'The Iconisation of Chandrababu: Sharing Sovereignty in India's Federal Market Economy', *Economic and Political Weekly*, Vol. XXVI(18), 5 May 2001, pp. 1541–52.

parties—at least the two dominant parties, the Congress and the BJP—have struggled to retain the confidence of their electorates by changes in leadership, goals and strategies. The Congress has not been as fast and as innovative as the BJP; the story of the Indian party system is the success of the BJP to displace, at least for now, the Congress as the dominant all-India party, which functions as an anchor for a ruling arrangement at the Centre.

No doubt the parties in India continue to perform traditional functions like setting collective goals, aggregating interests, becoming instruments of recruitment to political offices, and mobilising public opinion in favour of or against this or that politics.

Yet there are vast areas of contention outside the realm of 'economic reforms' that political parties must compete for; the invocation by 'smaller' political parties of emotional appeals like caste or religion or region can also be deemed to be a stratagem to try to get the better of dominant parties who acquire a stranglehold on the national imagination and national political discourse. In the first three decades, the Congress squeezed the other parties out of political imagination by invoking the non-sectarian appeal of the poor; now the Congress-BJP entente has appropriated the 'economic reforms', an emotion that has acquired an all-India appeal and has captured the imagination of an emerging pan-Indian middle class.

The party system in India is trying to adjust itself to the consequences and compulsions of the state's retreat from vast areas of public endeavour. Yet there would be no dearth of issues and emotions over which parties would have to engage themselves; after all it has been argued from the western experience that 'there is no reason at all to believe that there is any connection between the scope of government activity and the nature of party conflict'.[26]

The party system in India is experiencing the familiar 'central political tension between democracy and the market' in the era of globalisation and liberalisation. In the Indian context the tension has been succinctly put: 'The people who are excluded by the economics of markets are included by the politics of democracy. Hence, inclusion and exclusion are asymmetrical in politics and economics. The distribution of capabilities is also uneven in the economic and political spheres. The rich dominate the economy now more than earlier, but the poor have a strong voice in the polity now more than earlier. And there is a mismatch.'[27] And, this for the parties has produced the dilemma between 'winning and governing'.[28]

---

[26] Alan Ware, *Citizens, Parties and the State: A Re-appraisal*, Cambridge: Polity Press, 1987, p. 227.

[27] Deepak Nayyar, 'Economic Development and Political Democracy: Interaction of Economics and Politics in Independent India', in Nirja Gopal Jayal (ed.), *Democracy in India*, Delhi: Oxford University Press, 2001, pp. 361–90.

[28] Subrata Mitra, *Culture and Rationality: Politics of Social Change in Post-Colonial India*, New Delhi: Sage Publications, 1999), pp. 250–55.

The next phase in the evolution of the party system would be to find ways and means of carrying on legitimacy-generating and system-enforcing democratic competition; this would mean an insistence on a polity that is governable yet fair in its concern and inclusive in its reach and imagination. Only then would it be possible to strike a balance between the requirements of carrying on the reforms agenda and the compulsion to mediate conflicts over other issues, social, political and cultural. Political parties are learning the task of mediating and managing tensions between electoral compulsions and their egalitarian demands, and the harsh realities of economic liberalisation and equally harsh demands of globalisation.

16

LOCAL DEMOCRACY AND POLITICAL PARTIES IN INDIA

Sandeep Shastri

I

Any meaningful assessment of the structure, organisation and working of political parties in India and the nature of the party system that has evolved in this context, would necessarily involve an in-depth evaluation of the dynamics of party politics at the grassroot level. In consonance with the fact that the spotlight of attention in discussions on Indian politics has, more often than not, been on developments at the national and regional level, studies on political parties in India too, have tended to focus on party politics and party structures at the central and state level.[1] The 'big narrative' appears to have pushed to the sidelines the 'little narrative' of the finer nuances of party politics at the local level.

This chapter attempts an assessment of the interface between the party structures and the working of democracy at the local government level in India. The impact of the 73rd and 74th Amendment to the Constitution—

---

[1] See Myron Weiner, *Party Politics in India: The Development of a Multi-Party System*, Princeton: Princeton University Press, 1957; Paul Brass, *Factional Politics in an Indian State: The Congress in Uttar Pradesh*, Berkeley: University of California Press, 1965; Stanley Kochanek, *The Congress Party in India*, Princeton: Princeton University Press, 1968; Rajni Kothari, *Politics in India*, New Delhi: Orient Longman, 1970; Richard Sisson, *The Congress Party in Rajasthan: Political Integration and National Building in an Indian State*, Berkeley: University of California Press, 1972; Myron Weiner and J.O Fields (eds), *Electoral Politics in an Indian State*, Delhi: Manohar, 1975; M.P. Singh, 'The Crisis of the Indian State: From Quiet Developmentalism to Noisy Democracy', *Asian Survey*, 30:8, 1990; Richard Sisson and Ramashray Roy, *Diversity and Dominance in Indian Politics*, New Delhi: Sage Publications, 1990; Kohli, *Democracy and Discontent: India's Growing Crisis of Governability*, Cambridge: Cambridge University Press, 1990; Thomas Blom Hanson and Christophe Jafferelot, *The BJP and Compulsion of Politics in India*, New Delhi: Oxford University Press, 1998.

which resulted in the local bodies being accorded a constitutional status, making them the third tier in the federal system—needs to be taken into account in any study of local government and political parties. Keeping this in mind, the chapter is divided into three parts. The first section attempts to briefly outline the importance that political parties in India have accorded to local government institutions and politics. In the second section a study of the role of political parties in local government politics in the pre-73rd/74th Amendment phase is undertaken and in the last section the emerging issues in party politics and local government after the passage of the 73rd and 74th Amendments are examined.

It has often been stressed that the philosophy underlying the power sharing arrangement within a political system is mirrored in the power equations and relative importance of the multiple levels of organisation within the political parties that operate in the system. Political parties in India are no exception. While it is beyond a shadow of doubt that the process of democratisation within a political party and the participation of party functionaries at various levels in decision-making, is an essential pre-requisite for carrying forward the process of 'democratic deepening' in any political system,[2] the democracy project in many countries—including India—has faced serious challenges in actualising the same. The culture of hyper-centralisation, which seems to have defined the nature of power relations within the political system has undoubtedly influenced and shaped the internal structuring of power in political parties. A natural corollary to this development is the near non-involvement or at best the mere formal involvement of the lower levels of the organisational structure of political parties in the decision-making process. Such a trend has important and significant implications for local-level politics.

A perusal of the election manifestos of major political parties is clearly indicative of the lack of serious commitment on their part to truly empowering local bodies. The National Democratic Alliance (NDA) manifesto issued at the time of the 1999 Lok Sabha elections made out a strong case for the immediate implementation of constitutional and legal reforms. The need to activate 'Panchayats and local bodies' appears to have been included under this section

[2] See John Burnheim, *Is Democracy Possible?* Cambridge: Polity, 1990; Arend Lijphart, 'The South European Examples of Democratization', *Government and Opposition*, 25:1, 1990, pp. 68–84; William A. Galston, *Liberal Purposes: Goods, Virtues and Diversity in the Liberal State*, New York: Cambridge University Press, 1991; Guy Hermet, 'The Age of Democracy', *International Social Science Journal*, 43:128, 1991, pp. 249–58; Stanley Hoffman, 'Capitalist Democracies and Democratic States', *Political Studies*, 39, 1991, pp. 342–49; Giovanni Sartori, 'Rethinking Democracy: Bad Polity and Bad Politics', *International Social Science Journal*, 43:129, 1991, pp. 437–50; Alan Touraine, 'What Does Democracy Mean Today?', *International Social Science Journal*, 43:128, 1991, pp. 259–68; Lars Rudebeck (ed.), *When Democracy Makes Sense*, Stockholm: Akut, 1992.

as a belated afterthought.[3] The Congress manifesto merely stated that the party was 'deeply concerned at the level of general stagnation and lack of meaningful movement forward' in implementing the scheme of Panchayati Raj envisaged by the Constitution.[4] No concrete suggestions were offered on how best the constitutional provisions could be implemented in letter and spirit. Earlier, the Common Minimum Programme (CMP) of the United Front had complimented the Panchayati Raj institutions for providing much needed grassroot-level development and promised to 'strengthen this process further ... and devolve greater power and authority including financial to these bodies'.[5] Though the manifestos clearly record the commitment of the political parties to devolve power and strengthen the local government system, they are silent on the steps being taken to initiate matching changes in the party structure. Their lack of sincerity in this regard is clearly transparent.

The faith reposed by citizens in local government on the one hand and their apprehensions regarding the credibility of political parties on the other, was clearly evident in the National Election Study Survey.[6] The survey indicated that in the index of popular trust in institutions, political parties secured 39 points (out of a maximum of 100) while local governments secured 58 points.[7] The same survey also indicated that less than 10 per cent of the respondents felt that political parties were serving a useful purpose. Nearly 70 per cent of the respondents did not feel close to any political party.[8] The National Election Study, 1998 revealed that more than 45 per cent of the respondents felt that political parties do not care at all for the people.[9] A study undertaken in Karnataka during the 1999 elections indicated a similar trend. When respondents were asked to comment on the working of Panchayati Raj institutions in their area, more than 55 per cent expressed satisfaction with their functioning. The main reason for this optimism was the manner in which the local bodies had afforded an opportunity for their participation in decision-making and the success of these bodies in solving local problems. Among the 45 per cent who were unhappy with the working

---

[3] National Democratic Alliance, *For a Proud, Prosperous India: An Agenda.*, New Delhi: BJP Central Office, 1999, p. 7.
[4] The Congress spoke of stagnation in the process, merely three years after it was voted out of power at the national level. Indian National Congress, *Manifesto: Lok Sabha Elections 1999*, 1999, p. 27.
[5] Common Minimum Programme, 'United Front's Policy Statement', *Mainstream*, 34:28, 1996, pp. 13–18.
[6] National Election Study (NES), *Data Set*, Delhi: Centre for the Study of Developing Societies, 1996.
[7] Yogendra Yadav, 'The Maturing of a Democracy', *India Today*, 15 August 1996, p. 40.
[8] NES, *Data Set*.
[9] NES, *Data Set*, Delhi: Centre for the Study of Developing Societies, 1998. Also see Sandeep Shastri, 'Democracy as Global Entitlement' in *Democracy, Security and Human Rights*, Khanna and Kueck (eds), Delhi: Shipra, 2003.

of local government institutions, the reason they assigned for the same was revealing. More than 80 per cent of those who had expressed reservations about local bodies blamed political parties for vitiating the political atmosphere at the local level by injecting personality-based inter-party competition. The respondents also felt that intra-party rivalry often expressed at the local level, in the process, severely undermined the functioning of these bodies.[10]

Thus, while local government institutions have the potential to provide the basic services and amenities that citizens seek and also afford an opportunity for citizen participation in decision making, the political parties have tended to neglect this level of government, preferring to focus their attention on the management of power at the national and state levels.

II

For a purposeful assessment of the constitutional provisions relating to local government, it would be useful to review the Constituent Assembly debates on this issue. Such an evaluation affords an opportunity to examine the attitude of the founding fathers of the Constitution and more specifically, the dominant political party (Congress), on issues relating to local government structures.

Article 40[11] of the Indian Constitution clearly represented a gesture of tokenism—on the part of the members of the Constituent Assembly—towards local government. In spite of the fact that not a single day passed in the Constituent Assembly without the name Mahatma Gandhi (for whom Panchayats represented true democracy) being invoked, on the issue of local government structures the framers of the Constitution preferred to ignore the advice of the Father of the Nation. The symbolic concern for local government that the Constitution makers came to express was verily, a by-product of multi-track factors and forces. A few of them merit attention.

A factor of crucial significance, in this regard, was the unitary mindset that appeared to hold sway both in the Constituent Assembly and in the Congress Party.[12] Ambedkar summed up the dominant mood in the Constituent Assembly on issues relating to federalism and local government while introducing the provisions of the Draft Constitution. He categorically stated that

---

[10] Sandeep Shastri, *The Electoral Verdict in Karnataka*, Bangalore: Department of Political Science, 1999. Also see Shastri (2003), op cit.
[11] Article 40 of the Indian Constitution reads, 'The State shall take steps to organise village panchayats and endow them with such powers and authority as may be necessary to enable them to function as units of self-government'.
[12] See Sandeep Shastri, 'Indian Federalism and National Integration: A Critique', *Indian Journal of Political Science*, 51:2, 1990, pp. 1–14; and Sandeep Shastri, 'Nehru and Centre-State Relations: A Study in the Dynamics of Indian Federalism', *Détente*, 10:1, 1991, pp. 8–10.

though 'the country and the people may be divided into different States for convenience of administration, the country is one integral whole ... under a single *imperium* derived from a single source'.[13]

Second, the issue of state and local rights was accorded a secondary status by the Constitution founding fathers. As a result, it was felt that 'local government' could be placed in the 'State List', as such a step would in no way jeopardise the unity and integrity of the country. Consequently, it was left to the states to decide the structures, power and functions of local government.

Third, several among the decision makers in the Constituent Assembly (and the Congress Party) believed that the sociology of local politics inevitably encouraged divisive forces and fissiparous tendencies. Ambedkar's intervention in the Constituent Assembly when he characterised the love of the intellectual Indians for village community as both infinite and pathetic, is a case in point. He went on to add that the village republics were responsible for the ruination of India and the Indian village was a 'sink of localism, a den of ignorance, narrow-mindedness and communalism'.[14] Nehru too, tended to view extreme localism as a threat to the unity and progress of the nation. Even as the Constitution was being drafted, in one of his fortnightly letters to the chief ministers he remarked that the 'first priority must necessarily be to preserve unity, strength and stability.... Everything that comes in the way of that may prove harmful.'[15]

Finally, Article 40 appeared to be a minor and inevitable concession that had to be granted to those who favoured a powerful and vibrant local government system. In a bid to appease the 'Gandhians' who had projected an alternative model of governance[16] and in order to blunt the criticism that the Constitution makers had abandoned 'Gandhian' ideals, this article was included.[17] In the general discussion in the Constituent Assembly, on the

---

[13] *Constituent Assembly Debates* (hereinafter *CAD*) New Delhi: Lok Sabha Secretariat, 2nd Reprint, 7:43.

[14] *CAD*, 7:39.

[15] Jawaharlal Nehru, *Letters to Chief Ministers 1947–64*, Vol. 1, Delhi: Oxford University Press, 1986, p. 143.

[16] See Shriman Narayan Agarwal, *Gandhian Constitution for Free India*, Allahabad: Kitabistan, 1946.

[17] see Granville Austin, *The Indian Constitution: Cornerstone of a Nation*, Delhi: Oxford University Press, 1966, pp. 28–31.

[18] Those who raised the issue included: Laksminarayana Sahu, K. Hanumanthaiah, N.G. Ranga, K. Santhanam, S.L. Saksena, R.K. Sidwa, M.A. Ayyangar, H.V. Kamath, Damodar Swarup, Jaspat Roy Kapoor, Alagu Rai Shastri, A.K. Ghosh, P.S. Deshmukh, Lokanath Misra, Raj Bahadur, Upendranath Burman, R.V. Dhulekar, B.P. Jhunjhunwala, B.S. Mehta, O.V. Alagesan, Mahavir Tyagi and Krishnaswami Bharati (many among them were prominent Congressmen). If Shibban Lal Saksena asserted that strong local governments had the potential 'for holding the country together' (*CAD*, 7:264), Santhanam averred that local autonomy for each village must be 'considered the basic framework for the future' of India (*CAD*, 7:256). Damodar Swarup drew attention to the fact that by ignoring local

final draft of the Constitution, more than 30 members[18] made a reference to the glaring absence of any significant provision in the Constitution on local government structures.[19]

It is also relevant to note in this context that the Constituent Assembly did not think it necessary to make any provisions in the Constitution to regulate the organisation and functioning of political parties. It was only when the 52nd Amendment to the Constitution (Anti-Defection provisions) was passed, did the term 'political parties' find a reference in the Constitution document. The neglect of this important institutional dimension of parliamentary democracy by the Constitution framers is also reflective of their priorities. The Constitution founding fathers appeared to be more concerned about legitimising and formalising existing political structures and relationships, and given the role and position envisaged for the Congress Party in post-independence politics, it was never felt necessary to try and regulate and discipline the functioning of political parties.

With the inauguration of the Constitution, one of the first government initiatives with regard to local government, launched in the 1950s, was the Community Development Programme. Nehru asserted that the community development movement had its basis in the 'village Panchayat.[20] However, he underscored the fact that this movement focused more on the administrative and economic side of village life. A conscious attempt was made to insulate the programme from any form of political influence. Nehru advised chief ministers that the community development movement involved a new pattern of working, which bypassed 'considerations of caste and religion and even, to some extent, politics'.[21] Many commentators have opined that the attempt to divorce the community development movement from politics was largely responsible for the lack of public interest in the programme.[22]

By the late 1950s, on the basis of the recommendations of the Balwantrai Mehta Committee, several states created a three-tier Panchayati Raj system. Nehru referred to this development as the laying of the 'foundation of democracy' in India.[23] With the Congress being the dominant party in most of the

government, the Draft Constitution missed an opportunity to build a structure of governance 'reared from the bottom upward' (CAD, 7:212) and H.V. Kamath charged that the ignoring of local government by the Draft Constitution was typical of 'urban highbrow' (CAD, 7:219).

[19] CAD, 11:557–870.
[20] Jawaharlal Nehru, Letters to Chief Ministers 1947–64, Vol. 4, Delhi: Oxford University Press, 1988, p. 528.
[21] Ibid., p. 157, emphasis added.
[22] See W.H. Morris-Jones, The Government and Politics of India, Bombay: B.I. Publications, 1964; and George Mathew, Status of Panchayati Raj in the States of India, New Delhi: Concept, 1994.
[23] Nehru made this comment while inaugurating a Panchayat at Nagaur in Rajasthan on Gandhi Jayanti (2 October) in 1959, see The Times of India, 3 October 1959.

states, it attempted to ensure unanimity in the elections to the Panchyati Raj institutions. The basis of the Congress reasoning was that 'election would mean conflict and ... this would aggravate the already paralysing faction divisions of village life'.[24] A consensus choice was the more preferred option. More often than not, this resulted in the entrenched social groups continuing to monopolise power. It also served the interests of the ruling party, as the leaders at the local level could help mobilise support for the party at the time of the Assembly or Lok Sabha elections.[25] It has rightly been observed that it was the nexus between the dominant social group at the local level and the political leadership at the district and state level which resulted in the benefits of development not reaching the genuine beneficiaries.[26]

With the passage of time, when 'consensus elections' to the local bodies could not be managed, the Congress expressed itself in favour of party politics being kept out of these contests. The advantage that it enjoyed was that in view of its position as the dominant local party, it managed to ensure that candidates who won became 'Congress representatives if they were not so already'.[27]

With the political/electoral competition at the local level intensifying—often triggered by caste rivalries and also a reflection of the challenge to Congress domination at the state/district level—new political/social forces sought to occupy the political space created at the local level. Local politics then became the arena to settle scores between rival parties and leaders. Often, local politics became the site for resolving inter- and intra-party disputes.

Several states amended their Panchayati Raj Acts to permit electoral contests to be on a formal party basis. West Bengal is an interesting case in point.[28] With local elections being fought on a party basis, it was possible 'for a person to stand in opposition to the traditional village leadership and to draw upon external political resources to mobilize support'.[29] Based on the study of the working of two Panchayat bodies in West Bengal after the introduction of elections on a party basis, Webster concluded that the panchayat

---

[24] Morris-Jones, *The Government and Politics of India*, p. 227.

[25] Studies of local government politics in Karnataka during the chief ministership of Devraj Urs show that though Urs was successful in building a non-dominant backward caste coalition at the state level, he was unable to break the monopoly of power that the dominant castes enjoyed at the local level. See Amal Ray and Jayalaksmi Kumpatla, 'Zilla Parishad Presidents in Karnataka: Their Social Background and Implications for Development', *Economic and Political Weekly*, 32, 1987, pp. 42–43.

[26] See L.C. Jain (ed.), *Grass Without Roots*, New Delhi: Sage Publications, 1982, p. 205.

[27] Morris-Jones, *The Government and Politics of India*, p. 228; also, Neil Webster, 'Panchayat Raj in West Bengal: Popular Participation for the People or the Party?', *Development and Change*, 23:4, 1992, p. 135.

[28] In 1978, West Bengal reorganised its Panchayati Raj system and made elections open to party politics.

[29] Webster, 'Panchayat Raj in West Bengal', p. 136.

raj system 'does not need a strong party, but that the *party needs more than just electoral support if it is to continue the movement towards a people's democracy'.*[30]

As the initiative for creating and strengthening local government structures was left to the states, the nature, design and importance of local governments varied significantly from state to state.

III

It was only after more than four decades of independence—in 1989—that an attempt was made to accord a constitutional status to local government bodies and ensure uniformity in their structure all over the country. The 64th and 65th Constitutional Amendment Bills were introduced by the government in Parliament as an effort in this direction. The prime mover of the initiative, Rajiv Gandhi, stated that the Amendment had as its purpose vesting power 'in the only place where power rightfully belongs'.[31] While participating in the debate in the Lok Sabha on the 64th Amendment Bill, Rajiv Gandhi asserted that as the Constitution had not made specific provisions for local government institutions, they had 'withered at the roots'.[32] He went on to add that by according a constitutional status to local government bodies, a constitutional obligation was being imposed on all concerned, an obligation that could not be flouted for 'reasons of expediency or indifference' (*ibidem*). However, the Amendments were defeated in the Rajya Sabha and it was left to the Congress government under Narasimha Rao's leadership to introduce the 73rd and 74th Amendment Bills—which more or less retained the provisions of the 64th and 65th Amendment Bills—and get them approved by Parliament and the requisite number of State Legislative Assemblies. As a result of the passing of the 73rd and 74th Amendments, Panchayats and Nagarpalikas have now been conferred a constitutional position and can legitimately claim their status as the third tier of the federal system.

After the passage of the 73rd and 74th Amendments, the political competition at the local government level witnessed crucial changes of a positive nature. Some of these shifts were a direct consequence of the Amendments while other changes were generated by important political developments at the national and regional levels. Their implications for the role of political parties at the local level were far reaching.

The constitutional amendments ushered in an element of uniformity in the structure of local bodies all over the country. They also attempted to

---

[30] Ibid., p. 161, emphasis added.
[31] *Lok Sabha Debates*, New Delhi: Lok Sabha Secretariat, 7 August 1989.
[32] Ibid.

ensure that across the states the local governments were entrusted similar responsibilities. However, the success achieved by local governments in fulfilling these functions varied significantly from state to state. The question of structures first. By mandating direction elections for all the three levels of rural local government, the Amendments changed the complection of political competition. The reservation of seats for women in local bodies drastically altered the composition of the local bodies. By permitting the states to make a provision for reservation for backward communities, the Amendments opened a window of opportunity for the non-dominant backward castes to assert their voice in local government decision making.

The end of one party domination and the emergence of a competitive party system has had a trickle down effect on local politics, especially with direct elections to local bodies. With the epicentre of politics shifting to the states, local issues have tended to influence citizen/voter choice and preference.[33] Even though at the national level the number of political parties competing for power may have registered a sharp increase, at the constituency/local level the competition is essentially bi-polar or at the most tri-polar. A significantly low rate of seat retention in the Lok Sabha and Assembly elections has resulted in the electoral battle at the constituency/local level assuming tremendous significance.[34] A survey conducted at the time of the local body elections in Karnataka in 1994–95, reveals that though the Gram Panchayat (lowest tier) elections were conducted on a non-party basis, only 7 per cent of the elected representatives were independents. Those who contest elections today, no longer hide their political affiliations.[35]

In spite of the above changes, political parties have not attempted to capitalise on these developments to build a strong grassroot support base. Little or no initiative has been taken, either by the party leadership or the party workers, to make use of the opportunities that are now emerging, to strengthen the forces of internal democracy in political parties. Two recent studies point to the nature and extent of internal democracy in parties and its impact on local politics. A study conducted by Lok Satta in Andhra Pradesh reveals that in none of the four major political parties in the state—Telugu Desam, Congress, the Communist Party of India (Marxist) (CPI [M]) and the Bharatiya Janata Party (BJP)—is there a genuine democratic process for choosing candidates for local body elections. In all cases, the local Member of the Legislative

---

[33] The National Election Studies, 1996, 1998 and 1999 have highlighted the fact that local issues have tended to dominate in the elections. Yogendra Yadav, 'India's Third Electoral System', *Economic and Political Weekly*, 35:34–35, 1999, pp. 2394–95.

[34] In the 1998 Lok Sabha elections, while the effective number of parties at the national level was around seven, at the constituency level it was around three. Ibid., pp. 2394–95.

[35] K. Subha, *Karnataka Panchayat Elections*, New Delhi: Concept, 1997, p. 65.

Assembly (MLA)/Member of Parliament (MP) played a decisive role.[36] A similar study conducted in Karnataka reveals that in the strongholds of both the Congress and the BJP, the grassroot party workers were rarely involved in the process of choosing candidates for local elections and the local MLAs/MPs had a major say in the decision.[37] It is also surprising therefore, that the biographical sketches of 156 of the 224 legislators elected in 1999 (to the Karnataka Legislative Assembly), make no mention of their being elected to or participating in elected local bodies prior to their becoming legislators.

Local initiative is further undermined, with MPs and MLAs being made ex-officio members of panchayati raj institutions. As a result, they tend to dominate the proceedings and prevent the local voice from asserting itself. In Karnataka, given the role that the ex-officio members played during the election of the Adhyaksha (Chairperson) of the Zilla Panchayat, the elected members threatened to resign in protest forcing the state government to amend the law. Though the state legislators and MPs from a district continue to be voting members of panchayats, they are now not allowed to vote when the Adhyaksha is to be elected or a motion of no-confidence against the Adhyaksha is being considered.

Yet another indicator of the approach of some of the political parties to the empowerment of local governments is the proposal initiated by them to amend

---

[36] The study revealed that in all the four parties there was no formal mechanism for securing public opinion/party workers' opinion on candidates. *Lok Satta*, Hyderabad: Lok Satta Publications, 1999.

Congress (I): As far as selection of candidates to local bodies and other representatives bodies is concerned, there is no procedure for taking opinion of their own party members by the leaders. It is the local senior leaders along with the MLAs who choose the party candidates for election to local bodies.

Telugu Desam Party: As far as selection of candidates to elected public office in TDP is concerned, the senior party functionaries along with the MLA decide the candidates for local bodies.

BJP: As far as the election of candidates to public office are concerned it is the senior level leaders along with MLAs who chose the party candidates for election to the local bodies which are to be finally approved by the State Election Committee.

CPI (M): As far as selection of candidates for public office is concerned, units of the party are consulted. But there is a unanimous mode of choice of the party candidates decided by the district leadership for the local bodies.

[37] Researchers in the Department of Political Science, Bangalore University, conducted the study on the eve of the 1999 Lok Sabha elections. Two Lok Sabha constituencies, one a strong hold of the Congress (Kolar) and the other a stronghold of the BJP (Bangalore South) were selected for the study. The researchers interviewed party workers and office bearers in the district/*taluk* and ward offices. In the case of both parties, the party workers admitted that they were informed of the party choice of candidates (and asked to work for their success) and had little role to play in deciding who the candidate would be. Party workers also conceded that the prospective candidates had to secure the support of the local MLA in order to secure the party ticket. Sandeep Shastri, 'Parties Lack Internal Democracy', *Deccan Herald*, 12 July 1999.

the constitutional provisions relating to local government structures. The proposed constitutional amendment bill seeks to empower state legislatures to decide on the mode of election of members and chairpersons of the block- and district-level Panchayati Raj institutions. The implications of such an amendment would be far reaching. If implemented, it could result in indirect elections to or exclusively ex-officio membership in block- and district-level local bodies. Such a change would run counter to the original intentions of the 73rd and 74th Amendments and would seriously erode local government autonomy and initiative. Political parties would largely welcome this move as it would provide them direct access to manipulating and managing power at the local government level, given the near absence of internal democracy and the high level of centralisation in most of them. It is important to note that besides the BJP, important regional parties like the Telugu Desam, Akali Dal, Dravida Munnetra Kazhagam (DMK) and Indian National Lok Dal all favour the proposed amendment. Such an amendment eminently suits the interests of regional parties, whose power centre is located at the state capital and any move towards indirect elections to block- and district-level local bodies will further empower the party leadership. Such an amendment would be favoured by most political parties, as it would permit them to exercise greater control over local governments as decision-making on local issues would not be on the basis of deliberations at the local bodies, but the preference of those holding important positions in the political party hierarchy.

Party competition at the state level having an impact on the nature and direction of local government politics was clearly evident in recent developments in Kerala. The decision of the government to legislate on banning defections in local bodies, when viewed in isolation, can be commended as a step in the right direction to arrest floor crossing in local bodies. However, in reality, the anti-defection reform was introduced in view of the intense rivalry between the Left Democratic Front (LDF) and United Democratic Front (UDF) percolating down to the local body level. This is clearly evident from the stand adopted by the different political parties on the reform measure. While the opposition welcomes the initiative, it expressed its serious reservations on the true intent of the ruling alliance.[38]

In recent years caste polarisation at the local and state level has played a critical role in determining the composition of both local and state-level elected bodies. With provisions having been made for reservations for non-dominant backward castes in local bodies in most states, these sections are today represented in significant numbers in the local bodies. However, in the State Legislative Assemblies the dominant castes continue to retain control. Karnataka is chosen as an example to illustrate this point. The caste background of the members of the State Assembly and Panchayat bodies are mentioned in

---

[38] *The Hindu*, 24 October 1998.

Table 16.1. In the local bodies, the dominant castes in the state—Vokkaligas and Lingayats (who account for 36 per cent of the state's population)—account for one-third of the members. However, in the State Legislative Assembly they constitute more than half the members. On the other hand, the non-dominant backward castes (around one-third of the state population), account for 37 per cent of the members of the local bodies and less than 22 per cent of the members of the State Legislative Assembly. While in the local bodies, the non-dominant backward castes have been accorded fair representation, they continue to be grossly under-represented in the crucial State Legislature and in the state council of ministers,[39] where the dominant castes continue to be the majority.

Thus, an analysis of recent trends with regard to the interface between local democracies and political parties clearly demonstrates the fact that political parties have not been in a position to benefit from the political empowerment that local bodies have an opportunity to benefit from. In the process, they have also contributed to preventing the local bodies from developing to their fullest potential. Federal systems which have been witness to an overcentralisation of power (like India), have, as a natural and inevitable consequence, had local governments which have limited autonomy and very

Table 16.1: Representation to Different Castes in Karnataka Legislative Assembly and Local Bodies

Caste	Percentage of State Population	Percentage of Seats Won in the Assembly (1994)	Percentage of Seats Won in the Local Bodies (1994–95)
Lingayat	15.3	28.57	17.0
Vokkaliga	10.8	24.11	16.0
Brahmin	3.5	4.46	2.5
Scheduled Caste	16.7	15.63	15.3
Scheduled Tribe	6.7	2.68	7.0
Kuruba	3.6	4.46	7.5
Other OBC's	29.1	17.41	29.5
Minority	14.3	2.68	5.2
	100.00	100.00	100.00

Source: For Legislature: Shastri, *Towards Explaining the Voters Mandate*, Bangalore: Vinayaka, 1994, pp. 54–57; Shastri, 'Twilight of Congress Hegemony: Emergence of a Bi-Polar Alliance System is Karnataka', *Economic and Political Weekly*, Aug-Sept 1999, 34: 34–35, pp. 2440–48. For Local Bodies: Subha. K., *Karnataka Panchayat Elections 1995*, New Delhi: Concept, 1997: 71.

---

[39] See R.L.M. Patil and Sandeep Shastri, 'Administrative Acumen Should Determine Composition of the Ministry', *The Indian Express*, 21 July 1997; also Mary Latha, 'Politics of Ministry Making in Karnataka', unpublished M.Phil Dissertation submitted to the Department of Political Science, Bangalore University. Bangalore, 1994.

few opportunities for translating into reality the autonomy guaranteed to them. In the first place, local government institutions get a raw deal in the conflict for power and jurisdiction between the central and state governments. Second, the state governments which have been already rendered more or less powerless by the Centre, obsessively hold on to whatever limited power they continue to enjoy, refusing to share the same with the local authorities. A linked development is the nature of the party system in India. The 'culture of centralisation' which dictates the nature and dynamics of the federal system appears to have become the defining character of the party system. Given the absence of internal democracy in parties and the increasing importance of the party leadership in decision making, the meaning empowerment of local authorities remains unfulfilled and limited success has been achieved in realising the lofty goals as enshrined in the constitution.

ABOUT THE EDITORS AND CONTRIBUTORS

The Editors

Dr Ajay K. Mehra is Director (Honorary), Centre for Public Affairs. He teaches Indian politics at the Shaheed Bhagat Singh College (Eve.), University of Delhi. A keen student of processes and institutions in Indian politics, his research areas include national security issues, politics of urbanisation and institutions and issues in Indian politics. A prolific writer, he has authored two books, co-authored three, contributed chapters to several books and scholarly papers to journals. He is a regular contributor to Indian media on issues of public affairs.

Prof. D.D. Khanna, former Professor and Head, Department of Defence and Strategic Studies, University of Allahabad is currently Director, Society for Peace, Security and Development Studies, Allahabad. He has authored and edited several books and contributed to journals on security and development problems related to South Asian countries.

Prof. Gert W. Kueck is the Resident Representative of the Konrad Adenauer Foundation (Germany) to India. He has specialised in international and developmental economics and political affairs. He has specialised in international conferences, many of them within the framework of the United Nations, has authored books and contributed to journals, particularly related to North–South and South–South relations.

The Contributors

Prof. Balveer Arora is currently Rector, Jawaharlal Nehru University, New Delhi. He teaches government and politics at the Centre for Political Studies. He obtained his doctorate from the University of Paris I Pantheon-Sorbonne. He has held visiting assignments at the Institut d'Edudes Politiques and the Maison des Sciences de l'Homme in Paris, and at the Centre for the Advanced Study of India, University of Pennsylvania. He has written extensively on India's federal institutions and processes of centre–state relations. He is currently working on the impact of coalitions on federal governance.

Prof. Bidyut Chakrabarty teaches in the Department of Political Science, University of Delhi.

Prof. S.K. Chaube retired as Professor of Indian politics in the Department of Political Science, University of Delhi after 45 years in teaching and research. He has authored *Constituent Assembly of India: Springboard of Revolution, Hill Politics in Northeast India, Politics and Constitution in China, Colonialism, Freedom Struggle and Nationalism in India*, besides contributing more than a 100 articles in periodicals and newspapers home and abroad. He is at present a Fellow in the Lok Sabha Secretariat.

Pran Chopra is a senior journalist. At various times, he was Visiting Professor at the Centre for Policy Research, New Delhi; Editorial Director of the Press Foundation of Asia; and Chief Editor of The Statesman of Calcutta and New Delhi.

Muchkund Dubey is a retired career diplomat. Currently he is President of the Council for Social Development, New Delhi.

Dr Partha S. Ghosh is currently a Director at the Indian Council of Social Science Research, New Delhi, was earlier a Visiting Fellow at the Centre for Policy Research, New Delhi, a Humboldt Fellow at the South Asia Institute of the Heidelberg University, Germany, and a Ford Visiting Scholar in the Program in Arms Control, Disarmament and International Security (ACDIS) at the University of Illinois at Urbana-Champaign, USA. He has many publications to his credit. His latest book is: *BJP and the Evolution of Hindu Nationalism* (1999). He is also associated with the Centre for Public Affairs.

Dr Madhav Godbole, a Ph.D. in Industrial Economics, is a civil servant. He was Union Home Secretary before he took voluntary retirement in 1993. He was the chairman of the energy review committee on Enron power generation project and power sector reforms and also of the renegotiation committee on Enron project appointed by the Government of Maharashtra. *Unfinished Innings—Recollections and Reflections of a Civil Servant,* and *The Changing Times—A Commentary on Current Affairs* latest of the nine books he has authored in English and Marathi. He was given Chinmulgund Public Administration Award and Dr M. Visvesvaraya Memorial Lifetime Achievement Award.

Dr Harish Khare, a Ph.D. in Political Science from Yale is Associate Editor, *The Hindu,* based in New Delhi. He has written extensively on political institutions and specialises in the Congress Party affairs.

Prof. Karl-Rudolf Korte, is Professor of Political Science at the University of Cologne and he is Director of the Research Group on German Affairs at the Center for Applied Policy Research (C.A.P.) in Munich. He has authored a number of books, most recently on political leadership, political party systems and Bundestag elections. His other works focus on the politics of German unification, European integration, German and Japan foreign policy and the integration process in East Asia. His most recent book is *Aufstieg und Fall von Regierungen. Machterwerb and Machterosionen in westlichen Demokratien* (2001).

Prof. Pradeep Kumar taught Political Science at Punjab University, Chandigarh, till his sad and untimely demise in early 2002. His scholarship and research were on Indian politics with particular reference to State politics. His publications include *Studies on Indian Federalism* (1988), *The Uttarakhand Movement: Construction of a Regional Identity* (2000). He also edited two books, *Regional Political Parties* (1988) and *Some Issues in Contemporary Indian Politics* (1997), besides contributing to professional journals.

Dr Sajal Nag teaches Modern History at Assam Central University, Silchar. He is the author of *Roots of Ethnic Conflict: Nationality Question in North East India* (1990), *India and North East India: Mind, Politics and the Process of Integration 1946–50,* (1998), *Nationalism, Sepratism and Sessionism* (1999), *Rejecting India: Ethnicity, Insurgence and Nationality Question in North East India,* (2001). He is the recipient of Senior Fellowship from Nehru Memorial Museum and Library, New Delhi 2001.

Prof. Suhas Palshikar teaches at the Department of Politics and Public Administration, University of Pune. He has published in English and Marathi. His area of specialisation is political process in India. He has been associated with the series of election studies conducted by CSDS, Delhi, from 1995. Presently engaged in an extensive study of society and politics in Pune city.

Dr Amit Prakash (Ph.D., School of Oriental and African Studies, University of London) is presently Associate Professor in Law and Governance at the Jawaharlal Nehru University, New Delhi. He has authored *Jharkhand: Politics of Development of Identity* (2001), *Good Governance and Development Policies: A Comparative Study of Uttar Pradesh and Maharashtra* (to be published under the auspices of the Centre for Policy Research, New Delhi). He has published widely in national and international journals.

Dr Sandeep Shastri teaches Political Science at Bangalore University. He specialises in the area of electoral and federal studies. He is the India Coordinator of the World Values Survey Project and a Fellow of the Salzburg Seminar. He is also a Member of the Executive Board of International Political Science Association's Research Committee on Structure and Organisation of Government.

INDEX

accountability, 99

adaptability, 98, 381

Adenauer, Konrad, 103

Advani, Lal Krishna, 36, 89, 182, 197, 231, 232, 233–34, 239, 252, 255, 260, 315, 352

Africa: parliament democracy, 163

Agnivesh, Swami, 193

ahimsa, 66

Ahirs: benefited by Mandal Commission Report, 260

Ahom, home land demand for, 349

Aiyer, Subramania, 62

AJGAR, 260

Akali Dal, akalis, 28, 258, 303, 308, 313, 314, 317, 394

Akhil Bharatiya Hindu Mahasabha, *see* Hindu Mahasabha

Akhil Bharatiya Sena, 193

Alagesan, O.V., 388n

Alamati dispute, 268n

Ali, Amir, 73

All Assam Students' Union (AASU), 350, 351, 352

All India Anna Dravida Munnetra Kazhagam (AIADMK), 154, 273, 302, 308, 313, 317–19

All India Congress Committee (AICC), *see* Indian National Congress

All India Forward Bloc, *see* Forward Bloc

All India Kisan Sabha, *see* Kisan Sabha

All India Trade Union Congress (AITUC), 77, 218

All India Worker's and Peasant's Party (AIWPP), 77

All Party Hill Leaders Conference (APHLC), 349, 358–59

allegiance, 236

alternative voting system, 170

Ambedkar, B.R., 88n, 215, 387–88

ambiguity, 185

Amsterdam Treaty, 128

Anand, A.S., 209

Anandpur sahib resolution, 365

Andaman Nicobar: cultural dimension of state reorganisation, 340

Andhra Mahasabha, 341

Andhra Pradesh, 307, 332, 364; cultural dimension of state reorganisation, 340; dominant caste groups, 300; Indira Gandhi's confrontational politics, 33; land reforms, 66; lingual assertion, 154; non-Congress governments, 249; regional parties, 311, 313, 316, 324–26, 333; sub-national assertions, 153; *see also* Telugu Desam Party

Angami, T.N., 359, 360

Angamis, 360

Anglophiles, 163

animism, 340

Annadurai, C.M., 31

anti-colonialism, 49, 58, 152

anti-Defection Act, 94, 168, 178, 196, 389

anti-poverty programmes, 285

antiquity with continuity, 288–89

anti-Sikh riots, 33, 230

antyodaya, 230

Aos, 360

Arunachal Congress, 361

Arunachal Pradesh, 363; upgraded to statehood, 360;—categorised as a small state, 338

Arya Samaj, 79

Asom Gana Parishad (AGP), 250, 257, 302, 306, 308, 313, 351–53, 365

Asom Jatiya Mahasangha, 344

Asom Jatiyabadi Dal (AJD), 350–51
Assam Accord, 33, 350, 351
Assam Association, 341
Assam Gana Sangram Parishad
    (AGSP), 350
Assam Pradesh Congress Committee
    (APCC), 342–43, 349, 350
Assam, Assamese, 45, 307, 363; agita-
    tion, 230; categorised as a large state,
    337–38; Congress, corrupt rule,
    352;—retained power in Assembly
    elections, 1967, 30; economic neglect,
    350; identity, 348, 350, 353; illegal
    Bengali immigrants, 341–42, 348, 349,
    352;— dominance, 342;— move-
    ment to deport, 350; Indira Gandhi's
    confrontational politics, 33; nation-
    ality, 341–43; regional parties, 316;
    sub-national assertions, 153; see also
    North East
assertiveness, 269
ASSOCHAM, 373
associations, politics, 55–59, 60, 61
Australia Club, 279
authoritarianism, 252
Autonomous District Council (ADC), 356
autonomy, 40, 94, 314, 364, 395–96
Ayodhya controversy, 36, 168, 210,
    215, 216, 217, 219, 242, 256, 260,
    270, 373; see also Babri Masjid
Ayyangar, M.A., 388n

Babri Masjid issue, 209, 216, 220, 221,
    223, 231, 234, 233, 270–71
backwardness, 260, 314
Baden-Württemberg, Germany: hold
    of Christian Democrats, 104
Bahadur, Raj, 388n
Bahujan Mahasangh (BMS),
    Maharashtra, 315
Bahujan Samaj Party (BSP), 85n, 194,
    221, 234, 266, 301, 303, 307, 309, 315,
    365; caste-based mobilisations, 142;
    rural support base, 134; voters, eco-
    nomic class of, 146–47;—educational
    level, 137;—occupation, 137, 139
Bajrang Dal, 215, 221, 231, 271

Balwantrai Mehta Committee, 389
Banerjea, Surendranath, 27, 60
Banerjee, Mamata, 297, 327
Bang Congress, 293
Bangladesh war, 228
Bansi Lal, 95n
bar on contesting more than one
    constituency, 197
Barzel, Rainer, 119
Basu, Chitta, 188
Basu, Jyoti, 34, 244n, 272
Bavarian Party (Bayern Partei [BP]),
    Germany, 102, 104, 119
Bawun-Chetri nexus, 357
behaviours, 23
Bengal British India Society, 55
Bengal, Bengal Presidency: partition,
    63, 64, 74; political activities, 56;
    renaissance, 225
Bengalis, 336; identity, 326–27; Muslims,
    341; refugees, 228; see also Assam,
    North East, Tripura
Bentinck, Lord, 52n, 54
Besant, Annie, 60
Bhagwati, 350
Bhandari, Nar Bahadur, 357
Bharatiya Janata Party (BJP), 21–22, 32,
    33, 34, 35, 36, 37, 39, 40, 42, 43, 45,
    46, 79n, 87, 89, 151n, 194, 209, 216–
    17, 219, 244–46, 249, 250, 255, 257–
    59, 262, 263, 264, 266, 267, 268, 269,
    271, 274–75, 284–85, 296, 309, 310,
    316, 319, 321, 323, 320, 326–27, 328,
    329–31, 332, 335, 352, 370–71, 379,
    380, 382, 392–93; caste-based
    mobilisation, 142–43; Chennai
    declaration, 98, 370–72; consolida-
    tion drive, 232–34; economic class
    of voters, 146–49; educational level
    of voters, 135–37; gender-based
    mobilisation, 131–32; occupation of
    voters, 137–40; positive evolution
    of coalition politics, 92–93, 247–48,
    250–51; pro-Sc stand, 238; religion of
    voters, 144–45; urban versus rural
    support base, 132–34, 137; see also
    National Democratic alliance (NDA)

Bharatiya Jan Sangh (BJS), 28, 32, 35, 42, 79, 81, 89, 225, 228, 229, 236, 241, 244, 295, 353

Bharatiya Lok Dal, *see* Lok Dal

Bhave, Vinoba, 210

Bhils: socio-religious movements, 152

Bhujbal, Chhagan, 209

Bhutiyas, 346, 357

Bidwai, Praful, 272*n*

Biedenkopf, Kurt, 119–20

Bihar, 42, 258, 297, 301, 307, 332, 363; caste identity, 159; caste war, 281; coalition government, 250; Congress lost Assembly elections, 1967, 30; Hindu factor, 224; land reforms, 66; leftist politics, 153; non-Congress governments, 249; regional parties, 311, 316, 320–22, 333; reservations for OBCs, 259*n*; *see also* Rashtriya Janata Dal, Yadav Laloo Prasad

Biju Janata Dal (BJD), Orissa, 301, 319–20, 328

BIMARU (Bihar, Madhya Pradesh, Rajasthan and Uttar Pradesh), 199, 203

bi-nodal party system, 42, 43, 84

bio-diversity, 277

black money, role in Indian political system, 187

Blavstsky, Madame, 60

Bodo, Thaneshwar, 351

Bodoland movement, 154, 365

Bodos, 351

Bofors scandal, 207, 233

Bolshevik revolution, 215

Bombay Presidency Association, 55, 61

Bombay Presidency: social and political activities, 55

Bommai, S.R., 266

Bongal Kheda, 346

Bonn Republic, Germany: role of political parties, 100

Bonnerjee, N.C., 62

booth-capturing, 183, 221, 298

Bordoloi, Gopinath, 342

Bose, Subhash Chandra, 27, 71, 72

Bosu, Jyotirmoy, 188

bourgeois, bourgeoisie, 78, 218, 236

Brahmanical order, 238

Brahmo Samaj, 26, 54

Brandenburg, Germany: hold of Social Democratic Party, 104

British India Society, 54

British Indian Association, 54, 55, 56–57

British Labour Party, 219

British Liberal Party, 210–11, 217

British: colonial power and imperialism, 24, 175, 224; political divisions in terms of class, 210; politics, 211–12; trade union, 217

Buddhism, 226

Bundesrat (the first chamber of the German Parliament), 102, 108

Bundestag (Federal Council, the second chamber of the German Parliament), 102, 103, 104, 105, 106, 107, 112, 119

Bundestagswahl, 106–8

bureaucracy, 215, 219, 241, 367, 372, 374–75

Burman, Upendranath, 388*n*

Cabinet Mission Plan, 76, 342–43

Cachar, 342; Bengali immigration, 343

candidates: number of children, 202; with criminal records, 193–95; independent, 196; minimum educational qualification for, 201–2; non-serious, 196–97; socio-economic background, 215

capitalism, 49, 334, 341

caretaker government in the period leading to elections, 198–99

Carstens, Karl, 119

caste, caste-based political mobilisations, polarisation, 29, 45, 85, 88, 89, 141–43, 149, 154, 176, 214, 218, 219, 245, 248, 266, 280, 283, 299–300, 315, 329–30, 357, 389, 394–95; groups, 301–2; hierarchy, 35; identity, 159

catch-all–parties' *see Volksparteien*

Catholic Centre Party, Germany, 103

Catholics, 105

Cauvery dispute, 268*n*

Cawasjee, Framjee, 50n
Census, 1971, 199
Central Board of Direct Taxes (CBDT),
190
Central Bureau of Investigation (CBI),
167, 269
Central Intelligence Agency (CIA),
United States of America, 188
centralism, 215
Centre for Media Studies, 204
Centre–state relations, 331
Chagla, M.C., 187
Chakma issue, 360, 361
Chakraborty, Nripen, 355
Chaliha, 350
Chamling, Pawan Kumar, 357
Chandrashekhar, 34, 244n, 252, 253,
255, 261, 265, 307
Charan Singh, 32, 188, 256, 300
charismatic leadership, 332
Chatterjee, Somnath, 182
Chautala, Om Prakash, 183, 254–55
Chavan, Y.B., 187
Chawla, Amarnath, 193
Chennai Declaration, 98, 370–72
Chenoy, Anuradha, 272n
Chhattisgarh Mukti Morcha (CMM),
314
Chhattisgarh, 42, 337n, 365; chief-
ministerial issue, 241; Hindu
factor, 224
Chogyal, Namgyal, 347, 357
Chola Empire, 224
Chhotanagpur, 52n
Christian Democratic Union
(Christlich Demokratische Union)
[CDU], Germany, 102, 103, 104,
105, 106, 107, 108, 109, 111, 112–13,
115, 117, 121; revitalisation, 118–20
Christian social values, 114, 116
Christian Socialist Union (Christlich
Soziale Union) [CSU], Germany,
102, 103, 104, 105, 107, 108, 109
Christians, 42, 224, 237–78, 240; ‹
electoral support, 145; violence
against, 215, 221, 223
Churchill, Winston, 212

citizen rights, violation, 216
citizens' panel, 195
citizenship, 214
Civil Disobedience movement, 66, 67,
78, 163
civil society, 40, 41, 210–11, 219–20,
372; collousness, 212; and the
Constitution of India, 221–22
civilisational values, 41
class mobilisations, 21, 34, 35, 89, 176,
217, 248, 299
coalescence, 23, 27, 46
coalition government, coalition politics,
22, 23, 31, 37, 40, 42, 43, 92, 93, 96, 97,
172, 174, 175, 179, 180, 232, 235, 249,
251, 264, 266, 272, 274, 283, 287, 294,
301, 304, 306, 329; in Germany, 112
cohesion, 112, 271, 290
collaboration, 26
colonial discourse and the nationalists,
155–59
colonialism, 49–50, 52
commitment, 272, 274, 386
Committee on State Funding of
Elections (Indrajit Gupta Committee), 191
Common Cause, 189, 190
communal leaning, 286
communalism, communal nationalism, 88, 225, 231, 287, 330, 388
communion, 33
communism in Germany, 112
Communist movement, 76–77, 172
Communist Party of Germany
(Kommunistische Partie
Deutschlands [KPD]), Federal
Republic of Germany, 101, 103
Communist Party of Great Britain, 77
Communist Party of India (CPI), 28, 70,
76–78, 81, 215, 240, 252, 257, 270, 271,
279–84, 286, 301, 307, 346, 349, 353
Communist Party of India (Marxist)
(CPM), 34, 43, 84n, 95, 191, 244, 246,
249n, 250, 252, 258, 262, 263, 265, 266–
68, 270, 271, 272, 273, 279, 281, 282,
283, 284, 286, 301, 307, 352, 353–56,
359, 363, 365, 366, 392, 393n, 394

communities, 89, 214, 218, 315
community consideration, 283
community development movement,
    389
competition, competing framework of
    politics, 83, 329–31, 366, 368, 382, 392
Comprehensive Test Ban Treaty
    (CTBT), 279, 282
Confederation of Indian Industry
    (CII), 373
conflicts, conflicting interests, 27, 46,
    368, 382
Congress, Congress (I), 21, 26, 27,
    28–29, 32, 33, 34, 37, 40, 42, 43, 44,
    45, 47, 50–51, 54, 56, 58–68, 69,
    70–73, 77–79, 81, 92, 95, 129, 207,
    215, 216–17, 218, 219, 244–46, 255,
    257–59, 262, 268, 269, 274–75, 279,
    281, 282–84, 285, 304n, 328, 335,
    336–37, 342, 346, 347, 353, 355, 368,
    378, 381, 382, 387, 393; Allahabad
    Session, 1888, 73; in Arunachal
    Pradesh, 360; in Assam, 354,
    356–57, 363; Bangalore resolution,
    1951, 46; Bangalore session, 2001,
    98, 380; bourgeois, 78; bungling the
    tribal issues, 349–50; caste-based
    mobilisation, 142–43; centralisation,
    94; decline and degeneration,
    loosing power, 39, 41, 87, 88, 151,
    173, 174, 208, 235, 245, 247–49, 263,
    264, 274, 306, 329–31, 372;
    deinstitutionalisation, 32;
    destablished governments at
    Centre, 179; dominance, 29, 85, 88,
    151, 171, 173, 174–76, 264, 294, 295,
    300, 389–90; election manifesto,
    1951, 368–69;—1999, 386;
    federalisation, 292–93; Gaya
    session, 1922, 68 ; gender-based
    mobilisation, 131; hegemony, 252;
    in Hill states, 341, 358–62; role in
    independence, 60, 174;
    institutionalisation, 24–25, 27;
    Karachi Session, 70; Lahore
    session, 1929, 67; in Manipur, 361;
    mass movement, 64; in Mizoram,

362; and Muslims, 74–75, 238–39;
    Nagpur session, 337; preeminence,
    227–28; poor governance, 98;
    power struggle, 31; Ramgarh
    Session, 1939, 71; received dona-
    tions from abroad for election,
    188–89; regional factions, 297–302;
    social base, 66; split, 30, 64; and the
    state reorganisation, 341–44, 348;
    Surat session, 1906, 64; Tripura
    Session, 71, 72; urban versus rural
    support base, 132–33; voters,
    economic class, 146–48;—educa-
    tional level, 135–37;—occupation,
    138–40;—religion, 144–45; in west
    Bengal, 326
Congress (O), 295
Congress (R), 304n
Congress (S), 252, 296
Congress for Democracy, 295, 355
Congress Socialist Party, 27, 69–72
conscience vote, 94
consensus, 168, 213, 217, 274, 379, 390
conservatism, 79
Conservative Party, United Kingdom,
    212
constituencies, size, discrepancy, 200
Constituent Assembly of India, 215,
    305, 387–88
Constitution of India, 21, 28, 37, 158, 165,
    183–84, 198–99, 201, 206, 207, 210, 213,
    221–22, 230, 265, 294, 305, 357, 386,
    387–89; 42nd Amendment, 1976, 199;
    64th and 65th Amendment, 391; 73rd
    and 74th Amendment, 22, 24, 37, 99,
    277, 384–85, 391–92, 394; Directive
    Principles of State Policy, 219
convenience versus democracy, 169–71
convergence, 39, 69, 217; in European
    Union, 127
conversions, 239
cooperation, 23, 283, 368
corruption, 98, 270, 274, 282–83, 287, 357
Cow Belt, 224
cow slaughter issue, 228, 231, 242
crime, politicisation, criminals in
    politics, 41, 182, 193, 282

cronyism, 285
cross-voting, 211, 212
crystallisation process, 22, 25, 143, 290
cultural identity and nationalism, 227, 302, 336
cultural imperialism, 278
Curzon, Lord, 63

dalit, 42, 43, 285, 298, 301, 328, 334; *see also* caste, other backward classes
Damodar Swarup, 388*n*
Dangs: socio-religious movements, 152
Das, Chita Ranjan, 68
decentralisation, 97
decision-making process, 278, 370, 385, 392, 396; citizen participation, 387
decolonisation, 50
decriminalising Indian politics, 193–96
deflection, 46
delegitimation, 98
democracy, democratic institutions, 26, 41, 46, 64, 67, 82, 92, 94, 99, 101, 162–64, 198; commitment, 168; erosion, 277; governance, 196; in Germany, 116, 121; intra party, 98; and market, 382; massification, 292; mockery of 206; Muslim vote bank, 298; three-tier system, 165
Democratic Party of Nagaland (DPN), 359
democratisation process, 37, 45, 297, 330, 331–32, 385; in European Union, 125–26
Deora, Murali S., 377
Derozio, Henry, 53
Desai, Morarji, 224, 251, 296
Deshmukh, P.S., 388*n*
despotism, 215
Dev, Narendra, *see* Narendra Dev, Acharya
Deve Gowda, H.D., 224, 244*n*, 257, 258, 264*n*, 265, 296
development, de-bureaucratisation, 371; process and socio-economic considerations, 152
Development Block Councils, 280
Devi Lal, 253, 254–55, 259, 265

Dhodia: socio-religious movements, 152
Dhulekar, R.V., 388*n*
Dimasas, 351
Direct Taxes Enquiry Committee, 187
disagreements, 366
disintegration, 85
dislocations, political costs, 378
disorder, 84
disputes, 366
dissatisfaction, 366
distrust, 366, 372
diversity, 162–63, 174–76, 288, 291
domestic savings, 276
dominance, domination, 84, 86–87, 335
Dorzee, Kazi Lendup, 347
Dravida identity, 315
Dravida Munnetra Kazhagam (DMK), 31, 34, 88*n*, 154, 252, 257, 264*n*, 273, 287, 296, 297, 302, 306, 308, 313, 314, 317–19, 388, 365, 394
duality role, 335
Dubey, Muchkund, 272*n*
Dunn, Mrs, 348
Dutt, Rajani Palme, 77
dynamism, 41, 117

East India Company, 26, 51–52, 54*n*, 55
Eastern India Tribal Union, 349
economic: class of voters, 146–50; crisis, 1991–92, 275, 369; inequalities, 180; reforms, 284; restructuring, 335
education, educational: and the franchise, 162–63; level of voters, 135–37; and proliferating societies, linkage, 56–57; qualification for contestants, 201–2; western style, 52–53
Election Commission (EC), 37, 94–96, 129, 169, 171, 183–85, 195, 201, 205–6, 207, 262, 265, 301
elections, electoral, electorate, 172; base, erosion in Germany, 108; equality, incongruity, 166; expenditure, ceiling, 187;—government, 181;—should be made public, 192;—unaccounted, 187; fragmentation, 171; funding, 186–93;—

business and industry, funding for elections, 190;—private, 169;—state, 169, 191–92, 197, 213; increasing frequency, implications, 181; malpractices, 183, 198; manifesto, source of power, 215–16; petitions, 200–201; purity and integrity, 192, 196; reforms, 187;—neglect in, 182–83; results and socio-political reality, nexus, 172; rising cost, 41; socialism, 298; system, credibility, 196; see also general elections
Election Symbols (Reservation and Allotment) Order, 1968, 95
Elphinston Institution, 54
emancipation, 345
Emergency, 31, 33, 43, 173, 253, 294
empowerment, 47, 395, 396
English education in India, 52, 53n
English Utilitarianism, 156
Enlightenment, 156
equality before law, 217
Eskimo, 291
ethno-cultural plurality, 336
Eucken, 115
Europe: liberalisation, 381; market transition, 377
European Democratic Alliance, 125
European Integration, party for, 115–16
European Parliament (EP), 122–23, 126, 128; party system, 124
European People's Party (EPP), 123, 124–25, 126, 127
European Union, 21, 22; emerging party system, 39
Europeanisation, 113
exaggeration, 171
exit polls, 165, 204–6, 234

FICCI, 373
factionalism, 36, 94, 98, 172, 242
Fait accompli, 260
'false consciousness', 215
Faraizi movement, 52n
Farraka Agreement, 282–83

Federal Republic of Germany (FRG), see Germany
federalism, federal structure, 37, 92, 277, 288–89, 294, 302; cultural dimension, 339
federalisation, 47, 286, 287; of political parties, 36–37, 40, 41
first-past-the-post vs list system, 202
fiscal deficit, 370
fiscal reforms, 367
flexibility, 92, 98, 248n
fodder scam case, 258
Foreign Contribution Regulation Act (FCRA), 188–89
foreign money in election funding, 188–90
Foreign National Movement, 350
foreign policy, 281
Forward Block (FB), 27, 72, 307
Forza Europa, 127
fragmentation, 23, 37, 41, 85, 94, 99, 129, 154, 161
Free Democratic Party (Freie Demokratische Partei [FDP]), Germany, 102, 103, 104, 105, 106, 107; as a role model, 120–21
freedom, 222
freedom movement, peasants' role, 218

Gadak Y.K. vs Balasaheb Vikhe Patil, 187
Gamit: socio-religious movements, 152
Gana Mukti Parishad (GMP), 354, 355
Ganatantra Parishad, Orissa, 313
Gandhi, Indira, 30–33, 44, 72, 97, 151, 173, 188, 194, 197, 214–15, 228, 229, 231, 237, 244, 253, 256, 264, 304, 350, 355, 372; assassination, 230
Gandhi, M.K., 65–68, 69, 70, 72, 163, 166, 174, 216, 219, 225, 226, 342–43, 387; assassination, 67
Gandhi, Rajiv, 32, 33, 184, 207, 233, 245, 252, 253, 270, 332, 372, 376, 391; assassination, 34, 35
Gandhi, Sanjay, 253
Gandhi, Sonia, 34, 169, 197, 240, 243, 267n, 302, 332
Gandhian movement, 219, 230

Gandhians, 162–63
Gandhi-Irwin Pact (1931), 70
Garos, 358
Gates, Bill, 375
Gawli, Arun, 193
Geißler, Heiner, 120
gender: distinction, 35; the support
    base of political parties, 131–32
general elections, 227; 1st (1952), 28, 173,
    346; 2nd (1957), 173; 3rd(1962), 354;
    4th (1967), 30; 5th (1971), 244, 294,
    304, 354, 355; 6th (1977), 173–74, 308;
    7th, 308; 8th (1984), 173, 295; 9th
    (1989), 181, 245, 256, 266, 295; 10th
    (1991), 36; 11th (1996), 21, 36, 39, 130n,
    131–36, 138–40, 142, 144–45, 146–49,
    150, 174, 196, 235, 245, 256, 264, 304,
    309;—candidates with criminal
    records, 194;—number of candidates
    contested, 171;—manifesto, 279;—
    regional formations, 295; 12th (1998),
    21, 22, 36, 89, 130n 131–34, 136, 138–
    40, 142, 144–45, 147–49, 150, 174, 196,
    235, 264;—candidates with criminal
    records, 193;—average expenditure
    of a candidate, 187;—voters, 181;
    13th (1999), 21, 22, 39, 85, 89, 96, 130n,
    132–34, 143, 149, 174, 181, 235, 266;—
    average expenditure of a candidate,
    187;—malpractices, 183
'general will', 216
geographical factors, 227
German Democratic Republic, see
    Germany
German Party (Deutsche Partei [DP]),
    Germany, 103
German People's Union (Deutsche
    Volksunion [DVU]), 104, 107
Germany, 21, 22, 106, 213; basic law,
    38, 41, 101, 103, 207; citizen rights
    movement, 105; Constitutional
    Court ruling, 1952 and 1956, 103;
    electoral system, effect on party
    system, 106–8; Federal Constitu-
    tional Court, 38; government and
    the 1998 Parliamentary Election
    (Bundetagswah), 106–8; party funds

scandal, 117–18; party system struc-
    ture, 41, 102–6; peace movement,
    104; political parties, 38; Political Party
    Act, 1967, 38, 102; political system,
    100–101, 214; reunification, 103, 104,
    106, 107, 109, 114
Gestation (period), 51
Ghosh, A.K., 388n
Gill, M.S., 204
globalisation and liberalisation, 46,
    113, 114, 248n, 270, 271, 280, 282,
    284, 286–87, 333–34, 366–67, 371,
    375, 376, 381–83; irreversibility, 374
Godesberg Reforms, Germany, 105
Gokhale, Gopal Krishna, 65
Golpara, Assam: demand for a
    Kamata State, 349
Golwalkar, M.S., 80, 227
Gorkha National Liberation Front
    (GNLF), 152
Gorkhaland, demand for, 365
Goswami Committee on Electoral
    Reforms (1990), 182, 185, 191
governance, 174–76, 178, 180, 239,
    248; disorder, 96; unaccountability,
    277–78
Government of India Act, 1919, 76
Govindacharya, K.N., 238
Greens, Germany, 104, 105–6, 107, 121
group mobility, 366
Group of 15 (G-15), 279
Gujarat, 364; cultural dimension of state
    reorganisation, 340; dominant caste
    groups, 300; factionalism, 242; land
    reforms, 66; regional parties, 310;
    socio-religious movements, 152
Gujarat Sabha, 341
Gujars, benefited by Mandal Commis-
    sion report, 260
Gujral, I.K., 188, 244n, 258, 265, 272n
Gupta, Indrajit, 191, 272n
Gupta, Kanwar Lal, 188
Guptas, 224
Gurung, D.B., 347

Hamburg, Germany: hold of social
    democratic party, 104

Hanumanthaiah, K., 388n
Hare, David, 53
Harit Pradesh, movement for
    independent state, 337n
Haryana, 42, 332; categorised as a large
    state, 338; Congress retained power
    in Assembly elections, 1967, 30;
    dominant caste groups, 300; Hindu
    factor, 224; regional parties, 311, 333
Haryana Vikas Party (HVP), 95n
Hastings, Warren, 51
Hedgewar, Keshav Baliram, 80
Hegde, Rama Krishna, 95n
hegemony, 356
Hessen, Germany: hold of Christian
    Democrats, 104
heterogeneous society, 26, 31
Hill State Peoples Democratic Party
    (HSPDP), 358–59
Hills Union, 348
Himachal Pradesh, 42, 233; BJP
    government, 234–35; Congress
    government, 234; Hindu factor, 224
Hindi speaking belt, 339, 365; the BJS
    platform, 228
Hindu, Hindus, Hinduism, 42, 54, 73,
    151n, 216, 218, 224, 226, 227, 228,
    232, 236, 339; chauvinism, 33;
    communalism, 329; majoritarian
    view, 271; nationalism, 43, 225, 226,
    229; orthodoxy, 172, 176; 'right'
    consolidation, 36; sectarian parties,
    28; traditionalist, 226; vote bank,
    144, 230–31, 233; see also Hindutva
Hindu Code Bill, 219
Hindu College, 53, 55
Hindu Jagran Manch, 221
Hindu Mahasabha, 28, 79, 80, 81, 226,
Hinduja, S.P., 189
Hindutva, Hindutva ideology, 215, 217,
    220, 226, 230, 231, 234–35, 250, 257,
    271, 301, 314, 334; limits of, 237–39
Hispanic, 291
Hitler, 78
homogeneous community, 256; India
    lacked, 163
hostility, 372

human rights movement, 223
Hume, Allan Octavian, 25, 60, 61, 62, 74n
hypercentralisation, 385

identities, identity questions, 314,
    341–45, 363; articulation, 151–55,
    159–61; formation and party
    formation, 341
ideological consistency, 98
ideological orientation, 239
Illegal Migrant Detection Tribunal
    (IMDT) Act, 1983, 351–52
illiteracy and the electorate, 173
Imperial Legislative Council, 65
imperialism, 51, 52
incoherence, 94, 215
Income Tax Act, 189, 190, 192
Income Tax Department, 189
independent candidates, see candidates
India Economic Summit, 373–74
Indian Association, Calcutta, 27, 56–57,
    59, 60–61, 62n
Indian League, 56
Indian National Congress (INC), see
    Congress
Indian National Trade Union Con-
    gress (INTUC), 215
Indian Penal Code (IPC), 195, 197
Indian Union Muslim League, 219,
    227, 308
Indrajit Gupta Committee on State
    Funding of Elections, see Commit-
    tee on State Funding of Elections
industrial capitalism, 217
industrialisation, 159, 289, 299
inefficiency, 274
inequality, 276, 376
inexperience and the electorate, 173
Initiative for National Renewal and
    Empowerment of people (INREP),
    44, 272, 273
inner party democracy, 240–41
innovations, 99, 381
instability, 84, 178–79
institutionalisation of Indian party
    system, 28–36, 50
Intelligence Bureau (IB), 188

Interim Government, 64
International Monetary Fund (IMF), 262
inter-party competition, personality
    based, 387; rivalries, 178
inter-religious empathy, 56
intimidation, 183, 298
Iranian revolution, 230
Irula: socio-religious movements, 152
Islam, international, resurgence, 230
Islamic fundamentalism, 80
Israel: power sharing processes, 87
Italy: power sharing processes, 87

Jagjivan Ram, 214
Jahrkhand; chief-ministerial issue, 241
Jainism, 226
Jaintia Darbar, 341
Jaintia, 358
Jammu and Kashmir, 283, 307, 365;
    Article 370, 283; categorised as a
    small state, 338; Indira Gandhi's
    confrontational politics, 33;
    Kashmiri identity, 153; Muslims,
    230; regional parties, 311
Jan Morcha (People's Front), 253
Jana Congress, 293
Janata Dal (JD), 35, 43, 95, 154, 209,
    234, 245, 249n, 252–53, 255, 256,
    257, 258, 262, 270, 271, 280, 281,
    282, 296–97, 301, 310, 316, 319, 322
Janata Dal (G), 308
Janata Dal (Secular), 301, 309
Janata Dal (Socialist), 263n
Janata Dal (United), 87n, 91n, 264n,
    267, 273, 301, 309
Janata Party (JP), 31, 33, 43, 79n, 87,
    229, 244, 251–53, 271, 295, 308, 350,
    355, 360; collapse, 229; fragmenta-
    tion, 32, 35, 89, 96n
Jats, 300; benefited by Mandal
    Commission report, 260
Jayalalitha, J., 297
Jayaprakash Narayan, 71, 229
Jethmalani, Ram, 209
Jharkhand, 42, 337n; Hindu factor, 224
Jharkhand Mukti Morcha (JMM), 97,
    154, 314

Jharkhand Party, 28, 319
Jhumias, 355
Jhunjhunwala, B.P., 388n
Jinnah, Mohammad Ali, 215, 217
Jitendra Prasad, 240
Joshi, Murli Manohar, 239
judiciary, judicial system, 167, 215;
    activism 269; reforms, 371
jurisdiction, 94
justice, 248n

Kaka Kalelkar Commission, 259n
Kalani, Pappu, 194
Kamata state, demand for, 349
Kamath, H.V., 388n
Kammas, 326
Kamraj, K., 292n
Kapoor, Jaspat Roy, 388n
Karat, Prakash, 272n
Karbis, 351
Karnataka Ekikaran Sangh, 341
Karnataka, 301, 364; caste back-
    grounds of State Assembly and
    Panchayat bodies members, 394–
    95; Congress retained power in
    Assembly elections, 1967, 30;
    cultural dimension of state
    reorganisation, 340; dominant caste
    groups, 300; Indira Gandhi's
    confrontational politics, 33; lingual
    assertion, 154, 159; non-Congress
    governments, 249; Panchayati Raj
    Institutions, 386–87; party
    competition, impact on local body
    elections, 392–94; regional parties,
    313, 316
Kathodi: socio-religious movements,
    152
Kayastha Mahasangha, 219
Kerala, 301, 307, 363; categorised as a
    small state, 338; Congress lost
    Assembly elections, 1967, 30;
    coalition government, 250;— non-
    Congress, 29; cultural dimension of
    state reorganisation, 340; party
    competition, impact on local
    government, 394; regional parties,

310, 316; secularism, 172; social coalition, 266
Kerala Congress, 293, 308
Kesri, Sitaram, 188, 189, 258
Khalistan movement, 153, 230
KHAM (Kshatriya, Harijan, Adivasi, Muslim) alliances, 300
Khan, Arif Mohammad, 255
Kharkongor, McDonald, 348
Khasi Jaintia Federated, 348
Khasi National Darbar, 341, 358
Khasi State People Union, 348
Khasi Students' Union, 359; Public Demand and Implementation Convention (PDIC), 359; Hills People Union, 359
Khasis, 348, 358
Khilafat movement, 67, 74, 218
Kisan Mazdoor Praja Party (KMPP), 28, 240
knowledge society in Germany, 113, 116
Koeris, 298; benefited by Mandal Commission report, 260
Kohl, Helmut, 107, 119
'Kok Borok', 355, 356
Kokna: socio-religious movements, 152
Konrad Adenauer Foundation, 22
Koya: socio-religious movements, 152
Krishnamurthy, G.V.G., 193
Krishnamurthy, K. Jana, 377
Krishnaswami Bharati, 388n
Kunbis, 324
Kurmis, 298, 320; benefited by Mandal Commission report, 260

labour laws reforms, 379
labour market in Germany, 112
Labour Party, United Kingdom, 212
Laender (federal states), 102, 104–5, 111, 113, 114
laissez faire, 368
Lajpat Rai, Lala, 63, 79
Laldenga, , 362
land ceilings, land reforms, 175–76, 178, 217, 299; impact on party system, 176
land politics in Germany, 104, 106
Landholders' Society, 55

landlordism, 347
landownership, 176
Landtag, 108
language issue, 73, 218, 231, 314, 365; see also linguistic
Latif, Abdul, 73
Latin America: liberalisation, 381; market transition, 377; parliamentary democracy, 163
law and order, 287
Law Commission of India, 185, 186, 192, 195, 196, 197, 200, 202, 221; Report on Reforms of Electoral Law, 1999, 191
lawlessness, 181
laxity, 169
Laxman, Bangaru, 238
leadership crisis, 257
Left Front (LF), 34, 89, 257, 326, 330; economic class of voters, 146; gender-based support, 132
Left Democratic Front (LDF), 394
leftism, 77
legislature, size and redrawing of constituencies, 199–200
Lenin, V.I., 214–15
Lepcha, D.S., 347
Lepchas, 346, 357
liberal democracy, 215–16
liberalisation, see globalisation and liberalisation
Liberation Tigers of Tamil Eelam (LTTE), 34
Licence-Permit Quota Raj, 381
Lingayats, 316, 395
lingual assertion, 154
linguistic: diversity, 153, 227; identity, 159; reorganisation of states, 177, 289, 337
local democracies, institutionalisation, 46
local self-government, 46, 57, 58
localism, 388
locality, 149, 218, 332
Lodhas, benefited by Mandal Commission report, 260
Lok Ayukta Bill, 278

Lok Dal, 295, 394
Lok Pal Bill, 278, 283
Lok Shakti, Karnataka, 87n, 96n, 170, 309, 316, 324, 328
London Club, 279
Lucknow Pact, 1916, 27, 65, 75
Lyngdoh, B.B., 358

Maastricht Treaty, 122, 123, 128
Macaulay, 52
Machtwechsel (change in government), 107
Mackba, M.I., 53n
Madhya Pradesh (MP) 42, 363; BJP government, 234; Congress government, 234;—retained power in Assembly elections, 1967, 30; Hindu factor, 224; reservations for OBCs, 259n, 260
Madras Native Association, 55
Mahabaleshwar Giristhan Nagar Parishad, 196
Mahajan Sabha, Madras, 62n
Maharashtra, 291, 301, 364; coalition government, 250; Congress retained power in Assembly elections, 1967, 30; cultural dimension of state reorganisation, 340; dominant caste groups, 300; lingual assertion, 154; non-Congress governments, 249; regional parties, 311, 323–24, 333
Maharashtrawadi Gomantak Party (MGP), Goa, 313
majoritarianism 230
Majumdar, Sudhir Ranjan, 356
Malaviya, Madan Mohan, 79
Malaylis, 336; socio-religious movements, 152
Malis, 315
Mandai massacre, Tripura, 355
Mandal Commission, 35, 232, 255
Mandal issue, 35, 233, 256, 259–61, 373
Mandal, B.P., 259n
Mandir issue, *see* Ayodhya controversy
Manipur: identity question, 344–45; political configurations, 361; political instability, 361; regional parties, 311; sub-national assertions, 153
Manipur People's Party (MPP), 361
Manusmriti, 238
Marathas, 224, 300, 315, 324
Marathi, 314
Marathwada University, renaming controversy, 238
marginalised groups, participation, 276
Marumalarchi Dravida Munnetra Kazhagam (MDMK), 303
Marxism, 69, 77, 214, 251
Marxist parties, 28
mass awakening and political education, 54, 163
Mauryas, 224
Media, and the caretaker government, 198–99
mediation, tools for, 378–81
Meenakshipuram, conversions, 230
Meerut Conspiracy, 77
Meghalaya: birth of, 358; cultural dimension of state reorganisation, 340; plan for the hill state, 350; regional parties, 311; sub-national assertions, 153
Mehta, B.S., 388n
Mehta, Pherozeshah, 57, 61
members of parliament: factionalism, 242; political power, 339
Members of Parliament Local Area Development Scheme (MPLADS), 192
Merkel, Angela, 120
Merz, Friedrich, 119
Microsoft, 375
middle class, 50, 176, 274, 335, 373
middle space, 330–31
migration, 217
minorities, empowerment, 287
minorityism, 234
Misra, Lokanath, 388n
Missile Transfer Control Regime (MTCR), 279
Mitra, Kamal, 272n
Mizo Accord, 1986, 362
Mizo National Front (MNF), 154, 349, 362

Mizo Union (MU), 341, 347, 362
Mizoram, 363; sub-national assertions, 153, 154
Mizoram People's Conference (PC), 362
Mizos, 347–48
mobilisation, 300, 329–30
Model Code of Conduct (MCC), 185
modernism, modernisation, 53, 115
Mohanta, P.K., 351
Montague-Chelmsford, 76
Mookerjee, Syama Prasad, 79, 81
Moplah uprisings (1849–55), 52n
moral authority, 171
Mouvement Républicain Populaire, 217
Moynihan, Daniel P., 188
Mughals, 224
Muhammadan Literary and Scientific of Calcutta, 73
Müller-Armack, 115
multi party parliamentary system, 174, 175, 252
multi-culturalism, 291
multiparty democracy, 233, 248
Muslim(s), 42, 43, 237, 240, 298, 321, 322, 324; deserted Congress, 229; electoral support, 144–45; Indian politics and party system, 72–76, 217; literacy level, 204; representation in Lok Sabha, 203–4; traditionalists, 232, 226
Muslim Anglo-Oriental College, Aligarh, 74
Muslim League, 26, 27, 28, 60, 64–65, 67, 72–73, 74–75, 76, 79, 81, 215, 217, 342, 343
Muslim Personal Law Board, 219
Mustafa, Seema, 272n

Naga National Council (NNC), 341, 347, 359, 360
Naga Peoples' Convention (NPC), 359, 360
Nagaland: cultural dimension of state reorganisation, 340; ethnic composition, 360; secessionist movement, 359; sub-national assertions, 153

Nagas, 154, 347–48
Naidu, Chand, 297
Naidu, Chandrababu, 325–26
Naik: socio-religious movements, 152
Naoroji, Dadabhai, 55, 64
Narasimha Rao, P.V., 34, 36, 45, 97, 182, 224, 234, 241, 270, 308, 372, 373, 376, 379–80
Narayan, Jayaprakash; *see* Jayaprakash Narayan
Narcotics Drugs and Psychotropic Substances Act, 1985, 195
Narendra Dev, Acharya, 70
narrow-mindedness, 388
National Commission of Minorities, 215
National Conference, 313
National Conference, Calcutta, 1885, 57, 58, 59, 60
national consciousness, 51
National Democratic alliance (NDA), 36, 43, 242, 244, 249, 250, 262, 264, 267, 309, 325, 370, 378, 380, 385; caste-based mobilisations, 143, 216, 239
national discourse and socio-cultural identities, 159–61
National Election Study Survey, 386
National Front (NF), 34, 35, 36, 43, 45, 89, 237, 245, 252, 253n, 255, 259, 261, 268, 296–97, 308; caste-based mobilisation, 142; economic class of voters, 146–49; educational level of voters, 136–37; gender-based mobilisation, 132; occupation of voters, 138–40; religion of voters, 144–45; urban versus rural support base, 134
National Institute of Public Finance and Policy, 187
National Mohammedan Association, 57, 73
national movement, 50, 69, 76, 77–78, 336
national parties, 42–44, 150, 181, 363–64
National Security Council, 282
National Socialist Council of Nagaland (NSCN) (IM), 360
National Telegraph Union, 62n

National-Democratic Party of Germany (National-Demokratische Partei Deutschlands [NPD]), Federal Republic of Germany, 103, 104
nationalism, 26, 51, 52, 56, 58, 59, 67, 70, 158–59, 225, 231, 290, 291; religion-based, 81
Nationalist Congress Party (NCP), 95, 302, 316, 323–24
Naxalite politics, 153
Nayyar, Deepak, 272n
Nazi period, 100
Nehru, Arun, 255
Nehru, Jawaharlal, 29, 30, 66, 79, 80, 81, 174, 194, 214–15, 219, 350, 368, 372, 388–89
Nehru, Motilal, 68
Nehruvian politics, 369–70
Nepalis, 346
nepotism, 357
Neun Union, 114, 116
neutrality, 215
new states, creation and power politics, 243
Nicholas Roy, J. J.M., 348, 358
Nijalingappa, S., 292n
Nikhil Manipuri Sabha, 341, 344
Non-aligned Movement (NAM), 278
non-cooperation, 67, 74, 76n
non-government organisations (NGOs), 279
Non-Proliferation Treaty (NPT), 279, 282
norms, 284; individualistic and collectivist, 212
North East: Christians, 230; demography, 348; refugees, influx, 348; party formation and politics, 336–48; in the period of Parliamentary democracy, 348–58; sub-national identity articulation, 153–54
North East Frontier Agency (NEFA), 349
North East Reorganisation Bill, 1972, 355, 358
Northrhine-Westphalia, Germany: hold of social democratic party, 104

OBC, see other backward classes
votes, 285
obsolescence, 94
occupational inter-linkage with political support, 137–40
Official Language Bill, 349
Oil Shock, 1972, 228
Olcott, Colonel, 60
opinion polls, see exit poll
opposition, 23, 26
Orissa, 301, 332; regional parties, 333; Congress lost Assembly elections, 1967, 30; lingual assertion, 159; regional parties, 311, 313, 319–20
Oriyas, 336
Osborne, Robert, 57
Other Backward Classes (OBCs), 237, 256, 259, 281, 298, 314, 315, 317, 319, 320–21, 323, 324, 325–26, 328, 330–31, 333: political mobilisations, 142; reservation in jobs, 222, 232; see also Mandal issue
Outlook, 195

Pal, Bipin Chandra, 60, 63, 219
Palatinate, Rhineland, 119
Panchayati Raj Institutions (PRIs), 24, 46, 99, 280, 283, 386, 390, 393–94
Pande, B.D., 303
Paniyan: socio-religious movements, 152
Paradigm shift, 373
parliamentarianism, 26
Parliamentary Group of the Party of European Socialists, 125
parliamentary system, 59; moral authority, 167; see also democracy
parochial considerations, 245
parties, see political parties
partition, 162, 348, 345
Party of European Socialists (PESs), 123, 127
Party of Socialist Democracy (Partei des Demokratischen Sozialismus [PDS]), Germany, 102, 104, 105, 106
Paswan, Ramvilas, 380

Patel, Sardar Vallabhbhai, 227, 232n
Patels (Patidars), 300
Patil, Blasaheb Vikhe, 187
Patil, S.K., 292n
Patnaik, Biju, 319
Patnaik, Navin, 319
patron-client relationship, 220
Pattal Makkal Katchi (PMK), Tamil
    Nadu, 301, 303, 314
Pawar, Sharad, 302, 324
peasants, 217–18
Peasants' and Workers' Party (PWP),
    Maharashtra, 307, 323
People's Party of Arunachal (PPA), 360
permanent settlement, 176
personal freedom, 217
personality based conglomeration, 265
plebiscitarian democracy, 49, 332
Polenz, Ruprecht, 120
police, politicisation, 181
political alliances, see coalition
    government, coalition politics
political attitudes, 23
political capacity, 377
political cohabitation, 64
political concessions, 377
political consciousness, 26, 55, 63, 163,
    300
political disputes, 373
political economy, 333–35, 372
political equations, 246
political hegemony, 156
political identification, 321
political instability, 161
political institution, 49
political mobilisations, 25, 50–51, 129,
    219
political order, 366
political party system, 240–42;
    crystallisation, 63; federalisation,
    22; institutionalisation, 60; four
    parameters, 47
political parties, 185–86; and the civil
    society, 213–14; decentralisation and
    institutes; decentralised relationship,
    93–94; fragmentation in European
    Union, 122–28; in colonial India, 218–

19; in independent India, 219–21; in
    political theory, 210–11; insensitive to
    public opinion, 190; interactions, 23
interrelationships, 23, 26; and their
    members, 211–13; polarisation,
    185–86; politics in European Union,
    125–26; and representation, 214–17;
    structures and institutional
    framework, 40–42
political powers, 224
political recognition, 160–61
political reforms, 42, 371
political rivals, 28
political sociology, 21
political stability, 155
political system's legitimacy, 378
politicians, 172
politicisation, 300
'politics of mendicancy', 27
politics: criminalisation, 41;
    Mandalisation, 232; and nation
    building, 225; regionalism, 43, 44,
    248
polity, 41, 48, 155, 164, 166, 167, 168,
    170, 172, 173, 176, 242, 257, 258, 291,
    377; federalisation, 331; fragmenta-
    tion, 222
polluting industrial units, relocation, 284
Poona Sarvajanik Sabha, 62n
populism, 180, 370
poverty, 214, 276, 370, 378; and
    politics, 163
power, 268, 277, 285, 335; and authority,
    386; compulsions, 23, 242; devolution
    of, 283; equations, 385; management,
    387; overcentralisation, 395; politics,
    41; sharing processes, 87, 92–93, 385;
    shift, 47; structure, 248
Praja Socialist party (PSP), 349, 353
Prasad, Kamala, 272n
presidencies, political consciousness,
    55–59
Presidential system, 162, 170
Press Club of India, 272
Press Council of India (PCI), 205
Princely states, integration into the
    Indian union, 337

privatisation, 280
proliferation, 185
Provincial Assembly elections, 1937, 76
Provincial Legislative Council, 65
proxy voting, 182
public attitudes and behaviour, 165, 284
public biases, 165
public interest litigation, 188
Pudiya Tamizhagam (PT), Tamil
    Nadu, 301
punishment for electoral offences,
    197–98
Punjab, 228, 307, 364; aristocracy, 236;
    categorised as a large state, 338; coa-
    lition government, 250; Congress
    lost Assembly elections, 1967, 30;
    cultural dimension of state reorgan-
    isation, 340; dominant caste groups,
    300; Indira Gandhi's confrontational
    politics, 33; Khalistani identity ques-
    tion, 153; regional parties, 311, 313,
    316, 317, 333
Punjab Accord, 33
Punjab Hindu Sabha, 79
Punjab Infrastructure Development
    Board, 375
Punjab, Haryana and Delhi Chambers
    of Commerce (PHDCCI), 375
Punjabi identity, 314
Purbanchal Lok Parishad (PLP), 350–51
Purna Swaraj, 67

Quit India movement, 67, 78, 80

racial factors, 217, 227
radicalisation, 286
Rainbow Group, 125
raison d'etre, 268n, 286, 368, 373
Raj Krishna, 187
Raj Kumar, Dr, 220
Raja, D., 273
Rajasthan, 42, 307, 363; BJP government,
    234; Congress lost Assembly elec-
    tions, 1967, 30; factionalism, 242;
    Hindu factor, 224; non-Congress
    governments, 249; political power,
    339; regional parties, 310

Rajputs, 321; benefited by Mandal
    Commission report, 260
Rajya Sabha, 170; elections, some
    issues, 206–8
Ram Janmabhoomi issue, see Ayodhya
    controversy
Ram Rajya Parishad, 28
Rama Rao, N.T., 325
Ramjanmabhoomi/temle issue
Ranga, N.G., 388n
Rao, Bhaskar, 204
Rashtriya Janata Dal (RJD), 154, 258,
    267n, 270n, 273, 301, 307, 315,
    320–22, 329
Rashtriya Swayamsevak Sangh (RSS),
    32, 33, 89, 98, 219, 226, 227, 229,
    231–32, 236, 239, 271; and the
    Hindu right, 78–81
Rast Goftar, fortnightly, 55
rath yatra, 232
rationalism, 156–57
reconciliation, 73
Red Indian, 291
Reddy, Jaipal, 257
Reddys, 300
reform movements, 51
region and nation, relationship, 44
regional identities, 175, 313; in
    Germany, 114–15
regional parties emergence, 34, 40,
    44–46, 150, 177, 181, 363–64
regionalism, 44, 45, 88, 268n, 302,
    314–15, 324, 333, 334
religion, religious, 149, 217, 245, 277, 389;
    communalism, 314; conversions, 223;
    factors, 227; politicisation, 230; of
    voters, 143–46
representation, 26
Representation of People Act (RPA),
    1951, 96, 185, 192, 193, 194, 197
Republican Party of India (RPI),
    Maharashtra, 88n, 315, 323
Republicans (Die Republikaner), 104
reservation issue, 218, 220, 222,
    259–61, 277, 281
Revolt of 1857, 25
Revolutionary Socialist Party (RSP),
    307, 355

right, rights, 179; to contest, 173; to
    form a party, 162, 164, 173, 221; to
    information, 278; to vote, 213
Ripon, Lord, 58, 61
rivalry, 172
Rousseau, 216, 222
Rowlatt *satyagraha*, 67
Roy, M.N., 76
Roy, Raja Ram Mohun, 26, 52, 54
rule of law, 209, 220, 277
ruling classes, 333, 334
rural-urban divide, 35, 165, 259
ryots and zamindars, relation, 56

Sahu, Laksminarayana, 388*n*
Saikia, Hiteswar, 352
Saksena, Shibban Lal, 388*n*
Samajwadi Party (SP), 154, 221, 234,
    246, 257, 258, 266, 270, 272, 279*n*,
    280, 281, 298, 301, 303, 307, 315,
    322–23, 365
Samata Party, 84*n*, 87*n*, 194, 258, 266,
    270, 279*n*, 281, 301, 303, 307, 309,
    316, 320–22, 329
Sangh Parivar, 34, 79*n*, 266
Sanghavi, Abhishek Manu, 188
Sangma, Purno, 364
Sangma, Williamson, 358
Sanjeeva Reddy, N., 292*n*
Santhal rebellion (1855–56)
Santhanam, K., 388*n*
Sanyasi rebellion, Bengal, 52*n*
Sastry, Peri, 184
sati, 54
Satpathy, Nadini, 319
Satya Bhakta, 76
satyagraha, 66
Savarkar, Vinayak Damodar, 79, 80,
    226
Saxony-Anhalt, Germany: hold of
    social democratic party, 104
Sayeed, Mufti Mohammad, 220*n*
Sayeed, Rubaiya, 220
scaffolding, 97
Scandinavia: women representation,
    203
Schäuble, Wolfgang, 120

Scheduled Castes and Scheduled
    Tribes, 215; political mobilisations,
    142; protective discrimination, 259*n*
schism, 26
Schleswig-Holstein, Germany: hold of
    Social Democratic Party of Ger-
    many (Sozialdemokratische Partie
    Deutschlands [SPD]), 105
Scottish Plan, 350
sectarian conflicts, 217
sectarian diversity, 291
secularism, secularisation, 172, 172,
    214, 229, 231, 238, 270, 277, 283, 284,
    286, 351; in Germany, 109
Securities and Exchange Board of
    India (SEBI), 205
self-conscious political identity, 151
self-reliance, 278
Sema, Hokishe, 359
Semas, 360
Sengupta, Sukhomoy, 354, 355
separatism, 177
Seshan, T.N., 183
Shah Bano case, 231, 232, 270
Shaivites, 291
Shakdhar, S.L., 183, 186, 187
Shankarseth, Jagannath, 53*n*
Sharma, Shankar Dayal, 206
Shastri, Alagu Rai, 388*n*
Shilu Ao, P., 359, 360
Shiromani Akali Dal, 219
Shiv Sena, 185, 194, 198, 209, 212, 219,
    238, 301, 303, 314, 320, 323–24, 365
Shivaji, 314
Shukla, S.P., 272*n*
Sibsagar, Assam, demand for Ahom
    homeland, 349
Sidwa, R.K., 388*n*
Sikh Gurudwara Prabandhak Com-
    mittee (SGPC), 219, 303
Sikhs, Sikhism, 42, 145, 226, 230, 317
Sikkim, 363; cultural dimension of
    state reorganisation, 340; identity
    question, 346–47; Indira Gandhi's
    confrontational politics, 33; lower
    caste rebellion, 357; Nepali mi-
    grants, discrimination, 347;
    regional parties, 311

Sikkim Congress, 357
Sikkim Democratic Front, 357–58
Sikkim Janata Parishad, 357
Sikkim National Party, 347
Sikkim Sangram Parishad (SSP), 308,
     357–58
Sikkim State Congress, 341, 347
Simon Commission report, 348
sine qua non, 286
Singh, Ajit, 255
Singh, Charan, *See* Charan Singh
Singh, Kanwaljit, 375
Singh, Kuldeep, 193
Singh, Manmohan, 207, 369–70, 371,
     377, 380
Singh, N.K., 374
Singh, V.P., 34, 35, 43, 45, 182, 184, 232,
     233, 244n, 245, 251–53, 254, 255,
     256, 259, 261, 268n, 271, 272, 296
Sinha, S.K., 352
Sinha, Yashwant, 379
Sitaramayya, Pattabhi, 72
scepticism, 373
Smadja, Claude, 374
social: awareness, 53; backwardness in
     Germany, 110; base of Indian
     politics, 34, 36, 236–37;—of regional
     parties, 316–28; behaviour, 284;
     change in Germany, 109–10;
     classes, 236, 275; cleavages, 49, 149,
     150–51;—in Germany, 114,—
     politicisation, 249; development,
     280; diversity, 299; groups, 24, 151,
     160, 236, 240, 246, 261, 274, 300;—
     local level and district level, nexus,
     390; identification, 236; indiscipline,
     370; institutions, 49; integration,
     159, 232; justice, 154, 209, 261;
     market economy in Germany, 115;
     morality, 166; order, 368; realign-
     ment, 32; reality, 305; reform
     movement, 52, 58, 59, 158;
     resilience, 49; resources, 366; rights,
     368; stability, 376n; transformation,
     51, 285;—in Germany, 116
Social Democratic Party of Germany
     (Sozialdemokratische Partei [SPD]),

102, 103, 104, 105, 107, 108, 109, 111,
     115, 121
socialism, 33, 214, 229, 351; collapse in
     Germany, 112
Socialist and Social Democratic move-
     ments in European Union, 125
Socialist Party, 28
Socialist Riech Party (Sozialistiche
     Reichspartei [SRP]), Germany, 101,
     103
Socialist Unity Party of Germany
     (Sozialistische Einheitpartei
     Deutschlands [SED]), Germany,
     102, 106
Society for the Acquisition of General
     Knowledge, 53
society, 23; disorientation in Germany,
     113, 116; *see also* civil society
socio-cultural processes, 44, 46
socio-economic: groups, 245; hetero-
     geneity, 260; inequality, 289;
     interests, 39; mosaics, 178; process,
     246; reality, 172
socio-political groups, 248; multiplicity,
     251; reality, 172
socio-religious movements, 50, 152
Solanki, Madhavsinh, 259n
solidarity, 109
Somnath temple, 232n
'Sonar Asom', 351
South Africa: National Assembly,
     women representation, 203; racial
     bigotry, 65
Southeast Asia: parliament democ-
     racy, 163
splintering, 185
stability, 181, 388
Staines, *Father*, 239
state: autonomy, 248n; capitalism, 274;
     and civil society, 30, 217–18; and
     individual relationship, 367; and
     market relationship, 46, 367, 372–75
and religion, 277; role, reorientation,
     370; to state relationship, 367
State Reorganisation Commission,
     280, 337, 349, 353–54, 366–67
statehood, movements for, 314, 364

STATT-Party, 105
status quo, 285
Strauß, Fraz-Joseph, 119
Students' Literary and Scientific
    Society, 55
sub-national movements, 364
self-assertion, 364
Sultanate, 224
Surendra Mohan, 272n
Surjit, Harkishan, 272n
swadeshi movement, 64, 78
Swadeshi Jagran Manch, 271
Swamy, Subramaniam, 96n, 307
Swaraj Party, 27, 68–69
Swatantra Party, 319
Swell, G.G., 348, 364
Syed Ahmad, 73–74, 218
Sylhet, Assam, 342; transfer to
    Pakistan, 343, 348
Symbol allocation to parties, 95, 185

Tagore, Debendranath, 54
Tagore, Dwarkanath, 54
Tamang-Gurung-Rai, 357
Tamil Manila Congress (TMC), 257,
    264n, 301, 303
Tamil Nadu, Tamil, 332; coalition
    government, 250; Congress lost
    Assembly elections, 1967, 30;
    consolidation of Dravidian politics,
    34; cultural dimension of state
    reorganisation, 340; culture,
    Hinduisation, 318; lingual asser-
    tion, 154, 159; regional parties, 311,
    313, 316, 317–19, 333
Tamilnad Congress, 28
Tata Electoral Trust, 191
Tata Sons, 190
Tatvabodhini Sabha, 54
Tayabji, Badruddin, 62
Tehering, Tashi, 347
Telang, K.T., 62
Telengana movement, 77, 78, 337n
Telugu Desam Party (TDP), 154, 252,
    257, 258, 264n, 296, 297, 302, 306,
    308, 313, 324–26, 330, 365, 381, 392,
    393n, 394

Telugus, 336
Thackerey, Bal, 194, 198, 201, 209, 212
Thakur, Karpoori, 259n
Theosophical Society, 60
Third Front, 22, 43–44, 282–85; as an
    ideology, 273–79; significance as a
    political force, 258–62; as a reality,
    279–82
Thomas, R.R., 348
Thomson, George, 53
Thuringia, Germany: hold of Christian
    Democrats, 104
Tibetan Lamas, 346
Tilak, Balganghadhar, 63, 65
tolerance, 215
Trade Union movement and politics,
    77, 217
transformation, 21, 47, 48, 49, 332, 333
transnational parties in European
    Union, 123, 126
transparency, 278
Tribal Advisory Council, 355
tribes, tribal, 315; autonomy, 152;
    loyalties supersede the party
    ideology, 364; votes, 285; see also
    Tripura, North East, Nagaland,
    Meghalay, Manipur
Trinamool Congress, 258, 301, 307,
    326–27, 328, 330, 365
Tripura, 301, 307, 363, 365; Bengali
    refugees, 346, 355 ; communal
    tension, 355; cultural dimension of
    state reorganisation, 340; effected
    by partition, 353; identity question,
    344, 345; monopoly of CPM, 249n;
    sub-national assertions, 153, 154
Tripura Areas Autonomuos District
    Council Act (TAADC), 1979, 355–56
Tripura (States Reorganisation Act,
    1956) Act, 354
Tripura Land Revenue and Land
    Reforms Act, 1960, 354, 355;
    (second amendment), 1974, 355
Tripura National Volunteers (TNV), 356
Tripura Rajya Gana Parishad, 341, 345
Tripura Rajya Mukti Parishad, 341, 345
Tripura Rajya Praja Mondol, 345

Tripura State Committee of All India Kisan Sabha, 218, 355
Tripura Territorial Council, 354
Tripura Upajati Juba Samiti (TUJS), 354, 355, 356
trusteeship, 70
Tshering, Sonam, 347
Tuensang Regional Council, 359
two-party system, 171, 249n
two-nation theory, 217
Tyabji, Badruddin, 74n
Tyagi, Mahavir, 388n

Umaruddin, 349
underprivileged, higher turnout in elections, 168
Uniform Civil Code, 231, 232, 242
United Bengal Hindu Movement, 79
United Democratic Front (UDF), 311, 359
United Front (UF), 36, 43, 89, 245, 256–58, 262, 268, 273, 308, 309, 319, 378, 380, 394; caste-based mobilisation, 142; economic class of voters, 147–49; educational level of voters, 136–37; gender-based mobilisation, 132; occupation of voters, 138–40; religion of voters, 144–45; urban versus rural support base, 132, 134
United Goan Party (UGP), 313
United Liberation Front of Assam (ULFA), 351–52, 353
United Nations, 215, 279
unity, 33
unity in diversity, 291
universal adult franchise, 162–63, 164–65, 171, 173, 180
Unlawful Activities (Prevention) Act, 1967, 195
urban middle class dominance, 173, 335
urban versus rural voters, 132–35, 137
Urs, Devraj, 300, 390
Utkal Congress, 313, 319
Uttar Pradesh, 42, 301, 307, 363; BJP government, 234; caste identity, 159; Congress lost Assembly elections, 1967, 30; factionalism, 242; Hindu

factor, 224; land reforms, 66; non-Congress governments, 249; political instability, 181; political mobilisation, 35; political power, 339; regional parties, 311, 322–23, 333; social coalition, 266; success, of Samajwadi party, 246
Uttarakhand, demand for separate state, 297
Uttaranchal, 337n; chief-ministerial issue, 241; role in electoral battle for New Delhi, 42; Hindu factor, 224

Vaishnavaites, 291
Vajpayee, Atal Behari, 33, 87, 88, 89, 93, 96, 168, 182, 184, 216, 232, 239, 241, 332, 352, 378, 381
values, 29, 284, 366
Vanaik, Achin, 272n
vandalism, 221
Vanjara, 300
Veerappan, 220n
Venkataraman, R., 85n, 188
Vidarbha, movement for independent state, 337n
Vijayanagar Empire, 224
village economy, 49
Village Panchayat, 389
village republics, 388
Vinayak cult, 318
violations, 167
violence, 85, 181, 183, 221, 223, 277, 287, 298
Vishal Haryana Parishad, 314
Vishwa Hindu Parishad (VHP), 33–34, 215, 216, 219, 221, 239, 271
Vizol, 359, 360
Vokkaligas, 300, 301, 316, 395
volatility, 93
Volksparteien, 38, 39, 103, 109–11, 113, 127; crisis, 108; reasons for decline, 109–11
voters: mobilisation, 23; impersonation, 183; fragmentation, 37; frustration, 99; growth, 181; rights, 214; rural vs urban, 165

Wahabi movement, 52*n*
Waigel, Theodor, 107
Wanchoo Committee, *see* Direct Taxes
  Enquiry Committee
Warli tribe, socio-religious movement,
  152
Washington, George, 210
Weimar Republic, Germany: role of
  political parties, 100, 103
welfarism, 276
West Bengal, 301, 307, 308, 363, 365; coalition government, 250, 304; Congress lost Assembly elections, 1967,
  30; government cooperation, 283;
  Indira Gandhi's confrontational politics, 33; monopoly of CPM, 34, 249*n*;
  Panchayati raj system, 390–91; politics, 326; regional parties, 313, 316;
  social coalition, 266
Westminster, 55
White Anglo Saxon Protestant
  (WASP), 291
women: representation in Lok Sabha,
  202–3, reservation for, 99; voting
  behaviour, 131

working class movement, 215
World Bank, 261, 262
World Economic Forum, 373–74
World Trade Organisation (WTO), 262,
  375, 380; Agreement on Agricul-
  ture, 280, 284
World War I, 218
World War II, 78, 100, 103

Yadav, Laloo Prasad, 209, 255, 258,
  315, 320–21
Yadav, Mulayam Singh, 197, 257, 266,
  273, 330
Yadav, Pappu, 194
Yadav, Sharad, 301, 380
Yadavs, 298, 301, 315, 321, 322–23
Yechuri, Sitaram, 250*n*
Young Bengal, 53
Young India, 54
'Young Turk', 253

zamindari abolition, 299
Zila Parishads, 280
Zilla Panchayat, 393